The Pattern
Almanac
2000

The Software Patterns Series

Series Editor: John M. Vlissides

The Software Patterns Series (SPS) comprises pattern literature of lasting significance to software developers. Software patterns document general solutions to recurring problems in all software-related spheres, from the technology itself, to the organizations that develop and distribute it, to the people who use it. Books in the series distill experience from one or more of these areas into a form that software professionals can apply immediately. *Relevance* and *impact* are the tenets of the SPS. Relevance means each book presents patterns that solve real problems. Patterns worthy of the name are intrinsically relevant; they are borne of practitioners' experiences, not theory or speculation. Patterns have impact when they change how people work for the better. A book becomes a part of the series not just because it embraces these tenets, but because it has demonstrated it fulfills them for its audience.

Titles in the series:

The Design Patterns Smalltalk Companion, Sherman Alpert/Kyle Brown/Bobby Woolf

The Pattern Almanac, Linda Rising

Pattern Hatching: Design Patterns Applied, John Vlissides

Pattern Languages of Program Design, edited by James O. Coplien/Douglas C. Schmidt

Pattern Languages of Program Design 2, edited by John M. Vlissides/James O. Coplien/
 Norman L. Kerth

Pattern Languages of Program Design 3, edited by Robert Martin/Dirk Riehle/
 Frank Buschmann

Pattern Languages of Program Design 4, edited by Neil Harrison/Brian Foote/
 Hans Rohnert

Please see our web site at http://www.awl.com/cseng/swpatterns
for more information on these titles.

The Pattern
Almanac
2000

Linda Rising

ADDISON-WESLEY

Boston • San Francisco • New York • Toronto • Montreal
London • Munich • Paris • Madrid
Capetown • Sydney • Tokyo • Singapore • Mexico City

The publisher offers discounts on this book when ordered in quantity for special sales. For more information, please contact:

Pearson Education Corporate Sales Division
One Lake Street
Upper Saddle River, NJ 07458
(800) 382-3419
corpsales@pearsontechgroup.com

Visit us on the Web at www.awl.com/cseng/

Library of Congress Card Number: 99-067056

Text printed on recycled and acid-free paper.
ISBN 0-201-61567-3
1 2 3 4 5 6 7 8 9 10 – CRS – 04 03 02 01 00
First printing, May 2000

To AG Communication Systems—for one brief, shining moment, it was Camelot!

Credits

Adams, M., J.O. Coplien, R. Gamoke, R. Hanmer, F. Keeve, and K. Nicodemus, "Fault-Tolerant Tele-communication System Patterns," *Pattern Languages of Program Design 2,* J.M. Vlissides, J. O. Coplien, and N. L. Kerth, eds., Addison-Wesley, 1996, pp. 549–562. Copyright © 1996, AT&T, used by permission.

van den Broecke, J., J.O. Coplien, "Using Design Patterns to Build a Framework for Multimedia Net-working," *Bell Labs Technical Journal,* Winter 1997, pp. 166-187. Copyright © 1997, Lucent Technolo-gies, used by permission.

Coplien, J.O., "Curiously Recurring Template Patterns," *C++ Report,* Feb. 1995, pp. 24–27. Copyright © 1995, Lucent Technologies, used by permission.

Coplien, J.O., "A Generative Development-Process Pattern Language," *Pattern Languages of Program Design 1,* J.O. Coplien and D.C. Schmidt, eds., Addison-Wesley, 1995, pp. 183–238. Copyright © 1995, Lucent Technologies, used by permission.

Coplien, J.O., "C++ Idioms," *Pattern Languages of Program Design 4*, N.B. Harrison, B. Foote, and H. Rohnert, eds., Addison-Wesley, 2000, pp. 167-197. Copyright © 2000, Lucent Technologies, used by permission.

Coplien, J.O., and B. Woolf, "A Pattern Language for Writers' Workshops," *Pattern Languages of Program Design 4,* N.B. Harrison, B. Foote, and H. Rohnert, eds., Addison-Wesley, 2000. Copyright © 2000, Lucent Technologies, used by permission.

DeBruler, D., "A Generative Pattern Language for Distributed Processing," *Pattern Languages of Program Design 1,* J. O. Coplien and D.C. Schmidt, eds., Addison-Wesley, 1995, pp. 69–89. Copyright © 1995, Lucent Technologies, used by permission.

Harrison, N.B., "Organizational Patterns for Teams," *Pattern Languages of Program Deisgn 2,* J. Vlis-sides, J.O. Coplien, and N. Kerth, eds., Addison-Wesley, 1996, pp. 345–352. Copyright © 1996, Lucent Technologies, used by permission.

Harrison, N.B., "Patterns for Logging Diagnostic Messages," *Pattern Languages of Program Design 3,* R. C. Martin, D. Riehle, and F. Buschmann, eds., Addison-Wesley, 1997, pp. 277–289. Copyright © 1997, Lucent Technologies, used by permission.

Hanmer, R., and G. Stymfal, "An Input and Output Pattern Language, Lessons from Telecommunica-tions," *Pattern Languages of Program Design 4,* N. B. Harrison, B. Foote, and H. Rohnert, eds., Addi-son-Wesley, 2000, pp. 503-536. Copyright © 2000, Lucent Technologies & AG Communications, used by permission.

Contents

Preface ix

List of Almanac Entries xi

Categories xxiii

Almanac Entries 1

Bibliography 181

Index 201

Preface

This book organizes and describes published patterns to help you find the pattern(s) you need. It contains two kinds of patterns: those that stand alone (*patterns*), and those that work within a collection (*subpatterns*). The collections may be pattern languages, or they may be patterns published as a unit that solve problems in a particular domain. In other words, collections comprise interdependent patterns that work together to one degree or another. Standalone patterns and collections of patterns are generically termed *entries* of the Almanac.

The first section you encounter, the *List of Almanac Entries*, is just that: an exhaustive list of all entry titles and their starting page numbers. Patterns and subpatterns are denoted by a ♦, and a ❖ denotes collections. Next comes the *Categories* section, which lists categories of patterns in alphabetical order. Each category is followed by the patterns, collections, and experience reports that pertain to it. After Categories comes the heart of the book, the *Almanac Entries*, containing descriptions of the patterns and collections themselves. Next comes the *Bibliography*, which contains references for all entries and experience reports. Finally, there is an *Index* of entries, subpatterns, authors, and citations.

If you know the name of a pattern or collection and want to know more about it, use the List of Almanac Entries to find the page number of its entry. If you're not sure of the exact title but know a keyword or two, use the Index. If you're interested in patterns for a given domain, look the domain up in the Categories section. With time, you will develop your own technique for using the Almanac effectively.

I'm sure you'll also discover areas for improvement. If you find that I have missed a book, article, or URL that harbors patterns, by all means let me know. References to publications that show patterns in action are also welcome. And of course, corrections or additions of any kind are greatly appreciated, especially regarding misinterpretation of pattern intent or characterization, misspellings, annoying habits— you name it!

A sticky topic that I hesitated to tackle, at least for now, is pattern evaluation. For those who know Christopher Alexander's work, he labels his patterns with asterisks that indicate how successfully each pattern captures a "deep and inescapable property of a well-formed environment" [Alexander+77, xiv]. In that vein, I'd love to hear stories about patterns that have or have not worked for you, as well as insights regarding pattern evaluation and categorization. Please send everything to risingl@acm.org, and thanks in advance for your input!

Acknowledgments

This has been an exhilarating project! It couldn't have happened without the hard work of many people— first and foremost, the pattern writers. Thank you all. I am honored to be a proxy for your contributions to the pattern literature.

Thanks to John Vlissides for believing I could really pull this off. He made a significant contribution to the project.

Thanks to Paul Becker, Mike Hendrickson, and Sarah Weaver at Addison-Wesley for their support in bringing the book to fruition.

Thanks to Ross Venables for collating all those files!

Thanks to Luci Crackau for her work on the categories and for allowing me to take over her office.

Thanks to Patrick Chan, the *Java Developers Almanac* author and Frame guru who has been a tireless co-developer of this book. Thanks also to Arthur Ogawa, TEX wizard, for contributing his valuable skills to the layout.

Thanks to Rosemary Michelle Simpson, indexer extraordinaire, who also made many valuable suggestions for this book.

Thanks to Joel Jones, a former fellow grad student, who jumped in to ferret out experience papers and write up summaries.

Thanks to all the reviewers who spent valuable time coming up with improvements to this work.

Thanks to Charlie Schultz and Jeff Seigel, my original supporters at AG Communication Systems, and to Paul Narula, my most recent coach, for allowing me to spend time on this effort.

Finally, thanks to Karl Rehmer, who reminds me, when I forget, that I have everything I need. Thanks, you dear heart!

L.R.
Phoenix, Arizona
January 2000
risingl@acm.org

List of Almanac Entries

ABSTRACT CLASS ♦ 2
ABSTRACT CLIENT ♦ 2
ABSTRACT FACTORY ♦ 2
ABSTRACT SESSION ♦ 2
ACCEPTOR ♦ 3
ACCESSING RELATIONAL DATABASES ❖ 3
   RELATIONAL DATABASE ACCESS LAYER ♦ 3
   HIERARCHICAL VIEW ♦ 3
   PHYSICAL VIEW ♦ 3
   QUERY BROKER ♦ 4
ACCOUNT NUMBER ♦ 4
ACCOUNTABILITY AND
   ORGANIZATIONAL STRUCTURES ❖ 4
   PARTY ♦ 4
   RECURSIVE STRUCTURES FOR ORGANIZATIONS ♦ 4
   ABSTRACT MODELS WITH
      CONSTRAINTS IN SUBTYPES ♦ 4
   MULTIPLE HIERARCHIC ASSOCIATIONS ♦ 4
   ORGANIZATIONAL STRUCTURE-TYPED
      RELATIONSHIP ♦ 5
   OBJECTIFY ASSOCIATIONS ♦ 5
   TYPED RELATIONSHIP ♦ 5
   ACCOUNTABILITY ABSTRACTION ♦ 5
   ACCOUNTABILITY KNOWLEDGE LEVEL ♦ 5
   PUT FREQUENTLY VARYING
      STRUCTURES IN INSTANCES ♦ 5
   KNOWLEDGE LEVEL ♦ 5
ACTIVE OBJECT ♦ 6
ACYCLIC VISITOR ♦ 6
ADAPTER ♦ 6
ANALYSIS PATTERNS ❖ 6
   PARTY ♦ 6
   ORGANIZATION HIERARCHIES ♦ 7
   ORGANIZATION STRUCTURE ♦ 7
   ACCOUNTABILITY ♦ 7
   ACCOUNTABILITY KNOWLEDGE LEVEL ♦ 7
   PARTY TYPE GENERALIZATIONS ♦ 7
   HIERARCHIC ACCOUNTABILITY ♦ 7
   OPERATING SCOPE ♦ 7
   POST ♦ 7
   QUANTITY ♦ 8

CONVERSION RATIO ♦ 8
COMPOUND UNITS ♦ 8
MEASUREMENT ♦ 8
OBSERVATION ♦ 8
SUBTYPING OBSERVATION CONCEPTS ♦ 8
PROTOCOL ♦ 8
DUAL TIME RECORD ♦ 9
REJECTED OBSERVATION ♦ 9
ACTIVE OBSERVATION, HYPOTHESIS,
   AND PROJECTION ♦ 9
ASSOCIATED OBSERVATION ♦ 9
PROCESS OF OBSERVATION ♦ 9
ENTERPRISE SEGMENT ♦ 9
MEASUREMENT PROTOCOL ♦ 9
RANGE ♦ 9
PHENOMENON WITH RANGE ♦ 10
NAME ♦ 10
IDENTIFICATION SCHEME ♦ 10
OBJECT MERGE ♦ 10
OBJECT EQUIVALENCE ♦ 10
ACCOUNT ♦ 10
TRANSACTION ♦ 10
SUMMARY ACCOUNT ♦ 11
MEMO ACCOUNT ♦ 11
POSTING RULES ♦ 11
INDIVIDUAL INSTANCE METHOD ♦ 11
POSTING RULE EXECUTION ♦ 11
POSTING RULES FOR MANY ACCOUNTS ♦ 11
CHOOSING ENTRIES ♦ 11
ACCOUNTING PRACTICE ♦ 12
SOURCES OF AN ENTRY ♦ 12
BALANCE SHEET AND INCOME STATEMENT ♦ 12
CORRESPONDING ACCOUNT ♦ 12
SPECIALIZED ACCOUNT MODEL ♦ 12
BOOKING ENTRIES TO MULTIPLE ACCOUNTS ♦ 12
PROPOSED AND IMPLEMENTED ACTION ♦ 12
COMPLETED AND ABANDONED ACTIONS ♦ 12
SUSPENSION ♦ 12
PLAN ♦ 13
PROTOCOL ♦ 13
RESOURCE ALLOCATION ♦ 13

OUTCOME AND START FUNCTIONS ♦ 13
CONTRACT ♦ 13
PORTFOLIO ♦ 13
QUOTE ♦ 13
SCENARIO ♦ 13
FORWARD CONTRACTS ♦ 13
OPTIONS ♦ 14
PRODUCT ♦ 14
SUBTYPE STATE MACHINES ♦ 14
PARALLEL APPLICATION AND
    DOMAIN HIERARCHIES ♦ 14
MULTIPLE ACCESS LEVELS TO A PACKAGE ♦ 14
MUTUAL VISIBILITY ♦ 14
SUBTYPING PACKAGES ♦ 14
TWO-TIER ARCHITECTURE ♦ 14
THREE-TIER ARCHITECTURE ♦ 15
PRESENTATION AND APPLICATION LOGIC ♦ 15
DATABASE INTERACTION ♦ 15
IMPLEMENTING ASSOCIATIONS ♦ 15
IMPLEMENTING GENERALIZATIONS ♦ 15
OBJECT CREATION ♦ 15
OBJECT DESTRUCTION ♦ 15
ENTRY POINT ♦ 16
IMPLEMENTING CONSTRAINTS ♦ 16
ASSOCIATIVE TYPE ♦ 16
KEYED MAPPING ♦ 16
HISTORIC MAPPING ♦ 16
APPROACHES FOR SEPARATING
    CLIENTS FROM SERVERS ❖ 16
INTELLIGENT CHILDREN ♦ 16
ABSTRACT SERVER ♦ 16
ADAPTED SERVER ♦ 17
ARCHITECTURAL PATTERNS FOR ENABLING
    APPLICATION SECURITY ❖ 17
SINGLE ACCESS POINT ♦ 17
CHECK POINT ♦ 17
ROLES ♦ 17
SESSION ♦ 17
FULL VIEW WITH ERRORS ♦ 18
LIMITED VIEW ♦ 18
SECURE ACCESS LAYER ♦ 18
ARCHITECTURE PATTERNS FOR
    BUSINESS SYSTEMS ❖ 18
ONLINE ENGINEERING MODEL ♦ 18
MESSAGING ENGINEERING MODEL ♦ 18
BATCH ENGINEERING MODEL ♦ 19
STREAM I-O ENGINEERING MODEL ♦ 19
ASYNCHRONOUS COMPLETION TOKEN ♦ 19
BACKUP ♦ 19
BASIC RELATIONSHIP PATTERNS ❖ 19
RELATIONSHIP AS ATTRIBUTE ♦ 20
RELATIONSHIP OBJECT ♦ 20

COLLECTION OBJECT ♦ 20
ACTIVE VALUE ♦ 20
MUTUAL FRIENDS ♦ 20
BIG BALL OF MUD PATTERN LANGUAGE ❖ 20
BIG BALL OF MUD ♦ 21
THROWAWAY CODE ♦ 21
PIECEMEAL GROWTH ♦ 21
KEEP IT WORKING ♦ 21
SHEARING LAYERS ♦ 21
SWEEPING IT UNDER THE RUG ♦ 21
RECONSTRUCTION ♦ 21
BLACKBOARD ♦ 22
BODYGUARD ♦ 22
BRIDGE ♦ 22
BROKER ♦ 22
BUILDER ♦ 23
BUREAUCRACY ♦ 23
BUSINESS PATTERNS OF
    ASSOCIATION OBJECTS ❖ 23
ASSOCIATION OBJECT ♦ 23
CUSTOMER CONTACT ♦ 23
3-LEVEL ORDER ♦ 24
C++ IDIOMS ❖ 24
HANDLE/BODY ♦ 24
COUNTED BODY ♦ 24
DETACHED COUNTED BODY ♦ 24
HANDLE/BODY HIERARCHY ♦ 24
ENVELOPE/LETTER ♦ 25
VIRTUAL CONSTRUCTOR ♦ 25
CONCRETE DATA TYPE ♦ 25
ALGEBRAIC HIERARCHY ♦ 25
HOMOGENEOUS ADDITION ♦ 25
PROMOTE AND ADD ♦ 26
PROMOTION LADDER ♦ 26
NON-HIERARCHICAL ADDITION ♦ 26
TYPE PROMOTION ♦ 26
CAPABLE, PRODUCTIVE, AND SATISFIED ❖ 26
PRODUCTION POTENTIAL ♦ 26
BOOTSTRAPPING ♦ 26
PROBLEM-ORIENTED TEAM ♦ 27
ROUND PEGS FOR ROUND HOLES ♦ 27
PULSE ♦ 27
DELIVERABLES TO GO ♦ 27
TEAM SPACE ♦ 27
EFFECTIVE HANDOVER ♦ 27
ARRANGING THE FURNITURE ♦ 27
CASCADE ♦ 28
CATERPILLAR'S FATE: A PATTERN
    LANGUAGE FOR THE TRANSFORMATION
    FROM ANALYSIS TO DESIGN ❖ 28
CONCURRENT THREADS OF EXECUTION ♦ 28

SYNCHRONIZATION OF
    CONCURRENT THREADS ♦ 28
COLLABORATIVE WORK PACKETS ♦ 28
WORK PACKET CONTENTS ♦ 28
WORK PACKET STATUS REPORT ♦ 29
WORK PACKET COMPLETION REPORT ♦ 29
WORK PACKET PRIORITY ♦ 29
WORK PACKET SECURITY ♦ 29
SHAPE OF PROGRAM ♦ 29
SYSTEM CITIZEN'S ROLE ♦ 29
DECISION MAKER'S ROLE ♦ 30
WORKERS' ROLE ♦ 30
INTERFACE'S ROLE ♦ 30
INFORMATIONAL ROLE ♦ 30
SMALL FAMILY SYSTEMS ♦ 30
WORK ACCOMPLISHED THROUGH DIALOGS ♦ 30
CRITICAL REGION PROTECTION ♦ 31
EVENT ACQUISITION ♦ 31
EVENT ROUTING ♦ 31
HUMAN INTERFACE ROLE IS A
    SPECIAL INTERFACE ROLE ♦ 31
DATA KNOWS ITS ROOTS ♦ 31
CHAIN OF RESPONSIBILITY ♦ 32
CHECKS: A PATTERN LANGUAGE OF
    INFORMATION INTEGRITY ❖ 32
WHOLE VALUE ♦ 32
EXCEPTIONAL VALUE ♦ 32
MEANINGLESS BEHAVIOR ♦ 32
ECHO BACK ♦ 32
VISIBLE IMPLICATION ♦ 33
DEFERRED VALIDATION ♦ 33
INSTANT PROJECTION ♦ 33
HYPOTHETICAL PUBLICATION ♦ 33
FORECAST CONFIRMATION ♦ 33
DIAGNOSTIC QUERY ♦ 33
CLIENT-DISPATCHER-SERVER ♦ 34
CLIENT-SPECIFIED SELF ♦ 34
COLLECTION OF HISTORY PATTERNS ❖ 34
EDITION ♦ 34
CHANGE LOG ♦ 34
HISTORY ON ASSOCIATION ♦ 34
POSTING ♦ 35
HISTORY ON SELF ♦ 35
MEMENTO CHILD ♦ 35
HISTORY ON TREE ♦ 35
COMMAND ♦ 35
COMMAND PROCESSOR ♦ 36
COMMUNICATING PROCESSES ♦ 36
COMPOSING MULTIMEDIA
    ARTIFACTS FOR REUSE ❖ 36
GLUE ♦ 36
COMPONENTS LAYOUT ♦ 36

TEMPLATE ♦ 36
DEFINE AND RUN PRESENTATION ♦ 36
SYNCHRONIZE CHANNELS ♦ 37
COMPOSITE ♦ 37
CONCURRENT PROGRAMMING IN
    JAVA, SECOND EDITION: DESIGN
    PRINCIPLES AND PATTERNS ❖ 37
METHOD ADAPTERS ♦ 37
SESSION ♦ 37
DOUBLE CHECK ♦ 38
OPEN CALLS ♦ 38
PASS-THROUGH HOST ♦ 38
COPY-ON-WRITE ♦ 38
ATOMIC COMMITMENT ♦ 38
OPEN CONTAINERS ♦ 38
ROLLBACK ♦ 38
ROLL-FORWARD ♦ 39
MULTIPHASE CANCELLATION ♦ 39
CONFLICT SETS ♦ 39
READERS AND WRITERS ♦ 39
VETOABLE CHANGES ♦ 39
THREAD-PER-MESSAGE ♦ 39
WORKER THREADS ♦ 39
EVENT-DRIVEN I/O ♦ 39
FLOW NETWORKS ♦ 40
FUTURES ♦ 40
FORK/JOIN ♦ 40
CONNECTOR ♦ 40
COUNTED POINTER ♦ 40
CREATING REPORTS WITH QUERY OBJECTS ❖ 40
REPORT OBJECTS ♦ 41
QUERY OBJECTS ♦ 41
COMPOSABLE QUERY OBJECTS ♦ 41
FORMULA OBJECTS ♦ 41
CONSTRAINT OBSERVER ♦ 41
CROSSING CHASMS: A PATTERN LANGUAGE FOR
    OBJECT-RDBMS INTEGRATION ❖ 41
TABLE DESIGN TIME ♦ 42
REPRESENTING OBJECTS AS TABLES ♦ 42
REPRESENTING OBJECT RELATIONSHIPS ♦ 42
REPRESENTING INHERITANCE IN
    A RELATIONAL DATABASE ♦ 42
REPRESENTING COLLECTIONS IN
    A RELATIONAL DATABASE ♦ 42
OBJECT IDENTIFIER ♦ 42
FOREIGN KEY REFERENCES ♦ 43
FOREIGN KEY VERSUS DIRECT REFERENCE ♦ 43
CURIOUSLY RECURRING TEMPLATE ♦ 43
CUSTOMER INTERACTION PATTERNS ❖ 43
IT'S A RELATIONSHIP, NOT A SALE ♦ 43
KNOW THE CUSTOMER ♦ 43
BUILD TRUST ♦ 43

LISTEN, LISTEN, LISTEN ♦ 44
BE RESPONSIVE ♦ 44
CUSTOMER MEETINGS: GO EARLY, STAY LATE ♦ 44
SHOW PERSONAL INTEGRITY ♦ 44
TAKE YOUR LICKS ♦ 44
BE AWARE OF BOUNDARIES ♦ 44
MIND YOUR MANNERS ♦ 44
DECISION DEFERRAL AND CAPTURE
    PATTERN LANGUAGE ❖ 45
DECISION-BASED MODELS ♦ 45
APPROPRIATE LIVING MODELS ♦ 45
EXECUTABLE MODELS ♦ 45
UPWARD TRACEABILITY ♦ 45
DOWNWARD CHANGES ♦ 45
DECORATOR ♦ 46
DEFAULT VISITOR ♦ 46
DEMO PREP: A PATTERN LANGUAGE
    FOR THE PREPARATION OF
    SOFTWARE DEMONSTRATIONS ❖ 46
ELEMENT IDENTIFICATION ♦ 46
CATALYTIC SCENARIOS ♦ 47
MUTABLE CODE ♦ 47
PROTOTYPING LANGUAGES ♦ 47
LIGHTWEIGHT USER INTERFACES ♦ 47
JUDICIOUS FIREWORKS ♦ 47
ARCHIVE SCENARIOS ♦ 48
DESIGN PATTERNS FOR OBJECT-ORIENTED
    HYPERMEDIA APPLICATIONS ❖ 48
NAVIGATIONSTRATEGY ♦ 48
NAVIGATIONOBSERVER ♦ 48
DETACHABLE INSPECTOR ♦ 49
DISPLAY MAINTENANCE ❖ 49
DISPLAY LIST ♦ 49
REQUEST UPDATE ♦ 49
GLOBAL UPDATE ♦ 49
PAINTER'S ALGORITHM ♦ 50
CONSOLIDATE REQUESTS ♦ 50
LAZY REDRAW ♦ 50
CLIP REQUESTS ♦ 50
DOUBLE BUFFER ♦ 50
PAGE FLIP ♦ 50
DISTRIBUTED PROCESSES ♦ 51
DOUBLE-CHECKED LOCKING ♦ 51
DRIVER DUTY ♦ 51
DRIVER DUTY CONSTRUCTOR ♦ 51
EPISODES: A PATTERN LANGUAGE
    OF COMPETITIVE DEVELOPMENT ❖ 51
PRODUCT INITIATIVE ♦ 52
MARKET WALK-THROUGH ♦ 52
IMPLIED REQUIREMENTS ♦ 52
WORK QUEUE ♦ 52
WORK GROUP ♦ 52

WORK QUEUE REPORT ♦ 52
COMPARABLE WORK ♦ 52
COMPLETION HEADROOM ♦ 53
DEVELOPMENT EPISODE ♦ 53
INFORMAL LABOR PLAN ♦ 53
WORK SPLIT ♦ 53
RECOMMITMENT MEETING ♦ 53
REQUIREMENT WALK-THROUGH ♦ 54
TECHNICAL MEMO ♦ 54
REFERENCE DATA ♦ 54
PROGRAMMING EPISODE ♦ 54
ESSENCE ♦ 54
EVENT NOTIFICATION ♦ 54
EVENTHANDLER ♦ 55
EVOLUTION, ARCHITECTURE,
    AND METAMORPHOSIS ❖ 55
SOFTWARE TECTONICS ♦ 55
FLEXIBLE FOUNDATIONS ♦ 55
METAMORPHOSIS ♦ 55
EXTENSION OBJECT ♦ 55
EXTERNAL POLYMORPHISM ♦ 56
EXTRINSIC VISITOR ♦ 56
FACADE ♦ 56
FACTORY METHOD ♦ 56
FAULT-TOLERANT TELECOMMUNICATION
    SYSTEM PATTERNS ❖ 57
MINIMIZE HUMAN INTERVENTION ♦ 57
PEOPLE KNOW BEST ♦ 57
FIVE MINUTES OF NO ESCALATION MESSAGES ♦ 57
RIDING OVER TRANSIENTS ♦ 57
LEAKY BUCKET COUNTERS ♦ 57
SICO FIRST AND ALWAYS ♦ 58
TRY ALL HARDWARE COMBOS ♦ 58
FOOL ME ONCE ♦ 58
FEATURE EXTRACTION—A PATTERN
    FOR INFORMATION RETRIEVAL ♦ 58
FINITE STATE MACHINE PATTERNS ❖ 58
BASIC FSM ♦ 58
STATE-DRIVEN TRANSITION ♦ 59
INTERFACE ORGANIZATION ♦ 59
LAYERED ORGANIZATION ♦ 59
MEALLY ♦ 59
MOORE ♦ 59
HYBRID ♦ 59
ENCAPSULATED STATE ♦ 60
DYNAMIC STATE INSTANTIATION ♦ 60
FLEXIBLE COMMAND INTERPRETER ♦ 60
FLYWEIGHT ♦ 60
FORWARDER-RECEIVER ♦ 60
FROM PROTOTYPE TO REALITY ♦ 61
FUNCTIONALITY ALA CARTE ♦ 61

G++: A PATTERN LANGUAGE FOR COMPUTER-INTEGRATED MANUFACTURING ❖ 61
HIERARCHY OF CONTROL LAYERS ♦ 61
VISIBILITY AND COMMUNICATION BETWEEN CONTROL MODULES ♦ 61
CATEGORIZE OBJECTS FOR CONCURRENCY ♦ 62
ACTIONS TRIGGERED BY EVENTS ♦ 62
SERVICES "WAITING FOR" ♦ 62
CLIENT/SERVER/SERVICE ♦ 62
IMPLEMENTATION OF "MULTIPLE KINDS OF SERVICES" CONTROL MODULES ♦ 62
INTERFACE TO CONTROL MODULES ♦ 62
PROTOTYPE AND REALITY ♦ 63
DISTRIBUTION OF CONTROL MODULES ♦ 63
GENERATION GAP ♦ 63
GENERATIVE DEVELOPMENT-PROCESS PATTERN LANGUAGE ❖ 63
SIZE THE ORGANIZATION ♦ 63
SELF-SELECTING TEAM ♦ 63
SOLO VIRTUOSO ♦ 64
SIZE THE SCHEDULE ♦ 64
FORM FOLLOWS FUNCTION ♦ 64
DOMAIN EXPERTISE IN ROLES ♦ 64
PHASING IT IN ♦ 64
APPRENTICE ♦ 64
ORGANIZATION FOLLOWS LOCATION ♦ 64
ORGANIZATION FOLLOWS MARKET ♦ 65
DEVELOPER CONTROLS PROCESS ♦ 65
PATRON ♦ 65
ARCHITECT CONTROLS PRODUCT ♦ 65
CONWAY'S LAW ♦ 65
ARCHITECT ALSO IMPLEMENTS ♦ 65
REVIEW THE ARCHITECTURE ♦ 65
CODE OWNERSHIP ♦ 66
APPLICATION DESIGN IS BOUNDED BY TEST DESIGN ♦ 66
ENGAGE QA ♦ 66
ENGAGE CUSTOMERS ♦ 66
GROUP VALIDATION ♦ 66
SCENARIOS DEFINE PROBLEM ♦ 66
MERCENARY ANALYST ♦ 67
FIRE WALLS ♦ 67
GATEKEEPER ♦ 67
SHAPING CIRCULATION REALMS ♦ 67
MOVE RESPONSIBILITIES ♦ 67
BUFFALO MOUNTAIN ♦ 67
WORK FLOWS INWARD ♦ 68
THREE TO SEVEN HELPERS PER ROLE ♦ 68
NAMED STABLE BASES ♦ 68
DIVIDE AND CONQUER ♦ 68
DECOUPLE STAGES ♦ 68

HUB, SPOKE, AND RIM ♦ 68
AESTHETIC PATTERN ♦ 68
COUPLING DECREASES LATENCY ♦ 69
PROTOTYPE ♦ 69
TAKE NO SMALL SLIPS ♦ 69
DEVELOPING IN PAIRS ♦ 69
INTERRUPTS UNJAM BLOCKING ♦ 69
DON'T INTERRUPT AN INTERRUPT ♦ 69
COMPENSATE SUCCESS ♦ 69
GENERATIVE PATTERN LANGUAGE FOR DISTRIBUTED PROCESSING ❖ 70
DEFINE THE DATA STRUCTURE ♦ 70
IDENTIFY THE NOUNS ♦ 70
FACTOR OUT COMMON ATTRIBUTES ♦ 70
NORMALIZE THE ROLES ♦ 70
IDENTIFY PROBLEM DOMAIN RELATIONSHIPS ♦ 70
INTRODUCE VIRTUAL ATTRIBUTES ♦ 70
ANIMATE THE DATA ♦ 70
TIME THREAD ANALYSIS ♦ 71
DETERMINE THE ACTORS ♦ 71
HALF-OBJECT + PROTOCOL ♦ 71
HALF-SYNC/HALF-ASYNC ♦ 71
HIGH-LEVEL AND PROCESS PATTERNS FROM THE MEMORY PRESERVATION SOCIETY ❖ 71
THINK SMALL ♦ 72
MEMORY BUDGET ♦ 72
MEMORY OVERDRAFT ♦ 72
MAKE THE USER WORRY ♦ 72
PARTIAL FAILURE ♦ 72
CAPTAIN OATES ♦ 72
EXHAUSTION TEST ♦ 73
MEMORY PERFORMANCE ASSESSMENT ♦ 73
HOOK METHOD ♦ 73
IDENTIFY THE CHAMPION PATTERN LANGUAGE ❖ 73
IDENTIFY THE CHAMPION ♦ 73
EXPERTS REVIEW PAPERS ♦ 73
CHAMPIONS REVIEW PAPERS ♦ 74
MAKE CHAMPIONS EXPLICIT ♦ 74
IDENTIFY THE CONFLICTS ♦ 74
IDENTIFY MISSING CHAMPIONS ♦ 74
CHAMPIONS SPEAK FIRST ♦ 74
CONSENSUS ON PC PAPERS ♦ 74
IMPLEMENTATION PATTERNS FOR THE OBSERVER PATTERN ❖ 74
CONDUIT OF SUBJECT CHANGE ♦ 75
ONE MESSAGE PER CHANGE REQUEST ♦ 75
ONE MESSAGE PER AFFECTED OBJECT ♦ 75
OPTIMIZED MESSAGES PER CHANGE REQUEST ♦ 75
MESSAGE PACKET ♦ 75
OBSERVER UPDATE MESSAGE ♦ 75

IMPROVING RESPONSIVENESS IN INTERACTIVE APPLICATIONS USING QUEUES ❖ 76
EVENT QUEUE ♦ 76
MERGE COMPATIBLE EVENTS ♦ 76
HANDLE ARTIFICIAL EVENTS ♦ 76
DECOUPLE EXECUTION AND OUTPUT ♦ 76
INPUT AND OUTPUT PATTERN LANGUAGE ❖ 76
MML ♦ 77
IO GATEKEEPER ♦ 77
MIND YOUR OWN BUSINESS ♦ 77
IO TRIAGE ♦ 77
TIMESTAMP ♦ 77
WHO ASKED? ♦ 78
GEORGE WASHINGTON IS STILL DEAD ♦ 78
BOTTOM LINE ♦ 78
FIVE MINUTES OF NO ESCALATION MESSAGES ♦ 78
SHUT UP AND LISTEN ♦ 79
PSEUDO-IO ♦ 79
BELTLINE TERMINAL ♦ 79
AUDIBLE ALARM ♦ 79
ALARM GRID ♦ 79
OFFICE ALARMS ♦ 79
DON'T LET THEM FORGET ♦ 79
STRING A WIRE ♦ 80
RAW IO ♦ 80
INTERPRETER ♦ 80
ITERABLE CONTAINER ♦ 80
ITERATOR ♦ 80
JUDGE ♦ 81
LAYERS ♦ 81
LAZY OPTIMIZATION: PATTERNS FOR EFFICIENT SMALLTALK PROGRAMMING ❖ 81
PERFORMANCE ASSESSMENT ♦ 81
LAZY OPTIMIZATION ♦ 81
PERFORMANCE CRITERIA ♦ 82
THRESHOLD SWITCH ♦ 82
PERFORMANCE MEASUREMENT ♦ 82
HOT SPOT ♦ 82
EXPERIMENT ♦ 82
CACHEABLE EXPRESSION ♦ 82
CACHING TEMPORARY VARIABLE ♦ 83
CACHING ARGUMENT ♦ 83
CACHING STATE VARIABLE ♦ 83
SIMPLIFICATION ♦ 83
TRANSIENT REDUCTION ♦ 83
OBJECT TRANSFORMATION ♦ 83
HYPOTH-A-SIZED COLLECTION ♦ 84
CONCATENATING STREAM ♦ 84
LIFE CYCLE AND REFACTORING PATTERNS THAT SUPPORT EVOLUTION AND REUSE ❖ 84
PROTOTYPE A FIRST-PASS DESIGN ♦ 84
EXPAND THE INITIAL PROTOTYPE ♦ 84

CONSOLIDATE THE PROGRAM TO SUPPORT EVOLUTION AND REUSE ♦ 85
EVOLVE AGGREGATIONS FROM INHERITANCE HIERARCHIES ♦ 85
CREATE ABSTRACT SUPERCLASS ♦ 85
LOCALIZED OWNERSHIP: MANAGING DYNAMIC OBJECTS IN C++ ❖ 85
CREATOR AS SOLE OWNER ♦ 85
SEQUENCE OF OWNERS ♦ 85
SHARED OWNERSHIP ♦ 86
MANAGER ♦ 86
MASTER-SLAVE ♦ 86
MEDIATOR ♦ 86
MEMBER CONTAINER ♦ 86
MEMENTO ♦ 87
MICROKERNEL ♦ 87
MODEL-VIEW-CONTROLLER ♦ 87
MOODS: MODELS FOR OBJECT-ORIENTED DESIGN OF STATE ❖ 87
TO SIMPLIFY COMPLEX BEHAVIOR, USE DECOMPOSITION ♦ 88
FOR OBJECTS WITH MOODS, USE STATE CLASSES ♦ 88
WHEN EVENTS CAUSE MOODS, USE STATE MACHINE ♦ 88
FOR STATE MACHINES, USE TRANSITION METHODS ♦ 88
WHEN STATES ARE CONDITIONS, USE PREDICATIVE STATE CLASSES ♦ 88
WHEN STATES ARE ASSOCIATIONS, USE STATE OBJECTS ♦ 89
FOR COMPLEX MOODS, USE A MOOD ALTERNATOR ♦ 89
WHEN THERE ARE MANY MOODS, USE MOOD CLASSIFIER ♦ 89
NEW CLIENTS WITH OLD SERVERS: A PATTERN LANGUAGE FOR CLIENT/SERVER FRAMEWORKS ❖ 89
EXCEPTION ♦ 89
SOLITAIRE ♦ 89
OBJECTS FROM RECORDS ♦ 90
REQUEST ♦ 90
MATERIALIZATION ♦ 90
FINALIZATION ♦ 90
IDENTITY MANAGEMENT ♦ 90
MEGA-SCROLLING ♦ 90
SEARCHING FOR BUSINESS OBJECTS ♦ 90
DEPENDENCY ♦ 91
CREATING AND UPDATING BUSINESS OBJECTS ♦ 91
FACTORY METHOD ♦ 91
WINDOW-KEEPING ♦ 91
VIEWING ♦ 91
CLIENT/SERVER FRAMEWORK ♦ 91

NULL OBJECT ♦ 91
OBJECT RECOVERY ♦ 92
OBJECT RECURSION ♦ 92
OBJECT SYNCHRONIZER ♦ 92
OBJECT-ORIENTED DESIGN PATTERNS
    IN REACTIVE SYSTEMS ❖ 92
  OBJECT-ORIENTED SIMULATION ♦ 93
  OBJECTIFY THE EVENTS ♦ 93
  OBJECTIFY SYSTEM STATE ♦ 93
  OBJECTS WITH REMOTE CONTROL ♦ 93
  EVENT-DRIVEN RPC ♦ 93
OBSERVER ♦ 94
ORGANIZATIONAL MULTIPLEXING: PATTERNS
    FOR PROCESSING SATELLITE TELEMETRY
    WITH DISTRIBUTED TEAMS ❖ 94
  LOOSE INTERFACES ♦ 94
  PARSER/BUILDER ♦ 94
  HIERARCHY OF FACTORIES ♦ 94
  HANDLERS ♦ 95
ORGANIZATIONAL PATTERNS FOR TEAMS ❖ 95
  DESIGN BY TEAM ♦ 95
  UNITY OF PURPOSE ♦ 95
  DIVERSITY OF MEMBERSHIP ♦ 95
  LOCK 'EM UP TOGETHER ♦ 95
  VALIDATION BY TEAMS ♦ 96
PANEL STATES ♦ 96
PARTIES & MEDIA AS FIRST
    CLASS CITIZENS ♦ 96
PARTITIONING SMALLTALK CODE INTO
    ENVY/DEVELOPER COMPONENTS ❖ 96
  LAYERED AND SECTIONED ARCHITECTURE ♦ 96
  LAYER IN AN APPLICATION ♦ 96
  SECTION IN A SUBAPPLICATION ♦ 97
  TWO APPLICATIONS ♦ 97
  NO SUBAPPLICATIONS ♦ 97
PATTERN AS A CLASS ♦ 97
PATTERN FOR SEPARATING
    ASSEMBLY AND PROCESSING ♦ 97
PATTERN LANGUAGE FOR AN
    ESSAY-BASED WEB SITE ❖ 97
  NATURAL TEXT FLOW ♦ 98
  NATURAL TEXT HYPERLINKS ♦ 98
  NATURAL TEXT DIRECTORIES ♦ 98
  REFERENCE SECTION ♦ 98
  EXPOSABLE GUTS ♦ 98
  WORKSHEET DOCUMENTS ♦ 98
  NEW DOCUMENT NOTIFICATION ♦ 99
  14.4 KBPS TESTING ♦ 99
PATTERN LANGUAGE FOR DEVELOPING
    FORM STYLE WINDOWS ❖ 99
  SUBFORM ♦ 99
  ALTERNATIVE SUBFORMS ♦ 99

SUBFORM SELECTION ♦ 99
SUBFORM MATCH ♦ 100
SUBFORM MISMATCH ♦ 100
PATTERN LANGUAGE FOR IMPROVING THE
    CAPACITY OF REACTIVE SYSTEMS ❖ 100
  CAPACITY BOTTLENECK ♦ 100
  PROCESSING CAPACITY ♦ 100
  OPTIMIZE HIGH-RUNNER CASES ♦ 100
  SHED LOAD ♦ 101
  FINISH WORK IN PROGRESS ♦ 101
  FRESH WORK BEFORE STALE ♦ 101
  MATCH PROGRESS WORK WITH NEW ♦ 101
  SHARE THE LOAD ♦ 101
  WORK SHED AT PERIPHERY ♦ 102
  LEAKY BUCKET OF CREDITS ♦ 102
PATTERN LANGUAGE FOR
    PATTERN WRITING ❖ 102
  PATTERN ♦ 102
  PATTERN LANGUAGE ♦ 102
  MANDATORY ELEMENTS PRESENT ♦ 102
  OPTIONAL ELEMENTS WHEN HELPFUL ♦ 103
  VISIBLE FORCES ♦ 103
  SINGLE-PASS READABLE ♦ 103
  SKIPPABLE SECTIONS ♦ 103
  FINDABLE SECTIONS ♦ 103
  RELATIONSHIPS TO OTHER PATTERNS ♦ 103
  READABLE REFERENCES TO PATTERNS ♦ 104
  PATTERN THUMBNAIL ♦ 104
  EVOCATIVE PATTERN NAME ♦ 104
  NOUN PHRASE NAME ♦ 104
  MEANINGFUL METAPHOR NAME ♦ 104
  INTENT CATALOG ♦ 104
  CLEAR TARGET AUDIENCE ♦ 104
  TERMINOLOGY TAILORED TO AUDIENCE ♦ 105
  UNDERSTOOD NOTATIONS ♦ 105
  CODE SAMPLES ♦ 105
  CODE SAMPLES AS BONUS ♦ 105
  PATTERN LANGUAGE SUMMARY ♦ 105
  PROBLEM/SOLUTION SUMMARY ♦ 105
  COMMON PROBLEMS HIGHLIGHTED ♦ 106
  RUNNING EXAMPLE ♦ 106
  DISTINCTIVE HEADINGS
    CONVEY STRUCTURE ♦ 106
  GLOSSARY ♦ 106
PATTERN LANGUAGE FOR SMALLTALK
    & RELATIONAL DATABASES ❖ 106
  FOUR-LAYER ARCHITECTURE ♦ 106
  TABLE DESIGN TIME ♦ 107
  REPRESENTING OBJECTS AS TABLES ♦ 107
  OBJECT IDENTIFIER ♦ 107
  REPRESENTING OBJECT RELATIONSHIPS ♦ 107
  REPRESENTING COLLECTIONS ♦ 107

FOREIGN KEY REFERENCES ♦ 108
BROKER ♦ 108
OBJECT METADATA ♦ 108
QUERY OBJECT ♦ 108
CLIENT SYNCHRONIZATION ♦ 109
CACHE MANAGEMENT ♦ 109
PATTERN LANGUAGE FOR TOOL CONSTRUCTION
    AND INTEGRATION BASED ON THE TOOLS
    AND MATERIALS METAPHOR ❖ 109
MATERIALS ♦ 109
TOOLS ♦ 109
ASPECTS ♦ 109
ENVIRONMENT ♦ 110
TOOL AND MATERIAL COUPLING ♦ 110
TOOL COMPOSITION ♦ 110
SEPARATION OF POWERS ♦ 110
EVENT MECHANISM ♦ 110
IP/FP PLUG IN ♦ 111
MATERIAL CONTAINER ♦ 111
TOOL COORDINATOR ♦ 111
PATTERN LANGUAGE FOR
    WRITERS' WORKSHOPS ❖ 111
OPEN REVIEW ♦ 111
SAFE SETTING ♦ 111
AUTHORS ARE EXPERTS ♦ 111
WORKSHOP COMPRISES AUTHORS ♦ 112
COMMUNITY OF TRUST ♦ 112
MODERATOR GUIDES THE WORKSHOP ♦ 112
SITTING IN A CIRCLE ♦ 112
AUTHORS' CIRCLE ♦ 112
READING JUST BEFORE REVIEWING ♦ 112
AUTHOR READS SELECTION ♦ 112
FLY ON THE WALL ♦ 112
VOLUNTEER SUMMARIZES THE WORK ♦ 113
POSITIVE FEEDBACK FIRST ♦ 113
SUGGESTIONS FOR IMPROVEMENT ♦ 113
AUTHOR ASKS FOR CLARIFICATION ♦ 113
POSITIVE CLOSURE ♦ 113
THANK THE AUTHOR ♦ 113
CLEARING THE PALATE ♦ 113
SELECTIVE CHANGES ♦ 114
PATTERN LANGUAGE OF TRANSPORT
    SYSTEMS (POINT AND ROUTE) ❖ 114
POINT ♦ 114
ROUTE ♦ 114
PATTERN SYSTEM FOR NETWORK
    MANAGEMENT INTERFACES ❖ 114
MANAGER-AGENT ♦ 114
MANAGED OBJECT ♦ 115
REMOTE OPERATION ♦ 115
PATTERN-BASED INTEGRATION
    ARCHITECTURES ❖ 115

(LEGACY) WRAPPER ♦ 115
WORK FLOW MANAGER ♦ 115
BROKER ♦ 115
SHARED REPOSITORY ♦ 115
PATTERNS FOR CLASSROOM EDUCATION ❖ 116
ITERATIVE COURSE DEVELOPMENT ♦ 116
CHICKEN AND EGG ♦ 116
MIX NEW AND OLD ♦ 116
PITFALL DIAGNOSIS AND PREVENTION ♦ 116
MODULE'S STORY ♦ 116
SEVEN PARTS ♦ 116
VISIBLE CHECKLIST ♦ 117
ACQUAINTANCE EXAMPLES ♦ 117
EXAMPLE LASTS ONE WEEK ♦ 117
REFERENCE EXAMPLES ♦ 117
COLORFUL ANALOGY ♦ 117
SIMULATION GAMES ♦ 117
QUIZ GAMES ♦ 118
DEBRIEF AFTER ACTIVITIES ♦ 118
PATTERNS FOR DESIGNING IN TEAMS ❖ 118
MULTIPLE COMPETING DESIGNS ♦ 118
DECISION DOCUMENT ♦ 118
CREATOR-REVIEWER ♦ 119
MASTER-JOURNEYMAN ♦ 119
AD-HOC CORRECTIONS ♦ 119
PATTERNS FOR DESIGNING NAVIGABLE
    INFORMATION SPACES ❖ 119
SET-BASED NAVIGATION ♦ 119
NODES IN CONTEXT ♦ 119
ACTIVE REFERENCE ♦ 120
NEWS ♦ 120
LANDMARK ♦ 120
BASKET ♦ 120
PATTERNS FOR ENCAPSULATING
    CLASS TREES ❖ 120
CLASS RETRIEVAL ♦ 120
LATE CREATION ♦ 120
CLASS CLAUSE ♦ 121
CLASS SPECIFICATION ♦ 121
CLASS SEMANTICS ♦ 121
PATTERNS FOR EVOLVING FRAMEWORKS ❖ 121
THREE EXAMPLES ♦ 121
WHITE-BOX FRAMEWORKS ♦ 121
COMPONENT LIBRARY ♦ 122
HOT SPOTS ♦ 122
PLUGGABLE OBJECTS ♦ 122
FINE-GRAINED OBJECTS ♦ 122
BLACK-BOX FRAMEWORK ♦ 122
VISUAL BUILDER ♦ 123
LANGUAGE TOOLS ♦ 123
PATTERNS FOR GENERATING A
    LAYERED ARCHITECTURE ❖ 123

PEDESTAL ♦ 123
BRIDGE ♦ 123
SYMMETRICAL REUSE ♦ 123
ELEVATE REFERENCES TO ENHANCE REUSE ♦ 124

PATTERNS FOR LOGGING DIAGNOSTIC MESSAGES ❖ 124
DIAGNOSTIC LOGGER ♦ 124
DIAGNOSTIC CONTEXT ♦ 124
TYPED DIAGNOSTICS ♦ 124

PATTERNS FOR SOFTWARE ARCHITECTURES ❖ 124
PIPELINE ♦ 125
DATA ABSTRACTION OR OBJECT-ORIENTED ♦ 125
IMPLICIT INVOCATION OR EVENT-BASED ♦ 125
REPOSITORY ♦ 125
INTERPRETER ♦ 125
MAIN PLUS SUBROUTINES ♦ 125
LAYERED ARCHITECTURE ♦ 125

PATTERNS FOR SYSTEM TESTING ❖ 126
TESTER'S MORE IMPORTANT THAN THE TEST CASES ♦ 126
DESIGNERS ARE OUR FRIENDS ♦ 126
GET INVOLVED EARLY ♦ 126
TIME TO TEST ♦ 126
TAKE TIME ♦ 126
"UNCHANGED" INTERFACES ♦ 127
AMBIGUOUS DOCUMENTATION ♦ 127
USE OLD PROBLEM REPORTS ♦ 127
PROBLEM AREA ♦ 127
BUSY SYSTEM ♦ 127
DON'T TRUST SIMULATIONS ♦ 127
END USER VIEWPOINT ♦ 127
UNUSUAL TIMING ♦ 128
MULTIPLE PROCESSORS ♦ 128
SCRATCH 'N SNIFF ♦ 128
STRANGE BEHAVIOR ♦ 128
KILLER TEST ♦ 128
DOCUMENT THE PROBLEM ♦ 128
ADOPT-A-PROBLEM ♦ 128
PET PEEVE ♦ 129

PATTERNS OF EVENTS ❖ 129
EVENT-CENTERED ARCHITECTURE ♦ 129
CLASSES OF EVENT OBJECTS ♦ 129
FINE-GRAINED CLASSIFICATION OF EVENTS ♦ 129
OBJECT-ORIENTED STATE MACHINE ♦ 129

PATTERNS ON THE FLY ❖ 130
TRAIN HARD FIGHT EASY ♦ 130
TRAIN THE TRAINER ♦ 130
TRIAL PROJECT ♦ 130
CASUAL DUTY ♦ 130
GURU DOES ALL ♦ 130
CULT OF PERSONALITY ♦ 130

CARGO CULT ♦ 131
CONTAINMENT BUILDING ♦ 131
DOORMAT ♦ 131
LET'S PLAY TEAM ♦ 131
LONG POLE IN THE TENT ♦ 131
PEACEMAKER ♦ 131
SACRIFICIAL LAMB ♦ 131
SCHEDULE CHICKEN ♦ 132

PIPES & FILTERS ♦ 132
PLUGGABLE FACTORY ♦ 132
PLUGGABLE FACTORY ♦ 132
PLUGGABLE VIEW CONTROLLER ♦ 132
POCKET-SIZED BROKER ❖ 133
TRANSCEIVER-PARCEL ♦ 133
BROKER AS INTERMEDIARY ♦ 133
BROKER AS DIVORCE ATTORNEY ♦ 133
BROKER AS MATCHMAKER ♦ 133

POINTS AND DEVIATIONS: PATTERN LANGUAGE OF FIRE ALARM SYSTEMS ❖ 133
DEVIATION ♦ 134
POINT ♦ 134
POOL ♦ 134
LAZY STATE ♦ 134
PERIODIC OBJECT ♦ 134
DATA PUMP ♦ 135

PRESENTATION-ABSTRACTION-CONTROL ♦ 135
PRIORITIZING FORCES IN SOFTWARE DESIGN ❖ 135
PROTECTED VARIATIONS ♦ 135
PERSISTENCE ACCESSORS ♦ 135
SKILL MIX ♦ 135
THREE SUBSYSTEMS ♦ 135
GENERIC UI, SPECIFIC UI ♦ 136
GENERICS AND SPECIFICS ♦ 136
APPLICATION BOUNDARY ♦ 136
SPLIT VALIDATION ♦ 136
EDITS INSIDE ♦ 136
SUBCLASS PER TEAM ♦ 136
MODEL HIERARCHY ♦ 136
FACADE ♦ 137
DOMAIN INTERCEPTS ♦ 137

PROACTOR ♦ 137
PROCESS CONTROL ♦ 137
PRODUCT TRADER ♦ 138
PROPAGATOR: A FAMILY OF PATTERNS ❖ 138
STRICT PROPAGATOR ♦ 138
STRICT PROPAGATOR WITH FAILURE ♦ 138
LAZY PROPAGATOR ♦ 138
ADAPTIVE PROPAGATOR ♦ 138

PROTOTYPE ♦ 138
PROTOTYPE-BASED OBJECT SYSTEM ♦ 139

PROXY ♦ 139
PROXY DESIGN PATTERN REVISITED ♦ 139
PUBLISHER-SUBSCRIBER ♦ 139
RAPPeL: A REQUIREMENTS-ANALYSIS
    PROCESS PATTERN LANGUAGE FOR
    OBJECT-ORIENTED DEVELOPMENT ❖ 140
  BUILDING THE RIGHT THINGS ♦ 140
  MANAGING AND MEETING
      CUSTOMER EXPECTATIONS ♦ 140
  CUSTOMER RAPPORT ♦ 140
  SPONSOR OBJECTIVES ♦ 140
  DEFINING REQUIREMENTS ♦ 140
  PROBLEM DOMAIN ANALYSIS ♦ 141
  INFORMATION NEEDS ♦ 141
  FINDING AND DEFINING THE
      DOMAIN OBJECTS ♦ 141
  CLASSIFYING, ASSOCIATING, AND
      GROUPING THE DOMAIN OBJECTS ♦ 141
  ELABORATION OF THE DOMAIN OBJECTS ♦ 141
  OBJECT AGING ♦ 141
  OBJECT STEREOTYPES ♦ 141
  BEHAVIORAL REQUIREMENTS ♦ 142
  ENVISIONING ♦ 142
  REQUIREMENTS SPECIFICATION ♦ 142
  BUSINESS RULES ♦ 142
  PRAGMATIC EXTERNAL REQUIREMENTS ♦ 142
  USER INTERFACE REQUIREMENTS ♦ 142
  PROTOTYPES ♦ 142
  REQUIREMENTS VALIDATION ♦ 143
REACTOR ♦ 143
RECOVERABLE DISTRIBUTOR ♦ 143
RECURSIVE CONTROL ♦ 143
REFLECTION ♦ 144
REMOTE CONTROL ♦ 144
REQUEST SCREEN MODIFICATION ♦ 144
RESOURCE EXCHANGER ♦ 144
REUSABILITY THROUGH
    SELF-ENCAPSULATION ❖ 145
  DEFINE CLASSES BY BEHAVIOR, NOT STATE ♦ 145
  IMPLEMENT BEHAVIOR WITH
      ABSTRACT STATE ♦ 145
  IDENTIFY MESSAGE LAYERS ♦ 145
  DEFER IDENTIFICATION OF
      STATE VARIABLES ♦ 145
  ENCAPSULATE CONCRETE STATE ♦ 145
  USE LAZY INITIALIZATION ♦ 145
  DEFINE DEFAULT VALUES VIA
      EXPLICIT PROTOCOL ♦ 146
ROLE OBJECT ♦ 146
ROUTER ♦ 146

SCRUM: A PATTERN LANGUAGE
    FOR HYPERPRODUCTIVE
    SOFTWARE DEVELOPMENT ❖ 146
  SPRINT ♦ 146
  BACKLOG ♦ 146
  SCRUM MEETINGS ♦ 147
SELECTING LOCKING DESIGNS FOR
    PARALLEL PROGRAMS ❖ 147
  SEQUENTIAL PROGRAM ♦ 147
  CODE LOCKING ♦ 147
  DATA LOCKING ♦ 147
  DATA OWNERSHIP ♦ 147
  PARALLEL FASTPATH ♦ 147
  READER/WRITER LOCKING ♦ 147
  HIERARCHICAL LOCKING ♦ 148
  ALLOCATOR CACHES ♦ 148
  CRITICAL-SECTION FUSING ♦ 148
  CRITICAL-SECTION PARTITIONING ♦ 148
SELECTING LOCKING PRIMITIVES FOR
    PARALLEL PROGRAMMING ❖ 148
  TEST-AND-SET LOCK ♦ 148
  QUEUED LOCK ♦ 149
  QUEUED READER/WRITER LOCK ♦ 149
  COUNTER READER/WRITER LOCK ♦ 149
  DISTRIBUTED READER/WRITER LOCK ♦ 149
SELFISH CLASS PATTERN LANGUAGE ❖ 149
  SELFISH CLASS ♦ 150
  WORKS OUT OF THE BOX ♦ 150
  LOW SURFACE-TO-VOLUME RATIO ♦ 150
  GENTLE LEARNING CURVE ♦ 150
  PROGRAMMING-BY-DIFFERENCE ♦ 150
  FIRST ONE'S FREE ♦ 151
  WINNING TEAM ♦ 151
SERIALIZER ♦ 151
SERVICE CONFIGURATOR ♦ 151
SESSION CONTROL & OBSERVATION ♦ 151
SHOPPER ♦ 152
SINGLETON ♦ 152
SMALLTALK BEST PRACTICE PATTERNS ❖ 152
  COMPOSED METHOD ♦ 152
  CONSTRUCTOR METHOD ♦ 152
  CONSTRUCTOR PARAMETER METHOD ♦ 152
  SHORTCUT CONSTRUCTOR METHOD ♦ 152
  CONVERSION ♦ 153
  CONVERTER METHOD ♦ 153
  CONVERTER CONSTRUCTOR METHOD ♦ 153
  QUERY METHOD ♦ 153
  COMPARING METHOD ♦ 153
  REVERSING METHOD ♦ 153
  METHOD OBJECT ♦ 153
  EXECUTE AROUND METHOD ♦ 154
  DEBUG PRINTING METHOD ♦ 154

METHOD COMMENT ♦ 154
MESSAGE ♦ 154
CHOOSING MESSAGE ♦ 154
DECOMPOSING MESSAGE ♦ 154
INTENTION REVEALING MESSAGE ♦ 154
INTENTION REVEALING SELECTOR ♦ 154
DISPATCHED INTERPRETATION ♦ 155
DOUBLE DISPATCH ♦ 155
MEDIATING PROTOCOL ♦ 155
SUPER ♦ 155
EXTENDING SUPER ♦ 155
MODIFYING SUPER ♦ 155
DELEGATION ♦ 155
SIMPLE DELEGATION ♦ 155
SELF DELEGATION ♦ 155
PLUGGABLE BEHAVIOR ♦ 156
PLUGGABLE SELECTOR ♦ 156
PLUGGABLE BLOCK ♦ 156
COLLECTING PARAMETER ♦ 156
COMMON STATE ♦ 156
VARIABLE STATE ♦ 156
EXPLICIT INITIALIZATION ♦ 156
LAZY INITIALIZATION ♦ 157
DEFAULT VALUE METHOD ♦ 157
CONSTANT METHOD ♦ 157
DIRECT VARIABLE ACCESS ♦ 157
INDIRECT VARIABLE ACCESS ♦ 157
GETTING METHOD ♦ 157
SETTING METHOD ♦ 157
COLLECTION ACCESSOR METHOD ♦ 157
ENUMERATION METHOD ♦ 158
BOOLEAN PROPERTY SETTING METHOD ♦ 158
ROLE SUGGESTING INSTANCE
    VARIABLE NAME ♦ 158
TEMPORARY VARIABLE ♦ 158
COLLECTING TEMPORARY VARIABLE ♦ 158
CACHING TEMPORARY VARIABLE ♦ 158
EXPLAINING TEMPORARY VARIABLE ♦ 158
REUSING TEMPORARY VARIABLE ♦ 158
ROLE SUGGESTING TEMPORARY
    VARIABLE NAME ♦ 158
COLLECTION ♦ 159
ORDERED COLLECTION ♦ 159
RUN ARRAY ♦ 159
SET ♦ 159
EQUALITY METHOD ♦ 159
HASHING METHOD ♦ 159
DICTIONARY ♦ 159
SORTED COLLECTION ♦ 159
ARRAY ♦ 159
BYTE ARRAY ♦ 159
INTERVAL ♦ 160

IS EMPTY ♦ 160
INCLUDES: ♦ 160
CONCATENATION ♦ 160
ENUMERATION ♦ 160
DO ♦ 160
COLLECT ♦ 160
SELECT/REJECT ♦ 160
DETECT ♦ 160
INJECT:INTO: ♦ 161
DUPLICATE REMOVING SET ♦ 161
TEMPORARILY SORTED COLLECTION ♦ 161
STACK ♦ 161
QUEUE ♦ 161
SEARCHING LITERAL ♦ 161
LOOKUP CACHE ♦ 161
PARSING STREAM ♦ 161
CONCATENATING STREAM ♦ 162
SIMPLE SUPERCLASS NAME ♦ 162
QUALIFIED SUBCLASS NAME ♦ 162
INLINE MESSAGE PATTERN ♦ 162
TYPE SUGGESTING PARAMETER NAME ♦ 162
INDENTED CONTROL FLOW ♦ 162
RECTANGULAR BLOCK ♦ 162
GUARD CLAUSE ♦ 162
CONDITIONAL EXPRESSION ♦ 163
SIMPLE ENUMERATION PARAMETER ♦ 163
CASCADE ♦ 163
YOURSELF ♦ 163
INTERESTING RETURN VALUE ♦ 163
SMALLTALK SCAFFOLDING PATTERNS ❖ 163
EXTENSIBLE ATTRIBUTES ♦ 163
ARTIFICIAL ACCESSORS ♦ 163
GENERATED ACCESSORS ♦ 164
ARTIFICIAL DELEGATION ♦ 164
CACHED EXTENSIBILITY ♦ 164
SELECTOR SYNTHESIS ♦ 164
SPONSOR-SELECTOR ♦ 164
**STARS: A PATTERN LANGUAGE FOR
    QUERY-OPTIMIZED SCHEMAS** ❖ 164
QUERY OPTIMIZED DATABASE ♦ 165
WHOLE BUSINESS ENTITIES ♦ 165
KEY BUSINESS ACTIVITIES AND INFLUENCES ♦ 165
TRANSACTION HISTORY ♦ 165
PEOPLE, PLACES, AND THINGS ♦ 165
TIME ♦ 165
DIMENSION ROLL-UP ♦ 165
STATE ♦ 166
STATE PATTERNS ❖ 166
STATE OBJECT ♦ 166
STATE MEMBER ♦ 166
PURE STATE ♦ 166
EXPOSED STATE ♦ 166

STATE-DRIVEN TRANSITIONS ♦ 167
OWNER-DRIVEN TRANSITIONS ♦ 167
DEFAULT STATE ♦ 167
STATE TRANSITION SYSTEMS ♦ 167
STRATEGY ♦ 167
STREAMS ♦ 167
SURROGATE ♦ 168
**SURVIVING OBJECT-ORIENTED PROJECTS:
  A MANAGER'S GUIDE** ❖ 168
CLEAR THE FOG ♦ 168
EARLY AND REGULAR DELIVERY ♦ 168
PROTOTYPE ♦ 168
MICROCOSM ♦ 168
HOLISTIC DIVERSITY ♦ 169
GOLD RUSH ♦ 169
OWNER PER DELIVERABLE ♦ 169
FUNCTION OWNERS/COMPONENT OWNERS ♦ 169
SOMEONE ALWAYS MAKES PROGRESS ♦ 169
TEAM PER TASK ♦ 169
SACRIFICE ONE PERSON ♦ 170
DAY CARE ♦ 170
**TEAMWORK AND CONFIGURATION
  MANAGEMENT** ❖ 170
PRIVATE VERSIONING ♦ 170
INCREMENTAL INTEGRATION ♦ 170
INDEPENDENT WORKSPACES ♦ 171
TEMPLATE METHOD ♦ 171
TEMPORAL PATTERNS ❖ 171
TEMPORAL PROPERTY ♦ 171
TEMPORAL ASSOCIATION ♦ 172
SNAPSHOT ♦ 172
THREAD-SPECIFIC STORAGE ♦ 172
THREE-LEVEL FSM ♦ 172
TRANSACTIONS AND ACCOUNTS ❖ 172
BUSINESS TRANSACTIONS ♦ 173
SEPARATE TRANSACTION PROCESSING
  FROM ARCHIVAL ♦ 173
BUSINESS ACCOUNTS ♦ 173
COMPOSITE TRANSACTIONS ♦ 173
ADJUSTING TRANSACTIONS ♦ 173
MONTH END CLOSING ♦ 173
EXPLICIT BUSINESS RULES ♦ 173
CONTINUOUS PROCESSING ♦ 174
**TROPYC: A PATTERN LANGUAGE FOR
  CRYPTOGRAPHIC SOFTWARE** ❖ 174
SECURE-CHANNEL COMMUNICATION ♦ 174
INFORMATION SECRECY ♦ 174

MESSAGE INTEGRITY ♦ 174
SENDER AUTHENTICATION ♦ 174
SIGNATURE ♦ 175
SECRECY WITH INTEGRITY ♦ 175
SECRECY WITH SENDER AUTHENTICATION ♦ 175
SECRECY WITH SIGNATURE ♦ 175
SIGNATURE WITH APPENDIX ♦ 175
SECRECY WITH SIGNATURE WITH APPENDIX ♦ 175
TYPE OBJECT ♦ 176
**UNDERSTANDING AND USING THE
  VALUEMODEL FRAMEWORK IN
  VISUALWORKS SMALLTALK** ❖ 176
USE A VALUEMODEL TO GENERALIZE
  AN OBJECT'S ASPECT ♦ 176
USE A VALUEMODEL TO SHARE A VALUE ♦ 176
USE ONCHANGESEND:TO: TO REGISTER
  INTERESTS ON A VALUE ♦ 176
USE VALUEMODEL CHAINS INSTEAD
  OF ONCHANGESEND:TO: ♦ 176
ENCAPSULATE SENDERS OF
  VALUE AND VALUE: ♦ 177
ENSURE THAT ALL OBJECTS SHARING A VALUE
  USE THE SAME VALUEMODEL ♦ 177
MAINTAIN CONSISTENT
  VALUEMODELVALUE TYPES ♦ 177
USE A VALUEHOLDER TO HOLD A
  STAND-ALONE OBJECT ♦ 177
USE AN ASPECTADAPTOR TO HOLD
  AN ASPECT OF AN OBJECT ♦ 177
USE A BUFFEREDVALUEHOLDER TO DELAY
  THE COMMIT OF A NEW VALUE ♦ 177
USE A RANGEADAPTOR TO CHANNEL
  A NUMBER'S RANGE ♦ 177
USE AN INDEXEDADAPTOR TO HOLD A
  SINGLE INDEX IN A COLLECTION ♦ 177
USE A SLOTADAPTOR TO HOLD A
  SINGLE INSTANCE VARIABLE ♦ 178
USE A PLUGGABLEADAPTOR TO HOLD
  SOME PART OF AN OBJECT ♦ 178
USE A TYPECONVERTER TO CONVERT
  A VALUE BETWEEN TYPES ♦ 178
USE A SCROLLVALUEHOLDER TO HOLD A
  POSITION IN n-DIMENSIONAL SPACE ♦ 178
USE SELECTIONINLIST TO HOLD A
  LIST AND ITS SELECTION ♦ 178
VIEW HANDLER ♦ 178
VISITOR ♦ 179
WHOLE-PART ♦ 179
WRAPPER FACADE ♦ 179
WRITE A LOOP ONCE ♦ 179

Categories

Categories of entries appear in alphabetical order, each category followed by patterns and sub-patterns (both denoted by ♦) and collections (denoted by ❖). These categories come from the patterns themselves; I don't override the classifications of pattern authors.

Often I hear developers complain that when they read a pattern, the target domain is one they don't understand or care about. I have tried to address that complaint by including experience papers that describe real pattern uses. So in addition to the categories of the *GoF* text (creational, behavioral, structural) and those of other authors, I've made categories of the application domains themselves. If you are interested in telecommunications, for example, you can read through the list of patterns, subpatterns, and experience reports that treat that domain.

Accounting
Air Defense
Analysis
Architectural
Automated Manufacturing
Banking
Behavioral
Business Computation
Business Planning
Business Process
C++ Idioms
Client-Server
Communications
Concurrent Systems
Configuration Management
Creational
Cryptography
Customer Interaction
Database
Decision Tree
   Learning Systems
Design Process
Distributed Systems

Event-Driven Systems
Fault-Tolerant Systems
Finite State Machines
Fire Alarm Systems
Frameworks
GUI Development
Health Care
Hypermedia
Integration
Interactive Systems
Inventory Control Systems
Java Idioms
Memory Management
Multimedia
Networks
Order Management
Organization and Process
Parallel Programming
Pattern Writing
Performance
Persistence
Propagation
Reactive and
   Real-Time Systems

Refactoring
Security
Smalltalk ENVY/Developer
   Idioms
Smalltalk Idioms
Smalltalk ValueModel
   Idioms
Speech Recognition
Structural
System Modelling
Technical Paper Review
Telecommunications
Telemetry Processing
Testing
Time
Trading
Training
Transaction Processing
Transportation
Visualization and
   Monitoring
Web Site Development
Writers' Workshops

Accounting

ACCOUNT ♦ 10
ACCOUNT NUMBER ♦ 4
ACCOUNTING PRACTICE ♦ 12
ADJUSTING TRANSACTIONS ♦ 174
BALANCE SHEET AND INCOME STATEMENT ♦ 12
BOOKING ENTRIES TO MULTIPLE ACCOUNTS ♦ 12
BUSINESS ACCOUNTS ♦ 174
BUSINESS TRANSACTIONS ♦ 174
CHOOSING ENTRIES ♦ 11
COMPOSITE TRANSACTIONS ♦ 174
CONTINUOUS PROCESSING ♦ 175
CORRESPONDING ACCOUNT ♦ 12
EXPLICIT BUSINESS RULES ♦ 174
INDIVIDUAL INSTANCE METHOD ♦ 11
MEMO ACCOUNT ♦ 11
MONTH END CLOSING ♦ 174
POSTING RULE EXECUTION ♦ 11
POSTING RULES ♦ 11
POSTING RULES FOR MANY ACCOUNTS ♦ 11
SEPARATE TRANSACTION PROCESSING FROM
    ARCHIVAL ♦ 174
SOURCES OF AN ENTRY ♦ 12
SPECIALIZED ACCOUNT MODEL ♦ 12
SUMMARY ACCOUNT ♦ 11
TRANSACTION ♦ 10
TRANSACTIONS AND ACCOUNTS ❖ 173

Air Defense

REENGINEERING A LEGACY SYSTEM USING DESIGN
    PATTERNS AND ADA-95 OBJECT-ORIENTED FEATURES
    [Barkataki+98]

Analysis

3-LEVEL ORDER ♦ 24
ABSTRACT MODELS WITH CONSTRAINTS IN
    SUBTYPES ♦ 4
ACCOUNTABILITY ♦ 7
ACCOUNTABILITY ABSTRACTION ♦ 5
ACCOUNTABILITY AND ORGANIZATIONAL
    STRUCTURES ❖ 4
ACCOUNTABILITY KNOWLEDGE LEVEL ♦ 7
ACCOUNTABILITY KNOWLEDGE LEVEL ♦ 5
ACTIVE OBSERVATION, HYPOTHESIS, AND
    PROJECTION ♦ 9
ANALYSIS PATTERNS ❖ 6
Analysis Patterns [Fowler98]
ASSOCIATED OBSERVATION ♦ 9
ASSOCIATION OBJECT ♦ 23
BEHAVIORAL REQUIREMENTS ♦ 142
BUILDING THE RIGHT THINGS ♦ 141

BUSINESS PATTERNS OF ASSOCIATION
    OBJECTS ❖ 23
COMPOUND UNITS ♦ 8
CONVERSION RATIO ♦ 8
CUSTOMER CONTACT ♦ 23
DATABASE INTERACTION ♦ 15
DEFINING REQUIREMENTS ♦ 141
DUAL TIME RECORD ♦ 9
ENTERPRISE SEGMENT ♦ 9
FINDING AND DEFINING THE DOMAIN
    OBJECTS ♦ 142
HIERARCHIC ACCOUNTABILITY ♦ 7
INFORMATION NEEDS ♦ 142
KNOWLEDGE LEVEL ♦ 5
MANAGING AND MEETING CUSTOMER
    EXPECTATIONS ♦ 141
MEASUREMENT ♦ 8
MEASUREMENT PROTOCOL ♦ 9
MULTIPLE HIERARCHIC ASSOCIATIONS ♦ 4
OBJECTIFY ASSOCIATIONS ♦ 5
OBSERVATION ♦ 8
OPERATING SCOPE ♦ 7
ORGANIZATION HIERARCHIES ♦ 7
ORGANIZATION STRUCTURE ♦ 7
ORGANIZATIONAL STRUCTURE-TYPED
    RELATIONSHIP ♦ 5
PARTY ♦ 6
PARTY ♦ 4
PARTY TYPE GENERALIZATIONS ♦ 7
PHENOMENON WITH RANGE ♦ 10
POST ♦ 7
PRAGMATIC EXTERNAL REQUIREMENTS ♦ 143
PRESENTATION AND APPLICATION LOGIC ♦ 15
PROBLEM DOMAIN ANALYSIS ♦ 141
PROCESS OF OBSERVATION ♦ 9
PROTOCOL ♦ 8
PROTOCOL ♦ 13
PUT FREQUENTLY VARYING STRUCTURES IN
    INSTANCES ♦ 5
QUANTITY ♦ 8
RANGE ♦ 9
RAPPeL: A REQUIREMENTS-ANALYSIS PROCESS
    PATTERN LANGUAGE FOR OBJECT-ORIENTED
    DEVELOPMENT ❖ 140
RECURSIVE STRUCTURES FOR ORGANIZATIONS ♦ 4
REJECTED OBSERVATION ♦ 9
REQUIREMENTS SPECIFICATION ♦ 143
REQUIREMENTS VALIDATION ♦ 143
SNAPSHOT ♦ 173

Subtyping Observation Concepts ♦ 8
Temporal Association ♦ 173
Temporal Patterns ❖ 172
Temporal Property ♦ 172
Three-Tier Architecture ♦ 15
Two-Tier Architecture ♦ 14
Typed Relationship ♦ 5
User Interface Requirements ♦ 143

Architectural
Architectural Patterns for Enabling
    Application Security ❖ 17
Architecture Patterns for Business
    Systems ❖ 18
Batch Engineering Model ♦ 19
Big Ball of Mud ♦ 21
Big Ball of Mud Pattern Language ❖ 20
Blackboard ♦ 22
Bridge ♦ 124
Broker ♦ 22
Broker as Divorce Attorney ♦ 134
Broker as Intermediary ♦ 133
Broker as Matchmaker ♦ 134
Check Point ♦ 17
Classes of Event Objects ♦ 129
Communicating Processes ♦ 36
Data Abstraction or Object-Oriented ♦ 125
Database Interaction ♦ 15
Distributed Processes ♦ 51
Domain Intercepts ♦ 137
Event-Centered Architecture ♦ 129
Facade ♦ 137
Four-Layer Architecture ♦ 107
Full View with Errors ♦ 18
Generics and Specifics ♦ 136
Half-Sync/Half-Async ♦ 71
Implicit Invocation or Event-Based ♦ 125
Interpreter ♦ 125
Layered and Sectioned Architecture ♦ 97
Layered Architecture ♦ 126
Layers ♦ 81
Limited View ♦ 18
Loose Interfaces ♦ 95
Main Plus Subroutines ♦ 126
Master-Slave ♦ 86
Messaging Engineering Model ♦ 18
Microkernel ♦ 87
Model Hierarchy ♦ 137
Model-View-Controller ♦ 88
Object Recovery ♦ 92

Online Engineering Model ♦ 18
Pattern Language for Smalltalk &
    Relational Databases ❖ 106
Patterns for Generating a Layered
    Architecture ❖ 123
Patterns for Software Architectures ❖ 125
Patterns of Events ❖ 129
Pedestal ♦ 123
Persistence Accessors ♦ 136
Piecemeal Growth ♦ 21
Pipeline ♦ 125
Pipes & Filters ♦ 132
Pocket-Sized Broker ❖ 133
Pocket-Sized Broker [Olson98b]
Presentation and Application Logic ♦ 15
Presentation-Abstraction-Control ♦ 135
Prioritizing Forces in Software
    Design ❖ 136
Process Control ♦ 138
Protected Variations ♦ 136
Prototype-Based Object System ♦ 139
Recursive Control ♦ 144
Reflection ♦ 145
Relational Database Access Layer ♦ 3
Repository ♦ 125
Roles ♦ 17
Secure Access Layer ♦ 18
Session ♦ 17
Shape of Program ♦ 29
Single Access Point ♦ 17
Software Architecture [Shaw+96]
Some Patterns for Software Architectures
    [Shaw96]
Sponsor-Selector ♦ 165
State Transition Systems ♦ 168
Stream I-O Engineering Model ♦ 19
Streams ♦ 168
Symmetrical Reuse ♦ 124
Table Design Time ♦ 42
Three Subsystems ♦ 136
Three-Tier Architecture ♦ 15
Throwaway Code ♦ 21
Transceiver-Parcel ♦ 133
Two-Tier Architecture ♦ 14

Automated Manufacturing
Actions Triggered by Events ♦ 62
Categorize Objects for Concurrency ♦ 62
Client/Server/Service ♦ 62

Creating Applications from Components: A
Manufacturing Framework Design [Schmid96]

Creating the Architecture of a Manufacturing
Framework by Design Patterns [Schmid95]

DISTRIBUTION OF CONTROL MODULES ◆ 63

G++: A PATTERN LANGUAGE
FOR COMPUTER-INTEGRATED
MANUFACTURING ❖ 61

HIERARCHY OF CONTROL LAYERS ◆ 61

IMPLEMENTATION OF "MULTIPLE KINDS OF
SERVICES" CONTROL MODULES ◆ 63

INTERFACE TO CONTROL MODULES ◆ 63

PROTOTYPE AND REALITY ◆ 63

SERVICES "WAITING FOR" ◆ 62

VISIBILITY AND COMMUNICATION BETWEEN
CONTROL MODULES ◆ 62

Banking

Framework Development for Large Systems
[Bäumer+97]

ROLE OBJECT ◆ 147

Behavioral

ACTIVE VALUE ◆ 20

ACYCLIC VISITOR ◆ 6

ASPECTS ◆ 110

BASIC RELATIONSHIP PATTERNS ❖ 19

BUREAUCRACY ◆ 23

CHAIN OF RESPONSIBILITY ◆ 32

COLLECTION OBJECT ◆ 20

COMMAND ◆ 35

COMMAND PROCESSOR ◆ 36

Command Processor [Sommerlad96]

CONDUIT OF SUBJECT CHANGE ◆ 75

Default and Extrinsic Visitor [Nordberg98]

DEFAULT STATE ◆ 168

DEFAULT VISITOR ◆ 46

ENVIRONMENT ◆ 110

EVENT MECHANISM ◆ 111

EVENTHANDLER ◆ 55

EXPOSED STATE ◆ 167

EXTENSION OBJECT ◆ 55

EXTRINSIC VISITOR ◆ 56

FLEXIBLE COMMAND INTERPRETER ◆ 60

HOOK METHOD ◆ 73

IMPLEMENTATION PATTERNS FOR THE OBSERVER
PATTERN ❖ 75

INTERPRETER ◆ 80

IP/FP PLUG IN ◆ 111

ITERATOR ◆ 81

MANAGER ◆ 86

MATERIAL CONTAINER ◆ 111

MATERIALS ◆ 109

MEDIATOR ◆ 87

MEMENTO ◆ 87

MESSAGE PACKET ◆ 75

MUTUAL FRIENDS ◆ 20

NULL OBJECT ◆ 92

OBJECT RECURSION ◆ 92

OBSERVER ◆ 94

OBSERVER UPDATE MESSAGE ◆ 76

ONE MESSAGE PER AFFECTED OBJECT ◆ 75

ONE MESSAGE PER CHANGE REQUEST ◆ 75

OPTIMIZED MESSAGES PER CHANGE
REQUEST ◆ 75

OWNER-DRIVEN TRANSITIONS ◆ 168

PATTERN LANGUAGE FOR TOOL CONSTRUCTION
AND INTEGRATION BASED ON THE TOOLS AND
MATERIALS METAPHOR ❖ 109

PUBLISHER-SUBSCRIBER ◆ 140

PURE STATE ◆ 167

REACTOR ◆ 144

Reactor: An Object Behavioral Pattern for
Concurrent Event Demultiplexing and Event
Handler Dispatching [Schmidt95]

RELATIONSHIP AS ATTRIBUTE ◆ 20

RELATIONSHIP OBJECT ◆ 20

SEPARATION OF POWERS ◆ 110

SHOPPER ◆ 153

STATE ◆ 167

STATE MEMBER ◆ 167

STATE OBJECT ◆ 167

STATE PATTERNS ❖ 167

STATE-DRIVEN TRANSITIONS ◆ 168

STRATEGY ◆ 168

TEMPLATE METHOD ◆ 172

THREAD-SPECIFIC STORAGE ◆ 173

TOOL AND MATERIAL COUPLING ◆ 110

TOOL COMPOSITION ◆ 110

TOOL COORDINATOR ◆ 111

TOOLS ◆ 110

TYPE OBJECT ◆ 177

VISITOR ◆ 180

Business Computation

CHECKS: A PATTERN LANGUAGE OF
INFORMATION INTEGRITY ❖ 32

DEFERRED VALIDATION ◆ 33

DIAGNOSTIC QUERY ◆ 33

ECHO BACK ◆ 32

EXCEPTIONAL VALUE ♦ 32
Financial Software Design Patterns [Zhang+96a]
Financial Software Design Patterns [Zhang+96b]
Financial Software Design Patterns [Zhang+96c]
FORECAST CONFIRMATION ♦ 33
FORMULA OBJECTS ♦ 41
HYPOTHETICAL PUBLICATION ♦ 33
INSTANT PROJECTION ♦ 33
MEANINGLESS BEHAVIOR ♦ 32
MEASUREMENT PROTOCOL ♦ 9
PHENOMENON WITH RANGE ♦ 10
RANGE ♦ 9
VISIBLE IMPLICATION ♦ 33
WHOLE VALUE ♦ 32

Business Planning
COMPLETED AND ABANDONED ACTIONS ♦ 12
ENTERPRISE SEGMENT ♦ 9
OUTCOME AND START FUNCTIONS ♦ 13
PLAN ♦ 13
PROPOSED AND IMPLEMENTED ACTION ♦ 12
PROTOCOL ♦ 8
PROTOCOL ♦ 13
RESOURCE ALLOCATION ♦ 13
SUSPENSION ♦ 12

Business Process
ACCOUNTABILITY ♦ 7
ACCOUNTABILITY KNOWLEDGE LEVEL ♦ 7
HIERARCHIC ACCOUNTABILITY ♦ 7
OPERATING SCOPE ♦ 7
ORGANIZATION HIERARCHIES ♦ 7
ORGANIZATION STRUCTURE ♦ 7
PARTY ♦ 6
PARTY TYPE GENERALIZATIONS ♦ 7
POST ♦ 7

C++ Idioms
ABSTRACT CLIENT ♦ 2
Advanced C++ Programming Styles and Idioms
    [Coplien92]
ALGEBRAIC HIERARCHY ♦ 25
C++ IDIOMS ❖ 24
CONCRETE DATA TYPE ♦ 25
COUNTED BODY ♦ 24
COUNTED POINTER ♦ 40
CREATOR AS SOLE OWNER ♦ 86
CURIOUSLY RECURRING TEMPLATE ♦ 43
DETACHED COUNTED BODY ♦ 24
Discovering Patterns in Existing Applications
    [Martin95b]

ENVELOPE/LETTER ♦ 25
HANDLE/BODY ♦ 24
HANDLE/BODY HIERARCHY ♦ 24
HOMOGENEOUS ADDITION ♦ 25
ITERABLE CONTAINER ♦ 81
LOCALIZED OWNERSHIP: MANAGING DYNAMIC
    OBJECTS IN C++ ❖ 86
MEMBER CONTAINER ♦ 87
More on the Geometry of C++ Objects, Part 1
    [Coplien99a]
More on the Geometry of C++ Objects, Part 2
    [Coplien99b]
NON-HIERARCHICAL ADDITION ♦ 26
PROMOTE AND ADD ♦ 26
PROMOTION LADDER ♦ 26
SEQUENCE OF OWNERS ♦ 86
Setting the Stage [Coplien94b]
SHARED OWNERSHIP ♦ 86
Software Design Patterns: Common Questions
    and Answers [Coplien94a]
THREE-LEVEL FSM ♦ 173
TYPE PROMOTION ♦ 26
VIRTUAL CONSTRUCTOR ♦ 25
WRITE A LOOP ONCE ♦ 180

Client-Server
ABSTRACT SERVER ♦ 16
ABSTRACT SESSION ♦ 2
ADAPTED SERVER ♦ 17
APPROACHES FOR SEPARATING CLIENTS FROM
    SERVERS ❖ 16
CACHE MANAGEMENT ♦ 109
CLIENT SYNCHRONIZATION ♦ 109
CLIENT-DISPATCHER-SERVER ♦ 34
CLIENT/SERVER FRAMEWORK ♦ 92
CREATING AND UPDATING BUSINESS
    OBJECTS ♦ 91
DEPENDENCY ♦ 91
EXCEPTION ♦ 90
FACTORY METHOD ♦ 91
FINALIZATION ♦ 90
FOUR-LAYER ARCHITECTURE ♦ 107
IDENTITY MANAGEMENT ♦ 91
INTELLIGENT CHILDREN ♦ 16
MATERIALIZATION ♦ 90
MEGA-SCROLLING ♦ 91
NEW CLIENTS WITH OLD SERVERS: A
    PATTERN LANGUAGE FOR CLIENT/SERVER
    FRAMEWORKS ❖ 90
OBJECTS FROM RECORDS ♦ 90

PERSISTENCE ACCESSORS ♦ 136
RECURSIVE CONTROL ♦ 144
REMOTE OPERATION ♦ 115
REQUEST ♦ 90
RESOURCE EXCHANGER ♦ 145
SEARCHING FOR BUSINESS OBJECTS ♦ 91
SOLITAIRE ♦ 90
TABLE DESIGN TIME ♦ 42
TWO-TIER ARCHITECTURE ♦ 14
Using the Mediator Design Pattern to Perform
    Multiplexing [Cerwin98]
VIEWING ♦ 91
WINDOW-KEEPING ♦ 91

Communications
ABSTRACT SESSION ♦ 2
ACCEPTOR ♦ 3
ACTIVE OBJECT ♦ 6
Applying Design Patterns to Simplify Signal
    Handling [Schmidt98a]
ASYNCHRONOUS COMPLETION TOKEN ♦ 19
CLIENT-DISPATCHER-SERVER ♦ 34
CONNECTOR ♦ 40
DIAGNOSTIC CONTEXT ♦ 124
DIAGNOSTIC LOGGER ♦ 124
Family of Design Patterns for Application-Level
    Gateways [Schmidt96b]
Family of Design Patterns for Flexibly
    Configuring Network Services in Distributed
    Systems [Schmidt96a]
FORWARDER-RECEIVER ♦ 60
HALF-SYNC/HALF-ASYNC ♦ 71
MANAGED OBJECT ♦ 115
MANAGER-AGENT ♦ 115
PATTERN SYSTEM FOR NETWORK MANAGEMENT
    INTERFACES ❖ 114
PATTERNS FOR LOGGING DIAGNOSTIC
    MESSAGES ❖ 124
PROACTOR ♦ 138
REMOTE OPERATION ♦ 115
ROUTER ♦ 147
TYPED DIAGNOSTICS ♦ 125
Using Design Patterns to Evolve System Software
    from Unix to Windows NT [Schmidt+95]

Concurrent Systems
ACCEPTOR ♦ 3
ACTIONS TRIGGERED BY EVENTS ♦ 62
ACTIVE OBJECT ♦ 6
ASYNCHRONOUS COMPLETION TOKEN ♦ 19
ATOMIC COMMITMENT ♦ 38

CATEGORIZE OBJECTS FOR CONCURRENCY ♦ 62
CATERPILLAR'S FATE: A PATTERN LANGUAGE
    FOR THE TRANSFORMATION FROM ANALYSIS TO
    DESIGN ❖ 28
CLIENT/SERVER/SERVICE ♦ 62
COLLABORATIVE WORK PACKETS ♦ 28
CONCURRENT PROGRAMMING IN JAVA, SECOND
    EDITION: DESIGN PRINCIPLES AND
    PATTERNS ❖ 37
CONCURRENT THREADS OF EXECUTION ♦ 28
CONFLICT SETS ♦ 39
CONNECTOR ♦ 40
COPY-ON-WRITE ♦ 38
CRITICAL REGION PROTECTION ♦ 31
DATA KNOWS ITS ROOTS ♦ 31
DATA PUMP ♦ 135
DECISION MAKER'S ROLE ♦ 30
Designing Concurrent and Distributed Control
    Systems [Aarsten+96a]
DETERMINE THE ACTORS ♦ 71
DEVIATION ♦ 134
DOUBLE CHECK ♦ 38
DOUBLE-CHECKED LOCKING ♦ 51
EVENT-DRIVEN I/O ♦ 39
EVENT-DRIVEN RPC ♦ 94
FLOW NETWORKS ♦ 40
FORK/JOIN ♦ 40
FROM PROTOTYPE TO REALITY ♦ 61
FUTURES ♦ 40
G++: A PATTERN LANGUAGE
    FOR COMPUTER-INTEGRATED
    MANUFACTURING ❖ 61
HALF-SYNC/HALF-ASYNC ♦ 71
HIERARCHY OF CONTROL LAYERS ♦ 61
HUMAN INTERFACE ROLE IS A SPECIAL
    INTERFACE ROLE ♦ 31
IMPLEMENTATION OF "MULTIPLE KINDS OF
    SERVICES" CONTROL MODULES ♦ 63
INFORMATIONAL ROLE ♦ 30
INTERFACE TO CONTROL MODULES ♦ 63
INTERFACE'S ROLE ♦ 30
LAZY STATE ♦ 135
METHOD ADAPTERS ♦ 37
MULTIPHASE CANCELLATION ♦ 39
OBJECT SYNCHRONIZER ♦ 93
OBJECT-ORIENTED DESIGN PATTERNS IN
    REACTIVE SYSTEMS ❖ 93
OBJECT-ORIENTED SIMULATION ♦ 93
OBJECTIFY SYSTEM STATE ♦ 94

OBJECTIFY THE EVENTS ♦ 93
OBJECTS WITH REMOTE CONTROL ♦ 94
OPEN CALLS ♦ 38
OPEN CONTAINERS ♦ 38
PASS-THROUGH HOST ♦ 38
PERIODIC OBJECT ♦ 135
POINT ♦ 134
POINTS AND DEVIATIONS: PATTERN LANGUAGE
    OF FIRE ALARM SYSTEMS ❖ 134
POOL ♦ 135
PROACTOR ♦ 138
PROTOTYPE AND REALITY ♦ 63
READERS AND WRITERS ♦ 39
REMOTE CONTROL ♦ 145
RESOURCE EXCHANGER ♦ 145
ROLL-FORWARD ♦ 39
ROLLBACK ♦ 38
SERVICES "WAITING FOR" ♦ 62
SESSION ♦ 37
SHAPE OF PROGRAM ♦ 29
SMALL FAMILY SYSTEMS ♦ 30
SYNCHRONIZATION OF CONCURRENT
    THREADS ♦ 28
SYSTEM CITIZEN'S ROLE ♦ 29
THREAD-PER-MESSAGE ♦ 39
THREAD-SPECIFIC STORAGE ♦ 173
TIME THREAD ANALYSIS ♦ 71
VETOABLE CHANGES ♦ 39
VISIBILITY AND COMMUNICATION BETWEEN
    CONTROL MODULES ♦ 62
WORK ACCOMPLISHED THROUGH DIALOGS ♦ 30
WORK PACKET COMPLETION REPORT ♦ 29
WORK PACKET CONTENTS ♦ 28
WORK PACKET PRIORITY ♦ 29
WORK PACKET SECURITY ♦ 29
WORK PACKET STATUS REPORT ♦ 29
WORKER THREADS ♦ 39
WORKERS' ROLE ♦ 30

Configuration Management
INCREMENTAL INTEGRATION ♦ 171
INDEPENDENT WORKSPACES ♦ 172
LAYER IN AN APPLICATION ♦ 97
NAMED STABLE BASES ♦ 68
NO SUBAPPLICATIONS ♦ 97
PARTITIONING SMALLTALK CODE INTO
    ENVY/DEVELOPER COMPONENTS ❖ 97
PRIVATE VERSIONING ♦ 171
SECTION IN A SUBAPPLICATION ♦ 97

TEAMWORK AND CONFIGURATION
    MANAGEMENT ❖ 171
TWO APPLICATIONS ♦ 97
Creational
ABSTRACT FACTORY ♦ 2
BUILDER ♦ 23
FACTORY METHOD ♦ 57
LATE CREATION ♦ 121
PATTERNS FOR ENCAPSULATING CLASS
    TREES ❖ 120
PLUGGABLE FACTORY ♦ 133
PRODUCT TRADER ♦ 138
PROTOTYPE ♦ 139
SINGLETON ♦ 153
Cryptography
INFORMATION SECRECY ♦ 175
MESSAGE INTEGRITY ♦ 175
SECRECY WITH INTEGRITY ♦ 176
SECRECY WITH SENDER AUTHENTICATION ♦ 176
SECRECY WITH SIGNATURE ♦ 176
SECRECY WITH SIGNATURE WITH APPENDIX ♦ 176
SECURE-CHANNEL COMMUNICATION ♦ 175
SENDER AUTHENTICATION ♦ 175
SIGNATURE ♦ 176
SIGNATURE WITH APPENDIX ♦ 176
TROPYC: A PATTERN LANGUAGE FOR
    CRYPTOGRAPHIC SOFTWARE ❖ 175
Customer Interaction
ARCHIVE SCENARIOS ♦ 48
BE AWARE OF BOUNDARIES ♦ 44
BE RESPONSIVE ♦ 44
BUILD TRUST ♦ 43
CATALYTIC SCENARIOS ♦ 47
CUSTOMER INTERACTION PATTERNS ❖ 43
CUSTOMER MEETINGS: GO EARLY, STAY
    LATE ♦ 44
CUSTOMER RAPPORT ♦ 141
DEMO PREP: A PATTERN LANGUAGE
    FOR THE PREPARATION OF SOFTWARE
    DEMONSTRATIONS ❖ 46
DESIGNERS ARE OUR FRIENDS ♦ 126
ELEMENT IDENTIFICATION ♦ 46
ENGAGE CUSTOMERS ♦ 66
FUNCTIONALITY ALA CARTE ♦ 61
GET INVOLVED EARLY ♦ 126
IT'S A RELATIONSHIP, NOT A SALE ♦ 43
JUDICIOUS FIREWORKS ♦ 47
KNOW THE CUSTOMER ♦ 43
LIGHTWEIGHT USER INTERFACES ♦ 47

LISTEN, LISTEN, LISTEN ♦ 44

MANAGING AND MEETING CUSTOMER
EXPECTATIONS ♦ 141

MIND YOUR MANNERS ♦ 44

MUTABLE CODE ♦ 47

PROTOTYPING LANGUAGES ♦ 47

SHOW PERSONAL INTEGRITY ♦ 44

SPONSOR OBJECTIVES ♦ 141

TAKE YOUR LICKS ♦ 44

Database

ACCESSING RELATIONAL DATABASES ❖ 3

ACCOUNT NUMBER ♦ 4

BROKER ♦ 108

CACHE MANAGEMENT ♦ 109

CLIENT SYNCHRONIZATION ♦ 109

COMPOSABLE QUERY OBJECTS ♦ 41

CONSTRAINT OBSERVER ♦ 41

CREATING REPORTS WITH QUERY OBJECTS ❖ 40

CROSSING CHASMS: A PATTERN LANGUAGE FOR
OBJECT-RDBMS INTEGRATION ❖ 41

DIMENSION ROLL-UP ♦ 166

FEATURE EXTRACTION—A PATTERN FOR
INFORMATION RETRIEVAL ♦ 58

FOREIGN KEY REFERENCES ♦ 43

FOREIGN KEY REFERENCES ♦ 108

FOREIGN KEY VERSUS DIRECT REFERENCE ♦ 43

FORMULA OBJECTS ♦ 41

HIERARCHICAL VIEW ♦ 3

JUDGE ♦ 81

KEY BUSINESS ACTIVITIES AND
INFLUENCES ♦ 166

OBJECT IDENTIFIER ♦ 42

OBJECT IDENTIFIER ♦ 107

OBJECT METADATA ♦ 108

OBJECT RECOVERY ♦ 92

PATTERN LANGUAGE FOR SMALLTALK &
RELATIONAL DATABASES ❖ 106

Pattern of Inheritance and Polymorphism for
Persistent Objects Stored in a Relational
Database [Pang99]

PEOPLE, PLACES, AND THINGS ♦ 166

PHYSICAL VIEW ♦ 3

QUERY BROKER ♦ 4

QUERY OBJECT ♦ 109

QUERY OBJECTS ♦ 41

QUERY OPTIMIZED DATABASE ♦ 166

RELATIONAL DATABASE ACCESS LAYER ♦ 3

REPORT OBJECTS ♦ 41

REPRESENTING COLLECTIONS ♦ 108

REPRESENTING COLLECTIONS IN A RELATIONAL
DATABASE ♦ 42

REPRESENTING INHERITANCE IN A RELATIONAL
DATABASE ♦ 42

REPRESENTING OBJECT RELATIONSHIPS ♦ 42

REPRESENTING OBJECT RELATIONSHIPS ♦ 107

REPRESENTING OBJECTS AS TABLES ♦ 42

REPRESENTING OBJECTS AS TABLES ♦ 107

STARS: A PATTERN LANGUAGE FOR
QUERY-OPTIMIZED SCHEMAS ❖ 165

SURROGATE ♦ 169

TABLE DESIGN TIME ♦ 42

TABLE DESIGN TIME ♦ 107

TIME ♦ 166

TRANSACTION HISTORY ♦ 166

WHOLE BUSINESS ENTITIES ♦ 166

Decision Tree Learning Systems

Applying Design Patterns to Decision Tree
Learning System [Masuda+98]

Design Process

ABSTRACT CLASS ♦ 2

AD-HOC CORRECTIONS ♦ 119

ANIMATE THE DATA ♦ 71

ARRAY ♦ 160

ASSOCIATIVE TYPE ♦ 16

BOOLEAN PROPERTY SETTING METHOD ♦ 159

BYTE ARRAY ♦ 160

CACHING TEMPORARY VARIABLE ♦ 159

CASCADE ♦ 164

CHOOSING MESSAGE ♦ 155

CLASSIFYING, ASSOCIATING, AND GROUPING THE
DOMAIN OBJECTS ♦ 142

COLLECT ♦ 161

COLLECTING PARAMETER ♦ 157

COLLECTING TEMPORARY VARIABLE ♦ 159

COLLECTION ♦ 160

COLLECTION ACCESSOR METHOD ♦ 158

COMMON STATE ♦ 157

COMPARING METHOD ♦ 154

COMPOSED METHOD ♦ 153

CONCATENATING STREAM ♦ 163

CONCATENATION ♦ 161

CONDITIONAL EXPRESSION ♦ 164

CONDUIT OF SUBJECT CHANGE ♦ 75

CONSOLIDATE THE PROGRAM TO SUPPORT
EVOLUTION AND REUSE ♦ 85

CONSTANT METHOD ♦ 158

CONSTRUCTOR METHOD ♦ 153

CONSTRUCTOR PARAMETER METHOD ♦ 153

CONVERSION ♦ 154

CONVERTER CONSTRUCTOR METHOD ♦ 154

CONVERTER METHOD ♦ 154

CREATE ABSTRACT SUPERCLASS ♦ 85

CREATOR-REVIEWER ♦ 119

DEBUG PRINTING METHOD ♦ 155

DECISION DOCUMENT ♦ 119

DECOMPOSING MESSAGE ♦ 155

DEFAULT VALUE METHOD ♦ 158

DEFER IDENTIFICATION OF STATE VARIABLES ♦ 146

DEFINE CLASSES BY BEHAVIOR, NOT STATE ♦ 146

DEFINE DEFAULT VALUES VIA EXPLICIT PROTOCOL ♦ 147

DEFINE THE DATA STRUCTURE ♦ 70

DELEGATION ♦ 156

DETECT ♦ 161

DETERMINE THE ACTORS ♦ 71

DICTIONARY ♦ 160

DIRECT VARIABLE ACCESS ♦ 158

DISPATCHED INTERPRETATION ♦ 156

DO ♦ 161

DOUBLE DISPATCH ♦ 156

DUPLICATE REMOVING SET ♦ 162

ELABORATION OF THE DOMAIN OBJECTS ♦ 142

ELEVATE REFERENCES TO ENHANCE REUSE ♦ 124

ENCAPSULATE CONCRETE STATE ♦ 146

ENTRY POINT ♦ 16

ENUMERATION ♦ 161

ENUMERATION METHOD ♦ 159

EQUALITY METHOD ♦ 160

EVOLUTION, ARCHITECTURE, AND METAMORPHOSIS ❖ 55

EVOLVE AGGREGATIONS FROM INHERITANCE HIERARCHIES ♦ 85

EXECUTE AROUND METHOD ♦ 155

EXPAND THE INITIAL PROTOTYPE ♦ 85

EXPLAINING TEMPORARY VARIABLE ♦ 159

EXPLICIT INITIALIZATION ♦ 157

EXTENDING SUPER ♦ 156

FACTOR OUT COMMON ATTRIBUTES ♦ 70

FINDING AND DEFINING THE DOMAIN OBJECTS ♦ 142

FINE-GRAINED CLASSIFICATION OF EVENTS ♦ 130

FIRST ONE'S FREE ♦ 152

FLEXIBLE FOUNDATIONS ♦ 55

FOR COMPLEX MOODS, USE A MOOD ALTERNATOR ♦ 89

FOR OBJECTS WITH MOODS, USE STATE CLASSES ♦ 88

FOR STATE MACHINES, USE TRANSITION METHODS ♦ 89

Framework Development for Large Systems [Bäumer+97]

GENERATIVE PATTERN LANGUAGE FOR DISTRIBUTED PROCESSING ❖ 70

GENTLE LEARNING CURVE ♦ 151

GETTING METHOD ♦ 158

GUARD CLAUSE ♦ 163

HASHING METHOD ♦ 160

HISTORIC MAPPING ♦ 16

IDENTIFICATION SCHEME ♦ 10

IDENTIFY MESSAGE LAYERS ♦ 146

IDENTIFY PROBLEM DOMAIN RELATIONSHIPS ♦ 70

IDENTIFY THE NOUNS ♦ 70

IMPLEMENT BEHAVIOR WITH ABSTRACT STATE ♦ 146

IMPLEMENTATION PATTERNS FOR THE OBSERVER PATTERN ❖ 75

IMPLEMENTING ASSOCIATIONS ♦ 15

IMPLEMENTING CONSTRAINTS ♦ 16

IMPLEMENTING GENERALIZATIONS ♦ 15

INCLUDES: ♦ 161

INDENTED CONTROL FLOW ♦ 163

INDIRECT VARIABLE ACCESS ♦ 158

INFORMATIONAL ROLE ♦ 30

INJECT:INTO: ♦ 162

INLINE MESSAGE PATTERN ♦ 163

INTENTION REVEALING MESSAGE ♦ 155

INTENTION REVEALING SELECTOR ♦ 155

INTERESTING RETURN VALUE ♦ 164

INTERFACE'S ROLE ♦ 30

INTERVAL ♦ 161

INTRODUCE VIRTUAL ATTRIBUTES ♦ 71

IS EMPTY ♦ 161

KEYED MAPPING ♦ 16

LAZY INITIALIZATION ♦ 158

LIFE CYCLE AND REFACTORING PATTERNS THAT SUPPORT EVOLUTION AND REUSE ❖ 85

LOOKUP CACHE ♦ 162

LOW SURFACE-TO-VOLUME RATIO ♦ 151

MASTER-JOURNEYMAN ♦ 119

MEDIATING PROTOCOL ♦ 156

MEMORY PERFORMANCE ASSESSMENT ♦ 73

MESSAGE ♦ 155

MESSAGE PACKET ♦ 75

METAMORPHOSIS ♦ 55

METHOD COMMENT ♦ 155
METHOD OBJECT ♦ 154
MODIFYING SUPER ♦ 156
MOODS: MODELS FOR OBJECT-ORIENTED
    DESIGN OF STATE ❖ 88
MULTIPLE COMPETING DESIGNS ♦ 118
NAME ♦ 10
NORMALIZE THE ROLES ♦ 70
OBJECT AGING ♦ 142
OBJECT CREATION ♦ 15
OBJECT DESTRUCTION ♦ 15
OBJECT EQUIVALENCE ♦ 10
OBJECT MERGE ♦ 10
OBJECT STEREOTYPES ♦ 142
OBJECT-ORIENTED STATE MACHINE ♦ 130
OBSERVER UPDATE MESSAGE ♦ 76
ONE MESSAGE PER AFFECTED OBJECT ♦ 75
ONE MESSAGE PER CHANGE REQUEST ♦ 75
OPTIMIZED MESSAGES PER CHANGE
    REQUEST ♦ 75
ORDERED COLLECTION ♦ 160
PARSING STREAM ♦ 162
PATTERN AS A CLASS ♦ 97
PATTERNS FOR DESIGNING IN TEAMS ❖ 118
PLUGGABLE BEHAVIOR ♦ 157
PLUGGABLE BLOCK ♦ 157
PLUGGABLE SELECTOR ♦ 157
PROGRAMMING-BY-DIFFERENCE ♦ 151
PROTOTYPE A FIRST-PASS DESIGN ♦ 85
QUALIFIED SUBCLASS NAME ♦ 163
QUERY METHOD ♦ 154
QUEUE ♦ 162
RECTANGULAR BLOCK ♦ 163
REUSABILITY THROUGH
    SELF-ENCAPSULATION ❖ 146
REUSING TEMPORARY VARIABLE ♦ 159
REVERSING METHOD ♦ 154
ROLE OBJECT ♦ 147
ROLE SUGGESTING INSTANCE VARIABLE
    NAME ♦ 159
ROLE SUGGESTING TEMPORARY VARIABLE
    NAME ♦ 159
RUN ARRAY ♦ 160
SEARCHING LITERAL ♦ 162
SELECT/REJECT ♦ 161
SELF DELEGATION ♦ 156
SELFISH CLASS ♦ 151
SELFISH CLASS PATTERN LANGUAGE ❖ 150
SET ♦ 160

SETTING METHOD ♦ 158
SHEARING LAYERS ♦ 21
SHORTCUT CONSTRUCTOR METHOD ♦ 153
SIMPLE DELEGATION ♦ 156
SIMPLE ENUMERATION PARAMETER ♦ 164
SIMPLE SUPERCLASS NAME ♦ 163
SMALLTALK BEST PRACTICE PATTERNS ❖ 153
SOFTWARE TECTONICS ♦ 55
SORTED COLLECTION ♦ 160
STACK ♦ 162
SUPER ♦ 156
SWEEPING IT UNDER THE RUG ♦ 21
TEMPORARILY SORTED COLLECTION ♦ 162
TEMPORARY VARIABLE ♦ 159
TIME THREAD ANALYSIS ♦ 71
TO SIMPLIFY COMPLEX BEHAVIOR, USE
    DECOMPOSITION ♦ 88
TYPE SUGGESTING PARAMETER NAME ♦ 163
USE LAZY INITIALIZATION ♦ 146
VARIABLE STATE ♦ 157
WHEN EVENTS CAUSE MOODS, USE STATE
    MACHINE ♦ 89
WHEN STATES ARE ASSOCIATIONS, USE STATE
    OBJECTS ♦ 89
WHEN STATES ARE CONDITIONS, USE
    PREDICATIVE STATE CLASSES ♦ 89
WHEN THERE ARE MANY MOODS, USE MOOD
    CLASSIFIER ♦ 89
WINNING TEAM ♦ 152
WORK ACCOMPLISHED THROUGH DIALOGS ♦ 30
WORKS OUT OF THE BOX ♦ 151
YOURSELF ♦ 164

Distributed Systems

ACCEPTOR ♦ 3
ACTIVE OBJECT ♦ 6
ASYNCHRONOUS COMPLETION TOKEN ♦ 19
BODYGUARD ♦ 22
BROKER ♦ 22
BROKER AS DIVORCE ATTORNEY ♦ 134
BROKER AS INTERMEDIARY ♦ 133
BROKER AS MATCHMAKER ♦ 134
CLIENT-DISPATCHER-SERVER ♦ 34
CONNECTOR ♦ 40
DATA PUMP ♦ 135
DEFINE THE DATA STRUCTURE ♦ 70
DESIGNING CONCURRENT AND DISTRIBUTED CONTROL
    SYSTEMS [Aarsten+96a]
DEVIATION ♦ 134
DISTRIBUTED PROCESSES ♦ 51

DISTRIBUTION OF CONTROL MODULES ♦ 63

DOVE: A Distributed Object Visualization Environment [Kircher+99]

Dynamically Configuring Communication Services [Jain+97]

ESSENCE ♦ 54

Essential Design Pattern for Fault-Tolerant Distributed State Sharing [Islam+96]

EVENT-DRIVEN RPC ♦ 94

Family of Design Patterns for Flexibly Configuring Network Services in Distributed Systems [Schmidt96a]

FORWARDER-RECEIVER ♦ 60

FROM PROTOTYPE TO REALITY ♦ 61

GENERATIVE PATTERN LANGUAGE FOR DISTRIBUTED PROCESSING ❖ 70

HALF-OBJECT + PROTOCOL ♦ 71

HALF-SYNC/HALF-ASYNC ♦ 71

LAZY STATE ♦ 135

MANAGED OBJECT ♦ 115

MANAGER-AGENT ♦ 115

OBJECT RECOVERY ♦ 92

PATTERN SYSTEM FOR NETWORK MANAGEMENT INTERFACES ❖ 114

PERIODIC OBJECT ♦ 135

POCKET-SIZED BROKER ❖ 133

Pocket-Sized Broker [Olson98b]

POINT ♦ 134

POINTS AND DEVIATIONS: PATTERN LANGUAGE OF FIRE ALARM SYSTEMS ❖ 134

POOL ♦ 135

PROACTOR ♦ 138

REACTOR ♦ 144

Reactor: An Object Behavioral Pattern for Concurrent Event Demultiplexing and Event Handler Dispatching [Schmidt95]

RECOVERABLE DISTRIBUTOR ♦ 144

REMOTE CONTROL ♦ 145

REMOTE OPERATION ♦ 115

RESOURCE EXCHANGER ♦ 145

SERVICE CONFIGURATOR ♦ 152

TRANSCEIVER-PARCEL ♦ 133

Using the Facade Pattern with CORBA [Price+99]

Event-Driven Systems

Adapting Observer for Event-Driven Design [Piehler99]

CLASSES OF EVENT OBJECTS ♦ 129

CONSOLIDATE REQUESTS ♦ 50

DECOUPLE EXECUTION AND OUTPUT ♦ 77

DETERMINE THE ACTORS ♦ 71

EVENT ACQUISITION ♦ 31

EVENT NOTIFICATION ♦ 54

EVENT QUEUE ♦ 76

EVENT ROUTING ♦ 31

EVENT-CENTERED ARCHITECTURE ♦ 129

EVENT-DRIVEN RPC ♦ 94

FINE-GRAINED CLASSIFICATION OF EVENTS ♦ 130

HANDLE ARTIFICIAL EVENTS ♦ 76

IMPLICIT INVOCATION OR EVENT-BASED ♦ 125

IMPROVING RESPONSIVENESS IN INTERACTIVE APPLICATIONS USING QUEUES ❖ 76

MERGE COMPATIBLE EVENTS ♦ 76

OBJECT-ORIENTED DESIGN PATTERNS IN REACTIVE SYSTEMS ❖ 93

OBJECT-ORIENTED SIMULATION ♦ 93

OBJECT-ORIENTED STATE MACHINE ♦ 130

OBJECTIFY SYSTEM STATE ♦ 94

OBJECTIFY THE EVENTS ♦ 93

OBJECTS WITH REMOTE CONTROL ♦ 94

PATTERN FOR SEPARATING ASSEMBLY AND PROCESSING ♦ 98

PATTERNS OF EVENTS ❖ 129

REACTOR ♦ 144

Reactor: An Object Behavioral Pattern for Concurrent Event Demultiplexing and Event Handler Dispatching [Schmidt95]

RECURSIVE CONTROL ♦ 144

SERVICES "WAITING FOR" ♦ 62

TIME THREAD ANALYSIS ♦ 71

Fault-Tolerant Systems

ALARM GRID ♦ 79

AUDIBLE ALARM ♦ 79

BACKUP ♦ 19

BELTLINE TERMINAL ♦ 79

BOTTOM LINE ♦ 78

Development of an Object-Oriented Framework for Vessel Control Systems [Dagermo+98]

DON'T LET THEM FORGET ♦ 80

ESSENCE ♦ 54

Essential Design Pattern for Fault-Tolerant Distributed State Sharing [Islam+96]

FAULT-TOLERANT TELECOMMUNICATION SYSTEM PATTERNS ❖ 57

FIVE MINUTES OF NO ESCALATION MESSAGES ♦ 79

Five Minutes of No Escalation
   Messages ♦ 57
Fool Me Once ♦ 58
George Washington Is Still Dead ♦ 78
Input and Output Pattern Language ❖ 77
Input and Output Pattern Language [Hanmer+99]
IO Gatekeeper ♦ 77
IO Triage ♦ 78
Leaky Bucket Counters ♦ 58
Mind Your Own Business ♦ 77
Minimize Human Intervention ♦ 57
MML ♦ 77
Object Recovery ♦ 92
Office Alarms ♦ 80
People Know Best ♦ 57
Pseudo-IO ♦ 79
Raw IO ♦ 80
Recoverable Distributor ♦ 144
Riding Over Transients ♦ 57
Shut Up and Listen ♦ 79
SICO First and Always ♦ 58
String a Wire ♦ 80
Timestamp ♦ 78
Try All Hardware Combos ♦ 58
Who Asked? ♦ 78

Finite State Machines
Basic FSM ♦ 59
Curiously Recurring Template ♦ 43
Default State ♦ 168
Dynamic State Instantiation ♦ 60
Encapsulated State ♦ 60
Exposed State ♦ 167
Finite State Machine Patterns ❖ 58
For Complex MOODS, Use a MOOD
   Alternator ♦ 89
For Objects with MOODS, Use State
   Classes ♦ 88
For State Machines, Use Transition
   Methods ♦ 89
Hybrid ♦ 60
Interface Organization ♦ 59
Layered Organization ♦ 59
Meally ♦ 59
MOODS: Models for Object-Oriented
   Design of State ❖ 88
Moore ♦ 59
Object-Oriented State Machine ♦ 130
Owner-Driven Transitions ♦ 168
Pure State ♦ 167

State ♦ 167
State Member ♦ 167
State Object ♦ 167
State Patterns ❖ 167
State-Driven Transition ♦ 59
State-Driven Transitions ♦ 168
Three-Level FSM ♦ 173
To Simplify Complex Behavior, Use
   Decomposition ♦ 88
When Events Cause MOODS, Use State
   Machine ♦ 89
When States Are Associations, Use State
   Objects ♦ 89
When States Are Conditions, Use
   Predicative State Classes ♦ 89
When There Are Many MOODS, Use MOOD
   Classifier ♦ 89

Fire Alarm Systems
Data Pump ♦ 135
Deviation ♦ 134
Lazy State ♦ 135
Periodic Object ♦ 135
Point ♦ 134
Points and Deviations: Pattern Language
   of Fire Alarm Systems ❖ 134
Pool ♦ 135

Frameworks
Black-Box Framework ♦ 123
Component Library ♦ 122
Fine-Grained Objects ♦ 122
Hot Spots ♦ 122
Language Tools ♦ 123
Patterns for Evolving Frameworks ❖ 121
Pluggable Objects ♦ 122
Three Examples ♦ 121
Visual Builder ♦ 123
White-Box Frameworks ♦ 122

GUI Development
Adapting Observer for Event-Driven Design
   [Piehler99]
Alternative Subforms ♦ 100
Application Boundary ♦ 137
CHECKS: A Pattern Language of
   Information Integrity ❖ 32
Clip Requests ♦ 50
Command Processor [Sommerlad96]
Consolidate Requests ♦ 50
Decouple Execution and Output ♦ 77

Deferred Validation ♦ 33

Display List ♦ 49

Display Maintenance ❖ 49

Double Buffer ♦ 50

Echo Back ♦ 32

Event Queue ♦ 76

Generation Gap ♦ 63

Generic UI, Specific UI ♦ 136

Global Update ♦ 49

Handle Artificial Events ♦ 76

Heading Off Tragedy: Using Design Patterns
Against a Moving Target [Woodward96]

Human Interface Role Is a Special
Interface Role ♦ 31

Hypothetical Publication ♦ 33

Improving Responsiveness in Interactive
Applications Using Queues ❖ 76

Instant Projection ♦ 33

Lazy Redraw ♦ 50

Merge Compatible Events ♦ 76

Object Recovery ♦ 92

Page Flip ♦ 50

Painter's Algorithm ♦ 50

Panel States ♦ 96

Panel States: A User Interface Design Pattern
[Spall98]

Pattern Hatching [Vlissides98a]

Pattern Language for Developing Form
Style Windows ❖ 99

Pattern Language for Developing Form Style
Windows [Bradac+98]

Pluggable View Controller ♦ 133

Request Screen Modification ♦ 145

Request Update ♦ 49

Split Validation ♦ 137

Subform ♦ 99

Subform Match ♦ 100

Subform Mismatch ♦ 100

Subform Selection ♦ 100

Three Subsystems ♦ 136

User Interface Requirements ♦ 143

View Handler ♦ 179

Viewing ♦ 91

Visible Implication ♦ 33

Window-Keeping ♦ 91

Health Care

Active Observation, Hypothesis, and
Projection ♦ 9

Analysis Patterns [Fowler98]

Associated Observation ♦ 9

Completed and Abandoned Actions ♦ 12

Dual Time Record ♦ 9

Judge ♦ 81

Measurement ♦ 8

Object Equivalence ♦ 10

Object Merge ♦ 10

Observation ♦ 8

Operating Scope ♦ 7

Outcome and Start Functions ♦ 13

Party Type Generalizations ♦ 7

Plan ♦ 13

Post ♦ 7

Process of Observation ♦ 9

Proposed and Implemented Action ♦ 12

Protocol ♦ 8

Protocol ♦ 13

Rejected Observation ♦ 9

Resource Allocation ♦ 13

Subtyping Observation Concepts ♦ 8

Suspension ♦ 12

Hypermedia

Active Reference ♦ 120

Basket ♦ 120

Design Patterns for Object-Oriented
Hypermedia Applications ❖ 48

Landmark ♦ 120

NavigationObserver ♦ 48

NavigationStrategy ♦ 48

News ♦ 120

Nodes in Context ♦ 120

Patterns for Designing Navigable
Information Spaces ❖ 119

Set-based Navigation ♦ 119

Integration

(Legacy) Wrapper ♦ 115

Broker ♦ 116

Pattern-Based Integration
Architectures ❖ 115

Shared Repository ♦ 116

Work Flow Manager ♦ 115

Interactive Systems

Aspects ♦ 110

Decouple Execution and Output ♦ 77

Environment ♦ 110

Event Mechanism ♦ 111

Event Queue ♦ 76

HANDLE ARTIFICIAL EVENTS ♦ 76
IMPROVING RESPONSIVENESS IN INTERACTIVE
    APPLICATIONS USING QUEUES ❖ 76
IP/FP PLUG IN ♦ 111
MATERIAL CONTAINER ♦ 111
MATERIALS ♦ 109
MERGE COMPATIBLE EVENTS ♦ 76
PATTERN LANGUAGE FOR TOOL CONSTRUCTION
    AND INTEGRATION BASED ON THE TOOLS AND
    MATERIALS METAPHOR ❖ 109
SEPARATION OF POWERS ♦ 110
TOOL AND MATERIAL COUPLING ♦ 110
TOOL COMPOSITION ♦ 110
TOOL COORDINATOR ♦ 111
TOOLS ♦ 110

Inventory Control Systems
ACCOUNT ♦ 10
ACCOUNTING PRACTICE ♦ 12
BALANCE SHEET AND INCOME STATEMENT ♦ 12
BOOKING ENTRIES TO MULTIPLE ACCOUNTS ♦ 12
CHOOSING ENTRIES ♦ 11
CORRESPONDING ACCOUNT ♦ 12
INDIVIDUAL INSTANCE METHOD ♦ 11
MEMO ACCOUNT ♦ 11
POSTING RULE EXECUTION ♦ 11
POSTING RULES ♦ 11
POSTING RULES FOR MANY ACCOUNTS ♦ 11
SOURCES OF AN ENTRY ♦ 12
SPECIALIZED ACCOUNT MODEL ♦ 12
SUMMARY ACCOUNT ♦ 11
TRANSACTION ♦ 10

Java Idioms
ATOMIC COMMITMENT ♦ 38
CONCURRENT PROGRAMMING IN JAVA, SECOND
    EDITION: DESIGN PRINCIPLES AND
    PATTERNS ❖ 37
CONFLICT SETS ♦ 39
COPY-ON-WRITE ♦ 38
DOUBLE CHECK ♦ 38
EVENT-DRIVEN I/O ♦ 39
FLOW NETWORKS ♦ 40
FORK/JOIN ♦ 40
FUTURES ♦ 40
METHOD ADAPTERS ♦ 37
MULTIPHASE CANCELLATION ♦ 39
OPEN CALLS ♦ 38
OPEN CONTAINERS ♦ 38
PASS-THROUGH HOST ♦ 38

READERS AND WRITERS ♦ 39
ROLL-FORWARD ♦ 39
ROLLBACK ♦ 38
SESSION ♦ 37
THREAD-PER-MESSAGE ♦ 39
VETOABLE CHANGES ♦ 39
WORKER THREADS ♦ 39

Memory Management
CAPTAIN OATES ♦ 73
EXHAUSTION TEST ♦ 73
HIGH-LEVEL AND PROCESS PATTERNS FROM THE
    MEMORY PRESERVATION SOCIETY ❖ 72
MAKE THE USER WORRY ♦ 72
MEMORY BUDGET ♦ 72
MEMORY OVERDRAFT ♦ 72
MEMORY PERFORMANCE ASSESSMENT ♦ 73
PARTIAL FAILURE ♦ 72
THINK SMALL ♦ 72

Multimedia
COMPONENTS LAYOUT ♦ 36
COMPOSING MULTIMEDIA ARTIFACTS FOR
    REUSE ❖ 36
DEFINE AND RUN PRESENTATION ♦ 36
GLUE ♦ 36
PARTIES & MEDIA AS FIRST CLASS CITIZENS ♦ 96
PLUGGABLE FACTORY ♦ 133
REQUEST SCREEN MODIFICATION ♦ 145
SESSION CONTROL & OBSERVATION ♦ 152
SYNCHRONIZE CHANNELS ♦ 37
TEMPLATE ♦ 36
Using Design Patterns to Build a Framework for
    Multimedia Networking [VandenBroecke+97]

Networks
ABSTRACT SESSION ♦ 2
CASCADE ♦ 28
DRIVER DUTY ♦ 51
DRIVER DUTY CONSTRUCTOR ♦ 51
Driver Duty Constructor: A Pattern for Public
    Transport Systems [Zhao+99]
Driver Duty: A Pattern for Public Transport
    Systems [Zhao+98a]
Experience in Applying Design Patterns to
    Decouple Object Interactions in the Ingage™
    IP Prototype [Duell98]
Framework for Network Protocol Software
    [Hüni+95]
LAYERS ♦ 81

MANAGED OBJECT ♦ 115

MANAGER-AGENT ♦ 115

Modeling Transport Objects with Patterns [Foster+98]

PATTERN LANGUAGE OF TRANSPORT SYSTEMS (POINT AND ROUTE) ❖ 114

Pattern Language of Transport Systems (Point and Route) [Foster+97]

Pattern Language of Transport Systems (Point and Route) [Zhao+98b]

PATTERN SYSTEM FOR NETWORK MANAGEMENT INTERFACES ❖ 114

POINT ♦ 114

REMOTE OPERATION ♦ 115

ROUTE ♦ 114

Order Management

3-LEVEL ORDER ♦ 24

Experiencing Patterns at the Design Level [Brown96]

Organization and Process

AD-HOC CORRECTIONS ♦ 119

AESTHETIC PATTERN ♦ 69

APPLICATION DESIGN IS BOUNDED BY TEST DESIGN ♦ 66

APPRENTICE ♦ 65

ARCHITECT ALSO IMPLEMENTS ♦ 66

ARCHITECT CONTROLS PRODUCT ♦ 65

ARRANGING THE FURNITURE ♦ 27

BACKLOG ♦ 148

BE AWARE OF BOUNDARIES ♦ 44

BE RESPONSIVE ♦ 44

BOOTSTRAPPING ♦ 26

BUFFALO MOUNTAIN ♦ 68

BUILD TRUST ♦ 43

BUSINESS RULES ♦ 143

CAPABLE, PRODUCTIVE, AND SATISFIED ❖ 26

CARGO CULT ♦ 131

CASUAL DUTY ♦ 131

CLEAR THE FOG ♦ 169

CODE OWNERSHIP ♦ 66

COMPARABLE WORK ♦ 52

COMPENSATE SUCCESS ♦ 70

COMPLETION HEADROOM ♦ 53

CONTAINMENT BUILDING ♦ 131

CONWAY'S LAW ♦ 65

COUPLING DECREASES LATENCY ♦ 69

CREATOR-REVIEWER ♦ 119

CULT OF PERSONALITY ♦ 131

CUSTOMER INTERACTION PATTERNS ❖ 43

CUSTOMER MEETINGS: GO EARLY, STAY LATE ♦ 44

CUSTOMER RAPPORT ♦ 141

DAY CARE ♦ 171

DECISION DOCUMENT ♦ 119

DECOUPLE STAGES ♦ 68

DELIVERABLES TO GO ♦ 27

DESIGN BY TEAM ♦ 95

DESIGNERS ARE OUR FRIENDS ♦ 126

DEVELOPER CONTROLS PROCESS ♦ 65

DEVELOPING IN PAIRS ♦ 69

DEVELOPMENT EPISODE ♦ 53

DIVERSITY OF MEMBERSHIP ♦ 96

DIVIDE AND CONQUER ♦ 68

DOMAIN EXPERTISE IN ROLES ♦ 64

DON'T INTERRUPT AN INTERRUPT ♦ 69

DOORMAT ♦ 131

EARLY AND REGULAR DELIVERY ♦ 169

EFFECTIVE HANDOVER ♦ 27

ENGAGE CUSTOMERS ♦ 66

ENGAGE QA ♦ 66

ENVISIONING ♦ 143

EPISODES: A PATTERN LANGUAGE OF COMPETITIVE DEVELOPMENT ❖ 51

FIRE WALLS ♦ 67

FORM FOLLOWS FUNCTION ♦ 64

FUNCTION OWNERS/COMPONENT OWNERS ♦ 170

GATEKEEPER ♦ 67

GENERATIVE DEVELOPMENT-PROCESS PATTERN LANGUAGE ❖ 63

GENERIC UI, SPECIFIC UI ♦ 136

GENERICS AND SPECIFICS ♦ 136

GET INVOLVED EARLY ♦ 126

GOLD RUSH ♦ 170

GROUP VALIDATION ♦ 67

GURU DOES ALL ♦ 131

HOLISTIC DIVERSITY ♦ 170

HUB, SPOKE, AND RIM ♦ 68

IMPLIED REQUIREMENTS ♦ 52

INFORMAL LABOR PLAN ♦ 53

INTERRUPTS UNJAM BLOCKING ♦ 69

IT'S A RELATIONSHIP, NOT A SALE ♦ 43

KEEP IT WORKING ♦ 21

KNOW THE CUSTOMER ♦ 43

LET'S PLAY TEAM ♦ 131

LISTEN, LISTEN, LISTEN ♦ 44

LOCK 'EM UP TOGETHER ♦ 96

LONG POLE IN THE TENT ♦ 132

Managing and Meeting Customer Expectations ♦ 141
Market Walk-through ♦ 52
Master-Journeyman ♦ 119
Mercenary Analyst ♦ 67
Microcosm ♦ 169
Mind Your Manners ♦ 44
Move Responsibilities ♦ 67
Multiple Competing Designs ♦ 118
Named Stable Bases ♦ 68
Organization Follows Location ♦ 65
Organization Follows Market ♦ 65
Organizational Patterns for Teams ❖ 95
Owner per Deliverable ♦ 170
Patron ♦ 65
Patterns for Designing in Teams ❖ 118
Patterns on the Fly ❖ 130
Peacemaker ♦ 132
Phasing It In ♦ 64
Problem-Oriented Team ♦ 27
Product Initiative ♦ 52
Production Potential ♦ 26
Programming Episode ♦ 54
Prototype ♦ 169
Prototype ♦ 69
Prototypes ♦ 143
Pulse ♦ 27
Recommitment Meeting ♦ 53
Reconstruction ♦ 21
Reference Data ♦ 54
Requirement Walk-through ♦ 54
Review the Architecture ♦ 66
Round Pegs for Round Holes ♦ 27
Sacrifice One Person ♦ 171
Sacrificial Lamb ♦ 132
Scenarios Define Problem ♦ 67
Schedule Chicken ♦ 132
Scrum Meetings ♦ 148
Scrum: A Pattern Language for Hyperproductive Software Development ❖ 147
Self-Selecting Team ♦ 64
Shaping Circulation Realms ♦ 67
Show Personal Integrity ♦ 44
Size the Organization ♦ 64
Size the Schedule ♦ 64
Skill Mix ♦ 136
Solo Virtuoso ♦ 64
Someone Always Makes Progress ♦ 170

Sponsor Objectives ♦ 141
Sprint ♦ 147
Subclass per Team ♦ 137
Surviving Object-Oriented Projects: A Manager's Guide ❖ 169
Sweeping It Under the Rug ♦ 21
Take No Small Slips ♦ 69
Take Time ♦ 127
Take Your Licks ♦ 44
Team per Task ♦ 170
Team Space ♦ 27
Technical Memo ♦ 54
Tester's More Important Than the Test Cases ♦ 126
Three to Seven Helpers per Role ♦ 68
Time to Test ♦ 127
Train Hard Fight Easy ♦ 130
Train the Trainer ♦ 130
Trial Project ♦ 130
Unity of Purpose ♦ 96
Validation by Teams ♦ 96
Work Flows Inward ♦ 68
Work Group ♦ 52
Work Queue ♦ 52
Work Queue Report ♦ 52
Work Split ♦ 53

Parallel Programming

Allocator Caches ♦ 149
Code Locking ♦ 148
Communicating Processes ♦ 36
Counter Reader/Writer Lock ♦ 150
Critical-Section Fusing ♦ 149
Critical-Section Partitioning ♦ 149
Data Locking ♦ 148
Data Ownership ♦ 148
Distributed Reader/Writer Lock ♦ 150
Hierarchical Locking ♦ 149
Parallel Fastpath ♦ 148
Queued Lock ♦ 150
Queued Reader/Writer Lock ♦ 150
Reader/Writer Locking ♦ 149
Selecting Locking Designs for Parallel Programs ❖ 148
Selecting Locking Primitives for Parallel Programming ❖ 149
Sequential Program ♦ 148
Test-and-Set Lock ♦ 150

Pattern Writing
CLEAR TARGET AUDIENCE ♦ 105
CODE SAMPLES ♦ 105
CODE SAMPLES AS BONUS ♦ 105
COMMON PROBLEMS HIGHLIGHTED ♦ 106
DISTINCTIVE HEADINGS CONVEY
    STRUCTURE ♦ 106
EVOCATIVE PATTERN NAME ♦ 104
FINDABLE SECTIONS ♦ 104
GLOSSARY ♦ 106
INTENT CATALOG ♦ 105
MANDATORY ELEMENTS PRESENT ♦ 103
MEANINGFUL METAPHOR NAME ♦ 104
NOUN PHRASE NAME ♦ 104
OPTIONAL ELEMENTS WHEN HELPFUL ♦ 103
PATTERN ♦ 102
PATTERN LANGUAGE ♦ 103
PATTERN LANGUAGE FOR PATTERN
    WRITING ❖ 102
Pattern Language for Pattern Writing
    [Meszaros+98]
PATTERN LANGUAGE SUMMARY ♦ 105
PATTERN THUMBNAIL ♦ 104
PROBLEM/SOLUTION SUMMARY ♦ 106
READABLE REFERENCES TO PATTERNS ♦ 104
RELATIONSHIPS TO OTHER PATTERNS ♦ 104
RUNNING EXAMPLE ♦ 106
SINGLE-PASS READABLE ♦ 103
SKIPPABLE SECTIONS ♦ 103
TERMINOLOGY TAILORED TO AUDIENCE ♦ 105
UNDERSTOOD NOTATIONS ♦ 105
VISIBLE FORCES ♦ 103
Performance
CACHEABLE EXPRESSION ♦ 83
CACHING ARGUMENT ♦ 83
CACHING TEMPORARY VARIABLE ♦ 83
EXPERIMENT ♦ 83
FUNCTIONALITY ALA CARTE ♦ 61
HOT SPOT ♦ 83
LAZY OPTIMIZATION ♦ 82
LAZY OPTIMIZATION: PATTERNS FOR EFFICIENT
    SMALLTALK PROGRAMMING ❖ 82
OBJECT TRANSFORMATION ♦ 84
PERFORMANCE ASSESSMENT ♦ 82
PERFORMANCE CRITERIA ♦ 82
PERFORMANCE MEASUREMENT ♦ 82
SIMPLIFICATION ♦ 84
THRESHOLD SWITCH ♦ 82
TRANSIENT REDUCTION ♦ 84

Persistence
DOMAIN INTERCEPTS ♦ 137
MODEL HIERARCHY ♦ 137
OBJECT RECOVERY ♦ 92
PARSER/BUILDER ♦ 95
PERSISTENCE ACCESSORS ♦ 136
SERIALIZER ♦ 152
Propagation
ADAPTIVE PROPAGATOR ♦ 139
LAZY PROPAGATOR ♦ 139
PROPAGATOR: A FAMILY OF PATTERNS ❖ 138
STRICT PROPAGATOR ♦ 139
STRICT PROPAGATOR WITH FAILURE ♦ 139

Reactive and Real-Time Systems
BRIDGE ♦ 124
CAPACITY BOTTLENECK ♦ 100
CLASSES OF EVENT OBJECTS ♦ 129
DECOUPLE EXECUTION AND OUTPUT ♦ 77
Development of an Object-Oriented Framework
    for Vessel Control Systems [Dagermo+98]
EDITION ♦ 34
EVENT ACQUISITION ♦ 31
EVENT QUEUE ♦ 76
EVENT ROUTING ♦ 31
EVENT-CENTERED ARCHITECTURE ♦ 129
EVENT-DRIVEN RPC ♦ 94
FINISH WORK IN PROGRESS ♦ 101
FRESH WORK BEFORE STALE ♦ 101
HANDLE ARTIFICIAL EVENTS ♦ 76
HISTORY ON SELF ♦ 35
IMPROVING RESPONSIVENESS IN INTERACTIVE
    APPLICATIONS USING QUEUES ❖ 76
LEAKY BUCKET OF CREDITS ♦ 102
MATCH PROGRESS WORK WITH NEW ♦ 102
MERGE COMPATIBLE EVENTS ♦ 76
OBJECT-ORIENTED DESIGN PATTERNS IN
    REACTIVE SYSTEMS ❖ 93
OBJECT-ORIENTED SIMULATION ♦ 93
OBJECTIFY SYSTEM STATE ♦ 94
OBJECTIFY THE EVENTS ♦ 93
OBJECTS WITH REMOTE CONTROL ♦ 94
OPTIMIZE HIGH-RUNNER CASES ♦ 101
PATTERN LANGUAGE FOR IMPROVING THE
    CAPACITY OF REACTIVE SYSTEMS ❖ 100
Pattern Language for Improving the Capacity of
    Reactive Systems [Meszaros96]
PATTERNS FOR GENERATING A LAYERED
    ARCHITECTURE ❖ 123

PATTERNS OF EVENTS ❖ 129
PEDESTAL ♦ 123
PROCESSING CAPACITY ♦ 101
RECURSIVE CONTROL ♦ 144
SHARE THE LOAD ♦ 102
SHED LOAD ♦ 101
SYMMETRICAL REUSE ♦ 124
WORK SHED AT PERIPHERY ♦ 102

Refactoring
ATOMIC COMMITMENT ♦ 38
CONSOLIDATE THE PROGRAM TO SUPPORT
    EVOLUTION AND REUSE ♦ 85
COPY-ON-WRITE ♦ 38
CREATE ABSTRACT SUPERCLASS ♦ 85
DOUBLE CHECK ♦ 38
ENCAPSULATE CONCRETE STATE ♦ 146
EVENT-DRIVEN I/O ♦ 39
EVOLVE AGGREGATIONS FROM INHERITANCE
    HIERARCHIES ♦ 85
IDENTIFY MESSAGE LAYERS ♦ 146
LIFE CYCLE AND REFACTORING PATTERNS THAT
    SUPPORT EVOLUTION AND REUSE ❖ 85
OPEN CALLS ♦ 38
OPEN CONTAINERS ♦ 38
PASS-THROUGH HOST ♦ 38
SHEARING LAYERS ♦ 21

Security
ARCHITECTURAL PATTERNS FOR ENABLING
    APPLICATION SECURITY ❖ 17
CHECK POINT ♦ 17
FULL VIEW WITH ERRORS ♦ 18
INFORMATION SECRECY ♦ 175
LIMITED VIEW ♦ 18
MESSAGE INTEGRITY ♦ 175
ROLES ♦ 17
SECRECY WITH INTEGRITY ♦ 176
SECRECY WITH SENDER AUTHENTICATION ♦ 176
SECRECY WITH SIGNATURE ♦ 176
SECRECY WITH SIGNATURE WITH APPENDIX ♦ 176
SECURE ACCESS LAYER ♦ 18
SECURE-CHANNEL COMMUNICATION ♦ 175
SENDER AUTHENTICATION ♦ 175
SESSION ♦ 17
SIGNATURE ♦ 176
SIGNATURE WITH APPENDIX ♦ 176
SINGLE ACCESS POINT ♦ 17
TROPYC: A PATTERN LANGUAGE FOR
    CRYPTOGRAPHIC SOFTWARE ❖ 175

Smalltalk ENVY/Developer Idioms
LAYER IN AN APPLICATION ♦ 97
LAYERED AND SECTIONED ARCHITECTURE ♦ 97
NO SUBAPPLICATIONS ♦ 97
PARTITIONING SMALLTALK CODE INTO
    ENVY/DEVELOPER COMPONENTS ❖ 97
SECTION IN A SUBAPPLICATION ♦ 97
TWO APPLICATIONS ♦ 97

Smalltalk Idioms
ARRAY ♦ 160
ARTIFICIAL ACCESSORS ♦ 164
ARTIFICIAL DELEGATION ♦ 165
BOOLEAN PROPERTY SETTING METHOD ♦ 159
BYTE ARRAY ♦ 160
CACHEABLE EXPRESSION ♦ 83
CACHED EXTENSIBILITY ♦ 165
CACHING ARGUMENT ♦ 83
CACHING STATE VARIABLE ♦ 84
CACHING TEMPORARY VARIABLE ♦ 83
CACHING TEMPORARY VARIABLE ♦ 159
CASCADE ♦ 164
CHOOSING MESSAGE ♦ 155
CLIENT-SPECIFIED SELF ♦ 34
COLLECT ♦ 161
COLLECTING PARAMETER ♦ 157
COLLECTING TEMPORARY VARIABLE ♦ 159
COLLECTION ♦ 160
COLLECTION ACCESSOR METHOD ♦ 158
COMMON STATE ♦ 157
COMPARING METHOD ♦ 154
COMPOSED METHOD ♦ 153
CONCATENATING STREAM ♦ 163
CONCATENATING STREAM ♦ 84
CONCATENATION ♦ 161
CONDITIONAL EXPRESSION ♦ 164
CONSTANT METHOD ♦ 158
CONSTRUCTOR METHOD ♦ 153
CONSTRUCTOR PARAMETER METHOD ♦ 153
CONVERSION ♦ 154
CONVERTER CONSTRUCTOR METHOD ♦ 154
CONVERTER METHOD ♦ 154
DEBUG PRINTING METHOD ♦ 155
DECOMPOSING MESSAGE ♦ 155
DEFAULT VALUE METHOD ♦ 158
DELEGATION ♦ 156
DETECT ♦ 161
DICTIONARY ♦ 160
DIRECT VARIABLE ACCESS ♦ 158
DISPATCHED INTERPRETATION ♦ 156

Do ◆ 161
Double Dispatch ◆ 156
Duplicate Removing Set ◆ 162
Enumeration ◆ 161
Enumeration Method ◆ 159
Equality Method ◆ 160
Execute Around Method ◆ 155
Experiment ◆ 83
Explaining Temporary Variable ◆ 159
Explicit Initialization ◆ 157
Extending Super ◆ 156
Extensible Attributes ◆ 164
Generated Accessors ◆ 165
Getting Method ◆ 158
Guard Clause ◆ 163
Hashing Method ◆ 160
Hot Spot ◆ 83
Hypoth-A-Sized Collection ◆ 84
Includes: ◆ 161
Indented Control Flow ◆ 163
Indirect Variable Access ◆ 158
Inject:into: ◆ 162
Inline Message Pattern ◆ 163
Intention Revealing Message ◆ 155
Intention Revealing Selector ◆ 155
Interesting Return Value ◆ 164
Interval ◆ 161
Is Empty ◆ 161
Lazy Initialization ◆ 158
Lazy Optimization ◆ 82
Lazy Optimization: Patterns for Efficient
    Smalltalk Programming ❖ 82
Lookup Cache ◆ 162
Mediating Protocol ◆ 156
Message ◆ 155
Method Comment ◆ 155
Method Object ◆ 154
Modifying Super ◆ 156
Object Transformation ◆ 84
Ordered Collection ◆ 160
Parsing Stream ◆ 162
Performance Assessment ◆ 82
Performance Criteria ◆ 82
Performance Measurement ◆ 82
Pluggable Behavior ◆ 157
Pluggable Block ◆ 157
Pluggable Selector ◆ 157
Qualified Subclass Name ◆ 163
Query Method ◆ 154

Queue ◆ 162
Rectangular Block ◆ 163
Reusing Temporary Variable ◆ 159
Reversing Method ◆ 154
Role Suggesting Instance Variable
    Name ◆ 159
Role Suggesting Temporary Variable
    Name ◆ 159
Run Array ◆ 160
Searching Literal ◆ 162
Select/Reject ◆ 161
Selector Synthesis ◆ 165
Self Delegation ◆ 156
Set ◆ 160
Setting Method ◆ 158
Shortcut Constructor Method ◆ 153
Simple Delegation ◆ 156
Simple Enumeration Parameter ◆ 164
Simple Superclass Name ◆ 163
Simplification ◆ 84
Smalltalk Best Practice Patterns ❖ 153
Smalltalk Scaffolding Patterns ❖ 164
Sorted Collection ◆ 160
Stack ◆ 162
Super ◆ 156
Temporarily Sorted Collection ◆ 162
Temporary Variable ◆ 159
Threshold Switch ◆ 82
Transient Reduction ◆ 84
Type Suggesting Parameter Name ◆ 163
Variable State ◆ 157
Yourself ◆ 164

Smalltalk ValueModel Idioms

Encapsulate Senders of value and
    value: ◆ 178
Ensure That All Objects Sharing a Value
    Use the Same ValueModel ◆ 178
Maintain Consistent ValueModel Value
    Types ◆ 178
Understanding and Using the
    ValueModel Framework in VisualWorks
    Smalltalk ❖ 177
Use a BufferedValueHolder to Delay the
    Commit of a New Value ◆ 178
Use a PluggableAdaptor to Hold Some
    Part of an Object ◆ 179
Use a RangeAdaptor to Channel a
    Number's Range ◆ 178

Use a ScrollValueHolder to Hold a
Position in n-Dimensional Space ♦ 179

Use a SlotAdaptor to Hold a Single
Instance Variable ♦ 179

Use a TypeConverter to Convert a Value
Between Types ♦ 179

Use a ValueHolder to Hold a Stand-Alone
Object ♦ 178

Use a ValueModel to Generalize an
Object's Aspect ♦ 177

Use a ValueModel to Share a Value ♦ 177

Use an AspectAdaptor to Hold an Aspect of
an Object ♦ 178

Use an IndexedAdaptor to Hold a Single
Index in a Collection ♦ 178

Use onChangeSend:to: to Register
Interests on a Value ♦ 177

Use SelectionInList to Hold a List and Its
Selection ♦ 179

Use ValueModel Chains Instead of
onChangeSend:to: ♦ 177

Speech Recognition
Design Patterns in Object-Oriented Frameworks
[Srinivasan99]

Structural
Adapter ♦ 6
Aspects ♦ 110
Bridge ♦ 22
Class Clause ♦ 121
Class Retrieval ♦ 120
Class Semantics ♦ 121
Class Specification ♦ 121
Composite ♦ 37
Decorator ♦ 46
Detachable Inspector ♦ 49
Environment ♦ 110
Event Mechanism ♦ 111
External Polymorphism ♦ 56
External Polymorphism [Cleeland+98b]
Facade ♦ 56
Flyweight ♦ 60
IP/FP Plug In ♦ 111
Material Container ♦ 111
Materials ♦ 109
Pattern Language for Tool Construction
and Integration Based on the Tools and
Materials Metaphor ❖ 109
Patterns and Java Class Libraries [White96]

Patterns for Encapsulating Class
Trees ❖ 120

Proxy ♦ 140
Proxy Design Pattern Revisited ♦ 140
Separation of Powers ♦ 110
Tool and Material Coupling ♦ 110
Tool Composition ♦ 110
Tool Coordinator ♦ 111
Tools ♦ 110
Whole-Part ♦ 180
Wrapper Facade ♦ 180

System Modelling
Abstract Models with Constraints in
Subtypes ♦ 4

Accountability Knowledge Level ♦ 7
Accountability Knowledge Level ♦ 5
Appropriate Living Models ♦ 45
Architecture Patterns for Business
Systems ❖ 18

Batch Engineering Model ♦ 19
Decision Deferral and Capture Pattern
Language ❖ 45

Decision-Based Models ♦ 45
Downward Changes ♦ 45
Executable Models ♦ 45
Knowledge Level ♦ 5
Messaging Engineering Model ♦ 18
Model Hierarchy ♦ 137
Online Engineering Model ♦ 18
Organization Hierarchies ♦ 7
Put Frequently Varying Structures in
Instances ♦ 5

Stream I-O Engineering Model ♦ 19
Upward Traceability ♦ 45

Technical Paper Review
Champions Review Papers ♦ 74
Champions Speak First ♦ 74
Consensus on PC Papers ♦ 74
Experts Review Papers ♦ 74
Identify Missing Champions ♦ 74
Identify the Champion ♦ 73
Identify the Champion Pattern
Language ❖ 73

Identify the Conflicts ♦ 74
Make Champions Explicit ♦ 74

Telecommunications
Alarm Grid ♦ 79
Audible Alarm ♦ 79

BELTLINE TERMINAL ♦ 79

BOTTOM LINE ♦ 78

CAPACITY BOTTLENECK ♦ 100

DIAGNOSTIC CONTEXT ♦ 124

DIAGNOSTIC LOGGER ♦ 124

DON'T LET THEM FORGET ♦ 80

FAULT-TOLERANT TELECOMMUNICATION SYSTEM
    PATTERNS ❖ 57

FINISH WORK IN PROGRESS ♦ 101

FIVE MINUTES OF NO ESCALATION
    MESSAGES ♦ 79

FIVE MINUTES OF NO ESCALATION
    MESSAGES ♦ 57

FOOL ME ONCE ♦ 58

FRESH WORK BEFORE STALE ♦ 101

GEORGE WASHINGTON IS STILL DEAD ♦ 78

INPUT AND OUTPUT PATTERN LANGUAGE ❖ 77

Input and Output Pattern Language [Hanmer+99]

IO GATEKEEPER ♦ 77

IO TRIAGE ♦ 78

LEAKY BUCKET COUNTERS ♦ 58

LEAKY BUCKET OF CREDITS ♦ 102

MATCH PROGRESS WORK WITH NEW ♦ 102

MIND YOUR OWN BUSINESS ♦ 77

MINIMIZE HUMAN INTERVENTION ♦ 57

MML ♦ 77

OFFICE ALARMS ♦ 80

OPTIMIZE HIGH-RUNNER CASES ♦ 101

PATTERN LANGUAGE FOR IMPROVING THE
    CAPACITY OF REACTIVE SYSTEMS ❖ 100

Pattern Language for Improving the Capacity of
    Reactive Systems [Meszaros96]

PATTERNS FOR LOGGING DIAGNOSTIC
    MESSAGES ❖ 124

PEOPLE KNOW BEST ♦ 57

PROCESSING CAPACITY ♦ 101

PSEUDO-IO ♦ 79

RAW IO ♦ 80

RIDING OVER TRANSIENTS ♦ 57

SHARE THE LOAD ♦ 102

SHED LOAD ♦ 101

SHUT UP AND LISTEN ♦ 79

SICO FIRST AND ALWAYS ♦ 58

STRING A WIRE ♦ 80

TIMESTAMP ♦ 78

TRY ALL HARDWARE COMBOS ♦ 58

TYPED DIAGNOSTICS ♦ 125

WHO ASKED? ♦ 78

WORK SHED AT PERIPHERY ♦ 102

Telemetry Processing

HANDLERS ♦ 95

HIERARCHY OF FACTORIES ♦ 95

LOOSE INTERFACES ♦ 95

ORGANIZATIONAL MULTIPLEXING: PATTERNS
    FOR PROCESSING SATELLITE TELEMETRY WITH
    DISTRIBUTED TEAMS ❖ 94

PARSER/BUILDER ♦ 95

PATTERN FOR SEPARATING ASSEMBLY AND
    PROCESSING ♦ 98

Testing

14.4 KBPS TESTING ♦ 99

"UNCHANGED" INTERFACES ♦ 127

ADOPT-A-PROBLEM ♦ 129

AMBIGUOUS DOCUMENTATION ♦ 127

APPLICATION DESIGN IS BOUNDED BY TEST
    DESIGN ♦ 66

BUSY SYSTEM ♦ 128

DESIGNERS ARE OUR FRIENDS ♦ 126

DOCUMENT THE PROBLEM ♦ 129

DON'T TRUST SIMULATIONS ♦ 128

END USER VIEWPOINT ♦ 128

ENGAGE QA ♦ 66

EXHAUSTION TEST ♦ 73

GET INVOLVED EARLY ♦ 126

KILLER TEST ♦ 129

MULTIPLE PROCESSORS ♦ 128

PATTERNS FOR SYSTEM TESTING ❖ 126

PET PEEVE ♦ 129

PROBLEM AREA ♦ 127

SCRATCH 'N SNIFF ♦ 128

STRANGE BEHAVIOR ♦ 128

TAKE TIME ♦ 127

TESTER'S MORE IMPORTANT THAN THE TEST
    CASES ♦ 126

TIME TO TEST ♦ 127

UNUSUAL TIMING ♦ 128

USE OLD PROBLEM REPORTS ♦ 127

Time

CHANGE LOG ♦ 34

COLLECTION OF HISTORY PATTERNS ❖ 34

Collection of History Patterns [Anderson99]

DUAL TIME RECORD ♦ 9

EDITION ♦ 34

HISTORIC MAPPING ♦ 16

HISTORY ON ASSOCIATION ♦ 34

HISTORY ON SELF ♦ 35

HISTORY ON TREE ♦ 35

MEMENTO CHILD ♦ 35

POSTING ♦ 35
PROPOSED AND IMPLEMENTED ACTION ♦ 12
SNAPSHOT ♦ 173
TEMPORAL ASSOCIATION ♦ 173
TEMPORAL PATTERNS ❖ 172
TEMPORAL PROPERTY ♦ 172

Trading
CONTRACT ♦ 13
FORWARD CONTRACTS ♦ 13
MULTIPLE ACCESS LEVELS TO A PACKAGE ♦ 14
MUTUAL VISIBILITY ♦ 14
OPTIONS ♦ 14
PARALLEL APPLICATION AND DOMAIN
    HIERARCHIES ♦ 14
PORTFOLIO ♦ 13
PRODUCT ♦ 14
QUOTE ♦ 13
SCENARIO ♦ 13
SUBTYPE STATE MACHINES ♦ 14
SUBTYPING PACKAGES ♦ 14

Training
ACQUAINTANCE EXAMPLES ♦ 117
CHICKEN AND EGG ♦ 116
COLORFUL ANALOGY ♦ 118
DEBRIEF AFTER ACTIVITIES ♦ 118
EXAMPLE LASTS ONE WEEK ♦ 117
ITERATIVE COURSE DEVELOPMENT ♦ 116
MIX NEW AND OLD ♦ 116
MODULE'S STORY ♦ 117
PATTERNS FOR CLASSROOM EDUCATION ❖ 116
PITFALL DIAGNOSIS AND PREVENTION ♦ 116
QUIZ GAMES ♦ 118
REFERENCE EXAMPLES ♦ 117
SEVEN PARTS ♦ 117
SIMULATION GAMES ♦ 118
VISIBLE CHECKLIST ♦ 117

Transaction Processing
ADJUSTING TRANSACTIONS ♦ 174
BUSINESS ACCOUNTS ♦ 174
BUSINESS TRANSACTIONS ♦ 174
CLIENT SYNCHRONIZATION ♦ 109
COMPOSITE TRANSACTIONS ♦ 174
CONTINUOUS PROCESSING ♦ 175
DIAGNOSTIC CONTEXT ♦ 124
DIAGNOSTIC LOGGER ♦ 124
EDITS INSIDE ♦ 137
EXPLICIT BUSINESS RULES ♦ 174
MONTH END CLOSING ♦ 174

PATTERNS FOR LOGGING DIAGNOSTIC
    MESSAGES ❖ 124
POSTING ♦ 35
SEPARATE TRANSACTION PROCESSING FROM
    ARCHIVAL ♦ 174
TRANSACTIONS AND ACCOUNTS ❖ 173
TYPED DIAGNOSTICS ♦ 125

Transportation
CASCADE ♦ 28
DRIVER DUTY ♦ 51
DRIVER DUTY CONSTRUCTOR ♦ 51
Driver Duty Constructor: A Pattern for Public
    Transport Systems [Zhao+99]
Driver Duty: A Pattern for Public Transport
    Systems [Zhao+98a]
Modeling Transport Objects with Patterns
    [Foster+98]
PATTERN LANGUAGE OF TRANSPORT SYSTEMS
    (POINT AND ROUTE) ❖ 114
Pattern Language of Transport Systems (Point
    and Route) [Foster+97]
Pattern Language of Transport Systems (Point
    and Route) [Zhao+98b]
POINT ♦ 114
ROUTE ♦ 114

Visualization and Monitoring
DOVE: A Distributed Object Visualization
    Environment [Kircher+99]

Web Site Development
14.4 KBPS TESTING ♦ 99
EXPOSABLE GUTS ♦ 99
NATURAL TEXT DIRECTORIES ♦ 98
NATURAL TEXT FLOW ♦ 98
NATURAL TEXT HYPERLINKS ♦ 98
NEW DOCUMENT NOTIFICATION ♦ 99
PATTERN LANGUAGE FOR AN ESSAY-BASED WEB
    SITE ❖ 98
REFERENCE SECTION ♦ 98
WORKSHEET DOCUMENTS ♦ 99

Writers' Workshops
AUTHOR ASKS FOR CLARIFICATION ♦ 113
AUTHOR READS SELECTION ♦ 113
AUTHORS ARE EXPERTS ♦ 112
AUTHORS' CIRCLE ♦ 112
CLEARING THE PALATE ♦ 114
COMMUNITY OF TRUST ♦ 112
FLY ON THE WALL ♦ 113

Almanac Entries

The information for each pattern includes several components, as outlined in the following diagram.

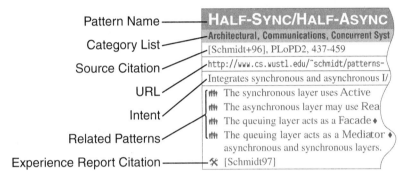

Related patterns are preceded by a 🎎. Experience report citations are preceded by a 🛠. Experience reports present examples in a given domain that illustrate how one or more patterns solve a real problem. A full reference for the citation of an experience report appears in the Bibliography.

Collections of patterns appear together and contain the information outlined in the diagram below. This information is followed by the subpatterns in order of appearance in the source.

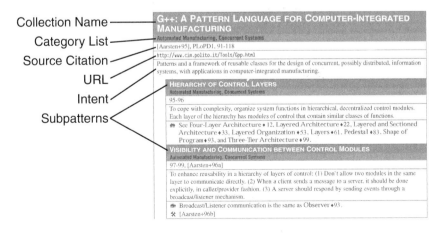

ABSTRACT CLASS

Design Process

[Woolf99a], *PLoPD4*, 5-14

When you're designing a class hierarchy, define the interface and general implementation in an abstract class and defer implementation to the subclasses.

- This pattern presents the same solution as CREATE ABSTRACT SUPERCLASS ♦ 85.

ABSTRACT CLIENT

C++ Idioms

[Martin95b], *PLoPD1*, 389-391

Servers need to send messages to their clients. This is difficult in C++ because the server must use an interface that is part of the client, making the server depend on the client. Instead, create abstract client interfaces that have the required interfaces and are inherited by the client.

ABSTRACT FACTORY

Creational

[Gamma+95], *GoF*, 87-95

[Alpert+98], *Design Patterns Smalltalk Companion*, 31-46

Provide an interface for creating families of related or dependent objects without specifying their concrete classes.

- ABSTRACT FACTORY ♦ 2 classes often use FACTORY METHOD ♦ 56 or PROTOTYPE ♦ 138.
- A concrete factory is often a SINGLETON ♦ 152.
- [Kircher+99], [Masuda+98], [Schmidt96a], [Woodward96], [Zhang+96c]

ABSTRACT SESSION

Client-Server, Communications, Networks

[Pryce99], *PLoPD4*, 95-109

`http://www-dse.doc.ic.ac.uk/~np2/patterns/`

When an object's services are invoked by clients, the server object may have to maintain state for each client. The server creates a session object that encapsulates state information for the client. The server returns a pointer to the session object.

- This pattern is an implementation of SESSION ♦ 37.
- The server uses FACTORY METHOD ♦ 56 to create sessions.
- The server uses MEDIATOR ♦ 86 to control interactions among clients. Session objects control interactions of the server and a single client.
- ACCEPTOR ♦ 3 and CONNECTOR ♦ 40 use this pattern.
- This pattern can implement ADAPTER ♦ 6.

ACCEPTOR

Communications, Concurrent Systems, Distributed Systems

[Schmidt98b], *PLoPD3*, 191-229

http://www.cs.wustl.edu/~schmidt/report-art.html

Decouple service initialization from the services provided. This pattern is for passive initialization.

- ꜛ CONNECTOR ♦ 40 is for active initialization.
- ꜛ This pattern can be used with ACTIVE OBJECT ♦ 6, REACTOR ♦ 143, and SERVICE CONFIGURATOR ♦ 151.
- ꜛ This pattern uses FACTORY METHOD ♦ 56 and TEMPLATE METHOD ♦ 171
- ✘ [Schmidt+95], [Schmidt96a], [Schmidt97]

ACCESSING RELATIONAL DATABASES

Database

[Keller+98b], *PLoPD3*, 313-343

Defines relational database access layers for database application design, either data-driven or representational.

RELATIONAL DATABASE ACCESS LAYER

Architectural, Database

317-326

To access a relational database, use a layered architecture. A logical access layer provides the interface to the stable application kernel, while a physical access layer accesses the database. The latter can adapt to changing performance needs.

- ꜛ Use QUERY BROKER ♦ 4 to decouple the layers.
- ꜛ This pattern is an application of LAYERED ARCHITECTURE ♦ 125, LAYERED AND SECTIONED ARCHITECTURE ♦ 96, and LAYERS ♦ 81.
- ꜛ HIERARCHY OF CONTROL LAYERS ♦ 61, PEDESTAL ♦ 123, FOUR-LAYER ARCHITECTURE ♦ 106, LAYERED ORGANIZATION ♦ 59, SHAPE OF PROGRAM ♦ 29, THREE-TIER ARCHITECTURE ♦ 15
- ꜛ CROSSING CHASMS ❖ 41 describes how to extend this pattern to an object-oriented view of a relational database.

HIERARCHICAL VIEW

Database

317-332

You're using RELATIONAL DATABASE ACCESS LAYER ♦ 3. The database access layer should present an interface expressed in terms of the domain's problem space to the application kernel.

- ꜛ Use QUERY BROKER ♦ 4 to decouple HIERARCHICAL VIEW ♦ 3 from the underlying PHYSICAL VIEW ♦ 3.

PHYSICAL VIEW

Database

332-335

You're using RELATIONAL DATABASE ACCESS LAYER ♦ 3 and HIERARCHICAL VIEW ♦ 3. To provide an easy-to-use interface to your physical database tables, encapsulate every table and every view with a ConcretePhysicalView class. Use these classes to encapsulate overflow tables and other database optimization techniques.

QUERY BROKER
Database

336-341

You're using RELATIONAL DATABASE ACCESS LAYER ♦ 3, HIERARCHICAL VIEW ♦ 3, and PHYSICAL VIEW ♦ 3. Use a broker to connect the hierarchical view and the physical view for reading and writing. The hierarchical view becomes the client side, and the physical view becomes the server.

♦♦♦ This pattern is an extension of BROKER ♦ 22.

♦♦♦ Brown and Whitenack also describe a BROKER ♦ 108.

ACCOUNT NUMBER
Accounting, Database

[Wake95], *PLoPD1*, 157-162

In a collection of account information, a name may be associated with many people, and a single person may have several different names. Assign exactly one account number to each person, and assign each account number only once.

ACCOUNTABILITY AND ORGANIZATIONAL STRUCTURES
Analysis

[Fowler96], *PLoPD2*, 353-370

Patterns for analysis and design.

PARTY
Analysis

359

Define a party object as a supertype for a person or an organization. This allows relationships to be established between a person or an organization by relating to a party.

♦♦♦ PARTY ♦ 6

RECURSIVE STRUCTURES FOR ORGANIZATIONS
Analysis

359-361

You need to describe an organization with a strict hierarchy. The levels change but not frequently. Use a recursive relationship on organization.

♦♦♦ This is an implementation of ABSTRACT MODELS WITH CONSTRAINTS IN SUBTYPES ♦ 4.

ABSTRACT MODELS WITH CONSTRAINTS IN SUBTYPES
Analysis, System Modelling

361-362

Should you choose a more abstract model or a more specific one? Create an abstract model for flexibility, and use subtypes to enforce the rules.

♦♦♦ RECURSIVE STRUCTURES FOR ORGANIZATIONS ♦ 4 is an implementation of this pattern.

MULTIPLE HIERARCHIC ASSOCIATIONS
Analysis

362-363

The enterprise is a matrix organization with more than one hierarchy. Apply RECURSIVE STRUCTURES FOR ORGANIZATIONS ♦ 4 for each hierarchy. Each hierarchy gets an association on organization and a partition of subtypes for the levels.

ORGANIZATIONAL STRUCTURE-TYPED RELATIONSHIP

Analysis

363-364

There are many links in the enterprise and the links may change frequently. You may need to keep a history of past structures. Add an association type and an organizational structure type. Each instance of an organizational structure type represents a kind of organizational relationship. Time may be added to a structure to record history.

OBJECTIFY ASSOCIATIONS

Analysis

364-365

You need to add a feature to an association, but it's inappropriate to add it to either type. Turn the association into a type with associations to the participating types and add the feature to the association.

> ♦♦♦ BASIC RELATIONSHIP PATTERNS ❖ 19 and BUSINESS PATTERNS OF ASSOCIATION OBJECTS ❖ 23 expand this pattern.

TYPED RELATIONSHIP

Analysis

365

Many similar associations are bloating a type. Use OBJECTIFY ASSOCIATIONS ♦ 5 and add an association type attribute; one instance is created for each association in this structure.

ACCOUNTABILITY ABSTRACTION

Analysis

366-367

Similar structural relationships exist between organizations, between people, and between people and organizations. Use TYPED RELATIONSHIP ♦ 5 to abstract the relationships and create an accountability type.

ACCOUNTABILITY KNOWLEDGE LEVEL

Analysis, System Modelling

367

Separate an organizational model into operational and knowledge levels. The operational level comprises accountability, party, and their interrelationships. The knowledge level comprises accountability type, party type, and their interrelationships.

> ♦♦♦ ACCOUNTABILITY KNOWLEDGE LEVEL ♦ 7

PUT FREQUENTLY VARYING STRUCTURES IN INSTANCES

Analysis, System Modelling

367-368

It isn't easy to change a model. Design the model so frequent changes affect instances of types in the same type structure.

KNOWLEDGE LEVEL

Analysis, System Modelling

369-370

Changes in the structure of types occur with changes in the business practice. A model for the day-to-day operational aspects of the problem has been developed. Create a knowledge level for the model. Each type on the operational level has a corresponding type on the knowledge level. An association links the operational type to its corresponding knowledge type. Relationships between knowledge types define the possible links between the operational types.

ACTIVE OBJECT

Communications, Concurrent Systems, Distributed Systems

[Lavender+96], *PLoPD2*, 483-499

http://www.cs.wustl.edu/~schmidt/patterns-ace.html

Decouple method execution from method invocation to simplify synchronized access to a shared resource.

- ♙ HALF-SYNC/HALF-ASYNC ♦ 71 decouples synchronous I/O from asynchronous I/O and typically uses ACTIVE OBJECT ♦ 6 to implement the synchronous layer.
- ✕ [Schmidt97], [Srinivasan99]

ACYCLIC VISITOR

Behavioral

[Martin98], *PLoPD3*, 93-103

Allow new functions to be added to class hierarchies without affecting those hierarchies and without creating the troublesome dependency cycles inherent to VISITOR ♦ 179.

ADAPTER

Structural

[Gamma+95], *GoF*, 139-150

[Alpert+98], *Design Patterns Smalltalk Companion*, 105-119

Convert the interface of a class to one expected by clients. This lets classes work together that couldn't otherwise because of incompatible interfaces.

- ♙ An adapter can be a command, translating messages between the client and adaptee.
- ♙ BRIDGE ♦ 22 has a similar structure but a different intent. BRIDGE ♦ 22 separates interface from implementation; ADAPTER ♦ 6 changes the interface to an object.
- ♙ DECORATOR ♦ 46 enhances another object without changing its interface, so it is more transparent to the application than this pattern. DECORATOR ♦ 46 also supports recursive composition.
- ♙ FACADE ♦ 56 defines a new interface, while this pattern reuses an old interface.
- ♙ PROXY ♦ 139 defines a representative or surrogate for another object but does not change its interface.
- ✕ [Brown96], [Carmichael98], [Gamma+99], [Hüni+95], [Keller+98a], [Piehler99], [Ramirez95], [Schmid95], [Schmidt97], [Schmidt98a], [Srinivasan99], [Woodward96]

ANALYSIS PATTERNS

Analysis

[Fowler97], *Analysis Patterns*

Analysis that reflects conceptual structures of business processes rather than actual software implementations. Patterns for various business domains.

> ### PARTY
>
> **Analysis, Business Process**
>
> 18-19
>
> Define a party object as a supertype for a person or an organization. This allows relationships to be established between a person or an organization by relating to a party.
>
> - ♙ PARTY ♦ 4

ORGANIZATION HIERARCHIES

Analysis, Business Process, System Modelling

19-20

Model organizational hierarchies with a recursive structure. Enforce relationships between organizational entities with rules. It's easier to change rules than to change the model.

ORGANIZATION STRUCTURE

Analysis, Business Process

21-22

Use types to define relationships between organizational entities.

ACCOUNTABILITY

Analysis, Business Process

22-24

Abstract responsibilities of people or organizations to an accountability entity.

ACCOUNTABILITY KNOWLEDGE LEVEL

Analysis, Business Process, System Modelling

24-27

Separate an organizational model into operational and knowledge levels. The operational level comprises accountability, party, and their interrelationships. The knowledge level comprises accountability type, party type, and their interrelationships. At the operational level, the model records day-to-day events. At the knowledge level, the model records general rules that govern the structure. Some data modelers call the knowledge level a "meta level."

ACCOUNTABILITY KNOWLEDGE LEVEL ◆ 5

PARTY TYPE GENERALIZATIONS

Analysis, Business Process, Health Care

27-28

Allow party types to have sub- and supertype relationships.

HIERARCHIC ACCOUNTABILITY

Analysis, Business Process

28-30

Create a hierarchic accountability type that captures the responsibility of parties in a hierarchy.

OPERATING SCOPE

Analysis, Business Process, Health Care

30-32

Accountability has a number of operating scopes, each of which is a subtype that describes the actual characteristics.

POST

Analysis, Business Process, Health Care

32-33

Introduce a post type that contains the responsibilities of a position. This allows job responsibilities to be attached to the post, not the person. This should only be used when there are significant responsibilities that are static, and people change posts often.

QUANTITY
Analysis

36-38

Define an object type that comprises a number and units.

♦♦♦ Quantity is a WHOLE VALUE ♦ 32 that the user interface can interpret and display. Monetary values should be represented as quantities where the currency is the unit.

CONVERSION RATIO
Analysis

38-39

Define a conversion ratio object between units, and give QUANTITY ♦ 8 an operation, convertTo(Unit), that returns a new quantity in the unit.

COMPOUND UNITS
Analysis

39-41

A compound unit is a combination of atomic units, e.g., meters per second. A sophisticated conversion operation can use CONVERSION RATIO ♦ 8 on atomic units to convert compound units. COMPOUND UNITS ♦ 8 must know the atomic units and their powers or relationships.

MEASUREMENT
Analysis, Health Care

41-42

If a large number of possible measurements would make the interface for a person object too complex, define a phenomenon object. A person would then have one attribute for all measurements. Attributes could be added to a measurement, e.g., who took the measurement and when.

OBSERVATION
Analysis, Health Care

42-46

Some attributes are qualitative, e.g., blood group, whether a patient has diabetes. Define an observation type that links the object to a phenomenon. Each phenomenon is a value for some phenomenon type.

♦♦♦ MEASUREMENT ♦ 8 defines a phenomenon type.

♦♦♦ OBSERVER ♦ 94

SUBTYPING OBSERVATION CONCEPTS
Analysis, Health Care

46

Some phenomena are special cases of another phenomenon. Define an observation type that links the object to a phenomenon. Each phenomenon is a value for some phenomenon type.

♦♦♦ MEASUREMENT ♦ 8 defines a phenomenon type.

♦♦♦ OBSERVER ♦ 94

PROTOCOL
Analysis, Business Planning, Health Care

46-47

The method of observing can occasionally cause different interpretations when dealing with similar phenomena. Record the protocol used in a protocol object.

DUAL TIME RECORD
Analysis, Health Care, Time

47-48

An OBSERVATION ♦ 8 may have a limited period during which it can be applied, so use two time records for each observation, one when the observation is applicable and one when it is recorded.

REJECTED OBSERVATION
Analysis, Health Care

48

Sometimes mistakes are made when an OBSERVATION ♦ 8 is made. This record must be kept but it can be linked to an observation that replaces it.

ACTIVE OBSERVATION, HYPOTHESIS, AND PROJECTION
Analysis, Health Care

49-50

As observations are recorded, levels of assurance are reached. An active observation is the one currently adopted; a hypothesis requires further testing. Projections are observations that might be seen in the future.

ASSOCIATED OBSERVATION
Analysis, Health Care

50-51

To record the chain of evidence behind a diagnosis, treat the diagnosis as an OBSERVATION ♦ 8 with an association to the observations used in evidence.

PROCESS OF OBSERVATION
Analysis, Health Care

51-55

A clinician makes an OBSERVATION ♦ 8 and considers an ASSOCIATED OBSERVATION ♦ 9. The clinician proposes further observations and interventions as needed as well as reevaluation of contradictory observations. As these steps produce further observations, this leads to a continuous process of observation.

ENTERPRISE SEGMENT
Analysis, Business Planning

59-65

To decompose a large enterprise using different criteria for different segments with varying degrees of granularity, define each decomposition criterion as a dimension, and represent it as a hierarchy of elements. Define an enterprise segment as the combination of one element from each dimension.

MEASUREMENT PROTOCOL
Analysis, Business Computation

65-76

Corporate analysis involves measurement. Measurements are usually read from a database or calculated. Define a measurement protocol type so that this information is not lost.

RANGE
Analysis, Business Computation

76-77

To make sense of a collection of data, you can group measurements into categories. Describe ranges of measurements. Then use PHENOMENON WITH RANGE ♦ 10. Define a range type with upper and lower bounds and suitable operations.

PHENOMENON WITH RANGE
Analysis, Business Computation

77-81

Give a phenomenon an attribute of range, or create a range function that links the range to the phenomenon under conditions described by other phenomena.

NAME
Design Process

86-87

Give an object a string as its identifier.

IDENTIFICATION SCHEME
Design Process

88-89

In simple systems there is usually a single identifier for each object, while complex systems may have many identifiers for one object. Define schemes so each identifier refers to only one unit. An identifier then refers to only one object but different parties can refer to the object differently.

OBJECT MERGE
Design Process, Health Care

90-92

In a complex system, two objects may be considered the same. To avoid redundancy: (1) Copy the attributes of the first to the second, switch all references from the first to the second, and then delete the first. (2) Mark the first as superseded and give it a link to the second. (3) Link the two object appearances with an essence that indicates they are the same.

  ♔ BRIDGE ♦ 22, COUNTED BODY ♦ 24, ESSENCE ♦ 54

OBJECT EQUIVALENCE
Design Process, Health Care

92-93

Some people think two objects are the same but others may think they are different. Create an equivalence relationship for the two objects.

  ♔ BASIC RELATIONSHIP PATTERNS ❖ 19

ACCOUNT
Accounting, Inventory Control Systems

97-98

When you're recording a history of changes to some quantity, create an account object. Each change is recorded as an entry against the account. The balance of the account gives the current value.

  ✶ [Carmichael98]

TRANSACTION
Accounting, Inventory Control Systems

98-101

You're using ACCOUNT ♦ 10 to record the history of changes to some quantity and must check that entries do not get lost. Entries withdrawn from one account must be deposited in another. Entries cannot be created or destroyed. "Two-legged" transactions move an entry from one account to another, while "multi-legged" allow entries in several accounts as long as the complete transaction balances.

SUMMARY ACCOUNT

Accounting, Inventory Control Systems

101-103

Accounts can be grouped. Create a summary account object with the other accounts as children.

MEMO ACCOUNT

Accounting, Inventory Control Systems

103-104

Sometimes account entries are not intended to balance. Allow a quantity to be stored in a side account without using a transaction. Create a memo account that does not affect real transactions and does not hold real entries.

ACCOUNT ♦ 10, TRANSACTION ♦ 10

POSTING RULES

Accounting, Inventory Control Systems

104-105

To automate transfers between accounts, define posting rules. This allows the building of active networks of accounts that update each other and reflect business rules.

INDIVIDUAL INSTANCE METHOD

Accounting, Inventory Control Systems

106-111

To attach methods to instances, use SINGLETON ♦ 152, STRATEGY ♦ 167, a case statement, an interpreter, or a parameterized method.

POSTING RULE EXECUTION

Accounting, Inventory Control Systems

111-115

Separate the strategy of firing the posting rules from the rules themselves. Use: (1) Eager Firing, where rules are fired when a suitable entry is made in a trigger account; (2) give the ACCOUNT ♦ 10 the responsibility for firing the rules; (3) let an external agent be responsible for firing the rule; or (4) give accounts responsibility for firing their rules and the rules for all dependent accounts.

POSTING RULES FOR MANY ACCOUNTS

Accounting, Inventory Control Systems

116-118

Use ACCOUNTABILITY KNOWLEDGE LEVEL ♦ 7 where posting rules for more than one ACCOUNT ♦ 10 are linked to account types, or define a posting rule on a SUMMARY ACCOUNT ♦ 11.

CHOOSING ENTRIES

Accounting, Inventory Control Systems

118-119

POSTING RULES ♦ 11 may need a subset of entries from its trigger ACCOUNT ♦ 10. This can be done by: (1) having the account return all entries and selecting the required subset; (2) defining a method that selects the subset; or (3) using a filter—an object that encapsulates the query.

PORTFOLIO ♦ 13

ACCOUNTING PRACTICE
Accounting, Inventory Control Systems

119-122

A network of accounts with POSTING RULES ♦ 11 can become too complex. Define an accounting practice to be a subset of the network posting rules. Each account is assigned an accounting practice for a given function.

SOURCES OF AN ENTRY
Accounting, Inventory Control Systems

122-123

Each transaction should know which posting rule created it and which entries were input. This pattern forms a chain of entries and transactions across the network.

⚎ CHAIN OF RESPONSIBILITY ♦ 32, POSTING RULES ♦ 11, TRANSACTION ♦ 10

BALANCE SHEET AND INCOME STATEMENT
Accounting, Inventory Control Systems

123-124

When you're using ACCOUNT ♦ 10 to describe a system, distinguish between the balance sheet and income statement accounts.

CORRESPONDING ACCOUNT
Accounting, Inventory Control Systems

124-125

Two parties may have different views of the same ACCOUNT ♦ 10. Treat the views as separate accounts that correspond to each other.

SPECIALIZED ACCOUNT MODEL
Accounting, Inventory Control Systems

125-127

The general accounting patterns can be used for a domain by subtyping the patterns' types.

BOOKING ENTRIES TO MULTIPLE ACCOUNTS
Accounting, Inventory Control Systems

127-131

There may be more than one ACCOUNT ♦ 10 for an entry. (1) Treat one account as the real account and use MEMO ACCOUNT ♦ 11 for the other. (2) Treat one account as the real account and use a derived account for the other.

PROPOSED AND IMPLEMENTED ACTION
Business Planning, Health Care, Time

158-160

Divide the possible states of a planned action into two subtypes: the intention and what actually happened.

COMPLETED AND ABANDONED ACTIONS
Business Planning, Health Care

160-161

Describe the end of an action as "completed" or "abandoned."

SUSPENSION
Business Planning, Health Care

161-162

When an action is deferred, link a suspension object to the action.

PLAN
Business Planning, Health Care

162-164

A plan is a collection of proposed actions linked in some sequence.

PROTOCOL
Analysis, Business Planning, Health Care

165-168

Actions can be carried out according to a standard operating procedure, or protocol. A protocol can be divided into subprotocols linked by dependencies.

RESOURCE ALLOCATION
Business Planning, Health Care

168-172

In planning, a resource requirement is specified at a general level; then in the execution of the plan, a specific instance is allocated.

OUTCOME AND START FUNCTIONS
Business Planning, Health Care

172-174

Outcome and start functions link a protocol to the observation concepts that trigger it and may be the result of it.

CONTRACT
Trading

176-180

Describe each trade with a contract for buying or selling goods.

PORTFOLIO
Trading

180-184

A portfolio is a collection of CONTRACT ♦ 13 objects.

QUOTE
Trading

185-188

A quote represents two numbers: the buying price (the bid) and the selling price (the offer).

SCENARIO
Trading

188-196

Prices change over time. A scenario is a collection of QUOTE ♦ 13 objects that represent the state of the market at a point in time.

FORWARD CONTRACTS
Trading

198-200

A forward contract is an agreement to do a deal some time in the future. It represents separate trade and delivery dates for the CONTRACT ♦ 13.

OPTIONS

Trading

200-205

An option gives the holder the right to buy currency at a prearranged exchange rate if the holder wishes. Define option to be a subtype of CONTRACT ♦ 13, or define option as a separate object with a contract as an attribute.

PRODUCT

Trading

205-211

A combination option is seen as one item by the seller and as a collection of simpler contracts internally (or by the dealers). Define what the seller sells as a product and what is internally valued as a CONTRACT ♦ 13.

SUBTYPE STATE MACHINES

Trading

211-216

A barrier option has different behaviors from an option and so seems to be a subtype of option. Ensure that both sub- and supertype objects respond to the same events.

PARALLEL APPLICATION AND DOMAIN HIERARCHIES

Trading

216-223

When displaying a list of objects of various types, some properties should not be displayed. The user interface objects must not send messages to inappropriate objects: (1) check the type of the object before the message is sent; (2) provide a supertype interface that encompasses all subtype behaviors; (3) treat the properties as a run-time attribute; (4) use an intermediate object loaded by the user interface; or (5) raise an exception.

MULTIPLE ACCESS LEVELS TO A PACKAGE

Trading

226-230

Different clients of a package need different amounts of behavior. (1) Split the package into separate packages or (2) allow packages to have more than one interface.

MUTUAL VISIBILITY

Trading

230-233

Types in two packages need to see each other. (1) Combine the two packages, (2) have two mutually visible packages, or (3) do not allow one type to see the other.

SUBTYPING PACKAGES

Trading

233-234

When a subtype is used with a package, the subtype can be in a separate package. The subtype is visible to the supertype but not vice versa.

TWO-TIER ARCHITECTURE

Analysis, Architectural, Client-Server

240-242

In client-server applications, partition the system into a shared database that sits on a server and several clients with interfaces that allow direct access to the data.

⚜ ACCESSING RELATIONAL DATABASES ❖ 3, CROSSING CHASMS ❖ 41

THREE-TIER ARCHITECTURE
Analysis, Architectural

242-245

In a TWO-TIER ARCHITECTURE ♦ 14, the user interface is tightly coupled to the database. Partition the system into three logical layers: application, domain, and database.

♦♦♦ ACCESSING RELATIONAL DATABASES ❖ 3, CROSSING CHASMS ❖ 41

♦♦♦ HIERARCHY OF CONTROL LAYERS ♦ 61, FOUR-LAYER ARCHITECTURE ♦ 106, LAYERED ARCHITECTURE ♦ 125, LAYERED AND SECTIONED ARCHITECTURE ♦ 96, LAYERED ORGANIZATION ♦ 59, LAYERS ♦ 81, PEDESTAL ♦ 123, SHAPE OF PROGRAM ♦ 29

PRESENTATION AND APPLICATION LOGIC
Analysis, Architectural

245-251

The application layer in THREE-TIER ARCHITECTURE ♦ 15 has two responsibilities. Separate the application layer into presentation (user interface) and application logic. Structure the application layer as a set of FACADE ♦ 56 objects for the presentation subsystem.

♦♦♦ PRESENTATION-ABSTRACTION-CONTROL ♦ 135

DATABASE INTERACTION
Analysis, Architectural

251-255

You're using THREE-TIER ARCHITECTURE ♦ 15. Let domain classes be responsible for saving themselves in the database or create a separate layer to handle the interactions between the domain layer and the database.

IMPLEMENTING ASSOCIATIONS
Design Process

274-281

(1) Choose one direction in an association to implement, and use an operation and a pointer. (2) Put operations and pointers in both directions. (3) Put operations in both directions but a pointer only in one. Use lookup for the other direction or (4) put operations in both directions and use a table and lookup for the pointers.

♦♦♦ BASIC RELATIONSHIP PATTERNS ❖ 19

IMPLEMENTING GENERALIZATIONS
Design Process

281-288

(1) Use inheritance. (2) Use classes for each combination of subtypes with multiple inheritance. (3) Use an internal flag. (4) Delegate to a hidden class, STATE ♦ 166 or (5) copy and replace.

♦♦♦ ABSTRACT CLASS ♦ 2

OBJECT CREATION
Design Process

289

Use a creation method with arguments for all mandatory and immutable mappings.

♦♦♦ FACTORY METHOD ♦ 56

OBJECT DESTRUCTION
Design Process

290-291

Define a destruction method and define how far the method should cascade.

ENTRY POINT
Design Process

291-294

How can objects of a type be located? Let the class store and retrieve its instances, or define a registrar to do this.

ᛗ   MANAGER ◆ 86

IMPLEMENTING CONSTRAINTS
Design Process

294

Define an operation in each object to check its constraints. Call it at the end of modifiers when debugging.

ᛗ   TEMPLATE METHOD ◆ 171

ASSOCIATIVE TYPE
Design Process

298-301

Create an associative type when you want to treat an association as a separate type.

ᛗ   BASIC RELATIONSHIP PATTERNS ❖ 19

KEYED MAPPING
Design Process

301-303

Use a lookup table or dictionary to implement relationships.

HISTORIC MAPPING
Design Process, Time

303-307

Objects do not just represent objects that currently exist; they often represent the memories of objects that once existed but have since disappeared. Use a dictionary implementation with time period keys.

APPROACHES FOR SEPARATING CLIENTS FROM SERVERS
Client-Server

[Martin95c], *ROAD*, Nov.-Dec. 1995, 26-29

Two approaches for separating clients from servers in a simple application based on a table lamp.

INTELLIGENT CHILDREN
Client-Server

Manage dependencies between clients and servers by defining an abstract class whose implementers interact with specific servers.

ᛗ   ABSTRACT SERVER ◆ 16 and ADAPTED SERVER ◆ 17 present alternatives to breaking client-server
    dependencies.

ABSTRACT SERVER
Client-Server

Break dependencies between clients and servers by defining an abstract class referenced by the client with the server implementing the abstract class.

ᛗ   The introduction of the abstract class is an implementation of STRATEGY ◆ 167.

ᛗ   ADAPTED SERVER ◆ 17 and INTELLIGENT CHILDREN ◆ 16 present alternative solutions to this
    problem.

ADAPTED SERVER
Client-Server

Break dependencies between clients and servers by defining an abstract server class referenced by the client. A server is derived from the abstract server class that contains the actual server.

- The abstract server class is an implementation of ADAPTER ◆ 6.
- ABSTRACT SERVER ◆ 16 and INTELLIGENT CHILDREN ◆ 16 provide alternative solutions to this problem.

ARCHITECTURAL PATTERNS FOR ENABLING APPLICATION SECURITY
Architectural, Security

[Yoder+99], *PLoPD4*, 301-336

http://www.joeyoder.com/papers/

Early design decisions allow application security to be added later and enable system evolution to meet changing security requirements.

SINGLE ACCESS POINT
Architectural, Security
303-306

It's difficult to make an application secure when there are many entry points. Set up one and only one way to get into the system and, if necessary, create a mechanism for deciding which sub-applications to launch.

- SINGLETON ◆ 152 can implement this pattern.
- Use CHECK POINT ◆ 17 to verify user information.
- Use SESSION ◆ 17 to track global information about the user's interaction with the system.

CHECK POINT
Architectural, Security
307-312

You're using SINGLE ACCESS POINT ◆ 17. To verify user information, create an object that encapsulates the algorithm for the security policy to handle all security checks. Use SESSION ◆ 17 and ROLES ◆ 17.

- This pattern implements STRATEGY ◆ 167.

ROLES
Architectural, Security
312-316

Users have different security profiles. To manage different user-privilege relationships, create one or more role objects that define the permissions and access rights for different user groups.

SESSION
Architectural, Security
316-320

You're using CHECK POINT ◆ 17. Many objects need access to shared variables. Create a Session object that holds all global information for a current user's interaction with the system.

- THREAD-SPECIFIC STORAGE ◆ 172 allows multiple threads to use one logically global access point to retrieve thread-specific data.
- DOUBLE-CHECKED LOCKING ◆ 51 can be used with multitasking or parallelism.

FULL VIEW WITH ERRORS
Architectural, Security

320-323

You're using ROLES ♦ 17. Applications may provide many ways to view data. Some operations may not be legal in a given state. When a user performs an illegal operation, display an error message.

- ⋔ LIMITED VIEW ♦ 18 provides an alternative solution.
- ⋔ CHECKS ❖ 32 provides more information on error notification.

LIMITED VIEW
Architectural, Security

323-329

You're using ROLES ♦ 17. Applications may provide many ways to view data. Some operations may not be legal in a given state. Allow users to see only what they have access to. Provide only the selections and menus their privileges permit.

- ⋔ FULL VIEW WITH ERRORS ♦ 18 describes an alternate solution.
- ⋔ CHECKS ❖ 32 provides more on error notification.

SECURE ACCESS LAYER
Architectural, Security

329-332

Most applications are integrated with other systems. No application can be secure if it is not properly integrated with the security of the systems it uses. Build your application's security around operating system, networking, and database security mechanisms. Build a secure access layer for communicating with the program on a secure lower-level.

- ⋔ LAYERED ARCHITECTURE ♦ 125, LAYERS ♦ 81

ARCHITECTURE PATTERNS FOR BUSINESS SYSTEMS
Architectural, System Modelling

[Boyd98a], *C++ Report*, May 1998, 42-50

Primary architectural characteristics of business systems. Engineering models that define an overall software architecture.

ONLINE ENGINEERING MODEL
Architectural, System Modelling

44-45

You're developing a software architecture for a business system. How can the system provide highly interactive functions? Define an online engineering model that supports immediate response, interactive error recognition, flexible access, and thin clients.

- ⋔ Many patterns, for example, MODEL-VIEW-CONTROLLER ♦ 87 and TRANSACTION ♦ 10, are implementations of this model.

MESSAGING ENGINEERING MODEL
Architectural, System Modelling

45-47

You're developing a software architecture for a business system. How can the system provide functions that are less interactive and more process-intensive? Define a messaging engineering model that supports complex, asynchronous interactive processing. Use ONLINE ENGINEERING MODEL ♦ 18. Determine from user feedback which model is best for each requirement.

BATCH ENGINEERING MODEL
Architectural, System Modelling
47-48

How can a business system provide some functions that are interactive and others that support batch processing? Define a batch engineering model. Use ONLINE ENGINEERING MODEL ♦ 18 and MESSAGING ENGINEERING MODEL ♦ 18, and make all three available throughout the design process. Determine from user feedback which is best for each business requirement.

STREAM I-O ENGINEERING MODEL
Architectural, System Modelling
48-50

You're developing a software architecture for a business system. How can the system provide some functions that are interactive, others that support batch processing, and still others that have characteristics of both? Define a stream I-O engineering model to support processing initiated by external messages or events. Use ONLINE ENGINEERING MODEL ♦ 18, MESSAGING ENGINEERING MODEL ♦ 18, and BATCH ENGINEERING MODEL ♦ 19. Determine from user feedback which is best for each business requirement.

ASYNCHRONOUS COMPLETION TOKEN
Communications, Concurrent Systems, Distributed Systems
[Pyarali+98], *PLoPD3*, 245-260

`http://www.cs.wustl.edu/~schmidt/patterns-ace.html`

Allows applications to associate state with the completion of asynchronous operations.

ἤἤ An asynchronous completion token is typically treated as a MEMENTO ♦ 87 by the underlying framework.

ἤἤ This pattern is generally used with PROACTOR ♦ 137.

BACKUP
Fault-Tolerant Systems
[Subramanian+96], *PLoPD2*, 207-225

Switch to a backup mode of operation. This provides redundancy in software when you want to offer various alternatives for a function and to switch between them dynamically.

ἤἤ The ReliableHandler object in this pattern is similar to PROXY ♦ 139 with an ordered set of alternate RealSubject objects.

ἤἤ This pattern uses request forwarding similar to CHAIN OF RESPONSIBILITY ♦ 32. But here, the forwarding is handled centrally in the ReliableHandler object.

ἤἤ STATE ♦ 166 uses a switching mechanism, but it switches between different states. Here, the switches are between different modes of operation.

BASIC RELATIONSHIP PATTERNS
Behavioral
[Noble99a], *PLoPD4*, 73-89

How objects can model relationships in programs.

RELATIONSHIP AS ATTRIBUTE
Behavioral

76-78

To design a small, simple, one-to-one relationship, make an attribute to represent the relationship.

- RELATIONSHIP OBJECT ◆ 20 describes how to represent a complex relationship with extra objects: an ACTIVE VALUE ◆ 20 for a globally important one-to-one relationship and a COLLECTION OBJECT ◆ 20 for a one-to-many relationship.
- MUTUAL FRIENDS ◆ 20 describes how to represent two-way relationships.

RELATIONSHIP OBJECT
Behavioral

78-80

Use a relationship object to represent a large, complex relationship.

- ACTIVE VALUE ◆ 20 uses a specialized relationship object that models a one-to-one relationship.
- COLLECTION OBJECT ◆ 20 uses a specialized relationship object that models a one-to-many relationship.
- RELATIONSHIP AS ATTRIBUTE ◆ 20 describes how to represent one-to-one relationships efficiently.
- Relationship objects can record other information, such as the time span of the relationship as in ASSOCIATION OBJECT ◆ 23.

COLLECTION OBJECT
Behavioral

80-82

Use a Collection to design a one-to-many relationship.

- This pattern implements the same solution as COLLECTION ◆ 159.

ACTIVE VALUE
Behavioral

82-84

To design a globally important one-to-one relationship, make an active value, an object that reifies a single variable. It should have an attribute to hold the variable's value with an accessor and a set method.

MUTUAL FRIENDS
Behavioral

84-88

To represent a two-way relationship, make a consistent set of one-way relationships.

- This pattern typically uses RELATIONSHIP AS ATTRIBUTE ◆ 20 and COLLECTION OBJECT ◆ 20 to implement the subsidiary one-way relationships. Alternatively, RELATIONSHIP OBJECT ◆ 20 can model the complex relationship.

BIG BALL OF MUD PATTERN LANGUAGE
Architectural

[Foote+99], *PLoPD4*, 653-692

`http://www.laputan.org/mud/mud.html`

The problems that arise in a haphazardly structured system.

BIG BALL OF MUD
Architectural

658-665

You need to deliver quality software on time and under budget, but resources are often constrained. Focus first on functionality, then on architecture, then on performance.

THROWAWAY CODE
Architectural

665-668

You need a quick fix for a small problem, a prototype, or a proof of concept. You think you will have time to rewrite or replace the initial solution, but that never happens. Therefore, write simple, expedient, disposable code that solves the problem.

PIECEMEAL GROWTH
Architectural

668-675

Master plans are often rigid, misguided, and out of date. Users' needs change with time. Incrementally address forces that encourage change and growth. Allow opportunities for growth to be exploited locally, as they occur. Refactor relentlessly.

KEEP IT WORKING
Organization and Process

675-678

Maintenance needs of a system have accumulated, but an overhaul is unwise, since you might break the system. Do what it takes to keep the system going.

SHEARING LAYERS
Design Process, Refactoring

678-681

Software systems cannot stand still, but different components change at different rates. Factor the system so that components that change at similar rates are together.

ᴍᴍ LAYERS ♦ 81

SWEEPING IT UNDER THE RUG
Design Process, Organization and Process

681-683

Haphazard code is hard to understand and tends to become worse if it is not controlled. If you can't make a mess go away, at least you can hide it. This restricts the chaos to a fixed area and can set the stage for future refactoring.

RECONSTRUCTION
Organization and Process

684-687

Your code has deteriorated to the point where it is beyond comprehension or repair. Throw it away and start over.

BLACKBOARD
Architectural
[Buschmann+96], *POSA*, 71-95

For problems with no deterministic solutions, use several specialized subsystems to assemble knowledge to build a partial solution.

✗ [Woodward96]

BODYGUARD
Distributed Systems
[DasNeves+98], *PLoPD3*, 231-244

Allow objects to be shared and access to them controlled in a distributed environment that lacks system-level support for distributed objects. Provide message dispatching validation and assignment of access rights to objects in non-local environments to prevent improper access to objects in collaborative applications.

- 👫 This pattern uses PROXY ♦ 139 with additional control and transport-related objects.
- 👫 This pattern is similar to ACCEPTOR ♦ 3 and REACTOR ♦ 143; however, REACTOR ♦ 143 is intended for a client/server architecture while this pattern is designed for a peer-to-peer environment.
- 👫 This pattern is a mid-level version of BROKER ♦ 22.

BRIDGE
Structural
[Gamma+95], *GoF*, 151-161

[Alpert+98], *Design Patterns Smalltalk Companion*, 121-135

Decouple an abstraction from its implementation so the two can vary independently.

- 👫 An ABSTRACT FACTORY ♦ 2 can create and configure a BRIDGE ♦ 22.
- 👫 ADAPTER ♦ 6 helps unrelated classes work together and is usually applied to existing systems. This pattern is applied up-front.
- ✗ [Schmidt96a], [Woodward96], [Zhang+96b]

BROKER
Architectural, Distributed Systems
[Buschmann+96], *POSA*, 99-124

Produce distributed software systems with decoupled components that interact by remote service invocations. The broker coordinates communication, e.g., forwards requests, transmits results and exceptions.

✗ [Barkataki+98], [Woodward96]

BUILDER
Creational

[Gamma+95], *GoF*, 97-106

[Alpert+98], *Design Patterns Smalltalk Companion*, 47-61

Separate construction of a complex object from its representation so that the same construction process can create different representations.

- ⚏ ABSTRACT FACTORY ◆ 2 is similar to this pattern. Both construct complex objects. BUILDER ◆ 23 focuses on constructing a complex object step by step, while ABSTRACT FACTORY ◆ 2 focuses on families of product objects. BUILDER ◆ 23 returns the complete product as a final step, while ABSTRACT FACTORY ◆ 2 returns each product object as it is created.

- �֎ [Masuda+98], [VandenBroecke+97], [Zhao+99]

BUREAUCRACY
Behavioral

[Riehle98], *PLoPD3*, 163-185

http://www.riehle.org/patterns/index.html

A composite pattern for building an hierarchical structure to interact with clients on every level but needs no external control and maintains internal consistency itself.

- ⚏ This pattern combines CHAIN OF RESPONSIBILITY ◆ 32, COMPOSITE ◆ 37, MEDIATOR ◆ 86, and OBSERVER ◆ 94.

BUSINESS PATTERNS OF ASSOCIATION OBJECTS
Analysis

[Boyd98b], *PLoPD3*, 395-408

http://www.riehle.org/BusinessPatterns/AssocObjects.html

Association objects represent something that happens at a point in time and have attributes inherent in the relationship (e.g., date, time, or cost) that change when a new association is formed.

ASSOCIATION OBJECT
Analysis

396-399

In business systems, static objects represent tangible things in the real world. How can the associations between these objects be identified? Define association objects with the date and time of the association. Association objects are needed if the association has behavior of its own over time.

- ⚏ Coad's Timed Association, Associative Type, and Historic Mapping are examples of this pattern [Coad95].

CUSTOMER CONTACT
Analysis

399-401

Use an object to represent an association between the business and the customer.

- ⚏ This pattern is a variation of ASSOCIATION OBJECT ◆ 23 and Coad's Event Logging [Coad95].

3-LEVEL ORDER
Analysis, Order Management
401-406
Many business systems are driven by the concept of an order. During the analysis phase, to create a simple order structure that still allows maximum flexibility, consider an order to be a series of association objects. Separate order responsibilities into a 3-level structure: rules, receivables, and costs.

C++ IDIOMS

C++ Idioms
[Coplien99c], *PLoPD4*, 167-197
`http://www.bell-labs.com/~cope/Patterns/C++Idioms/EuroPLoP98.html`
Recasting of idioms in [Coplien92] into a pattern language that treats algebraic types. See an earlier version in [Coplien99a] and [Coplien99b].

HANDLE/BODY

C++ Idioms
171-173
To separate interface from implementation in C++ objects, split a class into two implementation classes. One, the handle, becomes an identifier and is the user interface. The other, the body, is the implementation. The handle forwards member function calls to the body.

- ♔ This pattern doesn't address run-time dynamics. See COUNTED BODY ♦ 24, ENVELOPE/LETTER ♦ 25, and their subtending patterns.
- ♔ This pattern makes inheritance less useful. See HANDLE/BODY HIERARCHY ♦ 24.

COUNTED BODY

C++ Idioms
173-176
You're using HANDLE/BODY ♦ 24. Assignment in C++ is defined recursively as member-by-member assignment with copying at the termination of the recursion. It would be more efficient if copying were rebinding. Add a reference count to the body class. Memory management is added to the handle class. Any operation that modifies the state of the body must make its own copy of the body and decrement the reference count of the original body.

DETACHED COUNTED BODY

C++ Idioms
176-179
To overcome the overhead of an additional level of indirection when applying COUNTED BODY ♦ 24 to immutable classes, associate a shared count and a separate shared body with each instance of a common handle abstraction.

HANDLE/BODY HIERARCHY

C++ Idioms
179-182
You're using HANDLE/BODY ♦ 24. Some classes have subtyping relationships and implementation-sharing relationships that do not correspond with each other. C++ ties implementation inheritance and representation inheritance together, and you may want to inherit each separately. Maintain separate inheritance hierarchies for handle classes and body classes. The base interface class contains a reference to the base implementation class.

ENVELOPE/LETTER

C++ Idioms

182-184

You're using HANDLE/BODY ♦ 24 or COUNTED BODY ♦ 24 to support multiple implementations of a single ADT. Derive all solution body classes from a common base class. Use the handle class as the common base class for alternate bodies. Make handle member functions virtual. Each alternative implementation derived from the handle class overrides suitable virtual functions.

ᛗ This pattern is the basis for VIRTUAL CONSTRUCTOR ♦ 25.

ᛗ In ALGEBRAIC HIERARCHY ♦ 25, this pattern is the basis for PROMOTION LADDER ♦ 26.

ᛗ To vary implementation at run-time, consider STATE ♦ 166.

VIRTUAL CONSTRUCTOR

C++ Idioms

184-185

You're using HANDLE/BODY ♦ 24. A client wants to create an object of an unspecified class in a class hierarchy. An object created from the classes in the hierarchy can be used interchangeably by the client. To create an object whose general type is known by the client but whose subtype characteristics must be chosen from context, use ENVELOPE/LETTER ♦ 25.

ᛗ When the letter class variations are algorithmic, use STRATEGY ♦ 167.

CONCRETE DATA TYPE

C++ Idioms

186-187

Your design enumerates system classes, and you need to establish the lifetime and scope of the objects for those classes. When should you use "new" to allocate an object? Objects that represent real-world entities that live outside the program should be instantiated using "new."

ᛗ For dynamically allocated representations, see COUNTED BODY ♦ 24.

ᛗ For user-defined types that behave like built-in algebraic types, see ALGEBRAIC HIERARCHY ♦ 25.

ALGEBRAIC HIERARCHY

C++ Idioms

187-189

To construct the inheritance hierarchy for algebraic types, use BRIDGE ♦ 22 to separate interface from implementation. The visible part is class Number. It contains a pointer to a representation part, which contains the representation and operations of the type, e.g., Complex, Real, Integer, Imaginary. Use STATE ♦ 166 so Numbers can change type over time.

ᛗ HOMOGENEOUS ADDITION ♦ 25, NON-HIERARCHICAL ADDITION ♦ 26, PROMOTE AND ADD ♦ 26, PROMOTION LADDER ♦ 26, and TYPE PROMOTION ♦ 26 complete this pattern.

HOMOGENEOUS ADDITION

C++ Idioms

189-190

You're using ALGEBRAIC HIERARCHY ♦ 25. You need to distribute addition to the objects. How many addition operations are there, and where do they belong? Each type should only support homogeneous algebraic operations unless performance dictates otherwise. Use PROMOTE AND ADD ♦ 26.

PROMOTE AND ADD

C++ Idioms

190-192

You're using ALGEBRAIC HIERARCHY ♦ 25 and HOMOGENEOUS ADDITION ♦ 25. To do heterogeneous addition, use run-time type identification (RTTI) to determine which of the two object types is more general. Promote and add the more specific type to the more general type using PROMOTION LADDER ♦ 26. Then use HOMOGENEOUS ADDITION ♦ 25. If one type is not a proper subtype of the other, use NON-HIERARCHICAL ADDITION ♦ 26.

PROMOTION LADDER

C++ Idioms

192-193

You're using PROMOTE AND ADD ♦ 26. Where do you put the knowledge of type promotion? Each class should know how to promote itself to its own base class type. Promotions of more than two levels of the inheritance hierarchy can be handled by multiple successive promotions.

NON-HIERARCHICAL ADDITION

C++ Idioms

193-194

You're using PROMOTION LADDER ♦ 26 and HOMOGENEOUS ADDITION ♦ 25. Sometimes neither type is a subtype of the other, so neither can be promoted to the type of the other. Promote both to a more general type.

TYPE PROMOTION

C++ Idioms

195-196

Promotion between objects of different but related C++ types—zero or one of which is a built-in type or a type exported by a library for which you do not have the source—promote a class object type to a built-in type or a type exported from a library using a member conversion operator. Use constructors for all other promotions.

    ᛘ PROMOTION LADDER ♦ 26

CAPABLE, PRODUCTIVE, AND SATISFIED

Organization and Process

[Taylor99], *PLoPD4*, 611-636

For managers of teams using iterative development.

PRODUCTION POTENTIAL

Organization and Process

612-615

You see a lot of activity but little progress on deliverables. You must translate the activity to an assessment of the team's progress and its capacity to produce. Use BOOTSTRAPPING ♦ 26, PULSE ♦ 27, and ROUND PEGS FOR ROUND HOLES ♦ 27.

BOOTSTRAPPING

Organization and Process

615-618

Most team members are unfamiliar with the problem domain, the application, and each other. Partition some responsibilities and share others. Use ROUND PEGS FOR ROUND HOLES ♦ 27 to identify those team members with capabilities and experience. Then use PROBLEM-ORIENTED TEAM ♦ 27.

Problem-Oriented Team
Organization and Process
618-620

You've used Bootstrapping ♦ 26. Use the team's need to understand the problem to build team cohesion. If the problem space is highly complex and cannot be mastered by all team members quickly, choose a critical but manageable part.

Round Pegs for Round Holes
Organization and Process
621-623

You've used Bootstrapping ♦ 26. Now you must assign tasks to people. Individual capabilities and preferred work modes must be observed over time. Discover each individual's preferences for working, and allocate tasks accordingly.

Pulse
Organization and Process
623-625

A software development team is capable of bursts of higher productivity to meet production demands, but you must handle the timing, length, and frequency of these peaks with care. Determine the team's delivery rhythm by putting the team through periods of higher-pressure release cycles. You'll establish a project rhythm of peaks and troughs aligned with project plans and deliverables.

Deliverables To Go
Organization and Process
625-627

You must scope and time the team's deliverables so that they will be used. Don't release until users are ready to consume.

Team Space
Organization and Process
627-630

If productivity is to be maintained over time, a holistic, healthy work environment must recognize the natural rhythm of human work. Productivity peaks interleave with nonproductive periods during an average day. Create a physical space for casual, unplanned interactions between team members.

Effective Handover
Organization and Process
630-632

A critical team member is leaving. The departing developer should handover to a continuing developer, setting the replacement free to do new work. If the continuing developer is now overloaded, using the departure as an opportunity to shuffle and reallocate everyone's tasks and responsibilities.

Arranging the Furniture
Organization and Process
632-635

Your established team is entering a transition period where members are replaced by newcomers who must quickly come to grips with large and complex software modules. People are territorial and need to mark their intellectual territory to establish a feeling of ownership. Newcomers should move in by cosmetically arranging code. This must be a background, incremental task and should not be used as an excuse to trash the backyard.

CASCADE

Networks, Transportation

[Foster+99], *JOOP*, Feb. 1999, 18-24

Layer and order the parts of a complex whole. Each layer is an instance of COMPOSITE ♦ 37. Cascade is part of a pattern language for transport systems.

- ♦♦♦ DRIVER DUTY ♦ 51, Driver Duty Builder, and ROUTE ♦ 114 are implementations of this pattern.
- ♦♦♦ ROLE OBJECT ♦ 146 presents a way of representing multiple concurrent roles a component can play and provides a setting for considering the interaction between whole-part hierarchies and roles.
- ✗ [Zhao+98a], [Zhao+99]

CATERPILLAR'S FATE: A PATTERN LANGUAGE FOR THE TRANSFORMATION FROM ANALYSIS TO DESIGN

Concurrent Systems

[Kerth95], *PLoPD1*, 297-320

http://c2.com/ppr/catsfate.html

Transformation from analysis to a design in a concurrent processing environment.

CONCURRENT THREADS OF EXECUTION

Concurrent Systems

295-296

When a system contains processes that run simultaneously or pseudo-simultaneously, identify threads of execution that can exist independently. Then use COLLABORATIVE WORK PACKETS ♦ 28 and SYNCHRONIZATION OF CONCURRENT THREADS ♦ 28. If there's only one concurrent thread, use SHAPE OF PROGRAM ♦ 29.

SYNCHRONIZATION OF CONCURRENT THREADS

Concurrent Systems

296-297

You've used CONCURRENT THREADS OF EXECUTION ♦ 28. Review each thread throughout its life cycle and identify those points where a signal is sent to or received from another thread. Name the signal for the situation it represents, identifying the sender and the receiver.

COLLABORATIVE WORK PACKETS

Concurrent Systems

297-298

You're using CONCURRENT THREADS OF EXECUTION ♦ 28. Review the life cycle of each thread in a pair of concurrent threads, and identify work initiated by one and continued by the other. Name the work packet for the information and work unit it manages or hides. For each work packet, identify possible producer and consumer concurrent threads.

WORK PACKET CONTENTS

Concurrent Systems

298-299

You're using COLLABORATIVE WORK PACKETS ♦ 28. For each work packet, document all information necessary for the work to be done. Then use WORK PACKET COMPLETION REPORT ♦ 29, WORK PACKET PRIORITY ♦ 29, WORK PACKET SECURITY ♦ 29 and WORK PACKET STATUS REPORT ♦ 29.

WORK PACKET STATUS REPORT
Concurrent Systems

299-301

You're using COLLABORATIVE WORK PACKETS ♦ 28 and WORK PACKET CONTENTS ♦ 28. Now decide whether to generate a report for the producer on the work packet's status. Keep this part of the design as simple as possible. Your system needs to produce status reports, but that's not its primary goal.

WORK PACKET COMPLETION REPORT
Concurrent Systems

301-302

You're using SYNCHRONIZATION OF CONCURRENT THREADS ♦ 28, COLLABORATIVE WORK PACKETS ♦ 28, and WORK PACKET CONTENTS ♦ 28. When a work packet completes its processing in the consumer's concurrent thread of execution, keep the completion report simple. Ensure SHAPE OF PROGRAM ♦ 29 addresses the receipt of every completion report identified.

WORK PACKET PRIORITY
Concurrent Systems

302-303

You're using COLLABORATIVE WORK PACKETS ♦ 28, and transforming the general SHAPE OF PROGRAM ♦ 29 to a specific one. Determine a policy for selecting waiting work packets. "First come, first served" might be sufficient, but there may be hidden requirements.

WORK PACKET SECURITY
Concurrent Systems

303-304

You're using WORK PACKET CONTENTS ♦ 28 and looking at work packet security issues. If security is crucial, stop all design activities, return to analysis, and develop effective security models.

SHAPE OF PROGRAM
Architectural, Concurrent Systems

305-307

You're using SYNCHRONIZATION OF CONCURRENT THREADS ♦ 28, and COLLABORATIVE WORK PACKETS ♦ 28. You're ready to apply a specific form to the general shape of your program. A tiered structure is a good starting point. Objects on each tier can request services from components on the same or lower tiers but not on higher tiers. When the tiered shape begins to fail, use SMALL FAMILY SYSTEMS ♦ 30 and WORK ACCOMPLISHED THROUGH DIALOGS ♦ 30.

   👣 HIERARCHY OF CONTROL LAYERS ♦ 61, FOUR-LAYER ARCHITECTURE ♦ 106, LAYERED ARCHITECTURE ♦ 125, LAYERED AND SECTIONED ARCHITECTURE ♦ 96, LAYERED ORGANIZATION ♦ 59, LAYERS ♦ 81, PEDESTAL ♦ 123, THREE-TIER ARCHITECTURE ♦ 15

SYSTEM CITIZEN'S ROLE
Concurrent Systems

307-308

You're using CONCURRENT THREADS OF EXECUTION ♦ 28, and the SHAPE OF PROGRAM ♦ 29 is moving from general to specific. Most programs reside on platforms where several applications are running concurrently. Design a single object with the protocol that applications must follow to be good citizens in a community of applications. Use EVENT ACQUISITION ♦ 31 and EVENT ROUTING ♦ 31.

   👣 The responsible object may be a SINGLETON ♦ 152.

DECISION MAKER'S ROLE
Concurrent Systems

308-309

When the SHAPE OF PROGRAM ♦ 29 begins to move from the general to the specific, and the system citizen's role becomes defined, create an object responsible for decision-making activities. Separate policy-making activities from those that carry out policy. Then connect objects defined in HUMAN INTERFACE ROLE IS A SPECIAL INTERFACE ROLE ♦ 31, INTERFACE'S ROLE ♦ 30, and WORKERS' ROLE ♦ 30.

ⵜⵜ   The responsible object may be a STRATEGY ♦ 167.

WORKERS' ROLE
Concurrent Systems

309

When the SHAPE OF PROGRAM ♦ 29 begins to move from the general to the specific, you're ready to design objects to move the application closer to its goal. Build objects to carry out policy- and decision-making responsibilities.

INTERFACE'S ROLE
Concurrent Systems, Design Process

309-310

When the SHAPE OF PROGRAM ♦ 29 begins to move from the general to the specific, you're ready to design objects that hide the behavior of external entities. Hide the behavior of these entities in an object that provides high-level abstract services to the system.

ⵜⵜ   Both BRIDGE ♦ 22 and FACADE ♦ 56 support high-level abstract services.

INFORMATIONAL ROLE
Concurrent Systems, Design Process

310-311

When the SHAPE OF PROGRAM ♦ 29 begins to move from the general to the specific, you're ready to design objects that move through the system, visiting interface objects. Create objects to deliver specific information without exposing the structure of the information. These objects are found by noting how information flows on an event-partitioned data-flow diagram.

ⵜⵜ   INTERFACE'S ROLE ♦ 30

ⵜⵜ   VISITOR ♦ 179 can implement polymorphic operations on objects external to their classes.

SMALL FAMILY SYSTEMS
Concurrent Systems

311-312

When the SHAPE OF PROGRAM ♦ 29 begins to move from the general to the specific and the tiered system is awkward, don't discard the program shape; just augment it with another "mini" shape for the portions of the system you're considering.

ⵜⵜ   The internal design from HUMAN INTERFACE ROLE IS A SPECIAL INTERFACE ROLE ♦ 31 benefits from this pattern.

WORK ACCOMPLISHED THROUGH DIALOGS
Concurrent Systems, Design Process

312-313

When the SHAPE OF PROGRAM ♦ 29 is moving from the general to the specific and you see two objects that need to call each other's operations. Allow the two objects to carry on a dialog with each other. Avoid controlling dialogs or dialogs that involve more than one object.

CRITICAL REGION PROTECTION
Concurrent Systems

313-314

You're using CONCURRENT THREADS OF EXECUTION ♦ 28 and the SHAPE OF PROGRAM ♦ 29 for each thread has moved from general to specific. Look for potential critical region problems. For each concurrent thread, identify the shared objects. For each shared object, if needed, develop a protection mechanism that ensures safe use.

♦♦♦ SELECTING LOCKING DESIGNS FOR PARALLEL PROGRAMS ❖ 147 and SELECTING LOCKING PRIMITIVES FOR PARALLEL PROGRAMMING ❖ 148 give insight into critical region protection in parallel programs, much of which generalizes to concurrent systems.

♦♦♦ Concurrent Programming in Java: Design Principles and Patterns [Lea00]

EVENT ACQUISITION
Event-Driven Systems, Reactive and Real-Time Systems

314-315

When the SHAPE OF PROGRAM ♦ 29 begins to move from the general to the specific and the system citizen's role is being considered, choose the event-acquisition capabilities that make sense for your application and refine the shape of the program. Return to SHAPE OF PROGRAM ♦ 29 to transform the general shape into a specific one.

♦♦♦ PATTERNS OF EVENTS ❖ 129 describes event processing in a distributed real-time control and information system.

EVENT ROUTING
Event-Driven Systems, Reactive and Real-Time Systems

315

When the SHAPE OF PROGRAM ♦ 29 begins to move from the general to the specific, and the system citizen's role is being considered, use this pattern and EVENT ACQUISITION ♦ 31 to resolve design issues. Return to SHAPE OF PROGRAM ♦ 29 and continue to transform the general shape into a specific one.

♦♦♦ PATTERNS OF EVENTS ❖ 129 describes event processing in a distributed real-time control and information system.

HUMAN INTERFACE ROLE IS A SPECIAL INTERFACE ROLE
Concurrent Systems, GUI Development

316-317

When the SHAPE OF PROGRAM ♦ 29 begins to move from the general to the specific, you will see how decision-making objects get direction from humans. Create an interface object that hides human interface-specific design decisions.

♦♦♦ Both BRIDGE ♦ 22 and FACADE ♦ 56 support interface objects to hide human interface-specific design decisions.

DATA KNOWS ITS ROOTS
Concurrent Systems

317-318

Once you've identified collaborative work packets, informational role-oriented objects, or any other entity that contains information, determine if their history should be known. Design the entity so it records all relevant information.

CHAIN OF RESPONSIBILITY

Behavioral

[Gamma+95], *GoF*, 223-232

[Alpert+98], *Design Patterns Smalltalk Companion*, 225-244

Avoid coupling the sender of a request to its receiver by giving more than one object a chance to handle the request. Chain the receiving objects and pass the request along the chain until an object handles it.

- ♦♦♦ This pattern is often applied with COMPOSITE ♦ 37, where a component's parent is its successor.
- ♦♦♦ EVENTHANDLER ♦ 55 is an adaptation of this pattern that avoids cyclic link time dependencies.
- ♦♦♦ This pattern employs OBJECT RECURSION ♦ 92.

CHECKS: A PATTERN LANGUAGE OF INFORMATION INTEGRITY

Business Computation, GUI Development

[Cunningham95], *PLoPD1*, 145-155

http://c2.com/ppr/checks.html

Make validity checks on data.

WHOLE VALUE

Business Computation

146-147

Reuse the literal values in a programming language and construct new objects that represent the meaningful quantities of your business. Use these values as the arguments of their messages and the units of input and output. Be sure these objects capture the whole quantity, not just magnitude.

EXCEPTIONAL VALUE

Business Computation

147-148

Including all business possibilities in a class hierarchy can be confusing, difficult, or inappropriate, so extend the range of an attribute beyond that offered in WHOLE VALUE ♦ 32. Use one or more distinguished values to represent exceptional circumstances and simplify the domain model hierarchy and method structure.

MEANINGLESS BEHAVIOR

Business Computation

148-149

Whole Values can exhibit subtle variations in behavior, and Exceptional Values can appear throughout the computations. Methods may stumble in circumstances you cannot foresee. Write methods without concern for possible failure. Expect the input/output widgets that initiate computation to recover from failure and continue processing.

ECHO BACK

Business Computation, GUI Development

149-150

Users enter data in small batches. The cycle is repeated but not always with the same batch boundaries. Inform users of their success in entering values as each field or cell is processed. Echo back field and cell values immediately.

VISIBLE IMPLICATION

Business Computation, GUI Development

151-152

Combine ECHO BACK ♦ 32 with methods that compute attributes to simplify some entries and improve the effectiveness of visual review for others. Compute derived or redundant quantities implied by those already entered. Display the computed values in fields or cells alongside those that are changed. Expect MEANINGLESS BEHAVIOR ♦ 32 when something is incompletely specified.

DEFERRED VALIDATION

Business Computation, GUI Development

152-153

You're using WHOLE VALUE ♦ 32 and ECHO BACK ♦ 32. These checks are immediate on entry. Delay detailed validation until action is requested.

INSTANT PROJECTION

Business Computation, GUI Development

153

As you collect information for future use, you can use VISIBLE IMPLICATION ♦ 33 for user entries. Offer to project the consequences before the publication is made.

♦♦♦ HYPOTHETICAL PUBLICATION ♦ 33 offers a versatile but cumbersome alternative.

HYPOTHETICAL PUBLICATION

Business Computation, GUI Development

153-154

A complicated domain model might pass DEFERRED VALIDATION ♦ 33 but still in be doubt. Consider an elaborate mechanism for detecting mistakes. Allow the user to make any number of hypothetical publications that can be released in a controlled way.

♦♦♦ This pattern can substitute for INSTANT PROJECTION ♦ 33 when forecasting tools are available for published models.

FORECAST CONFIRMATION

Business Computation

154

When real-world events can be anticipated, generate appropriate computer models and publish them for public use. Adjust and confirm values associated with mechanically published events.

DIAGNOSTIC QUERY

Business Computation

155

When you use WHOLE VALUE ♦ 32 and EXCEPTIONAL VALUE ♦ 32, you accumulate useful information. Incorporate mechanisms for the diagnostic tracing of every value in the system. Where rules and formulas have been applied, make them retrievable from the system.

CLIENT-DISPATCHER-SERVER

Client-Server, Communications, Distributed Systems

[Buschmann+96], *POSA*, 323-337

[Sommerlad+96], *PLoPD2*, 475-482

A dispatcher component is an intermediary between clients and servers. The dispatcher provides location transparency with a name service and hides details of the communication connection.

- ⚏ FORWARDER-RECEIVER ♦ 60 can be combined with this pattern to hide details of interprocess communication.
- ⚏ ACCEPTOR ♦ 3 and CONNECTOR ♦ 40 decouple connection set-up from connection processing.

CLIENT-SPECIFIED SELF

Smalltalk Idioms

[Viljamaa95], *PLoPD1*, 495-504

Replaces message to "self" with messages to an argument. Using the sender as the argument lets it inherit methods from others besides its superclasses.

COLLECTION OF HISTORY PATTERNS

Time

[Anderson99], *PLoPD4*, 263-297

Record an object's history by associating the state with the event that caused it.

- ⚏ HISTORIC MAPPING ♦ 16

EDITION

Reactive and Real-Time Systems, Time

267-270

An event causes an object to change the value of a variable. Audit information must be attached to the new value recording the time of the change and the responsible user. To represent the relationship between the new state and the event, use MEMENTO ♦ 87 and capture the relationship by an edition, which provides the association between the event and the state.

CHANGE LOG

Time

271-276

The value of a simple variable has changed. The previous value is to be recorded for audit purposes. To store the previous value and keep the previous state accessible, assign a change log to those objects whose simple variables will be tracked over time.

HISTORY ON ASSOCIATION

Time

276-280

The value of a variable that references a complex object has changed. The previous value is recorded for audit purposes. To maintain the historical values of a complex variable, replace the pointer to the complex object with an instance of history. When the value of the variable is changed, a new edition is added to the history.

POSTING
Time, Transaction Processing
280-285

The value of an accumulated total has been changed via the posting of a transaction. The amounts that contribute to the total should be recorded for audit purposes. To record the contribution of each transaction to the total, resolve the many-to-many relationship between account and transaction with a posting subtype of edition. This provides a historical wrapper around the transaction.

ᛗ ACCOUNT ♦ 10, POSTING RULES ♦ 11, TRANSACTION ♦ 10

HISTORY ON SELF
Reactive and Real-Time Systems, Time
285-289

To associate all the changes of state that may have occurred on an object as the result of a single event, instead of applying history to individual variables, apply it to the object as a whole. Before changing any state as a result of a single event, a new edition is written to history.

MEMENTO CHILD
Time
289-293

A member has changed containers. To remove an object from a collection, yet retain the reference, use HISTORY ON SELF ♦ 35 before changing the originator's parent. Replace the originator with the memento in the memento's container. After a predetermined duration, remove mementos from the children of the container.

HISTORY ON TREE
Time
293-296

For some major business transactions, you must treat a component as the sum of its parts and create a snapshot of an entire collection of nodes. To implement this treatment of the whole, recursively apply it to the descendants of the subject node.

ᛗ This pattern is based on COMPOSITE ♦ 37.

COMMAND
Behavioral
[Gamma+95], *GoF*, 233-242
[Alpert+98], *Design Patterns Smalltalk Companion*, 245-259

Encapsulate a request as an object, allowing the parameterization of clients with different requests, queue or log requests, and support undoable operations.

ᛗ COMPOSITE ♦ 37 can implement MacroCommands.

ᛗ MEMENTO ♦ 87 can keep state for an undo.

ᛗ A command copied before being placed on the history list is a PROTOTYPE ♦ 138.

ᛗ COMMAND PROCESSOR ♦ 36 adds scaffolding for multilevel undo and redo.

ᛗ Commands can represent transactions. See TRANSACTIONS AND ACCOUNTS ❖ 172.

✗ [Gamma+99], [Hüni+95], [Long99], [Masuda+98], [Schmid95], [VandenBroecke+97]

COMMAND PROCESSOR
Behavioral

[Buschmann+96], *POSA*, 277-290
[Sommerlad96], *PLoPD2*, 63-74

Separates the request for a service from its execution, manages requests as separate objects, schedules their execution, and provides additional services, e.g., storing request objects for a later undo.

♦♦♦ This pattern extends COMMAND ♦ 35.

COMMUNICATING PROCESSES
Architectural, Parallel Programming

[Shaw96], *PLoPD2*, 261

For applications with a collection of distinct, largely independent computations whose execution should proceed independently, computations coordinate data or control at discrete points in time.

COMPOSING MULTIMEDIA ARTIFACTS FOR REUSE
Multimedia

[Cybulski+99], *PLoPD4*, 461-488

Defines a multimedia authoring environment capable of producing and applying multimedia components or artifacts.

GLUE
Multimedia

466-471

You need to combine multimedia artifacts into a composite artifact. Apply glue to join them into a composite object. The glue also determines which of the artifact properties must match for the components to stay together. To extract a component from a composite artifact, remove the glue.

COMPONENTS LAYOUT
Multimedia

471-475

You need to arrange multimedia artifacts with respect to their audio-visual properties. Compose the artifacts into a layout and use glue to associate each component with its position in the layout.

TEMPLATE
Multimedia

475-482

You need to produce a collection of composite multimedia artifacts that are similar in structure and content. Define a template, a special kind of composite that contains all shared components and gap components. The template can generate instances by filling in or replacing the gaps with non-common artifacts.

DEFINE AND RUN PRESENTATION
Multimedia

482-485

You need to show an organized collection of artifacts to the user in sequence. Plan the presentation by organizing artifacts into a partial order using glue. Define a delivery channel to carry the multimedia message as a series of artifacts. The delivery can happen through one or more channels.

| **SYNCHRONIZE CHANNELS** |
| Multimedia |
| 485-487 |
| You need to synchronize continuous and non-continuous multimedia artifacts sent through multiple channels into a multi-channel presentation. For non-continuous artifacts, define delay artifacts. Delays define the sequence of temporal positions in the composites of continuous and non-continuous artifacts. |

COMPOSITE

| Structural |
| [Gamma+95], *GoF*, 163-173 |
| [Alpert+98], *Design Patterns Smalltalk Companion*, 137-159 |
| Compose objects into tree structures to represent part-whole hierarchies. Clients can then treat individual objects and compositions of objects uniformly. |
| ⋔ Often the component-parent link is used in CHAIN OF RESPONSIBILITY ♦ 32.
 ⋔ This pattern can implement MacroCommands.
 ⋔ DECORATOR ♦ 46 is often used with this pattern, usually with a common parent class.
 ⋔ ITERATOR ♦ 80 can traverse a Composite structure.
 ⋔ VISITOR ♦ 179 localizes operations and behavior that would otherwise be distributed across Composite and Leaf classes.
 ✄ [Brown96], [Foster+99], [Gamma+99], [Hüni+95], [Johnson94a], [Johnson94b], [Johnson95], [Keller+98a], [Masuda+98], [Vlissides98a], [Zhao+98a] |

CONCURRENT PROGRAMMING IN JAVA, SECOND EDITION: DESIGN PRINCIPLES AND PATTERNS

| Concurrent Systems, Java Idioms |
| [Lea00], *Concurrent Programming in Java, Second Edition: Design Principles and Patterns* |
| Assumes object-oriented background but little knowledge of concurrency. Chapter 1 provides a conceptual basis for concurrent object-oriented programming. The three subsequent chapters describe the use of concurrency constructs in Java. |

| **METHOD ADAPTERS** |
| Concurrent Systems, Java Idioms |
| 64-65, 150-151 |
| To exercise "before" and "after" control on an activity, define a class whose sole purpose is to invoke a particular method on a particular object. |
| **SESSION** |
| Concurrent Systems, Java Idioms |
| 101 |
| A hand-off protocol ensures that at any point at most one actively executing method can access an object. Many hand-offs are structured as sessions in which objects are constructed that will be confined to a sequence of operations comprising a service. |

DOUBLE CHECK
Concurrent Systems, Java Idioms, Refactoring

120-121

When an illegal value has been read, reaccess the field under synchronization, determine its current value and take appropriate action. When locking causes liveness or performance problems, you can refactor the design using this pattern.

OPEN CALLS
Concurrent Systems, Java Idioms, Refactoring

121-123, 287

When you don't need to synchronize stateless parts of methods, use open calls or messages sent without holding locks. They eliminate bottlenecks but are useful only when clients know enough to use an approach that permits independent execution.

PASS-THROUGH HOST
Concurrent Systems, Java Idioms, Refactoring

125, 287

When a class can be partitioned into independent subsets, refactor the Host class to produce Helper classes whose actions are delegated by the Host. In the most extreme case, a Pass-Through Host simply relays all messages using simple unsynchronized methods to a Helper.

　　♦ This pattern is a special case of OPEN CALLS ♦ 38 where no state in the Host needs to be updated before the call.

COPY-ON-WRITE
Concurrent Systems, Java Idioms, Refactoring

136-141

In copy-on-write updates, state changes don't directly update fields. Instead, new representation objects are constructed and attached.

　　♦ You can also use ATOMIC COMMITMENT ♦ 38.

ATOMIC COMMITMENT
Concurrent Systems, Java Idioms, Refactoring

140-141

Replace assignment statements with an optimistic update technique that conditionally swaps in a new state representation only if the existing state representation is the one the caller expects.

OPEN CONTAINERS
Concurrent Systems, Java Idioms, Refactoring

142-145

Most classes in concurrent programs undergo iterative refactorings to address locking issues. Ordered hierarchical locking techniques can be applied when you have layered containment but the parts are not hidden from other clients.

ROLLBACK
Concurrent Systems, Java Idioms

163

In response to a failure in some part of the system, maintain state representations that allow a return to a consistent state.

　　♦ If ROLLBACK ♦ 38 is impossible, consider ROLL-FORWARD ♦ 39.

　　♦ Before attempting an action, the current state can be recorded using MEMENTO ♦ 87.

ROLL-FORWARD
Concurrent Systems, Java Idioms

164

When ROLLBACK ♦ 38, as well as full continuation, is impossible or undesirable, push ahead conservatively to reestablish a guaranteed legal, consistent state.

MULTIPHASE CANCELLATION
Concurrent Systems, Java Idioms

175-176

Try to cancel a task in the least disruptive manner first. If this fails, try a more disruptive strategy.

CONFLICT SETS
Concurrent Systems, Java Idioms

203-206

A conflict set contains pairs of actions that cannot co-occur. (1) For each action: (1) declare a counter to be set if the action is in progress; (2) isolate each action in a non-public method; (3) Write public versions of the methods in (2) to surround the action with "before" and "after" control.

READERS AND WRITERS
Concurrent Systems, Java Idioms

207-210

Block Readers if there are waiting Writers. Waiting Writers are identified by the order in which the underlying JVM scheduler resumes unblocked threads. There are no downgrade mechanisms.

VETOABLE CHANGES
Concurrent Systems, Java Idioms

261-263

A host with a set of objects that support vetoable set methods sends vetoable change events to listeners. If any listener responds with a veto, the set operation is cancelled.

THREAD-PER-MESSAGE
Concurrent Systems, Java Idioms

288-289

Concurrency can be introduced into one-way messaging designs by issuing a message in its own thread. This strategy improves throughput when multiple parallel tasks can run faster than a sequence of them.

WORKER THREADS
Concurrent Systems, Java Idioms

290-303

A worker thread or background thread (or thread pool) executes many unrelated tasks. Each worker thread continually accepts new Runnable commands from hosts, holding them in a Channel until they can be run.

EVENT-DRIVEN I/O
Concurrent Systems, Java Idioms, Refactoring

299-303

To handle many sessions without using many threads, refactor tasks into an event-driven style. (1) Isolate basic per-command functionality in a "run" task that reads one command and performs the associated action. (2) Define "run" to be repeatedly triggered by input or an I/O exception. (3) Manually maintain completion status.

FLOW NETWORKS
Concurrent Systems, Java Idioms

305-324

A flow network is a collection of objects that all pass one-way messages along paths from sources to sinks in one or more stages. Each stage is a producer and/or a consumer.

FUTURES
Concurrent Systems, Java Idioms

332-336

Futures are virtual data objects that automatically block when clients try to invoke their field accessors before their computation is complete. A Future acts as an IOU for a given data object.

FORK/JOIN
Concurrent Systems, Java Idioms

344-357

A parallel version of the divide-and-conquer technique from sequential approaches, implemented by forking and later joining tasks.

CONNECTOR
Communications, Concurrent Systems, Distributed Systems

[Schmidt98b], *PLoPD3*, 191-229

http://www.cs.wustl.edu/~schmidt/report-art.html

Decouple service initialization from the services provided. This pattern is for active initialization.

- ♦♦♦ ACCEPTOR ♦ 3 is for passive initialization.
- ♦♦♦ This pattern can be used with ACTIVE OBJECT ♦ 6, REACTOR ♦ 143, and SERVICE CONFIGURATOR ♦ 151.
- ♦♦♦ This pattern uses FACTORY METHOD ♦ 56 and TEMPLATE METHOD ♦ 171.
- ♦♦♦ This pattern is similar to CLIENT-DISPATCHER-SERVER ♦ 34 (CDS). This pattern addresses both synchronous and asynchronous service initializations, while CDS focuses on synchronous connection.

COUNTED POINTER
C++ Idioms

[Buschmann+96], *POSA*, 353-358

Improves memory management of dynamically allocated, shared objects in C++ by introducing a reference counter to a body class updated by handle objects. Clients access body class objects only through handles. This pattern was first described in [Coplien92] and later expanded in [Coplien99c].

CREATING REPORTS WITH QUERY OBJECTS
Database

[Brant+99], *PLoPD4*, 375-390

http://www.joeyoder.com/papers/

Dynamic creation of formulas and queries for database-reporting applications. A Smalltalk perspective, but still generally applicable.

Entries

REPORT OBJECTS

Database

376-378

You need to create a configurable reporting application. Information will be given in a formula based on a database query. Define objects that represent the report that are made up of objects that process and view the data. A report is created by attaching processing objects to viewing objects. Use QUERY OBJECTS ◆ 41 to select data from the database and FORMULA OBJECTS ◆ 41 to operate on the data.

QUERY OBJECTS

Database

378-381

You're using REPORT OBJECTS ◆ 41 and need to create queries for reports at run-time. Create objects that represent queries. Define operations on these objects and a method to return query results.

COMPOSABLE QUERY OBJECTS

Database

381-384

You're using QUERY OBJECTS ◆ 41 to build dynamic queries. Many reports have similar queries. Build queries out of composable parts. Define one class to represent tables in the database. Define a class that performs each query.

- ⋔ Use COMPOSITE ◆ 37 and DECORATOR ◆ 46 to compose new objects.
- ⋔ Consider each operation as a parse node and use INTERPRETER ◆ 80.
- ⋔ Use OBSERVER ◆ 94 to maintain internal consistency.

FORMULA OBJECTS

Business Computation, Database

384-386

You're using REPORT OBJECTS ◆ 41 where some values are computed. You want the user to create or modify formulas at run-time. Define an object to represent the results of a computed formula. Use CONSTRAINT OBSERVER ◆ 41 so the result object is consistent with its inputs.

CONSTRAINT OBSERVER

Database

387-389

You're using FORMULA OBJECTS ◆ 41 and need to update results when input values change. Create a constraint object responsible for the computation. Use OBSERVER ◆ 94 to update the constraint when input values change. When the constraint is updated, it evaluates the formula and assigns the result.

CROSSING CHASMS: A PATTERN LANGUAGE FOR OBJECT-RDBMS INTEGRATION

Database

[Brown+96b], *PLoPD2*, 227-238

Crossing Chasms contains architectural patterns, static patterns that define tables and object models, dynamic patterns that resolve run-time problems of object-table mapping, and client-server patterns.

TABLE DESIGN TIME
Architectural, Database, Client-Server

229

Design a relational database schema after a first-pass object model done with a behavioral modeling technique. It may be prudent to wait until after an architectural prototype has been built. Doing things in reverse order often leads to a poorly factored OO design with separate function and data objects. See TABLE DESIGN TIME ◆ 107.

♦♦♦ REPRESENTING COLLECTIONS ◆ 107, REPRESENTING INHERITANCE IN A RELATIONAL DATABASE ◆ 42, REPRESENTING OBJECT RELATIONSHIPS ◆ 107, REPRESENTING OBJECTS AS TABLES ◆ 42

REPRESENTING OBJECTS AS TABLES
Database

230

To map objects into a relational database, start with a table for each persistent object. Determine the type of each instance variable and create a column in the table.

♦♦♦ If the instance variable contains a collection, use REPRESENTING COLLECTIONS ◆ 107. If it contains any other value, use FOREIGN KEY REFERENCES ◆ 43. Finally, use OBJECT IDENTIFIER ◆ 42 to create a column containing the object identifier.

♦♦♦ REPRESENTING OBJECTS AS TABLES ◆ 107

REPRESENTING OBJECT RELATIONSHIPS
Database

230-231

To represent object relationships in a relational database, one-to-one mappings become FOREIGN KEY REFERENCES ◆ 43. One-to-many mappings can use a relationship table. Many-to-many relationships become relationship tables.

♦♦♦ REPRESENTING OBJECT RELATIONSHIPS ◆ 107

REPRESENTING INHERITANCE IN A RELATIONAL DATABASE
Database

232-233

To represent a set of classes in an inheritance hierarchy in a relational database, for each class, create a table that has a column for each attribute in the class and an additional column for the common key shared with all subclass tables. An instance of a concrete subclass is retrieved by performing a JOIN of all tables in a path to the root with the common key as the join parameter.

REPRESENTING COLLECTIONS IN A RELATIONAL DATABASE
Database

233-234

To represent Smalltalk collections in a relational database, for each collection, create a relationship table that maps the primary keys of the containing objects to the primary keys of the contained objects.

OBJECT IDENTIFIER
Database

234-235

To preserve an object's identity in a relational database, assign an object identifier to each persistent object, typically a long integer guaranteed to be unique for a class of objects.

♦♦♦ OBJECT IDENTIFIER ◆ 107

♦♦♦ This pattern is an extension of IDENTIFICATION SCHEME ◆ 10.

FOREIGN KEY REFERENCES

Database

235-236

To represent objects in a relational database that reference other objects that are not base datatypes, assign each object a unique identifier. Add a column for each instance variable that is not a base datatype or a collection. Store the identifier of the referenced object in the column. Declare the column a foreign key. See FOREIGN KEY REFERENCES ♦ 108.

FOREIGN KEY VERSUS DIRECT REFERENCE

Database

236-238

In the domain object model, when should you use FOREIGN KEY REFERENCES ♦ 43 and when should you use a direct reference with pointers? Use direct references as much as possible. This permits fast over the object structures. Build the object network piece by piece, using PROXY ♦ 139 objects to minimize storage. Make associations only as complex as necessary.

CURIOUSLY RECURRING TEMPLATE

C++ Idioms, Finite State Machines

[Coplien95a], *C++ Report*, Feb. 1995, 24-27

A class is derived from a base class instantiated from a template. The derived class is passed as a parameter to the template instantiation. This pattern captures a circular dependency using inheritance in one direction and templates in the other.

🛠 [Piehler99]

CUSTOMER INTERACTION PATTERNS

Customer Interaction, Organization and Process

[Rising99], *PLoPD4*, 585-609

For developers who interact with customers.

IT'S A RELATIONSHIP, NOT A SALE

Customer Interaction, Organization and Process

587-589

Develop a rapport with your customer. Focus on your relationship, not the current transaction. Use KNOW THE CUSTOMER ♦ 43 and BUILD TRUST ♦ 43.

KNOW THE CUSTOMER

Customer Interaction, Organization and Process

589-592

You're using IT'S A RELATIONSHIP, NOT A SALE ♦ 43 and trying to establish rapport with a customer. Learn as much as possible about the customer. Use BE RESPONSIVE ♦ 44, CUSTOMER MEETINGS: GO EARLY, STAY LATE ♦ 44; and LISTEN, LISTEN, LISTEN ♦ 44.

BUILD TRUST

Customer Interaction, Organization and Process

592-595

You're using IT'S A RELATIONSHIP, NOT A SALE ♦ 43 and trying to establish rapport with a customer. Every contact with the customer is a chance to build trust. Take advantage of it. Use BE RESPONSIVE ♦ 44, CUSTOMER MEETINGS: GO EARLY, STAY LATE ♦ 44; and LISTEN, LISTEN, LISTEN ♦ 44.

LISTEN, LISTEN, LISTEN
Customer Interaction, Organization and Process

595-597

You're using IT'S A RELATIONSHIP, NOT A SALE ♦ 43, KNOW THE CUSTOMER ♦ 43, and BUILD TRUST ♦ 43. Listen to the customer with intent to understand. BE AWARE OF BOUNDARIES ♦ 44, MIND YOUR MANNERS ♦ 44, and SHOW PERSONAL INTEGRITY ♦ 44.

BE RESPONSIVE
Customer Interaction, Organization and Process

597-599

You're using IT'S A RELATIONSHIP, NOT A SALE ♦ 43, KNOW THE CUSTOMER ♦ 43, and BUILD TRUST ♦ 43. When you receive a request from the customer, let the customer know you received it and how you plan to resolve it. If you can't get resolution as promised, contact the customer and say what you've done thus far. BE AWARE OF BOUNDARIES ♦ 44, MIND YOUR MANNERS ♦ 44, and SHOW PERSONAL INTEGRITY ♦ 44.

CUSTOMER MEETINGS: GO EARLY, STAY LATE
Customer Interaction, Organization and Process

600-601

You're using IT'S A RELATIONSHIP, NOT A SALE ♦ 43, KNOW THE CUSTOMER ♦ 43, and BUILD TRUST ♦ 43. Arrive at customer meetings early enough to meet other attendees and spend time socializing. After the meeting, allow a little time to talk to others with common business interests.

SHOW PERSONAL INTEGRITY
Customer Interaction, Organization and Process

602-603

You're using IT'S A RELATIONSHIP, NOT A SALE ♦ 43, KNOW THE CUSTOMER ♦ 43, and BUILD TRUST ♦ 43. Don't withhold important information from the customer. BE AWARE OF BOUNDARIES ♦ 44.

TAKE YOUR LICKS
Customer Interaction, Organization and Process

603-604

You're using IT'S A RELATIONSHIP, NOT A SALE ♦ 43, KNOW THE CUSTOMER ♦ 43, and BUILD TRUST ♦ 43. Don't argue. Try to understand how the customer's business is impacted. Don't try to appease the customer by making promises you can't keep. BE AWARE OF BOUNDARIES ♦ 44.

BE AWARE OF BOUNDARIES
Customer Interaction, Organization and Process

605-606

You're using IT'S A RELATIONSHIP, NOT A SALE ♦ 43, KNOW THE CUSTOMER ♦ 43, and BUILD TRUST ♦ 43. In your interactions with the customer, treat every conversation with the customer as part of a negotiation. Don't discuss commercial considerations, e.g., price, cost, schedule, and content, that aren't your responsibility. MIND YOUR MANNERS ♦ 44 and SHOW PERSONAL INTEGRITY ♦ 44.

MIND YOUR MANNERS
Customer Interaction, Organization and Process

606-608

You're using IT'S A RELATIONSHIP, NOT A SALE ♦ 43, KNOW THE CUSTOMER ♦ 43, and BUILD TRUST ♦ 43. In your interactions with the customer, be polite, dress appropriately, and show respect for everyone, including competitors. Be especially careful with your interaction with others from your company in front of the customer. SHOW PERSONAL INTEGRITY ♦ 44.

DECISION DEFERRAL AND CAPTURE PATTERN LANGUAGE

System Modelling

[Hopley96], *PLoPD2*, 335-343

Models for designing an object-oriented call processing system.

DECISION-BASED MODELS

System Modelling

336-337

You're defining a system by successive refinement of models. Define model content on the basis of decisions captured in that model or deferred to refining models. These decisions are often based on what is being done, who is doing it, and how it is being done.

♦♦♦ APPROPRIATE LIVING MODELS ♦ 45 helps decide which decision-based model should be maintained.

APPROPRIATE LIVING MODELS

System Modelling

337-338

You're using DECISION-BASED MODELS ♦ 45. Choose an appropriate number of models so you don't spend all your time developing the models instead of developing the system. Models should be independent of decisions likely to change. A model can capture or be independent of multiple decisions.

EXECUTABLE MODELS

System Modelling

338-340

You're using DECISION-BASED MODELS ♦ 45. To ensure that a model is a correct or consistent representation of a solution to a problem, build an executable version of a model. This is a form of prototyping for model builders.

♦♦♦ PROTOTYPE ♦ 168, PROTOTYPE ♦ 69, PROTOTYPE A FIRST-PASS DESIGN ♦ 84, PROTOTYPES ♦ 142, PROTOTYPING LANGUAGES ♦ 47

UPWARD TRACEABILITY

System Modelling

340-341

You're developing a system represented by two or more levels of models, with different groups maintaining the different models. To ensure that information is not lost in moving from one model to another, maintain upward traceability between models and downward approval of that traceability. Designers of the refining model own and maintain the traceability to the refined model. Designers of the refined model give approval of that traceability.

DOWNWARD CHANGES

System Modelling

341-342

You're designing a system where problems are often encountered at more detailed levels of abstraction. These problems require changes. For multiple models at various levels of abstraction, to develop and make changes to those models, make changes from the highest level of abstraction to the lowest level, maintaining traceability all the way.

DECORATOR
Structural

[Gamma+95], *GoF*, 175-184

[Alpert+98], *Design Patterns Smalltalk Companion*, 161-177

Attach additional responsibilities to an object dynamically. This provides a flexible alternative to subclassing for extending functionality.

- ⵌ This pattern only changes an object's responsibilities, not its interface. ADAPTER ♦ 6 provides a new interface for an object.
- ⵌ This pattern can be considered a degenerate COMPOSITE ♦ 37 with one component; however, this pattern adds additional responsibilities and is not intended for object aggregation.
- ⵌ This pattern can be confused with PROXY ♦ 139. A Proxy doesn't generally change the subject's behavior except to make it available or unavailable.
- ✖ [Bäumer+97], [Johnson94b]

DEFAULT VISITOR
Behavioral

[Nordberg98], *PLoPD3*, 105-112

This pattern adds another level of inheritance to VISITOR ♦ 179, providing a default implementation that takes advantage of the inheritance relationships in a polymorphic hierarchy of elements.

- ⵌ See EXTRINSIC VISITOR ♦ 56 for a different implementation of VISITOR ♦ 179.

DEMO PREP: A PATTERN LANGUAGE FOR THE PREPARATION OF SOFTWARE DEMONSTRATIONS
Customer Interaction

[Coram96], *PLoPD2*, 407-416

http://patriot.net/~maroc/papers/demopatlang.html

Preparation for customer demonstrations.

ELEMENT IDENTIFICATION
Customer Interaction

408-409

You're preparing a customer demonstration. Identifying exactly what should be demonstrated is a critical part of instilling customer confidence. Identify the key areas that concern the customer. Present demonstrations to alleviate the customer's concern that what is being developed is correct and will work the way the customer expects.

- ⵌ Once you've applied this pattern, use CATALYTIC SCENARIOS ♦ 47.
- ⵌ The user interface can be demonstrated using LIGHTWEIGHT USER INTERFACES ♦ 47.
- ⵌ Functionality can be demonstrated using PROTOTYPING LANGUAGES ♦ 47.

CATALYTIC SCENARIOS
Customer Interaction
409-410

You're ready to start a project. Requirements have been agreed upon. The customer has specified what he thinks he wants, but use demonstrable scenarios to be sure you and the customer agree on what is being built. Keep the demonstration uncomplicated and succinct.

- JUDICIOUS FIREWORKS ♦ 47 describes the dangers of demonstrations that hint at future possibilities you may not want to implement.

MUTABLE CODE
Customer Interaction
411

You've used CATALYTIC SCENARIOS ♦ 47 and evaluating the effort to develop them. The level of coding for developing a demonstration is unclear, especially if the code will be usable in the development effort. GUI builders and scripting languages will help with the demonstration. Write only the code necessary for a successful demonstration.

- If you develop a lot of screens, see LIGHTWEIGHT USER INTERFACES ♦ 47.
- PROTOTYPING LANGUAGES ♦ 47 discusses how you might integrate the code developed for the demonstration into the end product, as well as reduce the amount of code written.

PROTOTYPING LANGUAGES
Customer Interaction
411-412

You're using CATALYTIC SCENARIOS ♦ 47. If you can't implement the end product in a language that supports rapid prototyping, then consider using a prototyping/scripting language (e.g., Tcl, Perl, XLisp) that works with your implementation language. Often such prototyping languages can be embedded in the implementation language and even become an extension language for the product.

- A flexible prototyping language can demonstrate the product's functionality. You can fake it using JUDICIOUS FIREWORKS ♦ 47 in LIGHTWEIGHT USER INTERFACES ♦ 47.

LIGHTWEIGHT USER INTERFACES
Customer Interaction
412-413

Your customer demonstration must show some level of interactivity. Spend minimal effort on the user interface. If possible, use tools to facilitate easy modification of the interface without writing a lot of code. The customer should realize that the prototype interface is part of a demonstration, not part of the end product. Intentionally leave parts of the display incomplete; don't spend time making it just right.

JUDICIOUS FIREWORKS
Customer Interaction
413-414

You want the customer demonstration to excite the customer but not give unrealistic expectations. Dazzle the customer with just enough spectacular functionality to leave them wanting more. Use LIGHTWEIGHT USER INTERFACES ♦ 47. Pick a part of the interface to put on the best show and concentrate on it. Don't demonstrate extras that will not appear in the end product.

- Once you've coded your best fireworks, use ARCHIVE SCENARIOS ♦ 48 to be sure they are saved.

ARCHIVE SCENARIOS
Customer Interaction
415
You've prepared a successful customer demonstration and are returning to product development. Never believe that you've given all the demonstrations. Archive the demonstration. Code, scripts, results, and bugs should be saved. New scenarios will be developed or enhanced, but old demonstrations should be easy to repeat.

DESIGN PATTERNS FOR OBJECT-ORIENTED HYPERMEDIA APPLICATIONS

Hypermedia
[Rossi+96], *PLoPD2*, 177-191
Design patterns for object-oriented applications with hypermedia functionality.

NAVIGATIONSTRATEGY
Hypermedia
180-185
In conventional hypermedia applications, links are hard-coded from the source node to the target. Define a family of algorithms that decouples the activation of hypermedia links from the computation of their endpoints, allowing different means of obtaining the endpoints and their lazy creation.
⁂ This pattern is similar to STRATEGY ♦ 167 in that it allows the designer to define a family of algorithms, making them interchangeable and allowing the Link class to be extended independently of those algorithms. It differs from STRATEGY ♦ 167 by including a subhierarchy of factories where the strategy algorithm behaves as FACTORY METHOD ♦ 56, which allows lazy creation of endpoints and navigation strategies.
⁂ AbstractStrategyFactory is similar to ACCEPTOR ♦ 3 in that both establish connections lazily. AbstractStrategyFactory is similar to ABSTRACT FACTORY ♦ 2, while ACCEPTOR ♦ 3 is not.
⁂ This pattern uses TEMPLATE METHOD ♦ 171 to define the abstract algorithm for performing navigation.

NAVIGATIONOBSERVER
Hypermedia
185-189
Hypermedia applications should record navigation in a user-perceptible way. Decouple navigation from the perceivable record of the process, and simplify the construction of navigation history viewers by separating the hypermedia components (nodes and links) from the objects that implement both the record of navigation and its appearance.
⁂ The relationship between viewers and history resembles OBSERVER ♦ 94.
⁂ History may be implemented with SINGLETON ♦ 152.
⁂ MEDIATOR ♦ 86 can decouple hypermedia components from a history when dealing with multiple browsing sessions.

DETACHABLE INSPECTOR
Structural

[Sane+96a], *PLoPD2*, 159-175

http://choices.cs.uiuc.edu/sane/home.html#dp

Meta-facilities for instrumentation or debugging are commonly implemented by statements interspersed in program code. As a result, program modules become difficult to reuse in contexts where the meta-facilities may be absent or have incompatible implementations. Decouple and segregate meta-facilities so they can be changed or removed without affecting the program.

- This pattern is similar to DECORATOR ♦ 46 in that it adds responsibilities and can withdraw them. DECORATOR ♦ 46 alters object behavior; this pattern does not.
- VISITOR ♦ 179 is similar to this pattern. Here objects call the meta-facilities directly instead of an intermediate visitor object.
- The global inspector is implemented with SINGLETON ♦ 152.
- LAYERS ♦ 81

DISPLAY MAINTENANCE
GUI Development

[Towell99], *PLoPD4*, 489-502

Patterns for designing display architecture.

DISPLAY LIST
GUI Development

491-492

Visible component occlusion is important to the GUI, but components shouldn't have this responsibility. Maintain a list of all visual components and let the order dictate occlusion.

- Use PAINTER'S ALGORITHM ♦ 50 to render a display list.
- REQUEST UPDATE ♦ 49 can decide when rendering should occur.

REQUEST UPDATE
GUI Development

492-493

Visual components may be occluded by others in a GUI, complicating display updates. Request display update rather than redraw directly.

- This pattern provides the context for honoring update requests. Use CLIP REQUESTS ♦ 50, CONSOLIDATE REQUESTS ♦ 50, and LAZY REDRAW ♦ 50 to improve efficiency.
- GLOBAL UPDATE ♦ 49 offers an alternative solution.

GLOBAL UPDATE
GUI Development

493-494

You would use REQUEST UPDATE ♦ 49, but tracking many update requests slows the display. Instead of tracking individual update requests, update the entire display.

PAINTER'S ALGORITHM
GUI Development

494-496

Rendering a single visual component in a GUI with correct occlusion requires significant interobject knowledge of boundaries. Draw all components without regard to occlusion, back to front, so each visual object will replace any part of the image behind it. The display must be rewritable. This will exact a heavy penalty in display cost.

⚜ DOUBLE BUFFER ♦ 50 can reduce display flicker normally generated by this pattern.

CONSOLIDATE REQUESTS
Event-Driven Systems, GUI Development

496-497

Processing individual update requests from user events can be disruptive and inefficient. Consolidate update requests generated by a single user event. If transition times are lengthy, this pattern can give the impression the system has failed to respond.

⚜ This pattern is an optimization of REQUEST UPDATE ♦ 49.

LAZY REDRAW
GUI Development

497-498

Consecutive, similar redraws of a GUI may hinder interaction. Postpone redraws until time allows.

⚜ This pattern is an optimization of REQUEST UPDATE ♦ 49.

CLIP REQUESTS
GUI Development

498-499

Updating hidden regions of a GUI is unnecessary and inefficient. Exclude opaque foreground regions from update requests.

⚜ This is an optimization of REQUEST UPDATE ♦ 49.

DOUBLE BUFFER
GUI Development

500-501

Updating components directly to the display causes display flicker. Render visible components to a hidden display, then use a single operation to update the visible display.

⚜ PAGE FLIP ♦ 50 may be appropriate if large areas of the display will be updated each frame.

PAGE FLIP
GUI Development

501

You're using GLOBAL UPDATE ♦ 49. You would use DOUBLE BUFFER ♦ 50, but it's inefficient. Swap the active display buffer. Rendering will alternate between the two buffers. While one is visible, the other can be redrawn.

DISTRIBUTED PROCESSES

Architectural, Distributed Systems

[Shaw+96], *Software Architecture*, 31

There are several architectures for distributed systems. Some can be characterized by their topological features (e.g., ring and star organizations). Others can be characterized by the kinds of interprocess protocols used for communication (e.g., heartbeat algorithms). Client-server is a common form of distributed system architecture.

DOUBLE-CHECKED LOCKING

Concurrent Systems

[Schmidt+98], *PLoPD3*, 363-375

http://www.cs.wustl.edu/~schmidt/patterns-ace.html

Reduce contention and synchronization overhead when critical sections of code should be executed just once but must be thread-safe when they do acquire locks.

DRIVER DUTY

Networks, Transportation

[Zhao+98a], *JOOP*, July/Aug. 1998, 35-39, 77

Use a tree structure for ordering and layering the components that define a Driver Duty (a normal working day for drivers in a transport system).

  This pattern is an application of CASCADE ♦ 28 and COMPOSITE ♦ 37.

DRIVER DUTY CONSTRUCTOR

Networks, Transportation

[Zhao+99], *JOOP*, May 1999, 45-51, 77

This pattern comprises three other patterns: Driver Duty Builder, Driver Duty Director, and DRIVER DUTY ♦ 51. The first two patterns build and assemble the components of the third.

  Driver Duty Builder uses CASCADE ♦ 28 to build DRIVER DUTY ♦ 51 objects.

  Driver Duty Builder and Driver Duty Director work together as the components of BUILDER ♦ 23.

  Driver Duty Director is an application of STRATEGY ♦ 167.

EPISODES: A PATTERN LANGUAGE OF COMPETITIVE DEVELOPMENT

Organization and Process

[Cunningham96], *PLoPD2*, 371-388

http://c2.com/ppr/episodes.html

Organization and process for software development in small teams that describes mental states or episodes.

PRODUCT INITIATIVE
Organization and Process

374-375

When a wish list of features and functions is created for a product, clearly define an initiative for product improvement and be sure everyone understands the initiative. When this pattern has been followed, use MARKET WALK-THROUGH ♦ 52.

MARKET WALK-THROUGH
Organization and Process

375

When PRODUCT INITIATIVE ♦ 52 has been followed, hold a walkthrough of program and product concepts with both the development and business sides of an organization. When this pattern has been followed, use IMPLIED REQUIREMENTS ♦ 52.

IMPLIED REQUIREMENTS
Organization and Process

375-376

When MARKET WALK-THROUGH ♦ 52 has been followed, it's time to name functionality. Use names that have meaning for customers and that are consistent with the product initiative. When this pattern has been followed, use WORK QUEUE ♦ 52.

WORK QUEUE
Organization and Process

377

Use the implied requirements to create a schedule. Order the requirements by priority. When work can be factored from two or more items, give the common element a name that establishes its position on the list. Be prepared to reorder the list as new priorities arise. When this pattern has been followed, use WORK GROUP ♦ 52.

WORK GROUP
Organization and Process

377-378

When you've completed a work queue that (a) describes product initiative-relevant work, (b) is ordered by priority, and (c) shifts up as completed work is removed from the top, then allocate roughly two month's work from the top of the work queue. Be sure the team assigned to this work is committed to work together to complete their assignment. When this pattern has been followed, use WORK QUEUE REPORT ♦ 52.

WORK QUEUE REPORT
Organization and Process

378

It's difficult to detect schedule slips in a weekly status meeting. Collect status reports from weekly personal interviews. Request estimates of days of remaining effort (in terms of uninterrupted days) using comparisons with related previous work. Use these estimates along with individual dilution factors (usual number of uninterrupted days per week) to predict days to completion for each deliverable. When this pattern has been followed, use COMPLETION HEADROOM ♦ 53.

COMPARABLE WORK
Organization and Process

379-380

Ask developers to estimate by analogy to comparable tasks. A task half as complex as some previous task will probably take half the time.

COMPLETION HEADROOM
Organization and Process
380

Estimate completion dates using the remaining effort estimates in the work queue report. Calculate each contributor's earliest possible completion date, find the latest of these, and compare that to the hard delivery date for the project. The difference is the completion headroom. The headroom may fluctuate, but steady evaporation of headroom requires management to reorder the work queue, possibly deferring items to a later release date, creating a work split that removes poorly understood or difficult pieces, or holding a RECOMMITMENT MEETING ♦ 53.

♦♦♦ See TAKE NO SMALL SLIPS ♦ 69 for a discussion of schedule tracking.

DEVELOPMENT EPISODE
Organization and Process
380-381

Don't emphasize an individual's special skills. Treat all development as a group activity. This will produce better design decisions and will have a positive effect on the participants. Expertise is shared and everyone in the group learns.

♦♦♦ See DEVELOPING IN PAIRS ♦ 69 for a discussion of joint development.

INFORMAL LABOR PLAN
Organization and Process
381-382

Allow individuals to create their own short-term work plans. Realize that most of the group activity in a development episode will take place in pairs that find the time to work together. Don't call a meeting to schedule a development episode. Let individuals make their own plans.

♦♦♦ DEVELOPING IN PAIRS ♦ 69, DEVELOPMENT EPISODE ♦ 53, PROGRAMMING EPISODE ♦ 54

WORK SPLIT
Organization and Process
382

Divide each task into urgent and deferred pieces. (No more than half should be urgent.) Defer more work if necessary to have sufficient headroom. Defer analysis and design for parts that won't be implemented. Both halves of the split should appear in the work queue with different priorities.

♦♦♦ COMPLETION HEADROOM ♦ 53, WORK QUEUE ♦ 52

RECOMMITMENT MEETING
Organization and Process
382-383

When a product initiative is in jeopardy because implied requirements cannot be met, even with schedule and work queue adjustments, schedule a meeting with all management and key developers. Show that simple adjustments will not help. Eventually a solution will appear, usually as the question: "What is the least amount of work required to do X?" Give an answer based on a recent work queue report. This may be repeated for Y and Z. Ultimately a plan will be developed.

♦♦♦ PRODUCT INITIATIVE ♦ 52, WORK QUEUE ♦ 52, WORK QUEUE REPORT ♦ 52

REQUIREMENT WALK-THROUGH
Organization and Process
383-384
When any member of the work group begins to consider any part of an implied requirement, assemble the entire group. This is a good time to sketch the first informal work plan for that requirement, and it can lead to staffing changes.
ᚙ IMPLIED REQUIREMENTS ♦ 52, WORK GROUP ♦ 52

TECHNICAL MEMO
Organization and Process
384
Develop a series of well-formatted technical memoranda. Focus each memo on a single subject. Keep it short. Carefully selected, well-written memos can substitute for comprehensive design documentation.

REFERENCE DATA
Organization and Process
384
A requirement walk-through will identify relevant information sources, which will be retrieved, reviewed, and absorbed as the development episode begins. Collect these information sources as machine-readable examples. Annotate documents so the sources of information will not be lost.
ᚙ DEVELOPMENT EPISODE ♦ 53, REQUIREMENT WALK-THROUGH ♦ 54

PROGRAMMING EPISODE
Organization and Process
385
Programming should be done in discrete episodes. Select appropriate deliverables for an episode and commit sufficient resources to deliver them. Push for the decisions that can be made. Code the decisions and review the code.

ESSENCE
Distributed Systems, Fault-Tolerant Systems
[Carlson99], *PLoPD4*, 33-40
Many classes, particularly persistent ones, require that a certain subset of their attributes be valid before an instance can be considered valid. How can this be guaranteed in component-based or distributed environments where the client that creates the instances is outside your design control? Use an essence object for the compulsory properties of the object being created—the CreationTarget. There should be an essence class for each CreationTarget class.

EVENT NOTIFICATION
Event-Driven Systems
[Riehle96a], *TAPOS*, Vol. 2, No. 1, 1996, 43-52
http://www.riehle.org/papers/1996/tapos-1996-event.html
Changes in one object often require changes in dependent objects. Requiring objects to inform dependents about state changes explicitly couples object interfaces and implementations. Use implicit invocation. State changes, dependencies, and links among these objects become first-class objects.

EVENTHANDLER
Behavioral

[Jackson99], *C++ Report*, Jan. 1999, 38-45

An adaptation of CHAIN OF RESPONSIBILITY ♦ 32 that improves the functionality of the original pattern by avoiding cyclic link time dependencies.

EVOLUTION, ARCHITECTURE, AND METAMORPHOSIS
Design Process

[Foote+96], *PLoPD2*, 295-314

http://www.laputan.org/metamorphosis/metamorphosis.html

Shows how the forces that drive software development lead to more reflective systems.

SOFTWARE TECTONICS
Design Process

298-302

Build systems to adapt to changing user requirements. Allow people to tailor systems to meet their needs. Allow systems to change in a series of small, controlled steps to stay the potential upheaval resulting from massive changes too long deferred. Use FLEXIBLE FOUNDATIONS ♦ 55.

♦♦♦ METAMORPHOSIS ♦ 55 encourages construction of systems that retain enough run-time mechanics to allow themselves to be dynamic instruments of their own evolution.

FLEXIBLE FOUNDATIONS
Design Process

302-306

Building software with a flexible foundation helps resolve the need for the continual, incremental evolution described in SOFTWARE TECTONICS ♦ 55. Allow tools, languages, or frameworks to manipulate themselves; that is, build them out of first-class objects. This allows them to co-evolve with the system.

METAMORPHOSIS
Design Process

307-312

Provide mechanisms for augmenting the behavior of an object or system without changing its fundamental interface or behavior. When applications and substrates are built from objects, they can evolve together as requirements change.

EXTENSION OBJECT
Behavioral

[Gamma98], *PLoPD3*, 79-88

Add interfaces to a class without changing the class, and allow clients to access the interfaces they need.

♦♦♦ This pattern is similar to DECORATOR ♦ 46 and VISITOR ♦ 179 in that it addresses the problem of extending class functionality.

♦♦♦ ADAPTER ♦ 6 lets you adapt an interface to work like another. This pattern supports adding interfaces, sometimes dynamically.

EXTERNAL POLYMORPHISM
Structural

[Cleeland+98a], *C++ Report*, Sept. 1998, 28-43

[Cleeland+98b], *PLoPD3*, 377-390

`http://www.cs.wustl.edu/~schmidt/report-art.html`

Allow classes that are not related by inheritance and/or have no virtual methods to be treated polymorphically.

- ⚓ DECORATOR ♦ 46 dynamically extends an object transparently without using subclassing and assumes that the classes it adorns are abstract (i.e., having virtual member functions in C++) that are overridden by a Decorator. Because a Decorator is derived from the class it adorns, it must define *all* the methods it inherits. This pattern adds polymorphism to concrete classes having nonvirtual methods, letting you define just the polymorphic methods.
- ⚓ ADAPTER ♦ 6 converts an interface to something expected by a client. EXTERNAL POLYMORPHISM ♦ 56 extends interfaces so similar functionality may be accessed polymorphically. This pattern creates an entire class hierarchy outside the scope of the concrete classes.

EXTRINSIC VISITOR
Behavioral

[Nordberg98], *PLoPD3*, 112-122

Trade the performance overhead of a small number of run-time type tests for reduced complexity and coupling in the visitor and element classes by testing the feasibility of a visit operation before performing it.

- ⚓ This pattern is a different implementation of VISITOR ♦ 179.
- ⚓ DEFAULT VISITOR ♦ 46 has a straightforward specialization of VISITOR ♦ 179.
- ⚓ ACYCLIC VISITOR ♦ 6 has an implementation that avoids cyclic dependencies.

FACADE
Structural

[Gamma+95], *GoF*, 185-193

[Alpert+98], *Design Patterns Smalltalk Companion*, 179-188

Provide a unified interface to a set of interfaces in a subsystem. A facade defines a higher-level interface that makes the subsystem easier to use.

- ⚓ ABSTRACT FACTORY ♦ 2 can be used with this pattern to provide an interface for creating subsystem objects in a subsystem-independent way.
- ⚓ This pattern defines a new interface, while ADAPTER ♦ 6 reuses an old one.
- ✗ [Barkataki+98], [Price+99], [Ramirez95], [Srinivasan99], [VandenBroecke+97]

FACTORY METHOD
Creational

[Gamma+95], *GoF*, 107-116

[Alpert+98], *Design Patterns Smalltalk Companion*, 63-76

Define an interface for creating an object, but let subclasses decide which class to instantiate. This allows a class to defer instantiation to subclasses.

- ⚓ ABSTRACT FACTORY ♦ 2 classes often use FACTORY METHOD ♦ 56.
- ✗ [Bäumer+97], [Masuda+98], [Schmidt96a], [Spall98], [Zhang+96c]

FAULT-TOLERANT TELECOMMUNICATION SYSTEM PATTERNS

Fault-Tolerant Systems, Telecommunications

[Adams+96], *PLoPD2*, 549-562

http://www.bell-labs.com/people/cope/patterns/telecom/PLoP95_telecom.html

Addresses reliability and human factors issues in telecommunications software, which must be highly reliable and continuously running.

MINIMIZE HUMAN INTERVENTION

Fault-Tolerant Systems, Telecommunications

551-552

Downtime, human-induced or otherwise, must be minimized. History has shown that people cause the majority of problems in these systems, so let the machine try to do everything, deferring to a human only as a last resort.

🙌 Note the conflict with PEOPLE KNOW BEST ♦ 57.

PEOPLE KNOW BEST

Fault-Tolerant Systems, Telecommunications

552-553

The system must try to recover from all error conditions on its own. To balance automation with human authority and responsibility allow knowledgeable users to override automatic controls.

🙌 MINIMIZE HUMAN INTERVENTION ♦ 57

FIVE MINUTES OF NO ESCALATION MESSAGES

Fault-Tolerant Systems, Telecommunications

553-554

The human-machine interface is saturated with error reports. Display a message when taking the first action in a series that could lead to an excess number of messages. If the abnormal condition ends, display a message that everything is back to normal. Don't display a message for every change in state. People can't do anything about the messages except watch them anyway. So don't bother printing. This pattern is expanded in FIVE MINUTES OF NO ESCALATION MESSAGES ♦ 78.

🙌 Note the conflict with PEOPLE KNOW BEST ♦ 57

RIDING OVER TRANSIENTS

Fault-Tolerant Systems, Telecommunications

554-555

Some errors may be transient. To determine if a problem will work itself out, don't react immediately to detected conditions. Be sure a condition really exists by checking it several times, perhaps using LEAKY BUCKET COUNTERS ♦ 57.

LEAKY BUCKET COUNTERS

Fault-Tolerant Systems, Telecommunications

555-556

To handle transient faults, keep a counter for each failure group. Initialize the counter to a predetermined value. Decrement the counter for each error or event and increment it periodically (but never beyond its initial value). If the leak rate is faster than the fill rate, then an error condition is indicated.

🙌 This pattern is an extension of RIDING OVER TRANSIENTS ♦ 57.

Entries

SICO FIRST AND ALWAYS
Fault-Tolerant Systems, Telecommunications

557-558

Give the System Integrity Control Program (SICO) the ability and power to reinitialize the system when system sanity is threatened by error conditions. This program should oversee both the initialization process and the normal application functions so initialization can be restarted if it runs into errors.

TRY ALL HARDWARE COMBOS
Fault-Tolerant Systems, Telecommunications

558-560

The central controller has several configurations with many paths through the subsystems depending on the configuration. To select a workable configuration when there is a faulty subsystem, maintain a configuration counter in hardware and a table that maps from that counter to a configuration state. When the system fails to get through a configuration to a predetermined level of stability, it restarts the system with the configuration that corresponds to the next value of the counter.

FOOL ME ONCE
Fault-Tolerant Systems, Telecommunications

560-562

You're using TRY ALL HARDWARE COMBOS ♦ 58. A latent error can cause a system fault after the configuration counter has been reset. The system then no longer knows that it is in configuration escalation and retries the same configuration that has already failed. The first time the application tells the processor configuration that "all is well," believe it and reset the configuration counter. After that, ignore the request.

FEATURE EXTRACTION—A PATTERN FOR INFORMATION RETRIEVAL
Database

[Manolescu99], *PLoPD4*, 391-412

Many applications must search for similarities in large amounts of information in digital libraries. To keep this information under control, work with an alternative, simpler representation of the data. The representation should contain some information unique to each data item.

FINITE STATE MACHINE PATTERNS
Finite State Machines

[Yacoub+99], *PLoPD4*, 413-440

An extension of STATE PATTERNS ❖ 166 and THREE-LEVEL FSM ♦ 172 to implement a state machine in an object-oriented design.

BASIC FSM
Finite State Machines

417-420

An object's state changes in response to events in the system. To implement the correct object behavior, use STATE ♦ 166 and add one of the state transition mechanisms of STATE PATTERNS ❖ 166.

State-Driven Transition
Finite State Machines

421-423

To get a state object to change when the owning object's state changes, have the state object initiate the transition from itself (the current state) to the new state object. This ensures that transitions are atomic and removes state-dependent code.

- ⚜ This is the same pattern as STATE-DRIVEN TRANSITIONS ♦ 167.
- ⚜ This pattern is a refinement of STATE ♦ 166.

Interface Organization
Finite State Machines

423-426

To enable communication between entities when the behavior of one is described by an FSM, encapsulate the state classes and state-transition logic in the machine, and provide a simple interface that receives events.

- ⚜ This motives you to use STATE-DRIVEN TRANSITION ♦ 59 to simplify tasks required by the interface by delegating state transition logic to the states themselves.

Layered Organization
Finite State Machines

426-428

You're using an FSM. To make your design maintainable, structure the system in layers that decouple the logic of state transition from object behavior.

- ⚜ This pattern is an extension of THREE-LEVEL FSM ♦ 172.
- ⚜ HIERARCHY OF CONTROL LAYERS ♦ 61, FOUR-LAYER ARCHITECTURE ♦ 106, LAYERED ARCHITECTURE ♦ 125, LAYERED AND SECTIONED ARCHITECTURE ♦ 96, LAYERS ♦ 81, PEDESTAL ♦ 123, SHAPE OF PROGRAM ♦ 29, THREE-TIER ARCHITECTURE ♦ 15

Meally
Finite State Machines

428-430

To begin FSM output, make the concrete event method of each state call the output action method.

- ⚜ HYBRID ♦ 59 and MOORE ♦ 59 offer solutions for related problems.

Moore
Finite State Machines

430-432

To begin FSM output produced only at state entry when each state has a specific set of outputs, implement an output method in each state that calls the required actions. Make the state transition mechanism call the output method of the next upcoming state.

- ⚜ HYBRID ♦ 59 and MEALLY ♦ 59 offer solutions for related problems.

Hybrid
Finite State Machines

433

If some FSM outputs are started on events and other outputs are started only in a given state, make the event method of each state produce the event-dependent outputs, and make the state transition mechanism call an output method of the upcoming state to produce the state-dependent output.

- ⚜ MEALLY ♦ 59 and MOORE ♦ 59 offer solutions for related problems.

Entries

ENCAPSULATED STATE
Finite State Machines

434

Your FSM should follow a sequence of state changes. To ensure that no other state changes are imposed, encapsulate the current state and keep the reference private.

ᛗ EXPOSED STATE ♦ 166 offers a different approach.

DYNAMIC STATE INSTANTIATION
Finite State Machines

435-437

Your application is large, with too many states. To instantiate them, don't initially create all states. Make each state knowledgeable of upcoming states, and create instances of them on state entry and delete them on state exit.

FLEXIBLE COMMAND INTERPRETER
Behavioral

[Portner95], *PLoPD1*, 43-50

An architecture for an interpreter system that allows for flexible extension of the command language's scope and independence from the actual grammar of the language.

ᛗ This pattern has the same intent as INTERPRETER ♦ 80.

ᛗ This pattern can be extended by using STRATEGY ♦ 167.

FLYWEIGHT
Structural

[Gamma+95], *GoF*, 195-206

[Alpert+98], *Design Patterns Smalltalk Companion*, 189-211

Use sharing to support large numbers of fine-grained objects efficiently.

ᛗ This pattern is often combined with COMPOSITE ♦ 37 to implement a hierarchical structure as a directed acyclic graph with shared leaf nodes.

ᛗ STATE ♦ 166 and STRATEGY ♦ 167 objects are often implemented as flyweights.

FORWARDER-RECEIVER
Communications, Distributed Systems

[Buschmann+96], *POSA*, 307-322

Provide transparent interprocess communication for software systems with a peer-to-peer interaction model. Forwarders and receivers decouple peers from the underlying communication mechanisms.

ᛗ CLIENT-DISPATCHER-SERVER ♦ 34 provides transparent interprocess communication when the distribution of components is not known at compile-time or may vary at run-time.

FROM PROTOTYPE TO REALITY

Concurrent Systems, Distributed Systems

[Aarsten+96a], *CACM*, Oct. 1996, 50-58

To ensure a seamless evolution from simulation to final implementation, maintain two versions of each object, the prototype and the reality object. When moving from simulation to reality, replace the prototype object with the reality object. Ensure consistent transition by having the implementations inherit from a common base class that defines their interface.

- ⚏ This pattern is the same as PROTOTYPE AND REALITY ♦ 63.
- ⚏ Keeping two distinct implementations of an entity and changing from one to the other is an application of BRIDGE ♦ 22.
- ⚏ A reality object that encapsulates external functionality is an ADAPTER ♦ 6.
- ✖ [Aarsten+96b]

FUNCTIONALITY ALA CARTE

Customer Interaction, Performance

[Adams95], *PLoPD1*, 7-8

Determine the incremental performance cost of each feature and present the customer with the aggregate cost of the features selected. This does not change the performance of the system, but it makes the customer aware of the performance consequences of the current configuration.

G++: A PATTERN LANGUAGE FOR COMPUTER-INTEGRATED MANUFACTURING

Automated Manufacturing, Concurrent Systems

[Aarsten+95], *PLoPD1*, 91-118

http://www.cim.polito.it/Tools/Gpp.html

Patterns and a framework of reusable classes for the design of concurrent, possibly distributed, information systems, with applications in computer-integrated manufacturing.

HIERARCHY OF CONTROL LAYERS

Automated Manufacturing, Concurrent Systems

95-96

To cope with complexity, organize system functions in hierarchical, decentralized control modules. Each layer of the hierarchy has modules of control that contain similar classes of functions.

- ⚏ FOUR-LAYER ARCHITECTURE ♦ 106, LAYERED ARCHITECTURE ♦ 125, LAYERED AND SECTIONED ARCHITECTURE ♦ 96, LAYERED ORGANIZATION ♦ 59, LAYERS ♦ 81, PEDESTAL ♦ 123, SHAPE OF PROGRAM ♦ 29, THREE-TIER ARCHITECTURE ♦ 15

VISIBILITY AND COMMUNICATION BETWEEN CONTROL MODULES

Automated Manufacturing, Concurrent Systems

97-99; [Aarsten+96a], 50-58

To enhance reusability in a hierarchy of layers of control: (1) Don't allow two modules in the same layer to communicate directly. (2) When a client sends a message to a server, it should be done explicitly, in caller/provider fashion. (3) A server should respond by sending events through a broadcast/listener mechanism.

- ⚏ Broadcast/Listener communication is the same as OBSERVER ♦ 94.
- ✖ [Aarsten+96b]

CATEGORIZE OBJECTS FOR CONCURRENCY
Automated Manufacturing, Concurrent Systems

99-101; [Aarsten+96a], 50-58

In a complex system, control modules perform services concurrently, and concurrency assumes different scales of granularity. Represent fine-grained activities as event-driven, atomic actions that access sequential objects. Let medium-grained activities run in a thread of control to share blocking objects. Large-grained activities are separate active objects.

ACTIONS TRIGGERED BY EVENTS
Automated Manufacturing, Concurrent Systems

101-102

Communication through events can be *intra*service, generating a small-grained concurrency, or *inter*service, creating a larger-grained concurrency. Use the broadcast/listening mechanism to raise and listen to events.

⋔   Broadcast/Listener communication is the same as OBSERVER ♦ 94.

SERVICES "WAITING FOR"
Automated Manufacturing, Concurrent Systems, Event-Driven Systems

102-103

Services of a control module must wait for a condition to occur or for data to be transferred before they can perform an action concurrently with others. Blocking objects can solve this problem. Define an abstract class Condition to define any blocking object. Timers, semaphores, event handlers, and shared queues can be derived by inheritance or encapsulation.

CLIENT/SERVER/SERVICE
Automated Manufacturing, Concurrent Systems

103-105; [Aarsten+96a], 50-58

Control modules must provide services concurrently; therefore provide a common representation at different levels of the hierarchy for standardization purposes, and encapsulate resources and the services that manipulate them. Use a Client/Server/Service model, with two classes: Service and Server. Service encapsulates a thread of execution and can have internal data. Server defines the common characteristics of all active objects.

IMPLEMENTATION OF "MULTIPLE KINDS OF SERVICES" CONTROL MODULES
Automated Manufacturing, Concurrent Systems

105-107

Control modules manage different pools of shared resources and can offer different kinds of services. Assuming a Server base class: (1) Identify resources the control module needs. Resources shared by the services of an active object can only be blocking objects or other active objects. (2) Identify the different services. Specify their behavior in terms of FSMs extended by sequential objects. (3) Use a graphical notation and SDL to specify service behavior. (4) Define a doService method as a switch statement.

INTERFACE TO CONTROL MODULES
Automated Manufacturing, Concurrent Systems

108-110

Control modules offer different kinds of services. Use an Interface object to access each server.

PROTOTYPE AND REALITY
Automated Manufacturing, Concurrent Systems

110-111

To ensure a seamless evolution from simulation to final implementation, maintain two versions of each object: the prototype and the reality object. When moving from simulation to reality, replace the prototype object with the reality object. Ensure consistent transition by having the implementations inherit from a common base class that defines their interface. See FROM PROTOTYPE TO REALITY ◆ 61.

- ᛟᛟ Keeping two distinct implementations of an entity and changing from one to the other is an application of BRIDGE ◆ 22.
- ᛟᛟ A reality object that encapsulates external functionality exemplifies ADAPTER ◆ 6.

DISTRIBUTION OF CONTROL MODULES
Automated Manufacturing, Distributed Systems

111-114; [Aarsten+96a], 50-58

Divide distributed objects into two parts: an interface proxy and the implementation. In the original system, replace objects that have been moved to other nodes with proxy objects to forward requests to the remote object they represent. On the remote node, add support for listening for requests and forwarding them to the correct object.

- ✖ [Aarsten+96b]

GENERATION GAP
GUI Development

[Vlissides98a], *Pattern Hatching*, 85-101

Modify or extend generated code just once no matter how many times it is regenerated.

GENERATIVE DEVELOPMENT-PROCESS PATTERN LANGUAGE
Organization and Process

[Coplien95b], *PLoPD1*, 183-238

http://www.bell-labs.com/people/cope/Patterns/Process/index.html

Generative patterns to shape a new organization and its development processes.

SIZE THE ORGANIZATION
Organization and Process

190-192

How big should the organization be? By default, choose ten people. Don't add people late in development.

SELF-SELECTING TEAM
Organization and Process

192-193

There are no perfect criteria for screening team members. Build self-selecting teams, doing limited screening on the basis of track records and broad interests.

- ᛟᛟ DEVELOPMENT EPISODE ◆ 53
- ✖ [Janoff98]

SOLO VIRTUOSO
Organization and Process

193-194

On small projects, do the entire design and implementation with one or two people.

SIZE THE SCHEDULE
Organization and Process

194-195

Reward developers for meeting schedules. Keep two schedules: an external one (negotiated with the customer) and an internal one (negotiated with the developers). The internal should be shorter than the external by 2-3 weeks for a moderate project.

- ⸱ If the schedules can't be reconciled, either customer needs or the organization's resource commitments or the schedule must be renegotiated. See RECOMMITMENT MEETING ◆ 53.
- ⸱ COMPLETION HEADROOM ◆ 53

FORM FOLLOWS FUNCTION
Organization and Process

195-196

When a project lacks well-defined roles, group closely related activities. Name the resulting abstractions and make them into roles. The activities become the responsibilities of the individuals who will adopt the roles.

DOMAIN EXPERTISE IN ROLES
Organization and Process

196-197

To match staff to roles, hire domain experts with proven track records. An individual may play several roles. Multiple players can fill a single role. Domain training is more important than process training. Local gurus are good in all areas.

- ✗ [Janoff98]

PHASING IT IN
Organization and Process

197

You need to hire long-term staff beyond the initial experts. Phase the hiring program. Start by hiring experts and gradually bring on new people as the project grows.

APPRENTICE
Organization and Process

197-198

You can't always hire the experts you need. Each new employee should work as an apprentice to an established expert. The expert must be more than a mentor. Most apprenticeship programs will last six months to a year—the amount of time it takes to make a paradigm shift.

ORGANIZATION FOLLOWS LOCATION
Organization and Process

198-199

You're assigning tasks and roles across a geographically distributed workforce. The architectural partitioning should reflect the geographic partitioning and vice versa. Assign architectural responsibilities so decisions can be made locally.

ORGANIZATION FOLLOWS MARKET

Organization and Process

199-200

There should be a clear role or organizational accountability to individual market segments. In an organization serving several distinct markets, reflect the market structure in the development organization. A core organization can support what is common across all market segments.

DEVELOPER CONTROLS PROCESS

Organization and Process

200-202

What role should be the focal point of project communication? The developer is the process information clearinghouse. Responsibilities of developers include understanding requirements, reviewing the design and algorithms, building the implementation, and unit testing.

⚒ [Janoff98]

PATRON

Organization and Process

202-203

To give a project continuity, provide access to a visible, high-level manager or patron who champions the project, removes project-level barriers, and is responsible for the organization's morale.

⚒ [Janoff98]

ARCHITECT CONTROLS PRODUCT

Organization and Process

203-204

A product designed by too many individuals lacks elegance and cohesiveness. An architect should advise, control and communicate closely with developers. The architect should also be close to the customer.

👫 CUSTOMER RAPPORT ♦ 140, CUSTOMER INTERACTION PATTERNS ❖ 43
⚒ [Janoff98]

CONWAY'S LAW

Organization and Process

204

The organization is compatible with the product architecture. At this point it is more likely that the architecture can drive the organization.

⚒ [Janoff98]

ARCHITECT ALSO IMPLEMENTS

Organization and Process

205-206

To preserve architectural vision through to implementation, architects must also implement as well as advise and communicate with developers.

REVIEW THE ARCHITECTURE

Organization and Process

206

There are always blind spots in the architecture, so architectural decisions should be reviewed by all architects. Architects should review each other's code. Reviews should be frequent, even daily, early in the project. Reviews should be informal, with minimal paperwork.

👫 CREATOR-REVIEWER ♦ 119, GROUP VALIDATION ♦ 66, VALIDATION BY TEAMS ♦ 96

CODE OWNERSHIP
Organization and Process

207-208

Developers can't keep up with a constantly changing base of implementation code, so each code module in the system should be owned by a single developer. Except in unusual, explicit circumstances, code may only be modified by its owner.

APPLICATION DESIGN IS BOUNDED BY TEST DESIGN
Organization and Process, Testing

208-209

When do you design and implement test plans and scripts? Scenario-driven test design starts when scenario requirements are first agreed to by the customer. Test design evolves along with software design in response to customer scenario changes. When developers decide that architectural interfaces have stabilized, low-level test design and implementation can proceed.

  ♔ GET INVOLVED EARLY ♦ 126

ENGAGE QA
Organization and Process, Testing

209-210

To guarantee product quality, make QA a central role. Couple it tightly to development when development has something to test. Development's test plan can proceed in parallel with coding, but developers must first declare the system ready for testing.

  ♔ DESIGNERS ARE OUR FRIENDS ♦ 126, TIME TO TEST ♦ 126

  � [Janoff98]

ENGAGE CUSTOMERS
Customer Interaction, Organization and Process

210-211

To maintain customer satisfaction, closely couple the customer role to the developer and architect roles, not just to the QA role.

  ♔ CUSTOMER RAPPORT ♦ 140, CUSTOMER INTERACTION PATTERNS ❖ 43

  ✖ [Janoff98]

GROUP VALIDATION
Organization and Process

211-212

To ensure product quality, even before engaging QA, development (with customer input) can validate the design. CRC cards and group debugging help socialize design issues and solve problems. A validation team can work with QA to attack root causes of classes of software faults.

  ♔ CREATOR-REVIEWER ♦ 119, REVIEW THE ARCHITECTURE ♦ 65, VALIDATION BY TEAMS ♦ 96

SCENARIOS DEFINE PROBLEM
Organization and Process

212-213

Design documents are often ineffective vehicles for communicating the customer's vision of how the system should work. Capture system functional requirements as use cases.

MERCENARY ANALYST
Organization and Process

213-214

Supporting a design notation and related project documentation is too tedious for people directly contributing to product artifacts. Use a tech writer who is proficient in the necessary domains but does not have a stake in the design. This person will capture the design using a suitable notation and will format and publish the design for reviews and consumption by the organization.

FIRE WALLS
Organization and Process

214-215

Project implementers are often distracted by outsiders who offer input and criticism. A manager should shield developers from interaction with external actors and "keep the pests away."

GATEKEEPER
Organization and Process

215-216

To foster communication with typically introverted engineering personalities, one project member, an extrovert, rises to the role of gatekeeper. This person disseminates leading edge and fringe information from outside the project, "translating" it into terms relevant to the project. The gatekeeper may also leak project information to outsiders, marketing and the corporate control center.

SHAPING CIRCULATION REALMS
Organization and Process

216-217

When interaction in an organization is not as it should be, as prescribed by other patterns, give people titles that create a hierarchy with a structure that reflects the desired taxonomy. Give people job responsibilities that suggest the appropriate interactions between roles. Physically co-locate people who should have close communication. People will usually try to respect your wishes if you are reasonable.

MOVE RESPONSIBILITIES
Organization and Process

217-218

Unscrutinized relationships between roles can lead to undesirable coupling at the organizational level. Move responsibilities from the role with undesirable coupling to roles coupled to it from other processes. Responsibilities should not be shifted arbitrarily.

BUFFALO MOUNTAIN
Organization and Process

218-220

You want to optimize communications in a large software development organization. For any significant project interaction, the sum of the distances of two collaborating roles from the "center" of the organization should be less than the shortest distance spanning the entire organization. Avoid coupling with neighbors if you're in the outlying 50% of the organization. The intensity of any collaboration should be inversely proportional to the sum of the interacting roles' distance from the center.

WORK FLOWS INWARD
Organization and Process

221-222

Work that adds value directly to the product should be done by authoritarian roles. Work should be generated by customers, filtered through supporting roles, and carried out by implementers at the center. Managers should not be at the center of the communication grid; they will become overloaded and make poor decisions.

✖ [Janoff98]

THREE TO SEVEN HELPERS PER ROLE
Organization and Process

222-224

If there is uneven communication distribution, ensure that each role has three to seven helpers.

NAMED STABLE BASES
Configuration Management, Organization and Process

224-225

How frequently do you integrate? Stabilize system interfaces no more than once a week. Other software can be changed and integrated more frequently.

ﾉﾙﾙ TEAMWORK AND CONFIGURATION MANAGEMENT ❖ 170

DIVIDE AND CONQUER
Organization and Process

225

Organizations grow to the point where they cannot easily manage themselves and the decision process breaks down. Identify clusters of roles that have strong mutual coupling but are loosely coupled to the rest of the organization. Form a separate organization and process around those clusters.

DECOUPLE STAGES
Organization and Process

225-226

To decouple stages (e.g., architecture and design) in a development process, for known and mature domains, serialize the steps. Handoffs between steps should take place via well-defined interfaces.

HUB, SPOKE, AND RIM
Organization and Process

226

To decouple stages (e.g., architecture, design, coding) in a serialized development process while maintaining responsiveness, link each role to a central role that orchestrates process activities. Parallelism can be reintroduced if the central role can pipeline activities.

AESTHETIC PATTERN
Organization and Process

227-228

When an organization has an irregular structure, ensure the organization has identifiable subdomains that can grow into departments of their own as the project grows.

COUPLING DECREASES LATENCY
Organization and Process

229-230

When the process is not responsive enough, development intervals are too long and market windows are not met. Open communication paths between roles to increase the overall coupling-to-role ratio, particularly for communication with central roles.

PROTOTYPE
Organization and Process

230-231

Requirements acquired early in the process are hard to validate without testing. Build a prototype to understand requirements and supplement use cases.

- ⋔ This pattern expresses the same intent as PROTOTYPE ♦ 168, PROTOTYPE A FIRST-PASS DESIGN ♦ 84, and PROTOTYPES ♦ 142.
- ⋔ This pattern has a different intent from PROTOTYPE ♦ 138, which is a creational pattern where objects clone themselves.

TAKE NO SMALL SLIPS
Organization and Process

231-232

Every week, measure the critical path of the schedule. If it's three days beyond schedule, track a delusion index of three days. When the delusion index becomes ridiculous, then slip the schedule.

- ⋔ COMPLETION HEADROOM ♦ 53, WORK QUEUE REPORT ♦ 52

DEVELOPING IN PAIRS
Organization and Process

232

Pair up compatible designers. They can produce more together than they can by working individually. A pair of people is less likely to be blindsided than a single individual.

- ⋔ INFORMAL LABOR PLAN ♦ 53

INTERRUPTS UNJAM BLOCKING
Organization and Process

232

Events and tasks are too complex to schedule development activities in a linear sequence. When you're about to block on a critical resource, interrupt the provider of the resource to keep you unblocked. If the overhead is small enough, it doesn't affect throughput. It will always improve latency.

DON'T INTERRUPT AN INTERRUPT
Organization and Process

233-234

You're doing work triggered by INTERRUPTS UNJAM BLOCKING ♦ 69 and it's causing thrashing. Turn away further interrupts until the current work is complete.

COMPENSATE SUCCESS
Organization and Process

234-236

To provide appropriate motivation for success, establish lavish rewards for individuals contributing to successful make-or-break projects. The entire team should receive comparable rewards.

GENERATIVE PATTERN LANGUAGE FOR DISTRIBUTED PROCESSING

Design Process, Distributed Systems

[DeBruler95], *PLoPD1*, 69-89

`http://www.bell-labs.com/people/cope/Patterns/DistributedProcessing/DeBruler/index.html`

Strategies for decomposing complex software systems across processing nodes.

DEFINE THE DATA STRUCTURE
Design Process, Distributed Systems

71-72

For a large, distributed programming problem, to begin architecture and design, ignore everything about the distributed nature of the hardware and do a data structure analysis. Use IDENTIFY THE NOUNS ♦ 70, FACTOR OUT COMMON ATTRIBUTES ♦ 70, NORMALIZE THE ROLES ♦ 70, and IDENTIFY PROBLEM DOMAIN RELATIONSHIPS ♦ 70.

IDENTIFY THE NOUNS
Design Process

72-73

You're using DEFINE THE DATA STRUCTURE ♦ 70. Brainstorm the values, attributes, and roles in the system, and give them precise names.

FACTOR OUT COMMON ATTRIBUTES
Design Process

73-77

You've applied IDENTIFY THE NOUNS ♦ 70. To maximize reuse, identify the role inheritance structure.

NORMALIZE THE ROLES
Design Process

77-79

You've applied FACTOR OUT COMMON ATTRIBUTES ♦ 70. Attributes are defined for one large role that should be defined for multiple related roles. Apply the normalization techniques developed for relational database models.

IDENTIFY PROBLEM DOMAIN RELATIONSHIPS
Design Process

79-81

You've applied NORMALIZE THE ROLES ♦ 70. Many relationships are implicitly identified as compound roles during IDENTIFY THE NOUNS ♦ 70, but pure relationships need more effort to capture. Convert many-to-many relationships to two functional mappings and a role.

INTRODUCE VIRTUAL ATTRIBUTES
Design Process

81-82

An implementation of the data model produced in DEFINE THE DATA STRUCTURE ♦ 70 has complicated navigation code. Use accessor methods for all attributes. If there is a unique path to an ancestor node, all attributes of all roles in the path are propagated as virtual attributes of the role under consideration.

ANIMATE THE DATA
Design Process

82-83

You're using DEFINE THE DATA STRUCTURE ♦ 70 and have reached the point of diminishing returns. Use TIME THREAD ANALYSIS ♦ 71 and DETERMINE THE ACTORS ♦ 71.

TIME THREAD ANALYSIS
Concurrent Systems, Design Process, Event-Driven Systems

83-84

You're ready for ANIMATE THE DATA ♦ 70. How are data created and changed? Use time thread analysis. List the events and transactions in the real world. For each event, trace the causality flow through the roles of the data structure and note actions performed by each role.

⑆ CATERPILLAR'S FATE ❖ 28

DETERMINE THE ACTORS
Concurrent Systems, Design Process, Event-Driven Systems

84-85

You've identified the actions each role should perform in response to events. To determine what code is to be executed when an event occurs, use objects, callbacks, and FSMs.

HALF-OBJECT + PROTOCOL
Distributed Systems

[Meszaros95], *PLoPD1*, 129-132

Sometimes an object must appear in more than one address space. Divide the object into two half-objects, one in each address space, with a protocol between them. In each address space, implement the functionality to interact efficiently with the other objects in that address space.

HALF-SYNC/HALF-ASYNC
Architectural, Communications, Concurrent Systems, Distributed Systems

[Schmidt+96], *PLoPD2*, 437-459

http://www.cs.wustl.edu/~schmidt/patterns-ace.html

Integrates synchronous and asynchronous I/O models in concurrent programming.

⑆ The synchronous layer uses ACTIVE OBJECT ♦ 6.

⑆ The asynchronous layer may use REACTOR ♦ 143 to demultiplex events from multiple sources.

⑆ The queuing layer acts as a FACADE ♦ 56 that simplifies the interface to the asynchronous layer.

⑆ The queuing layer acts as a MEDIATOR ♦ 86 that coordinates the exchange of data between the asynchronous and synchronous layers.

✗ [Schmidt97]

HIGH-LEVEL AND PROCESS PATTERNS FROM THE MEMORY PRESERVATION SOCIETY
Memory Management

[Noble+99], *PLoPD4*, 221-238

Patterns for memory-challenged systems.

THINK SMALL
Memory Management

225-228

You're developing a small system with stringent memory requirements. Imagine the system even smaller than it really is. Develop a culture where saving memory is a habit. Use design and code reviews to exorcise wasteful features and techniques. Use CAPTAIN OATES ♦ 72, EXHAUSTION TEST ♦ 73, MAKE THE USER WORRY ♦ 72, MEMORY BUDGET ♦ 72, MEMORY PERFORMANCE ASSESSMENT ♦ 73, and PARTIAL FAILURE ♦ 72.

MEMORY BUDGET
Memory Management

228-229

You're using THINK SMALL ♦ 72. Draw up a memory budget and worry about it a lot. Define targets for the system and for each component. Targets increase the predictability of the memory use. Developers with targets can make local decisions where it's easy to identify problem areas.

MEMORY OVERDRAFT
Memory Management

229-230

You're using MEMORY BUDGET ♦ 72, but memory requirements are unpredictable. As development proceeds, it's clear that some will need more than their budgeted memory allotment. Include overdraft provisions in the budget.

- ♔ Extra allotments may be exhausted at run-time; use EXHAUSTION TEST ♦ 73 to determine behavior when an overdraft is used.
- ♔ You can also MAKE THE USER WORRY ♦ 72.
- ♔ In CAPTAIN OATES ♦ 72, part of the program releases some memory if that part of the program has a memory overdraft.

MAKE THE USER WORRY
Memory Management

230-232

You're using MEMORY BUDGET ♦ 72, but it's difficult to predict memory requirements. A lot depends on the user. Make the memory model explicit in the user interface so that the user can worry about memory.

PARTIAL FAILURE
Memory Management

232-233

No matter how well you reduce the program's memory requirements, there will always be situations when the program runs out of resources. To handle unlimited memory requests, allow the program to fail partially or have behavior degrade, but not stop. Use EXHAUSTION TEST ♦ 73.

- ♔ This pattern describes what to do when the system runs out of memory. CAPTAIN OATES ♦ 72 describes what to do when one process in the system runs out of memory.

CAPTAIN OATES
Memory Management

234-235

To prioritize memory demands, when a system runs out of memory, surrender memory used by less vital components rather than have the most important tasks fail.

- ♔ This pattern describes what to do when one process in the system runs out of memory. PARTIAL FAILURE ♦ 72 describes what to do when the system itself runs out of memory.

EXHAUSTION TEST
Memory Management, Testing

235-236

To be sure the program will work correctly when out of memory, use testing that simulates memory exhaustion. Verify that the program uses PARTIAL FAILURE ♦ 72 or MAKE THE USER WORRY ♦ 72.

MEMORY PERFORMANCE ASSESSMENT
Design Process, Memory Management

237-238

To stop memory constraints from dominating the design process, implement the system, paying attention to memory requirements only where these have a significant effect on the design. Once the system is working, identify the most wasteful areas and optimize their use.

HOOK METHOD
Behavioral

[Pree94], *Design Patterns for Object-Oriented Software Development*, 107

[Alpert+98], *Design Patterns Smalltalk Companion*, 358

[Gamma+95], *GoF*, 328

Provides default behavior that subclasses can extend. Often the hook method does nothing. Hook methods are abstract methods, regular methods, or template methods.

♦♦♦ TEMPLATE METHOD ♦ 171 often uses hook methods.

✕ [Schmidt98a]

IDENTIFY THE CHAMPION PATTERN LANGUAGE
Technical Paper Review

[Nierstrasz99], *PLoPD4*, 539-556

`http://www.iam.unibe.ch/~oscar/cgi-bin/omnbib.cgi`

How a program committee can discuss and accept or reject submissions to a technical conference.

IDENTIFY THE CHAMPION
Technical Paper Review

540-543

You're the Program Committee (PC) Chair for a technical conference. Make the review and selection process efficient by focusing PC members' attention on whether they will champion a submission during the meeting.

EXPERTS REVIEW PAPERS
Technical Paper Review

543-544

You're using IDENTIFY THE CHAMPION ♦ 73. You're expecting 100-200 submissions, each of which should be evaluated by three to four PC members. To distribute papers to the PC, match papers to members' domain expertise.

CHAMPIONS REVIEW PAPERS
Technical Paper Review

544-545

You're using IDENTIFY THE CHAMPION ◆ 73. To distribute papers to PC members and maximize each paper's chance that it will find a champion, let PC members choose papers they want to review. Use MAKE CHAMPIONS EXPLICIT ◆ 74.

MAKE CHAMPIONS EXPLICIT
Technical Paper Review

546-548

You're using IDENTIFY THE CHAMPION ◆ 73. To see which papers will be championed in advance of the meeting, on the review form, ask PC members explicitly whether they intend to champion the paper.

IDENTIFY THE CONFLICTS
Technical Paper Review

548-550

You're using MAKE CHAMPIONS EXPLICIT ◆ 74. It's a week before the PC meeting, and most reviews are in. Order or group the papers before the meeting according to their highest and lowest scores. Do not attempt to rank papers numerically.

IDENTIFY MISSING CHAMPIONS
Technical Paper Review

550-552

You're using MAKE CHAMPIONS EXPLICIT ◆ 74. It's a week before the PC meeting, and most reviews are in. Identify which papers are likely to be championed by whom, and be sure that champions are prepared for the meeting. If a potential champion is not an expert or cannot attend the meeting, take some compensating action, e.g., soliciting an extra review.

CHAMPIONS SPEAK FIRST
Technical Paper Review

552-555

In the PC meeting, discuss the papers in groups, following IDENTIFY THE CONFLICTS ◆ 74. For each paper, invite a champion to introduce the paper and say why it should be accepted. Then invite detractors to say why it should not be accepted. Finally open the general discussion, and try to reach a consensus. If there is no champion, the paper should not be discussed.

CONSENSUS ON PC PAPERS
Technical Paper Review

555

You're using CHAMPIONS SPEAK FIRST ◆ 74. Papers authored by PC members should be accepted only if there is at least one champion and no expert detractors.

IMPLEMENTATION PATTERNS FOR THE OBSERVER PATTERN
Behavioral, Design Process

[Kim+96], *PLoPD2*, 75-86

Extensions to OBSERVER ◆ 94.

CONDUIT OF SUBJECT CHANGE

Behavioral, Design Process

76-78

You're using OBSERVER ♦ 94. Observer objects are receiving insufficient detail about the update. Send an update message that comprises four lists: Add (object creations), Remove (object deletions), Modify (object modifications), and Container (subject containment relationships).

🏛 For more detail, see OBSERVER UPDATE MESSAGE ♦ 75.

ONE MESSAGE PER CHANGE REQUEST

Behavioral, Design Process

79-80

You're using CONDUIT OF SUBJECT CHANGE ♦ 75. You want the simplest possible update design where the subject can simply store any and all state change information. When a change request is initiated, a message object is created. Use the message class defined in OBSERVER UPDATE MESSAGE ♦ 75. When the subject changes state, it stores affected objects in the appropriate list.

ONE MESSAGE PER AFFECTED OBJECT

Behavioral, Design Process

80-81

You're using CONDUIT OF SUBJECT CHANGE ♦ 75. You want a simple update design without the danger of false hits that can occur in ONE MESSAGE PER CHANGE REQUEST ♦ 75. Since a single change request can affect multiple objects, for each affected object generate an update message that relates the object, its containers, and the nature of the change.

OPTIMIZED MESSAGES PER CHANGE REQUEST

Behavioral, Design Process

81-83

You're using CONDUIT OF SUBJECT CHANGE ♦ 75. You want an update design with a minimal number of update messages without false hits. You do not have to worry about a containment relationship for the subject. Provide an algorithm for generating a minimal number of updates.

MESSAGE PACKET

Behavioral, Design Process

84

You're using OBSERVER ♦ 94. The system can generate multiple update messages. Some of these messages belong to a group. The message receiver must identify the beginning and end of a series of messages in the same group. Define a message generator that knows when a group of messages is generated. The message generator can package messages into a packet, usually a simple list, and send the packet. The receiver is free to process the messages as needed.

OBSERVER UPDATE MESSAGE

Behavioral, Design Process

85

You're using OBSERVER ♦ 94 or any of its refinements. The subject consists of many objects with nested containment relationships. The observer needs to be informed of the subject's state change information, but not depend on the subject's structure. Any state change in the subject can be characterized by a series of new object creations (Add), old object deletions (Remove), and object modifications (Modify) at certain locations. The subject update message consists of four lists: Add, Remove, Modify, and Container. (The Container list indicates the locations where the updates are to be made.)

IMPROVING RESPONSIVENESS IN INTERACTIVE APPLICATIONS USING QUEUES

Event-Driven Systems, GUI Development, Interactive Systems, Reactive and Real-Time Systems

[Wake+96], *PLoPD2*, 563-573

Design for the low-level structure of interactive applications.

EVENT QUEUE

Event-Driven Systems, GUI Development, Interactive Systems, Reactive and Real-Time Systems

564-566

You're working on an interactive application. The application receives input as events. Build the program around an event queue. For each event in the queue, store the type of event, a time stamp, and event data. Order events by time.

- MERGE COMPATIBLE EVENTS ♦ 76 and HANDLE ARTIFICIAL EVENTS ♦ 76 improve program responsiveness. DECOUPLE EXECUTION AND OUTPUT ♦ 76 apply the event queue structure to output.
- There is usually only one event queue, so use SINGLETON ♦ 152.
- Events are low-level entities. COMMAND ♦ 35 can encapsulate an event in an object.

MERGE COMPATIBLE EVENTS

Event-Driven Systems, GUI Development, Interactive Systems, Reactive and Real-Time Systems

566-568

You're using EVENT QUEUE ♦ 76 but events are arriving faster than the program can handle. At each fetch, see if other events are pending. See whether the next event is compatible with the current one and combine them into a compound event. Repeat to merge all compatible events.

HANDLE ARTIFICIAL EVENTS

Event-Driven Systems, GUI Development, Interactive Systems, Reactive and Real-Time Systems

568-570

You're using EVENT QUEUE ♦ 76 but the program has too much to do in response to some events. Add artificial events to the queue. The program handles these events by doing background processing. This may speed up future interaction.

DECOUPLE EXECUTION AND OUTPUT

Event-Driven Systems, GUI Development, Interactive Systems, Reactive and Real-Time Systems

570-571

You're using EVENT QUEUE ♦ 76. Display is expensive or time-critical. Rather than strictly alternating command execution and result display, separate the two by introducing an output event. Output events can be kept on the regular event queue or a separate queue. Idle events can schedule output event processing.

- This pattern is a variation on OBSERVER ♦ 94. This pattern divorces view updating from model changes.
- MERGE COMPATIBLE EVENTS ♦ 76 and HANDLE ARTIFICIAL EVENTS ♦ 76 can be applied to output events.

INPUT AND OUTPUT PATTERN LANGUAGE

Fault-Tolerant Systems, Telecommunications

[Hanmer+99], *PLoPD4*, 503-536

Solves problems in interaction between a telecommunications switching system and humans.

MML
Fault-Tolerant Systems, Telecommunications
507-509

To make human communication with a large and complex machine easier and more reliable, use a standard messaging format. MML (huMan-Machine Language, an international standard) and PDS (Program Documentation Standard) are two examples.

- Sometimes a computer can monitor the system. PSEUDO-IO ◆ 79 can help by having the monitoring computer use the MML messages intended for humans.
- Use BOTTOM LINE ◆ 78 and GEORGE WASHINGTON IS STILL DEAD ◆ 78 to handle a lot of IO.
- Use MIND YOUR OWN BUSINESS ◆ 77, WHO ASKED? ◆ 78 and IO TRIAGE ◆ 77 to support different users.

IO GATEKEEPER
Fault-Tolerant Systems, Telecommunications
509-510

To use MML ◆ 77 for a large community of users, use a central communication point or gatekeeper and design and use an internal interface language that supports the MML ◆ 77.

- Now you can use AUDIBLE ALARM ◆ 79, FIVE MINUTES OF NO ESCALATION MESSAGES ◆ 78, GEORGE WASHINGTON IS STILL DEAD ◆ 78, IO TRIAGE ◆ 77, PSEUDO-IO ◆ 79, BOTTOM LINE ◆ 78, TIMESTAMP ◆ 77, and WHO ASKED? ◆ 78.

MIND YOUR OWN BUSINESS
Fault-Tolerant Systems, Telecommunications
511-512

You're using IO GATEKEEPER ◆ 77. Who should see the output? Define different output classifications. The gatekeeper should mark different terminal/console connections to receive output for only some classifications or logical channels.

- BELTLINE TERMINAL ◆ 79 can redirect output to a different device.

IO TRIAGE
Fault-Tolerant Systems, Telecommunications
512-514

You're using IO GATEKEEPER ◆ 77. Important information is hidden or delayed by less important information. A lot is output to workers even after applying GEORGE WASHINGTON IS STILL DEAD ◆ 78 and BOTTOM LINE ◆ 78. Prioritize messages. Display higher priority messages before lower priority messages. The alarm system should use the priority tag to sound the appropriate alarm. Use TIMESTAMP ◆ 77 to convey a better understanding of the system state.

- Use AUDIBLE ALARM ◆ 79 if people may not be watching their terminals when something important is being reported.

TIMESTAMP
Fault-Tolerant Systems, Telecommunications
514-515

You're using IO TRIAGE ◆ 77 but messages may not come out in the order requested by subsystems. Use a sequence number for all messages when the gatekeeper receives them.

WHO ASKED?
Fault-Tolerant Systems, Telecommunications

515-517

You're using MIND YOUR OWN BUSINESS ♦ 77. To decide what logical channel receives the results of a specific manual input request, display the output to the logical channel that made the request. A worker usually uses one terminal at a time. Send it to terminals monitoring the logical channel. Use IO TRIAGE ♦ 77.

GEORGE WASHINGTON IS STILL DEAD
Fault-Tolerant Systems, Telecommunications

517-518

You're using IO GATEKEEPER ♦ 77. To avoid too many messages that say the same thing, the gatekeeper should track messages and send only announcements that represent a real change of state. A problem might be detected hundreds of times, but if the state isn't changing frequently, the messages might be overkill.

- Use IO TRIAGE ♦ 77 to keep important information coming out even when the output channels are flooded.
- Use FIVE MINUTES OF NO ESCALATION MESSAGES ♦ 78 when workers can't perform any actions in response to a change in system state.
- Use SHUT UP AND LISTEN ♦ 79 so that humans can input a message against a flood of output.
- BOTTOM LINE ♦ 78 is similar to this pattern but deals with multiples of the same report.

BOTTOM LINE
Fault-Tolerant Systems, Telecommunications

518-520

You're using IO GATEKEEPER ♦ 77. Many messages about the same type of event are flooding the output. The gatekeeper should group messages about a common event, and display just a summary message that includes the number of occurrences. Provide the entire output upon request, as it may be essential to identify problems. Use SHUT UP AND LISTEN ♦ 79 so humans can input a message.

- This pattern deals with aggregation of nearly identical messages. GEORGE WASHINGTON IS STILL DEAD ♦ 78 deals with state change reports.
- Use FIVE MINUTES OF NO ESCALATION MESSAGES ♦ 78 when aggregation delays can only partly be tolerated. That pattern causes messages to be printed out periodically as well as in summary.

FIVE MINUTES OF NO ESCALATION MESSAGES
Fault-Tolerant Systems, Telecommunications

520-521

The human-machine interface is saturated with error reports, even though you're using BOTTOM LINE ♦ 78, GEORGE WASHINGTON IS STILL DEAD ♦ 78, or IO TRIAGE ♦ 77. Display a message when taking the first action in a series that could lead to an excess number of messages. If the abnormal condition ends, display a message that everything is back to normal. Do not display a message for every change in state. People can't do anything about the messages except watch them anyway. So don't bother printing. Use AUDIBLE ALARM ♦ 79 if something can't wait five minutes. This pattern is an extension of FIVE MINUTES OF NO ESCALATION MESSAGES ♦ 57.

SHUT UP AND LISTEN

Fault-Tolerant Systems, Telecommunications

522

You're using IO TRIAGE ♦ 77. Humans should be heard by the system. Users should be able to disable output. The gatekeeper is flooding the output stream even though you're using GEORGE WASHINGTON IS STILL DEAD ♦ 78 and BOTTOM LINE ♦ 78. The gatekeeper should give human input a higher priority than displaying output information, but not lose output messages. Human input messages should have a priority level comparable to critical output messages.

PSEUDO-IO

Fault-Tolerant Systems, Telecommunications

523-524

You're using MIND YOUR OWN BUSINESS ♦ 77. When one subsystem allows humans to access information, another subsystem may need the information. Allow a subsystem to insert a message into the input message stream to be processed just like any other input message.

BELTLINE TERMINAL

Fault-Tolerant Systems, Telecommunications

524-525

You're using MIND YOUR OWN BUSINESS ♦ 77. The terminal isn't near the worker. Provide remote terminal connections so that workers can always plug in a terminal IO device and create a "beltline terminal." Allow workers to redirect output to their beltline terminals.

AUDIBLE ALARM

Fault-Tolerant Systems, Telecommunications

525-527

You're using IO TRIAGE ♦ 77 and PEOPLE KNOW BEST ♦ 57. To notify workers immediately about a significant problem, report alarms audibly in the office. Remote visual indicators, such as colored lights, should also be used.

🏛 Use OFFICE ALARMS ♦ 79 to customize alarms to a specific customer site.

ALARM GRID

Fault-Tolerant Systems, Telecommunications

527-529

You're using AUDIBLE ALARM ♦ 79 and PEOPLE KNOW BEST ♦ 57. Workers need to know where to look for problems. Divide the office into small grids to locate the error. Tie alarm circuits together to report to the main office. When an alarmable situation occurs in a grid, alert all concerned personnel.

OFFICE ALARMS

Fault-Tolerant Systems, Telecommunications

529-530

You're using ALARM GRID ♦ 79. Design the alarm system to allow easy insertion of new office-specific alarms unique to a field site.

DON'T LET THEM FORGET

Fault-Tolerant Systems, Telecommunications

530-531

You're using AUDIBLE ALARM ♦ 79. Act on all requests to silence an alarm, but don't remember them. When the system detects an alarmed condition, sound the alarm regardless of how recently the silence request was received.

🏛 This pattern deals with alarmed situations. GEORGE WASHINGTON IS STILL DEAD ♦ 78 targets less-critical information.

STRING A WIRE
Fault-Tolerant Systems, Telecommunications

531-533

You're using IO GATEKEEPER ♦ 77. Critically important information must get to other computer systems. Sometimes the gatekeeper is too slow or is in a partial capability mode, or the system can't afford the resources to send a message to a nearby system. Provide a hard-wired messaging connection.

♦♦♦ Use RAW IO ♦ 80 if more information is needed.

RAW IO
Fault-Tolerant Systems, Telecommunications

533-534

You're using IO GATEKEEPER ♦ 77. Sometimes the gatekeeper is too slow or is in a partial capability mode, or the system can't afford the resources to do IO. STRING A WIRE ♦ 80 does not provide enough information. Display output via brute force mechanisms such as writing directly to a logical channel, thereby avoiding the IO system.

INTERPRETER
Behavioral

[Gamma+95], *GoF*, 243-255

[Alpert+98], *Design Patterns Smalltalk Companion*, 261-286

Given a language, define a representation for its grammar along with an interpreter that uses the representation to interpret sentences in the language.

♦♦♦ The abstract syntax tree example in this pattern is a COMPOSITE ♦ 37.

♦♦♦ FLYWEIGHT ♦ 60 can share terminal symbols in the abstract syntax tree.

♦♦♦ An ITERATOR ♦ 80 to traverse the interpreter structure.

♦♦♦ VISITOR ♦ 179 can maintain the behavior in each node of the abstract syntax tree.

ITERABLE CONTAINER
C++ Idioms

[Martin95b], *PLoPD1*, 372-377

Containers need to be iterated by clients that don't know the kind of container they are using. Arrange all containers into a common inheritance hierarchy that can be linearly iterated. Use PROTOTYPE ♦ 138, STRATEGY ♦ 167, and FACTORY METHOD ♦ 56 to create a concrete class that can iterate over any container in the hierarchy.

ITERATOR
Behavioral

[Gamma+95], *GoF*, 257-271

[Alpert+98], *Design Patterns Smalltalk Companion*, 273-286

Provide a way to access the elements of an aggregate object sequentially without exposing its underlying representation.

♦♦♦ ITERATOR ♦ 80 can traverse a Composite structure.

✖ [White96]

JUDGE
Database, Health Care

[Metsker98], *JOOP*, Nov./Dec. 1998, 49-59

Class diagrams depend as much on the relationships between the classes as the classes themselves. A Judge class acts as a third party, maintaining order in the relationships between pairs of problem domain classes.

⚶ This pattern is a special case of STRATEGY ♦ 167.

LAYERS
Architectural, Networks

[Buschmann+96], *POSA*, 31-51

Structure an application to be decomposed into groups of subtasks where each group is at a given level of abstraction.

⚶ MICROKERNEL ♦ 87 is a specialized layered architecture.

⚶ PRESENTATION-ABSTRACTION-CONTROL ♦ 135 also emphasizes levels of increasing abstraction, but the overall structure is a tree of nodes rather than a vertical line of nodes layered on top of each other.

⚶ HIERARCHY OF CONTROL LAYERS ♦ 61, FOUR-LAYER ARCHITECTURE ♦ 106, LAYERED ARCHITECTURE ♦ 125, LAYERED ORGANIZATION ♦ 59, LAYERED AND SECTIONED ARCHITECTURE ♦ 96, PEDESTAL ♦ 123, SHAPE OF PROGRAM ♦ 29, THREE-TIER ARCHITECTURE ♦ 15

✘ [VandenBroecke+97]

LAZY OPTIMIZATION: PATTERNS FOR EFFICIENT SMALLTALK PROGRAMMING
Performance, Smalltalk Idioms

[Auer+96], *PLoPD2*, 19-42

`http://www.rolemodelsoft.com/patterns/`

Creation of efficient Smalltalk programs. Most patterns could be applied in most languages.

PERFORMANCE ASSESSMENT
Performance, Smalltalk Idioms

21-23

To begin early program development, confident that performance won't be a problem, write a short (e.g., two-page) performance assessment of the system. Identify critical resources outside the programming language. Estimate how big and fast the final system will be. Develop prototypes for areas of concern if absolutely necessary.

⚶ PERFORMANCE CRITERIA ♦ 82 can be applied directly from this assessment.

LAZY OPTIMIZATION
Performance, Smalltalk Idioms

23-25

To achieve acceptable performance with the least cost, ignore efficiency through most of the development cycle. Tune performance once the program is running correctly and the design reflects your best understanding of how the cost should be structured. The changes will be limited in scope or will illuminate opportunities for better design.

⚶ Use PERFORMANCE CRITERIA ♦ 82 to be sure you and your client agree.

⚶ Use PERFORMANCE MEASUREMENT ♦ 82 to see if the suspect parts really are running too slowly.

PERFORMANCE CRITERIA
Performance, Smalltalk Idioms

25

Work with your client to get estimates for response time or throughput criteria for the system. Revise this list as the system matures.

- Use THRESHOLD SWITCH ♦ 82 to set a concrete goal.
- Use PERFORMANCE MEASUREMENT ♦ 82 for each criterion.

THRESHOLD SWITCH
Performance, Smalltalk Idioms

26

You've applied PERFORMANCE CRITERIA ♦ 82 and started to improve the problem areas. To determine when you've satisfied the performance requirements, you and your client should agree that when you've reached the performance criteria, you will stop tuning. Once you've agreed, begin actual tuning. Use PERFORMANCE MEASUREMENT ♦ 82.

PERFORMANCE MEASUREMENT
Performance, Smalltalk Idioms

26-28

You've used THRESHOLD SWITCH ♦ 82. To consistently measure performance and ensure that the system keeps running while you're tuning and know when you've triggered the threshold switches, write a routine that automatically tests and times apparent performance problems. Use a profiler to identify the biggest bottlenecks in the problem areas.

HOT SPOT
Performance, Smalltalk Idioms

28-29

You've used PERFORMANCE CRITERIA ♦ 82 and identified several areas that don't meet requirements. Profile most or all performance problems before putting a lot of energy into prioritizing, assigning, and fixing them. Identify where the majority of time is spent for each problem. These are the hot spots. Multiple performance problems may be the result of an approach that spans multiple areas.

- After a hot spot has been fixed, use PERFORMANCE MEASUREMENT ♦ 82 to see if performance has actually improved.

EXPERIMENT
Performance, Smalltalk Idioms

29-30

You've used HOT SPOT ♦ 82. To find the best performance solution, treat each performance improvement as an experiment. If it doesn't get you the desired result, make a note of what you did and what it gave you, and undo it. Keep only the experiments that help you reach your goal, using PERFORMANCE CRITERIA ♦ 82. You may have to apply several to get desired results.

CACHEABLE EXPRESSION
Performance, Smalltalk Idioms

30-32

The profiler has identified an expression as a significant contributor to execution time. The expression is executed many times, often with the same result. Use the lowest-overhead variable to alleviate the redundancy.

CACHING TEMPORARY VARIABLE
Performance, Smalltalk Idioms

32-33

You're using CACHEABLE EXPRESSION ♦ 82, and it's causing a Hot Spot because it occurs in a loop. For each expensive expression in the loop that returns the same value each time through, add a temporary variable initialized before the loop begins to the value of the expression. Replace all occurrences of the expression with the temporary variable. If this doesn't solve the performance problem, try Caching Instance Variable.

🏘 CACHING TEMPORARY VARIABLE ♦ 158

CACHING ARGUMENT
Performance, Smalltalk Idioms

33-34

You're having performance problems. Similar transient objects are being created to represent parts of the end result. Reduce the number of transient objects. Keep a single transient object and pass it around as an argument.

CACHING STATE VARIABLE
Smalltalk Idioms

34-37

You're using CACHEABLE EXPRESSION ♦ 82 and causing a Hot Spot. The expression is needed in varied contexts, so you can't use CACHING ARGUMENT ♦ 83 or CACHING TEMPORARY VARIABLE ♦ 83. To improve performance, identify the behavioral environment (Class, Class hierarchy, MetaClass) that encapsulates all the contexts where the expression is shared. Add a corresponding state variable and give it the name of the message to be cached. Rename the message to be cached by prepending "compute" to the corresponding selector. Use LAZY INITIALIZATION ♦ 157 to compute the value of the variable. This value should be reset when an event occurs that could make this value obsolete.

SIMPLIFICATION
Performance, Smalltalk Idioms

37-38

Several methods are Hot Spots in a certain context that cannot be simplified without compromising the integrity of the system for all instances of the same class. To improve the Hot Spots without causing undesirable side effects, examine the features of a class actually used by an instance or group of instances. Determine if there is another class that could provide the desired features more efficiently.

TRANSIENT REDUCTION
Performance, Smalltalk Idioms

38-39

You're improving the performance of a system and you have a set of objects, A, and would like to have a different set, B. To move from A to B in the most efficient manner, reduce the number of transient objects in an operation. Use CACHING ARGUMENT ♦ 83, CONCATENATING STREAM ♦ 84, and OBJECT TRANSFORMATION ♦ 83.

OBJECT TRANSFORMATION
Performance, Smalltalk Idioms

39

You're using TRANSIENT REDUCTION ♦ 83. Instead of creating new objects to replace the old ones, transform the old objects into the new objects.

HYPOTH-A-SIZED COLLECTION
Smalltalk Idioms

40

In a HOT SPOT ♦ 82, the program is spending time adding objects to a collection. When you realize that a significant number of objects will be added to a collection, be sure the collection is large enough to hold the end result.

CONCATENATING STREAM
Smalltalk Idioms

41

You want to improve the performance of a Smalltalk system. To concatenate several collections efficiently, use a Stream. See CONCATENATING STREAM ♦ 162.

♦♦♦ This pattern can be combined with HYPOTH-A-SIZED COLLECTION ♦ 84 to create a Stream whose collection won't grow.

LIFE CYCLE AND REFACTORING PATTERNS THAT SUPPORT EVOLUTION AND REUSE
Refactoring, Design Process

[Foote+95], *PLoPD1*, 239-257

http://www.laputan.org/lifecycle/Lifecycle.html

Software development comprises recurring prototype phases, expansion phases, and consolidation phases. These are patterns for evolving from inheritance hierarchies to aggregations and creating abstract classes.

PROTOTYPE A FIRST-PASS DESIGN
Design Process

242-244

The initial design of a system should focus on the requirements at hand, with broader applicability as a secondary concern. Get something running quickly to obtain design feedback. Build a prototype. Apply: Nouns in the Specification Imply Objects, Verbs Imply Operations; Build on Existing Objects Using Inheritance; Get it Running Now, Polish It Later; Avoid Premature Generality.

♦♦♦ This pattern has the same intent as PROTOTYPE ♦ 168, PROTOTYPE ♦ 69, and PROTOTYPES ♦ 142.

♦♦♦ This pattern has a different intent from PROTOTYPE ♦ 138, which is a creational pattern where objects clone themselves.

EXPAND THE INITIAL PROTOTYPE
Design Process

244-245

Add code to subclasses to maintain design integrity when changes are made. Apply: Subclass Existing Code Instead of Modifying It; Build on Existing Objects Using Inheritance; Defer Encapsulation for Shared Resources; Avoid Premature Generality; Get It Running Now, Polish It Later.

CONSOLIDATE THE PROGRAM TO SUPPORT EVOLUTION AND REUSE
Refactoring, Design Process

245-247

As objects evolve, design insights emerge. Refactor objects to reflect these insights: use consistent names; eliminate case analysis; reduce the number of arguments; reduce the size of methods; class hierarchies should be deep and narrow; the top of the class hierarchy should be abstract; minimize access to variables; subclasses should be specializations; split large classes; factor implementation differences into subcomponents; separate methods that do not communicate; send messages to components instead of to self; reduce implicit parameter passing.

EVOLVE AGGREGATIONS FROM INHERITANCE HIERARCHIES
Refactoring, Design Process

248-252

Class hierarchies developed in early phases are often functional but neither elegant nor reusable. Convert inheritance to aggregation by factoring parts of a class into a new component class.

CREATE ABSTRACT SUPERCLASS
Refactoring, Design Process

252-254

Clean up inheritance hierarchies by defining abstract classes that capture behavior common to one or more classes.

🏤 This pattern presents the same solution as ABSTRACT CLASS ♦ 2.

LOCALIZED OWNERSHIP: MANAGING DYNAMIC OBJECTS IN C++
C++ Idioms

[Cargill96], *PLoPD2*, 5-18

Management of dynamic object lifetimes in C++.

CREATOR AS SOLE OWNER
C++ Idioms

8-12

When a dynamic object is created in C++, the creator can determine the object's lifetime. If there is a narrow purpose for a dynamic object, let the creator control its lifetime. A narrow purpose does not imply that the object is short-lived or that the creator has exclusive access to it.

SEQUENCE OF OWNERS
C++ Idioms

12-13

You're creating a dynamic object in C++ and can't use CREATOR AS SOLE OWNER ♦ 85. Transfer ownership from the creator to another owner. Ownership may be transferred any number of times. This transfer must be an explicit part of the interface between the two. At any time, ownership rests with only one owner.

🏤 See SHARED OWNERSHIP ♦ 86 if a single owner cannot be identified.

SHARED OWNERSHIP
C++ Idioms
14-16
You're creating a dynamic object in C++ and can't use CREATOR AS SOLE OWNER ♦ 85 or SEQUENCE OF OWNERS ♦ 85. An object that defies simple characterization and management of its lifetime is likely to be long-lived. Allow arbitrary owners to declare unilateral interest in the dynamic object. The lifetime of the object continues until all the owners have relinquished their interest in it.

MANAGER

Behavioral

[Sommerlad98], *PLoPD3*, 19-28

Encapsulate management of the instances of a class into a separate manager object. This allows variation of management functionality independent of the class and reuse of the manager for different object classes.

⌖ BROKER ♦ 22 and CLIENT-DISPATCHER-SERVER ♦ 34 (CDS) provide access to a collection of server objects on behalf of clients. MANAGER ♦ 86, however, is responsible for the life of the server objects, while BROKER ♦ 22 and CDS are only responsible for server objects that already exist and are registered.

MASTER-SLAVE

Architectural

[Buschmann+96], *POSA*, 245-260

[Buschmann95], *PLoPD1*, 133-144

Handle computation of replicated services in a system to achieve fault tolerance and robustness. Separate independent slave components that together provide the same service to a master component, which is responsible for invoking them and for selecting a result. Clients communicate only with the master.

MEDIATOR

Behavioral

[Gamma+95], *GoF*, 273-282

[Alpert+98], *Design Patterns Smalltalk Companion*, 287-296

Define an object that encapsulates how a set of objects interact. Promote loose coupling by keeping objects from referring to each other explicitly.

⌖ FACADE ♦ 56 abstracts a subsystem to provide an improved interface. Its protocol is unidirectional—the Facade makes requests of the subsystem. MEDIATOR ♦ 86 can implement cooperative behavior not provided by colleague objects, and the protocol is multidirectional.

⌖ Colleagues can communicate with the mediator using OBSERVER ♦ 94.

✖ [Brown96], [Cerwin98], [Duell98], [Keller+98a], [Schmid95], [Vlissides98a]

MEMBER CONTAINER

C++ Idioms

[Martin95b], *PLoPD1*, 377-383

Many containers have membership semantics. These containers can have set operations. Clients need to perform these operations without knowing the kind of container they are using. Create an inheritance and containment hierarchy for all containers that exhibit membership semantics.

MEMENTO
Behavioral

[Gamma+95], *GoF*, 283-291

[Alpert+98], *Design Patterns Smalltalk Companion*, 297-304

Without violating encapsulation, capture and externalize an object's internal state so the object can be restored to the state.

֎ This pattern can keep state for an undo in COMMAND ♦ 35.

✕ [Brown96], [Vlissides98a]

MICROKERNEL
Architectural

[Buschmann+96], *POSA*, 171-191

For software systems that must adapt to changing system requirements, separate a minimal functional core from extended functionality and customer-specific parts. The microkernel is a socket for plugging in these extensions and coordinating their collaboration.

֎ BROKER ♦ 22 is applicable for distributed systems comprising interacting, decoupled components. Clients access services using remote procedure calls or message passing. BROKER ♦ 22 focuses on distribution across a network. The coupling of components with BROKER ♦ 22 is not as tight as in this pattern. BROKER ♦ 22 and MICROKERNEL ♦ 87 could be used in a distributed system.

֎ REFLECTION ♦ 144 provides a two-tiered architecture. The base level corresponds to a combination of this pattern and internal servers.

MODEL-VIEW-CONTROLLER
Architectural

[Buschmann+96], *POSA*, 125-143

Divide an interactive application into three components. The model contains the core functionality and data. Views display information to the user. Controllers handle user input. Views and controllers together comprise the user interface. A change-propagation mechanism ensures consistency between the user interface and the model.

֎ In PRESENTATION-ABSTRACTION-CONTROL ♦ 135, the abstraction component corresponds to the model in Model-View-Controller (MVC), and the view and controller are combined into a presentation component. Communication between abstraction and presentation components is decoupled by the control component. The interaction between presentation and abstraction is not limited to calling an update procedure, as it is in MVC.

֎ SESSION CONTROL & OBSERVATION ♦ 151 is a specialization of MVC that controls and maintains the state of a networked multimedia session and notifies those interested in that state.

✕ [Johnson95]

MOODS: MODELS FOR OBJECT-ORIENTED DESIGN OF STATE
Design Process, Finite State Machines

[Ran96], *PLoPD2*, 119-142

Design and implementation of objects with complex, state-dependent representation and behavior, or "moods."

֎ FINITE STATE MACHINE PATTERNS ❖ 58, STATE ♦ 166, STATE OBJECT ♦ 166, STATE PATTERNS ❖ 166

TO SIMPLIFY COMPLEX BEHAVIOR, USE DECOMPOSITION
Design Process, Finite State Machines

122-123

To make specification of behavior simpler, decompose each object with complex behavior by distributing its responsibilities among several simpler objects. When the complex object cannot be simply decomposed, when the complexity of its behavior is due to control, or when it has a number of abstract states, decompose the class into a cluster of state classes. If the complexity is due not to control but to processing, decompose each complex method separately.

FOR OBJECTS WITH MOODS, USE STATE CLASSES
Design Process, Finite State Machines

123-126

When an object's behavior depends significantly on its state, it behaves as if it had moods. The complex behavior can usually be traced to a set of conditions. When the same conditions affect a number of behaviors, identifying these conditions with abstract states may simplify specification of the object's behavior. Abstract states are conditions that guarantee more specific behavior of an object. When the object's behavior depends on additional conditions, substates may be identified to guarantee simpler behavior in each substate.

WHEN EVENTS CAUSE MOODS, USE STATE MACHINE
Design Process, Finite State Machines

126-127

When the current complex behavior of an object cannot be determined from the values of its attributes, it must be explicitly represented and tracked. Use an FSM to specify the tracking logic.

- ♦♦♦ FINITE STATE MACHINE PATTERNS ❖ 58 and THREE-LEVEL FSM ♦ 172 address issues in FSM design and implementation.

FOR STATE MACHINES, USE TRANSITION METHODS
Design Process, Finite State Machines

127-128

Reactive objects often respond to events and update the current state. To separate the reaction and the state transition, implement a state machine using dedicated transition methods for state classes. These transition methods can be called by the reactive methods.

- ♦♦♦ FINITE STATE MACHINE PATTERNS ❖ 58 and THREE-LEVEL FSM ♦ 172 address issues in FSM design and implementation.

WHEN STATES ARE CONDITIONS, USE PREDICATIVE STATE CLASSES
Design Process, Finite State Machines

128-129

Explicitly implementing state transitions may be inappropriate. To maintain the object-to-state relation without explicitly modeling state transitions, use Predicative State Classes to specify conditions for complex behaviors of an object.

WHEN STATES ARE ASSOCIATIONS, USE STATE OBJECTS

Design Process, Finite State Machines

129-131

When you have applied FOR OBJECTS WITH MOODS, USE STATE CLASSES ◆ 88, the representation and behavior are jointly specified by a cluster of classes. Normally, each object is identified with one class that determines its representation and behavior. To allow an object to follow behavior specified by different classes in different states, delegate the service to different objects. A change in the object's state can be conceptualized as a change in its association to a collaborator object.

🏃 STATE ◆ 166, STATE OBJECT ◆ 166

FOR COMPLEX MOODS, USE A MOOD ALTERNATOR

Design Process, Finite State Machines

132-134

To allow one object in different states to reflect the behavior and attributes specified by different state classes, the object must be an instance of all these classes. This is the MOOD Alternator class. Its instances include the attributes needed in all states. Each method of the MOOD Alternator delegates to a method of the state class corresponding to the mood of the alternator's instance.

WHEN THERE ARE MANY MOODS, USE MOOD CLASSIFIER

Design Process, Finite State Machines

134-136

To create a generic classification mechanism to use with different, complex, and changing hierarchies of predicative state classes, sequentially apply the predicates of the leaf states to the object.

NEW CLIENTS WITH OLD SERVERS: A PATTERN LANGUAGE FOR CLIENT/SERVER FRAMEWORKS

Client-Server

[Wolf+95], *PLoPD1*, 51-64

Patterns in object-oriented frameworks for Smalltalk workstations communicating with legacy host business systems.

EXCEPTION

Client-Server

53

Abnormal or unusual conditions often occur far from the point in the execution stack where a program would naturally respond to the condition. Defining these conditions as specializations of class Exception classifies the conditions into hierarchies.

SOLITAIRE

Client-Server

54

Some objects occur once in an application. This should be explicit in a framework, to help developers and users.

🏃 SINGLETON ◆ 152 addresses this problem for classes.

Objects from Records
Client-Server

54-55

Exchanging data between object-oriented clients and relational databases is complicated. Move the data access responsibility from the Business Object to a Record Object. The class Record is responsible for getting, setting, and committing field objects to/from a string of bytes.

Request
Client-Server

55

Client/server frameworks use different communications interfaces. These should be invisible to client applications. Clients use a request object, which atomically exchanges a collection of input records for a set of output records.

Materialization
Client-Server

55-56

An object-oriented client/server framework renders objects at the client from the server, whether or not the server supports objects. The client should be unaware of how or when this rendering occurs. Use Request ♦ 90 and Objects from Records ♦ 90 to transform host data to and from objects using Proxy ♦ 139.

Finalization
Client-Server

56-57

Maintain a dependency count for an object. When the last dependent is lost, use a finalization phase.

♦♦♦ Dependency ♦ 91

Identity Management
Client-Server

57

To prevent a multiplicity of business objects, use an abstract File class to manage the identity of business objects. If two lookups produce the same business object, the second merely references the object instead of producing another copy of it.

Mega-Scrolling
Client-Server

58

A request may return a collection of objects too large to materialize on the client, so limit the size of the returned collection. The limited subcollection may satisfy the user; if not, issue another request for the adjoining subcollection.

Searching for Business Objects
Client-Server

58-59

Searching for business objects can be reified by defining an abstract class called Search. Search objects define the criteria that govern a search and persist after the search, available for modification and reuse.

DEPENDENCY
Client-Server
59
To provide loose coupling between model objects and their views, use MODEL-VIEW-CONTROLLER ♦ 87 (MVC). The original MVC usually appears as just MV.
♦♦♦ This pattern has the same intent as OBSERVER ♦ 94.

CREATING AND UPDATING BUSINESS OBJECTS
Client-Server
59-60
You're using MATERIALIZATION ♦ 90 to apply changes to business objects. Updates must also propagate to dependent objects using DEPENDENCY ♦ 91. The objects are not views, but behave as views.

FACTORY METHOD
Client-Server
60
An extension of FACTORY METHOD ♦ 56.

WINDOW-KEEPING
Client-Server, GUI Development
60-61
When the user dismisses a window, the window-keeper simulates closing it, then caches it. If an object subsequently requires a window of this class, the window-keeper disinters the cached window and opens it on the object.
♦♦♦ WindowKeeper is a SOLITAIRE ♦ 89.

VIEWING
Client-Server, GUI Development
61
Viewing generally uses the functions provided by a user interface toolkit. Viewing also requires FACTORY METHOD ♦ 91, DEPENDENCY ♦ 91, and WINDOW-KEEPING ♦ 91 to overcome the problems of burdening the client with knowledge of the views of a model.

CLIENT/SERVER FRAMEWORK
Client-Server
61-62
An object-oriented client/server framework for communicating with a legacy host must let users locate, examine, and change or create objects. This pattern is an aggregation of CREATING AND UPDATING BUSINESS OBJECTS ♦ 91, SEARCHING FOR BUSINESS OBJECTS ♦ 90, and VIEWING ♦ 91.

NULL OBJECT

Behavioral
[Woolf98], *PLoPD3*, 5-18
A Null Object is a surrogate for another object with the same interface, but the Null Object does nothing.
♦♦♦ When a Null Object does not require any internal state, use SINGLETON ♦ 152.
♦♦♦ This pattern is similar to PROXY ♦ 139, which provides a level of indirection when accessing a real object. A Null Object replaces the real object.

OBJECT RECOVERY

Architectural, Database, Distributed Systems, Fault-Tolerant Systems, GUI Development, Persistence

[Silva+98], *PLoPD3*, 261-276

http://albertina.inesc.pt/~ars/dasco.html

Define a generic object recovery algorithm and decouple the recovery portion from the object's functionality to support different algorithms. Isolate recovery from persistence and object synchronization issues, allowing the recovery of transient objects to a previously defined state. This can also implement user undo and redo models of interaction.

- MEMENTO ♦ 87 can store the recovery state.
- DECORATOR ♦ 46 can add recovery responsibilities.
- STRATEGY ♦ 167 can provide recovery policies.
- COMMAND ♦ 35 and COMMAND PROCESSOR ♦ 36 also support undo/redo.

OBJECT RECURSION

Behavioral

[Woolf99b], *PLoPD4*, 41-51

Handle a request over a structure by delegating it polymorphically. A request can be decomposed repeatedly into smaller parts. An initiator makes a request of a handler. The handler does what it needs to do, then passes the request on to its successor—another handler—and returns a result based on the successor's result.

- CHAIN OF RESPONSIBILITY ♦ 32 uses this pattern.
- In INTERPRETER ♦ 80, the interpret() message traverses an abstract syntax tree using this pattern.
- ITERATOR ♦ 80 on a branching structure can be implemented recursively. If the terminating points are objects, then this is Object Recursion.
- PROXY ♦ 139 is an example of one-level-deep Object Recursion.

OBJECT SYNCHRONIZER

Concurrent Systems

[Silva+99], *PLoPD4*, 111-132

http://albertina.inesc.pt/~ars/dasco.html

Decouple object synchronization from object functionality. Invocations on an object are intercepted by a synchronization interface to allow them to proceed, delay, or reject them.

- ACTIVE OBJECT ♦ 6 decouples operation invocation from execution to simplify synchronized access to shared resources.
- When this pattern is combined with OBJECT RECOVERY ♦ 92, it allows specialization of synchronization policies that need to recover the object's state.
- This pattern uses PROXY ♦ 139 and STRATEGY ♦ 167.

OBJECT-ORIENTED DESIGN PATTERNS IN REACTIVE SYSTEMS

Concurrent Systems, Event-Driven Systems, Reactive and Real-Time Systems

[Aarsten+96b], *PLoPD2*, 537-548

Control of reactive and event-driven systems, with emphasis on evolution from simulation to a real system. An extension of G++: A PATTERN LANGUAGE FOR COMPUTER-INTEGRATED MANUFACTURING ❖ 61. Summarizes the G++ pattern language, the result of 10 years' experience in developing concurrent and distributed control systems and an application involving cooperative autonomous mobile robots.

Entries

OBJECT-ORIENTED SIMULATION

Concurrent Systems, Event-Driven Systems, Reactive and Real-Time Systems

540-542

You're developing software to control a reactive, event-driven system. You want to separate logical and physical design but also want to exploit an evolutionary development process. What architecture do you select for the logical design, and move from prototype to reality? Maintain two representations of the objects that will later interface to the external system so changes made during evolution remain local. To perform the transition from prototype to reality, replace the simulated objects of the prototype with the objects that will interface to the external system.

　The "glue" layer in this pattern is a continuation of ADAPTER ♦ 6. Instead of an Adapter object, there is a framework of objects that perform the adaptation.

OBJECTIFY THE EVENTS

Concurrent Systems, Event-Driven Systems, Reactive and Real-Time Systems

542-543

You're applying OBJECT-ORIENTED SIMULATION ♦ 93. Objects in the prototype communicate by exchanging events and method calls. To associate the external event objects with the logical events in the prototype, create a class Event to wrap real-system events.

　OBJECTS WITH REMOTE CONTROL ♦ 93 shows how the objectified events control the external system.

OBJECTIFY SYSTEM STATE

Concurrent Systems, Event-Driven Systems, Reactive and Real-Time Systems

543-544

You're applying OBJECT-ORIENTED SIMULATION ♦ 93. In the simulation, variables that characterize the external system state are implemented as usual programming language variables. Create a class for each type of data with get and set methods for the variable it wraps. Each class should know how to convert its own data type between the internal and external formats.

　This pattern is an application of PROTOTYPE AND REALITY ♦ 63.

OBJECTS WITH REMOTE CONTROL

Concurrent Systems, Event-Driven Systems, Reactive and Real-Time Systems

545-546

You're using OBJECTIFY THE EVENTS ♦ 93 and OBJECTIFY SYSTEM STATE ♦ 93. The software control objects must be interfaced to the external entities they control. Define a new class with a callback method.

　This pattern is an extension of PROTOTYPE AND REALITY ♦ 63.

EVENT-DRIVEN RPC

Concurrent Systems, Event-Driven Systems, Reactive and Real-Time Systems, Distributed Systems

547

You're using OBJECT-ORIENTED SIMULATION ♦ 93. You need to make distributed method calls through the external system. For each object that will receive remote method calls, define a compatible stub class. In the stub class, define two Events for each method, one to represent the call and the other for method return.

　This pattern is a different implementation of DISTRIBUTION OF CONTROL MODULES ♦ 63.

OBSERVER
Behavioral
[Gamma+95], *GoF*, 293-303

[Alpert+98], *Design Patterns Smalltalk Companion*, 305-326

Define a one-to-many dependency between objects so that when one object changes state, the others are notified and updated automatically.

- **ŧŧŧ** Colleagues can use this pattern to communicate with a MEDIATOR ♦ 86.
- **ŧŧŧ** IMPLEMENTATION PATTERNS FOR THE OBSERVER PATTERN ❖ 74, OBSERVATION ♦ 8, OBSERVER UPDATE MESSAGE ♦ 75, PUBLISHER-SUBSCRIBER ♦ 139
- **✘** [Dagermo+98], [Johnson95], [Kircher+99], [Piehler99], [Srinivasan99], [VandenBroecke+97], [Vlissides98a]

ORGANIZATIONAL MULTIPLEXING: PATTERNS FOR PROCESSING SATELLITE TELEMETRY WITH DISTRIBUTED TEAMS
Telemetry Processing
[Berczuk96], *PLoPD2*, 193-206

`http://world.std.com/~berczuk/pubs/PLoP95/HTML/BerczukPLoP95.html`

Development of ground software for satellite telemetry systems that considers organizational issues in architecture.

LOOSE INTERFACES
Architectural, Telemetry Processing
197

To help the development of a system with many teams proceeding at a reasonable pace, keep interfaces between subsystems loose. Limit the number of explicit, static interfaces. Use callbacks, PARSER/BUILDER ♦ 94 and HIERARCHY OF FACTORIES ♦ 94.

PARSER/BUILDER
Persistence, Telemetry Processing
198-199

Many systems need to read data from a stream and classify elements in the stream as objects. When the data stream contains tags that identify the raw data, convert the stream into object form. Use a Parser/Builder object that reads the tags and creates an object of the appropriate type.

- **ŧŧŧ** In this pattern, the Factory reads from a stream and the client doesn't know what type of object will be returned. This is not the case in BUILDER ♦ 23 or FACTORY METHOD ♦ 56.
- **ŧŧŧ** This pattern can be the front end to INTERPRETER ♦ 80.

HIERARCHY OF FACTORIES
Telemetry Processing
199-202

Once you decide to use PARSER/BUILDER ♦ 94, you need to partition the details of how to construct objects of various classes into the various groups responsible for this construction. Use a hierarchy of factories where each factory understands the criteria for making a packet of its type.

- **ŧŧŧ** This pattern is similar to BUILDER ♦ 23, which also has a hierarchy of factories. However, in this pattern, the data stream (instead of the application) defines what is made.

HANDLERS
Telemetry Processing

202-204

After you assemble packets from a telemetry data stream, you process them, generating data products. You need a way to direct this processing. Use a callback mechanism to define connections between the assembly process and the processing process. Provide a mechanism for assigning a handler object to which a completed entity will be forwarded.

᛭ This pattern is adapted from PATTERN FOR SEPARATING ASSEMBLY AND PROCESSING ♦ 97.

᛭ This pattern is an implementation of PIPES & FILTERS ♦ 132.

ORGANIZATIONAL PATTERNS FOR TEAMS
Organization and Process

[Harrison96], *PLoPD2*, 345-352

Solves problems of designing in teams.

DESIGN BY TEAM
Organization and Process

345-346

How can people work together to design and develop software? Use UNITY OF PURPOSE ♦ 95, DIVERSITY OF MEMBERSHIP ♦ 95, LOCK 'EM UP TOGETHER ♦ 95, and VALIDATION BY TEAMS ♦ 96.

UNITY OF PURPOSE
Organization and Process

346-347

To get different people pointed in the same direction, the project leader must instill a common vision and purpose in all members of the team.

᛭ SELF-SELECTING TEAM ♦ 63 describes how a team should come together. When a leader with a vision emerges, people with similar visions will gravitate to that leader.

DIVERSITY OF MEMBERSHIP
Organization and Process

348-349

To determine your product's required capabilities, the resources for its completion, and other information, create a team to specify user requirements. The team should include a developer, a user or user's representative, and a system tester.

᛭ Early involvement of system test is addressed in GET INVOLVED EARLY ♦ 126.

LOCK 'EM UP TOGETHER
Organization and Process

349-350

How can a team of different people come up with a single, coherent architecture? Gather the team in a room and require that every person commit to total participation until the architecture is complete or complete enough that a clear picture emerges.

᛭ ARCHITECT ALSO IMPLEMENTS ♦ 65, ARCHITECT CONTROLS PRODUCT ♦ 65, REVIEW THE ARCHITECTURE ♦ 65

VALIDATION BY TEAMS
Organization and Process

351-352

You're using UNITY OF PURPOSE ♦ 95 and DIVERSITY OF MEMBERSHIP ♦ 95. To ensure that designs are valid, hold a design review. Don't use formal design documents. Have the designer explain the design to the rest of the team. Each team member should check internal interfaces for consistency. The team should execute the design orally.

⛶ CREATOR-REVIEWER ♦ 119, GROUP VALIDATION ♦ 66, REVIEW THE ARCHITECTURE ♦ 65

PANEL STATES
GUI Development

[Spall98], *Java Report*, Feb. 1998, 23-25, 28-32

Present a collection of user interface panels in a sequence. Each panel displays different information, captures user input, and determines the next panel based on user choices.

⛶ This pattern interacts with PLUGGABLE VIEW CONTROLLER ♦ 132 and an application of STATE ♦ 166.

PARTIES & MEDIA AS FIRST CLASS CITIZENS
Multimedia

[VandenBroecke+97], *BLTJ*, Winter 1997, 166-187

Have each session maintain the parties and media in the session. Use a third object to maintain the state for each party associated with the medium. Parties and media thus become first class citizens in a session.

PARTITIONING SMALLTALK CODE INTO ENVY/DEVELOPER COMPONENTS
Configuration Management, Smalltalk ENVY/Developer Idioms

[Woolf96], *PLoPD2*, 43-58

`http://c2.com/ppr/envy/`

ENVY/Developer is a configuration management system for Smalltalk development. How to partition source code using ENVY.

LAYERED AND SECTIONED ARCHITECTURE
Architectural, Smalltalk ENVY/Developer Idioms

46-52

Develop a system with a layered and sectioned architecture to reduce dependencies between components.

⛶ FOUR-LAYER ARCHITECTURE ♦ 106, HIERARCHY OF CONTROL LAYERS ♦ 61, LAYERED ARCHITECTURE ♦ 125, LAYERED ORGANIZATION ♦ 59, LAYERS ♦ 81, PEDESTAL ♦ 123, SHAPE OF PROGRAM ♦ 29, THREE-TIER ARCHITECTURE ♦ 15

LAYER IN AN APPLICATION
Configuration Management, Smalltalk ENVY/Developer Idioms

52-54

You're using LAYERED AND SECTIONED ARCHITECTURE ♦ 96 to develop a Smalltalk program. Store each layer in an application.

SECTION IN A SUBAPPLICATION

Configuration Management, Smalltalk ENVY/Developer Idioms

54-55

You're using LAYERED AND SECTIONED ARCHITECTURE ♦ 96. Store each section in a subapplication so you can manage it as a section.

TWO APPLICATIONS

Configuration Management, Smalltalk ENVY/Developer Idioms

55-56

You're implementing Smalltalk code in an ENVY image. Start a (sub)system with two applications. One of the applications will contain the domain model layer(s), and the other will contain the application model layer(s). As the need for other layers arises, create applications for those.

NO SUBAPPLICATIONS

Configuration Management, Smalltalk ENVY/Developer Idioms

57

You're implementing Smalltalk code in an ENVY image. Each piece of code must be stored in an application. Start an application with no subapplications. As the need for sections becomes apparent, create subapplications to represent them.

PATTERN AS A CLASS

Design Process

[Soukup95], *PLoPD1*, 408-412

Use pattern classes to represent patterns as objects.

PATTERN FOR SEPARATING ASSEMBLY AND PROCESSING

Event-Driven Systems, Telemetry Processing

[Berczuk95], *PLoPD1*, 521-528

`http://world.std.com/~berczuk/pubs/PLoP94/callback.html`

To decouple the work done by geographically distributed teams, upstream components need not be concerned with downstream processing. The paper describes a Telemetry application, but the pattern applies to any system where interfaces between producers and consumers must be cleanly separated.

♦♦♦ A generic constructor to classify and build objects is a variant of ABSTRACT FACTORY ♦ 2.

PATTERN LANGUAGE FOR AN ESSAY-BASED WEB SITE

Web Site Development

[Orenstein96], *PLoPD2*, 417-431

`http://www.anamorph.com/docs/patterns/default.html`

How to write and organize essays on a Web site.

NATURAL TEXT FLOW
Web Site Development

419

Many Web documents contain words and phrases that call attention to their location on the Web. This is unnecessary. Write text that reflects the content of the document, in your native tongue, and avoid phrases that call attention to the "Webness" of the document.

ᴍ NATURAL TEXT HYPERLINKS ♦ 98 describes a method for writing hyperlink text.

ᴍ NATURAL TEXT DIRECTORIES ♦ 98 is a pattern for creating navigational tools for a document tree.

NATURAL TEXT HYPERLINKS
Web Site Development

419-420

You're using NATURAL TEXT FLOW ♦ 98. One of the useful features of the Web is hyperlinks to other documents, yet the wording of these links can distract readers from the natural flow of the text. Write your text document as if you were creating printed text in your native tongue, and look for the natural hyperlink phrase in the text you've written. It will almost always be there.

NATURAL TEXT DIRECTORIES
Web Site Development

420-421

You're using NATURAL TEXT FLOW ♦ 98 and NATURAL TEXT HYPERLINKS ♦ 98. To organize your documents, provide a series of natural text hyperlinks in your headers and footers. Reading from left to right, users should know exactly where they are in your document tree, with the leftmost position representing the current document and the rightmost position representing the site's home page.

REFERENCE SECTION
Web Site Development

424

You're using NATURAL TEXT FLOW ♦ 98. There may be many documents on the Web that discuss material related to your essays. To point interested readers to these pages, at the end of your essay, provide a Reference Section, formatted as an HTML unordered list. Supply links to related Web pages along with a description of these pages. Write the links using NATURAL TEXT HYPERLINKS ♦ 98.

EXPOSABLE GUTS
Web Site Development

425-426

When valuable information is found, users will want to know about the creation of the information itself. Provide meta information that explains how you gathered and presented your work. The meta information should never be the first thing the user sees, but it should be easily accessible from the primary information.

WORKSHEET DOCUMENTS
Web Site Development

426-427

You're using EXPOSABLE GUTS ♦ 98 and REFERENCE SECTION ♦ 98. You want to publish a document on the Web, but it isn't finished yet. For each unfinished page, create a separate Worksheet Document. In this document, state why the page is unfinished and what you expect to add. Provide a link to the Worksheet Document from the incomplete document's Reference Section.

NEW DOCUMENT NOTIFICATION
Web Site Development

428

You're using EXPOSABLE GUTS ♦ 98 to provide meta information for readers. When you add new essays to your site, previous readers won't know about the new material unless they visit your site to see what's changed. On the opening page of your Web site, close to the bottom, include a form with a single field for collecting readers' e-mail addresses. Send out notices when new documents are added to the site. If the site contains documents of different topics or subtopics, include checkboxes so that readers can choose the information they care about.

14.4 KBPS TESTING
Testing, Web Site Development

429-430

Documents at some Web sites can take a minute or longer to load at 14.4 kbps. When creating a Web site, test pages with large images on slower-speed systems. Near the development machines, set up a computer that is connected via a 14.4 kbps modem, and test all pages from this machine.

PATTERN LANGUAGE FOR DEVELOPING FORM STYLE WINDOWS
GUI Development

[Bradac+98], *PLoPD3*, 347-357

A form organizes a collection of widgets to perform an operation. Nontrivial applications may use many specialized forms.

SUBFORM
GUI Development

348-349

To minimize development and maintenance when designing form style windows in a GUI application, divide a form into subforms to construct the window. These subforms will contain groups of widgets to control related data. Any subform can be further divided into subforms.

ALTERNATIVE SUBFORMS
GUI Development

350

You're using SUBFORM ♦ 99 where different sets of data will be gathered based on a user response. To design a window where different sets of widgets are needed, compose a form using smaller subforms. Create one subform for each variation of the widgets that change and select the appropriate subform based on state data. Use SUBFORM SELECTION ♦ 99.

SUBFORM SELECTION
GUI Development

351-353

You're using ALTERNATIVE SUBFORMS ♦ 99. To choose from a collection of subforms that become active based on state data, have the parent subform maintain a collection of all child subforms. When there is a change in state data, the parent polls each child using SUBFORM MATCH ♦ 100. The most frequently used forms should be at the front of the collection for efficient performance.

SUBFORM MATCH
GUI Development

353-355

You're using SUBFORM SELECTION ♦ 99. How does the parent subform select the appropriate child subform based on state data in the parent? When there is a change in state data, poll the collection of subforms and let them identify themselves as a match for the state data.

  ♦♦♦ This pattern is similar to STATE ♦ 166 in that only one subform will match the state data.

SUBFORM MISMATCH
GUI Development

355-356

You're using SUBFORM MATCH ♦ 100 where state data resides in the child subform. How can the parent subform determine when a child subform no longer applies based on a change of state data in the child? Have the child subform notify its parent when there is a mismatch.

PATTERN LANGUAGE FOR IMPROVING THE CAPACITY OF REACTIVE SYSTEMS
Reactive and Real-Time Systems, Telecommunications

[Meszaros96], *PLoPD2*, 575-591

Improve the capacity and reliability of real-time reactive systems.

CAPACITY BOTTLENECK
Reactive and Real-Time Systems, Telecommunications

578-579

In a reactive system with a limited capacity, to improve the capacity of the system, learn what determines the system's capacity and what affects it. Optimize elements that truly limit system capacity. Engineer the system so that these limits can be avoided automatically, or ensure the system can withstand circumstances in which the demands on its resources are exceeded.

  ♦♦♦ Use PROCESSING CAPACITY ♦ 100, Memory Capacity, or Messaging Capacity if the limiting factor is the processing cost, the memory required, or the messaging systems' ability.

PROCESSING CAPACITY
Reactive and Real-Time Systems, Telecommunications

579-581

In a reactive system where capacity is limited by processing power, and work arrives in a stochastic fashion, apply the following. If a small number of request types constitute a large part of the processing cost, use OPTIMIZE HIGH-RUNNER CASES ♦ 100. If a large amount of processing capacity must be kept in reserve to handle peak loads, use SHED LOAD ♦ 101. Further tune the capacity at the expense of latency with Max Headroom. If the necessary increase in capacity exceeds what can be recovered from these techniques, use SHARE THE LOAD ♦ 101.

OPTIMIZE HIGH-RUNNER CASES
Reactive and Real-Time Systems, Telecommunications

581-583

In a reactive system with limited processing power, the average processing cost of service requests can be too high. In most systems, 80% or more of the processing power is consumed by 20% of the use cases. Measure or project the high-runner transactions and optimize only those that contribute significantly to the cost.

SHED LOAD

Reactive and Real-Time Systems, Telecommunications

583-585

In a processing-bound reactive system with more requests than it can handle, overloads must not cause it to become unavailable. Large numbers of requests can cause the system to thrash. In extreme situations, the entire system can crash. Use triage to shed some requests so that others can be served properly. Requests that cannot be handled properly should be shed before processing is wasted on them. Any request that will take longer than a specified time-out can be shed without any visible change in system behavior.

- FINISH WORK IN PROGRESS ♦ 101 maximizes the return on investment of processing cycles.
- MATCH PROGRESS WORK WITH NEW ♦ 101 prevents the deadlock that could be caused by throwing away the wrong work.
- FRESH WORK BEFORE STALE ♦ 101 maximizes the number of customers who get acceptable service.
- WORK SHED AT PERIPHERY ♦ 102 maximizes system throughput by reducing or eliminating the cost of shedding work in a bottleneck processor.

FINISH WORK IN PROGRESS

Reactive and Real-Time Systems, Telecommunications

585-586

In a reactive system where user requests are dependent on one another, which requests should be accepted and which should be rejected to improve system throughput? Categorize requests into new and progress categories. Process all progress requests before new requests.

FRESH WORK BEFORE STALE

Reactive and Real-Time Systems, Telecommunications

586-587

In a reactive system that can't satisfy all requests, to maximize the number of customers who get good service, give good service to as many customers as possible and give the remainder poor or no service. Put all new requests in a LIFO queue. Serve most recently received requests first. Serve stale requests after all fresh ones have been served.

- MATCH PROGRESS WORK WITH NEW ♦ 101 describes how to eliminate work entirely when the user cancels a request.

MATCH PROGRESS WORK WITH NEW

Reactive and Real-Time Systems, Telecommunications

587-588

You're using SHED LOAD ♦ 101 and FRESH WORK BEFORE STALE ♦ 101. Some users are giving up because their requests are not served immediately. This creates "undo" work the system cannot really afford. When related requests are received, pair them up. If the second request is a cancel, then the work request can be removed before any processing is done.

SHARE THE LOAD

Reactive and Real-Time Systems, Telecommunications

588-589

In a processing-bound reactive system that can't meet its target capacity and all means of increasing processing capacity have been exhausted, the cost of processing all the requests may exceed the capacity of a single processor at a specified system capacity. To increase available processing power, shift some of the processing to another processor. Select the functions to be moved that are clearly partitionable from those left behind.

WORK SHED AT PERIPHERY
Reactive and Real-Time Systems, Telecommunications
589-590
You're using SHED LOAD ♦ 101. To shed work at a minimum additional cost, move the detection of new work as close to the periphery of the system as possible. Give this part of the system information about the available processing capacity of the most limiting part of the system.
♦♦♦ LEAKY BUCKET OF CREDITS ♦ 102 describes how to communicate the status of the system's bottleneck processor.

LEAKY BUCKET OF CREDITS
Reactive and Real-Time Systems, Telecommunications
590-591
In a reactive system, one processor needs to be aware of the overload state of another processor. The bottleneck processor tells other processors when it can accept more work by sending them credits. Each of the other processors holds a leaky bucket of these credits. The buckets gradually leak until they are empty. When a processor sends work to other processors, it must track the credits from each.
♦♦♦ This pattern is a variation on LEAKY BUCKET COUNTERS ♦ 57.

PATTERN LANGUAGE FOR PATTERN WRITING

Pattern Writing

[Meszaros+98], *PLoPD3*, 529-574

What worked well in patterns or pattern languages reviewed at PLoP '95. The guidelines have been reviewed and updated.

PATTERN
Pattern Writing
532-533
You're an experienced practitioner, and you've noticed a certain solution to a commonly occurring problem. You would like to share your experience with others. Write the solution using the pattern form. Use MANDATORY ELEMENTS PRESENT ♦ 102 and OPTIONAL ELEMENTS WHEN HELPFUL ♦ 103.

PATTERN LANGUAGE
Pattern Writing
533-534
You're using PATTERN ♦ 102 to describe a procedure with many steps or a complex solution to a complex problem. Some steps may not apply in some circumstances. There may be alternate solutions to parts of the problem, depending on the circumstances. A single pattern can't handle the complexity. Factor the problem and its solution into a number of related problem-solution pairs. Capture each as a pattern in a collection of patterns or pattern language.

MANDATORY ELEMENTS PRESENT
Pattern Writing
535-537
You're using PATTERN ♦ 102. To capture the necessary information, include Name, Context, Problem, Forces, Solution.

OPTIONAL ELEMENTS WHEN HELPFUL

Pattern Writing

537

You've applied MANDATORY ELEMENTS PRESENT ♦ 102. To communicate other information, if they make the pattern easier to understand or if they provide better connections to other patterns, include Indications, Resulting Context, Related Patterns, Examples, Code Samples, Rationale, Aliases, Acknowledgements.

VISIBLE FORCES

Pattern Writing

539

You're using PATTERN ♦ 102 or PATTERN LANGUAGE ♦ 102 and are trying to capture a problem with several solutions. To be sure the reader understands the proper choice for a solution, be sure the forces are highly visible. Name each force and visually set it off.

SINGLE-PASS READABLE

Pattern Writing

539-541

You're using MANDATORY ELEMENTS PRESENT ♦ 102 and want the reader to understand your pattern in the least amount of time. Strive to make your pattern readable in a single pass. Use EVOCATIVE PATTERN NAME ♦ 104 or PATTERN THUMBNAIL ♦ 104 for referenced patterns. Use FINDABLE SECTIONS ♦ 103, VISIBLE FORCES ♦ 103, SKIPPABLE SECTIONS ♦ 103, PATTERN LANGUAGE SUMMARY ♦ 105, and GLOSSARY ♦ 106.

SKIPPABLE SECTIONS

Pattern Writing

541-542

You're using OPTIONAL ELEMENTS WHEN HELPFUL ♦ 103 and SINGLE-PASS READABLE ♦ 103. To make it easy for the reader to get the essence of a pattern while still providing enough information to apply it, identify the Problem, Context, and Solution so that the reader can quickly see if the pattern applies. Put more detailed information in sections that can be skipped.

FINDABLE SECTIONS

Pattern Writing

543-544

You're using SKIPPABLE SECTIONS ♦ 103. To make it easy to find key elements of the pattern, determine the sections a reader will want to see. Clearly mark the beginning of each of these sections. Use fonts, underlining, headings, graphics—whatever is appropriate for your pattern form.

RELATIONSHIPS TO OTHER PATTERNS

Pattern Writing

544-546

To make your pattern part of a larger collection of patterns, use the Related Patterns section to capture the pattern's relationship to other patterns. The pattern may lead to other patterns, may be set up by other patterns, may specialize a more general pattern, or may generalize a domain-specific pattern. There may be alternate patterns that solve similar problems.

READABLE REFERENCES TO PATTERNS
Pattern Writing

546-547

To reference other patterns in your pattern, weave pattern names into the narrative. Augment the pattern name with a reference. You can use PATTERN THUMBNAIL ♦ 104 for the reference. Set off the pattern name by highlighting it typographically.

PATTERN THUMBNAIL
Pattern Writing

547-549

To reference other patterns to maximize the reader's understanding and minimize the reader's effort, use EVOCATIVE PATTERN NAME ♦ 104. The first time the other pattern is referenced, use a tag or footnote with a brief thumbnail description of the essence of that pattern.

EVOCATIVE PATTERN NAME
Pattern Writing

549

To name the pattern to make it easy to remember and reference, choose a name to convey the essence of the solution. Imagine using the name in conversation or referring to the pattern from other patterns. Test the name by having people who are unfamiliar with the pattern guess at the solution based on its name. Use NOUN PHRASE NAME ♦ 104 or MEANINGFUL METAPHOR NAME ♦ 104.

NOUN PHRASE NAME
Pattern Writing

551-552

You're using EVOCATIVE PATTERN NAME ♦ 104 and are struggling to create a name that is easy to remember. Name the pattern after the result it creates.

ⵜ MEANINGFUL METAPHOR NAME ♦ 104 describes another way to solve this problem.

MEANINGFUL METAPHOR NAME
Pattern Writing

552-554

You're using EVOCATIVE PATTERN NAME ♦ 104, and you're struggling to make the name useful and memorable. Find a meaningful metaphor for the pattern, and name it accordingly. The metaphor should be familiar and easily understood by the target audience.

ⵜ NOUN PHRASE NAME ♦ 104 provides another solution for this problem.

INTENT CATALOG
Pattern Writing

554-555

To make it easy for other pattern writers to reference your pattern, provide a catalog of intents that you can use in PATTERN THUMBNAIL ♦ 104. An intent should be one or two sentences that describe the essence of the pattern.

CLEAR TARGET AUDIENCE
Pattern Writing

555-556

To be sure your pattern will be read by the intended audience, identify the target audience for the pattern solution. Keep this audience in mind while writing the pattern. Test the pattern with representatives from the target audience.

TERMINOLOGY TAILORED TO AUDIENCE

Pattern Writing

556-557

You're applying CLEAR TARGET AUDIENCE ♦ 104. Use terminology tailored to the audience to improve understandability. Use terms that a typical member of the audience could understand. Use GLOSSARY ♦ 106 for terms that may be unfamiliar.

UNDERSTOOD NOTATIONS

Pattern Writing

558-559

You're applying CLEAR TARGET AUDIENCE ♦ 104. To be sure that any diagrams will be understood by your readers, use diagramming notations that are familiar to the target audience. The notation should be widely used and easily understood. If you're following a standard, provide the reference or a detailed explanation in an appendix.

CODE SAMPLES

Pattern Writing

559-560

You're applying CLEAR TARGET AUDIENCE ♦ 104. You're writing a solution to a software architecture or design problem. To clarify implementation details, provide one or more code samples, written in a programming language likely to be understood by the target audience.

ᛉᛉ CODE SAMPLES AS BONUS ♦ 105 ensures that the pattern can be understood without code examples.

CODE SAMPLES AS BONUS

Pattern Writing

560-561

You're writing a solution to a software architecture or design problem. To clarify implementation details, regardless of the programming language the target audience knows, be sure the pattern can stand on its own. Communicate essential concepts without code examples. Use CODE SAMPLES ♦ 105, but be sure these reinforce the solution and are not essential for understanding.

PATTERN LANGUAGE SUMMARY

Pattern Writing

562-563

You're using PATTERN LANGUAGE ♦ 102. To give the reader an overview of the patterns, write a summary that introduces the complex problem and the patterns that solve it.

ᛉᛉ This pattern can also introduce a RUNNING EXAMPLE ♦ 106.

ᛉᛉ In large pattern languages, use PROBLEM/SOLUTION SUMMARY ♦ 105.

PROBLEM/SOLUTION SUMMARY

Pattern Writing

563-564

You're using PATTERN LANGUAGE SUMMARY ♦ 105. To make it easy for a reader to find useful patterns in your language, in the summary, include a table that summarizes all the patterns, including a brief description of each problem and solution.

ᛉᛉ If you're using INTENT CATALOG ♦ 104, you can collect information already available for each pattern.

COMMON PROBLEMS HIGHLIGHTED
Pattern Writing

564-565

You're using PATTERN LANGUAGE ◆ 102. Several patterns in the language solve the same problem. To help readers choose an alternative solution: (1) Capture the common problem and forces in one place in a Separate Problem Description or Referenced Problem Description, or (2) repeat it for every solution.

RUNNING EXAMPLE
Pattern Writing

565-566

You're using PATTERN LANGUAGE ◆ 102. To help the reader understand the solution the language provides, use a single example in all the patterns in the language. Explain the example once, possibly in the introduction or language summary. Use the running example to illustrate how each pattern contributes to the overall solution. Use additional examples if the running example is not effective.

DISTINCTIVE HEADINGS CONVEY STRUCTURE
Pattern Writing

567-568

You're using PATTERN LANGUAGE ◆ 102. To help readers understand how individual patterns fit into the language, make individual pattern headings visibly different from all other document headings. Prefix pattern headings with hierarchical section numbers where the numbering parallels the language structure.

GLOSSARY
Pattern Writing

568-569

You're using PATTERN LANGUAGE ◆ 102. Some terms may not be familiar to the target audience. To clarify this terminology without interrupting the flow of the language, provide a glossary of terms as part of the pattern language.

PATTERN LANGUAGE FOR SMALLTALK & RELATIONAL DATABASES
Architectural, Database

[Brown+96a], *Object Magazine*, Sept. 1996, 51-55

When and how to define a database schema to support an object model. The identity of the objects, their relationships, and their state must be preserved in the tables of a relational database; a continuation of CROSSING CHASMS ❖ 41.

FOUR-LAYER ARCHITECTURE
Architectural, Client-Server

53

What is the appropriate structure for classes in a Smalltalk client-server system? Use a four-layer architecture: View, Application Model, Domain Model, and Supporting Infrastructure. Determine interfaces between layers in advance and keep communication paths well defined.

ᛏᛏᛏ HIERARCHY OF CONTROL LAYERS ◆ 61, LAYERED ARCHITECTURE ◆ 125, LAYERED ORGANIZATION ◆ 59, LAYERED AND SECTIONED ARCHITECTURE ◆ 96, LAYERS ◆ 81, PEDESTAL ◆ 123, SHAPE OF PROGRAM ◆ 29, THREE-TIER ARCHITECTURE ◆ 15

Entries

TABLE DESIGN TIME

Database

53

Design a relational database schema after a first-pass object model done with a behavioral modeling technique. It may be prudent to wait until after an architectural prototype has been built. Doing things in reverse order often leads to a poorly factored OO design with separate function and data objects.

- ⚐ TABLE DESIGN TIME ♦ 42
- ⚐ REPRESENTING COLLECTIONS ♦ 107, REPRESENTING INHERITANCE IN A RELATIONAL DATABASE ♦ 42, REPRESENTING OBJECT RELATIONSHIPS ♦ 107, REPRESENTING OBJECTS AS TABLES ♦ 107

REPRESENTING OBJECTS AS TABLES

Database

53

To map objects into a relational database, start with a table for each persistent object. Determine the type of each instance variable and create a column in the table. If the instance variable contains a collection,

- ⚐ Use REPRESENTING COLLECTIONS ♦ 107. If it contains any other value, use FOREIGN KEY REFERENCES ♦ 108. Finally, use OBJECT IDENTIFIER ♦ 107 to create a column containing the object identifier.
- ⚐ REPRESENTING OBJECTS AS TABLES ♦ 42

OBJECT IDENTIFIER

Database

53

To preserve an object's identity in a relational database, assign an object identifier to each persistent object, typically a long integer guaranteed to be unique for a class of objects.

- ⚐ OBJECT IDENTIFIER ♦ 42
- ⚐ This pattern is an extension of IDENTIFICATION SCHEME ♦ 10.

REPRESENTING OBJECT RELATIONSHIPS

Database

53

To represent object relationships in a relational database, one-to-one mappings become FOREIGN KEY REFERENCES ♦ 108. One-to-many mappings can use a relationship table. Many-to-many relationships become relationship tables.

- ⚐ REPRESENTING OBJECT RELATIONSHIPS ♦ 42
- ⚐ REPRESENTING INHERITANCE IN A RELATIONAL DATABASE ♦ 42 and REPRESENTING COLLECTIONS ♦ 107

REPRESENTING COLLECTIONS

Database

53

To represent Smalltalk collections in a relational database, create a relationship table for each collection. A relationship table maps the primary keys of the containing objects to the primary keys of the contained objects. The relationship table may store other information as well.

- ⚐ REPRESENTING COLLECTIONS IN A RELATIONAL DATABASE ♦ 42

FOREIGN KEY REFERENCES
Database

53

To represent objects in a relational database that reference other objects that are not base datatypes, assign each object a unique identifier. Add a column for each instance variable that is not a base datatype or a collection. Store the identifier of the referenced object in the column. Declare the column a foreign key.

♠ FOREIGN KEY REFERENCES ♦ 43

BROKER
Database

54

To separate the domain-specific parts of an application from the database-specific parts, connect the database-specific classes and the domain-specific classes with an intermediate layer of broker objects.

♠ QUERY OBJECT ♦ 108 combined with BROKER ♦ 108 and OBJECT METADATA ♦ 108 produces a powerful mini-architecture. Each domain object will have a set of map objects that represent its object relationships as metadata. Broker classes save and restore objects that use QUERY OBJECT ♦ 108 to generate SQL from the data in the maps. This preserves proper layering.

♠ PROXY ♦ 139 can be used as a placeholder for information not yet read in from the database.

OBJECT METADATA
Database

54

To define the mapping between the elements of an object class and the corresponding parts of a relational scheme, reify the mapping into a set of map classes that map object relationships into relational equivalents. Map classes also map column names to instance variable selectors in domain objects.

♠ QUERY OBJECT ♦ 108 combined with BROKER ♦ 108 and OBJECT METADATA ♦ 108 produces a powerful mini-architecture. Each domain object will have a set of map objects that represent its object relationships as metadata. Broker classes save and restore objects that use QUERY OBJECT ♦ 108 to generate SQL from the data in the maps.

♠ This preserves proper layering. PROXY ♦ 139 can be used as a placeholder for information not yet read in from the database.

QUERY OBJECT
Database

54

To handle the generation and execution of common SQL statements and minimize the amount of duplicated code between broker classes, define a set of generic classes that generate SQL statements from common data. A hierarchy of classes representing SQL statements can generate the appropriate SQL given a domain object and its map object metadata representation.

♠ QUERY OBJECT ♦ 108 combined with BROKER ♦ 108 and OBJECT METADATA ♦ 108 produces a powerful mini-architecture. Each domain object will have a set of map objects that represent its object relationships as metadata. Broker classes save and restore objects that use QUERY OBJECT ♦ 108 to generate SQL from the data in the maps. This preserves proper layering. PROXY ♦ 139 can be used as a placeholder for information not yet read in from the database.

CLIENT SYNCHRONIZATION
Client-Server, Database, Transaction Processing
54-55

To handle client image and database synchronization when there are errors, mark objects as "deleted," "added," or "updated" during the session. If the database update succeeds, then remove the mark. If it fails, retry the transaction. If it continually fails, note the error and flush the cache. When changed objects are marked, you can return to the original state by storing changed objects locally and performing recovery later.

CACHE MANAGEMENT
Client-Server, Database
55

To manage the lifetime of persistent objects in a relational database, use a session object that has a bounded lifetime and is responsible for identity cache management of a limited set of objects. Balance speed versus space by flushing the cache as appropriate. Use a query-before-write (timestamp) technique to keep caches accurate.

PATTERN LANGUAGE FOR TOOL CONSTRUCTION AND INTEGRATION BASED ON THE TOOLS AND MATERIALS METAPHOR
Behavioral, Structural, Interactive Systems
[Riehle+95], *PLoPD1*, 9-42

http://www.riehle.org/papers/1994/plop-1994-tools.html

In the Tools and Materials Metaphor, people have the necessary skills for their work, so there is no need to define a fixed work flow. People decide how to organize their work and their environment.

MATERIALS
Behavioral, Structural, Interactive Systems
13-14

Professionals use tools to work on materials. Materials are the objects of work, the focus of attention. The separation of tools from materials lets you flexibly combine tools with materials so the same tool can work on different materials and different tools can work on the same material.

⚑ ASPECTS ♦ 109, TOOLS ♦ 109

TOOLS
Behavioral, Structural, Interactive Systems
15

Tools are the means of work. Unless a tool breaks down, it is peripheral to the user; the material is the focus. However, a tool always mediates the presentation of material to a user, thereby determining what a user may see. Separating tools from materials allows you to combine tools and materials flexibly.

⚑ ASPECTS ♦ 109, TOOL COMPOSITION ♦ 110

ASPECTS
Behavioral, Structural, Interactive Systems
16

Tools access materials through aspects. An aspect represents the qualities of a material that make it manipulable by a tool.

⚑ MATERIALS ♦ 109, TOOL AND MATERIAL COUPLING ♦ 110, TOOLS ♦ 109

ENVIRONMENT
Behavioral, Structural, Interactive Systems

17

Users organize tools and materials in an environment. The environment (for example, a visual desktop) provides the spatial and logical dimensions in which to grab, put down, store, and retrieve tools and materials.

🏢 MATERIALS ◆ 109, TOOLS ◆ 109

TOOL AND MATERIAL COUPLING
Behavioral, Structural, Interactive Systems

20-22

Assume tools and materials are represented as distinct objects. An aspect becomes an interface that provides the functionality a tool requires to handle a material according to the tasks defined by the aspect. This interface, called an "aspect class," is the simplest way to express the functionality of an aspect formally. This ensures that tools can be combined with materials flexibly.

🏢 ASPECTS ◆ 109

TOOL COMPOSITION
Behavioral, Structural, Interactive Systems

22-24

Build software tools from a hierarchy of tool components. Have the tool components communicate using MEDIATOR ◆ 86, OBSERVER ◆ 94, and CHAIN OF RESPONSIBILITY ◆ 32. Structure the hierarchy using COMPOSITE ◆ 37. A parent tool delegates work to its child tool components. Child tool components notify their parent when they change state.

🏢 BUREAUCRACY ◆ 23 updates this pattern.

🏢 EVENT MECHANISM ◆ 110, SEPARATION OF POWERS ◆ 110, TOOLS ◆ 109

SEPARATION OF POWERS
Behavioral, Structural, Interactive Systems

24-26

Structure a tool component into a functional part and one or more interface parts.

🏢 TOOL COMPOSITION ◆ 110

EVENT MECHANISM
Behavioral, Structural, Interactive Systems

26-28

Make a source object (for example the functional part of a tool component), and provide information about possible state changes to clients. Let clients register their interest in these state changes and make the source object send events to clients when the changes occur.

🏢 EVENT NOTIFICATION ◆ 54

🏢 This pattern is similar to OBSERVER ◆ 94 but allows registering interest in event types.

🏢 Java's delegation event model, http://java.sun.com/products/jdk/1.1/docs/guide/awt/designspec/events.html

IP/FP PLUG IN
Behavioral, Structural, Interactive Systems
28-30
Have the functional part of a tool component create the functional parts of its child components. Have each interface part create the interface parts of its child components. Have the functional part of a tool component notify its interface parts to create the interface parts of the child components. Each tool is thus composed of a hierarchy of tool components.
♦♦♦ TOOL COMPOSITION ♦ 110

MATERIAL CONTAINER
Behavioral, Structural, Interactive Systems
33-35
Group dependent materials into a single material container that acts as an enclosure so that constraints can be maintained in one place, independent from tools.

TOOL COORDINATOR
Behavioral, Structural, Interactive Systems
35-36
If a constraint changes a material's state, the tools's state and the material's visual presentation can become inconsistent. Notify tools about changes to their materials due to constraints.
♦♦♦ MATERIALS ♦ 109, TOOLS ♦ 109

PATTERN LANGUAGE FOR WRITERS' WORKSHOPS

Writers' Workshops
[Coplien99d], *PLoPD4*, 557-580
http://www.bell-labs.com/~cope/Patterns/WritersWorkshops/
The structures and practices that support writers' workshops, a continuation of [Coplien97].

OPEN REVIEW
Writers' Workshops
559-560
Pattern writers need a review process. An open review forum supports the most effective communication between authors and reviewers, supporting dialogue yet limiting vulnerability and bad feelings. Use SAFE SETTING ♦ 111 and COMMUNITY OF TRUST ♦ 112.

SAFE SETTING
Writers' Workshops
560-561
You're using OPEN REVIEW ♦ 111. Provide a safe setting where the author can receive useful feedback directed at the work, not the author, with the goal of preserving the dignity of the author. Use WORKSHOP COMPRISES AUTHORS ♦ 112, AUTHORS' CIRCLE ♦ 112, MODERATOR GUIDES THE WORKSHOP ♦ 112, POSITIVE FEEDBACK FIRST ♦ 113, SUGGESTIONS FOR IMPROVEMENT ♦ 113, POSITIVE CLOSURE ♦ 113, and THANK THE AUTHOR ♦ 113.

AUTHORS ARE EXPERTS
Writers' Workshops
561-563
You're using OPEN REVIEW ♦ 111 and SAFE SETTING ♦ 111. To balance the assessment of content and expression in the work, treat the authors as experts in their domain. Review the form more than content.

WORKSHOP COMPRISES AUTHORS
Writers' Workshops

563-564

You're using OPEN REVIEW ♦ 111 and SAFE SETTING ♦ 111. To deal with feelings of mistrust for outsiders who aren't stakeholders, let the workshop members be other authors who are interested in the material, who have a stake in the material, or who will contribute to improving the work.

COMMUNITY OF TRUST
Writers' Workshops

564-565

You're using OPEN REVIEW ♦ 111 and SAFE SETTING ♦ 111. Organize writers' workshops by areas of interest that tie together the works of the authors.

MODERATOR GUIDES THE WORKSHOP
Writers' Workshops

565-566

You're using OPEN REVIEW ♦ 111 and SAFE SETTING ♦ 111. To keep things moving and be sure the workshop guidelines are followed, each session should be led by an experienced moderator who guides the discussion.

SITTING IN A CIRCLE
Writers' Workshops

566-567

You're using OPEN REVIEW ♦ 111 and SAFE SETTING ♦ 111. To facilitate paths of communication, have reviewers sit in a circle that includes the author and moderator. Don't use tables. All participants should present an equally vulnerable and supportive face to the circle as a whole.

AUTHORS' CIRCLE
Writers' Workshops

567

You're using SITTING IN A CIRCLE ♦ 112. Have two circles, the inner for authors and the moderator, the outer for non-authors.

READING JUST BEFORE REVIEWING
Writers' Workshops

568-569

You're using OPEN REVIEW ♦ 111 and SAFE SETTING ♦ 111. To avoid under- or over-preparation, reviewers should read the pattern just before reviewing it.

AUTHOR READS SELECTION
Writers' Workshops

569-570

You're using READING JUST BEFORE REVIEWING ♦ 112. How can the group get to know the author a little? The author stands and reads a selection of the material, verbatim, to the reviewers.

FLY ON THE WALL
Writers' Workshops

570-571

You're using AUTHOR READS SELECTION ♦ 112. To keep the author engaged yet at an objective distance, move the author out of the circle to become a fly on the wall. When you're using VOLUNTEER SUMMARIZES THE WORK ♦ 113, POSITIVE FEEDBACK FIRST ♦ 113, and SUGGESTIONS FOR IMPROVEMENT ♦ 113, refer to the author as "the author." No one should make eye contact with the author.

VOLUNTEER SUMMARIZES THE WORK
Writers' Workshops

571-572

You're using SITTING IN A CIRCLE ♦ 112 and FLY ON THE WALL ♦ 112. How can the group communicate their understanding of the work to the author? The moderator asks a volunteer to summarize the work in his or her own words.

POSITIVE FEEDBACK FIRST
Writers' Workshops

572-573

You've applied VOLUNTEER SUMMARIZES THE WORK ♦ 113. How can the reviewers provide feedback so that it has the best chance of being successful? Start by accentuating the positives—what the author should leave unchanged in future iterations of the work.

SUGGESTIONS FOR IMPROVEMENT
Writers' Workshops

573-575

You've applied POSITIVE FEEDBACK FIRST ♦ 113. To point out problems without attacking the author, provide constructive feedback to the author. Offer no criticism unless it is accompanied by a well-considered, actionable suggestion for improvement.

AUTHOR ASKS FOR CLARIFICATION
Writers' Workshops

575

You've applied POSITIVE CLOSURE ♦ 113 and the feedback has ended. How can the author have a chance to speak without starting a debate? The moderator calls for the author to ask for clarification on any reviewer comments. The author will not defend his work or clarify his position.

POSITIVE CLOSURE
Writers' Workshops

576

You've applied SUGGESTIONS FOR IMPROVEMENT ♦ 113. To leave the author with a positive feeling at the end of the feedback, the moderator asks a single reviewer to recap an important positive aspect of the work or describe some part of the work that makes it shine. Make the author feel special.

THANK THE AUTHOR
Writers' Workshops

576-577

You've applied AUTHOR ASKS FOR CLARIFICATION ♦ 113, and the workshop has finished. End the workshop by thanking the author. Typically the author remains seated while all reviewers stand and applaud. Reviewers should make eye contact with the author.

CLEARING THE PALATE
Writers' Workshops

577-578

After one writers' workshop has been completed, to get ready for the next one, the moderator should ask for a volunteer to tell an irrelevant story, joke, or any other bit of unrelated topic matter.

SELECTIVE CHANGES
Writers' Workshops
578-579
At the end of a writers' workshop, how should the author incorporate feedback into the work? The author is not bound to the verbatim advice from the reviewers. All changes to be made are at the author's discretion.

PATTERN LANGUAGE OF TRANSPORT SYSTEMS (POINT AND ROUTE)

Networks, Transportation
[Zhao+98b], *PLoPD3*, 409-430
Point and Route are part of a pattern language for building transport systems.

POINT
Networks, Transportation
411-416
A point is a node in a transportation network. A point's role in the network is changeable. Represent a point as a domain-specific application of STATE ♦ 166, where the different roles or states can be used in different applications.

ROUTE
Networks, Transportation
417-429
A route is a path through a transport network. A route can be represented as a domain-specific application of COMPOSITE ♦ 37.

PATTERN SYSTEM FOR NETWORK MANAGEMENT INTERFACES

Communications, Distributed Systems, Networks
[Keller+98a], *CACM*, Sept. 1998, 86-93
http://www.iro.umontreal.ca/labs/gelo/layla/
Example uses of patterns in a framework for network management interfaces—the middle layer of a network management system.

MANAGER-AGENT
Communications, Distributed Systems, Networks
In a large system of collaborating components, a central manager often controls the components. To reduce complexity, isolate management functionality in one or more manager objects, partition the set of components into subsets, and define individual agent objects that represent each subset. Each manager will interact with several agents and each agent can report to more than one manager.
﬩ MANAGER ♦ 86
﬩ An agent functions as an ADAPTER ♦ 6 for its subset of components.
﬩ Use MEDIATOR ♦ 86 to maintain the relationships between managers and agents.
﬩ BROKER ♦ 22 or REMOTE OPERATION ♦ 115 can provide location transparency.

MANAGED OBJECT
Communications, Distributed Systems, Networks

You have to manage a collection of entities that may have different interfaces with different features. There may be a hierarchical or containment relationship among the entities. To create a uniform interface for representing and controlling the resources, for each entity use a managed object to translate its interface to one that is shared by all the entities.

REMOTE OPERATION
Client-Server, Communications, Distributed Systems, Networks

To minimize location dependencies in a distributed system, encapsulate all network interactions in stub objects on the client and server sides. The client stub and the server stub communicate with each other using connection and message instances specific to the network under consideration. The invoker and performer interact with their respective stubs.

ᛉᛉᛉ This pattern is a refinement of PROXY ♦ 139.

PATTERN-BASED INTEGRATION ARCHITECTURES
Integration

[Mularz95], *PLoPD1*, 441-452

Scheme for a paradigm shift from custom development to component integration.

(LEGACY) WRAPPER
Integration

444-445

Provide continued access to a legacy application while extending its capability and user base, eventually leading to its replacement.

ᛉᛉᛉ To support a heterogeneous, distributed user base, use BROKER ♦ 22.

ᛉᛉᛉ This pattern is similar to FACADE ♦ 56 and ADAPTER ♦ 6.

WORK FLOW MANAGER
Integration

445-448

Provide an integration component to automatically perform a user-defined task based on a known, repeatable execution sequence performed by stand-alone components. Use scripts to start and control the execution context for an integrated suite of applications.

BROKER
Integration

448-449

This pattern provides communication and location transparency for interoperating applications.

ᛉᛉᛉ This pattern is an implementation of BROKER ♦ 22 for integration problems.

SHARED REPOSITORY
Integration

449-450

Provide an integration scheme that allows individual components to process information in an internal form while sharing information with other components. Define a shared information model that captures all the data that can potentially be exchanged between components. Build an importer and an exporter for each component for the common data.

PATTERNS FOR CLASSROOM EDUCATION
Training

[Anthony96], *PLoPD2*, 391-406

How to teach difficult technical topics.

ITERATIVE COURSE DEVELOPMENT
Training

392-393

To develop a course that considers the needs of all kinds of students, develop courses iteratively. Create your best effort in isolation, then present it. As audiences change, the course will grow and improve.

CHICKEN AND EGG
Training

393-394

Two concepts are each a prerequisite of the other. The student who doesn't know A won't understand B, and the student who doesn't know B won't understand A. Give students the illusion of understanding by explaining A and B superficially. Iterate the explanations over and over, each time going into more detail. Maintain the illusion of understanding at each step.

MIX NEW AND OLD
Training

394

Basic concepts must be reviewed over and over, but that gets boring. New concepts must be introduced, but few students can handle more than 10-15% new material at a time. Iterate over a concept several times. Each time, present the material in a different way to accommodate a different learning style and mix in new material with the old.

PITFALL DIAGNOSIS AND PREVENTION
Training

394-395

Some concepts are pitfalls and are missed by many students. To keep students from falling into these traps, use an ounce of prevention. If something was a problem in one session, place extra emphasis on that topic when it comes up later.

- ♦♦♦ Use ITERATIVE COURSE DEVELOPMENT ♦ 116 to record pitfalls.
- ♦♦♦ COLORFUL ANALOGY ♦ 117, SIMULATION GAMES ♦ 117, and VISIBLE CHECKLIST ♦ 117 provide ways to highlight difficult concepts and prevent pitfalls.

MODULE'S STORY
Training

395-396

To make a module feel like a coherent whole, create an example, exercise, or goal that uses all the topics in the module. Make the flow of the module into a story. Keeping the story in mind will help the module flow this way. You may not actually have to tell the story to the students for this to be effective.

- ♦♦♦ ACQUAINTANCE EXAMPLES ♦ 117 will help you choose an example or exercise topic.
- ♦♦♦ VISIBLE CHECKLIST ♦ 117 can support the story flow of a module. If the module has sufficient cohesion, a checklist alone can provide the story.

SEVEN PARTS
Training

396-397

If you divide each module into about seven steps or subtopics, it will seem about right to most people.

VISIBLE CHECKLIST
Training

397-398

To relate the preview and review of a module to each other and to the material presented in between, when previewing the modules, use a visual aid as a checklist. Keep the checklist visible throughout the module. When you go to a new topic, refer to the checklist. At the end, use the checklist for review.

- ♔ SEVEN PARTS ♦ 116 recommends the number of things to include in the checklist.
- ♔ MODULE'S STORY ♦ 116 suggests an alternate way to organize a module.

ACQUAINTANCE EXAMPLES
Training

398-399

The examples for a training class should be familiar to students but not in their area of expertise. For example, choose business examples that students patronize but don't operate, such as a hotel or a video store.

- ♔ REFERENCE EXAMPLES ♦ 117 provides one way to give students a greater variety of example domains than you will have time to cover in the course.

EXAMPLE LASTS ONE WEEK
Training

399-400

How long should you use an example in a training course? When should you introduce a new one? Continue to use an example throughout a week-long course. Over a weekend, details of an example are forgotten, so introduce a new one the next week.

- ♔ ACQUAINTANCE EXAMPLES ♦ 117 explains how to choose the domain of examples in a class.

REFERENCE EXAMPLES
Training

400

A course must fit into tight time constraints but still cover the required material. To provide examples even though you can't spend time on them, give references to examples that students can use after the session ends.

COLORFUL ANALOGY
Training

400-401

Some important concepts involve boring details that aren't suitable for SIMULATION GAMES ♦ 117. A dry concept can still be illustrated with a colorful analogy.

SIMULATION GAMES
Training

401-402

You'll need to explain tricky concepts and provide interaction. Playing a simulation of a complex activity often gives students a much better understanding than a straight explanation. These activities also provide an opportunity for interaction.

- ♔ QUIZ GAMES ♦ 118 also provides interaction when no suitable topic for simulation is planned.

QUIZ GAMES

Training

402-403

Review is necessary but can be boring. Testing students' comprehension is useful but makes students nervous. When a section of the material is not suitable for SIMULATION GAMES ♦ 117, but you still want to provide interaction, use a quiz game, modeled on sports, board games, or TV game shows. These are entertaining as well as a familiar, safe format.

ᛉ This pattern can identify pitfalls for use in PITFALL DIAGNOSIS AND PREVENTION ♦ 116.

ᛉ VISIBLE CHECKLIST ♦ 117 can provide material for quiz game questions.

DEBRIEF AFTER ACTIVITIES

Training

403

You're using SIMULATION GAMES ♦ 117 or you've just completed an exercise. Some students haven't grasped the concepts the activity was intended to convey. To ensure that students still get the maximum value out of the experience, after the activity, lead a discussion of what the students learned. Ask open-ended questions (without a yes/no answer) to draw out comments and insights from each student. Students will value one another's discoveries more than what is simply told to them by the instructor.

PATTERNS FOR DESIGNING IN TEAMS

Design Process, Organization and Process

[Weir98], *PLoPD3*, 487-501

Techniques for using teams effectively in software design.

ᛉ CAPABLE, PRODUCTIVE, AND SATISFIED ❖ 26

MULTIPLE COMPETING DESIGNS

Design Process, Organization and Process

488-491

A team of designers can think itself into a cul-de-sac. Once the team has reached a conclusion, ego and inertia make it difficult to consider other possibilities. Have several designers work individually or in pairs to produce a different design to solve the same problem. The entire team then evaluates the designs in a series of reviews. Finally, a lead designer combines the different solutions into a single design.

ᛉ DECISION DOCUMENT ♦ 118 can identify the best elements in the competing designs.

ᛉ CREATOR-REVIEWER ♦ 119 can be applied to the product of the lead designer.

DECISION DOCUMENT

Design Process, Organization and Process

491-494

Teams typically make arbitrary design decisions. Have the team meet with a facilitator to produce a decision document, comparing and contrasting two design approaches. This is a short document, usually just a couple of pages.

ᛉ This pattern can be used when applying MULTIPLE COMPETING DESIGNS ♦ 118.

CREATOR-REVIEWER
Design Process, Organization and Process

494-496

People make mistakes. It's difficult to see problems and errors in your own work. When one or two designers are producing a design, there is a strong likelihood of undetected errors. Have each designer produce a draft or a complete design. Each of one or more reviewers receives a copy and provides feedback.

♦♦♦ GROUP VALIDATION ♦ 66, REVIEW THE ARCHITECTURE ♦ 65, VALIDATION BY TEAMS ♦ 96

MASTER-JOURNEYMAN
Design Process, Organization and Process

496-499

You need to partition the design work for a large system. There must be a chief architect or small team to provide design integrity. Yet in a large development project, it might be impossible for this core team to do all the design work. The core team should provide an overview of the system architecture and divide the system into independent components. Journeymen architects then design the components and act as chief architects for the components.

♦♦♦ See ARCHITECT CONTROLS PRODUCT ♦ 65 for more information on the chief architect role.

AD-HOC CORRECTIONS
Design Process, Organization and Process

499-500

It's difficult to keep documents up to date. Keep a master hard copy of the design accessible to the entire team. Anyone who updates the design must make corrections in the margin, delete sections that no longer apply, or write a description of the change. Ultimately, one team member should update online copies to reflect the corrections. This can be a learning experience for newcomers.

PATTERNS FOR DESIGNING NAVIGABLE INFORMATION SPACES
Hypermedia

[Rossi+99], *PLoPD4*, 445-460

For hypermedia in stand-alone applications, dynamic Web sites, or information systems.

SET-BASED NAVIGATION
Hypermedia

446-448

Hypermedia applications deal with collections of nodes that may be explored in different ways. Group nodes into meaningful sets, called navigational contexts, and provide inter- and intra-set navigation.

NODES IN CONTEXT
Hypermedia

448-451

You're using SET-BASED NAVIGATION ♦ 119. To allow the same node to be reached by different paths and reflect different perspectives, let the node appear in different navigational contexts. Modify its appearance and connections to other nodes according to the current context.

ACTIVE REFERENCE
Hypermedia
451-454
In hypermedia applications, users need to know where they are and decide where to go next. Use one navigational object as an index to other navigational objects. This object is perceivable together with target objects, allowing users to explore those objects or select another target.
NEWS
Hypermedia
454-455
The information space of most large Web sites is hardly ever navigated by users. Highlight the newest information, for example, a headline that changes to reflect the latest update.
⋔ NEW DOCUMENT NOTIFICATION ♦ 99 provides an extension of this solution.
LANDMARK
Hypermedia
455-457
You're building a Web-Information System for electronic shopping. If you explicitly specify a navigational link between every pair of navigation objects, you'll have a complex spaghetti-like topology. Define a set of landmarks accessible from every node. The interface of links to a landmark should be uniform to give users consistent visual clues about the landmark.
BASKET
Hypermedia
457-459
You want to keep track of user selections in an e-commerce Web site. Ask the user to select products to buy as they are traversed. Provide a persistent store for these items (e.g., a basket) to be accessed like any other navigation object.

PATTERNS FOR ENCAPSULATING CLASS TREES
Creational, Structural
[Riehle96b], *PLoPD2*, 87-104
`http://www.riehle.org/papers/1995/plop-1995-trading.html`
Encapsulation of class hierarchies behind their root classes.
CLASS RETRIEVAL
Structural
92-94
Clients of an encapsulated class tree need to retrieve classes from that tree. Have the clients create a specification for classes they are interested in. The client requests all classes from the class tree that meet the specification.
LATE CREATION
Creational
94-95
An encapsulated class tree is of no use unless objects of its internal classes can be created. Clients only know the interface class and a property that unambiguously identifies the class they are interested in. The client of a class creates a specification that unambiguously identifies a single class, then requests a new instance of a class that fits the specification.
⋔ CLASS CLAUSE ♦ 121 can be used in class specification.

CLASS CLAUSE

Structural

95-98

A class clause makes an atomic statement about a class property that is true or false. It is represented by an object and can be compared to other clauses. It provides a basis for class specifications and first-class representations of class semantics.

CLASS SPECIFICATION

Structural

98-99

Clients use specifications to retrieve classes from a class tree. A class specification is a formula from propositional calculus with clauses as its basic constituents. Clients build a specification by creating clauses and using them in a formula.

 CLASS CLAUSE ♦ 121, CLASS RETRIEVAL ♦ 120, LATE CREATION ♦ 120

CLASS SEMANTICS

Structural

99-101

Provide a set of clause instances for each class. Each clause makes a statement about the class. The set of clauses represents the semantics of the class. A class can be matched against a specification, which is realized by comparing clauses and evaluating the formula.

 CLASS CLAUSE ♦ 121, CLASS RETRIEVAL ♦ 120, CLASS SPECIFICATION ♦ 121, LATE CREATION ♦ 120

PATTERNS FOR EVOLVING FRAMEWORKS

Frameworks

[Roberts+98], *PLoPD3*, 471-486

`http://st-www.cs.uiuc.edu/users/droberts/evolve.html`

A common path that frameworks take.

THREE EXAMPLES

Frameworks

472-474

To start designing a framework for a particular domain, develop three applications the framework should support.

 Initial versions will probably follow WHITE-BOX FRAMEWORKS ♦ 121.

WHITE-BOX FRAMEWORKS

Frameworks

474-476

You're using THREE EXAMPLES ♦ 121 and have started to build your second application. Some frameworks rely heavily on inheritance, others on polymorphic composition. Use inheritance. Build a white-box framework by generalizing from classes in individual applications. Don't worry if the applications don't share any concrete classes.

 Use TEMPLATE METHOD ♦ 171 and FACTORY METHOD ♦ 56 to increase the amount of reusable code in the superclasses from which you're inheriting.

 BLACK-BOX FRAMEWORK ♦ 122 addresses the same problem as this pattern but with a different context.

COMPONENT LIBRARY

Frameworks

476-477

You're using WHITE-BOX FRAMEWORKS ♦ 121 and developing the second and subsequent examples. Similar objects must be implemented for each problem the framework solves. To avoid writing similar objects for each instantiation of the framework, start with a simple library of the obvious objects and add additional objects as you need them.

⚓ As components are added to the library, you will see recurring code. Use HOT SPOTS ♦ 122 for code that changes from application to application.

HOT SPOTS

Frameworks

478-479

You're using COMPONENT LIBRARY ♦ 122. As you develop applications based on your framework, you will see similar code. Pree calls these "Hot Spots" [Pree94]. To eliminate this common code, separate code that changes from code that remains stable. The changing code should be encapsulated in objects. Variation can then be achieved by composing the desired objects rather than creating subclasses and writing methods.

⚓ You may have to use FINE-GRAINED OBJECTS ♦ 122 to encapsulate the hot spots.

⚓ This may lead you to use BLACK-BOX FRAMEWORK ♦ 122.

⚓ HOT SPOT ♦ 82 describes code that's executed a lot, not code that's prone to change as in this pattern.

PLUGGABLE OBJECTS

Frameworks

479-480

You're using COMPONENT LIBRARY ♦ 122. Most of the subclasses you've written differ in trivial ways—for example, only one method is overridden. To avoid creating trivial subclasses when you use the framework, design adaptable subclasses to parameterize with messages to send, for example, indexes to access, blocks to evaluate, whatever distinguishes the subclasses.

⚓ Creating pluggable objects improves encapsulation when you're using HOT SPOTS ♦ 122.

FINE-GRAINED OBJECTS

Frameworks

481-482

You're using COMPONENT LIBRARY ♦ 122, and refactoring components to make them more reusable. Continue dividing objects until you would produce objects that have no meaning in the problem domain.

⚓ As you're using this pattern, you will begin applying BLACK-BOX FRAMEWORK ♦ 122.

BLACK-BOX FRAMEWORK

Frameworks

482-483

You're using PLUGGABLE OBJECTS ♦ 122, HOT SPOTS ♦ 122, and FINE-GRAINED OBJECTS ♦ 122. Some frameworks rely heavily on inheritance, others on polymorphic composition. Use inheritance to organize your component library and composition to combine components in applications. When it isn't clear which is better, favor composition.

⚓ This pattern provides the context for VISUAL BUILDER ♦ 123.

VISUAL BUILDER
Frameworks

483-485

You're using BLACK-BOX FRAMEWORK ♦ 122 and can make an application by connecting objects. A single application comprises two parts: (1) the script that connects the objects of the framework and turns them on and (2) the behavior of the objects. The connection script is usually similar for each application, but the specific objects are different. To simplify the creation of these scripts, create a graphical program that lets you specify the objects in your application and how they are connected. The program should generate code for an application from these specifications.

 ▥ When you use this pattern, you will create a visual programming language. Next use LANGUAGE TOOLS ♦ 123.

LANGUAGE TOOLS
Frameworks

485-486

You're using VISUAL BUILDER ♦ 123. The program creates complex composite objects. To inspect and debug these, create specialized inspecting and debugging tools.

PATTERNS FOR GENERATING A LAYERED ARCHITECTURE
Architectural, Reactive and Real-Time Systems

[Rubel95], *PLoPD1*, 119-128

Provide a natural decomposition of system requirements into a layered architecture. Mechanical control systems are used as an example.

PEDESTAL
Architectural, Reactive and Real-Time Systems

120-124

To create a layered architecture: (1) Select and order a set of domains. (2) Reflect the real-world domains in the software domain to form a model of the real world. The real-world domains form architectural layers. (3) Add a layer on the software model with objects that organize the behavior of the model. (4) Add another layer that connects the previous layers to a client.

 ▥ HIERARCHY OF CONTROL LAYERS ♦ 61, FOUR-LAYER ARCHITECTURE ♦ 106, LAYERED ARCHITECTURE ♦ 125, LAYERED ORGANIZATION ♦ 59, LAYERED AND SECTIONED ARCHITECTURE ♦ 96, LAYERS ♦ 81, SHAPE OF PROGRAM ♦ 29, THREE-TIER ARCHITECTURE ♦ 15

BRIDGE
Architectural, Reactive and Real-Time Systems

124

Given the layered architecture that results from using PEDESTAL ♦ 123, what can you do with the components that are part of different layers? Create a separate world for each domain. Information transfer between domains is enabled by a communication channel.

SYMMETRICAL REUSE
Architectural, Reactive and Real-Time Systems

125-127

Layers of the architecture in PEDESTAL ♦ 123 support reuse. Encapsulation hides the details of how components use objects in lower layers.

ELEVATE REFERENCES TO ENHANCE REUSE
Design Process

127-128

To model a relationship between two objects, implement the relationships in an object in a higher layer in the architecture.

- ⚘ See WORK ACCOMPLISHED THROUGH DIALOGS ♦ 30 for a view of relationships between objects.
- ⚘ See BASIC RELATIONSHIP PATTERNS ❖ 19 for a more complete treatment.

PATTERNS FOR LOGGING DIAGNOSTIC MESSAGES
Communications, Telecommunications, Transaction Processing

[Harrison98], *PLoPD3*, 277-289

Transaction-oriented systems lend themselves to common approaches to logging diagnostic messages.

DIAGNOSTIC LOGGER
Communications, Telecommunications, Transaction Processing

278-281

To report diagnostic information in a consistent manner, use a diagnostic logger as a single point for all messages to flow through. The diagnostic logger has two functions: (1) control of logging in general, e.g., specifying the output destination, error thresholds, debugging levels; and (2) other functions that allow the rest of the system to output diagnostic messages.

- ⚘ Use SINGLETON ♦ 152 for the diagnostic logger.

DIAGNOSTIC CONTEXT
Communications, Telecommunications, Transaction Processing

281-285

You're using DIAGNOSTIC LOGGER ♦ 124. If an error occurs in processing a set of discrete inputs, to associate error messages with the responsible input, while a transaction is processed, a diagnostic object identifies the transaction. The diagnostic logger will associate the error message with the context information in the associated diagnostic context.

- ⚘ This pattern is similar to COMMAND PROCESSOR ♦ 36, with the diagnostic logger playing the role of the command processor. Of course, a diagnostic context object is not executed as commands are.

TYPED DIAGNOSTICS
Communications, Telecommunications, Transaction Processing

285-288

You're using DIAGNOSTIC CONTEXT ♦ 124 and logging many different messages (e.g., errors, warnings, debugging messages). To be sure they are handled consistently, create an inheritance hierarchy of diagnostic message types. Each type encapsulates the characteristics of that category of diagnostics and parameterizes the variations. Details of diagnostic messages are embedded in the classes.

PATTERNS FOR SOFTWARE ARCHITECTURES
Architectural

[Shaw95], *PLoPD1*, 453-462

Architectural patterns. Continued in [Shaw96].

PIPELINE
Architectural

455; [Shaw96], 259

Apply when a series of independent computations are to be performed on ordered data, particularly when the computations can be performed incrementally on a data stream. The computations or filters incrementally transform one or more input streams to one or more output streams.

DATA ABSTRACTION OR OBJECT-ORIENTED
Architectural

455; [Shaw+96], 22-23; [Shaw96], 260

Data representations and their associated primitive operations are encapsulated in an abstract data type or object. The components of this architecture are instances of abstract data types or objects.

IMPLICIT INVOCATION OR EVENT-BASED
Architectural, Event-Driven Systems

456; [Shaw+96], 23-24; [Shaw96], 262

Components typically interact by announcing or broadcasting one or more events. Other components can register an interest in an event by associating a procedure with it. When the event is announced, the system invokes all registered procedures.

REPOSITORY
Architectural

456; [Shaw+96], 26-27; [Shaw96], 263

There are two kinds of components: a central data structure that represents the current state, and a collection of independent components that operate on the central data structure.

♦♦♦ BLACKBOARD ♦ 22 is an example of this pattern.

INTERPRETER
Architectural

456; [Shaw+96], 27; [Shaw96], 264

This solution generally has four components: (1) an interpretation engine to do the work; (2) the pseudocode to be interpreted; (3) the control state of the interpretation engine; and (4) the current state of the program being simulated.

♦♦♦ This pattern has a different intent from INTERPRETER ♦ 80.

MAIN PLUS SUBROUTINES
Architectural

456; [Shaw+96], 31-32; [Shaw96], 265

Architectures implemented in languages without support for modularization usually result in a main program and a collection of subroutines. The main program is a driver, typically providing a control loop for sequencing the subroutines.

LAYERED ARCHITECTURE
Architectural

457; [Shaw+96], 25; [Shaw96], 266

Suitable for applications with distinct classes of services that can be arranged hierarchically.

♦♦♦ HIERARCHY OF CONTROL LAYERS ♦ 61, FOUR-LAYER ARCHITECTURE ♦ 106, LAYERED ORGANIZATION ♦ 59, LAYERED AND SECTIONED ARCHITECTURE ♦ 96, LAYERS ♦ 81, PEDESTAL ♦ 123, SHAPE OF PROGRAM ♦ 29, THREE-TIER ARCHITECTURE ♦ 15

PATTERNS FOR SYSTEM TESTING
Testing

[DeLano+98], *PLoPD3*, 503-525. See also *PHand*, 97-119.

Testing patterns for developers and managers, as well as testers.

TESTER'S MORE IMPORTANT THAN THE TEST CASES
Organization and Process, Testing

506-507

Assign tasks to testers based on their experience and talent. No matter how effective the test cases are, the testing results are dependent on the tester.

DESIGNERS ARE OUR FRIENDS
Customer Interaction, Organization and Process, Testing

507-508

How should testers work with designers? Build rapport with designers. Approach designers with the attitude that the system has problems that require cooperation to resolve. Designers and testers have a common goal. Use GET INVOLVED EARLY ♦ 126 and DOCUMENT THE PROBLEM ♦ 128.

♦♦♦ DESIGN BY TEAM ♦ 95 stresses the importance of working together to develop and design software.

GET INVOLVED EARLY
Customer Interaction, Organization and Process, Testing

508-509

You're a system tester working on a large software project. To maximize support from the design community, establish a working relationship with the designers early in the project, for example, learn the system and the features along with the designers or attend reviews of requirements and design documentation. Invite designers to reviews of test plans. Use DESIGNERS ARE OUR FRIENDS ♦ 126. Don't wait until you need to interact with a designer; by that time it's too late. Trust must be built over time.

♦♦♦ This pattern is similar to the customer interaction patterns IT'S A RELATIONSHIP, NOT A SALE ♦ 43 and BUILD TRUST ♦ 43. Designers are customers for the support system testers provide.

♦♦♦ PRAGMATIC EXTERNAL REQUIREMENTS ♦ 142, REQUIREMENTS VALIDATION ♦ 143

TIME TO TEST
Organization and Process, Testing

509-510

Start testing when an area is available, but not before. Reach agreement with designers that the area is ready for testing.

♦♦♦ Agreement is easier if you've applied GET INVOLVED EARLY ♦ 126 and DESIGNERS ARE OUR FRIENDS ♦ 126.

♦♦♦ You may have to use TAKE TIME ♦ 126.

TAKE TIME
Organization and Process, Testing

510

You're using GET INVOLVED EARLY ♦ 126 and DESIGNERS ARE OUR FRIENDS ♦ 126. When designers are behind schedule, give them the time they ask for. Use TIME TO TEST ♦ 126 on other areas. You'll save effort in the long run; testing a poorer-quality system takes more time.

"UNCHANGED" INTERFACES

Testing

511-512

How should testing of third-party interfaces be scheduled? Don't fall into the trap of assuming that unchanged interfaces will function correctly in the new system. Test the third-party interface independently when it is chosen. When the project is ready to include the third-party software, immediately test to ensure the third-party functionality behaves as expected.

AMBIGUOUS DOCUMENTATION

Testing

512-513

To pinpoint possible problem areas, study the documentation. Look for areas that seem ambiguous or poorly defined. If the designers can tell you everything you need to know about a feature, it probably works. It's what they can't tell you that needs attention.

➤ Use GET INVOLVED EARLY ♦ 126 and DESIGNERS ARE OUR FRIENDS ♦ 126 to obtain this information early and point it out to designers.

USE OLD PROBLEM REPORTS

Testing

513

Examine the old problem reports to find areas that should be targeted for testing. You can't test for all old problems, so concentrate on those from the last valid snapshot.

PROBLEM AREA

Testing

514

What areas of the system should receive concentrated testing, regardless of the features being implemented? Keep a list of problem areas and the test cases to target them. These areas can be identified by: (1) talking to experienced system testers; (2) applying AMBIGUOUS DOCUMENTATION ♦ 127 and USE OLD PROBLEM REPORTS ♦ 127, and (3) looking for areas that designers avoid.

BUSY SYSTEM

Testing

515

What conditions should be considered for testing to find the most problems? Test in a busy environment, using simulators to provide levels of activity on the system. You don't need to stress the system; use a level of activity that the system could expect to experience regularly during busy times.

DON'T TRUST SIMULATIONS

Testing

515-516

You're using simulations in your test plans. To configure the testing environment, supplement simulations with real world testing. Testing is not complete without real-world scenarios. A simulator can run a test case successfully a hundred times, but the test may fail when performed by a human because of unpredictable behaviors that are introduced. Use END USER VIEWPOINT ♦ 127.

END USER VIEWPOINT

Testing

516-517

To test new features without repeating any testing, test outside the normal scope of features. Don't use tests already run for feature testing. Use END USER VIEWPOINT ♦ 127.

UNUSUAL TIMING

Testing

517

What additional testing should be done that might not be covered by the test plans for an area? Test unusual timing. Run tests more quickly or slowly than normal. Abort tests in the middle of execution. Use END USER VIEWPOINT ♦ 127. Some of these tests may be difficult to perform; those are exactly the ones that should be executed.

MULTIPLE PROCESSORS

Testing

518

When the system runs on multiple processors, test across all processors. A designer might have only considered one processor, assuming that it would work for all processors. Problems that occur on one processor will probably occur on other processors. Tests that pass one processor may fail on another.

SCRATCH 'N SNIFF

Testing

518-519

Once testing has started, what's a good strategy for determining the next test case to run? Test areas where problems have already been found. Problems tend to be found in clusters.

STRANGE BEHAVIOR

Testing

519

You've tested a feature on a previous release and on the new release the feature is working but not exactly as expected. Take any unusual behavior as an indication of a possible problem and follow up. This should be done even if the problem is not related to the current test. Be wary when familiar tests produce results that might be acceptable but not exactly what was expected.

KILLER TEST

Testing

519-520

Development is drawing to a close. The system is stable. To give a quick evaluation of the overall health of the system, use a favorite killer test to be run at any time. The test should provide good system coverage and be expected to fail, in some manner, most of the time.

DOCUMENT THE PROBLEM

Testing

520-521

You're using GET INVOLVED EARLY ♦ 126 and DESIGNERS ARE OUR FRIENDS ♦ 126. To communicate problems found in testing, write a problem report. Don't argue with the designer. Don't accept a well-intentioned promise or document the problem informally.

ADOPT-A-PROBLEM

Testing

522-523

You're using DESIGNERS ARE OUR FRIENDS ♦ 126. A problem has been uncovered without a clear-cut solution. Adopt the problem. Stick with it until it is resolved. Use DOCUMENT THE PROBLEM ♦ 128. Retest the problem periodically to gather data on it. Be aware of PET PEEVE ♦ 129.

PET PEEVE
Testing
523

You're using DESIGNERS ARE OUR FRIENDS ♦ 126, DOCUMENT THE PROBLEM ♦ 128, and ADOPT-A-PROBLEM ♦ 128. The validity of the problem has been debated to the point of holding up progress. Be sure the problem doesn't become a thorn in the designer's side. You might consider bringing in a third party (for example, the requirements writers) to resolve the impasse. At this point, stop following the status of the problem.

PATTERNS OF EVENTS
Architectural, Event-Driven Systems, Reactive and Real-Time Systems
[Ran95], *PLoPD1*, 547-553

Event processing in a distributed real-time control and information system.

EVENT-CENTERED ARCHITECTURE
Architectural, Event-Driven Systems, Reactive and Real-Time Systems
547-549

Product families minimize costs of concurrent evolution of similar products. This is possible if products are related by function and structure. Greater stability of program family architecture is possible if it is based on the major events that occur in the domain.

CLASSES OF EVENT OBJECTS
Architectural, Event-Driven Systems, Reactive and Real-Time Systems
549-550

When applying EVENT-CENTERED ARCHITECTURE ♦ 129, the events can become complex. Use classes to model events as system-level concepts. Event classes allow you to treat events as a group.

FINE-GRAINED CLASSIFICATION OF EVENTS
Design Process, Event-Driven Systems
550-551

An event's membership in different sets of interest may be determined more efficiently if the relationships between the sets are known in advance. Design a hierarchy of event classes that models the generalization/specialization relationship between events generated and expected by different components in the system. A component may register its interest in one or several classes of events.

OBJECT-ORIENTED STATE MACHINE
Design Process, Event-Driven Systems, Finite State Machines
551-552

You're using EVENT-CENTERED ARCHITECTURE ♦ 129. Reactive components are independent and often distributed and concurrent. Each reactive component is attached to some event class. A reactive component should provide the necessary interface for invocation by event objects. Specify the representation and behavior of a component by a cluster of classes. The root of the cluster specifies the public interface of the components and the state-independent part of its representation and behavior. Each state is represented as a class that directly or indirectly inherits the root of the state cluster.

PATTERNS ON THE FLY

Organization and Process

[Olson98a], *PHand*, 141-170

http://c2.com/cgi/wiki?DonOlson

Compares software development to fly fishing. Patterns and antipatterns for team structure.

TRAIN HARD FIGHT EASY

Organization and Process

145-147

Teams are thrown together and given a project without establishing team mentality or shared skills, knowledge, or vocabulary. Consequently, everyone learns "on the job" by trial and error. Train the team as a unit in relevant technologies to help give everyone the same tools and language.

✗ [Janoff98]

TRAIN THE TRAINER

Organization and Process

147-148

Training is expensive and time-consuming to give to entire teams. Just train one or two individuals in a classroom setting, and then use them to train the rest of the team. This is an antipattern.

♦♦♦ See TRAIN HARD FIGHT EASY ♦ 130.

TRIAL PROJECT

Organization and Process

149-150

A team of experienced software developers is formed, and TRAIN HARD FIGHT EASY ♦ 130 has been applied. Build a trial project together using the new technology. Make it a real project but a small one of no profound consequence.

CASUAL DUTY

Organization and Process

150-151

When a team is between projects and there is uncertainty about the next assignment, give the team some work on infrastructure, tools, process—something to benefit them and other teams in the future.

✗ [Janoff98]

GURU DOES ALL

Organization and Process

153-154

A newly formed team is given a project with a tight schedule, uncertain requirements, uneven distribution of skills, and new technologies. Let the most skilled and knowledgeable developer drive the design and implement the critical pieces. This can be an antipattern.

CULT OF PERSONALITY

Organization and Process

154-155

A tight schedule, poorly defined requirements, uneven distribution of skills among the development team, and new technologies has put a project in jeopardy. To save the day, bring in a legendary figure among the developers to take over the lead. Team members who are not impressed may need removal or reeducation.

CARGO CULT
Organization and Process

162-164

A project is in trouble and is very visible. Criticism is directed at the project, staff, and management. People on the project are beaten up by rumor, management interference, and demands for replans. The project is important and can't be scrapped. Redraw organization charts showing the troubled project in a new, larger context, possible demoting it in stature. You could use SACRIFICIAL LAMB ♦ 131, but don't make any real changes. This can be an antipattern.

CONTAINMENT BUILDING
Organization and Process

164-165

A project is failing and is too visible. People are leaving or are severely disgruntled. Much criticism is directed at the project, staff, and management. Add the failing project to another, larger project, changing its name if necessary and apparently altering its scope. This gives the team room to recover.

DOORMAT
Organization and Process

166

A doormat enables outside powers to manage the team without a reorganization. A rehabilitated SACRIFICIAL LAMB ♦ 131 can make a good doormat.

LET'S PLAY TEAM
Organization and Process

166-167

A tight schedule, uncertain requirements, uneven distribution of skills among developers, and new technologies have put a project in jeopardy. Pretend to be a team. Present a unified face through a team lead but otherwise do not collaborate. Be sure every team member has something to do but keep knowledge vertical, with little communication among members.

LONG POLE IN THE TENT
Organization and Process

167

A member of the team is the "long pole in the tent" if he is behind schedule or is suspected of being behind schedule, affecting other collaborating members.

PEACEMAKER
Organization and Process

168

A peacemaker is a placeholder in an organization who tries to calm and hold things together until a leader can be found or a reorganization is complete. The peacemaker should be someone who is well liked but who is not necessarily technically proficient. Usually this individual has many years with the company, knows the political ropes, and can buy time for a team as well as the team's management.

Usually PEACEMAKER ♦ 131 follows SACRIFICIAL LAMB ♦ 131 and precedes CULT OF PERSONALITY ♦ 130 or GURU DOES ALL ♦ 130.

SACRIFICIAL LAMB
Organization and Process

168-169

A project is visibly in trouble. Action must be taken. Select someone to be punished, whether through demotion, rescoping or removal of responsibility, or banishment to an area of no importance. Termination is rarely used if the action is primarily symbolic.

| **SCHEDULE CHICKEN** |
| **Organization and Process** |
| 169 |
| A project of some size with many sub-teams is underway. More than one team is slipping its schedule, but all are loathe to report problems, hoping that some other team will give in sooner and admit delay. It's best if the team that loses the game is one that other teams depend on; then the losing team will take the heat for slippages that would have occurred anyway. |

| **PIPES & FILTERS** |
| **Architectural** |
| [Buschmann+96], *POSA*, 53-70 |
| [Meunier95], *PLoPD1*, 427-440 |
| [Shaw+96], *Software Architecture*, 21-22 |
| For systems that process a stream of data. Each processing step is encapsulated in a filter component. Data passes through pipes that connect filters. Combining filters produces families of related systems. |
| ⋔ LAYERS ♦ 81 is better for systems that require reliable operation, since it is easier to implement error handling. However, LAYERS ♦ 81 does not support the easy recombination and reuse of components, the key feature of this pattern. |
| ✘ [Woodward96] |

| **PLUGGABLE FACTORY** |
| **Creational** |
| [Vlissides98b], *C++ Report*, Nov./Dec. 1998, 52-56, 68 |
| [Vlissides99], *C++ Report*, Feb. 1999, 51-55, 57 |
| Specify and change product types dynamically without replacing the factory instance, which allows clients to vary product types by varying the prototypes it copies. |
| ⋔ This pattern has a structure similar to that of ABSTRACT FACTORY ♦ 2 but with notable differences contributed by PROTOTYPE ♦ 138. |
| ⋔ PRODUCT TRADER ♦ 138 offers several variants of and alternatives to this pattern. |

| **PLUGGABLE FACTORY** |
| **Multimedia** |
| [VandenBroecke+97], *BLTJ*, Winter 1997, 166-187 |
| Create objects from a repository. When a client requests an object from the repository, a reseller object can instantiate a class in the repository by name. Clients can also query the repository for a list of class names. |
| ⋔ This pattern is an extension of FACTORY METHOD ♦ 56 and ABSTRACT FACTORY ♦ 2. |

| **PLUGGABLE VIEW CONTROLLER** |
| **GUI Development** |
| [Spall98], *Java Report*, Feb. 1998, 23-25, 28-32 |
| A Java panel groups the controls for a user interface and represents the view and controller components. A panel has a single reference to its model. Using this reference, a panel may communicate changes to, and request information from, the model. |
| ⋔ This pattern is an extension of MODEL-VIEW-CONTROLLER ♦ 87. |

POCKET-SIZED BROKER

Architectural, Distributed Systems

[Olson98b], *PHand*, 171-181

Extensions of BROKER ♦ 22.

TRANSCEIVER-PARCEL

Architectural, Distributed Systems

172-174

You want to decouple components of an application using BROKER ♦ 22. The architecture is peer-to-peer rather than client-server, and you don't care about efficiency but want an extensible system. All components should use the same mode of communication. Define each component as a transceiver to send or receive parcels. Parcels use VISITOR ♦ 179.

BROKER AS INTERMEDIARY

Architectural, Distributed Systems

174-177

You're using TRANSCEIVER-PARCEL ♦ 133, and you want the dumbest broker imaginable. Create a broker as another transceiver that understands two things: (1) use of a registrar to register a transceiver for the parcels it can receive and (2) routing parcels to transceivers based on information in the registrar.

BROKER AS DIVORCE ATTORNEY

Architectural, Distributed Systems

177-179

You're using BROKER AS INTERMEDIARY ♦ 133. Your application will be distributed across processes and/or processors. Use at least one broker per process. Each broker should use PROXY ♦ 139 for each kind of transceiver it supports in its address space. The Proxy receives parcels from other processes.

BROKER AS MATCHMAKER

Architectural, Distributed Systems

180-181

You're using BROKER AS INTERMEDIARY ♦ 133 or BROKER AS DIVORCE ATTORNEY ♦ 133, and the architecture is inefficient. Allow the broker to perform the first parcel routing between sending and receiving transceivers, supplying the address of the latter to the former and vice versa. The transceivers can then communicate directly.

POINTS AND DEVIATIONS: PATTERN LANGUAGE OF FIRE ALARM SYSTEMS

Concurrent Systems, Distributed Systems, Fire Alarm Systems

[Molin+98], *PLoPD3*, 431-435

Architecture of an object-oriented framework for a family of fire alarm systems.

DEVIATION

Concurrent Systems, Distributed Systems, Fire Alarm Systems

433-435

A fire alarm system must detect extraordinary events. To implement dependencies and information flow between alarm detection and actuators, user interfaces, and other outputs, represent deviations from normal states as a deviation with subclasses alarm, fault, and disturbance. Deviations are the unit of distribution in the system. Deviations are replicated to all control units. The set of deviations defines the system state.

- POINT ♦ 134 describes entities responsible for creating and deleting deviations.
- POOL ♦ 134 provides access to all deviation instances.

POINT

Concurrent Systems, Distributed Systems, Fire Alarm Systems

435-437

To separate the logical behavior of a fire alarm system from the variation among input sensors and output actuators, define the interface between the logical part and the input/output part as a set of points, InputPoints, or OutputPoints. A point has binary state—active or inactive.

- Use BRIDGE ♦ 22 to connect points to I/O Devices.
- PERIODIC OBJECT ♦ 134 allows points and devices to operate concurrently.
- DATA PUMP ♦ 135 enables points and devices to be synchronized efficiently.
- LAZY STATE ♦ 134 provides points with a compact implementation of state-dependent behavior.

POOL

Concurrent Systems, Distributed Systems, Fire Alarm Systems

437-438

You're using DEVIATION ♦ 134 and need a uniform way of accessing all instances regardless of their distribution on different nodes. To provide a standardized interface, collect all instances in pools—virtual containers that contain all instances of the class. A copy of each pool should be on each node in the system.

- A pool may be implemented using MANAGER ♦ 86.

LAZY STATE

Concurrent Systems, Distributed Systems, Fire Alarm Systems

439-440

You're using POINT ♦ 134. Most points have state-dependent behavior. Use STATE ♦ 166, but replace the state member variable with a member function. The current state is not stored explicitly but computed when state-dependent behavior is invoked.

- The state function can be implemented using POOL ♦ 134 to store disablements.

PERIODIC OBJECT

Concurrent Systems, Distributed Systems, Fire Alarm Systems

440-442

To preserve inherent concurrency and meet requirements for performance, demonstrability, and memory efficiency, while still separating scheduling strategies from task behavior, represent each periodic task as a periodic object, where an abstract class defines the pure virtual function tick. Different tasks are implemented as subclasses that define a tick operation. Define scheduling classes to iterate over a collection of periodic objects with different scheduling strategies.

- Using COMPOSITE ♦ 37 for periodic object and having schedulers inherit from the abstract class lets you modularize scheduling further by building a hierarchy of schedulers.
- DATA PUMP ♦ 135 describes how periodic objects can be combined with points and devices.

DATA PUMP
Concurrent Systems, Distributed Systems, Fire Alarm Systems

442-443

Designate devices as periodic objects. Let them pump/push data to points. Control flow follows data flow, and points are passive, so no buffers are needed between points and devices.

PRESENTATION-ABSTRACTION-CONTROL
Architectural

[Buschmann+96], *POSA*, 145-168

Define a hierarchy of cooperating agents to structure interactive software systems. Each agent is responsible for an aspect of the application's functionality and consists of three components: presentation, abstraction, and control. These components separate human-computer aspects of the agent from its functional core and its communication with other agents.

♦♦♦ MODEL-VIEW-CONTROLLER ♦ 87 also separates the functional core of a system from information display and user input handling.

PRIORITIZING FORCES IN SOFTWARE DESIGN
Architectural

[Cockburn96], *PLoPD2*, 317-333

General principles for software design.

PROTECTED VARIATIONS
Architectural

321-322

Protect system integrity from change by identifying areas of predicted variation and creating a stable interface around them.

PERSISTENCE ACCESSORS
Architectural, Client-Server, Persistence

322-324

When the interface to the persistence infrastructure is likely to change, use persistence accessor methods. These are owned by the infrastructure, not the domain, and may be regenerated at any time.

SKILL MIX
Organization and Process

324-325

When team membership is likely to change, separate subsystems by staff skill requirements. This allows specialists to work in their area of expertise and enables successors to see the results of these special abilities in isolation.

♦♦♦ CONWAY'S LAW ♦ 65 states that system design is a copy of the organization's communication structures.

THREE SUBSYSTEMS
Architectural, GUI Development

325

You're developing workstation application software. Create three subsystems: infrastructure, user interface, and application domain. User interface experts can concentrate on human factors and user interface programming; application domain experts can concentrate on application requirements, data needs, and model object behavior; and infrastructure experts can concentrate on system structure.

GENERIC UI, SPECIFIC UI
GUI Development, Organization and Process

325-326

When a team has a high percentage of novices, create two class layers in the user interface subsystem. Use highly skilled developers for the generic classes, and novices for the specific classes. Let the generic user interface developers create frameworks, and the specific user interface developers use them.

GENERICS AND SPECIFICS
Architectural, Organization and Process

326-327

When a team has a high percentage of novices, create two class layers for the problems in the system. Use experts to design the generic parts, and novices to design the specific parts.

APPLICATION BOUNDARY
GUI Development

327

To protect system integrity from changing external components, define the user interface to be outside the application proper. Make all functions of the application accessible through a program-driven interface.

SPLIT VALIDATION
GUI Development

328

Should input validation be performed before the application is called, or should it be performed by the application itself? Perform entry validation in two steps. Keystroke validation is performed in the user interface, and value validation is performed by the application.

♦♦♦ DEFERRED VALIDATION ♦ 33

EDITS INSIDE
Transaction Processing

328-329

When a user can cancel a transaction after making changes but before committing, the most efficient way of editing is to keep two copies of the object, the safe copy and the editing copy.

SUBCLASS PER TEAM
Organization and Process

329-330

When there are conflicting design issues for a class, assign designers in conflict to work on different layers of the class hierarchy.

MODEL HIERARCHY
Architectural, Persistence, System Modelling

330-331

Validation, domain, and persistence are the three parts of any persistent domain object. When they are designed by different teams following SKILL MIX ♦ 135, the class hierarchy for persistent domain classes consists of Model (for the common domain issues), ValidatedModel (for the validation issues), and PersistentModel (for the persistence issues). Model and ValidatedModel can be merged or broken apart, depending on the design.

FACADE
Architectural

331

Provide a single point of call to volatile interfaces. This protects developers from massive rework if an interface changes and provides a unified interface to a set of interfaces.

ᛜ This pattern is an extension of FACADE ♦ 56.

DOMAIN INTERCEPTS
Architectural, Persistence

331-332

To protect developers from massive rework due to persistence layer interface changes, the user interface should never call the persistent subsystem layer directly. Instead, it calls a domain object, whose superclass provides a single point of implementation for the service.

PROACTOR
Communications, Concurrent Systems, Distributed Systems

[Pyarali+99], *PLoPD4*, 133-163

http://www.cs.wustl.edu/~schmidt/patterns-ace.html

Integrate the demultiplexing of asynchronous completion events and the dispatching of their corresponding event handlers.

ᛜ ASYNCHRONOUS COMPLETION TOKEN ♦ 19 is generally used with this pattern.

ᛜ This pattern is related to OBSERVER ♦ 94. PROACTOR ♦ 137 is generally used to asynchronously demultiplex multiple sources of input to their associated event handler, while OBSERVER ♦ 94 is usually associated with a single source of events.

ᛜ This pattern can be considered an asynchronous variant of the synchronous REACTOR ♦ 143 pattern. Reactor demultiplexes and dispatches multiple event handlers when it is possible to initiate an operation synchronously without blocking. PROACTOR ♦ 137 supports demultiplexing and dispatching of multiple event handlers triggered by the completion of asynchronous events.

ᛜ This pattern is often used instead of ACTIVE OBJECT ♦ 6 to decouple a system's concurrency policy from the threading model.

ᛜ CHAIN OF RESPONSIBILITY ♦ 32 decouples events from event handlers, but there is no knowledge of which handler will be executed, if any. In this pattern, there is full disclosure of the target handler.

✗ [Schmidt97]

PROCESS CONTROL
Architectural

[Shaw+96], *Software Architecture*, 27-31

A process control system maintains specified properties of the outputs of the process at reference values called "set points."

PRODUCT TRADER

Creational

[Bäumer+98], *PLoPD3*, 29-46

`http://www.riehle.org/papers/1996/plop-1996-product-trader.html`

Allow clients to create objects by naming an abstract superclass and providing a specification. This decouples the client from the product.

🛠 [Bäumer+97]

PROPAGATOR: A FAMILY OF PATTERNS

Propagation

[Feiler+99], *Proc. TOOLS-23*, July 28 - Aug. 1, 1997

`http://www.sei.cmu.edu/publications/articles/propagator.html`

Consistent update of objects in a dependency network.

These patterns are similar to OBSERVER ♦ 94 or PUBLISHER-SUBSCRIBER ♦ 139, which follow a depth-first propagation. These patterns, however, operate in a dependency network that may be an acyclic or a cyclic graph and may implement different update strategies.

STRICT PROPAGATOR

Propagation

Define a network of objects so that when one object changes state, all directly and indirectly dependent objects are updated immediately.

STRICT PROPAGATOR WITH FAILURE

Propagation

Define a network of objects so that when one object changes state, dependent objects are updated or (in case of failure) marked as invalid.

This pattern extends STRICT PROPAGATOR ♦ 138 with a valid marker.

LAZY PROPAGATOR

Propagation

Define a network of objects so that when one object changes state, other objects can determine whether they are affected by the changes and can bring themselves up to date.

ADAPTIVE PROPAGATOR

Propagation

Define a network of objects so that when one object changes state, dependent objects are updated in a flexible manner. When an object changes, a forward propagation phase marks affected objects as invalid but does not actually update them.

PROTOTYPE

Creational

[Gamma+95], *GoF*, 117-126

[Alpert+98], *Design Patterns Smalltalk Companion*, 77-89

Specify the kinds of objects to create using a prototypical instance, and create objects by copying this prototype.

A command copied before being placed on the history list is a PROTOTYPE ♦ 138.

🛠 [Bäumer+97], [Hüni+95], [Johnson94b]

PROTOTYPE-BASED OBJECT SYSTEM
Architectural

[Noble99b], *PLoPD4*, 53-71

Some programs need dynamically extensible representations of objects that cannot be determined in advance. Have clients send messages to objects that search for a slot to handle the message and delegate messages to the slot.

♦♦ This pattern is related to REFLECTION ♦ 144. The implementation of the object system itself and any associated interpreter are the meta level for the object system.

♦♦ METAMORPHOSIS ♦ 55, TYPE OBJECT ♦ 176

PROXY
Structural

[Gamma+95], *GoF*, 207-217

[Alpert+98], *Design Patterns Smalltalk Companion*, 213-221

[Buschmann+96], *POSA*, 263-275

Provide a surrogate or placeholder for another object.

♦♦ ADAPTER ♦ 6 provides a different interface to an object; Proxy provides the same interface. A protection proxy might refuse to perform an operation that the subject will perform, so its interface may be a subset of the original object's.

♦♦ DECORATOR ♦ 46 is similar in structure to this pattern. The ConcreteComponent in DECORATOR ♦ 46 (the RealSubject in PROXY ♦ 139) implements a behavior invoked by a decorator (the Proxy in PROXY ♦ 139). The primary difference between DECORATOR ♦ 46 and PROXY ♦ 139 is intent. DECORATOR ♦ 46 adds functionality or provides options for dynamically choosing functionality in addition to the core functionality of ConcreteComponent.

✗ [Dagermo+98], [Keller+98a], [Vlissides98a]

PROXY DESIGN PATTERN REVISITED
Structural

[Rohnert96], *PLoPD2*, 105-118

Seven variants of PROXY ♦ 139, Remote Proxy, Protection Proxy, Cache Proxy, Synchronization Proxy, Counting Proxy, Virtual Proxy, and Firewall Proxy.

PUBLISHER-SUBSCRIBER
Behavioral

[Buschmann+96], *POSA*, 339-343

Keep the state of cooperating components synchronized by enabling one-way propagation of changes. One publisher notifies any number of subscribers about changes to its state.

♦♦ The publisher is the subject in OBSERVER ♦ 94. The subscribers are observers.

RAPPeL: A Requirements-Analysis Process Pattern Language for Object-Oriented Development

Analysis

[Whitenack95], *PLoPD1*, 259-291

http://www.bell-labs.com/people/cope/Patterns/Process/RAPPeL/rapel.html

For analysts, developers, and project managers engaged in defining requirements for business applications in an object-oriented environment.

Building the Right Things

Analysis

263-264

To capture, communicate, and validate software requirements, identify requirements sources. Devise a work plan for interviewing and examining the sources and produce a set of interview results. Capture and validate sponsor objectives as well as manage customer expectations. Prioritize requirements. Establish and keep customer rapport during this process.

Managing and Meeting Customer Expectations

Analysis, Customer Interaction, Organization and Process

264-265

To manage and meet customer expectations for a product, create a list of customer expectations, and classify each as a real requirement or wish. Classify each real requirement in the requirements specification using BEHAVIORAL REQUIREMENTS ♦ 142 or PRAGMATIC EXTERNAL REQUIREMENTS ♦ 142. These requirements must be prioritized. Use PROTOTYPES ♦ 142 to ensure system behavior will meet the customer expectations.

Customer Rapport

Customer Interaction, Organization and Process

265

To build a good relationship with a customer, first develop a good rapport with the customer, then move to specifying the customer's requirements. Focus on the user. Don't talk down to them. Don't use too much technical jargon. Use PROTOTYPES ♦ 142.

🏭 CUSTOMER INTERACTION PATTERNS ❖ 43

Sponsor Objectives

Customer Interaction, Organization and Process

266

Hold interviews to build consensus on the most important business objectives (no more than eight). Ask, "If the system will not substantially meet this objective, is that sufficient reason to stop system development?" If the answer is yes, then the objective is a solid one. Each goal should be measurable.

🏭 This pattern is closely related to MARKET WALK-THROUGH ♦ 52.

Defining Requirements

Analysis

266-269

Create and maintain a glossary of common business terms. Use BEHAVIORAL REQUIREMENTS ♦ 142 and PROBLEM DOMAIN ANALYSIS ♦ 141. Validate the requirements specification with the customer.

🏭 REQUIREMENTS VALIDATION ♦ 143

PROBLEM DOMAIN ANALYSIS
Analysis

269-271

To determine the essential nature of the system's problem domain, use problem domain analysis. Use FINDING AND DEFINING THE DOMAIN OBJECTS ♦ 141; INFORMATION NEEDS ♦ 141; CLASSIFYING, ASSOCIATING, AND GROUPING THE DOMAIN OBJECTS ♦ 141; BEHAVIORAL REQUIREMENTS ♦ 142; ELABORATION OF THE DOMAIN OBJECTS ♦ 141; BUSINESS RULES ♦ 142; ELABORATION OF THE DOMAIN OBJECTS ♦ 141; and OBJECT AGING ♦ 141.

INFORMATION NEEDS
Analysis

271-272

Identify the ways users will manipulate information. Use ENVISIONING ♦ 142, USER INTERFACE REQUIREMENTS ♦ 142, and PROTOTYPES ♦ 142.

FINDING AND DEFINING THE DOMAIN OBJECTS
Analysis, Design Process

272-273

To determine objects in the problem domain and define their roles and responsibilities, consider every process, transaction, piece of information, and problem domain entity an object. Use CRC cards. If possible, derive the initial domain model from use cases. Alternatively, a written description of the business process can be used.

👥 SCENARIOS DEFINE PROBLEM ♦ 66

CLASSIFYING, ASSOCIATING, AND GROUPING THE DOMAIN OBJECTS
Design Process

273-275

To capture the set of associations among domain objects, for each object identified in INFORMATION NEEDS ♦ 141, and for each responsibility, trace a simple scenario in which the object uses the behavior. Note all relationships with other objects.

ELABORATION OF THE DOMAIN OBJECTS
Design Process

275

Instead of assigning attributes, state that a responsibility of an object is to convey information that may be held by an attribute. Use INFORMATION NEEDS ♦ 141 to associate information with an object. Use BUSINESS RULES ♦ 142. To capture life cycle and states, use OBJECT AGING ♦ 141.

OBJECT AGING
Design Process

276

If an object changes state, define its life cycle, using BEHAVIORAL REQUIREMENTS ♦ 142. For each domain object, determine whether there are state changes. Name each state and build a state transition diagram, listing the use case event that causes each state change.

👥 FINITE STATE MACHINE PATTERNS ❖ 58, STATE ♦ 166, STATE PATTERNS ❖ 166

OBJECT STEREOTYPES
Design Process

276-278

To determine roles of the objects in the problem domain, Wirfs-Brock has created a list of behavioral stereotypes for objects [Wirfs-Brock93]. Use this as a starting point.

BEHAVIORAL REQUIREMENTS

Analysis

278-281

To determine the system's required behaviors, first consider behaviors in terms of use cases—how clients will use the system. For each client, list all use cases. This will capture the primary external behaviors of the system.

ENVISIONING

Organization and Process

281

Envisioning means: (1) imagining a system to support a set of business processes and (2) conceiving an entirely new set of business processes. Write the entire process, detailing each step. Each step of the process should be considered a potential use case.

REQUIREMENTS SPECIFICATION

Analysis

281-282

Use a basic template to specify requirements that organizes the information into sections that reflect the activities and types of deliverables needed. Use BEHAVIORAL REQUIREMENTS ♦ 142, PROBLEM DOMAIN ANALYSIS ♦ 141, and REQUIREMENTS VALIDATION ♦ 143.

BUSINESS RULES

Organization and Process

282-287

To define and capture business rules so they can be verified and used, James Odell [Martin98] describes a taxonomy that classifies business rules into six types. Divide these into two categories: three that constrain use cases and three that constrain objects and their states.

PRAGMATIC EXTERNAL REQUIREMENTS

Analysis

287-288

Use a template to capture most nonbehavioral requirements as well as the constraining behavioral requirements. Review the constraints with all groups involved in delivery, installation, training, and implementation.

   🏃 GET INVOLVED EARLY ♦ 126, REQUIREMENTS VALIDATION ♦ 143

USER INTERFACE REQUIREMENTS

Analysis, GUI Development

288

Use cases provide a way for verbalizing user tasks. Use PROTOTYPES ♦ 142 to examine the user's views.

PROTOTYPES

Organization and Process

288-290

Work with the customer to build low-fidelity prototypes using paper widgets, drawings, self-stick notes, and index cards. Alternate between prototyping and use case modeling. Prototyping involves users and use case modeling provides rigorous analysis.

   🏃 This pattern has the same intent as PROTOTYPE ♦ 168, PROTOTYPE ♦ 69, and PROTOTYPE A FIRST-PASS DESIGN ♦ 84.

   🏃 This pattern has a different intent from PROTOTYPE ♦ 138, which is a creational pattern where objects clone themselves.

REQUIREMENTS VALIDATION	
Analysis	
290	
To verify that behavioral requirements are correct and complete, have all interested parties read the requirements specification. Conduct review meetings. Follow up on all issues raised. Use PROTOTYPES ♦ 142. Continue requirements verification through each system development iteration.	
ᛝ GET INVOLVED EARLY ♦ 126, PRAGMATIC EXTERNAL REQUIREMENTS ♦ 142	

REACTOR

Behavioral, Distributed Systems, Event-Driven Systems

[Schmidt95], *PLoPD1*, 529-545

`http://www.cs.wustl.edu/~schmidt/patterns-ace.html`

Support the demultiplexing and dispatching of multiple event handlers triggered concurrently by multiple events, and simplify event-driven applications by integrating the demultiplexing of events and the dispatching of the corresponding event handlers.

- ᛝ This pattern provides a FACADE ♦ 56 for event demultiplexing.
- ᛝ Each virtual method provided by the Event_Handler base class is a TEMPLATE METHOD ♦ 171.
- ᛝ An event handler may be created using FACTORY METHOD ♦ 56.
- ᛝ This pattern can demultiplex messages and events that flow through a PIPES & FILTERS ♦ 132 architecture.
- ✗ [Schmidt+95], [Schmidt97], [Woodward96]

RECOVERABLE DISTRIBUTOR

Distributed Systems, Fault-Tolerant Systems

[Islam+96], *CACM*, Oct. 1996, 65-74

This pattern creates local views of global data in a distributed system, maintains consistency between the local and global data, detects processor failures, and recovers global state in the event of processor failures.

- ᛝ This pattern is similar to OBSERVER ♦ 94, where observers are updated automatically when a single subject changes. Here, global and (possibly) local state is updated on a local state change.
- ᛝ A local state manager acts as PROXY ♦ 139 for the global state manager.
- ᛝ This pattern is similar to STRATEGY ♦ 167 in that it provides a uniform interface for a family of protocols.
- ᛝ The relationship between the state-sharing and fault-tolerant components in this pattern follows BRIDGE ♦ 22. This allows the Recoverable Distributor to mix and match data-consistency and fault-tolerant protocols.

RECURSIVE CONTROL

Architectural, Client-Server, Event-Driven Systems, Reactive and Real-Time Systems

[Selic98], *PLoPD3*, 147-171

Separate real-time control aspects from application functionality and control mechanisms. Each component can then be recursively structured into the these three parts, hence the name of the pattern.

- ᛝ Separating control from function is an implementation of STRATEGY ♦ 167.
- ᛝ Structurally, this pattern is related to COMPOSITE ♦ 37.
- ᛝ Behaviorally, this pattern incorporates CHAIN OF RESPONSIBILITY ♦ 32.
- ᛝ OBJECT RECURSION ♦ 92

REFLECTION
Architectural

[Buschmann+96], *POSA*, 193-219

[Buschmann96], *PLoPD2*, 271-294

Split the application into two parts: (1) a meta level provides information about selected system properties and makes the software self-aware; (2) a base level builds on the meta level and includes the application logic. Changes to the meta level affect base level behavior. This allows the system to dynamically change structure and behavior.

- ₶ MICROKERNEL ♦ 87 supports adaptation and change by allowing additional functionality. The microkernel is a socket for plugging in extensions and coordinating their collaboration.
- ₶ PROTOTYPE-BASED OBJECT SYSTEM ♦ 139 takes this pattern to its logical conclusion.

REMOTE CONTROL
Concurrent Systems, Distributed Systems

[Aarsten+96a], *CACM*, Oct. 1996, 50-58

In a simulation, the control of a peripheral device uses variables and events. In reality, this is not the case. Make the data for accessing the peripheral state virtual by using a proxy. Create a class to encapsulate external events. Overload the method to broadcast logical events with a new method that takes an event as a parameter.

- ✕ [Aarsten+96b]

REQUEST SCREEN MODIFICATION
GUI Development, Multimedia

[Towell95], *PLoPD1*, 555-556

A common multimedia problem is the on-screen presentation of multiple actors. To give the impression of depth, objects are ordered. This allows an object to be partially covered by a closer object. Each object updates its appearance by requesting a third party to modify an area of the screen. The third party then requests that each object redraw the appropriate section of itself.

RESOURCE EXCHANGER
Client-Server, Concurrent Systems, Distributed Systems

[Sane+96b], *PLoPD2*, 461-473

`http://choices.cs.uiuc.edu/sane/home.html#dp`

In a concurrent system, servers do more work than clients, so they can become computation and communication bottlenecks. Further, servers on one machine compete for shared facilities, so one busy server can starve another. To manage resources shared among multiple processes, let processes act as generators or acceptors of resources. Acceptors register themselves with an exchanger. When an acceptor requests a resource, it must have a resource to exchange. Each acceptor has a pool of resources based on the credit it has with the system. If acceptors keep resources too long, its pool will eventually be exhausted.

REUSABILITY THROUGH SELF-ENCAPSULATION

Design Process

[Auer95], *PLoPD1*, 505-516

http://www.rolemodelsoft.com/patterns/

Use of inheritance in implementing new classes from scratch, but also useful in refactoring.

DEFINE CLASSES BY BEHAVIOR, NOT STATE

Design Process

506-507

When creating a new class, list the public message names, e.g., instance variables, class variables, and specify the behavior of the class without regard to data structure.

IMPLEMENT BEHAVIOR WITH ABSTRACT STATE

Design Process

507-508

You've applied DEFINE CLASSES BY BEHAVIOR, NOT STATE ♦ 145. To approach implementation without forcing data structure decisions on subclasses, identify state information needed to complete implementation details by defining a message that returns the state instead of defining a variable.

IDENTIFY MESSAGE LAYERS

Design Process, Refactoring

508-510

You've applied IMPLEMENT BEHAVIOR WITH ABSTRACT STATE ♦ 145, or a class has been fully defined. How can methods be factored to make the class efficient and simple to subclass? Identify a small subset of abstract state and behavior methods that all other methods can use as kernel methods. Alter other methods to use these kernel methods when possible.

DEFER IDENTIFICATION OF STATE VARIABLES

Design Process

510-511

You're applying IDENTIFY MESSAGE LAYERS ♦ 145, or a class has been fully defined, and specialization through subclassing is now desired. Once a data structure is defined and methods refer to it, subclasses inherit these assumptions. So, defer identification of state variables as long as possible. Make the base class stateless and let the subclasses add state. Developers of subclasses can choose to inherit state from one of the concrete subclasses or to build from the abstract class.

ENCAPSULATE CONCRETE STATE

Design Process, Refactoring

511-512

The data structure of a class has been identified and its behavior defined. To minimize the negative effect of these decisions on the flexibility of the class hierarchy, when adding state variables, only refer to them with get and set methods.

USE LAZY INITIALIZATION

Design Process

512-514

You're using ENCAPSULATE CONCRETE STATE ♦ 145. Use lazy initialization to set initial or default values of a state variable. To set a variable to its default value, send the set message with a nil argument.

♦♦♦ LAZY INITIALIZATION ♦ 157

DEFINE DEFAULT VALUES VIA EXPLICIT PROTOCOL
Design Process

514-516

Define initial or default values for class-specific variables in an explicit method. Use a selector that has "default" as its prefix and the capitalized variable name as its root.

🏛 DEFAULT VALUE METHOD ♦ 157

ROLE OBJECT
Banking, Design Process

[Bäumer+97], *CACM*, Oct. 1997, 52-59

[Bäumer+99], *PLoPD4*, 15-31

`http://www.riehle.org/papers/1997/plop-1997-role-object.html`

A role is a client-specific view of an object. An object can play several roles, and the same role can be played by different objects. This pattern is a collection of smaller patterns.

🏛 Using DECORATOR ♦ 46, a subclass is a role that decorates the abstract class.

🏛 PRODUCT TRADER ♦ 138 creates and manages role objects.

ROUTER
Communications

[Schmidt96b], *TAPOS*, Vol. 2, No. 1, 1996, 15-30

`http://www.cs.wustl.edu/~schmidt/patterns-experience.html`

Decouple multiple sources of input from multiple sources of output, and route messages without blocking on any I/O channel.

🏛 This pattern uses REACTOR ♦ 143 as a cooperative multitasking scheduler/dispatcher to initialize and route messages in a thread of control.

SCRUM: A PATTERN LANGUAGE FOR HYPERPRODUCTIVE SOFTWARE DEVELOPMENT
Organization and Process

[Beedle+99], *PLoPD4*, 637-651

Scrum is a software development process that assumes a chaotic environment. The goal is to incrementally develop software in short, time-boxed intervals, or sprints.

SPRINT
Organization and Process

640-643

To allocate project work to a team over the development life cycle, during a sprint of about 30 days, the team is shielded from outside chaos and allowed to produce a deliverable.

BACKLOG
Organization and Process

643-644

To organize the work remaining on a project, maintain a prioritized list, the Backlog. The list is dynamic and updated at the end of each SPRINT ♦ 146.

SCRUM MEETINGS
Organization and Process
644-649

To control an empirical and unpredictable development process, meet with the team in a short daily meeting where participants say: (1) what they have done since the last meeting, (2) what roadblocks were encountered, and (3) what they will be doing until the next meeting.

SELECTING LOCKING DESIGNS FOR PARALLEL PROGRAMS
Parallel Programming
[McKenney96a], *PLoPD2*, 501-535

http://c2.com/ppr/mutex/mutexpat.html

Locking designs for parallel programs.

SEQUENTIAL PROGRAM
Parallel Programming
510-511

To eliminate the complexity of parallelization, construct an entirely sequential program. Eliminate all synchronization primitives and the overhead and complexity associated with them.

CODE LOCKING
Parallel Programming
511-513

Use code locking when a small amount of execution time is spent in critical sections or when you only need modest scaling. This is the simplest locking design.

DATA LOCKING
Parallel Programming
511-513

To get better speedups than straightforward parallelizations such as CODE LOCKING ♦ 147, partition data structures so that each portion can be processed in parallel. Each portion has its own independent critical section.

DATA OWNERSHIP
Parallel Programming
515-519

Each CPU or thread should own its own data and shouldn't need locking primitives to access it, but must use a communication mechanism to access another CPU's or thread's data.

🏘 ACTIVE OBJECT ♦ 6 describes an object-oriented approach to this kind of communication.

PARALLEL FASTPATH
Parallel Programming
520-521

To get speedups in programs that can't use aggressive locking patterns throughout, use an aggressive locking pattern for most of the workload (the fastpath) and a more conservative approach for the rest.

READER/WRITER LOCKING
Parallel Programming
521-523

To speedup programs that rarely modify shared data, allow readers to proceed in parallel, but require writers to exclude readers and other writers.

HIERARCHICAL LOCKING
Parallel Programming

523-524

To speedup programs when updates are complex and expensive, but infrequent operations such as insertion and deletion require coarse-grained locking, partition data structures into coarse- and fine-grained portions. For example, use a single lock for the internal nodes and links of a search tree, but use a separate lock for each of the leaves.

   ⚭ If updates to the leaves are expensive compared to searches and synchronization primitives, this approach can produce better speedups than CODE LOCKING ♦ 147 or DATA LOCKING ♦ 147.

ALLOCATOR CACHES
Parallel Programming

524-527

To get speedups in global memory allocators, create a per-CPU or per-process cache of data structure instances. A CPU owns the instances in its cache, so it won't incur overhead and contention penalties to allocate and free them.

   ⚭ Use a global allocator with a less aggressive locking pattern (e.g., CODE LOCKING ♦ 147) when the per-CPU cache overflows or underflows.

CRITICAL-SECTION FUSING
Parallel Programming

527-529

To get speedups in programs with frequent, small critical sections on machines with high synchronization overheads, combine small critical sections into larger ones.

CRITICAL-SECTION PARTITIONING
Parallel Programming

529-530

To get speedups in programs with infrequent, large critical sections on machines with low synchronization overheads, split large critical sections into smaller ones.

SELECTING LOCKING PRIMITIVES FOR PARALLEL PROGRAMMING
Parallel Programming

[McKenney96b], *CACM*, Oct. 1996, 75-82

`http://c2.com/ppr/mutex/mutexpat.html`

Selection of locking primitives for parallel programs assuming a locking design has already been chosen

   ⚭ SELECTING LOCKING DESIGNS FOR PARALLEL PROGRAMS ❖ 147

TEST-AND-SET LOCK
Parallel Programming

78-79

In a parallel program where contention is low and fairness and performance are not crucial, but memory size is a limiting factor, use a locking primitive based on test-and-set.

   ⚭ The simplicity of this pattern pays off if your design enforces low contention, e.g., ALLOCATOR CACHES ♦ 148, DATA LOCKING ♦ 147, DATA OWNERSHIP ♦ 147, HIERARCHICAL LOCKING ♦ 148, or PARALLEL FASTPATH ♦ 147.

QUEUED LOCK

Parallel Programming

79-80

In a parallel program where contention is high and fair access to critical sections is important, use a queued-lock primitive. Since each CPU has its own queue element, only the CPU most recently granted the lock will consume memory bandwidth to access the new lock state.

↟ TEST-AND-SET LOCK ◆ 148 causes every CPU to consume memory bandwidth whenever any CPU releases the lock.

QUEUED READER/WRITER LOCK

Parallel Programming

80

In a parallel program where contention is high, read-to-write ratio is moderate or high, and where fair access to critical sections is important, use a queued reader/writer lock. When a reader is granted the lock, it first checks to see if the next element on the queue also corresponds to a reader. If so, it grants the lock to this next reader. When the last reader leaves the critical section, it grants the lock to the writer at the head of the queue.

COUNTER READER/WRITER LOCK

Parallel Programming

80-81

In a parallel program with a moderate-to-high read-to-write ratio, high contention, and coarse-grained parallelism, use a counter reader/writer lock primitive. The lock maintains the cumulative number of requests and completions for readers/writers. Each requester takes a snapshot of the number of requests so far, increments the appropriate request counter, and then waits for all prior conflicting requests to complete. A read request waits for all prior write requests to complete, while a write request waits for all prior requests to complete.

DISTRIBUTED READER/WRITER LOCK

Parallel Programming

81

In a parallel program with a high read-to-write ratio and high read-side contention, use a distributed reader/writer lock primitive. Use a per-CPU lock for readers and an additional lock to gate writers. A reader acquires only its CPU's lock, while a writer must acquire the writer-gate lock as well as each of the reader-side per-CPU locks.

SELFISH CLASS PATTERN LANGUAGE

Design Process

[Foote+98], *PLoPD3*, 452-470

http://www.laputan.org/selfish/selfish.html

What can be done to encourage reuse.

SELFISH CLASS
Design Process

453-455

Software is a pool of potentially reusable artifacts. For these artifacts to flourish, programmers must find them appealing, so, be sure they reliably solve a useful problem in a direct and comprehensible fashion. Make them widely available.

- ♦♦♦ Use WORKS OUT OF THE BOX ♦ 150 to create software artifacts that are immediately useful.
- ♦♦♦ When LOW SURFACE-TO-VOLUME RATIO ♦ 150 is used, artifacts are easier to understand and provide greater leverage.
- ♦♦♦ GENTLE LEARNING CURVE ♦ 150 recommends building artifacts that reveal their complexity and power gradually.
- ♦♦♦ PROGRAMMING-BY-DIFFERENCE ♦ 150 shows how code can evolve without jeopardizing its identity.
- ♦♦♦ FIRST ONE'S FREE ♦ 151 and WINNING TEAM ♦ 151 present strategies to find a broader audience for reuse.

WORKS OUT OF THE BOX
Design Process

455-459

If it's too much trouble to reuse an artifact, programmers may not bother. Design objects that exhibit reasonable behavior with default arguments. Provide everything a programmer needs to try out these objects. Make it as easy as possible for designers to see a working example.

LOW SURFACE-TO-VOLUME RATIO
Design Process

459-462

Objects with complex interfaces that conceal few of their internals are hard to understand and reuse. Design objects with low surface-to-volume ratios, that is, objects with small external interfaces, or surface areas, that encapsulate a large volume of internal complexity.

- ♦♦♦ GENTLE LEARNING CURVE ♦ 150 recommends that artifacts give new users the appearance of having a low surface area. The full interface is gradually exposed as users learn their way around the artifact.

GENTLE LEARNING CURVE
Design Process

462-464

Complex interfaces can overwhelm novices. Design artifacts to allow users to start with a simple subset of their capabilities and gradually master more complex capabilities as they go along.

- ♦♦♦ This pattern provides many of the same benefits as WORKS OUT OF THE BOX ♦ 150 does early on, while rewarding more experienced programmers with more advanced capabilities later.

PROGRAMMING-BY-DIFFERENCE
Design Process

464-466

You want an artifact to adapt to requirements while maintaining its integrity. Use translators, subclasses, and/or wrappers to supply new states or behavior while leaving the original artifact intact.

- ♦♦♦ ADAPTER ♦ 6, COMPOSITE ♦ 37, DECORATOR ♦ 46, FACADE ♦ 56, and INTERPRETER ♦ 80 describe ways to wrap an artifact to extend functionality.
- ♦♦♦ An artifact using LOW SURFACE-TO-VOLUME RATIO ♦ 150 is easier to wrap than one with a complex external interface.
- ♦♦♦ Artifacts that use WORKS OUT OF THE BOX ♦ 150 are more likely to be incorporated in new work.

FIRST ONE'S FREE		
Design Process		
466-467		
Even a well-designed software artifact will not survive if no one sees it. Give it away.		
🏛 WINNING TEAM ♦ 151 describes an alternate solution when you provide a popular platform.		
WINNING TEAM		
Design Process		
467-469		
Even a well-designed software artifact will not survive if no one sees it. Bundle it with a popular platform.		
🏛 Use FIRST ONE'S FREE ♦ 151 if you have no popular platform at hand.		

SERIALIZER

Persistence

[Riehle+98], *PLoPD3*, 293-312

http://www.riehle.org/patterns/index.html

Efficiently stream objects into data structures. Create objects from the data structures. Examples include writing and reading objects from flat files, relational database tables, network transport buffers, etc.

🏛 Use PRODUCT TRADER ♦ 138 or FACTORY METHOD ♦ 56 to implement the newByName operation in class Serializable.

🏛 The streaming policy can be implemented with STRATEGY ♦ 167.

SERVICE CONFIGURATOR

Distributed Systems

[Jain+97], *C++ Report*, June 1997, 29-42, 46

http://www.cs.wustl.edu/~schmidt/report-art.html

Decouple the behavior of services from the point when service implementations are configured in an application.

🏛 This pattern can use MANAGER ♦ 86 to create and delete services and maintain a repository of services.

🏛 Use with REACTOR ♦ 143 to perform event demultiplexing and dispatching for configured services.

🏛 Dynamically configured services that execute for long periods can use ACTIVE OBJECT ♦ 6.

🏛 The Service base class provides HOOK METHODS ♦ 73 that the Service Configurator uses to initiate, resume, and terminate services.

🗡 [Srinivasan99]

SESSION CONTROL & OBSERVATION

Multimedia

[VandenBroecke+97], *BLTJ*, Winter 1997, 166-187

Control and maintain the state of a networked multimedia session, and notify those interested in that state.

🏛 Session state uses PARTIES & MEDIA AS FIRST CLASS CITIZENS ♦ 96. COMMAND ♦ 35 controls the session state; BUILDER ♦ 23 realizes a session context local to the application.

🏛 This pattern is a specialization of MODEL-VIEW-CONTROLLER ♦ 87.

SHOPPER
Behavioral
[Doble96], *PLoPD2*, 143-145

A consumer creates a shopper object with a list of requests. The shopper traverses a set of objects and collects the requested items.

- ♦♦♦ STRATEGY ♦ 167 can allow mixing and matching of provider traversal and item selection strategies.
- ♦♦♦ Provider traversal can be implemented using ITERATOR ♦ 80.
- ♦♦♦ This pattern is similar to CHAIN OF RESPONSIBILITY ♦ 32, where the providers are the handlers and the shopping list is a composite request.

SINGLETON
Creational
[Gamma+95], *GoF*, 127-134

[Alpert+98], *Design Patterns Smalltalk Companion*, 91-101

Ensure a class only has one instance, and provide a global point of access to it.

- ✗ [Dagermo+98], [Piehler99], [Schmidt97], [Schmidt98a], [Vlissides98a], [Zhang+96a]

SMALLTALK BEST PRACTICE PATTERNS
Smalltalk Idioms, Design Process
[Beck97], *Smalltalk Best Practice Patterns*

Patterns used by experienced, successful Smalltalk developers.

COMPOSED METHOD
Smalltalk Idioms, Design Process
21-22

To divide a program into methods, realize that methods should perform one identifiable task. Keep all operations in a method at the same level of abstraction. This will produce programs with many small methods (a few lines long).

CONSTRUCTOR METHOD
Smalltalk Idioms, Design Process
23-24

To represent instance creation, provide methods to create well-formed instances and pass all required parameters to them.

CONSTRUCTOR PARAMETER METHOD
Smalltalk Idioms, Design Process
25-26

You're using CONSTRUCTOR METHOD ♦ 152. To set instance variables from the parameters, use a single method that sets all variables. Preface its name with "set" plus the names of the variables.

SHORTCUT CONSTRUCTOR METHOD
Smalltalk Idioms, Design Process
26-27

When CONSTRUCTOR METHOD ♦ 152 is too wordy, represent object creation as a message to one of the arguments of the constructor method. Add no more than three of these to a system.

CONVERSION
Smalltalk Idioms, Design Process

28

To convert information from one object format to another, convert from one object to another rather than overwhelm any object's protocol.

CONVERTER METHOD
Smalltalk Idioms, Design Process

28-29

To represent simple conversion of one object to another with the same protocol but different format, provide a method in the original object that performs the conversion. Name the method by prepending "as" to the class of the object returned.

CONVERTER CONSTRUCTOR METHOD
Smalltalk Idioms, Design Process

29-30

To represent the conversion of one object to another with a different protocol, use CONSTRUCTOR METHOD ♦ 152 with the object to be converted as an argument.

QUERY METHOD
Smalltalk Idioms, Design Process

30-32

To represent testing a property of an object, provide a method that returns a Boolean. Name it by prefacing the property name with a form of "be," e.g., is, was, will.

COMPARING METHOD
Smalltalk Idioms, Design Process

32-33

To order objects with respect to each other, implement "<=" to return true if the receiver should be ordered before the argument.

REVERSING METHOD
Smalltalk Idioms, Design Process

33-34

To code a smooth flow of messages, code a method on the parameter. Derive its name from the original message. Take the original receiver as a parameter to the new method. Implement the method by sending the original message to the original receiver.

METHOD OBJECT
Smalltalk Idioms, Design Process

34-37

To code a method where many lines of code share many arguments and temporary variables, create a class named after the method with an instance variable for the receiver of the original method, each argument, and each temporary variable. Use CONSTRUCTOR METHOD ♦ 152 and take the original receiver and the method arguments. Give it one instance method, #compute, implemented by copying the body of the original method. Replace the method with one that creates an instance of the new class and sends it #compute.

EXECUTE AROUND METHOD
Smalltalk Idioms, Design Process

37-39

To represent pairs of actions that have to be taken together, code a method that takes a Block as an argument. Name the method by appending "During: aBlock" to the name of the first method to be invoked. In the body of the Execute Around Method, invoke the first method, evaluate the block, then invoke the second method.

DEBUG PRINTING METHOD
Smalltalk Idioms, Design Process

39-40

To code the default printing method, override printOn: to provide information about an object's structure.

METHOD COMMENT
Smalltalk Idioms, Design Process

40-43

To comment methods, at the beginning of the method communicate important information not obvious in the code.

MESSAGE
Smalltalk Idioms, Design Process

43-44

To invoke computation, send a named message. Let the receiver decide what to do with it.

CHOOSING MESSAGE
Smalltalk Idioms, Design Process

45-47

To execute one of several alternatives, send a message to one of several objects. Each object executes one alternative.

DECOMPOSING MESSAGE
Smalltalk Idioms, Design Process

47-48

To invoke parts of a computation, send several messages to "self."

INTENTION REVEALING MESSAGE
Smalltalk Idioms, Design Process

48-49

To communicate your intent when the implementation is simple, send a message to "self." Name the message so it communicates what is to be done, not how it is to be done. Code a simple method for the message.

INTENTION REVEALING SELECTOR
Smalltalk Idioms, Design Process

49-51

Name methods after what they accomplish.

DISPATCHED INTERPRETATION

Smalltalk Idioms, Design Process

51-55

To allow two objects to cooperate when one wishes to conceal its representation, have the client send a message to the encoded object. Pass a parameter to which the encoded object will send decoded messages.

DOUBLE DISPATCH

Smalltalk Idioms, Design Process

55-57

To code a computation that has many cases—the cross product of two families of classes, send a message to the argument. Append the class name of the receiver to the selector and send the receiver as an argument.

MEDIATING PROTOCOL

Smalltalk Idioms, Design Process

57-59

To code the interaction between two objects that need to remain independent, refine the protocol between the objects to use consistent terms.

SUPER

Smalltalk Idioms, Design Process

59-60

To invoke superclass behavior, send a message to "super" instead of "self."

EXTENDING SUPER

Smalltalk Idioms, Design Process

60-62

To add to a superclass implementation of a method, override the method and send a message to "super" in the overriding method.

MODIFYING SUPER

Smalltalk Idioms, Design Process

62-64

To change part of the behavior of a superclass method without modifying it, override the method and invoke "super."

DELEGATION

Smalltalk Idioms, Design Process

65-65

To allow an object to share implementation without inheritance, send part of its work to another object.

SIMPLE DELEGATION

Smalltalk Idioms, Design Process

65-66

To invoke a disinterested delegate, delegate messages unchanged.

SELF DELEGATION

Smalltalk Idioms, Design Process

67-69

To implement delegation to an object that needs reference to the delegator, send the delegator in an additional parameter called "for:."

PLUGGABLE BEHAVIOR
Smalltalk Idioms, Design Process

69-70

To parameterize the behavior of an object, add a variable to trigger different behavior.

PLUGGABLE SELECTOR
Smalltalk Idioms, Design Process

70-73

To code simple instance-specific behavior, add a variable that contains a selector to be performed. Append "Message" to the ROLE SUGGESTING INSTANCE VARIABLE NAME ♦ 158. Use COMPOSED METHOD ♦ 152 to simply perform the selector.

✘ [Gamma+99]

PLUGGABLE BLOCK
Smalltalk Idioms, Design Process

73-75

To use PLUGGABLE BEHAVIOR ♦ 156 when the code is not worth a separate class, add an instance variable to store a Block. Append "Block" to the ROLE SUGGESTING INSTANCE VARIABLE NAME ♦ 158. Use COMPOSED METHOD ♦ 152 to evaluate the Block to invoke the PLUGGABLE BEHAVIOR ♦ 156.

COLLECTING PARAMETER
Smalltalk Idioms, Design Process

75-77

To return a collection that is the collaborative result of several methods, add a parameter to all the methods that collects the results.

✘ [Gamma+99]

COMMON STATE
Smalltalk Idioms, Design Process

80-81

To represent state that will have different values for all instances of a class, declare an instance variable in the class.

VARIABLE STATE
Smalltalk Idioms, Design Process

82-83

To represent state that might not be present in all instances of a class, put variables that only some instances will have in a Dictionary stored in an instance variable called "properties." Implement "propertyAt:aSymbol" and "propertyAt:aSymbol put:anObject" to access properties.

♦♦♦ This pattern has the same intent as EXTENSIBLE ATTRIBUTES ♦ 163.

EXPLICIT INITIALIZATION
Smalltalk Idioms, Design Process

83-85

To initialize instance variables to their default values, implement a method "initialize" that sets all values explicitly. Override the class message "new" to invoke it on new instances.

LAZY INITIALIZATION

Smalltalk Idioms, Design Process

85-86

To initialize instance variables to their default values, use GETTING METHOD ♦ 157 for each variable. Initialize it if necessary using DEFAULT VALUE METHOD ♦ 157.

♦♦♦ USE LAZY INITIALIZATION ♦ 145

DEFAULT VALUE METHOD

Smalltalk Idioms, Design Process

86-87

To represent the default value of a variable, create a method that returns the value. Prepend "default" to the name of the variable to form the name of the method.

♦♦♦ DEFINE DEFAULT VALUES VIA EXPLICIT PROTOCOL ♦ 146

CONSTANT METHOD

Smalltalk Idioms, Design Process

87-89

To code a constant, create a method that returns the constant value.

DIRECT VARIABLE ACCESS

Smalltalk Idioms, Design Process

89-91

To get and set an instance variable, access and set the variable directly.

INDIRECT VARIABLE ACCESS

Smalltalk Idioms, Design Process

91-93

To get and set an instance variable, use GETTING METHOD ♦ 157 and SETTING METHOD ♦ 157.

GETTING METHOD

Smalltalk Idioms, Design Process

93-95

To provide access to an instance variable, provide a method that returns the value of the variable. Give it the same name as the variable.

SETTING METHOD

Smalltalk Idioms, Design Process

95-96

To change the value of an instance variable, provide a method with the same name as the variable and a single parameter—the value to be set.

COLLECTION ACCESSOR METHOD

Smalltalk Idioms, Design Process

96-99

To provide access to an instance variable that holds a collection, provide methods implemented using DELEGATION ♦ 155 to the collection. To name the methods, add the name of the collection to the collection messages.

ENUMERATION METHOD
Smalltalk Idioms, Design Process

99-100

To provide safe, general access to collection elements, implement a method that executes a Block for each element of the collection. Name the method by concatenating the name of the collection and "Do:."

BOOLEAN PROPERTY SETTING METHOD
Smalltalk Idioms, Design Process

100-101

To set a Boolean property, create two methods with names beginning with "be." One has the property name and the other the negation. Add "toggle" if the client doesn't want to know the current state.

ROLE SUGGESTING INSTANCE VARIABLE NAME
Smalltalk Idioms, Design Process

102-103

Name an instance variable for the role it plays. Make it plural if the variable will hold a collection.

TEMPORARY VARIABLE
Smalltalk Idioms, Design Process

103-104

To save the value of an expression for use in a method, create a variable whose scope and extent is the method. Declare it just below the method selector. Assign it when the expression is valid.

COLLECTING TEMPORARY VARIABLE
Smalltalk Idioms, Design Process

105-106

Use a temporary variable to collect values to be used later in a method.

CACHING TEMPORARY VARIABLE
Smalltalk Idioms, Design Process

106-108

To improve the performance of a method, set a temporary variable to the value of the expression when it's valid, then use the variable instead of the expression.

⚶ CACHING TEMPORARY VARIABLE ♦ 83

EXPLAINING TEMPORARY VARIABLE
Smalltalk Idioms, Design Process

108-109

To simplify a complex expression in a method, remove a subexpression, assign its value to a temporary variable before the complex expression, then use the variable in the complex expression.

REUSING TEMPORARY VARIABLE
Smalltalk Idioms, Design Process

109-110

To reuse an expression in a method when its value may change, execute the expression once and set a temporary variable. Use the variable instead of the expression in the method.

ROLE SUGGESTING TEMPORARY VARIABLE NAME
Smalltalk Idioms, Design Process

110-111

Name a temporary variable after the role it plays.

COLLECTION
Smalltalk Idioms, Design Process

115-116

To represent a one-to-many relationship, use a Collection.

♦♦♦ This implements the same solution as COLLECTION OBJECT ♦ 20.

ORDERED COLLECTION
Smalltalk Idioms, Design Process

116-117

To code collections whose size can't be determined in advance, use an ordered collection as the default dynamically sized collection.

RUN ARRAY
Smalltalk Idioms, Design Process

118-119

To compactly code an ordered collection or array, use a run array to compress long runs of the same element.

SET
Smalltalk Idioms, Design Process

119-124

To code a collection whose elements are unique, use a set.

EQUALITY METHOD
Smalltalk Idioms, Design Process

124-126

To code equality for new objects, define a method called "=." Protect the implementation of the method so only objects of compatible classes will be tested.

HASHING METHOD
Smalltalk Idioms, Design Process

126-128

To ensure that new objects work correctly with hashed collections, if you override "=," override "hash."

DICTIONARY
Smalltalk Idioms, Design Process

128-131

To map one kind of object to another, use a dictionary.

SORTED COLLECTION
Smalltalk Idioms, Design Process

131-132

To sort a collection, use a sorted collection. Set its sort block to use a criterion other than "<=."

ARRAY
Smalltalk Idioms, Design Process

133-135

To code a collection with a fixed number of elements, use an array. Create it with "new:anInteger" so it has space for the number of elements it needs.

BYTE ARRAY
Smalltalk Idioms, Design Process

135-137

To code an array of numbers in the range 0..255 or -128..127, use a byte array.

INTERVAL
Smalltalk Idioms, Design Process

137-138

To code a collection of numbers in sequence, use an interval with start, stop, and an optional step value. Use methods Number»to: and to:by: (see SHORTCUT CONSTRUCTOR METHOD ♦ 152) to build Intervals.

IS EMPTY
Smalltalk Idioms, Design Process

139-141

To see if a collection is empty, send isEmpty. Use notEmpty to see if a collection has elements.

INCLUDES:
Smalltalk Idioms, Design Process

141-143

To search for an element in a collection, send includes: with the element as an argument.

CONCATENATION
Smalltalk Idioms, Design Process

143-144

To concatenate two collections, send "," to the first with the second as an argument.

ENUMERATION
Smalltalk Idioms, Design Process

144-145

To execute code across a collection, use enumeration messages.

DO
Smalltalk Idioms, Design Process

146-147

To execute code for each element in a collection, send do: to a collection to iterate over its elements. Pass a one argument block as the parameter. It will be evaluated once for each element.

COLLECT
Smalltalk Idioms, Design Process

147-149

To operate on the result of a message sent to each element of a collection, use collect: to create a new collection whose elements are the results of evaluating the block passed to collect:.

SELECT/REJECT
Smalltalk Idioms, Design Process

149-150

To filter out part of a collection, use select: and reject: to return new collections. Enumerate the new collection. Both take a one argument block that returns a Boolean. Select: returns elements where block returns true. Reject: returns elements where block returns false.

DETECT
Smalltalk Idioms, Design Process

150-152

To search a collection, send detect:. The first element for which the block argument evaluates to true will be returned.

Entries

INJECT:INTO:

Smalltalk Idioms, Design Process

152-153

To keep a running value over a collection, use inject:into:. Make the first argument the initial value and the second argument a two-element block. Call the block arguments "sum" and "each." Have the block evaluate to the next value of the running value.

DUPLICATE REMOVING SET

Smalltalk Idioms, Design Process

154

To remove duplicates from a collection, send "asSet" to the collection. The result will have all duplicates removed.

TEMPORARILY SORTED COLLECTION

Smalltalk Idioms, Design Process

155

To present a collection with one of many sort orders, send "asSortedCollection" to get a sorted copy of the collection. Send "asSortedCollection:aBlock" for custom sort requests.

STACK

Smalltalk Idioms, Design Process

156-157

To implement a stack, use ORDERED COLLECTION ♦ 159.

QUEUE

Smalltalk Idioms, Design Process

157-159

To implement a queue, use ORDERED COLLECTION ♦ 159.

SEARCHING LITERAL

Smalltalk Idioms, Design Process

159-161

To search for one of a few literal objects, ask a literal collection if it includes the element.

LOOKUP CACHE

Smalltalk Idioms, Design Process

161-163

To optimize complex DETECT ♦ 160 or SELECT/REJECT ♦ 160 loops, prepend "lookup" to the name of the search method. Add an instance variable holding a DICTIONARY ♦ 159 to cache results. Name the variable by appending "Cache" to the name of the search. Make the parameters of the search the keys of the dictionary and the results of the search the values.

PARSING STREAM

Smalltalk Idioms, Design Process

164-165

To write a simple parser, put the stream in an instance variable. Have all parsing methods work from the same stream.

CONCATENATING STREAM
Smalltalk Idioms, Design Process

165-166

You want to improve the performance of a Smalltalk system. To concatenate several collections efficiently, use a stream. See CONCATENATING STREAM ♦ 84.

♯♯♯ This pattern can be combined with HYPOTH-A-SIZED COLLECTION ♦ 84 to create a stream whose collection won't grow.

SIMPLE SUPERCLASS NAME
Smalltalk Idioms, Design Process

168-169

What do you call a class that is the root of an inheritance hierarchy? Use a single word that conveys its purpose in the design.

QUALIFIED SUBCLASS NAME
Smalltalk Idioms, Design Process

169-170

Name a new subclass, by prepending an adjective to the superclass name.

INLINE MESSAGE PATTERN
Smalltalk Idioms, Design Process

172-174

To format the message pattern, avoid explicit line breaks.

TYPE SUGGESTING PARAMETER NAME
Smalltalk Idioms, Design Process

174-175

Name a method parameter by using the most general expected class preceded by "a" or "an." If more than one parameter has the same expected class, precede the class name with a descriptive word.

INDENTED CONTROL FLOW
Smalltalk Idioms, Design Process

175-177

To indent messages, put zero or one argument messages on the same line as their receiver. For messages with two or more keywords, put each keyword/argument pair on its own line, indented one tab.

RECTANGULAR BLOCK
Smalltalk Idioms, Design Process

177-178

To format blocks, make blocks rectangular. Use the square brackets as the upper left and bottom right corners of the rectangle. If the statement is simple, the block can fit on one line. If the statement is compound, bring the block onto its own line and indent.

GUARD CLAUSE
Smalltalk Idioms, Design Process

178-179

To format code that shouldn't execute if a condition holds, format the one-branch conditional with an explicit return.

CONDITIONAL EXPRESSION
Smalltalk Idioms, Design Process

180-182

To format conditional expressions where both branches assign or return a value, format the expression so the value is used where it clearly expresses the intent of the method.

SIMPLE ENUMERATION PARAMETER
Smalltalk Idioms, Design Process

182-183

Name the parameter to an enumeration block "each." If there are nested enumeration blocks, append a descriptive word to all parameter names.

CASCADE
Smalltalk Idioms, Design Process

183-185

To format multiple messages to the same receiver, use a cascade to send several messages to the same receiver. Separate messages with a semicolon. Put each message on its own line and indent one tab. Use cascades for messages with zero or one argument.

YOURSELF
Smalltalk Idioms, Design Process

186-188

To use the value of a cascade if the last message doesn't return the receiver of the message, append the message "yourself" to the cascade.

INTERESTING RETURN VALUE
Smalltalk Idioms, Design Process

188-189

Explicitly return a value at the end of a method, when you want the sender to use the value.

SMALLTALK SCAFFOLDING PATTERNS
Smalltalk Idioms

[Doble+99], *PLoPD4*, 199-219

http://www.rolemodelsoft.com/patterns/

Support for rapid development of prototypes using Smalltalk.

EXTENSIBLE ATTRIBUTES
Smalltalk Idioms

202-204

You're creating a class in a prototype. Other designers will add attributes to your class. Add a dictionary attribute to your class to store additional attributes against symbol keys. Provide an accessor for the dictionary. Use ARTIFICIAL ACCESSORS ♦ 163 or CACHED EXTENSIBILITY ♦ 164.

ᛗ This pattern has the same intent as VARIABLE STATE ♦ 156.

ARTIFICIAL ACCESSORS
Smalltalk Idioms

204-206

You're using EXTENSIBLE ATTRIBUTES ♦ 163. To make accessing extended attributes easier, simulate the presence of accessors for extended attributes.

GENERATED ACCESSORS
Smalltalk Idioms

206-211

You're using EXTENSIBLE ATTRIBUTES ♦ 163. To make it easier for the attributes to be functional, write a code generator that generates standard missing accessors.

ARTIFICIAL DELEGATION
Smalltalk Idioms

211-213

You're creating a class in a prototype. Other designers will add attributes and operations to your class. Override the doesNotUnderstand: method of the delegator class to iterate through its attributes, looking for an attribute that supports the method selector that was not understood.

CACHED EXTENSIBILITY
Smalltalk Idioms

213-216

You're using ARTIFICIAL ACCESSORS ♦ 163 and/or ARTIFICIAL DELEGATION ♦ 164. To identify the implicit behavior and make it part of the explicit behavior of the class, override the doesNotUnderstand: method, substituting code to generate explicit methods for the virtual methods invoked the first time the implicit message is sent.

SELECTOR SYNTHESIS
Smalltalk Idioms

217-218

You're designing a class for a prototype. The class has state-based behavior. You expect additional states and events will be added to your class. Define states and events as symbols. For a given event/state pair, synthesize a method selector by concatenating the state and event symbols, then dispatch based on the resulting selector.

SPONSOR-SELECTOR
Architectural

[Wallingford98], *PLoPD3*, 67-78

Provide a mechanism for selecting the best resource for a task from a set of resources that changes dynamically. Allow a system to integrate new resources and new knowledge about resources at run-time without affecting clients.

♦♦♦ This pattern may use BROKER ♦ 22, PROXY ♦ 139, or STRATEGY ♦ 167.

♦♦♦ This pattern is similar to BLACKBOARD ♦ 22, CLIENT-DISPATCHER-SERVER ♦ 34, and REFLECTION ♦ 144.

STARS: A PATTERN LANGUAGE FOR QUERY-OPTIMIZED SCHEMAS
Database

[Peterson95], *PLoPD1*, 163-177

http://c2.com/ppr/stars.html

An easy-to-query schema for decision-support systems.

QUERY OPTIMIZED DATABASE

Database

164-166

Online transaction processing (OLTP) systems are usually optimized for recording business transactions. Develop a new database optimized for easy querying. The new database will probably be implemented on a different machine from the one that hosts the OLTP database.

✤ Once you have a list of reconstituted entities to model your business area, use KEY BUSINESS ACTIVITIES AND INFLUENCES ♦ 165 to focus on these events.

WHOLE BUSINESS ENTITIES

Database

166-168

To understand a schema for your business, use easily recognized names for the objects in QUERY OPTIMIZED DATABASE ♦ 165. Find entities in your domain that are directly relevant to your problem by examining the reports you use to monitor your business. Make a list of these entities.

KEY BUSINESS ACTIVITIES AND INFLUENCES

Database

168-170

You're using WHOLE BUSINESS ENTITIES ♦ 165. Characterize entities by how they are related to each other. By defining these relationships, you're defining the role of each entity.

TRANSACTION HISTORY

Database

170-173

You're using KEY BUSINESS ACTIVITIES AND INFLUENCES ♦ 165. For each activity, create a fact table with all the information and the transaction history for the activity.

PEOPLE, PLACES, AND THINGS

Database

173-175

You're using KEY BUSINESS ACTIVITIES AND INFLUENCES ♦ 165. Create a table for each person, place, or thing that has a part in the transactions you're examining. These tables should model the entity.

TIME

Database

175-176

To measure changes in business activity, data from a range of specified times must be analyzed. Create a dimension table containing units of time that correspond to some significant event in your business.

DIMENSION ROLL-UP

Database

176-177

You've applied TRANSACTION HISTORY ♦ 165. You want to roll up the level of activity in your business so you can see the big picture for some group of records in a table. Create a table to represent the larger organization to encompass your business dimension. This table should include all information related to the thing to be included on a report. These things should already be listed in WHOLE BUSINESS ENTITIES ♦ 165.

STATE

Behavioral, Finite State Machines

[Gamma+95], *GoF*, 305-313

[Alpert+98], *Design Patterns Smalltalk Companion*, 327-338

Allow an object to alter its behavior when its internal state changes. The object will appear to change its class.

- State objects are often implemented as FLYWEIGHT ♦ 60 objects.
- This pattern can be confused with STRATEGY ♦ 167. If the context will contain only one of several possible state/strategy objects, use STRATEGY ♦ 167. If the context may contain many different state/strategy objects, use STATE ♦ 166. An object is usually put into a state by an external client, while it will choose a strategy on its own.
- FINITE STATE MACHINE PATTERNS ❖ 58, MOODS ❖ 87, STATE PATTERNS ❖ 166
- ✘ [Brown96], [Dagermo+98], [Foster+97], [Hüni+95], [Schmidt97], [Spall98], [Zhang+96a]

STATE PATTERNS

Behavioral, Finite State Machines

[Dyson+98], *PLoPD3*, 125-142

Refinement and extension of STATE ♦ 166.

STATE OBJECT

Behavioral, Finite State Machines

128-130

To get different behavior from an object depending on its current state, encapsulate the state of the object in a "state" object. Delegate all state-dependent behavior to this state object.

- This pattern has the same intent as STATE ♦ 166.

STATE MEMBER

Behavioral, Finite State Machines

130-132

To decide whether a data member belongs in the owning class or in the state object class, if a data member is only required for a single state, place it in the corresponding state object class. If the data member is required for some but not all states, place it in a common superclass. If the data member is state-independent, place it in the owning class and pass it to the state object if necessary.

PURE STATE

Behavioral, Finite State Machines

133

You have a lot of state objects. To reduce the number required, when a state object has no state members, it represents pure state—nothing but state-specific behavior. A pure state object can be shared among any number of objects, reducing the number of state objects required.

EXPOSED STATE

Behavioral, Finite State Machines

134-136

To prevent the owning class from having too many state-specific, state-dependent methods, expose the state object by defining a method in the owning class that returns a reference to it. Make statement-specific inquiries directly to the state object.

STATE-DRIVEN TRANSITIONS
Behavioral, Finite State Machines

136-138

To get the state object to change when the owning object's state changes, have the state object initiate the transition from itself (the current state) to the new state object. This ensures that transitions are atomic and removes state-dependent code.

OWNER-DRIVEN TRANSITIONS
Behavioral, Finite State Machines

138-140

To reuse state object classes among owning classes with different state-transition profiles, if state object classes are used by more than one owning class, and those owning classes have different FSMs, have the owning class initiate the transition between states.

DEFAULT STATE
Behavioral, Finite State Machines

140-142

When creating a new owning object, to ensure it has the correct initial state object, use a method, called by the initialize method, that returns the default state object. Redefine this method in a subclass if a different default state is required.

STATE TRANSITION SYSTEMS
Architectural

[Shaw+96], *Software Architecture*, 32

This is a common structure for reactive systems. These systems are defined in terms of a set of states and a set of named transitions that move the system from one state to another.

STRATEGY
Behavioral

[Gamma+95], *GoF*, 315-323

[Alpert+98], *Design Patterns Smalltalk Companion*, 339-353

Define a family of algorithms, encapsulate each one, and make them interchangeable. Strategy lets the algorithm vary independently from clients that use it.

- 👫 Concrete strategies often make good FLYWEIGHT ♦ 60 objects.
- 👫 TEMPLATE METHOD ♦ 171 uses inheritance to vary part of an algorithm. STRATEGY ♦ 167 uses delegation to vary the entire algorithm.
- 👫 SPONSOR-SELECTOR ♦ 164 enhances this pattern to pick the best ConcreteStrategy at run-time.
- ✗ [Foster+97], [Hüni+95], [Johnson94b], [Johnson95], [Masuda+98], [Ramirez95], [Schmid95], [Schmidt96a], [Schmidt97], [Zhao+98a], [Zhao+99]

STREAMS
Architectural

[Edwards95], *PLoPD1*, 417-426

Allow designers to concentrate on the data flow of a complex system without concern for the techniques individual components use to distribute the computational burden.

- 👫 This pattern works naturally with PIPES & FILTERS ♦ 132.

SURROGATE

Database

[Pang99], *JOOP*, Feb. 1999, 41-44

Allow persistent objects whose data are stored in a relational database to retain inheritance and polymorphism features. Create a table for each class in the inheritance hierarchy. The tables will contain columns for each attribute defined in that class and an additional column representing the common key shared among all subclass tables. The base class has an attribute called subtype.

  ✛ This pattern is an extension of REPRESENTING INHERITANCE IN A RELATIONAL DATABASE ♦ 42.

SURVIVING OBJECT-ORIENTED PROJECTS: A MANAGER'S GUIDE

Organization and Process

[Cockburn98], *Surviving Object-Oriented Projects: A Manager's Guide*

`http://members.aol.com/acockburn/riskcata/riskbook.htm`

Strategies for managing, staffing, and building a development organization.

CLEAR THE FOG

Organization and Process

206-207

You don't know the issues well enough to put together a sound plan, so deliver something. This will tell you the real issues.

  ✛ This pattern has EARLY AND REGULAR DELIVERY ♦ 168, MICROCOSM ♦ 168, and PROTOTYPE ♦ 168 as specializations.

EARLY AND REGULAR DELIVERY

Organization and Process

208-209

You don't know what problems you will encounter during development, so deliver something early. Discover what you don't know you don't know. Deliver regularly and improve each time.

  ✛ CLEAR THE FOG ♦ 168 is the general expression of this strategy.

PROTOTYPE

Organization and Process

210-211

You don't know how some design decision will work out, so build an isolated solution and discover how it really works.

  ✛ CLEAR THE FOG ♦ 168 is the general expression of this strategy.

  ✛ This pattern expresses the same intent as PROTOTYPE ♦ 69, PROTOTYPE A FIRST-PASS DESIGN ♦ 84, and PROTOTYPES ♦ 142.

  ✛ This pattern has a different intent from PROTOTYPE ♦ 138, which is a creational pattern where objects clone themselves.

MICROCOSM

Organization and Process

212-213

You have to create a plan but have never done this sort of project, so run an 8- to 12-week instrumented pilot to get productivity and throughput data for your plan.

  ✛ CLEAR THE FOG ♦ 168 is the general expression of this strategy.

HOLISTIC DIVERSITY

Organization and Process

214-216

Development of a subsystem requires many skills, but people specialize, so create a team from multiple specialties.

- **ᛗ** OWNER PER DELIVERABLE ♦ 169 ensures that someone owns each required deliverable.
- **ᛗ** DIVERSITY OF MEMBERSHIP ♦ 95 ensures that a requirements gathering team includes users.

GOLD RUSH

Organization and Process

218-219

You don't have time to wait for requirements to settle, so start design and programming immediately. Adjust requirements weekly.

- **ᛗ** HOLISTIC DIVERSITY ♦ 169 is a prerequisite for fast, effective communication.

OWNER PER DELIVERABLE

Organization and Process

220-221

Be sure every deliverable has one and only one owner.

- **ᛗ** This is a general strategy with specializations: DAY CARE ♦ 170, FUNCTION OWNERS/COMPONENT OWNERS ♦ 169, and TEAM PER TASK ♦ 169.

FUNCTION OWNERS/COMPONENT OWNERS

Organization and Process

222-223

If you organize teams by components, functions suffer and vice versa, so be sure every function and every component has an owner.

- **ᛗ** OWNER PER DELIVERABLE ♦ 169 is the general expression of this strategy.

SOMEONE ALWAYS MAKES PROGRESS

Organization and Process

224-225

Distractions constantly interrupt your team's progress, so be sure that someone keeps moving toward the primary goal, no matter what happens.

- **ᛗ** This is a general strategy with specializations DAY CARE ♦ 170, SACRIFICE ONE PERSON ♦ 170, and TEAM PER TASK ♦ 169.

TEAM PER TASK

Organization and Process

226-228

A major diversion hits your team, so let a subteam handle the diversion and keep the main team going.

- **ᛗ** This strategy treats each task as both an activity and a deliverable. OWNER PER DELIVERABLE ♦ 169 is the general strategy for ownership and accountability.
- **ᛗ** FUNCTION OWNERS/COMPONENT OWNERS ♦ 169 recommends a team for each artifact in addition to the task of designing it.
- **ᛗ** SOMEONE ALWAYS MAKES PROGRESS ♦ 169 is the general distraction-management strategy.
- **ᛗ** SACRIFICE ONE PERSON ♦ 170 recommends losing only one person to a distraction.
- **ᛗ** DAY CARE ♦ 170 addresses training as a separate deliverable from the software.

SACRIFICE ONE PERSON

Organization and Process

230-231

A minor diversion hits the team, so assign one person to handle it.

- ♦♦♦ TEAM PER TASK ♦ 169 is the general expression of this strategy.
- ♦♦♦ OWNER PER DELIVERABLE ♦ 169 is the general strategy for ownership.
- ♦♦♦ SOMEONE ALWAYS MAKES PROGRESS ♦ 169 is the general distraction-management strategy.
- ♦♦♦ DAY CARE ♦ 170 addresses training as a separate deliverable.
- ♦♦♦ In FIRE WALLS ♦ 67, the distraction comes from requests outside the team. A project manager role protects the other team members.
- ♦♦♦ In MERCENARY ANALYST ♦ 67, documentation is the distraction. A technical writer protects the other team members.
- ♦♦♦ In GATEKEEPER ♦ 67, technical information is the distraction. One team member is designated to protect the other team members.
- ✘ [Janoff98]

DAY CARE

Organization and Process

232-235

Experts are spending all their time mentoring novices, so put one expert in charge of all the novices. The rest of the team keeps going.

- ♦♦♦ SOMEONE ALWAYS MAKES PROGRESS ♦ 169 is the general expression of this strategy.

TEAMWORK AND CONFIGURATION MANAGEMENT

Configuration Management

[Berczuk97], *C++ Report*, July/Aug. 1997, 29-33, 72

Configuration management patterns and how they relate to organization. A revised version may be found online at http://www.enteract.com/~bradapp/acme, along with Appleton's PLoP '98 paper "Streamed Lines," on branching patterns for parallel development, and Cabrera's PLoP '99 paper "Patterns for Software Reconstruction."

PRIVATE VERSIONING

Configuration Management

31-32

You want to checkpoint changes without making the changes available to the entire development team. You want to implement CODE OWNERSHIP ♦ 66, but subsystems never work entirely in isolation. Provide developers a local revision control area to checkpoint changes at a granularity they are comfortable with. Developers should migrate changes to the shared version at reasonable intervals.

INCREMENTAL INTEGRATION

Configuration Management

32

Some development projects have infrequent integration that reflects considerable change. This can make it difficult to use NAMED STABLE BASES ♦ 68. Allow developers to build current software periodically. Developers should be discouraged from having long intervals between check-ins. When you're using PRIVATE VERSIONING ♦ 170, the developer's private copy should be converted to a named stable base weekly.

INDEPENDENT WORKSPACES

Configuration Management

32-33

You're using NAMED STABLE BASES ♦ 68. To balance the need for developers to use current revisions with the desire to avoid having dependencies change constantly, provide developers an independent workspace where they can maintain control of their own environment.

TEMPLATE METHOD

Behavioral

[Gamma+95], *GoF*, 325-330

[Alpert+98], *Design Patterns Smalltalk Companion*, 355-369

Define the skeleton of an algorithm, deferring some steps to subclasses. This allows subclasses to redefine certain steps of an algorithm without changing the algorithm's structure.

- Factory Methods are often called by a Template Method.
- This pattern uses inheritance to vary part of an algorithm. STRATEGY ♦ 167 uses delegation to vary the entire algorithm.
- [Gamma+99], [Masuda+98], [Vlissides98a], [Zhang+96c]

TEMPORAL PATTERNS

Analysis, Time

[Carlson+99], *PLoPD4*, 241-262

For problems arising when objects change over time.

TEMPORAL PROPERTY

Analysis, Time

241-250

You want to track how a property has changed or is expected to change, or both. The property holds a number of discrete values for intervals of time, as opposed to properties such as temperature that can change continuously. Build a model to represent the validity period of each property value. Provide support for clients not concerned with the temporal aspects by adding methods that do not require a time parameter, and assume a default of the current time.

- This pattern is an extension of HISTORIC MAPPING ♦ 16.
- Time period abstraction is an example of RANGE ♦ 9.
- This pattern is closely related to TEMPORAL ASSOCIATION ♦ 172 when you're interested in the intermediate object in the relationship. When multiple relationships and/or properties change over time, use both TEMPORAL ASSOCIATION ♦ 172 and TEMPORAL PROPERTY ♦ 171.
- Use SNAPSHOT ♦ 172 to view one or more properties with time and historical information removed.

TEMPORAL ASSOCIATION

Analysis, Time

250-254

You need to track how the state of object relationships has changed or is expected to change, or both. There is always an intermediate object representing the relationship, so add time information directly to the intermediate object.

- ⵗ This pattern is similar to Boyd's ASSOCIATION OBJECT ♦ 23.
- ⵗ This pattern is closely related to TEMPORAL PROPERTY ♦ 171 when you're not interested in the intermediate object in the relationship.
- ⵗ When multiple relationships and/or properties change over time, use both TEMPORAL ASSOCIATION ♦ 172 and TEMPORAL PROPERTY ♦ 171.

SNAPSHOT

Analysis, Time

255-261

Modify a client interface by adding methods to allow provision of a snapshot object for a point in time. The snapshot object provides a view of one or more properties or relationships with time and history removed. The snapshot should provide the time to which it applies.

THREAD-SPECIFIC STORAGE

Behavioral, Concurrent Systems

[Schmidt+99], *C++ Report*, Nov./Dec. 1997, 33-47, 52

http://www.cs.wustl.edu/~schmidt/patterns-ace.html

Allow multiple threads to use one logically global access point to retrieve thread-specific data without incurring locking overhead for each access.

- ⵗ Objects implemented with this pattern are often used as a per-thread SINGLETON ♦ 152.
- ⵗ PROXY ♦ 139 can shield the libraries, frameworks, and applications from the implementation of thread-specific storage provided by OS thread libraries.
- ⵗ DOUBLE-CHECKED LOCKING ♦ 51 is commonly used by applications that employ THREAD-SPECIFIC STORAGE ♦ 172 to avoid constraining the order of initialization for thread-specific storage keys.

THREE-LEVEL FSM

C++ Idioms, Finite State Machines

[Martin95b], *PLoPD1*, 383-389

FSMs are often implemented as a mixture of control and behavior, which makes them hard to understand. Even when behavior and control are separated, as in STATE ♦ 166, it is difficult to derive new FSMs from old ones and difficult to override old behaviors or add new ones because of a cyclic dependency between behaviors and the control mechanisms. Use inheritance to break the dependency cycle.

TRANSACTIONS AND ACCOUNTS

Accounting, Transaction Processing

[Johnson96], *PLoPD2*, 239-249

Business transaction processing systems cause master files of accounts to be updated. These patterns describe how these systems work and how to improve them.

BUSINESS TRANSACTIONS

Accounting, Transaction Processing

242

Businesses need to prove that things are as they say they are, so they must turn everything into a transaction that can be recorded. The current state of a business should be apparent from the aggregate record.

♦♦♦ When this pattern has been applied, use SEPARATE TRANSACTION PROCESSING FROM ARCHIVAL ♦ 173.

SEPARATE TRANSACTION PROCESSING FROM ARCHIVAL

Accounting, Transaction Processing

242-243

You're using BUSINESS TRANSACTIONS ♦ 173. Use different representations of transactions during processing from those for archival purposes. Don't archive transactions until you've finished all processing related to a business event, including rerunning it and generating management information.

BUSINESS ACCOUNTS

Accounting, Transaction Processing

243-244

Keep a set of accounts that track the current state of the business. State variables are attributes of the accounts.

COMPOSITE TRANSACTIONS

Accounting, Transaction Processing

244

Some transactions are composite transactions, so post a transaction to several accounts; e.g., a sales transaction might be posted to a sales system, an inventory system, and an accounts receivable system.

ADJUSTING TRANSACTIONS

Accounting, Transaction Processing

244-245

Never change a transaction once it has been posted. Instead, post an "adjustment" transaction.

MONTH END CLOSING

Accounting, Transaction Processing

245-246

Finalize all transactions in a month-end closing. If accounts are out of balance, then transactions can be adjusted to fix the problems. After a month-end closing, transactions for that month cannot be changed. Closings can also occur weekly, quarterly, or yearly.

EXPLICIT BUSINESS RULES

Accounting, Transaction Processing

246-248

Separate business rules from transaction-processing software and store them in a database. Each rule must have a specified time during which it is valid. This allows you to stop programming in terms of the implementation language and start programming in the language of the rules themselves.

CONTINUOUS PROCESSING

Accounting, Transaction Processing

248

Process all transactions when they are entered into the system. This includes posting them to accounts, updating the attributes of those accounts, and checking for any dependencies on the updated attributes.

ᛗ This pattern makes it easier to use MONTH END CLOSING ◆ 173.

TROPYC: A PATTERN LANGUAGE FOR CRYPTOGRAPHIC SOFTWARE

Cryptography, Security

[Braga+99], *PLoPD4*, 337-371

Cryptographic software architecture addresses four fundamental services of information security: data confidentiality, data integrity, sender authentication, and sender nonrepudiation.

SECURE-CHANNEL COMMUNICATION

Cryptography, Security

342-345

To structure flexible and reusable cryptographic software for secure communication, define Codifier and Decodifier classes. The Codifier class has a HOOK METHOD ◆ 73 that performs a transformation on the sent message. The Decodifier class has a Hook Method that performs a transformation on the received message.

INFORMATION SECRECY

Cryptography, Security

346-349

To support the sending of sensitive messages so outsiders can't read them, have the sender and receiver share an encryption function and a secret key. The sender encrypts the message; the receiver decrypts it.

ᛗ This pattern does not provide data integrity, sender authentication, or nonrepudiation. Use SECRECY WITH INTEGRITY ◆ 175, SECRECY WITH SENDER AUTHENTICATION ◆ 175, and SECRECY WITH SIGNATURE ◆ 175 to address these issues.

MESSAGE INTEGRITY

Cryptography, Security

347-349

A receiver of long messages can determine whether a message is correct when cryptographic keys are not used, if the sender and receiver agree to use a Modification Detection Code (MDC). Sender computes the MDC of the message and sends it along with the message. Receiver compares the MDC of the message to the received MDC.

SENDER AUTHENTICATION

Cryptography, Security

349-351

The sender and receiver of messages can distinguish their communication from perhaps spurious ones when you're using a secret key and a secure channel if the sender and receiver use a cryptographic algorithm for generation of Message Authentication Codes (MACs). Sender computes the MAC of the message-plus-key. Receiver computes the MAC of the message-plus-key.

SIGNATURE

Cryptography, Security

351-353

The receiver of a message can convince himself and a third party of the identity of the sender, if the sender and receiver use a public-key digital-signature protocol. Sender applies the algorithm using the private key and sends the result (the signature). Receiver encrypts the message with the private key. Only the knowledge of the key by the sender could have produced the signature.

SECRECY WITH INTEGRITY

Cryptography, Security

353-355

To verify the integrity of an encrypted message without loss of secrecy, use a Modification Detection Code (MDC) to compute the MDC of the original message. The message is encrypted and sent, along with the MDC. The secret key to compute the MDC must be different from the public key used for encryption.

SECRECY WITH SENDER AUTHENTICATION

Cryptography, Security

355-356

To authenticate the sender of an encrypted message without the loss of secrecy, use INFORMATION SECRECY ♦ 174 and SENDER AUTHENTICATION ♦ 174. Use a Message Authentication Code (MAC). Compute the MAC over the original message. Both encrypted message and the MAC are sent. The secret key to compute the MAC must be different from the public key used for encryption.

SECRECY WITH SIGNATURE

Cryptography, Security

356-358

A receiver can prove to a third party the authorship of an encrypted message without loss of secrecy, by using INFORMATION SECRECY ♦ 174 and SIGNATURE ♦ 175. Sender signs a message, encrypts the signed message and sends it. Receiver encrypts the message and verifies the signed message.

SIGNATURE WITH APPENDIX

Cryptography, Security

358-359

To reduce the memory requirements for signed messages while increasing the performance of the protocol, use SIGNATURE ♦ 175 and MESSAGE INTEGRITY ♦ 174. Implement a signature protocol over a message hash value, which is a Modification Detection Code. Sender computes the hash value of the message, signs it, and sends both. Receiver decrypts the signature, recovers the hash value, and compares it to the one recovered from the signature.

SECRECY WITH SIGNATURE WITH APPENDIX

Cryptography, Security

359-361

To reduce the memory required to store a message signature while increasing system performance, without loss of secrecy, use INFORMATION SECRECY ♦ 174 and SIGNATURE WITH APPENDIX ♦ 175. Sender computes a hash value of the message and signs it. The original message is encrypted and sent with the signed hash value. Receiver decrypts the message and verifies the signature of the hash value with a computed hash value of the decrypted message.

TYPE OBJECT
Behavioral

[Johnson+98], *PLoPD3*, 47-65

Decouple instances from their classes so the classes can become instances of a class. Use two concrete classes, one whose instances represent the application's instances and one whose instances represent types. Each application instance has a pointer to its corresponding type.

- ⚑ This pattern is similar to STRATEGY ♦ 167 and STATE ♦ 166. All three break an object into pieces, and the real object delegates to the new object.
- ⚑ An object may seem to be acting as DECORATOR ♦ 46 for its Type Object. They have similar interfaces, but a Decorator does not behave like an instance of its Component.

UNDERSTANDING AND USING THE VALUEMODEL FRAMEWORK IN VISUALWORKS SMALLTALK
Smalltalk ValueModel Idioms

[Woolf95], *PLoPD1*, 467- 498

http://c2.com/ppr/vmodels.html

ValueModel is a framework in VisualWorks Smalltalk. Describes ValueModels and how to use them.

USE A VALUEMODEL TO GENERALIZE AN OBJECT'S ASPECT
Smalltalk ValueModel Idioms

471-473

To allow one object to retrieve and change a collaborator object in a uniform way, use a ValueModel to store the value. ValueModel is an abstract class, so you'll actually use an instance of one of its concrete subclasses.

USE A VALUEMODEL TO SHARE A VALUE
Smalltalk ValueModel Idioms

473-474

To allow two objects to share a common value so that both can access and change it, and when one object changes it, the other is notified automatically, place the common value in a shared ValueModel. The sharing objects can register their interest, and the ValueModel will notify them when the value changes.

USE ONCHANGESEND:TO: TO REGISTER INTERESTS ON A VALUE
Smalltalk ValueModel Idioms

474-477

To allow an object using the value in a ValueModel to be notified when the value changes, to register your interest, send the ValueModel "aValueModel onChangeSend: aSelector to: aDependent", in which aSelector is the name of the method to run when the value changes, and aDependent is the object that contains the method (usually "yourself").

USE VALUEMODEL CHAINS INSTEAD OF ONCHANGESEND:TO:
Smalltalk ValueModel Idioms

477-479

If the update performed when a change occurs is so simple that a separate "<something>Changed" method seems unnecessary, eliminate this step and use a ValueModel instead. This will connect the parent and dependent models using two ValueModels.

ENCAPSULATE SENDERS OF VALUE AND VALUE:

Smalltalk ValueModel Idioms

479-481

When should you use "value" and "value:"? Implement separate messages for accessing an object's aspects or values and the ValueModels that contain those aspects.

ENSURE THAT ALL OBJECTS SHARING A VALUE USE THE SAME VALUEMODEL

Smalltalk ValueModel Idioms

481

How can multiple objects that need to share the same value be assured of sharing a single ValueModel? When an instance variable holds a ValueModel, create a get method for it but not a set method, and initialize it in the initialize method. This will ensure that it will only be set once and never reset.

MAINTAIN CONSISTENT VALUEMODEL VALUE TYPES

Smalltalk ValueModel Idioms

481-483

When an object gets a value from a ValueModel, how does it know the type of object it will receive? When defining a variable's type as ValueModel, also specify the type of the ValueModel's value.

USE A VALUEHOLDER TO HOLD A STAND-ALONE OBJECT

Smalltalk ValueModel Idioms

483-484

To wrap ValueModel behavior around objects in instance variables, use a ValueHolder. It will wrap the object and give it ValueModel behavior. Store the ValueHolder in the instance variable.

USE AN ASPECTADAPTOR TO HOLD AN ASPECT OF AN OBJECT

Smalltalk ValueModel Idioms

484-486

How can ValueModel behavior be wrapped around a retrieval of an aspect of another model? Use an AspectAdaptor. Unlike a ValueHolder, the object itself won't be wrapped with ValueModel behavior. Retrieving and storing the object as an aspect of its container model will be wrapped as a ValueModel.

USE A BUFFEREDVALUEHOLDER TO DELAY THE COMMIT OF A NEW VALUE

Smalltalk ValueModel Idioms

486-487

When a view has a number of values, how can the user be allowed to change all of them without changing them in the ApplicationModel and then accept or cancel all the changes at once? Use a BufferedValueHolder as a layer of separation between the model and the ValueModel for a field. A regular ValueModel will immediately store a new value in the model, but the ValueModel stored inside a Buffered ValueHolder will suspend the new value until you tell it to commit to the model.

USE A RANGEADAPTOR TO CHANNEL A NUMBER'S RANGE

Smalltalk ValueModel Idioms

487

To convert a real-world quantity to a percentage so that when the quantity changes, the percentage is automatically recalculated, use a RangeAdaptor, a ValueModel that converts a number in a specified range into a percentage.

USE AN INDEXEDADAPTOR TO HOLD A SINGLE INDEX IN A COLLECTION

Smalltalk ValueModel Idioms

488

To wrap ValueModel behavior around an element in a collection, use an IndexedAdaptor to give a collection element the aspect value.

USE A SLOTADAPTOR TO HOLD A SINGLE INSTANCE VARIABLE
Smalltalk ValueModel Idioms

489-490

To wrap ValueModel behavior around an instance variable without changing the kind of object an instance variable holds, use SlotAdaptor to give an object's instance variable the aspect value. The SlotAdaptor will also allow the element to be shared by multiple dependents.

USE A PLUGGABLEADAPTOR TO HOLD SOME PART OF AN OBJECT
Smalltalk ValueModel Idioms

490-491

To wrap ValueModel behavior around an arbitrary portion of an object, use a PluggableAdaptor to hold an arbitrary portion of an object when no other kind of ValueModel will work.

    ADAPTER ♦ 6

USE A TYPECONVERTER TO CONVERT A VALUE BETWEEN TYPES
Smalltalk ValueModel Idioms

491-492

When two objects want to share a value but each wants a different type, how can the value appear as the appropriate type for each? Use a TypeConverter to convert the type of object.

USE A SCROLLVALUEHOLDER TO HOLD A POSITION IN N-DIMENSIONAL SPACE
Smalltalk ValueModel Idioms

492-493

You're using the ValueModel framework. What object should keep track of how much a point's position on a grid has changed? Use a ScrollValueHolder to hold the scroll position of a point. Set the grid to be the minimum size of each step the point must take when it moves.

USE SELECTIONINLIST TO HOLD A LIST AND ITS SELECTION
Smalltalk ValueModel Idioms

493-494

To set up a list so it can say which item is being used, use a SelectionInList to track a list and its current selection. When you register your interest in one of its aspects, it will notify you of changes.

VIEW HANDLER
GUI Development

[Buschmann+96], *POSA*, 291-303

Manage all views of a software system and allow clients to open, manipulate, and dispose of views. Coordinate dependencies between views and organize updates.

- MODEL-VIEW-CONTROLLER ♦ 87 provides an infrastructure for separating functionality from input and output behavior. This pattern is a refinement of the relationship between the model and its associated views.
- PRESENTATION-ABSTRACTION-CONTROL ♦ 135 (PAC) implements the coordination of multiple views following this pattern. An intermediate level PAC agent that creates and coordinates views, corresponds to View Handler. Lower-level PAC agents that present data to the user are view components.

VISITOR

Behavioral

[Gamma+95], *GoF*, 331-344

[Alpert+98], *Design Patterns Smalltalk Companion*, 371-385

Represent an operation to be performed on the elements of an object structure, letting you define a new operation without changing the classes of the elements on which it operates.

- Visitor can apply an operation over a COMPOSITE ♦ 37 structure.
- A visitor can implement behavior for each node of an INTERPRETER ♦ 80.
- ⚒ [Hüni+95], [Kircher+99], [Masuda+98], [Vlissides98a]

WHOLE-PART

Structural

[Buschmann+96], *POSA*, 225-242

An aggregate component (the whole) encapsulates constituent components (the parts), organizes their collaboration, and provides a common interface to the functionality. Direct access to the parts is not allowed.

- As a variant of this pattern, COMPOSITE ♦ 37 is applicable for representing whole-part hierarchies of objects when clients should ignore differences between compositions of objects and individual objects. Clients will treat all objects in the composite structure uniformly.
- FACADE ♦ 56 provides a simple interface to a complex subsystem. Clients use this interface instead of accessing subsystem components directly; however, FACADE ♦ 56 does not force encapsulation of the components. Clients can still access them directly.

WRAPPER FACADE

Structural

[Schmidt99], *C++ Report*, Feb. 1999, 40-50

`http://www.cs.wustl.edu/~schmidt/patterns-ace.html`

Encapsulate low-level functions and data structures with object-oriented class interfaces.

- This pattern is similar to FACADE ♦ 56, which simplifies the interface for a subsystem. This pattern provides concise, robust, portable, and maintainable class interfaces that encapsulate low-level functions and data structures.
- PATTERNS FOR ENCAPSULATING CLASS TREES ❖ 120

WRITE A LOOP ONCE

C++ Idioms

[Martin95b], *PLoPD1*, 391-393

Sometimes the same loop will appear over and over in different parts of the application. The loop will be similar, but the body will be different. If the looping structure changes once, it must be changed everywhere. Write the loop once. Use inheritance to implement different bodies.

Bibliography

This is an annotated bibliography of all patterns and experience reports mentioned in the Almanac. Experience reports list the patterns they applied (after the ✖ symbol).

Citation ——— [Schmidt96a] Schmidt, D.C., "A Family of Design
Distributed Systems," Proceedings of the Inter

URL ——— http://www.cs.wustl.edu/~schmidt/

Synopsis ——— { Application of a family of design patterns and the
Environment).

Patterns Applied ——— ✖ Acceptor ♦ 4, Abstract Factory ♦ 3,

[Aarsten+95] Aarsten, A., G. Elia, G. Menga, "G++: A Pattern Language for Computer-Integrated Manufacturing," *PLoPD1*, 91-118.
http://www.cim.polito.it/Tools/Gpp.html

Patterns and a framework of reusable classes for the design of concurrent, possibly distributed, information systems, with applications in computer-integrated manufacturing.

[Aarsten+96a] Aarsten, A., D. Brugali, G. Menga, "Designing Concurrent and Distributed Control Systems," *CACM*, Oct. 1996, 50-58.

Summary of G++, a pattern language for concurrent and distributed control systems, and an application in computer-integrated manufacturing.

[Aarsten+96b] Aarsten, A., G. Menga, L. Mosconi, "Object-Oriented Design Patterns in Reactive Systems," *PLoPD2*, 537-548.

Control of reactive and event-driven systems, with emphasis on evolution from simulation to a real system. An extension of [Aarsten+95]. Summarizes the G++ pattern language, the result of 10 years' experience in developing concurrent and distributed control systems and an application involving cooperative autonomous mobile robots.

✖ VISIBILITY AND COMMUNICATION BETWEEN CONTROL MODULES ♦ 61, OBJECTS AND CONCURRENCY [Aarsten+96a], FROM PROTOTYPE TO REALITY ♦ 61, DISTRIBUTION OF CONTROL MODULES ♦ 63, REMOTE CONTROL ♦ 144

[Adams+96] Adams, M., J.O. Coplien, R. Gamoke, R. Hanmer, F. Keeve, K. Nicodemus, "Fault-Tolerant Telecommunication System Patterns," *PLoPD2*, 549-562.
http://www.bell-labs.com/people/cope/patterns/telecom/PLoP95_telecom.html

Addresses reliability and human factors issues in telecommunications software.

[Adams95] Adams, S.S., "Functionality Ala Carte," *PLoPD1*, 7-8.

Determine the incremental performance cost of each feature and present the customer with the aggregate cost of the features selected. This does not change the performance of the system, but it makes the customer aware of the performance consequences of the current configuration.

[Alexander+75] Alexander, C.A., et al., *The Oregon Experiment,* Oxford University Press, 1975.

How Alexander applied his pattern language to the campus at the University of Oregon.

[Alexander+77] Alexander, C.A., et al., *A Pattern Language,* Oxford University Press, 1977.

253 patterns for regions, towns, communities, buildings, rooms, the smallest construction detail, entrances and chairs, for instance. The pictures capture the essence of these patterns and draw the reader in to learn more about the patterns. Brad Appleton has more information about Alexander's new work: `http://www.enteract.com/~bradapp/docs/NoNoO.html`

[Alexander79] Alexander, C.A., *The Timeless Way of Building,* Oxford University Press, 1979.

In this book Alexander describes the "quality without a name." A topic that has generated a lot of discussion on the patterns listserver. This quality is central to the notion of patterns and is closely tied to the goal of capturing patterns, to describe solutions that make us feel more alive.The following site gives more information about Alexander: `http://www.math.utsa.edu/sphere/salingar/Chris.text.html`

[Alpert+98] Alpert, S., K. Brown, B. Woolf, *The Design Patterns Smalltalk Companion,* Addison-Wesley, 1998.

A companion volume to *GoF* with additional information about the design patterns presented from a Smalltalk perspective.

[Anderson99] Anderson, F., "A Collection of History Patterns," *PLoPD4*, 263-297.

Record an object's history by associating the state with the event that caused it.

[Anthony96] Anthony, D.L., "Patterns for Classroom Education," *PLoPD2*, 391-406.

How to teach difficult technical topics.

[Auer+96] Auer, K., K. Beck, "Lazy Optimization: Patterns for Efficient Smalltalk Programming," *PLoPD2*, 19-42.

`http://www.rolemodelsoft.com/patterns/`

Creation of efficient Smalltalk programs. Most patterns could be applied in most languages.

[Auer95] Auer, K., "Reusability Through Self-Encapsulation," *PLoPD1*, 505-516.

`http://www.rolemodelsoft.com/patterns/`

Use of inheritance in implementing new classes from scratch, but also useful in refactoring.

[Barkataki+98] Barkataki, S., S. Harte, T. Dinh, "Reengineering A Legacy System Using Design Patterns and Ada-95 Object-Oriented Features," *Ada Letters*, Nov./Dec. 1998, ACM SIGAda Ann. Int. Conf. (SIGAda '98), Nov. 1998, 148-151.

Reengineering of a large air defense system, written in Ada-95, to improve performance and maintainability and to discover and create a set of reusable software components for future air defense projects.

⚒ BROKER ♦ 22, FACADE ♦ 56

[Beck97] Beck, K., *Smalltalk Best Practice Patterns,* Prentice Hall, 1997.

Patterns used by experienced, successful Smalltalk developers.

[Beedle+99] Beedle, M., M. Devos, Y. Sharon, K. Schwaber, J. Sutherland, "Scrum: A Pattern Language for Hyperproductive Software Development," *PLoPD4*, 637-651.

Scrum is a software development process that assumes a chaotic environment. The goal is to incrementally develop software in short, time-boxed intervals, or sprints.

[Berczuk95] Berczuk, S.P., "A Pattern for Separating Assembly and Processing," *PLoPD1*, 521-528.

`http://world.std.com/~berczuk/pubs/PLoP94/callback.html`

To decouple the work done by geographically distributed teams, upstream components need not be concerned with downstream processing. The paper describes a Telemetry application, but the pattern applies to any system where interfaces between producers and consumers must be cleanly separated.

[Berczuk96] Berczuk, S.P., "Organizational Multiplexing: Patterns for Processing Satellite Telemetry with Distributed Teams," *PLoPD2*, 193-206.

`http://world.std.com/~berczuk/pubs/PLoP95/HTML/BerczukPLoP95.html`

Development of ground software for satellite telemetry systems that considers organizational issues in architecture.

[Berczuk97] Berczuk, S.P., "Teamwork and Configuration Management," *C++ Report*, July/Aug. 1997, 29-33, 72.

Configuration management patterns and how they relate to organization. A revised version may be found online at `http://www.enteract.com/~bradapp/acme`, along with Appleton's PLoP '98 paper "Streamed Lines," on branching patterns for parallel development, and Cabrera's PLoP '99 paper "Patterns for Software Reconstruction."

[Boyd98a] Boyd, L.L., "Architecture Patterns for Business Systems," *C++ Report*, May 1998, 42-50.

Primary architectural characteristics of business systems. Engineering models that define an overall software architecture.

[Boyd98b] Boyd, L.L., "Business Patterns of Association Objects," *PLoPD3*, 395-408.
`http://www.riehle.org/BusinessPatterns/AssocObjects.html`

Association objects represent something that happens at a point in time and have attributes inherent in the relationship (e.g., date, time, or cost) that change when a new association is formed.

[Bradac+98] Bradac, M., B. Fletcher, "A Pattern Language for Developing Form Style Windows," *PLoPD3*, 347-357.

A form organizes a collection of widgets to perform an operation. Nontrivial applications may use many specialized forms.

[Braga+99] Braga, A.M., C.M.F. Rubira, R. Dahab, "Tropyc: A Pattern Language for Cryptographic Software," *PLoPD4*, 337-371.

Cryptographic software architecture addresses four fundamental services of information security: data confidentiality, data integrity, sender authentication, and sender nonrepudiation.

[Brant+99] Brant, J., J. Yoder, "Creating Reports with Query Objects," *PLoPD4*, 375-390.
`http://www.joeyoder.com/papers/`

Dynamic creation of formulas and queries for database-reporting applications. A Smalltalk perspective, but still generally applicable.

[Brown+96a] Brown, K., B. Whitenack, "A Pattern Language for Smalltalk & Relational Databases," *Object Magazine*, Sept. 1996, 51-55.

When and how to define a database schema to support an object model. The identity of the objects, their relationships, and their state must be preserved in the tables of a relational database, a continuation of [Brown+96b].

[Brown+96b] Brown, K., B. Whitenack, "Crossing Chasms: A Pattern Language for Object-RDBMS Integration," *PLoPD2*, 227-238.

Crossing Chasms contains architectural patterns, static patterns that define tables and object models, dynamic patterns that resolve run-time problems of object-table mapping, and client-server patterns.

[Brown96] Brown, K., "Experiencing Patterns at the Design Level," *Object Magazine*, Jan. 1996, 40-48.

Experience mentoring OO novices in the development of an order management system for a pharmaceutical company to allow employees to order resources by selecting type, subtype, and vendor of the resource, as well as the delivery date and other delivery details.

⚒ ADAPTER ♦ 6, COMPOSITE ♦ 37, MEDIATOR ♦ 86, MEMENTO ♦ 87, STATE ♦ 166

[Buschmann+96] Buschmann, F., R. Meunier, H. Rohnert, P. Sommerlad, M. Stal, *Pattern-Oriented Sofware Archicture—A System of Patterns,* Wiley, 1996.

A collection of patterns that spans several levels of abstraction but concentrates on software architecture.

[Buschmann95] Buschmann, F., "The Master-Slave Pattern," *PLoPD1*.

Handle computation of replicated services in a system to achieve fault tolerance and robustness. Separate independent slave components that together provide the same service to a master component, which is responsible for invoking them and for selecting a result. Clients communicate only with the master.

[Buschmann96] Buschmann, F., "Reflection," *PLoPD2*, 271-294.

> Split the application into two parts: (1) a meta level provides information about selected system properties and makes the software self-aware; (2) a base level builds on the meta level and includes the application logic. Changes to the meta level affect base level behavior. This allows the system to dynamically change structure and behavior.

[Bäumer+97] Bäumer, D., G. Cryczan, R. Knoll, C. Lilienthal, D. Riehle, H. Züllighoven, "Framework Development for Large Systems," *CACM*, Oct. 1997, 52-59.

> `http://www.riehle.org/papers/1997/plop-1997-role-object.html`

Experiences with successful large-scale industrial banking projects.

> ✘ DECORATOR ♦ 46, FACTORY METHOD ♦ 56, PRODUCT TRADER ♦ 138, PROTOTYPE ♦ 138

[Bäumer+98] Bäumer, D., D. Riehle, "Product Trader," *PLoPD3*, 29-46.

> `http://www.riehle.org/papers/1996/plop-1996-product-trader.html`

Allow clients to create objects by naming an abstract superclass and providing a specification. This decouples the client from the product.

[Bäumer+99] Bäumer, D., D. Riehle, W. Siberski, M. Wulf, "The Role Object Pattern," *PLoPD4*.

> `http://www.riehle.org/papers/1997/plop-1997-role-object.html`

A role is a client-specific view of an object. An object may play several roles, and the same role can be played by different objects. A Role Object is a collection of design patterns. Using DECORATOR ♦ 46, a subclass of an abstract class is defined as a role and decorates the abstract class.

[Cargill96] Cargill, T., "Localized Ownership: Managing Dynamic Objects in C++," *PLoPD2*, 5-18.

> Management of dynamic object lifetimes in C++.

[Carlson+99] Carlson, A., S. Estepp, M. Fowler, "Temporal Patterns," *PLoPD4*, 241-262.

> For problems arising when objects in a complex information system change over time.

[Carlson99] Carlson, A., "Essence," *PLoPD4*, 33-40.

> Many classes, particularly persistent ones, require that a certain subset of their attributes be valid before an instance can be considered valid. How can this be guaranteed in component-based or distributed environments where the client that creates the instances is outside your design control? Use an essence object for the compulsory properties of the object being created—the CreationTarget. There should be an essence class for each CreationTarget class.

[Carmichael98] Carmichael, A., "Applying Analysis Patterns in a Component Architecture," *Patterns for Distributed Components*, Unicom Seminars Ltd., May 1998.

> `http://www.objectuk.co.uk/Papers/Appat/ApplyingPatterns.html`

An example investment management system that shows how analysis patterns and an architectural pattern may be applied.

> ✘ ACCOUNT ♦ 10, ADAPTER ♦ 6

[Cerwin98] Cerwin, J., "Using the Mediator Design Pattern to Perform Multiplexing," *Java Report*, Feb. 1998, 35-44.

A generic way to manage client-side data requests by applying multiplexing.

> ✘ MEDIATOR ♦ 86

[Cleeland+98a] Cleeland, C., D.C. Schmidt, "External Polymorphism," *C++ Report*, Sept. 1998, 28-43.

> `http://www.cs.wustl.edu/~schmidt/report-art.html`

Allow classes that are not related by inheritance and/or have no virtual methods to be treated polymorphically.

[Cleeland+98b] Cleeland, C., D.C. Schmidt, T.H. Harrison, "External Polymorphism," *PLoPD3*, 377-390.

    `http://www.cs.wustl.edu/~schmidt/report-art.html`

Allow classes that are not related by inheritance and/or have no virtual methods to be treated polymorphically.

[Coad95] Coad, P., D. North, M. Mayfield, *Object Models: Strategies, Patterns, & Applications,* Prentice Hall, 1995.

Real-life examples to illustrate how to build effective object models.

[Cockburn96] Cockburn, A., "Prioritizing Forces in Software Design," *PLoPD2*, 317-333.

General principles for software design.

[Cockburn98] Cockburn, A., *Surviving Object-Oriented Projects: A Manager's Guide,* Addison-Wesley, 1998.

    `http://members.aol.com/acockburn/riskcata/riskbook.htm`

Strategies for managing, staffing, and building a development organization.

[Coplien92] Coplien, J.O., *Advanced C++ Programming Styles and Idioms,* Addison-Wesley, 1992.

To help programmers who have already learned C++ develop their expertise.

[Coplien94a] Coplien, J.O., "Software Design Patterns: Common Questions and Answers," *Proc. Object Expo*, June 1994, 39-42. See also *PHand*, 311-319.

Frequently asked questions about patterns and answers.

[Coplien94b] Coplien, J.O., "Setting the Stage," *C++ Report*, Oct. 1994, 8-16. See also *PHand*, 301-310.

A prelude to the series of C++ Report columns on patterns by Jim Coplien.

[Coplien95a] Coplien, J.O., "Curiously Recurring Template Patterns," *C++ Report*, Feb. 1995, 24-27.

A class is derived from a base class instantiated from a template. The derived class is passed as a parameter to the template instantiation. This pattern captures a circular dependency using inheritance in one direction and templates in the other.

[Coplien95b] Coplien, J.O., "A Generative Development-Process Pattern Language," *PLoPD1*, 183-238.

    `http://www.bell-labs.com/people/cope/Patterns/Process/index.html`

Generative patterns to shape a new organization and its development processes.

[Coplien97] Coplien, J.O., "A Pattern Language for Writers' Workshops," *C++ Report*, Apr. 1997, 51-60.

    `http://www.bell-labs.com/~cope/Patterns/WritersWorkshops/`

The structures and practices of pattern review sessions.

[Coplien99a] Coplien, J.O., "More on the Geometry of C++ Objects, Part 1," *C++ Report*, Jan. 1999, 53-57.

    `http://www.bell-labs.com/~cope/Patterns/C++Idioms/EuroPLoP98.html`

An extension of the pattern language initially described in [Coplien92].

[Coplien99b] Coplien, J.O., "More on the Geometry of C++ Objects, Part 2," *C++ Report*, Mar. 1999, 52-58.

    `http://www.bell-labs.com/~cope/Patterns/C++Idioms/EuroPLoP98.html`

An extension of the pattern language introduced in [Coplien99a], based on [Coplien92].

[Coplien99c] Coplien, J.O., "C++ Idioms," *PLoPD4*, 167-197.

    `http://www.bell-labs.com/~cope/Patterns/C++Idioms/EuroPLoP98.html`

Recasting of idioms in [Coplien92] into a pattern language that treats algebraic types. See an earlier version in [Coplien99a] and [Coplien99b].

[Coplien99d] Coplien, J.O., "A Pattern Language for Writers' Workshops," *PLoPD4*, 557-580.
`http://www.bell-labs.com/~cope/Patterns/WritersWorkshops/`

The structures and practices that support writers' workshops, a continuation of [Coplien97].

[Coram96] Coram, T., "Demo Prep: A Pattern Language for the Preparation of Software Demonstrations," *PLoPD2*, 407-416.
`http://patriot.net/~maroc/papers/demopatlang.html`

Preparation for customer demonstrations.

[Cunningham95] Cunningham, W., "CHECKS: A Pattern Language of Information Integrity," *PLoPD1*, 145-155.
`http://c2.com/ppr/checks.html`

Make validity checks on data.

[Cunningham96] Cunningham, W., "EPISODES: A Pattern Language of Competitive Development," *PLoPD2*, 371-388.
`http://c2.com/ppr/episodes.html`

Organization and process for software development in small teams that describes mental states or episodes.

[Cybulski+99] Cybulski, J.L., T. Linden, "Composing Multimedia Artifacts for Reuse," *PLoPD4*, 461-488.

Defines a multimedia authoring environment capable of producing and applying multimedia components or artifacts.

[Dagermo+98] Dagermo, P., J. Knutsson, "Development of an Object-Oriented Framework for Vessel Control Systems," *Workshop on Distributed Control Architectures*, IEEE International Conference on Robotics and Automation (ICRA), Apr. 1997.
`http://hillside.net/patterns/papers/`

A framework for control and maneuver of ships.

🛠 OBSERVER ♦ 94, PROXY ♦ 139, SINGLETON ♦ 152, STATE ♦ 166

[DasNeves+98] DasNeves, F., A. Garrido, "Bodyguard," *PLoPD3*, 231-244.

Allow objects to be shared and access to them controlled in a distributed environment that lacks system-level support for distributed objects. Provide message dispatching validation and assignment of access rights to objects in non-local environments to prevent improper access to objects in collaborative applications.

[DeBruler95] DeBruler, D.L., "A Generative Pattern Language for Distributed Processing," *PLoPD1*, 69-89.
`http://www.bell-labs.com/people/cope/Patterns/DistributedProcessing/DeBruler/index.html`

Strategies for decomposing complex software systems across processing nodes.

[DeLano+98] DeLano, D.E., L. Rising, "Patterns for System Testing," *PLoPD3*, 503-525. See also *PHand*, 97-119..

Testing patterns for developers and managers, as well as testers.

[Doble+99] Doble, J., K. Auer, "Smalltalk Scaffolding Patterns," *PLoPD4*, 199-219.
`http://www.rolemodelsoft.com/patterns/`

Support for rapid development of prototypes using Smalltalk.

[Doble96] Doble, J., "Shopper," *PLoPD2*, 143-145.

A consumer creates a shopper object with a list of requests. The shopper traverses a set of objects and collects the requested items.

[Duell98] Duell, M., "Experience in Applying Design Patterns to Decouple Object Interactions in the Ingage™ IP Prototype," *PHand*, 59-67.

`http://www.agcs.com/patterns/Papers/`

Application of MEDIATOR ♦ 86 to prevent changes in object interactions from propagating throughout related classes.

🛠 MEDIATOR ♦ 86

[Dyson+98] Dyson, P., B. Anderson, "State Patterns," *PLoPD3*, 125-142.

Refinement and extension of STATE ♦ 166.

[Edwards95] Edwards, S.H., "Streams: A Pattern for "Pull-Driven" Processing," *PLoPD1*, 417-426.

Allow designers to concentrate on the data flow of a complex system without concern for the techniques individual components use to distribute the computational burden.

[Feiler+99] Feiler, P., W. Tichy, "Propagator: A Family of Patterns," *Proc. TOOLS-23*, July 28 - Aug. 1, 1997.

`http://www.sei.cmu.edu/publications/articles/propagator.html`

Consistent update of objects in a dependency network.

[Foote+95] Foote, B., W.F. Opdyke, "Life cycle and Refactoring Patterns that Support Evolution and Reuse," *PLoPD1*, 239-257.

`http://www.laputan.org/lifecycle/Lifecycle.html`

Software development comprises recurring prototype phases, expansion phases, and consolidation phases. These are patterns for evolving from inheritance hierarchies to aggregations and creating abstract classes.

[Foote+96] Foote, B., J. Yoder, "Evolution, Architecture, and Metamorphosis," *PLoPD2*, 295-314.

`http://www.laputan.org/metamorphosis/metamorphosis.html`

Shows how the forces that drive software development lead to more reflective systems.

[Foote+98] Foote, B., J. Yoder, "The Selfish Class," *PLoPD3*, 452-470.

`http://www.laputan.org/selfish/selfish.html`

What can be done to encourage reuse.

[Foote+99] Foote, B., J. Yoder, "Big Ball of Mud," *PLoPD4*, 653-692.

`http://www.laputan.org/mud/mud.html`

The problems that arise in a haphazardly structured system.

[Foster+97] Foster, T., L. Zhao, "A Pattern Language of Transport Systems (Point and Route)," *PLoPD3*, 409-430.

Use of STATE ♦ 166 and STRATEGY ♦ 167 in a public transport model.

🛠 STATE ♦ 166, STRATEGY ♦ 167

[Foster+98] Foster, T., L. Zhao, "Modeling Transport Objects with Patterns," *JOOP*, Jan. 1998, 26-32.

Extension of [Foster+97].

[Foster+99] Foster, T., L. Zhao, "Cascade," *JOOP*, Feb. 1999, 18-24.

Layer and order the parts of a complex whole. Each layer is an instance of COMPOSITE ♦ 37. Cascade is part of a pattern language for transport systems.

🛠 COMPOSITE ♦ 37

[Fowler96] Fowler, M., "Accountability and Organizational Structures," *PLoPD2*, 353-370.

Patterns for analysis and design.

[Fowler97] Fowler, M., *Analysis Patterns,* Addison-Wesley, 1997.

Analysis that reflects conceptual structures of business processes rather than actual software implementations. Patterns for various business domains.

[Fowler98] Fowler, M., "Analysis Patterns," *Java Report*, Apr. 1998, 15-24.

A brief introduction to analysis patterns elaborated in [Fowler97].

[Gamma+95] Gamma, E., R. Helm, R. Johnson, J. Vlissides, *Design Patterns: Elements of Reusable Object-Oriented Systems,* Addison-Wesley, 1995.

Describes simple and elegant solutions to problems in object-oriented design.

[Gamma+99] Gamma, E., K. Beck, "JUnit: A Cook's Tour," *Java Report*, May 1999, 27-38.
`http://members.pingnet.ch/gamma/junit.htm`

JUnit is a framework for writing repeatable tests. The design of the framework is explained incrementally, applying patterns one after another.

🛠 ADAPTER ♦ 6, COLLECTING PARAMETER ♦ 156, COMMAND ♦ 35, COMPOSITE ♦ 37, PLUGGABLE SELECTOR ♦ 156, TEMPLATE METHOD ♦ 171

[Gamma98] Gamma, E., "Extension Object," *PLoPD3*, 79-88.

Add interfaces to a class without changing the class, and allow clients to access the interfaces they need.

[Hanmer+99] Hanmer, R., G. Stymfal, "An Input and Output Pattern Language," *PLoPD4*, 503-536.

Solves problems in interaction between a telecommunications switching system and humans.

[Harrison96] Harrison, N.B., "Organizational Patterns for Teams," *PLoPD2*, 345-352.

Solves problems of designing in teams.

[Harrison98] Harrison, N.B., "Patterns for Logging Diagnostic Messages," *PLoPD3*, 277-289.

Transaction-oriented systems lend themselves to common approaches to logging diagnostic messages.

[Hopley96] Hopley, A., "Decision Deferral and Capture Pattern Language," *PLoPD2*, 335-343.

Models for designing an object-oriented call processing system.

[Hüni+95] Hüni, H., R.E. Johnson, R. Engel, "A Framework for Network Protocol Software," *Proc. OOPSLA '95, SIGPLAN Notices*, Oct. 1995, 358-369.
`http://hillside.net/patterns/papers/`

A framework for network software that implements the signalling system of a multi-protocol ATM access switch. An earlier version implemented TCP/IP.

🛠 ADAPTER ♦ 6, COMMAND ♦ 35, COMPOSITE ♦ 37, PROTOTYPE ♦ 138, STATE ♦ 166, STRATEGY ♦ 167, VISITOR ♦ 179

[Islam+96] Islam, N., M. Devarakonda, "An Essential Design Pattern for Fault-Tolerant Distributed State Sharing," *CACM*, Oct. 1996, 65-74.

This pattern creates local views of global data in a distributed system, maintains consistency between the local and global data, detects processor failures, and recovers global state in the event of processor failures.

[Jackson99] Jackson, E.W., "EventHandler: The Chain of Responsibility Pattern without Cyclic Link Dependencies," *C++ Report*, Jan. 1999, 38-45.

An adaptation of CHAIN OF RESPONSIBILITY ♦ 32 that improves the functionality of the original pattern by avoiding cyclic link time dependencies.

[Jain+97] Jain, P., D.C. Schmidt, "Dynamically Configuring Communication Services," *C++ Report*, June 1997, 29-42, 46.
`http://www.cs.wustl.edu/~schmidt/report-art.html`

Decouple the behavior of services from the time service implementations configured in an application.

[Janoff98] Janoff, N., "Organizational Patterns at AG Communication Systems," *PHand*, 131-138.

Application of organizational patterns in one company's transition to self-directed work teams.

🛠 ARCHITECT CONTROLS PRODUCT ♦ 65, CASUAL DUTY ♦ 130, CONWAY'S LAW ♦ 65, DEVELOPER CONTROLS PROCESS ♦ 65, DOMAIN EXPERTISE IN ROLES ♦ 64, ENGAGE CUSTOMERS ♦ 66, ENGAGE QA ♦ 66, PATRON ♦ 65, SACRIFICE ONE PERSON ♦ 170, SELF-SELECTING TEAM ♦ 63, TRAIN HARD FIGHT EASY ♦ 130, WORK FLOWS INWARD ♦ 68

[Johnson+98] Johnson, R.E., B. Woolf, "Type Object," *PLoPD3*, 47-65.

Decouple instances from their classes so the classes can become instances of a class. Use two concrete classes, one whose instances represent the application's instances and one whose instances represent types. Each application instance has a pointer to its corresponding type.

[Johnson94a] Johnson, R.E., "Patterns of Thought: An Introduction to Patterns," *ROAD*, May-June 1994, 45-48. See also *PHand*, 353-359.

Use of COMPOSITE ♦ 37 in the RTL System, a compiler back-end written in Smalltalk.

🛠 COMPOSITE ♦ 37

[Johnson94b] Johnson, R.E., "Patterns of Thought: How Patterns Work in Teams," *ROAD*, Sept.-Oct. 1994, 52-54. See also *PHand*, 361-368.

Use of several design patterns in a document processing system.

🛠 COMPOSITE ♦ 37, DECORATOR ♦ 46, PROTOTYPE ♦ 138, STRATEGY ♦ 167

[Johnson95] Johnson, R.E., "Patterns of Thought: Patterns and Frameworks," *ROAD*, Mar.-Apr. 1995, 46-48. See also *PHand*, 375-382.

Shows how MODEL-VIEW-CONTROLLER ♦ 87 is composed of simpler design patterns.

🛠 COMPOSITE ♦ 37, MODEL-VIEW-CONTROLLER ♦ 87, OBSERVER ♦ 94, STRATEGY ♦ 167

[Johnson96] Johnson, R.E., "Transactions and Accounts," *PLoPD2*, 239-249.

Business transaction processing systems cause master files of accounts to be updated. These patterns describe how these systems work and how to improve them.

[Keller+98a] Keller, R.K., J. Tessier, G.von Bochmann, "A Pattern System for Network Management Interfaces," *CACM*, Sept. 1998, 86-93.

`http://www.iro.umontreal.ca/labs/gelo/layla/`

Example uses of patterns in a framework for network management interfaces—the middle layer of a network management system.

🛠 ADAPTER ♦ 6, COMPOSITE ♦ 37, MEDIATOR ♦ 86, PROXY ♦ 139

[Keller+98b] Keller, W., J. Coldewey, "Accessing Relational Databases," *PLoPD3*, 313-343.

Defines relational database access layers for database application design, either data-driven or representational.

[Kerth95] Kerth, N.L., "Caterpillar's Fate: A Pattern Language for the Transformation from Analysis to Design," *PLoPD1*, 297-320.

`http://c2.com/ppr/catsfate.html`

Transformation from analysis to a design in a concurrent processing environment.

[Kim+96] Kim, J.J., K.M. Benner, "Implementation Patterns for the Observer Pattern," *PLoPD2*, 75-86.

Extensions to OBSERVER ♦ 94.

[Kircher+99] Kircher, M., D.C. Schmidt, "DOVE: A Distributed Object Visualization Environment," *C++ Report*, Mar. 1999, 42-51.

Design and application of a distributed object visualization environment (DOVE) that supports monitoring and visualization of applications and services in heterogeneous distributed systems.

🛠 ABSTRACT FACTORY ♦ 2, OBSERVER ♦ 94, VISITOR ♦ 179

Bibliography

[Lavender+96] Lavender, R.G., D.C. Schmidt, "Active Object: An Object Behavioral Pattern for Concurrent Programming," *PLoPD2*, 483-499.

`http://www.cs.wustl.edu/~schmidt/patterns-ace.html`

Decouple method execution from method invocation to simplify synchronized access to a shared resource.

[Lea00] Lea, D., *Concurrent Programming in Java, Second Edition: Design Principles and Patterns,* Addison Wesley, 2000.

Assumes object-oriented background but little knowledge of concurrency. Chapter 1 provides a conceptual basis for concurrent object-oriented programming. The three subsequent chapters describe the use of concurrency constructs in Java.

[Lea95] Lea, D., "Christopher Alexander: An Introduction for Object-Oriented Designers," *Software Engineering Notes*, Dec. 1995, 73-77. See also *PHand*, 407-422..

`http://g.oswego.edu/dl/ca/`

An excellent introduction to the work of building architect Christopher Alexander. Alexander's work, like patterns, is not necessarily tied to object-oriented development, so the title is a little misleading.

[Long99] Long, P., "To Do Or Not To Do—That Is The Question," *Java Report*, May 1999, 39-50, 66.

`http://archive.javareport.com/9905/html/from_pages/ftp_feature.shtml`

Enhancement of a rudimentary drawing application, SimpleDraw, to incorporate undo and redo support.

⚒ COMMAND ♦ 35

[Manolescu99] Manolescu, D.A., "Feature Extraction—A Pattern for Information Retrieval," *PLoPD4*, 391-412.

Many applications must search for similarities in large amounts of information in digital libraries. To keep this information under control, work with an alternative, simpler representation of the data. The representation should contain some information unique to each data item.

[Martin+98] Martin, J., J.J. Odell, *Object-Oriented Methods: A Foundation,* Prentice Hall, 1998.

[Martin95a] Martin, R.C., "PLoP, PLoP, Fizz, Fizz," *JOOP*, Jan. 1995, 7-12. See also *PHand*, 423-434.

Report on the first PLoP.

[Martin95b] Martin, R.C., "Discovering Patterns in Existing Applications," *PLoPD1*, 365-393.

Patterns (most are C++ idioms) found in an application and a classification scheme.

[Martin95c] Martin, R.C., "Button, Button, Who's Got the Button?," *ROAD*, Nov.-Dec. 1995, 26-29.

Two approaches for separating clients from servers in a simple application based on a table lamp.

[Martin98] Martin, R.C., "Acyclic Visitor," *PLoPD3*, 93-103.

Allow new functions to be added to class hierarchies without affecting those hierarchies and without creating the troublesome dependency cycles inherent to VISITOR ♦ 179.

[Masuda+98] Masuda, G.N., G.N. Sakamoto, K. Ushijima, "Applying Design Patterns to Decision Tree Learning System," *ACM SIGSOFT 6th Int. Symp. on Found. of Software Engineering*, Nov. 1998, 111-120.

Design patterns applied to the development of a decision tree learning system.

⚒ ABSTRACT FACTORY ♦ 2, BUILDER ♦ 23, COMMAND ♦ 35, COMPOSITE ♦ 37, FACTORY METHOD ♦ 56, STRATEGY ♦ 167, TEMPLATE METHOD ♦ 171, VISITOR ♦ 179

[McKenney96a] McKenney, P.E., "Selecting Locking Designs for Parallel Programs," *PLoPD2*, 501-535.

`http://c2.com/ppr/mutex/mutexpat.html`

Locking designs for parallel programs.

[McKenney96b] McKenney, P.E., "Selecting Locking Primitives for Parallel Programming," *CACM*, Oct. 1996, 75-82.

    `http://c2.com/ppr/mutex/mutexpat.html`

Selection of locking primitives for parallel programs assuming a locking design has already been chosen (see SELECTING LOCKING DESIGNS FOR PARALLEL PROGRAMS ❖ 147).

[Meszaros+98] Meszaros, G., J. Doble, "A Pattern Language for Pattern Writing," *PLoPD3*, 529-574.

What worked well in patterns or pattern languages reviewed at PLoP '95. The guidelines have been reviewed and updated.

[Meszaros95] Meszaros, G., "Pattern: Half-Object + Protocol (HOPP)," *PLoPD1*, 129-132.

Sometimes an object must appear in more than one address space. Divide the object into two interdependent half-objects, one in each address space, with a protocol between them. In each address space, implement the functionality to interact efficiently with the other objects in that address space. Define the protocol to coordinate the activities of each half-object.

[Meszaros96] Meszaros, G., "A Pattern Language for Improving the Capacity of Reactive Systems," *PLoPD2*, 575-591.

Improve the capacity and reliability of real-time reactive systems.

[Metsker98] Metsker, S.J., "The Judge Pattern: Ensuring the Relational Integrity of Objects," *JOOP*, Nov./Dec. 1998, 49-59.

Class diagrams depend as much on the relationships between the classes as the classes themselves. A Judge class acts as a third party, maintaining order in the relationships between pairs of problem domain classes.

[Meunier95] Meunier, R., "The Pipes and Filters Architecture," *PLoPD1*.

An architecture for systems that process a stream of data. Each processing step is encapsulated in a filter component. Data is passed through pipes between adjacent filters. Combining filters allows building families of related systems.

[Molin+98] Molin, P., L. Ohlsson, "Points and Deviations: Pattern Language of Fire Alarm Systems," *PLoPD3*, 431-435.

Architecture of an object-oriented framework for a family of fire alarm systems.

[Mularz95] Mularz, D.E., "Pattern-Based Integration Architectures," *PLoPD1*, 441-452.

Scheme for a paradigm shift from custom development to component integration.

[Nierstrasz99] Nierstrasz, O., "Identify the Champion," *PLoPD4*, 539-556.

    `http://www.iam.unibe.ch/~oscar/cgi-bin/omnbib.cgi`

How a program committee can discuss and accept or reject submissions to a technical conference.

[Noble+99] Noble, J., C. Weir, "High-Level and Process Patterns from the Memory Preservation Society," *PLoPD4*, 221-238.

Patterns for memory-challenged systems.

[Noble99a] Noble, J., "Basic Relationship Patterns," *PLoPD4*, 73-89.

How objects can model relationships in programs.

[Noble99b] Noble, J., "The Prototype-Based Object System Pattern," *PLoPD4*, 53-71.

Some programs need dynamically extensible representations of objects that cannot be determined in advance. Have clients send messages to objects that search for a slot to handle the message and delegate messages to the slot.

[Nordberg98] Nordbeg, M., "Default and Extrinsic Visitor," *PLoPD3*, 105-123.

Variations on VISITOR ◆ 179.

[Olson98a] Olson, D.S., "Patterns on the Fly," *PHand*, 141-170.

    `http://c2.com/cgi/wiki?DonOlson`

Compares software development to fly fishing. Patterns and antipatterns for team structure.

Bibliography

[Olson98b] Olson, D.S., "A Pocket-Sized Broker," *PHand*, 171-181.

Extensions of BROKER ♦ 22.

[Orenstein96] Orenstein, R., "A Pattern Language for an Essay-Based Web Site," *PLoPD2*, 417-431.

`http://www.anamorph.com/docs/patterns/default.html`

How to write and organize essays on a Web site.

[Pang99] Pang, C., "A Pattern of Inheritance and Polymorphism for Persistent Objects Stored in a Relational Database," *JOOP*, Feb. 1999, 41-44.

Allow persistent objects whose data are stored in a relational database to retain inheritance and polymorphism features.

[Peterson95] Peterson, S., "Stars: A Pattern Language for Query-Optimized Schemas," *PLoPD1*, 163-177.

`http://c2.com/ppr/stars.html`

An easy-to-query schema for decision-support systems.

[PHand] Rising, L., ed., *The Patterns Handbook,* Cambridge University Press, 1998.

A collection of stories about one company's experience developing a patterns culture.

[Piehler99] Piehler, M., "Adapting Observer for Event-Driven Design," *C++ Report*, June 1999, 36-42.

Addresses the problem of event-propagation. The solution is a system of patterns, the center of which is a variant of OBSERVER ♦ 94.

🛠 ADAPTER ♦ 6, CURIOUSLY RECURRING TEMPLATE ♦ 43, OBSERVER ♦ 94, SINGLETON ♦ 152

[PLoPD1] Coplien, J.O., D.C. Schmidt, eds., *Pattern Languages of Program Design,* Addison-Wesley, 1995.

Papers from the first patterns conference, PLoP '94.

[PLoPD2] Vlissides, J., J.O. Coplien, N.L. Kerth, eds., *Pattern Languages of Program Design 2,* Addison-Wesley, 1996.

Papers from the second patterns conference, PLoP '95.

[PLoPD3] Martin, R.C., D. Riehle, F. Buschmann, eds., *Pattern Languages of Program Design 3,* Addison-Wesley, 1998.

Papers from PLoP '96 and EuroPLoP '96.

[PLoPD4] Harrison, N.B., B. Foote, H. Rohnert, eds., *Pattern Languages of Program Design 4,* Addison-Wesley, 2000.

Papers from PLoP '98, EuroPLoP '98 or any earlier PLoP or EuroPLoP, not previously published in the PLoPD series.

[Portner95] Portner, N., "Flexible Command Interpreter: A Pattern for an Extensible and Language-Independent Interpreter System," *PLoPD1*, 43-50.

An architecture for an interpreter system that allows for flexible extension of the command language's scope and independence from the actual grammar of the language.

[Pree94] Pree, W., *Design Patterns for Object-Oriented Software Development,* Addison-Wesley, 1994.

Introduces "meta patterns," which describe patterns at a high level of abstraction.

[Price+99] Price, M., D. Prantzalos, "Using the Facade Pattern with CORBA," *Distributed Computing*, Jan./Feb. 1999, 58-59.

Describes how FACADE ♦ 56 and CORBA manage aspects of distributed processing.

🛠 FACADE ♦ 56

[Pryce99] Pryce, N., "Abstract Session," *PLoPD4*, 95-109.
  http://www-dse.doc.ic.ac.uk/~np2/patterns/

When an object's services are invoked by clients, the server object may have to maintain state for each client. The server creates a session object that encapsulates state information for the client. The server returns a pointer to the session object.

[Pyarali+98] Pyarali, I., T.H. Harrison, D.C. Schmidt, "Asynchronous Completion Token," *PLoPD3*, 245-260.
  http://www.cs.wustl.edu/~schmidt/patterns-ace.html

Allows applications to associate state with the completion of asynchronous operations.

[Pyarali+99] Pyarali, I., T.H. Harrison, D.C. Schmidt, T.D. Jordan, "Proactor," *PLoPD4*, 133-163.
  http://www.cs.wustl.edu/~schmidt/patterns-ace.html

Integrate the demultiplexing of asynchronous completion events and the dispatching of their corresponding event handlers.

[Ramirez95] Ramirez, R.L., "A Design Patterns Experience Report," *ROAD*, Nov.-Dec. 1995, 53-55.

Application of patterns in developing an object-oriented framework for analyzing hardware errors.

✘ ADAPTER ♦ 6, FACADE ♦ 56, STRATEGY ♦ 167

[Ran95] Ran, A.S., "Patterns of Events," *PLoPD1*, 547-553.

Event processing in a distributed real-time control and information system.

[Ran96] Ran, A.S., "MOODS: Models for Object-Oriented Design of State," *PLoPD2*, 119-142.

Design and implementation of objects with complex, state-dependent representation and behavior, or "moods."

[Riehle+95] Riehle, D., H. Züllighoven, "A Pattern Language for Tool Construction and Integration Based on the Tools and Materials Metaphor," *PLoPD1*, 9-42.
  http://www.riehle.org/papers/1994/plop-1994-tools.html

In the Tools and Materials Metaphor, people have the necessary skills for their work, so there is no need to define a fixed work flow. People decide how to organize their work and their environment.

[Riehle+98] Riehle, D., W. Siberski, D. Bäumer, D. Megert, H. Züllighoven, "Serializer," *PLoPD3*, 293-312.
  http://www.riehle.org/patterns/index.html

Efficiently stream objects into data structures. Create objects from the data structures. Examples include writing and reading objects from flat files, relational database tables, network transport buffers, etc.

[Riehle96a] Riehle, D., "The Event Notification Pattern—Integrating Implicit Invocation with Object-Orientation," *TAPOS*, Vol. 2, No. 1, 1996, 43-52.
  http://www.riehle.org/papers/1996/tapos-1996-event.html

Changes in one object often require changes in dependent objects. Use implicit invocation. State changes, dependencies, and links among these objects become first-class objects.

[Riehle96b] Riehle, D., "Patterns for Encapsulating Class Trees," *PLoPD2*, 87-104.
  http://www.riehle.org/papers/1995/plop-1995-trading.html

Encapsulation of class hierarchies behind their root classes.

[Riehle98] Riehle, D., "Bureaucracy," *PLoPD3*, 163-185.
  http://www.riehle.org/patterns/index.html

A composite pattern for building an hierarchical structure to interact with clients on every level but needs no external control and maintains internal consistency itself.

[Rising99] Rising, L., "Customer Interaction Patterns," *PLoPD4*, 585-609.

For developers who interact with customers.

[Roberts+98] Roberts, D., R.E. Johnson, "Patterns for Evolving Frameworks," *PLoPD3*, 471-486.
`http://st-www.cs.uiuc.edu/users/droberts/evolve.html`

A common path that frameworks take.

[Rohnert96] Rohnert, H., "The Proxy Design Pattern Revisited," *PLoPD2*, 105-118.

Seven variants of PROXY ♦ 139, Remote Proxy, Protection Proxy, Cache Proxy, Synchronization Proxy, Counting Proxy, Virtual Proxy, and Firewall Proxy.

[Rossi+96] Rossi, G., A. Garrido, S. Carvalho, "Design Patterns for Object-Oriented Hypermedia Applications," *PLoPD2*, 177-191.

Design patterns for object-oriented applications with hypermedia functionality.

[Rossi+99] Rossi, G., D. Schwabe, F. Lyardet, "Patterns for Designing Navigable Information Spaces," *PLoPD4*, 445-460.

For hypermedia in stand-alone applications, dynamic Web sites, or information systems.

[Rubel95] Rubel, B., "Patterns for Generating a Layered Architecture," *PLoPD1*, 119-128.

Provide a natural decomposition of system requirements into a layered architecture. Mechanical control systems are used as an example.

[Sane+96a] Sane, A., R. Campbell, "Detachable Inspector/Removable cout: A Structural Pattern for Designing Transparent Layered Services," *PLoPD2*, 159-175.
`http://choices.cs.uiuc.edu/sane/home.html#dp`

Decouple and segregate meta-facilities so they can be changed or removed without affecting the program.

[Sane+96b] Sane, A., R. Campbell, "Resource Exchanger: A Behavioral Pattern for Low-Overhead Concurrent Resource Management," *PLoPD2*, 461-473.
`http://choices.cs.uiuc.edu/sane/home.html#dp`

To manage resources shared among multiple processes, let processes act as generators or acceptors of resources. Acceptors register themselves with an Exchanger.

[Schmid95] Schmid, H.A., "Creating the Architecture of a Manufacturing Framework by Design Patterns," *Proc. OOPSLA '95*, Oct. 1995, 370-384. See also *PHand*, 443-470.

Design process of a framework for the control of automated manufacturing systems, performed as a sequence of transformation steps, guided using design patterns.

⚒ ADAPTER ♦ 6, COMMAND ♦ 35, MEDIATOR ♦ 86, STRATEGY ♦ 167

[Schmid96] Schmid, H.A., "Creating Applications from Components: A Manufacturing Framework Design," *IEEE Software*, Nov. 1996, 67-75.

Extension of [Schmid95].

[Schmidt+95] Schmidt, D.C., P. Stephenson, "Using Design Patterns to Evolve System Software from Unix to Windows NT," *C++ Report*, Mar./Apr. 1995, 47-60. See also *PHand*, 471-504.
`http://www.cs.wustl.edu/~schmidt/report-art.html`

Use of design patterns to port systems software between UNIX and Windows NT on a telecommunication switch management project at Ericsson/GE Mobile Communications.

⚒ ACCEPTOR ♦ 3, REACTOR ♦ 143

[Schmidt+96] Schmidt, D.C., C.D. Cranor, "Half-Sync/Half-Async: An Architectural Pattern for Efficient and Well-Structured Concurrent I/O," *PLoPD2*, 437-459.
`http://www.cs.wustl.edu/~schmidt/patterns-ace.html`

Integrates synchronous and asynchronous I/O models in concurrent programming.

[Schmidt+98] Schmidt, D.C., T.H. Harrison, "Double-Checked Locking," *PLoPD3*, 363-375.
`http://www.cs.wustl.edu/~schmidt/patterns-ace.html`

Reduce contention and synchronization overhead when critical sections of code should be executed just once but must be thread-safe when they do acquire locks.

[Schmidt+99] Schmidt, D.C., T.H. Harrison, N. Pryce, "Thread-Specific Storage for C/C++: An Object Behavioral Pattern for Accessing per-Thread State Efficiently," *C++ Report*, Nov./Dec. 1997, 33-47, 52.

`http://www.cs.wustl.edu/~schmidt/patterns-ace.html`

Allow multiple threads to use one logically global access point to retrieve thread-specific data without incurring locking overhead for each access.

[Schmidt95] Schmidt, D.C., "Reactor: An Object Behavioral Pattern for Concurrent Event Demultiplexing and Event Handler Dispatching," *PLoPD1*, 529-545.

`http://www.cs.wustl.edu/~schmidt/patterns-ace.html`

Support the demultiplexing and dispatching of multiple event handlers triggered concurrently by multiple events, and simplify event-driven applications by integrating the demultiplexing of events and the dispatching of the corresponding event handlers.

[Schmidt96a] Schmidt, D.C., "A Family of Design Patterns for Flexibly Configuring Network Services in Distributed Systems," *Proc. Int. Conf. Configurable Distributed Systems*, May 1996.

`http://www.cs.wustl.edu/~schmidt/patterns-experience.html`

Application of a family of design patterns and the implementation of ACCEPTOR ♦ 3 in ACE (Adaptive Communications).

🛠 ACCEPTOR ♦ 3, ABSTRACT FACTORY ♦ 2, BRIDGE ♦ 22, FACTORY METHOD ♦ 56, STRATEGY ♦ 167

[Schmidt96b] Schmidt, D.C., "A Family of Design Patterns for Application-Level Gateways," *TAPOS*, Vol. 2, No. 1, 1996, 15-30.

`http://www.cs.wustl.edu/~schmidt/patterns-experience.html`

Decouple multiple sources of input from multiple sources of output, and route messages without blocking on any I/O channel.

[Schmidt97] Schmidt, D.C., "Applying Design Patterns and Frameworks to Develop Object-Oriented Communication Software," *Handbook of Programming Languages*, Vol. I, P. Salus, ed., MacMillan Computer Publishing, 1997.

`http://www.cs.wustl.edu/~schmidt/ACE-papers.html`

Describes the development of high-performance concurrent Web servers using the ACE framework.

🛠 ACCEPTOR ♦ 3, ACTIVE OBJECT ♦ 6, HALF-SYNC/HALF-ASYNC ♦ 71, REACTOR ♦ 143, PROACTOR ♦ 137, ADAPTER ♦ 6, SINGLETON ♦ 152, STATE ♦ 166, STRATEGY ♦ 167

[Schmidt98a] Schmidt, D.C., "Applying Design Patterns to Simplify Signal Handling," *C++ Report*, Apr. 1998, 43-47.

`http://www.cs.wustl.edu/~schmidt/report-art.html`

Use of patterns to simplify the development of components that avoid traps and pitfalls associated with signals and signal handling.

🛠 ADAPTER ♦ 6, HOOK METHOD ♦ 73, SINGLETON ♦ 152

[Schmidt98b] Schmidt, D.C., "Acceptor and Connector," *PLoPD3*, 191-229.

`http://www.cs.wustl.edu/~schmidt/report-art.html`

Decouple service initialization from the services provided for active or passive initialization.

[Schmidt99] Schmidt, D.C., "Wrapper Facade," *C++ Report*, Feb. 1999, 40-50.

`http://www.cs.wustl.edu/~schmidt/patterns-ace.html`

Encapsulate low-level functions and data structures with object-oriented class interfaces.

[Selic98] Selic, B., "Recursive Control," *PLoPD3*, 147-171.

Separate real-time control aspects from application functionality and control mechanisms. Each components can then be recursively structured into these three parts, hence the name of the pattern.

[Shaw+96] Shaw, M., D. Garlan, *Software Architecture,* Prentice Hall, 1996.

Useful abstractions of system design. Extension of [Shaw95] and [Shaw96].

[Shaw95] Shaw, M., "Patterns for Software Architectures," *PLoPD1*, 453-462.

Architectural patterns. Continued in [Shaw96].

[Shaw96] Shaw, M., "Some Patterns for Software Architectures," *PLoPD2*, 252-269.

Guidance for high-level system design. Continuation of [Shaw95].

[Silva+98] Silva, A.R., J.D. Pereira, J.A. Marques, "Object Recovery," *PLoPD3*, 261-276.

http://albertina.inesc.pt/~ars/dasco.html

Define a generic object recovery algorithm and decouple the recovery portion from the object's functionality to support different algorithms.

[Silva+99] Silva, A.R., J.D. Pereira, J.A. Marques, "Object Synchronizer: A Design Pattern for Object Synchronization," *PLoPD4*, 111-132.

http://albertina.inesc.pt/~ars/dasco.html

Decouple object synchronization from object functionality. Invocations on an object are intercepted by a synchronization interface to allow them to proceed, delay, or reject them.

[Sommerlad+96] Sommerlad, P., M. Stal, "The Client-Dispatcher-Server Design Pattern," *PLoPD2*.

A dispatcher component is an intermediary between clients and servers. The dispatcher provides location transparency with a name service and hides details of the communication connection.

[Sommerlad96] Sommerlad, P., "Command Processor," *PLoPD2*, 63-74.

Separates the request for a service from its execution, manages requests as separate objects, schedules their execution, and provides additional services, e.g., storing request objects for a later undo.

[Sommerlad98] Sommerlad, P., "Manager," *PLoPD3*, 19-28.

Encapsulate management of the instances of a class into a separate manager object. This allows variation of management functionality independent of the class and reuse of the manager for different object classes.

[Soukup95] Soukup, J., "Implementing Patterns," *PLoPD1*, 408-412.

Use pattern classes to represent patterns as objects.

[Spall98] Spall, R., "Panel States: A User Interface Design Pattern," *Java Report*, Feb. 1998, 23-25, 28-32.

Application of a framework of patterns to present user interface panels in a sequence.

✄ FACTORY METHOD ♦ 56, STATE ♦ 166

[Srinivasan99] Srinivasan, S., "Design Patterns in Object-Oriented Frameworks," *Computer*, Feb. 1999, 24-32.

Experience developing an object-oriented framework for speech recognition applications.

✄ ACTIVE OBJECT ♦ 6, ADAPTER ♦ 6, FACADE ♦ 56, OBSERVER ♦ 94, SERVICE CONFIGURATOR ♦ 151

[Subramanian+96] Subramanian, S., W. Tsai, "Backup Pattern: Designing Redundancy in Object-Oriented Software," *PLoPD2*, 207-225.

Switch to a backup mode of operation. This provides redundancy in software when you want to offer various alternatives for a function and to switch between them dynamically.

[Taylor99] Taylor, P., "Capable, Productive, and Satisfied," *PLoPD4*, 611-636.

How the ability to produce and evolve software can be created and maintained.

[Towell95] Towell, D., "Request Screen Modification," *PLoPD1*, 555-556.

A common multimedia problem is the on-screen presentation of multiple actors. Each object updates its appearance by requesting a third party to modify an area of the screen. The third party then requests that each object redraw the appropriate section of itself.

[Towell99] Towell, D., "Display Maintenance," *PLoPD4*, 489-502.

Patterns for designing display architecture.

[VandenBroecke+97] Broecke, J.A.vanden, J.O. Coplien, "Using Design Patterns to Build a Framework for Multimedia Networking," *BLTJ*, Winter 1997, 166-187.

Experience with MediaBuilder, a framework for networked multimedia applications, to build a conferencing application that adapts to different multimedia and network standards.

⚒ BUILDER ♦ 23, COMMAND ♦ 35, FACADE ♦ 56, LAYERS ♦ 81, OBSERVER ♦ 94

[Viljamaa95] Viljamaa, P., "Client-Specified Self," *PLoPD1*, 495-504.

Replaces message to "self" with messages to an argument. Using the sender as the argument lets it inherit methods from others besides its superclasses.

[Vlissides95] Vlissides, J., "Pattern Hatching—Perspectives from the 'Gang of Four'," *C++ Report*, Mar./Apr. 1995, 36-39. See also *PHand*, 505-513.

`http://lib.stat.cmu.edu/~lamj/sigs/c++-report/cppr9503v.html`

Perspectives on *GoF* from a member of the GoF.

[Vlissides98a] Vlissides, J., *Pattern Hatching,* Addison-Wesley, 1998.

Use of several patterns in the design of a hierarchical file system.

⚒ COMPOSITE ♦ 37, MEDIATOR ♦ 86, MEMENTO ♦ 87, OBSERVER ♦ 94, PROXY ♦ 139, SINGLETON ♦ 152, TEMPLATE METHOD ♦ 171, VISITOR ♦ 179

[Vlissides98b] Vlissides, J., "Pluggable Factory, Part 1," *C++ Report*, Nov./Dec. 1998, 52-56, 68.

Specify and change product types dynamically without replacing the factory instance, which allows clients to vary product types by varying the prototypes it copies.

[Vlissides99] Vlissides, J., "Pluggable Factory, Part 2," *C++ Report*, Feb. 1999, 51-55, 57.

Extension of [Vlissides98b].

[Wake+96] Wake, W.C., B.D. Wake, E.A. Fox, "Improving Responsiveness in Interactive Applications Using Queues," *PLoPD2*, 563-573.

Design for the low-level structure of interactive applications.

[Wake95] Wake, W.C., "Account Number: A Pattern," *PLoPD1*, 157-162.

Assign exactly one account number to each person, and assign each account number only once.

[Wallingford98] Wallingford, E., "Sponsor-Selector," *PLoPD3*, 67-78.

Provide a mechanism for selecting the best resource for a task from a set of resources that changes dynamically. Allow a system to integrate new resources and new knowledge about resources at run-time without affecting clients.

[Weir98] Weir, C., "Patterns for Designing in Teams," *PLoPD3*, 487-501.

Techniques for using teams effectively in software design.

[White96] White, I., "Patterns and Java Class Libraries," *Java Report*, Oct. 1996, 41-45.

Describes how Dictionary and Enumeration of java.util implement ITERATOR ♦ 80.

⚒ ITERATOR ♦ 80

[Whitenack95] Whitenack, B., "RAPPeL: A Requirements-Analysis Process Pattern Language for Object-Oriented Development," *PLoPD1*, 259-291.

`http://www.bell-labs.com/people/cope/Patterns/Process/RAPPeL/rapel.html`

For analysts, developers, and project managers engaged in defining requirements for business applications in an object-oriented environment.

[Wirfs-Brock93] Wirfs-Brock, R., "Characterizing Your Objects," *Smalltalk Report*, Feb. 1993, 7-9.

Bibliography

[Wolf+95] Wolf, K., C. Liu, "New Clients with Old Servers: A Pattern Language for Client/Server Frameworks," *PLoPD1*, 51-64.

Patterns in object-oriented frameworks for Smalltalk workstations communicating with legacy host business systems.

[Woodward96] Woodward, K.G., "Heading Off Tragedy: Using Design Patterns Against a Moving Target," *Second World Conference on Integrated Design and Process Technology*, Dec. 1996.

`http://hillside.net/patterns/papers/`

Development of a GUI simulator.

🛠 ABSTRACT FACTORY ♦ 2, ADAPTER ♦ 6, BLACKBOARD ♦ 22, BRIDGE ♦ 22, BROKER ♦ 22, PIPES & FILTERS ♦ 132, REACTOR ♦ 143

[Woolf95] Woolf, B., "Understanding and Using the ValueModel Framework in VisualWorks Smalltalk," *PLoPD1*, 467- 498.

`http://c2.com/ppr/vmodels.html`

ValueModel is a framework in VisualWorks Smalltalk. This collection describes ValueModels and how to use them.

[Woolf96] Woolf, B., "Partitioning Smalltalk Code into ENVY/Developer Components," *PLoPD2*, 43-58.

`http://c2.com/ppr/envy/`

ENVY/Developer is a configuration management system for Smalltalk development. How to partition source code using ENVY.

[Woolf98] Woolf, B., "Null Object," *PLoPD3*, 5-18.

A Null Object is a surrogate for another object with the same interface, but the Null Object does nothing.

[Woolf99a] Woolf, B., "The Abstract Class Pattern," *PLoPD4*, 5-14.

When you're designing a class hierarchy, define the interface and general implementation in an abstract class and defer implementation to the subclasses.

[Woolf99b] Woolf, B., "Object Recursion," *PLoPD4*, 41-51.

Handle a request over a structure by delegating it polymorphically. A request can be decomposed repeatedly into smaller parts.

[Yacoub+99] Yacoub, S., H. Anmar, "Finite State Machine Patterns," *PLoPD4*, 413-440.

An extension of STATE PATTERNS ❖ 166 and THREE-LEVEL FSM ♦ 172 to implement a state machine in an object-oriented design.

[Yoder+99] Yoder, J., J. Barcalow, "Architectural Patterns for Enabling Application Security," *PLoPD4*, 301-336.

`http://www.joeyoder.com/papers/`

Early design decisions allow application security to be added later and enable system evolution to meet changing security requirements.

[Zhang+96a] Zhang, J.Q., E. Sternbach, "Financial Software Design Patterns," *JOOP*, Jan. 1996, 6-12.

Use of patterns in a bond yield calculator. Starting with a U.S. Treasury bond calculator, the authors show how other types of bond calculators can be added without modifying code.

🛠 SINGLETON ♦ 152, STATE ♦ 166

[Zhang+96b] Zhang, J.Q., E. Sternbach, "Financial Software Design Patterns," *JOOP*, Feb. 1996, 6-12.

By decoupling mathematical and financial models, designers can reuse option models in different option markets and add new option models. A legacy option model is also adapted.

🛠 BRIDGE ♦ 22

[Zhang+96c] Zhang, J.Q., E. Sternbach, "Financial Software Design Patterns," *JOOP*, Mar./Apr. 1996, 6-14.

A yield curve structure supporting new curve construction techniques that can be plugged in without modifying code. Also supports selecting the desired yield curve algorithm at run-time.

⚒ Abstract Factory ◆ 2, Factory Method ◆ 56, Template Method ◆ 171

[Zhao+98a] Zhao, L., T. Foster, "Driver Duty: A Pattern for Public Transport Systems," *JOOP*, July/Aug. 1998, 35-39, 77.

Introduces Driver Duty in the pattern language of transport systems.

⚒ Cascade ◆ 28, Composite ◆ 37, Strategy ◆ 167

[Zhao+98b] Zhao, L., T. Foster, "A Pattern Language of Transport Systems (Point and Route)," *PLoPD3*, 409-430.

Point and Route are part of a pattern language for building transport systems.

[Zhao+99] Zhao, L., T. Foster, "Driver Duty Constructor: A Pattern for Public Transport Systems," *JOOP*, May 1999, 45-51, 77.

Introduces the Driver Duty Constructor in the pattern language of transport systems.

⚒ Builder ◆ 23, Cascade ◆ 28, Strategy ◆ 167

Bibliography

Index

14.4 Kbps Testing ♦ **99**
3-Level Order ♦ **24**

Aarsten, A.
[Aarsten+95]; 181
  G++: A Pattern Language for Computer-Integrated
    Manufacturing ❖ 61
[Aarsten+96a]; 181
  From Prototype to Reality ♦ 61
[Aarsten+96b]; 181
  Object-Oriented Design Patterns in Reactive
    Systems ❖ 92
  Remote Control ♦ 144
abandonment
  as action termination description; Completed and
    Abandoned Actions ♦ 12
  Completed and Abandoned Actions ♦ 12
Abrams, D.
[Alexander+75]; 181
Abstract Class ♦ **2**
[Woolf99a]; 198
Abstract Client ♦ **2**
[Martin95b]; 190
Abstract Factory ♦ **2**
[Alpert+98]; 182
[Gamma+95]; 188
Abstract Models with Constraints in Subtypes ♦ **4**
Abstract Server ♦ **16**
Abstract Session ♦ **2**
[Pryce99]; 193
abstract/abstraction(s)
  See Also encapsulation; isolation
  Abstract Class ♦ 2
    See Also Create Abstract Superclass
    Create Abstract Superclass relationship to; Create
      Abstract Superclass ♦ 85
    Implementing Generalizations relationship to;
      Implementing Generalizations ♦ 15
  Abstract Client ♦ 2
  Abstract Factory ♦ 2
    See Also Singleton
    Bridge relationship to; Bridge ♦ 22
    Builder relationship to; Builder ♦ 23
    Facade relationship to; Facade ♦ 56
    Factory Method relationship to; Abstract Factory ♦ 2
    NavigationStrategy relationship to;
      NavigationStrategy ♦ 48

  Pattern for Separating Assembly and Processing
    relationship to; Pattern for Separating Assembly and
    Processing ♦ 97
  Pluggable Factory relationship to; Pluggable
    Factory ♦ 132
  Prototype relationship to; Abstract Factory ♦ 2
Abstract Models with Constraints in Subtypes ♦ 4
  Recursive Structures for Organizations relationship
    to; Recursive Structures for Organizations ♦ 4
Abstract Server ♦ 16
  Adapted Server relationship to; Abstract Server ♦ 16,
    Adapted Server ♦ 17
  Intelligent Children relationship to; Intelligent
    Children ♦ 16, Abstract Server ♦ 16
  Strategy relationship to; Abstract Server ♦ 16
Abstract Session ♦ 2
  See Also Adapter
  Acceptor relationship to; Abstract Session ♦ 2
  Connector relationship to; Abstract Session ♦ 2
  Factory Method relationship to; Abstract Session ♦ 2
  Mediator relationship to; Abstract Session ♦ 2
  Session relationship to; Abstract Session ♦ 2
Accountability Abstraction ♦ 5
associations, into types; Objectify Associations ♦ 5
classes
  creating; Life Cycle and Refactoring Patterns that
    Support Evolution and Reuse ♦ 84
  inheritance hierarchy cleanup use; Create Abstract
    Superclass ♦ 85
  managing client-server dependencies with; Intelligent
    Children ♦ 16, Abstract Server ♦ 16, Adapted
    Server ♦ 17
Create Abstract Superclass ♦ 85
Data Abstraction or Object-Oriented ♦ 125
data types
  data representation by; Data Abstraction or
    Object-Oriented ♦ 125
  multiple implementations, handling;
    Envelope/Letter ♦ 25
decomposing software into levels of; Layers ♦ 81
decoupling from implementation; Bridge ♦ 22
Implement Behavior with Abstract State ♦ 145
implementing; Implementing Generalizations ♦ 15
interface as; Interface's Role ♦ 30
levels in model design
  communication among the model levels; Upward
    Traceability ♦ 45

abstract/abstraction(s) *continued*
  levels in model design *continued*
    making consistent changes; DOWNWARD CHANGES ♦ 45
  models
    domain rule enforcement with subtypes; ABSTRACT MODELS
      WITH CONSTRAINTS IN SUBTYPES ♦ 4
    of relationships between two objects; ELEVATE REFERENCES
      TO ENHANCE REUSE ♦ 124
  of object values, as object collaboration support; USE A
    VALUEMODEL TO GENERALIZE AN OBJECT'S ASPECT ♦ 176
  PRESENTATION-ABSTRACTION-CONTROL ♦ 135
  responsibilities, into a type; ACCOUNTABILITY ♦ 7
  state, behavior implementation with; IMPLEMENT BEHAVIOR
    WITH ABSTRACT STATE ♦ 145
  supertype definition; PARTY ♦ 4, PARTY ♦ 6
  syntax tree, language grammar representation use;
    INTERPRETER ♦ 80
ACCEPTOR ♦ 3
  See Also ACTIVE OBJECT; CONNECTOR; REACTOR; SERVICE
    CONFIGURATOR
  ABSTRACT SESSION relationship to; ABSTRACT SESSION ♦ 2
  BODYGUARD relationship to; BODYGUARD ♦ 22
  CLIENT-DISPATCHER-SERVER relationship to;
    CLIENT-DISPATCHER-SERVER ♦ 34
  CONNECTOR relationship to; CONNECTOR ♦ 40
  FACTORY METHOD relationship to; ACCEPTOR ♦ 3
  NAVIGATIONSTRATEGY relationship to;
    NAVIGATIONSTRATEGY ♦ 48
  [Schmidt98b]; 195
  TEMPLATE METHOD relationship to; ACCEPTOR ♦ 3
access(ing)
  ACCESSING RELATIONAL DATABASES ❖ 3
    THREE-TIER ARCHITECTURE relationship to; THREE-TIER
      ARCHITECTURE ♦ 15
  accessor methods, integrating data model into implementation;
    INTRODUCE VIRTUAL ATTRIBUTES ♦ 70
  ARTIFICIAL ACCESSORS ♦ 163
  attributes; GENERATED ACCESSORS ♦ 164
  COLLECTION ACCESSOR METHOD ♦ 157
  collections; COLLECTION ACCESSOR METHOD ♦ 157,
    ENUMERATION METHOD ♦ 158
  control
    check point use for; CHECK POINT ♦ 17
    distributed systems without system-level support;
      BODYGUARD ♦ 22
    handling multiple package access levels; MULTIPLE ACCESS
      LEVELS TO A PACKAGE ♦ 14
    secure access layer as security integration tool; SECURE
      ACCESS LAYER ♦ 18
    single access point use for; SINGLE ACCESS POINT ♦ 17
    to state objects; EXPOSED STATE ♦ 166
  database
    connecting the access layers; QUERY BROKER ♦ 4
    defining access layers in a relational database; ACCESSING
      RELATIONAL DATABASES pattern language ♦ 3,
      RELATIONAL DATABASE ACCESS LAYER ♦ 3
  DIRECT VARIABLE ACCESS ♦ 157
  extended attributes; ARTIFICIAL ACCESSORS ♦ 163
  GENERATED ACCESSORS ♦ 164

INDIRECT VARIABLE ACCESS ♦ 157
  instance variables, directly; DIRECT VARIABLE ACCESS ♦ 157
  of legacy software, wrappers use for; (LEGACY)
    WRAPPER ♦ 115
  MULTIPLE ACCESS LEVELS TO A PACKAGE ♦ 14
  of objects; ENTRY POINT ♦ 16
  PERSISTENCE ACCESSORS ♦ 135
  persistent accessors, client-server application use;
    PERSISTENCE ACCESSORS ♦ 135
  of physical database tables; PHYSICAL VIEW ♦ 3
  RELATIONAL DATABASE ACCESS LAYER ♦ 3
  rights, encapsulating as roles; ROLES ♦ 17
  SECURE ACCESS LAYER ♦ 18
  simultaneous, protection mechanisms; CRITICAL REGION
    PROTECTION ♦ 31
  SINGLE ACCESS POINT ♦ 17
  values, of variables; GETTING METHOD ♦ 157
  variables; GETTING METHOD ♦ 157
    indirectly; INDIRECT VARIABLE ACCESS ♦ 157
ACCESSING RELATIONAL DATABASES ❖ 3
  [Keller+98b]; 189
accomplishment
  WORK ACCOMPLISHED THROUGH DIALOGS ♦ 30
ACCOUNT ♦ 10
ACCOUNT NUMBER ♦ 4
  [Wake95]; 197
account(s)
  ACCOUNT ♦ 10
    BALANCE SHEET AND INCOME STATEMENT relationship to;
      BALANCE SHEET AND INCOME STATEMENT ♦ 12
    BOOKING ENTRIES TO MULTIPLE ACCOUNTS relationship to;
      BOOKING ENTRIES TO MULTIPLE ACCOUNTS ♦ 12
    CORRESPONDING ACCOUNT relationship to; CORRESPONDING
      ACCOUNT ♦ 12
    MEMO ACCOUNT relationship to; MEMO ACCOUNT ♦ 11
    POSTING relationship to; POSTING ♦ 35
    POSTING RULE EXECUTION relationship to; POSTING RULE
      EXECUTION ♦ 11
    POSTING RULES FOR MANY ACCOUNTS relationship to;
      POSTING RULES FOR MANY ACCOUNTS ♦ 11
    TRANSACTION relationship to; TRANSACTION ♦ 10
  ACCOUNT NUMBER ♦ 4
  establishing unique references with; ACCOUNT NUMBER ♦ 4
  ACCOUNTABILITY ♦ 7
  ACCOUNTABILITY ABSTRACTION ♦ 5
  ACCOUNTABILITY AND ORGANIZATIONAL STRUCTURES ♦ 4
  ACCOUNTABILITY KNOWLEDGE LEVEL ♦ 5, ♦ 7
    POSTING RULES FOR MANY ACCOUNTS relationship to;
      POSTING RULES FOR MANY ACCOUNTS ♦ 11
  ACCOUNTING PRACTICE ♦ 12
    POSTING RULES relationship to; ACCOUNTING
      PRACTICE ♦ 12
  accounting practice, creating; ACCOUNTING PRACTICE ♦ 12
  BOOKING ENTRIES TO MULTIPLE ACCOUNTS ♦ 12
  business, tracking the state of the business with; BUSINESS
    ACCOUNTS ♦ 173
  BUSINESS ACCOUNTS ♦ 173
  closing, month-end; MONTH END CLOSING ♦ 173
  CORRESPONDING ACCOUNT ♦ 12

creating; ACCOUNT ♦ 10

entries

recording for a transaction; SOURCES OF AN ENTRY ♦ 12

selecting; CHOOSING ENTRIES ♦ 11

memo, creating; MEMO ACCOUNT ♦ 11

MEMO ACCOUNT ♦ 11

multiple

booking entries to; BOOKING ENTRIES TO MULTIPLE
ACCOUNTS ♦ 12

grouping; SUMMARY ACCOUNT ♦ 11

posting rule handling; POSTING RULES FOR MANY
ACCOUNTS ♦ 11

posting rules for, handling many; POSTING RULES FOR MANY
ACCOUNTS ♦ 11

POSTING RULES FOR MANY ACCOUNTS ♦ 11

SPECIALIZED ACCOUNT MODEL ♦ 12

SUMMARY ACCOUNT ♦ 11

transactions, creating; TRANSACTION ♦ 10

TRANSACTIONS AND ACCOUNTS ♦ 172

transfering between, rules for; POSTING RULES ♦ 11

updating, in transaction processing systems; TRANSACTIONS
AND ACCOUNTS ♦ 172

views, equivalence relationship between; CORRESPONDING
ACCOUNT ♦ 12

ACCOUNTABILITY ♦ 7

accountability

HIERARCHIC ACCOUNTABILITY ♦ 7

ACCOUNTABILITY ABSTRACTION ♦ 5

ACCOUNTABILITY AND ORGANIZATIONAL STRUCTURES ♦ 4

[Fowler96]; 187

ACCOUNTABILITY KNOWLEDGE LEVEL ♦ 7

ACCOUNTING PRACTICE ♦ 12

ACQUAINTANCE EXAMPLES ♦ 117

EXAMPLE LASTS ONE WEEK relationship to; EXAMPLE LASTS
ONE WEEK ♦ 117

MODULE'S STORY relationship to; MODULE'S STORY ♦ 116

REFERENCE EXAMPLES relationship to; ACQUAINTANCE
EXAMPLES ♦ 117

acquisition

EVENT ACQUISITION ♦ 31

of events, design issues; EVENT ACQUISITION ♦ 31

actions

ACTIONS TRIGGERED BY EVENTS ♦ 62

COMPLETED AND ABANDONED ACTIONS ♦ 12

decoupling proposed and implemented; PROPOSED AND
IMPLEMENTED ACTION ♦ 12

plan relationship to; PLAN ♦ 13

role, identifying with time-thread analysis; TIME THREAD
ANALYSIS ♦ 71

suspending; SUSPENSION ♦ 12

termination, description of; COMPLETED AND ABANDONED
ACTIONS ♦ 12

ACTIONS TRIGGERED BY EVENTS ♦ 62

activation link

decoupling from endpoint computation;
NAVIGATIONSTRATEGY ♦ 48

active

ACTIVE OBJECT ♦ 6

See Also HALF-SYNC/HALF-ASYNC

CONNECTOR relationship to; CONNECTOR ♦ 40

DATA OWNERSHIP relationship to; DATA OWNERSHIP ♦ 147

HALF-SYNC/HALF-ASYNC relationship to;
HALF-SYNC/HALF-ASYNC ♦ 71

OBJECT SYNCHRONIZER relationship to; OBJECT
SYNCHRONIZER ♦ 92

PROACTOR relationship to; PROACTOR ♦ 137

ACTIVE OBSERVATION, HYPOTHESIS, AND PROJECTION ♦ 9

ACTIVE REFERENCE ♦ 120

ACTIVE VALUE ♦ 20

RELATIONSHIP AS ATTRIBUTE relationship to; RELATIONSHIP
AS ATTRIBUTE ♦ 20

RELATIONSHIP OBJECT relationship to; RELATIONSHIP
OBJECT ♦ 20

categorizing objects with respect to activity, in complex
concurrent systems; CATEGORIZE OBJECTS FOR
CONCURRENCY ♦ 62

initialization, decoupling from services provided;
CONNECTOR ♦ 40

ACTIVE OBJECT ♦ 6

[Lavender+96]; 190

ACTIVE OBSERVATION, HYPOTHESIS, AND PROJECTION ♦ 9

ACTIVE REFERENCE ♦ 120

ACTIVE VALUE ♦ 20

activities

KEY BUSINESS ACTIVITIES AND INFLUENCES ♦ 165

actors

DETERMINE THE ACTORS ♦ 71

ACYCLIC VISITOR ♦ 6

EXTRINSIC VISITOR relationship to; EXTRINSIC VISITOR ♦ 56

[Martin98]; 190

AD-HOC CORRECTIONS ♦ 119

Adams, M.

[Adams+96]; 181

FAULT-TOLERANT TELECOMMUNICATION SYSTEM
PATTERNS ❖ 57

Adams, S. S.

[Adams95]; 181

FUNCTIONALITY ALA CARTE ♦ 61

ADAPTED SERVER ♦ 17

ADAPTER ♦ 6

[Alpert+98]; 182

[Gamma+95]; 188

adapters

ADAPTED SERVER ♦ 17

ABSTRACT SERVER relationship to; ABSTRACT SERVER ♦ 16,
ADAPTED SERVER ♦ 17

ADAPTER relationship to; ADAPTED SERVER ♦ 17

INTELLIGENT CHILDREN relationship to; INTELLIGENT
CHILDREN ♦ 16, ADAPTED SERVER ♦ 17

ADAPTER ♦ 6

ADAPTED SERVER relationship to; ADAPTED SERVER ♦ 17

BRIDGE relationship to; ADAPTER ♦ 6, BRIDGE ♦ 22

COMMAND relationship to; ADAPTER ♦ 6

DECORATOR relationship to; ADAPTER ♦ 6, DECORATOR ♦ 46

EXTERNAL POLYMORPHISM relationship to; EXTERNAL
POLYMORPHISM ♦ 56

FACADE relationship to; ADAPTER ♦ 6, FACADE ♦ 56

adapters *continued*
  ADAPTER *continued*
    FROM PROTOTYPE TO REALITY relationship to; FROM
      PROTOTYPE TO REALITY ♦ 61
    (LEGACY) WRAPPER relationship to; (LEGACY)
      WRAPPER ♦ 115
    MANAGER-AGENT relationship to; MANAGER-AGENT ♦ 114
    OBJECT-ORIENTED SIMULATION relationship to;
      OBJECT-ORIENTED SIMULATION ♦ 93
    PROGRAMMING-BY-DIFFERENCE relationship to;
      PROGRAMMING-BY-DIFFERENCE ♦ 150
    PROTOTYPE AND REALITY relationship to; PROTOTYPE AND
      REALITY ♦ 63
    PROXY relationship to; ADAPTER ♦ 6, PROXY ♦ 139
  ADAPTIVE PROPAGATOR ♦ 138
  method, before and after methods; METHOD ADAPTERS ♦ 37
  METHOD ADAPTERS ♦ 37
  USE A PLUGGABLEADAPTOR TO HOLD SOME PART OF AN
    OBJECT ♦ 178
  USE A RANGEADAPTOR TO CHANNEL A NUMBER'S
    RANGE ♦ 177
  USE A SLOTADAPTOR TO HOLD A SINGLE INSTANCE
    VARIABLE ♦ 178
  USE AN ASPECTADAPTOR TO HOLD AN ASPECT OF AN
    OBJECT ♦ 177
  USE AN INDEXEDADAPTOR TO HOLD A SINGLE INDEX IN A
    COLLECTION ♦ 177
ADAPTIVE PROPAGATOR ♦ 138
adaptor
  See adapters
addition
  See Also mathematics
  heterogeneous; PROMOTE AND ADD ♦ 26
  HOMOGENEOUS ADDITION ♦ 25
  non-hierarchical promotion; NON-HIERARCHICAL
    ADDITION ♦ 26
  operations, distributing; HOMOGENEOUS ADDITION ♦ 25
  PROMOTE AND ADD ♦ 26
address
  space, multiple, handling objects in; HALF-OBJECT +
    PROTOCOL ♦ 71
ADJUSTING TRANSACTIONS ♦ 173
adjustment
  ADJUSTING TRANSACTIONS ♦ 173
  transactions, handling; ADJUSTING TRANSACTIONS ♦ 173
ADOPT-A-PROBLEM ♦ 128
  DESIGNERS ARE OUR FRIENDS relationship to;
    ADOPT-A-PROBLEM ♦ 128
  DOCUMENT THE PROBLEM relationship to;
    ADOPT-A-PROBLEM ♦ 128
  PET PEEVE relationship to; ADOPT-A-PROBLEM ♦ 128
ADT (abstract data types)
  data types, data representation by; DATA ABSTRACTION OR
    OBJECT-ORIENTED ♦ 125
  multiple implementations; ENVELOPE/LETTER ♦ 25
AESTHETIC PATTERN ♦ 68
after methods
  concurrency control use; METHOD ADAPTERS ♦ 37

agents
  hierarchy of cooperating; PRESENTATION-ABSTRACTION-
    CONTROL ♦ 135
  MANAGER-AGENT ♦ 114
aggregations
  See Also collections
  cncapsulation of elements while sequentially processing;
    ITERATOR ♦ 80
  EVOLVE AGGREGATIONS FROM INHERITANCE
    HIERARCHIES ♦ 85
  evolving software from inheritance to; LIFE CYCLE AND
    REFACTORING PATTERNS THAT SUPPORT EVOLUTION AND
    REUSE ♦ 84, EVOLVE AGGREGATIONS FROM INHERITANCE
    HIERARCHIES ♦ 85
  relationship of parts to; WHOLE-PART ♦ 179
aging
  OBJECT AGING ♦ 141
alarms
  ALARM GRID ♦ 79
    AUDIBLE ALARM relationship to; ALARM GRID ♦ 79
    PEOPLE KNOW BEST relationship to; ALARM GRID ♦ 79
  audible, as fault-tolerant system notification mechanism;
    AUDIBLE ALARM ♦ 79
  AUDIBLE ALARM ♦ 79
  location strategies; ALARM GRID ♦ 79
  OFFICE ALARMS ♦ 79
  office-specific, in fault-tolerant systems; OFFICE ALARMS ♦ 79
  POINTS AND DEVIATIONS: PATTERN LANGUAGE OF FIRE
    ALARM SYSTEMS ♦ 133
  silenceing, error override of; DON'T LET THEM FORGET ♦ 79
Alexander, C.
  [Alexander+75]; 181
  [Alexander+77]; 182, 193
  [Alexander79]; 182
algebra
  See Also mathematics
  ALGEBRAIC HIERARCHY ♦ 25
    BRIDGE relationship to; ALGEBRAIC HIERARCHY ♦ 25
    CONCRETE DATA TYPE relationship to; CONCRETE DATA
      TYPE ♦ 25
    ENVELOPE/LETTER relationship to; ENVELOPE/LETTER ♦ 25
    HOMOGENEOUS ADDITION relationship to; ALGEBRAIC
      HIERARCHY ♦ 25, HOMOGENEOUS ADDITION ♦ 25
    NON-HIERARCHICAL ADDITION relationship to; ALGEBRAIC
      HIERARCHY ♦ 25
    PROMOTE AND ADD relationship to; ALGEBRAIC
      HIERARCHY ♦ 25, PROMOTE AND ADD ♦ 26
    PROMOTION LADDER relationship to; ALGEBRAIC
      HIERARCHY ♦ 25
    STATE relationship to; ALGEBRAIC HIERARCHY ♦ 25
    TYPE PROMOTION relationship to; ALGEBRAIC
      HIERARCHY ♦ 25
  data types, inheritance hierarchy for; ALGEBRAIC
    HIERARCHY ♦ 25
  heterogeneous addition; PROMOTE AND ADD ♦ 26
  operations, distributing; HOMOGENEOUS ADDITION ♦ 25
  types, C++ IDIOMS pattern language; C++ IDIOMS ♦ 24
ALGEBRAIC HIERARCHY ♦ 25

algorithms
See Also control, flow
family, defining; STRATEGY ◆ 167
information retrieval, feature extraction; FEATURE
EXTRACTION—A PATTERN FOR INFORMATION
RETRIEVAL ◆ 58
PAINTER'S ALGORITHM ◆ 50
rendering; PAINTER'S ALGORITHM ◆ 50
security check, encapsulating; CHECK POINT ◆ 17
template definition; TEMPLATE METHOD ◆ 171
understanding, as developer role; DEVELOPER CONTROLS
PROCESS ◆ 65
allocation
ALLOCATOR CACHES ◆ 148
CODE LOCKING relationship to; ALLOCATOR CACHES ◆ 148
TEST-AND-SET LOCK relationship to; TEST-AND-SET
LOCK ◆ 148
CODE LOCKING, ALLOCATOR CACHES relationship to;
ALLOCATOR CACHES ◆ 148
collection, as optimization technique; HYPOTH-A-SIZED
COLLECTION ◆ 84
of memory, performance strategies; ALLOCATOR
CACHES ◆ 148
RESOURCE ALLOCATION ◆ 13
of resources; RESOURCE ALLOCATION ◆ 13
ALLOCATOR CACHES ◆ 148
Alpert, S.
[Alpert+98]; 182
ABSTRACT FACTORY ◆ 2
ADAPTER ◆ 6
BRIDGE ◆ 22
BUILDER ◆ 23
CHAIN OF RESPONSIBILITY ◆ 32
COMMAND ◆ 35
COMPOSITE ◆ 37
DECORATOR ◆ 46
FACADE ◆ 56
FACTORY METHOD ◆ 56
FLYWEIGHT ◆ 60
HOOK METHOD ◆ 73
ITERATOR ◆ 80
MEDIATOR ◆ 86
MEMENTO ◆ 87
OBSERVER ◆ 94
PROTOTYPE ◆ 138
PROXY ◆ 139
SINGLETON ◆ 152
STATE ◆ 166
TEMPLATE METHOD ◆ 171
VISITOR ◆ 179
[Alpert+98], INTERPRETER ◆ 80
ALTERNATIVE SUBFORMS ◆ 99
alternatives
ALTERNATIVE SUBFORMS ◆ 99
SUBFORM relationship to; ALTERNATIVE SUBFORMS ◆ 99
SUBFORM SELECTION relationship to; ALTERNATIVE
SUBFORMS ◆ 99, SUBFORM SELECTION ◆ 99
AMBIGUOUS DOCUMENTATION ◆ 127
PROBLEM AREA relationship to; PROBLEM AREA ◆ 127

analogies
as teaching strategy; COLORFUL ANALOGY ◆ 117
analysis
abstracting either-or-both relationship into a supertype;
PARTY ◆ 4, PARTY ◆ 6
ANALYSIS PATTERNS ◆ 6
of big ball of mud systems, analysis and solutions; BIG BALL
OF MUD PATTERN LANGUAGE ◆ 20
of domain object relationships; CLASSIFYING, ASSOCIATING,
AND GROUPING THE DOMAIN OBJECTS ◆ 141
MERCENARY ANALYST ◆ 67
organizational, patterns for; ACCOUNTABILITY AND
ORGANIZATIONAL STRUCTURES pattern language ◆ 4
of performance bottlenecks; HOT SPOT ◆ 82
of problem domain; PROBLEM DOMAIN ANALYSIS ◆ 141
PROBLEM DOMAIN ANALYSIS ◆ 141
requirements, for object-oriented development; RAPPeL: A
REQUIREMENTS-ANALYSIS PROCESS PATTERN LANGUAGE
FOR OBJECT-ORIENTED DEVELOPMENT ◆ 140
TIME THREAD ANALYSIS ◆ 71
transformation from analysis; CATERPILLAR'S FATE: A
PATTERN LANGUAGE FOR THE TRANSFORMATION FROM
ANALYSIS TO DESIGN ◆ 28
ANALYSIS PATTERNS ◆ 6
[Fowler97]; 187
Anderson, B.
[Dyson+98]; 187
STATE PATTERNS ❖ 166
Anderson, F.
[Anderson99]; 182
COLLECTION OF HISTORY PATTERNS ◆ 34
Angel, S.
[Alexander+75]; 181
[Alexander+77]; 182
ANIMATE THE DATA ◆ 70
animation
ANIMATE THE DATA ◆ 70
DEFINE THE DATA STRUCTURE relationship to; ANIMATE
THE DATA ◆ 70
DETERMINE THE ACTORS relationship to; ANIMATE THE
DATA ◆ 70
TIME THREAD ANALYSIS relationship to; ANIMATE THE
DATA ◆ 70, TIME THREAD ANALYSIS ◆ 71
Anmar, H.
[Yacoub+99]; 198
FINITE STATE MACHINE PATTERNS ❖ 58
Anthony, D. L.
[Anthony96]; 182
PATTERNS FOR CLASSROOM EDUCATION ❖ 116
antipatterns
CARGO CULT; CARGO CULT ◆ 131
CULT OF PERSONALITY; CULT OF PERSONALITY ◆ 130
GURU DOES ALL; GURU DOES ALL ◆ 130
SACRIFICIAL LAMB; SACRIFICIAL LAMB ◆ 131
SCHEDULE CHICKEN; SCHEDULE CHICKEN ◆ 132
TRAIN THE TRAINER ◆ 130
appendix
SECRECY WITH SIGNATURE WITH APPENDIX ◆ 175
SIGNATURE WITH APPENDIX ◆ 175

APPLICATION BOUNDARY ◆ 136
APPLICATION DESIGN IS BOUNDED BY TEST DESIGN ◆ 66
applications
  APPLICATION BOUNDARY ◆ 136
  APPLICATION DESIGN IS BOUNDED BY TEST DESIGN ◆ 66
    GET INVOLVED EARLY relationship to; APPLICATION DESIGN
      IS BOUNDED BY TEST DESIGN ◆ 66
  ARCHITECTURAL PATTERNS FOR ENABLING APPLICATION
    SECURITY ◆ 17
  design, testing relationship to; APPLICATION DESIGN IS
    BOUNDED BY TEST DESIGN ◆ 66
  evolution of sections from; NO SUBAPPLICATIONS ◆ 97
  frameworks development based on; THREE EXAMPLES ◆ 121
  IMPROVING RESPONSIVENESS IN INTERACTIVE APPLICATIONS
    USING QUEUES ◆ 76
  layer, decoupling user interface from domain model;
    PRESENTATION AND APPLICATION LOGIC ◆ 15
  LAYER IN AN APPLICATION ◆ 96
  model
    decoupling from domain model; TWO APPLICATIONS ◆ 97
    as Smalltalk client-server system layer; FOUR-LAYER
      ARCHITECTURE ◆ 106
  PARALLEL APPLICATION AND DOMAIN HIERARCHIES ◆ 14
  PRESENTATION AND APPLICATION LOGIC ◆ 15
  storing layers in; LAYER IN AN APPLICATION ◆ 96
  storing sections in subapplications; SECTION IN A
    SUBAPPLICATION ◆ 97
  as three-tier application layer; THREE-TIER
    ARCHITECTURE ◆ 15
  TWO APPLICATIONS ◆ 97
APPRENTICE ◆ 64
apprenticeship
  APPRENTICE ◆ 64
  in team training strategy; APPRENTICE ◆ 64
APPROACHES FOR SEPARATING CLIENTS FROM SERVERS ◆ 16
  [Martin95c]; 190
APPROPRIATE LIVING MODELS ◆ 45
  DECISION-BASED MODELS relationship to; DECISION-BASED
    MODELS ◆ 45
ARCHITECT ALSO IMPLEMENTS ◆ 65
ARCHITECT CONTROLS PRODUCT ◆ 65
ARCHITECTURAL PATTERNS FOR ENABLING APPLICATION
  SECURITY ◆ 17
  [Yoder+99]; 198
architecture
  See Also geometry; shape; structure
  ARCHITECT ALSO IMPLEMENTS ◆ 65
    LOCK 'EM UP TOGETHER relationship to; LOCK 'EM UP
      TOGETHER ◆ 95
  ARCHITECT CONTROLS PRODUCT ◆ 65
    LOCK 'EM UP TOGETHER relationship to; LOCK 'EM UP
      TOGETHER ◆ 95
  architect's role, in relation to developers and customers;
    ARCHITECT CONTROLS PRODUCT ◆ 65
  ARCHITECTURAL PATTERNS FOR ENABLING APPLICATION
    SECURITY ◆ 17
  ARCHITECTURE PATTERNS FOR BUSINESS SYSTEMS ◆ 18
  business; ARCHITECTURE PATTERNS FOR BUSINESS
    SYSTEMS ◆ 18

database
  behavioral modeling role; TABLE DESIGN TIME ◆ 42
  connecting access layers; QUERY BROKER ◆ 4
  defining access layers; ACCESSING RELATIONAL DATABASES
    pattern language ◆ 3, RELATIONAL DATABASE ACCESS
    LAYER ◆ 3
  defining domain views; HIERARCHICAL VIEW ◆ 3
  defining physical views; PHYSICAL VIEW ◆ 3
development, by teams, strategies for ensuring coherence;
  LOCK 'EM UP TOGETHER ◆ 95
display, software design; DISPLAY MAINTENANCE ◆ 49
distributed systems; DISTRIBUTED PROCESSES ◆ 51
  creation; BROKER ◆ 22
event-centered; EVENT-CENTERED ARCHITECTURE ◆ 129
EVENT-CENTERED ARCHITECTURE ◆ 129
EVOLUTION, ARCHITECTURE, AND METAMORPHOSIS ◆ 55
extensible command interpreter; FLEXIBLE COMMAND
  INTERPRETER ◆ 60
finite state machine, layering use; LAYERED
  ORGANIZATION ◆ 59
FOUR-LAYER ARCHITECTURE ◆ 106
graph-based object-relationship design; SMALL FAMILY
  SYSTEMS ◆ 30
hypermedia navigation, strategies for;
  NAVIGATIONOBSERVER ◆ 48
implementation of, architects responsibilities for; ARCHITECT
  ALSO IMPLEMENTS ◆ 65
of interactive applications; MODEL-VIEW-CONTROLLER ◆ 87
interactive software systems; PRESENTATION-ABSTRACTION-
  CONTROL ◆ 135
layered; LAYERED ARCHITECTURE ◆ 125
  creation of; PEDESTAL ◆ 123
  generation of; PATTERNS FOR GENERATING A LAYERED
    ARCHITECTURE ◆ 123
LAYERED AND SECTIONED ARCHITECTURE ◆ 96
LAYERED ARCHITECTURE ◆ 125
layering
  as client-server class structure; FOUR-LAYER
    ARCHITECTURE ◆ 106
  of system functions into a hierarchy; HIERARCHY OF
    CONTROL LAYERS ◆ 61
  of programs; SHAPE OF PROGRAM ◆ 29
  reducing component dependencies with; LAYERED AND
    SECTIONED ARCHITECTURE ◆ 96
object-oriented, fire alarm system family; POINTS AND
  DEVIATIONS: PATTERN LANGUAGE OF FIRE ALARM
  SYSTEMS ◆ 133
PATTERN-BASED INTEGRATION ARCHITECTURES ◆ 115
PATTERNS FOR GENERATING A LAYERED ARCHITECTURE ◆ 123
PATTERNS FOR SOFTWARE ARCHITECTURES ◆ 124
project, workforce location impact on; ORGANIZATION
  FOLLOWS LOCATION ◆ 64
REVIEW THE ARCHITECTURE ◆ 65
reviewing strategies; REVIEW THE ARCHITECTURE ◆ 65
role relative to organization; CONWAY'S LAW ◆ 65
for satellite telemetry systems, software and organizational
  development strategies; ORGANIZATIONAL MULTIPLEXING:
  PATTERNS FOR PROCESSING SATELLITE TELEMETRY WITH
  DISTRIBUTED TEAMS ◆ 94

sectioning, reducing component dependencies with; LAYERED AND SECTIONED ARCHITECTURE ◆ 96

security, patterns for; ARCHITECTURAL PATTERNS FOR ENABLING APPLICATION SECURITY ◆ 17

software; PATTERNS FOR SOFTWARE ARCHITECTURES ◆ 124

  adapting to changing system requirements; MICROKERNEL ◆ 87

  big ball of mud system analysis and solutions; BIG BALL OF MUD PATTERN LANGUAGE ◆ 20

  for cryptography; TROPYC: A PATTERN LANGUAGE FOR CRYPTOGRAPHIC SOFTWARE ◆ 174

  development; EVOLUTION, ARCHITECTURE, AND METAMORPHOSIS ◆ 55

  flexible foundation importance; FLEXIBLE FOUNDATIONS ◆ 55

  non-deterministic design; BLACKBOARD ◆ 22

  stream-oriented; PIPES & FILTERS ◆ 132

  THREE-TIER ARCHITECTURE ◆ 15

  TWO-TIER ARCHITECTURE ◆ 14

  of workstation software; THREE SUBSYSTEMS ◆ 135

ARCHITECTURE PATTERNS FOR BUSINESS SYSTEMS ◆ 18

  [Boyd98a]; 183

ARCHIVE SCENARIOS ◆ 48

archiving

  ARCHIVE SCENARIOS ◆ 48

  objects; HISTORIC MAPPING ◆ 16

  scenarios; ARCHIVE SCENARIOS ◆ 48

  SEPARATE TRANSACTION PROCESSING FROM ARCHIVAL ◆ 173

arguments

  caching, as optimization technique; CACHING ARGUMENT ◆ 83

  CACHING ARGUMENT ◆ 83

ARRANGING THE FURNITURE ◆ 27

ARRAY ◆ 159

arrays

  ARRAY ◆ 159

  BYTE ARRAY ◆ 159

  of bytes, coding; BYTE ARRAY ◆ 159

  compressing; RUN ARRAY ◆ 159

  creating; ARRAY ◆ 159

  RUN ARRAY ◆ 159

artificial

  ARTIFICIAL ACCESSORS ◆ 163

    CACHED EXTENSIBILITY relationship to; CACHED EXTENSIBILITY ◆ 164

    EXTENSIBLE ATTRIBUTES relationship to; ARTIFICIAL ACCESSORS ◆ 163

  ARTIFICIAL DELEGATION ◆ 164

    CACHED EXTENSIBILITY relationship to; CACHED EXTENSIBILITY ◆ 164

  HANDLE ARTIFICIAL EVENTS ◆ 76

ARTIFICIAL ACCESSORS ◆ 163

ARTIFICIAL DELEGATION ◆ 164

ASPECTS ◆ 109

aspects

  ASPECTS ◆ 109

    MATERIALS relationship to; ASPECTS ◆ 109

    TOOL AND MATERIAL COUPLING relationship to; ASPECTS ◆ 109, TOOL AND MATERIAL COUPLING ◆ 110

    TOOLS relationship to; TOOLS ◆ 109, ASPECTS ◆ 109

  objects, retrieving and storing; USE AN ASPECTADAPTOR TO HOLD AN ASPECT OF AN OBJECT ◆ 177

  relationship to tools and materials; ASPECTS ◆ 109

  USE AN ASPECTADAPTOR TO HOLD AN ASPECT OF AN OBJECT ◆ 177

assembly

  PATTERN FOR SEPARATING ASSEMBLY AND PROCESSING ◆ 97

assessment

  See Also evaluation

  MEMORY PERFORMANCE ASSESSMENT ◆ 73

  PERFORMANCE ASSESSMENT ◆ 81

ASSOCIATED OBSERVATION ◆ 9

ASSOCIATION OBJECT ◆ 23

association(s)

  See Also collections; relationships

  ASSOCIATED OBSERVATION ◆ 9

    PROCESS OF OBSERVATION relationship to; PROCESS OF OBSERVATION ◆ 9

  ASSOCIATION OBJECT ◆ 23

    ASSOCIATIVE TYPE relationship to; ASSOCIATION OBJECT ◆ 23

    CUSTOMER CONTACT relationship to; CUSTOMER CONTACT ◆ 23

    HISTORIC MAPPING relationship to; ASSOCIATION OBJECT ◆ 23

    RELATIONSHIP OBJECT relationship to; RELATIONSHIP OBJECT ◆ 20

    TEMPORAL ASSOCIATION relationship to; TEMPORAL ASSOCIATION ◆ 172

    TIMED ASSOCIATION relationship to; ASSOCIATION OBJECT ◆ 23

  ASSOCIATIVE TYPE ◆ 16

    ASSOCIATION OBJECT relationship to; ASSOCIATION OBJECT ◆ 23

    BASIC RELATIONSHIP PATTERNS relationship to; ASSOCIATIVE TYPE ◆ 16

  between hierarchies in a matrix organization; MULTIPLE HIERARCHIC ASSOCIATIONS ◆ 4

  BUSINESS PATTERNS OF ASSOCIATION OBJECTS ◆ 23

  CLASSIFYING, ASSOCIATING, AND GROUPING THE DOMAIN OBJECTS ◆ 141

  creating types for; ASSOCIATIVE TYPE ◆ 16

  HISTORY ON ASSOCIATION ◆ 34

  implementing; IMPLEMENTING ASSOCIATIONS ◆ 15

  IMPLEMENTING ASSOCIATIONS ◆ 15

  MULTIPLE HIERARCHIC ASSOCIATIONS ◆ 4

  OBJECTIFY ASSOCIATIONS; OBJECTIFY ASSOCIATIONS ◆ 5, ◆ 5

  objects, time-based relationship representation by; BUSINESS PATTERNS OF ASSOCIATION OBJECTS ◆ 23

  representation of; ASSOCIATION OBJECT ◆ 23

  states as, management strategies; WHEN STATES ARE ASSOCIATIONS, USE STATE OBJECTS ◆ 89

  between system and real world objects, representation of; ASSOCIATION OBJECT ◆ 23

  TEMPORAL ASSOCIATION ◆ 172

  WHEN STATES ARE ASSOCIATIONS, USE STATE OBJECTS ◆ 89

ASSOCIATIVE TYPE ◆ 16

assurance level
in medical observations; Active Observation, Hypothesis,
and Projection ♦ 9
AST (abstract syntax tree)
language grammar representation use; Interpreter ♦ 80
asynchronous
Asynchronous Completion Token
Memento relationship to; Asynchronous Completion
Token ♦ 19
Proactor relationship to; Asynchronous Completion
Token ♦ 19, Proactor ♦ 137
completion events, demultiplexing; Proactor ♦ 137
I/O models, integrating synchronous and;
Half-Sync/Half-Async ♦ 71
initialization, decoupling from services provided;
Connector ♦ 40
interactive systems, architecture for; Messaging
Engineering Model ♦ 18
operations, associating state with; Asynchronous
Completion Token ♦ 19
processes, coordinating; Communicating Processes ♦ 36
Asynchronous Completion Token ♦ 19
[Pyarali+98]; 193
atomic
Atomic Commitment ♦ 38
Copy-on-Write relationship to; Copy-on-Write ♦ 38
commitment; Atomic Commitment ♦ 38
transitions, mechanisms for; State-Driven Transition ♦ 59
units, term description; Compound Units ♦ 8
Atomic Commitment ♦ 38
attributes
accessing; Artificial Accessors ♦ 163, Generated
Accessors ♦ 164
adding to measurement objects; Measurement ♦ 8
aspects, relationship to tools and materials; Aspects ♦ 109
domain object, identifying; Elaboration of the Domain
Objects ♦ 141
extensible, creating; Extensible Attributes ♦ 163
Extensible Attributes ♦ 163
factoring, for role inheritance structure design; Factor Out
Common Attributes ♦ 70
Introduce Virtual Attributes ♦ 70
naming, as system design task; Identify the Nouns ♦ 70
Relationship As Attribute ♦ 20
relationship modeling; Basic Relationship Patterns ♦ 19
representing one-to-one relationships with; Relationship As
Attribute ♦ 20
validation; Essence ♦ 54
virtual, navigation assistance; Introduce Virtual
Attributes ♦ 70
Audible Alarm ♦ 79
audience
Terminology Tailored to Audience ♦ 105
auditory
See Also multimedia
Audible Alarm ♦ 79
Alarm Grid relationship to; Alarm Grid ♦ 79
Don't Let Them Forget relationship to; Don't Let Them
Forget ♦ 79

IO Triage relationship to; IO Triage ♦ 77, Audible
Alarm ♦ 79
Office Alarms relationship to; Audible Alarm ♦ 79
People Know Best relationship to; Audible Alarm ♦ 79
Auer, K.
[Auer+96]; 182
Lazy Optimization: Patterns for Efficient Smalltalk
Programming ❖ 81
[Auer95]; 182
Reusability Through Self-Encapsulation ❖ 145
[Doble+99]; 186
Smalltalk Scaffolding Patterns ❖ 163
authentication
of message sender, as cryptographic strategy; Sender
Authentication ♦ 174
Secrecy with Sender Authentication ♦ 175
sender, secrecy preservation with; Secrecy with Sender
Authentication ♦ 175
Sender Authentication ♦ 174
Author Asks for Clarification ♦ 113
Author Reads Selection ♦ 112
authoring/authors
See Also writing/writers
Author Asks for Clarification ♦ 113
Positive Closure relationship to; Author Asks for
Clarification ♦ 113
Thank the Author relationship to; Thank the
Author ♦ 113
Author Reads Selection ♦ 112
Fly on the Wall relationship to; Fly on the Wall ♦ 112
Reading Just Before Reviewing relationship to; Author
Reads Selection ♦ 112
Authors are Experts ♦ 111
Open Review relationship to; Authors are Experts ♦ 111
Safe Setting relationship to; Authors are Experts ♦ 111
Authors' Circle ♦ 112
Safe Setting relationship to; Safe Setting ♦ 111
Sitting in a Circle relationship to; Authors'
Circle ♦ 112
environments, multimedia; Composing Multimedia
Artifacts for Reuse ♦ 36
pattern, reading selection before reviewing; Author Reads
Selection ♦ 112
role in pattern writers workshops; Workshop Comprises
Authors ♦ 112
Thank the Author ♦ 113
Workshop Comprises Authors ♦ 112
Authors are Experts ♦ 111
Authors' Circle ♦ 112

Backlog ♦ 146
Backup ♦ 19
backup
Backup ♦ 19
Chain of Responsibility relationship to; Backup ♦ 19
Proxy relationship to; Backup ♦ 19
State relationship to; Backup ♦ 19
Backup
[Subramanian+96]; 196

balance
  account, as current value; ACCOUNT ◆ 10
  BALANCE SHEET AND INCOME STATEMENT ◆ 12
    ACCOUNT relationship to; BALANCE SHEET AND INCOME
      STATEMENT ◆ 12
  sheet, distinguishing income statement from; BALANCE SHEET
    AND INCOME STATEMENT ◆ 12
BALANCE SHEET AND INCOME STATEMENT ◆ 12
Barcalow, J.
  [Yoder+99]; 198
    ARCHITECTURAL PATTERNS FOR ENABLING APPLICATION
      SECURITY ◆ 17
Barkataki, S.
  [Barkataki+98]; 182
barrier option
  option relationship to; SUBTYPE STATE MACHINES ◆ 14
basic
  BASIC FSM ◆ 58
    STATE PATTERNS relationship to; BASIC FSM ◆ 58
    STATE relationship to; BASIC FSM ◆ 58
  BASIC RELATIONSHIP PATTERNS ◆ 19
    ELEVATE REFERENCES TO ENHANCE REUSE relationship to;
      ELEVATE REFERENCES TO ENHANCE REUSE ◆ 124
    OBJECT EQUIVALENCE relationship to; OBJECT
      EQUIVALENCE ◆ 10
BASIC FSM ◆ 58
BASIC RELATIONSHIP PATTERNS ◆ 19
  [Noble99a]; 191
BASKET ◆ 120
batch
  BATCH ENGINEERING MODEL ◆ 19
    MESSAGING ENGINEERING MODEL relationship to; BATCH
      ENGINEERING MODEL ◆ 19
    ONLINE ENGINEERING MODEL relationship to; BATCH
      ENGINEERING MODEL ◆ 19
    STREAM I-O ENGINEERING MODEL relationship to; STREAM
      I-O ENGINEERING MODEL ◆ 19
  engineering model, for batch processing; BATCH ENGINEERING
    MODEL ◆ 19
  stream engineering model support of; STREAM I-O
    ENGINEERING MODEL ◆ 19
BATCH ENGINEERING MODEL ◆ 19
Baumer, D.
  [Baumer+97]; 184
    ROLE OBJECT ◆ 146
  [Baumer+98]; 184
    PRODUCT TRADER ◆ 138
  [Baumer+99]; 184
    ROLE OBJECT ◆ 146
  [Riehle+98]; 193
    SERIALIZER ◆ 151
BE AWARE OF BOUNDARIES ◆ 44
BE RESPONSIVE ◆ 44
BE XXX
  BE AWARE OF BOUNDARIES ◆ 44
    BE RESPONSIVE relationship to; BE RESPONSIVE ◆ 44
    BUILD TRUST relationship to; BE AWARE OF
      BOUNDARIES ◆ 44

    IT'S A RELATIONSHIP, NOT A SALE relationship to; BE
      AWARE OF BOUNDARIES ◆ 44
    KNOW THE CUSTOMER relationship to; BE AWARE OF
      BOUNDARIES ◆ 44
    LISTEN, LISTEN, LISTEN relationship to; LISTEN, LISTEN,
      LISTEN ◆ 44
    MIND YOUR MANNERS relationship to; BE AWARE OF
      BOUNDARIES ◆ 44
    SHOW PERSONAL INTEGRITY relationship to; BE AWARE OF
      BOUNDARIES ◆ 44, SHOW PERSONAL INTEGRITY ◆ 44
  BE RESPONSIVE ◆ 44
    BE AWARE OF BOUNDARIES relationship to; BE
      RESPONSIVE ◆ 44
    BUILD TRUST relationship to; BUILD TRUST ◆ 43, BE
      RESPONSIVE ◆ 44
    IT'S A RELATIONSHIP, NOT A SALE relationship to; BE
      RESPONSIVE ◆ 44
    KNOW THE CUSTOMER relationship to; KNOW THE
      CUSTOMER ◆ 43, BE RESPONSIVE ◆ 44
    MIND YOUR MANNERS relationship to; BE RESPONSIVE ◆ 44
    SHOW PERSONAL INTEGRITY relationship to; BE
      RESPONSIVE ◆ 44
Beck, K.
  [Auer+96]; 182
    LAZY OPTIMIZATION: PATTERNS FOR EFFICIENT SMALLTALK
      PROGRAMMING ❖ 81
  [Beck97]; 182
    SMALLTALK BEST PRACTICE PATTERNS ❖ 152
  [Gamma+99]; 188
Beedle, M.
  [Beedle+99]; 182
    SCRUM: A PATTERN LANGUAGE FOR HYPERPRODUCTIVE
      SOFTWARE DEVELOPMENT ❖ 146
before methods
  concurrency control use; METHOD ADAPTERS ◆ 37
behavior
  association object handling; ASSOCIATION OBJECT ◆ 23
  behavioral patterns (GOF)
    CHAIN OF RESPONSIBILITY; CHAIN OF RESPONSIBILITY ◆ 32
    COMMAND; COMMAND ◆ 35
    INTERPRETER; INTERPRETER ◆ 80
  BEHAVIORAL REQUIREMENTS; BEHAVIORAL
    REQUIREMENTS ◆ 142
    DEFINING REQUIREMENTS relationship to; DEFINING
      REQUIREMENTS ◆ 140
    MANAGING AND MEETING CUSTOMER EXPECTATIONS
      relationship to; MANAGING AND MEETING CUSTOMER
      EXPECTATIONS ◆ 140
    OBJECT AGING relationship to; OBJECT AGING ◆ 141
    PROBLEM DOMAIN ANALYSIS relationship to; PROBLEM
      DOMAIN ANALYSIS ◆ 141
    REQUIREMENTS SPECIFICATION relationship to;
      REQUIREMENTS SPECIFICATION ◆ 142
  caching, prototyping use; CACHED EXTENSIBILITY ◆ 164
  change mechanisms; METAMORPHOSIS ◆ 55
  complexity, simplification strategies; TO SIMPLIFY COMPLEX
    BEHAVIOR, USE DECOMPOSITION ◆ 88
  customer protocol, components of; MIND YOUR
    MANNERS ◆ 44

behavior *continued*
  decoupling from control, in finite state machines;
    THREE-LEVEL FSM ♦ 172
  DEFINE CLASSES BY BEHAVIOR, NOT STATE ♦ 145
  defining classes by; DEFINE CLASSES BY BEHAVIOR, NOT
    STATE ♦ 145
  of domain objects, as relationship analysis tool; CLASSIFYING,
    ASSOCIATING, AND GROUPING THE DOMAIN OBJECTS ♦ 141
  encapsulation, state classes use for; FOR OBJECTS WITH
    MOODS, USE STATE CLASSES ♦ 88
  event-based
    architecture modeling of; EVENT-CENTERED
      ARCHITECTURE ♦ 129
    finite state machine management of; WHEN EVENTS CAUSE
      MOODS, USE STATE MACHINE ♦ 88
  factoring, into an accountability relationship;
    ACCOUNTABILITY ABSTRACTION ♦ 5
  IMPLEMENT BEHAVIOR WITH ABSTRACT STATE ♦ 145
  implementing, with abstract state; IMPLEMENT BEHAVIOR
    WITH ABSTRACT STATE ♦ 145
  meaningless, designing for; MEANINGLESS BEHAVIOR ♦ 32
  MEANINGLESS BEHAVIOR ♦ 32
  modeling, database design role; TABLE DESIGN TIME ♦ 42
  object, change relative to state change; STATE ♦ 166
  parameterization of; PLUGGABLE BEHAVIOR ♦ 156,
    PLUGGABLE BLOCK ♦ 156
  pattern writers workshop protocols; PATTERN LANGUAGE FOR
    WRITERS' WORKSHOPS ♦ 111
  PLUGGABLE BEHAVIOR ♦ 156
  relationship between entities and, defining; KEY BUSINESS
    ACTIVITIES AND INFLUENCES ♦ 165
  representation of, for object manipulation; VISITOR ♦ 179
  requirements
    analysis; BEHAVIORAL REQUIREMENTS ♦ 142
    validation; REQUIREMENTS VALIDATION ♦ 143
  selective use; MULTIPLE ACCESS LEVELS TO A PACKAGE ♦ 14
  simple instance-specific, coding of; PLUGGABLE
    SELECTOR ♦ 156
  state change, modeling, FSM use; BASIC FSM ♦ 58
  state-based, prototype handling of; SELECTOR
    SYNTHESIS ♦ 164
  of state-dependent objects, design and implementation
    strategies; MOODS: MODELS FOR OBJECT-ORIENTED
    DESIGN OF STATE ♦ 87
  STRANGE BEHAVIOR; STRANGE BEHAVIOR ♦ 128
  TO SIMPLIFY COMPLEX BEHAVIOR, USE DECOMPOSITION ♦ 88
  unusual, as indication for system testing; STRANGE
    BEHAVIOR ♦ 128
  ValueModel, wrapping objects with; USE A VALUEHOLDER TO
    HOLD A STAND-ALONE OBJECT ♦ 177
BELTLINE TERMINAL ♦ 79
  MIND YOUR OWN BUSINESS relationship to; MIND YOUR OWN
    BUSINESS ♦ 77, BELTLINE TERMINAL ♦ 79
Benner, K. M.
  [Kim+96]; 189
    IMPLEMENTATION PATTERNS FOR THE OBSERVER
      PATTERN ❖ 74

Berczuk, S. P.
  [Berczuk95]; 182
    PATTERN FOR SEPARATING ASSEMBLY AND PROCESSING ♦ 97
  [Berczuk96]; 182
    ORGANIZATIONAL MULTIPLEXING: PATTERNS FOR
      PROCESSING SATELLITE TELEMETRY WITH DISTRIBUTED
      TEAMS ♦ 94
  [Berczuk97]; 183
    TEAMWORK AND CONFIGURATION MANAGEMENT ❖ 170
bid
  quote representation of; QUOTE ♦ 13
BIG BALL OF MUD PATTERN LANGUAGE ♦ 20
  BIG BALL OF MUD ♦ 21
  [Foote+99]; 187
BLACK-BOX FRAMEWORK ♦ 122
  FINE-GRAINED OBJECTS relationship to; FINE-GRAINED
    OBJECTS ♦ 122, BLACK-BOX FRAMEWORK ♦ 122
  HOT SPOTS relationship to; HOT SPOTS ♦ 122, BLACK-BOX
    FRAMEWORK ♦ 122
  PLUGGABLE OBJECTS relationship to; BLACK-BOX
    FRAMEWORK ♦ 122
  VISUAL BUILDER relationship to; BLACK-BOX
    FRAMEWORK ♦ 122, VISUAL BUILDER ♦ 123
  WHITE-BOX FRAMEWORKS relationship to; WHITE-BOX
    FRAMEWORKS ♦ 121
BLACKBOARD ♦ 22
  [Buschmann+96]; 183
  REPOSITORY relationship to; REPOSITORY ♦ 125
  SPONSOR-SELECTOR relationship to; SPONSOR-SELECTOR ♦ 164
blocking
  INTERRUPTS UNJAM BLOCKING ♦ 69
  objects, defining, in concurrent systems; SERVICES 'WAITING
    FOR' ♦ 62
blocks
  enumeration, parameters, naming; SIMPLE ENUMERATION
    PARAMETER ♦ 163
  formatting; RECTANGULAR BLOCK ♦ 162
  PLUGGABLE BLOCK ♦ 156
body
  HANDLE/BODY ♦ 24
  HANDLE/BODY HIERARCHY ♦ 24
BODYGUARD ♦ 22
  ACCEPTOR relationship to; BODYGUARD ♦ 22
  BROKER relationship to; BODYGUARD ♦ 22
  [DasNeves+98]; 186
  PROXY relationship to; BODYGUARD ♦ 22
  REACTOR relationship to; BODYGUARD ♦ 22
BOOKING ENTRIES TO MULTIPLE ACCOUNTS ♦ 12
  ACCOUNT relationship to; BOOKING ENTRIES TO MULTIPLE
    ACCOUNTS ♦ 12
  MEMO ACCOUNT relationship to; BOOKING ENTRIES TO
    MULTIPLE ACCOUNTS ♦ 12
boolean
  BOOLEAN PROPERTY SETTING METHOD ♦ 158
  properties, setting; BOOLEAN PROPERTY SETTING
    METHOD ♦ 158
BOOLEAN PROPERTY SETTING METHOD ♦ 158

Bootstrapping ♦ 26
　Problem-Oriented Team relationship to;
　　Bootstrapping ♦ 26
　Production Potential relationship to; Production
　　Potential ♦ 26
　Round Pegs for Round Holes relationship to;
　　Bootstrapping ♦ 26
bottlenecks
　capacity as, strategies for dealing with; Capacity
　　Bottleneck ♦ 100
　Capacity Bottleneck ♦ 100
Bottom Line ♦ 78
　Five Minutes of No Escalation Messages relationship to;
　　Bottom Line ♦ 78
　George Washington is Still Dead relationship to; George
　　Washington is Still Dead ♦ 78, Bottom Line ♦ 78
　IO Gatekeeper relationship to; Bottom Line ♦ 78
　IO Triage relationship to; IO Triage ♦ 77
　MML relationship to; MML ♦ 77
　Shut Up and Listen relationship to; Bottom Line ♦ 78,
　　Shut Up and Listen ♦ 79
boundaries
　Application Boundary ♦ 136
　Application Design is Bounded by Test Design ♦ 66
　respect for, importance in customer relations; Be Aware of
　　Boundaries ♦ 44
box
　Works Out of the Box ♦ 150
Boyd, L. L.
　[Boyd98a]; 183
　　Architecture Patterns for Business Systems ♦ 18
　[Boyd98b]; 183
　　Business Patterns of Association Objects ♦ 23
Bradac, M.
　[Bradac+98]; 183
　　Pattern Language for Developing Form Style
　　　Windows ❖ 99
Braga, A. M.
　[Braga+99]; 183
　　Tropyc: A Pattern Language for Cryptographic
　　　Software ❖ 174
Brant, J.
　[Brant+99]; 183
　　Creating Reports with Query Objects ♦ 40
Bridge ♦ 22, ♦ 123
　Abstract Factory relationship to; Bridge ♦ 22
　Adapter relationship to; Adapter ♦ 6, Bridge ♦ 22
　Algebraic Hierarchy relationship to; Algebraic
　　Hierarchy ♦ 25
　[Alpert+98]; 182
　From Prototype to Reality relationship to; From
　　Prototype to Reality ♦ 61
　[Gamma+95]; 188
　Interface's Role relationship to; Interface's Role ♦ 30
　Pedestal relationship to; Bridge ♦ 123
　Point relationship to; Point ♦ 134
　Prototype and Reality relationship to; Prototype and
　　Reality ♦ 63

　Recoverable Distributor relationship to; Recoverable
　　Distributor ♦ 143
Broadcast/Listener
　Visibility and Communication between Control
　　Modules relationship to; Visibility and Communication
　　between Control Modules ♦ 61
Broker ♦ 22, ♦ 108, ♦ 115
　[Buschmann+96]; 183
Broker as Divorce Attorney ♦ 133
Broker as Intermediary ♦ 133
Broker as Matchmaker ♦ 133
brokers
　Broker ♦ 22, ♦ 108, ♦ 115
　　Bodyguard relationship to; Bodyguard ♦ 22
　　(Legacy) Wrapper relationship to; (Legacy)
　　　Wrapper ♦ 115
　　Manager relationship to; Manager ♦ 86
　　Manager-Agent relationship to; Manager-Agent ♦ 114
　　Microkernel relationship to; Microkernel ♦ 87
　　Object Metadata relationship to; Object
　　　Metadata ♦ 108
　　Object Metatdata relationship to; Broker ♦ 108
　　Pocket-Sized Broker relationship to; Pocket-Sized
　　　Broker ♦ 133
　　Proxy relationship to; Broker ♦ 108
　　Query Broker relationship to; Query Broker ♦ 4
　　Query Object relationship to; Broker ♦ 108, Query
　　　Object ♦ 108
　　Sponsor-Selector relationship to; Sponsor-
　　　Selector ♦ 164
　Broker as Divorce Attorney ♦ 133
　　Broker as Intermediary relationship to; Broker as
　　　Divorce Attorney ♦ 133
　　Broker as Matchmaker relationship to; Broker as
　　　Matchmaker ♦ 133
　　Proxy relationship to; Broker as Divorce
　　　Attorney ♦ 133
　Broker as Intermediary ♦ 133
　　Broker as Divorce Attorney relationship to; Broker as
　　　Divorce Attorney ♦ 133
　　Broker as Matchmaker relationship to; Broker as
　　　Matchmaker ♦ 133
　　Transceiver-Parcel relationship to; Broker as
　　　Intermediary ♦ 133
　Broker as Matchmaker ♦ 133
　　Broker as Diverce Attorney relationship to; Broker as
　　　Matchmaker ♦ 133
　　Broker as Intermediary relationship to; Broker as
　　　Matchmaker ♦ 133
　connecting relational database views with; Query
　　Broker ♦ 4
　low overhead; Broker as Intermediary ♦ 133
　performance improvement; Broker as Matchmaker ♦ 133
　Pocket-Sized Broker; Pocket-Sized Broker ♦ 133
　　Broker relationship to; Pocket-Sized Broker ♦ 133
　Query Broker ♦ 4
Brown, K.
　[Alpert+98]; 182
　　Abstract Factory ♦ 2

Brown, K. *continued*
[Alpert+98]; 182 *continued*
   Adapter ♦ 6
   Bridge ♦ 22
   Builder ♦ 23
   Chain of Responsibility ♦ 32
   Command ♦ 35
   Composite ♦ 37
   Decorator ♦ 46
   Facade ♦ 56
   Factory Method ♦ 56
   Flyweight ♦ 60
   Hook Method ♦ 73
   Iterator ♦ 80
   Mediator ♦ 86
   Memento ♦ 87
   Observer ♦ 94
   Prototype ♦ 138
   Proxy ♦ 139
   Singleton ♦ 152
   State ♦ 166
   Template Method ♦ 171
   Visitor ♦ 179
[Alpert+98], Interpreter ♦ 80
[Brown+96a]; 183
   Pattern Language for Smalltalk & Relational Databases ❖ 106
[Brown+96b]; 183
   Crossing Chasms: A Pattern Language for Object-RDBMS Integration ♦ 41
[Brown96]; 183
Brugali, D.
[Aarsten+96a]; 181
   From Prototype to Reality ♦ 61
budget
memory, establishing for restricted memory software development; Memory Budget ♦ 72
Memory Budget ♦ 72
Buffalo Mountain ♦ 67
buffering
double, display update use; Double Buffer ♦ 50
Double Buffer ♦ 50
event queues with artificial events; Handle Artificial Events ♦ 76
Use a BufferedValueHolder to Delay the Commit of a New Value ♦ 177
Build Trust ♦ 43
Builder ♦ 23
[Alpert+98]; 182
Gamma+95]; 188
building
Build Trust ♦ 43
   Be Aware of Boundaries relationship to; Be Aware of Boundaries ♦ 44
   Be Responsive relationship to; Build Trust ♦ 43, Be Responsive ♦ 44
   Customer Meetings: Go Early, Stay Late relationship to; Build Trust ♦ 43, Customer Meetings: Go Early, Stay Late ♦ 44
   Get Involved Early relationship to; Get Involved Early ♦ 126
   Go Early, Stay Late relationship to; Build Trust ♦ 43
   It's a Relationship, Not a Sale relationship to; It's a Relationship, Not a Sale ♦ 43, Build Trust ♦ 43
   Listen, Listen, Listen relationship to; Build Trust ♦ 43, Listen, Listen, Listen ♦ 44
   Mind Your Manners relationship to; Mind Your Manners ♦ 44
   Show Personal Integrity relationship to; Show Personal Integrity ♦ 44
Builder
   Abstract Factory relationship to; Builder ♦ 23
   Hierarchy of Factories relationship to; Hierarchy of Factories ♦ 94
   Parser/Builder relationship to; Parser/Builder ♦ 94
   Session Control & Observation relationship to; Session Control & Observation ♦ 151
Building the Right Things ♦ 140
Containment Building ♦ 131
Driver Duty Builder, Cascade relationship to; Cascade ♦ 28
Parser/Builder ♦ 94
projects, as team training technique; Trial Project ♦ 130
software tools; Tool Composition ♦ 110
transportation systems; Pattern Language of Transport Systems (Point and Route) ♦ 114
trust
   in customer relationships; Build Trust ♦ 43
   in pattern writers workshops; Workshop Comprises Authors ♦ 112, Community of Trust ♦ 112
   between system designers and testers; Get Involved Early ♦ 126
Visual Builder ♦ 123
Building the Right Things ♦ 140
Bureaucracy ♦ 23
[Riehle98]; 193
Tool Composition relationship to; Tool Composition ♦ 110
Buschmann, F.
[Buschmann+96]; 183
   Blackboard ♦ 22
   Broker ♦ 22
   Client-Dispatcher-Server ♦ 34
   Command Processor ♦ 36
   Counted Pointer ♦ 40
   Forwarder-Receiver ♦ 60
   Layers ♦ 81
   Master-Slave ♦ 86
   Microkernel ♦ 87
   Model-View-Controller ♦ 87
   Pipes & Filters ♦ 132
   Presentation-Abstraction-Control ♦ 135
   Proxy ♦ 139
   Publisher-Subscriber ♦ 139
   Reflection ♦ 144
   View Handler ♦ 178
[Buschmann95]; 183
   Master-Slave ♦ 86

[Buschmann96]; 184
    REFLECTION ♦ 144
[PLoPD3]; 192
business
  architecture patterns for; ARCHITECTURE PATTERNS FOR
    BUSINESS SYSTEMS ♦ 18
  ARCHITECTURE PATTERNS FOR BUSINESS SYSTEMS ♦ 18
  BUSINESS ACCOUNTS ♦ 173
  BUSINESS PATTERNS OF ASSOCIATION OBJECTS ♦ 23
  BUSINESS RULES
    BUSINESS RULES ♦ 142
    ELABORATION OF THE DOMAIN OBJECTS relationship to;
      ELABORATION OF THE DOMAIN OBJECTS ♦ 141
    PROBLEM DOMAIN ANALYSIS relationship to; PROBLEM
      DOMAIN ANALYSIS ♦ 141
  BUSINESS TRANSACTIONS ♦ 173
    SEPARATE TRANSACTION PROCESSING FROM ARCHIVAL
      relationship to; BUSINESS TRANSACTIONS ♦ 173, SEPARATE
      TRANSACTION PROCESSING FROM ARCHIVAL ♦ 173
  CREATING AND UPDATING BUSINESS OBJECTS ♦ 91
  customer relationship, representation of; CUSTOMER
    CONTACT ♦ 23
  EXPLICIT BUSINESS RULES ♦ 173
  KEY BUSINESS ACTIVITIES AND INFLUENCES ♦ 165
  measurement protocols; MEASUREMENT PROTOCOL ♦ 9
  MIND YOUR OWN BUSINESS ♦ 77
  objectives, identifying; SPONSOR OBJECTIVES ♦ 140
  orders, representation of; 3-LEVEL ORDER ♦ 24
  rules
    decoupling from transaction-processing software; EXPLICIT
      BUSINESS RULES ♦ 173
    defining and capturing; BUSINESS RULES ♦ 142
  SEARCHING FOR BUSINESS OBJECTS ♦ 90
  state
    tracking with business accounts; BUSINESS ACCOUNTS ♦ 173
    transaction capture of; BUSINESS TRANSACTIONS ♦ 173
  transaction processing systems, strategies for; TRANSACTIONS
    AND ACCOUNTS ♦ 172
  WHOLE BUSINESS ENTITIES ♦ 165
BUSINESS ACCOUNTS ♦ 173
BUSINESS PATTERNS OF ASSOCIATION OBJECTS ♦ 23
  [Boyd98b]; 183
BUSINESS RULES ♦ 142
BUSINESS TRANSACTIONS ♦ 173
BUSY SYSTEM ♦ 127
buying
  contract use in; CONTRACT ♦ 13
  price, quote representation of; QUOTE ♦ 13
BYTE ARRAY ♦ 159
bytes
  array of, coding; BYTE ARRAY ♦ 159
  BYTE ARRAY ♦ 159

C++ IDIOMS pattern language ♦ 24
  [Coplien99c]; 185
C++ language
  C++ IDIOMS pattern language ♦ 24
  clients, decoupling from servers; ABSTRACT CLIENT ♦ 2

  dynamic object lifetime management; LOCALIZED
    OWNERSHIP: MANAGING DYNAMIC OBJECTS IN C++ ♦ 85
  membership semantics for containers; MEMBER
    CONTAINER ♦ 86
CACHE MANAGEMENT ♦ 109
CACHEABLE EXPRESSION ♦ 82
CACHED EXTENSIBILITY ♦ 164
caching
  ALLOCATOR CACHES ♦ 148
  arguments, as optimization technique; CACHING
    ARGUMENT ♦ 83
  behavior, prototyping use; CACHED EXTENSIBILITY ♦ 164
  CACHE MANAGEMENT ♦ 109
  CACHE PROXY, PROXY DESIGN PATTERN REVISITED
    relationship to; PROXY DESIGN PATTERN REVISITED ♦ 139
  CACHEABLE EXPRESSION ♦ 82
    CACHING STATE VARIABLE relationship to; CACHING STATE
      VARIABLE ♦ 83
  CACHED EXTENSIBILITY ♦ 164
    ARTIFICIAL ACCESSORS relationship to; CACHED
      EXTENSIBILITY ♦ 164
    ARTIFICIAL DELEGATION relationship to; CACHED
      EXTENSIBILITY ♦ 164
    EXTENSIBLE ATTRIBUTES relationship to; EXTENSIBLE
      ATTRIBUTES ♦ 163
  CACHING ARGUMENT ♦ 83
    CACHING STATE VARIABLE relationship to; CACHING STATE
      VARIABLE ♦ 83
    TRANSIENT REDUCTION relationship to; TRANSIENT
      REDUCTION ♦ 83
  CACHING STATE VARIABLE ♦ 83
    CACHEABLE EXPRESSION relationship to; CACHING STATE
      VARIABLE ♦ 83
    CACHING ARGUMENT relationship to; CACHING STATE
      VARIABLE ♦ 83
    CACHING TEMPORARY VARIABLE relationship to; CACHING
      STATE VARIABLE ♦ 83
    LAZY INITIALIZATION relationship to; CACHING STATE
      VARIABLE ♦ 83
  CACHING TEMPORARY VARIABLE ♦ 83, ♦ 158
    CACHING STATE VARIABLE relationship to; CACHING STATE
      VARIABLE ♦ 83
  as collection searching optimization technique; LOOKUP
    CACHE ♦ 161
  expressions, as optimization technique; CACHEABLE
    EXPRESSION ♦ 82
  LOOKUP CACHE ♦ 161
  management of, in a relational database; CACHE
    MANAGEMENT ♦ 109
  temporary variables; CACHING TEMPORARY VARIABLE ♦ 158
  variables
    state, as optimization technique; CACHING STATE
      VARIABLE ♦ 83
    temporary, as optimization technique; CACHING TEMPORARY
      VARIABLE ♦ 83
  windows, in legacy system/object-oriented framework
    interactions; WINDOW-KEEPING ♦ 91
CACHING ARGUMENT ♦ 83
CACHING STATE VARIABLE ♦ 83

CACHING TEMPORARY VARIABLE ♦ 83, ♦ 158
callbacks
    event handling use; DETERMINE THE ACTORS ♦ 71
    event-driven system use; OBJECTS WITH REMOTE
        CONTROL ♦ 93
    multi-team distributed system development use; LOOSE
        INTERFACES ♦ 94
calls
    open, stateless method use with; OPEN CALLS ♦ 38
    OPEN CALLS ♦ 38
    processing, designing an object-oriented system for; DECISION
        DEFERRAL AND CAPTURE PATTERN LANGUAGE ♦ 45
CAM (computer-aided manufacturing)
    G++ pattern language; G++: A PATTERN LANGUAGE FOR
        COMPUTER-INTEGRATED MANUFACTURING ♦ 61
Campbell, R.
    [Sane+96a]; 194
        DETACHABLE INSPECTOR ♦ 49
    [Sane+96b]; 194
        RESOURCE EXCHANGER ♦ 144
cancellation
    multiphase; MULTIPHASE CANCELLATION ♦ 39
    MULTIPHASE CANCELLATION ♦ 39
    of user requests, strategies for handling; MATCH PROGRESS
        WORK WITH NEW ♦ 101
CAPABLE, PRODUCTIVE, AND SATISFIED ♦ 26
    PATTERNS FOR DESIGNING IN TEAMS relationship to; PATTERNS
        FOR DESIGNING IN TEAMS ♦ 118
    [Taylor99]; 196
capacity
    CAPACITY BOTTLENECK ♦ 100
        PROCESSING CAPACITY relationship to; CAPACITY
            BOTTLENECK ♦ 100
    limited, strategies for dealing with; CAPACITY
        BOTTLENECK ♦ 100
    PATTERN LANGUAGE FOR IMPROVING THE CAPACITY OF
        REACTIVE SYSTEMS ♦ 100
    PROCESSING CAPACITY ♦ 100
    of reactive systems, improving; PATTERN LANGUAGE FOR
        IMPROVING THE CAPACITY OF REACTIVE SYSTEMS ♦ 100
    of real-time systems, improving; PATTERN LANGUAGE FOR
        IMPROVING THE CAPACITY OF REACTIVE SYSTEMS ♦ 100
CAPACITY BOTTLENECK ♦ 100
CAPTAIN OATES ♦ 72
    MEMORY OVERDRAFT relationship to; MEMORY
        OVERDRAFT ♦ 72
    PARTIAL FAILURE relationship to; PARTIAL FAILURE ♦ 72,
        CAPTAIN OATES ♦ 72
    THINK SMALL relationship to; THINK SMALL ♦ 72
Cargill, T.
    [Cargill96]; 184
    [Cargill96b], LOCALIZED OWNERSHIP: MANAGING DYNAMIC
        OBJECTS IN C++ ❖ 85
CARGO CULT ♦ 131
    SACRIFICIAL LAMB relationship to; CARGO CULT ♦ 131
Carlson, A.
    [Carlson+99]; 184
        TEMPORAL PATTERNS ❖ 171

[Carlson99]; 184
    ESSENCE ♦ 54
Carmichael, A.
    [Carmichael98]; 184
Carvalho, S.
    [Rossi+96]; 194
        DESIGN PATTERNS FOR OBJECT-ORIENTED HYPERMEDIA
            APPLICATIONS ❖ 48
CASCADE ♦ 28, ♦ 163
    DRIVER DUTY BUILDER relationship to; CASCADE ♦ 28
    DRIVER DUTY relationship to; CASCADE ♦ 28, DRIVER
        DUTY ♦ 51
    [Foster+99]; 187
    message, formatting; CASCADE ♦ 163
    ROLE OBJECT relationship to; CASCADE ♦ 28
    ROUTE relationship to; CASCADE ♦ 28
CASUAL DUTY ♦ 130
CATALYTIC SCENARIOS ♦ 47
    ELEMENT IDENTIFICATION relationship to; ELEMENT
        IDENTIFICATION ♦ 46
    JUDICIOUS FIREWORKS relationship to; CATALYTIC
        SCENARIOS ♦ 47
    PROTOTYPING LANGUAGES relationship to; PROTOTYPING
        LANGUAGES ♦ 47
categorization
    See Also classification
    CATEGORIZE OBJECTS FOR CONCURRENCY ♦ 62
CATEGORIZE OBJECTS FOR CONCURRENCY ♦ 62
CATERPILLAR'S FATE: A PATTERN LANGUAGE FOR THE
    TRANSFORMATION FROM ANALYSIS TO DESIGN ♦ 28
    [Kerth95]; 189
    TIME THREAD ANALYSIS relationship to; TIME THREAD
        ANALYSIS ♦ 71
Cerwin, J.
    [Cerwin98]; 184
CHAIN OF RESPONSIBILITY ♦ 32
    [Alpert+98]; 182
    BACKUP relationship to; BACKUP ♦ 19
    COMPOSITE relationship to; CHAIN OF RESPONSIBILITY ♦ 32,
        COMPOSITE ♦ 37
    EVENTHANDLER relationship to; CHAIN OF
        RESPONSIBILITY ♦ 32, EVENTHANDLER ♦ 55
    [Gamma+95]; 188
    OBJECT RECURSION relationship to; CHAIN OF
        RESPONSIBILITY ♦ 32, OBJECT RECURSION ♦ 92
    POSTING RULES relationship to; SOURCES OF AN ENTRY ♦ 12
    PROACTOR relationship to; PROACTOR ♦ 137
    SHOPPER relationship to; SHOPPER ♦ 152
    SOURCES OF AN ENTRY relationship to; SOURCES OF AN
        ENTRY ♦ 12
    TRANSACTION relationship to; SOURCES OF AN ENTRY ♦ 12
champions
    CHAMPIONS REVIEW PAPERS ♦ 74
        IDENTIFY THE CHAMPION relationship to; CHAMPIONS
            REVIEW PAPERS ♦ 74
        MAKE CHAMPIONS EXPLICIT relationship to; CHAMPIONS
            REVIEW PAPERS ♦ 74

CHAMPIONS SPEAK FIRST ♦ 74
  CONSENSUS ON PC PAPERS relationship to; CONSENSUS ON
    PC PAPERS ♦ 74
  IDENTIFY THE CONFLICTS relationship to; CHAMPIONS
    SPEAK FIRST ♦ 74
  IDENTIFY MISSING CHAMPIONS ♦ 74
  IDENTIFY THE CHAMPION ♦ 73
  IDENTIFY THE CHAMPION PATTERN LANGUAGE ❖ 73
  PC meeting priorities; CHAMPIONS SPEAK FIRST ♦ 74
  project, software development role; PATRON ♦ 65
  technical papers
    identifying; IDENTIFY THE CHAMPION ♦ 73
    strategies for encouraging champions; CHAMPIONS REVIEW
      PAPERS ♦ 74
    strategies for ensuring; IDENTIFY MISSING CHAMPIONS ♦ 74
CHAMPIONS REVIEW PAPERS ♦ 74
change(ing)
  CHANGE LOG ♦ 34
  consistent, making in multi-level models; DOWNWARD
    CHANGES ♦ 45
  of container, recording previous reference; MEMENTO
    CHILD ♦ 35
  data, analysis of; TIME THREAD ANALYSIS ♦ 71
  decoupling from commit; EDITS INSIDE ♦ 136
  DOWNWARD CHANGES ♦ 45
  history of, creating accounts to record; ACCOUNT ♦ 10
  independence, as model design guideline; APPROPRIATE
    LIVING MODELS ♦ 45
  isolating, from rest of the model; PUT FREQUENTLY VARYING
    STRUCTURES IN INSTANCES ♦ 5
  mechanisms, design issues; METAMORPHOSIS ♦ 55
  multiple value, ValueModel framework handling; USE A
    BUFFEREDVALUEHOLDER TO DELAY THE COMMIT OF A
    NEW VALUE ♦ 177
  notification, of objects; USE onChangeSend:to: TO
    REGISTER INTERESTS ON A VALUE ♦ 176
  object
    relationships, tracking; TEMPORAL ASSOCIATION ♦ 172
    tracking; TEMPORAL PROPERTY ♦ 171
  in objects, over time, strategies for handling; TEMPORAL
    PATTERNS ♦ 171
  ONE MESSAGE PER CHANGE REQUEST ♦ 75
  OPTIMIZED MESSAGES PER CHANGE REQUEST ♦ 75
  predicted, isolating; PROTECTED VARIATIONS ♦ 135
  requests
    handling optiminzation; OPTIMIZED MESSAGES PER CHANGE
      REQUEST ♦ 75
    strategies for handling; ONE MESSAGE PER CHANGE
      REQUEST ♦ 75
  requirements
    handling; SOFTWARE TECTONICS ♦ 55
    handling without destroying system architecture; PIECEMEAL
      GROWTH ♦ 21
    microkernel architecture as mechanism for handling;
      MICROKERNEL ♦ 87
  SELECTIVE CHANGES ♦ 114
  simple strategies for handling; USE VALUEMODEL CHAINS
    INSTEAD OF onChangeSend:to: ♦ 176

state
  behavior modeling, FSM use; BASIC FSM ♦ 58
  classification of classes; WHEN THERE ARE MANY MOODS,
    USE MOOD CLASSIFIER ♦ 89
  in domain objects, requirements analysis; OBJECT
    AGING ♦ 141
  encapsulating in a finite state machine; DYNAMIC STATE
    INSTANTIATION ♦ 60
  event notification; EVENT NOTIFICATION ♦ 54
  handling, in a software tools environment; EVENT
    MECHANISM ♦ 110
  mechanisms for; STATE-DRIVEN TRANSITION ♦ 59
  moderating reports about; FIVE MINUTES OF NO
    ESCALATION MESSAGES ♦ 78
  one-to-many dependency relationship management of;
    OBSERVER ♦ 94
  sending information to an observer; CONDUIT OF SUBJECT
    CHANGE ♦ 75
  strategies for detecting; GEORGE WASHINGTON IS STILL
    DEAD ♦ 78
  subform selection based on; SUBFORM MATCH ♦ 100
  values; SETTING METHOD ♦ 157
  vetoable, use with vetoable set methdos; VETOABLE
    CHANGES ♦ 39
  VETOABLE CHANGES ♦ 39
CHANGE LOG ♦ 34
channels
  SECURE-CHANNEL COMMUNICATION ♦ 174
  SYNCHRONIZE CHANNELS ♦ 37
  USE A RANGEADAPTOR TO CHANNEL A NUMBER'S
    RANGE ♦ 177
chaotic systems
  analysis and solutions; BIG BALL OF MUD PATTERN
    LANGUAGE ♦ 20
CHECK POINT ♦ 17
check(s)
  CHECK POINT ♦ 17
    ROLE relationship to; CHECK POINT ♦ 17
    SESSION relationship to; CHECK POINT ♦ 17
    SINGLE ACCESS POINT relationship to; SINGLE ACCESS
      POINT ♦ 17
  checklist, as teaching aid; VISIBLE CHECKLIST ♦ 117
  CHECKS
    FULL VIEW WITH ERRORS relationship to; FULL VIEW WITH
      ERRORS ♦ 18
    LIMITED VIEW relationship to; LIMITED VIEW ♦ 18
  CHECKS: PATTERN LANGUAGE OF INFORMATION
    INTEGRITY ♦ 32
  DOUBLE CHECK ♦ 38
  illegal values, synchronization of; DOUBLE CHECK ♦ 38
  VISIBLE CHECKLIST ♦ 117
CHECKS: PATTERN LANGUAGE OF INFORMATION
  INTEGRITY ♦ 32
[Cunningham95]; 186
chicken
  CHICKEN AND EGG ♦ 116
  SCHEDULE CHICKEN ♦ 132
CHICKEN AND EGG ♦ 116

child
 MEMENTO CHILD ♦ 35
choice
 CHOOSING ENTRIES ♦ 11
 CHOOSING MESSAGE ♦ 154
CHOOSING ENTRIES ♦ 11
CHOOSING MESSAGE ♦ 154
churn avoidance
 software development schedule management; TAKE NO SMALL
  SLIPS ♦ 69
circle
 pattern writers workshop structure
  communications role; SITTING IN A CIRCLE ♦ 112
  trust role; AUTHORS' CIRCLE ♦ 112
citizen
 See Also first-class citizens
 good citizenship, within systems, establishing protocols for;
  SYSTEM CITIZEN'S ROLE ♦ 29
 SYSTEM CITIZEN'S ROLE ♦ 29
CLASS CLAUSE ♦ 121
class(es)
 abstract
  creation of; LIFE CYCLE AND REFACTORING PATTERNS THAT
   SUPPORT EVOLUTION AND REUSE ♦ 84
  inheritance hierarchy cleanup use; CREATE ABSTRACT
   SUPERCLASS ♦ 85
 ABSTRACT CLASS ♦ 2
 adding interfaces to; EXTENSION OBJECT ♦ 55
 CLASS CLAUSE ♦ 121
  CLASS SEMANTICS relationship to; CLASS SEMANTICS ♦ 121
  CLASS SPECIFICATION relationship to; CLASS
   SPECIFICATION ♦ 121
  LATE CREATION relationship to; LATE CREATION ♦ 120
 CLASS RETRIEVAL ♦ 120
  CLASS SEMANTICS relationship to; CLASS SEMANTICS ♦ 121
  CLASS SPECIFICATION relationship to; CLASS
   SPECIFICATION ♦ 121
 CLASS SEMANTICS ♦ 121
  CLASS CLAUSE relationship to; CLASS SEMANTICS ♦ 121
  CLASS RETRIEVAL relationship to; CLASS SEMANTICS ♦ 121
  CLASS SPECIFICATION relationship to; CLASS
   SEMANTICS ♦ 121
  LATE CREATION relationship to; CLASS SEMANTICS ♦ 121
 CLASS SPECIFICATION ♦ 121
  CLASS CLAUSE relationship to; CLASS SPECIFICATION ♦ 121
  CLASS RETRIEVAL relationship to; CLASS
   SPECIFICATION ♦ 121
  CLASS SEMANTICS relationship to; CLASS SEMANTICS ♦ 121
  LATE CREATION relationship to; CLASS SPECIFICATION ♦ 121
 CLASSES OF EVENT OBJECTS ♦ 129
  EVENT-CENTERED ARCHITECTURE relationship to; CLASSES
   OF EVENT OBJECTS ♦ 129
 clause, class semantic representation use; CLASS
  CLAUSE ♦ 121
 decoupling objects from; TYPE OBJECT ♦ 176
 deferring operations to subclasses; FACTORY METHOD ♦ 56
 DEFINE CLASSES BY BEHAVIOR, NOT STATE ♦ 145
 FOR OBJECTS WITH MOODS, USE STATE CLASSES ♦ 88
 hierarchies, designing; ABSTRACT CLASS ♦ 2

 implementation of, inheritance use; REUSABILITY THROUGH
  SELF-ENCAPSULATION ♦ 145
 instance management, encapsulation of; MANAGER ♦ 86
 as instances of other classes, support for; TYPE OBJECT ♦ 176
 PATTERN AS A CLASS ♦ 97
 PATTERNS FOR ENCAPSULATING CLASS TREES ♦ 120
 properties, class clause representation of; CLASS
  CLAUSE ♦ 121
 relationships among, managing; JUDGE ♦ 81
 representing patterns as; PATTERN AS A CLASS ♦ 97
 retrieval of, class specification use; CLASS
  SPECIFICATION ♦ 121
 reuse strategies; SELFISH CLASS PATTERN LANGUAGE ♦ 149
 SELFISH CLASS ♦ 150
 SELFISH CLASS PATTERN LANGUAGE ♦ 149
 semantics, class clause representation of; CLASS
  SEMANTICS ♦ 121
 single instance guarantee; SINGLETON ♦ 152
 Smalltalk, client-server system structure; FOUR-LAYER
  ARCHITECTURE ♦ 106
 specification, retrieving classes with; CLASS
  SPECIFICATION ♦ 121
 state
  classification of; WHEN THERE ARE MANY MOODS, USE
   MOOD CLASSIFIER ♦ 89
  managing complex dynamic behavior with; FOR OBJECTS
   WITH MOODS, USE STATE CLASSES ♦ 88
 subclasses, naming; QUALIFIED SUBCLASS NAME ♦ 162
 super, communication with; SUPER ♦ 155
 superclasses, naming; SIMPLE SUPERCLASS NAME ♦ 162
 trees
  creating objects from; LATE CREATION ♦ 120
  encapsulation of; PATTERNS FOR ENCAPSULATING CLASS
   TREES ♦ 120
  retrieval of information from; CLASS RETRIEVAL ♦ 120
CLASS RETRIEVAL ♦ 120
CLASS SEMANTICS ♦ 121
CLASS SPECIFICATION ♦ 121
CLASSES OF EVENT OBJECTS ♦ 129
classification
 of business rules; BUSINESS RULES ♦ 142
 of classes that can be reused; SYMMETRICAL REUSE ♦ 123
 CLASSIFYING, ASSOCIATING, AND GROUPING THE DOMAIN
  OBJECTS ♦ 141
  INFORMATION NEEDS relationship to; CLASSIFYING,
   ASSOCIATING, AND GROUPING THE DOMAIN
   OBJECTS ♦ 141
  PROBLEM DOMAIN ANALYSIS relationship to; PROBLEM
   DOMAIN ANALYSIS ♦ 141
 of customer product expectations; MANAGING AND MEETING
  CUSTOMER EXPECTATIONS ♦ 140
 of errors, into condition hierarchies; EXCEPTION ♦ 89
 of events, fine-grained; FINE-GRAINED CLASSIFICATION OF
  EVENTS ♦ 129
 FINE-GRAINED CLASSIFICATION OF EVENTS ♦ 129
 of measurements; RANGE ♦ 9
 of objects, for concurrency; CATEGORIZE OBJECTS FOR
  CONCURRENCY ♦ 62

of output, in fault-tolerant systems; MIND YOUR OWN
BUSINESS ♦ 77
of relationships; TYPED RELATIONSHIP ♦ 5
of state classes; WHEN THERE ARE MANY MOODS, USE
MOOD CLASSIFIER ♦ 89
of user requests, as system throughput optimization strategy;
SHED LOAD ♦ 101
**CLASSIFYING, ASSOCIATING, AND GROUPING THE DOMAIN
OBJECTS ♦ 141**
classroom
PATTERNS FOR CLASSROOM EDUCATION ♦ 116
teaching, patterns for; PATTERNS FOR CLASSROOM
EDUCATION ♦ 116
clause
class, class semantic representation use; CLASS CLAUSE ♦ 121
clean start
See RECONSTRUCTION
CLEAR TARGET AUDIENCE ♦ 104
CLEAR THE FOG ♦ 168
clearing
CLEAR TARGET AUDIENCE ♦ 104
CODE SAMPLES AS BONUS relationship to; CODE SAMPLES AS
BONUS ♦ 105
CODE SAMPLES relationship to; CODE SAMPLES ♦ 105
TERMINOLOGY TAILORED TO AUDIENCE relationship to;
TERMINOLOGY TAILORED TO AUDIENCE ♦ 105
UNDERSTOOD NOTATIONS relationship to; UNDERSTOOD
NOTATIONS ♦ 105
CLEAR THE FOG ♦ 168
EARLY AND REGULAR DELIVERY relationship to; CLEAR THE
FOG ♦ 168, EARLY AND REGULAR DELIVERY ♦ 168
MICROCOSM relationship to; CLEAR THE FOG ♦ 168,
MICROCOSM ♦ 168
PROTOTYPE relationship to; CLEAR THE FOG ♦ 168,
PROTOTYPE ♦ 168
CLEARING THE PALATE ♦ 113
EARLY AND REGULAR DELIVERY, CLEAR THE FOG relationship
to; CLEAR THE FOG ♦ 168
CLEARING THE PALATE ♦ 113
Cleeland, C.
[Cleeland+98a]; 184
EXTERNAL POLYMORPHISM ♦ 56
[Cleeland+98b]; 185
EXTERNAL POLYMORPHISM ♦ 56
client(s)
ABSTRACT CLIENT ♦ 2
APPROACHES FOR SEPARATING CLIENTS FROM SERVERS ♦ 16
CLIENT SYNCHRONIZATION ♦ 109
CLIENT-DISPATCHER-SERVER ♦ 34
ACCEPTOR relationship to; CLIENT-DISPATCHER-
SERVER ♦ 34
CONNECTOR relationship to; CLIENT-DISPATCHER-
SERVER ♦ 34, CONNECTOR ♦ 40
FORWARDER-RECEIVER relationship to; CLIENT-
DISPATCHER-SERVER ♦ 34, FORWARDER-RECEIVER ♦ 60
MANAGER relationship to; MANAGER ♦ 86
SPONSOR-SELECTOR relationship to; SPONSOR-
SELECTOR ♦ 164

client-server applications, persistent accessor use;
PERSISTENCE ACCESSORS ♦ 135
CLIENT-SPECIFIED SELF ♦ 34
CLIENT/SERVER FRAMEWORK ♦ 91
CREATING AND UPDATING BUSINESS OBJECTS relationship
to; CLIENT/SERVER FRAMEWORK ♦ 91
SEARCHING FOR BUSINESS OBJECTS relationship to;
CLIENT/SERVER FRAMEWORK ♦ 91
VIEWING relationship to; CLIENT/SERVER FRAMEWORK ♦ 91
CLIENT/SERVER/SERVICE ♦ 62
decoupling, from servers; ABSTRACT CLIENT ♦ 2, APPROACHES
FOR SEPARATING CLIENTS FROM SERVERS ♦ 16
decoupling products from; PRODUCT TRADER ♦ 138
dispatcher as intermediary between servers and;
CLIENT-DISPATCHER-SERVER ♦ 34
encapsulating state for, in a Session object; ABSTRACT
SESSION ♦ 2
hierarchical database views as; QUERY BROKER ♦ 4
interaction with, creating a hierarchical structure for;
BUREAUCRACY ♦ 23
NEW CLIENTS WITH OLD SERVERS: A PATTERN LANGUAGE
FOR CLIENT/SERVER FRAMEWORKS ♦ 89
parameterization, COMMAND support of; COMMAND ♦ 35
rendering objects at, in object-oriented framework/legacy
system interactions; MATERIALIZATION ♦ 90
selective behavior; MULTIPLE ACCESS LEVELS TO A
PACKAGE ♦ 14
server architecture
as distributed system architecture; DISTRIBUTED
PROCESSES ♦ 51
four-tier; FOUR-LAYER ARCHITECTURE ♦ 106
frameworks, legacy system relationships with; NEW
CLIENTS WITH OLD SERVERS: A PATTERN LANGUAGE FOR
CLIENT/SERVER FRAMEWORKS ♦ 89
in legacy system/object-oriented framework interactions;
CLIENT/SERVER FRAMEWORK ♦ 91
partitioning, two-tier; TWO-TIER ARCHITECTURE ♦ 14
resource and service standardization;
CLIENT/SERVER/SERVICE ♦ 62
three-tier; THREE-TIER ARCHITECTURE ♦ 15
specific views, role objects as; ROLE OBJECT ♦ 146
synchronizing, with databases; CLIENT
SYNCHRONIZATION ♦ 109
thin, engineering model for; ONLINE ENGINEERING
MODEL ♦ 18
CLIENT SYNCHRONIZATION ♦ 109
CLIENT-DISPATCHER-SERVER ♦ 34
[Buschmann+96]; 183
[Sommerlad+96]; 196
CLIENT-SPECIFIED SELF ♦ 34
[Viljamaa95]; 197
CLIENT/SERVER FRAMEWORK ♦ 91
CLIENT/SERVER/SERVICE ♦ 62
CLIP REQUESTS ♦ 50
clipping
CLIP REQUESTS ♦ 50
REQUEST UPDATE relationship to; REQUEST UPDATE ♦ 49,
CLIP REQUESTS ♦ 50
hidden regions, in a display request; CLIP REQUESTS ♦ 50

closure
    of business accounts, month-end; MONTH END CLOSING ♦ 173
    pattern writers workshop; CLEARING THE PALATE ♦ 113
    POSITIVE CLOSURE ♦ 113
Coad, P.
    [Coad95]; 185
Cockburn, A.
    [Cockburn96]; 185
        PRIORITIZING FORCES IN SOFTWARE DESIGN ❖ 135
    [Cockburn98]; 185
        SURVIVING OBJECT-ORIENTED PROJECTS: A MANAGER'S
        GUIDE ❖ 168
code(ing)
    See Also programming
    CODE LOCKING ♦ 147
        DATA LOCKING relationship to; DATA LOCKING ♦ 147
        HIERARCHICAL LOCKING relationship to; HIERARCHICAL
        LOCKING ♦ 148
    CODE OWNERSHIP ♦ 66
        PRIVATE VERSIONING relationship to; PRIVATE
        VERSIONING ♦ 170
    CODE SAMPLES ♦ 105
        CLEAR TARGET AUDIENCE relationship to; CODE
        SAMPLES ♦ 105
        CODE SAMPLES AS BONUS relationship to; CODE
        SAMPLES ♦ 105, CODE SAMPLES AS BONUS ♦ 105
    CODE SAMPLES AS BONUS ♦ 105
        CLEAR TARGET AUDIENCE relationship to; CODE SAMPLES
        AS BONUS ♦ 105
        CODE SAMPLES relationship to; CODE SAMPLES AS
        BONUS ♦ 105
    common, factoring; HOT SPOTS ♦ 122
    debug print method; DEBUG PRINTING METHOD ♦ 154
    generated, modifying just once; GENERATION GAP ♦ 63
    locking; CODE LOCKING ♦ 147
    methods, that contain each other; EXECUTE AROUND
        METHOD ♦ 154
    minimizing amount required, for customer demonstrations;
        MUTABLE CODE ♦ 47
    modules, ownership guidelines; CODE OWNERSHIP ♦ 66
    MUTABLE CODE ♦ 47
    partitioning into ENVY/Developer components;
        PARTITIONING SMALLTALK CODE INTO ENVY/DEVELOPER
        COMPONENTS ♦ 96
    review, design validation use; GROUP VALIDATION ♦ 66
    samples, pattern writing importance; CODE SAMPLES ♦ 105
    source code formatting; INDENTED CONTROL FLOW ♦ 162,
        RECTANGULAR BLOCK ♦ 162
    THROWAWAY CODE ♦ 21
CODE LOCKING ♦ 147
CODE OWNERSHIP ♦ 66
CODE SAMPLES ♦ 105
CODE SAMPLES AS BONUS ♦ 105
coherance
    in module teaching; MODULE'S STORY ♦ 116
    of purpose, in teams, strategies for developing; UNITY OF
        PURPOSE ♦ 95
Coldewey, J.
    [Keller+98b]; 189

collaboration
    COLLABORATIVE WORK PACKETS ♦ 28
        CONCURRENT THREADS OF EXECUTION relationship
        to; CONCURRENT THREADS OF EXECUTION ♦ 28,
        COLLABORATIVE WORK PACKETS ♦ 28
        WORK PACKET COMPLETION REPORT relationship to; WORK
        PACKET COMPLETION REPORT ♦ 29
        WORK PACKET PRIORITY relationship to; WORK PACKET
        PRIORITY ♦ 29
        WORK PACKET SECURITY relationship to; WORK PACKET
        SECURITY ♦ 29
        WORK PACKET STATUS REPORT relationship to; WORK
        PACKET STATUS REPORT ♦ 29
    in distributed systems, without system-level support;
        BODYGUARD ♦ 22
    among objects, support for; USE A VALUEMODEL TO
        GENERALIZE AN OBJECT'S ASPECT ♦ 176
    between system test and design, strategies for managing;
        DESIGNERS ARE OUR FRIENDS ♦ 126, GET INVOLVED
        EARLY ♦ 126
    work packets, identifying; COLLABORATIVE WORK
        PACKETS ♦ 28
COLLABORATIVE WORK PACKETS ♦ 28
COLLECT ♦ 160
COLLECTING PARAMETER ♦ 156
COLLECTING TEMPORARY VARIABLE ♦ 158
COLLECTION ♦ 159
COLLECTION ACCESSOR METHOD ♦ 157
COLLECTION OBJECT ♦ 20
COLLECTION OF HISTORY PATTERNS ♦ 34
    [Anderson99]; 182
collection(s)
    See Also aggregation
    accessing; COLLECTION ACCESSOR METHOD ♦ 157,
        ENUMERATION METHOD ♦ 158
    COLLECT ♦ 160
    COLLECTING PARAMETER ♦ 156
    COLLECTING TEMPORARY VARIABLE ♦ 158
    COLLECTION ♦ 159
        COLLECTION OBJECT relationship to; COLLECTION
        OBJECT ♦ 20, COLLECTION ♦ 159
    COLLECTION ACCESSOR METHOD ♦ 157
    COLLECTION OBJECT ♦ 20
        COLLECTION relationship to; COLLECTION OBJECT ♦ 20,
        COLLECTION ♦ 159
        MUTUAL FRIENDS relationship to; MUTUAL FRIENDS ♦ 20
        RELATIONSHIP AS ATTRIBUTE relationship to; RELATIONSHIP
        AS ATTRIBUTE ♦ 20
        RELATIONSHIP OBJECT relationship to; RELATIONSHIP
        OBJECT ♦ 20
    COLLECTION OF HISTORY PATTERNS ♦ 34
    compressing; RUN ARRAY ♦ 159
    concatenating; CONCATENATION ♦ 160
    concatenating into streams; CONCATENATING STREAM ♦ 162
    display, restricting the size of; MEGA-SCROLLING ♦ 90
    dynamically sized; ORDERED COLLECTION ♦ 159
    executing code across; ENUMERATION ♦ 160
    filtering; SELECT/REJECT ♦ 160
    gathering values from; COLLECT ♦ 160

Hypoth-A-Sized Collection ◆ 84
iterating over; Do ◆ 160
Ordered Collection ◆ 159
removing duplicates from; Duplicate Removing Set ◆ 161
representation, in a relational database; Representing
    Collections in a Relational Database ◆ 42
representation of
    with a fixed number of elements; Array ◆ 159
    with unique elements; Set ◆ 159
Representing Collections ◆ 107
Representing Collections in a Relational
    Database ◆ 42
representing in a relational database; Representing
    Collections ◆ 107
returning; Collecting Parameter ◆ 156
running values over; Inject:into: ◆ 161
saving a snapshot of; History On Tree ◆ 35
searching; Detect ◆ 160
    optimization of; Lookup Cache ◆ 161
searching for elements in; Includes: ◆ 160
size, sufficient initial allocation, as optimization technique;
    Hypoth-A-Sized Collection ◆ 84
Sorted Collection ◆ 159
sorting; Sorted Collection ◆ 159
    providing multiple sort orders; Temporarily Sorted
    Collection ◆ 161
Temporarily Sorted Collection ◆ 161
testing, for emptiness; Is Empty ◆ 160
Use an IndexedAdaptor to Hold a Single Index in a
    Collection ◆ 177
of values, saving in temporary variables; Collecting
    Temporary Variable ◆ 158
wrapping ValueModel behavior around an element of; Use
    an IndexedAdaptor to Hold a Single Index in a
    Collection ◆ 177
Colorful Analogy ◆ 117
Pitfall Diagnosis and Prevention relationship to; Pitfall
    Diagnosis and Prevention ◆ 116
Simulation Games relationship to; Colorful
    Analogy ◆ 117
Command ◆ 35
[Alpert+98]; 182
[Gamma+95]; 188
Command Processor ◆ 36
[Buschmann+96]; 183
[Sommerlad96]; 196
command(s)
Command ◆ 35
    Adapter relationship to; Adapter ◆ 6
    Command Processor relationship to; Command ◆ 35,
        Command Processor ◆ 36
    Composite relationship to; Command ◆ 35
    Event Queue relationship to; Event Queue ◆ 76
    Memento relationship to; Command ◆ 35, Memento ◆ 87
    Object Recovery relationship to; Object Recovery ◆ 92
    Prototype relationship to; Command ◆ 35
    Session Control & Observation relationship to; Session
        Control & Observation ◆ 151

Transactions and Accounts relationship to;
    Command ◆ 35
Command Processor ◆ 36
    Command relationship to; Command ◆ 35, Command
        Processor ◆ 36
    Diagnostic Context relationship to; Diagnostic
        Context ◆ 124
    Object Recovery relationship to; Object Recovery ◆ 92
Flexible Command Interpreter ◆ 60
comments
Method Comment ◆ 154
methods; Method Comment ◆ 154
commitment
atomic; Atomic Commitment ◆ 38
Atomic Commitment ◆ 38
decoupling editing changes from; Edits Inside ◆ 136
Use a BufferedValueHolder to Delay the Commit of a
    New Value ◆ 177
common
Common Problems Highlighted ◆ 106
Common State ◆ 156
interests, in pattern writers workshops; Community of
    Trust ◆ 112
problems, factoring, when writing a pattern language;
    Common Problems Highlighted ◆ 106
Common Problems Highlighted ◆ 106
Common State ◆ 156
Communicating Processes ◆ 36
communication(s)
Active Object support for; Active Object ◆ 6
Communicating Processes ◆ 36
connection, encapsulation, dispatcher use for;
    Client-Dispatcher-Server ◆ 34
decoupling initialization, from services provided;
    Acceptor ◆ 3
between development and business sides of an organization,
    product walkthrough use; Market Walk-through ◆ 52
encapsulating client state, in a Session object; Abstract
    Session ◆ 2
through events, mechanisms for; Actions Triggered by
    Events ◆ 62
in a fire alarm system, representation of; Deviation ◆ 134
in a hierarchy of control layers; Visibility and
    Communication between Control Modules ◆ 61
human-machine, design strategies for large and complex
    systems; MML ◆ 77
I/O gatekeeper, in telecommunications system design; IO
    Gatekeeper ◆ 77
inter-process, providing transparency in;
    Forwarder-Receiver ◆ 60
inter-processor, of overload conditions; Leaky Bucket of
    Credits ◆ 102
interfaces, hiding from legacy clients; Request ◆ 90
among interoperating applications; Broker ◆ 115
among model levels; Upward Traceability ◆ 45
network management interfaces; Pattern System for
    Network Management Interfaces ◆ 114
between pairs of objects; Work Accomplished Through
    Dialogs ◆ 30

communication(s) *continued*
PATTERNS FOR LOGGING DIAGNOSTIC MESSAGES ♦ 124
SECURE-CHANNEL COMMUNICATION ♦ 174
among software development roles, as tool for increasing
responsiveness; COUPLING DECREASES LATENCY ♦ 69
software development team
managing unequal distribution of; THREE TO SEVEN
HELPERS PER ROLE ♦ 68
structures that support; SHAPING CIRCULATION
REALMS ♦ 67, BUFFALO MOUNTAIN ♦ 67
systems, asynchronous completion event demultiplexing;
PROACTOR ♦ 137
VISIBILITY AND COMMUNICATION BETWEEN CONTROL
MODULES ♦ 61
community
See Also organization; team
COMMUNITY OF TRUST ♦ 112
OPEN REVIEW relationship to; OPEN REVIEW ♦ 111,
COMMUNITY OF TRUST ♦ 112
SAFE SETTING relationship to; COMMUNITY OF TRUST ♦ 112
COMMUNITY OF TRUST ♦ 112
COMPARABLE WORK ♦ 52
COMPARING METHOD ♦ 153
comparison
See Also equality; ordering
COMPARABLE WORK ♦ 52
COMPARING METHOD ♦ 153
of objects; COMPARING METHOD ♦ 153
compatibility
MERGE COMPATIBLE EVENTS ♦ 76
COMPENSATE SUCCESS ♦ 69
competition
among designers, effective design strategy; MULTIPLE
COMPETING DESIGNS ♦ 118
among designs, decision making strategies; DECISION
DOCUMENT ♦ 118
EPISODES: A PATTERN LANGUAGE OF COMPETITIVE
DEVELOPMENT ♦ 51
MULTIPLE COMPETING DESIGNS ♦ 118
software development structures and strategies for;
EPISODES: A PATTERN LANGUAGE OF COMPETITIVE
DEVELOPMENT ♦ 51
COMPLETED AND ABANDONED ACTIONS ♦ 12
completion
as action termination description; COMPLETED AND
ABANDONED ACTIONS ♦ 12
asynchronous completion events, demultiplexing;
PROACTOR ♦ 137
ASYNCHRONOUS COMPLETION TOKEN ♦ 19
of asynchronous operations, associating state with;
ASYNCHRONOUS COMPLETION TOKEN ♦ 19
COMPLETED AND ABANDONED ACTIONS ♦ 12
COMPLETION HEADROOM ♦ 53
RECOMMITMENT MEETING relationship to; COMPLETION
HEADROOM ♦ 53
SIZE THE SCHEDULE relationship to; SIZE THE
SCHEDULE ♦ 64
TAKE NO SMALL SLIPS relationship to; COMPLETION
HEADROOM ♦ 53

WORK QUEUE REPORT relationship to; WORK QUEUE
REPORT ♦ 52
WORK SPLIT relationship to; WORK SPLIT ♦ 53
computation, Futures handling of; FUTURES ♦ 40
project, time estimation strategies; COMPLETION
HEADROOM ♦ 53
reports, work packets; WORK PACKET COMPLETION
REPORT ♦ 29
WORK PACKET COMPLETION REPORT ♦ 29
COMPLETION HEADROOM ♦ 53
complexity
behavior, simplification strategies; TO SIMPLIFY COMPLEX
BEHAVIOR, USE DECOMPOSITION ♦ 88
capability subsetting, as reusability strategy; GENTLE
LEARNING CURVE ♦ 150
encapsulation of, as reusability strategy; LOW
SURFACE-TO-VOLUME RATIO ♦ 150
as force, in relationship patterns; RELATIONSHIP OBJECT ♦ 20
handling, in event class design; CLASSES OF EVENT
OBJECTS ♦ 129
layering management of; CASCADE ♦ 28
parallelization, elimination of; SEQUENTIAL PROGRAM ♦ 147
reducing, in visitor operations; EXTRINSIC VISITOR ♦ 56
in software development, resource management strategies;
INTERRUPTS UNJAM BLOCKING ♦ 69
of state-dependent objects, design and implementation
strategies; MOODS: MODELS FOR OBJECT-ORIENTED
DESIGN OF STATE ♦ 87
system
avoiding redundancy in; OBJECT MERGE ♦ 10
controling through layering system functions into
hierarchies; HIERARCHY OF CONTROL LAYERS ♦ 61
TO SIMPLIFY COMPLEX BEHAVIOR, USE DECOMPOSITION ♦ 88
COMPONENT LIBRARY ♦ 122
components
attribute validation; ESSENCE ♦ 54
COMPONENT LIBRARY ♦ 122
FINE-GRAINED OBJECTS relationship to; FINE-GRAINED
OBJECTS ♦ 122
HOT SPOTS relationship to; COMPONENT LIBRARY ♦ 122,
HOT SPOTS ♦ 122
PLUGGABLE OBJECTS relationship to; PLUGGABLE
OBJECTS ♦ 122
WHITE-BOX FRAMEWORKS relationship to; COMPONENT
LIBRARY ♦ 122
COMPONENTS LAYOUT ♦ 36
decoupling, extensible mechanisms for;
TRANSCEIVER-PARCEL ♦ 133
FUNCTION OWNERS/COMPONENT OWNERS ♦ 169
graphical
updating request for display; REQUEST UPDATE ♦ 49
visibility, display list management of; DISPLAY LIST ♦ 49
integration of; PATTERN-BASED INTEGRATION
ARCHITECTURES ♦ 115
library, framework development use; COMPONENT
LIBRARY ♦ 122
ownership of; FUNCTION OWNERS/COMPONENT
OWNERS ♦ 169
query composition from; COMPOSABLE QUERY OBJECTS ♦ 41

reducing dependencies among; LAYERED AND SECTIONED
ARCHITECTURE ♦ 96
tools, building software tools from a hierarchy of; TOOL
COMPOSITION ♦ 110

COMPONENTS LAYOUT ♦ 36

COMPOSABLE QUERY OBJECTS ♦ 41

COMPOSED METHOD ♦ 152

COMPOSING MULTIMEDIA ARTIFACTS FOR REUSE ♦ 36
[Cybulski+99]; 186

COMPOSITE ♦ 37
[Alpert+98]; 182
[Gamma+95]; 188

COMPOSITE TRANSACTIONS ♦ 173

composition
See Also delegation
COMPOSABLE QUERY OBJECTS ♦ 41
COMPOSITE relationship to; COMPOSABLE QUERY
OBJECTS ♦ 41
DECORATOR relationship to; COMPOSABLE QUERY
OBJECTS ♦ 41
INTERPRETER relationship to; COMPOSABLE QUERY
OBJECTS ♦ 41
OBSERVER relationship to; COMPOSABLE QUERY
OBJECTS ♦ 41
QUERY OBJECTS relationship to; COMPOSABLE QUERY
OBJECTS ♦ 41
COMPOSED METHOD ♦ 152
PLUGGABLE BLOCK relationship to; PLUGGABLE
BLOCK ♦ 156
PLUGGABLE SELECTOR relationship to; PLUGGABLE
SELECTOR ♦ 156
COMPOSING MULTIMEDIA ARTIFACTS FOR REUSE ♦ 36
COMPOSITE ♦ 37
CHAIN OF RESPONSIBILITY relationship to; CHAIN OF
RESPONSIBILITY ♦ 32, COMPOSITE ♦ 37
COMMAND relationship to; COMMAND ♦ 35
COMPOSABLE QUERY OBJECTS relationship to; COMPOSABLE
QUERY OBJECTS ♦ 41
DECORATOR relationship to; COMPOSITE ♦ 37,
DECORATOR ♦ 46
DRIVER DUTY relationship to; DRIVER DUTY ♦ 51
HISTORY ON TREE relationship to; HISTORY ON TREE ♦ 35
INTERPRETER relationship to; INTERPRETER ♦ 80
ITERATOR relationship to; COMPOSITE ♦ 37
PERIODIC OBJECT relationship to; PERIODIC OBJECT ♦ 134
PROGRAMMING-BY-DIFFERENCE relationship to;
PROGRAMMING-BY-DIFFERENCE ♦ 150
ROUTE relationship to; ROUTE ♦ 114
VISITOR relationship to; COMPOSITE ♦ 37
WHOLE-PART relationship to; WHOLE-PART ♦ 179
COMPOSITE TRANSACTIONS ♦ 173
in framework development, inheritance vs.; BLACK-BOX
FRAMEWORK ♦ 122
framework development use; HOT SPOTS ♦ 122
of multimedia artifacts
glue use for; GLUE ♦ 36
for reusability; COMPOSING MULTIMEDIA ARTIFACTS FOR
REUSE ♦ 36
object, tree structure representation of; COMPOSITE ♦ 37

of queries, from components; COMPOSABLE QUERY
OBJECTS ♦ 41
TOOL COMPOSITION ♦ 110
of transactions, handling; COMPOSITE TRANSACTIONS ♦ 173

compound
COMPOUND UNITS ♦ 8
CONVERSION RATIO relationship to; COMPOUND UNITS ♦ 8
units, term description; COMPOUND UNITS ♦ 8

COMPOUND UNITS ♦ 8

compression
of common element runs, in arrays and collections; RUN
ARRAY ♦ 159

computation completion
Futures handling of; FUTURES ♦ 40

computer models
validation of; FORECAST CONFIRMATION ♦ 33

CONCATENATING STREAM ♦ 84, ♦ 162

CONCATENATION ♦ 160

concatenation
of collections; CONCATENATION ♦ 160
into streams; CONCATENATING STREAM ♦ 162
CONCATENATING STREAM ♦ 84, ♦ 162
HYPOTH-A-SIZED COLLECTION relationship to;
CONCATENATING STREAM ♦ 84, CONCATENATING
STREAM ♦ 162
TRANSIENT REDUCTION relationship to; TRANSIENT
REDUCTION ♦ 83
CONCATENATION ♦ 160
of streams, as optimization technique; CONCATENATING
STREAM ♦ 84

concepts
interdependent, teaching strategies; CHICKEN AND EGG ♦ 116
SUBTYPING OBSERVATION CONCEPTS ♦ 8
system-level, event class design use; CLASSES OF EVENT
OBJECTS ♦ 129
teaching, analogies use; COLORFUL ANALOGY ♦ 117

concrete
CONCRETE DATA TYPE ♦ 25
ALGEBRAIC HIERARCHY relationship to; CONCRETE DATA
TYPE ♦ 25
COUNTED BODY relationship to; CONCRETE DATA TYPE ♦ 25
data types, vs. abstract data types; CONCRETE DATA TYPE ♦ 25
ENCAPSULATE CONCRETE STATE ♦ 145

CONCRETE DATA TYPE ♦ 25

concurrency
See Also parallelism; threads
ACTIVE OBJECT support for; ACTIVE OBJECT ♦ 6
associating state with asynchronous operation completion;
ASYNCHRONOUS COMPLETION TOKEN ♦ 19
asynchronous completion event demultiplexing;
PROACTOR ♦ 137
atomic commitment; ATOMIC COMMITMENT ♦ 38
CATEGORIZE OBJECTS FOR CONCURRENCY ♦ 62
categorizing objects for; CATEGORIZE OBJECTS FOR
CONCURRENCY ♦ 62
client/server/service model use; CLIENT/SERVER/SERVICE ♦ 62
CONCURRENT PROGRAMMING IN JAVA: DESIGN PRINCIPLES
AND PATTERNS, 2ND ED. ❖ 37

concurrency *continued*
  CONCURRENT THREADS OF EXECUTION ♦ 28
    COLLABORATIVE WORK PACKETS relationship to;
      CONCURRENT THREADS OF EXECUTION ♦ 28,
      COLLABORATIVE WORK PACKETS ♦ 28
    CRITICAL REGION PROTECTION relationship to; CRITICAL
      REGION PROTECTION ♦ 31
    SHAPE OF PROGRAM relationship to; CONCURRENT THREADS
      OF EXECUTION ♦ 28
    SYNCHRONIZATION OF CONCURRENT THREADS relationship
      to; CONCURRENT THREADS OF EXECUTION ♦ 28,
      SYNCHRONIZATION OF CONCURRENT THREADS ♦ 28
    SYSTEM CITIZEN'S ROLE relationship to; SYSTEM CITIZEN'S
      ROLE ♦ 29
  decoupling initialization, from services provided;
    ACCEPTOR ♦ 3
  distributed control systems, software development strategies;
    OBJECT-ORIENTED DESIGN PATTERNS IN REACTIVE
    SYSTEMS ♦ 92
  identifying collaborative work packets; COLLABORATIVE
    WORK PACKETS ♦ 28
  Java patterns; CONCURRENT PROGRAMMING IN JAVA: DESIGN
    PRINCIPLES AND PATTERNS, 2ND ED. ♦ 37
  load sharing; RESOURCE EXCHANGER ♦ 144
  in manufacturing systems, G++ pattern language; G++:
    A PATTERN LANGUAGE FOR COMPUTER-INTEGRATED
    MANUFACTURING ♦ 61
  object-oriented architecture, fire alarm system family; POINTS
    AND DEVIATIONS: PATTERN LANGUAGE OF FIRE ALARM
    SYSTEMS ♦ 133
  one-way messaging designs; THREAD-PER-MESSAGE ♦ 39
  performance requirements relationship to; PERIODIC
    OBJECT ♦ 134
  SYNCHRONIZATION OF CONCURRENT THREADS ♦ 28
  system, controling complexity through layering system
    functions into hierarchies; HIERARCHY OF CONTROL
    LAYERS ♦ 61
  thread; SYNCHRONIZATION OF CONCURRENT THREADS ♦ 28
  transformation from analysis to design, pattern language for;
    CATERPILLAR'S FATE: A PATTERN LANGUAGE FOR THE
    TRANSFORMATION FROM ANALYSIS TO DESIGN ♦ 28
  work load sharing, as system throughput optimization; SHARE
    THE LOAD ♦ 101
CONCURRENT PROGRAMMING IN JAVA: DESIGN PRINCIPLES
  AND PATTERNS, 2ND ED. ❖ 37
  [Lea99]; 190
CONCURRENT THREADS OF EXECUTION ♦ 28
CONDITIONAL EXPRESSION ♦ 163
conditions
  CONDITIONAL EXPRESSION ♦ 163
  formating source code to reflect; GUARD CLAUSE ♦ 162
  handling, of complex behavior; FOR OBJECTS WITH MOODS,
    USE STATE CLASSES ♦ 88
  states as, management strategies; WHEN STATES ARE
    CONDITIONS, USE PREDICATIVE STATE CLASSES ♦ 88
  system testing; BUSY SYSTEM ♦ 127
  WHEN STATES ARE CONDITIONS, USE PREDICATIVE STATE
    CLASSES ♦ 88

CONDUIT OF SUBJECT CHANGE ♦ 75
  OBSERVER relationship to; CONDUIT OF SUBJECT
    CHANGE ♦ 75
  OBSERVER UPDATE MESSAGE relationship to; CONDUIT OF
    SUBJECT CHANGE ♦ 75
  ONE MESSAGE PER AFFECTED OBJECT relationship to; ONE
    MESSAGE PER AFFECTED OBJECT ♦ 75
  ONE MESSAGE PER CHANGE REQUEST relationship to; ONE
    MESSAGE PER CHANGE REQUEST ♦ 75
  OPTIMIZED MESSAGES PER CHANGE REQUEST relationship to;
    OPTIMIZED MESSAGES PER CHANGE REQUEST ♦ 75
conferences
  technical paper acceptance process; IDENTIFY THE CHAMPION
    PATTERN LANGUAGE ♦ 73
configuration
  CONFIGURATION MANAGEMENT, NAMED STABLE BASES
    relationship to; NAMED STABLE BASES ♦ 68
  knowledge level facilitation of; KNOWLEDGE LEVEL ♦ 5
  management
    application to organization management; TEAMWORK AND
      CONFIGURATION MANAGEMENT ♦ 170
    partitioning code for; PARTITIONING SMALLTALK CODE INTO
      ENVY/DEVELOPER COMPONENTS ♦ 96
  prototype-based object systems; PROTOTYPE-BASED OBJECT
    SYSTEM ♦ 139
  of reports, design strategies; REPORT OBJECTS ♦ 41
  SERVICE CONFIGURATOR ♦ 151
  of services; SERVICE CONFIGURATOR ♦ 151
  TEAMWORK AND CONFIGURATION MANAGEMENT ♦ 170
confirmation
  of computer models; FORECAST CONFIRMATION ♦ 33
  FORECAST CONFIRMATION ♦ 33
CONFLICT SETS ♦ 39
conflicts
  CONFLICT SETS ♦ 39
  design, handling; SUBCLASS PER TEAM ♦ 136
  IDENTIFY THE CONFLICTS ♦ 74
  technical paper selection, strategies for handling; IDENTIFY
    THE CONFLICTS ♦ 74
connections
  CONNECTOR ♦ 40
    ABSTRACT SESSION relationship to; ABSTRACT SESSION ♦ 2
    ACCEPTOR relationship to; CONNECTOR ♦ 40
    ACTIVE OBJECT relationship to; CONNECTOR ♦ 40
    CLIENT-DISPATCHER-SERVER relationship to;
      CLIENT-DISPATCHER-SERVER ♦ 34, CONNECTOR ♦ 40
    FACTORY METHOD relationship to; CONNECTOR ♦ 40
    REACTOR relationship to; CONNECTOR ♦ 40
    SERVICE CONFIGURATOR relationship to; CONNECTOR ♦ 40
    TEMPLATE METHOD relationship to; CONNECTOR ♦ 40
  remote, for error handling; BELTLINE TERMINAL ♦ 79
CONNECTOR ♦ 40
  [Schmidt98b]; 195
CONSENSUS ON PC PAPERS ♦ 74
  CHAMPIONS SPEAK FIRST relationship to; CONSENSUS ON PC
    PAPERS ♦ 74
conservation
  preservation of, transactions use for; TRANSACTION ♦ 10

consistency
Maintain Consistent ValueModelValueTypes ◆ 177
maintaining, for object value types; Maintain Consistent ValueModelValueTypes ◆ 177
as Mutual Friends force; Mutual Friends ◆ 20
Consolidate Requests ◆ 50
Consolidate the Program to Support Evolution and Reuse ◆ 85
consolidation
Consolidate Requests ◆ 50
Request Update relationship to; Request Update ◆ 49, Consolidate Requests ◆ 50
Consolidate the Program to Support Evolution and Reuse ◆ 85
of requests, for display update; Consolidate Requests ◆ 50
Constant Method ◆ 157
constants
coding; Constant Method ◆ 157
Constant Method ◆ 157
Constraint Observer ◆ 41
constraints
Abstract Models with Constraints in Subtypes ◆ 4
Constraint Observer ◆ 41
Formula Objects relationship to; Formula Objects ◆ 41, Constraint Observer ◆ 41
domain object, identifying; Elaboration of the Domain Objects ◆ 141
domain rule enforcement with, in abstract models; Abstract Models with Constraints in Subtypes ◆ 4
formula updating management; Constraint Observer ◆ 41
implementing; Implementing Constraints ◆ 16
Implementing Constraints ◆ 16
materials
coordinating changes in; Tool Coordinator ◆ 111
separating from tools; Material Container ◆ 111
construction
Constructor Method ◆ 152
Constructor Parameter Method relationship to; Constructor Parameter Method ◆ 152
Method Object relationship to; Method Object ◆ 153
#Constructor Method, Shortcut Constructor Method relationship to; Shortcut Constructor Method ◆ 152
Constructor Parameter Method ◆ 152
Constructor Method relationship to; Constructor Parameter Method ◆ 152
Converter Constructor Method ◆ 153
decoupling from representation; Builder ◆ 23
of instances; Constructor Method ◆ 152
off objects, messages use; Shortcut Constructor Method ◆ 152
Shortcut Constructor Method ◆ 152
Virtual Constructor ◆ 25
Constructor Parameter Method ◆ 152
containers
change of, recording previous reference; Memento Child ◆ 35
Containment Building ◆ 131
grouping materials into; Material Container ◆ 111
interation of; Iterable Container ◆ 80
Iterable Container ◆ 80
Material Container ◆ 111
Member Container ◆ 86
membership semantics for; Member Container ◆ 86
nested, managing relationships in; Observer Update Message ◆ 75
open, layering of; Open Containers ◆ 38
Open Containers ◆ 38
virtual, managing distributed system objects with; Pool ◆ 134
Containment Building ◆ 131
contention
high, locking primitives for; Queued Lock ◆ 149, Queued Reader/Writer Lock ◆ 149, Counter Reader/Writer Lock ◆ 149, Distributed Reader/Writer Lock ◆ 149
low, locking primitives for; Test-and-Set Lock ◆ 148
reduction, double-checked locking use; Double-Checked Locking ◆ 51
contents
Work Packet Contents ◆ 28
context(s)
alarm design consideration of, in fault-tolerant systems; Office Alarms ◆ 79
diagnostic, establishing; Diagnostic Context ◆ 124
Diagnostic Context ◆ 124
multiple, hypermedia navigation strategies for; Nodes in Context ◆ 119
navigation, set-based strategies for designing; Set-based Navigation ◆ 119
Nodes in Context ◆ 119
continuity
Continuous Processing ◆ 174
Month End Closing relationship to; Continuous Processing ◆ 174
project, high-level manager/champion role; Patron ◆ 65
Continuous Processing ◆ 174
Contract ◆ 13
contracts
Contract ◆ 13
Forward Contracts relationship to; Forward Contracts ◆ 13
Options relationship to; Options ◆ 14
Portfolio relationship to; Portfolio ◆ 13
Product relationship to; Product ◆ 14
forward, time dependencies; Forward Contracts ◆ 13
Forward Contracts ◆ 13
portfolio as collection of; Portfolio ◆ 13
term description; Contract ◆ 13
control
access
check point use for; Check Point ◆ 17
distributed systems without system-level support; Bodyguard ◆ 22
handling multiple package access levels; Multiple Access Levels to a Package ◆ 14
secure access layer as security integration tool; Secure Access Layer ◆ 18
single access point use for; Single Access Point ◆ 17
to state objects; Exposed State ◆ 166
Architect Controls Product ◆ 65

control *continued*

decoupling from behavior, in finite state machines;
THREE-LEVEL FSM ♦ 172

DISTRIBUTION OF CONTROL MODULES ♦ 63

flow

See Also algorithms

in an fire alarm system; DATA PUMP ♦ 135

main program use for; MAIN PLUS SUBROUTINES ♦ 125

source code indications; INDENTED CONTROL FLOW ♦ 162

HIERARCHY OF CONTROL LAYERS ♦ 61

INDENTED CONTROL FLOW ♦ 162

INTERFACE TO CONTROL MODULES ♦ 62

MODEL-VIEW-CONTROLLER ♦ 87

modules

in distributed systems; DISTRIBUTION OF CONTROL
MODULES ♦ 63

interface for; INTERFACE TO CONTROL MODULES ♦ 62

OBJECTS WITH REMOTE CONTROL ♦ 93

PLUGGABLE VIEW CONTROLLER ♦ 132

PRESENTATION-ABSTRACTION-CONTROL ♦ 135

PROCESS CONTROL ♦ 137

RECURSIVE CONTROL ♦ 143

REMOTE CONTROL ♦ 144

SESSION CONTROL & OBSERVATION ♦ 151

VISIBILITY AND COMMUNICATION BETWEEN CONTROL
MODULES ♦ 61

CONVERSION ♦ 153

conversion

See Also promotion

between units, defining the ratio for; CONVERSION RATIO ♦ 8

CONVERSION ♦ 153

CONVERSION RATIO ♦ 8

QUANTITY relationship to; CONVERSION RATIO ♦ 8

CONVERTER CONSTRUCTOR METHOD ♦ 153

CONVERTER METHOD ♦ 153

format; CONVERSION ♦ 153

number, automatic recalculation; USE A RANGEADAPTOR TO
CHANNEL A NUMBER'S RANGE ♦ 177

object

different protocol; CONVERTER CONSTRUCTOR
METHOD ♦ 153

same protocol; CONVERTER METHOD ♦ 153

type, in object value sharing; USE A TYPECONVERTER TO
CONVERT A VALUE BETWEEN TYPES ♦ 178

USE A TYPECONVERTER TO CONVERT A VALUE BETWEEN
TYPES ♦ 178

CONVERSION RATIO ♦ 8

CONVERTER CONSTRUCTOR METHOD ♦ 153

CONVERTER METHOD ♦ 153

CONWAY'S LAW ♦ 65

SKILL MIX relationship to; SKILL MIX ♦ 135

cooperating

methods, coding; EXECUTE AROUND METHOD ♦ 154

objects, message use; DISPATCHED INTERPRETATION ♦ 155

coordination

of independent processes; COMMUNICATING PROCESSES ♦ 36

of material constraint changes, with tools; TOOL
COORDINATOR ♦ 111

TOOL COORDINATOR ♦ 111

Coplien, J. O.

[Adams+96]; 181

FAULT-TOLERANT TELECOMMUNICATION SYSTEM
PATTERNS ❖ 57

[Coplien92]; 185

[Coplien94a]; 185

[Coplien94b]; 185

[Coplien95a]; 185

CURIOUSLY RECURRING TEMPLATE ♦ 43

[Coplien95b]; 185

GENERATIVE DEVELOPMENT-PROCESS PATTERN
LANGUAGE ❖ 63

[Coplien97]; 185

[Coplien99a]; 185

[Coplien99b]; 185

[Coplien99c]; 185

C++ IDIOMS pattern language ♦ 24, ❖ 24

[Coplien99d]; 186

PATTERN LANGUAGE FOR WRITERS' WORKSHOPS ♦ 111

[PLoPD1]; 192

[PLoPD2]; 192

[VandenBroecke+97]; 197

PARTIES & MEDIA AS FIRST CLASS CITIZENS ♦ 96

PLUGGABLE FACTORY ♦ 132

SESSION CONTROL & OBSERVATION ♦ 151

COPY-ON-WRITE ♦ 38

copying

COPY-ON-WRITE ♦ 38

ATOMIC COMMITMENT relationship to; COPY-ON-WRITE ♦ 38

reference counting use with; COUNTED BODY ♦ 24

Coram, T.

[Coram96]; 186

DEMO PREP: A PATTERN LANGUAGE FOR THE PREPARATION
OF SOFTWARE DEMONSTRATIONS ❖ 46

core

of software artifact, preserving; PROGRAMMING-BY-
DIFFERENCE ♦ 150

correction

AD-HOC CORRECTIONS ♦ 119

of errors, diagnostic query mechanism for; DIAGNOSTIC
QUERY ♦ 33

CORRESPONDING ACCOUNT ♦ 12

ACCOUNT relationship to; CORRESPONDING ACCOUNT ♦ 12

costs

as business order component, representation of; 3-LEVEL
ORDER ♦ 24

COUNTED BODY ♦ 24

COUNTED POINTER ♦ 40

[Buschmann+96]; 183

COUNTER READER/WRITER LOCK ♦ 149

counting

COUNTED BODY ♦ 24

CONCRETE DATA TYPE relationship to; CONCRETE DATA
TYPE ♦ 25

ENVELOPE/LETTER relationship to; ENVELOPE/LETTER ♦ 25

HANDLE/BODY relationship to; HANDLE/BODY ♦ 24

COUNTED POINTER ♦ 40

COUNTER READER/WRITER LOCK ♦ 149

COUNTING PROXY, PROXY DESIGN PATTERN REVISITED
  relationship to; PROXY DESIGN PATTERN REVISITED ◆ 139
DETACHED COUNTED BODY ◆ 24
LEAKY BUCKET COUNTERS ◆ 57
reference
  copying use of; COUNTED BODY ◆ 24
  copying use with immutable classes; DETACHED COUNTED
    BODY ◆ 24
  garbage collectin use; FINALIZATION ◆ 90
  memory management use; COUNTED POINTER ◆ 40
transient errors, as fault-tolerant system buffering mechanism;
    LEAKY BUCKET COUNTERS ◆ 57
coupling
  See Also decoupling; encapsulation
  COUPLING DECREASES LATENCY ◆ 69
  loose, among interacting objects; MEDIATOR ◆ 86
  related roles, in organizational restructuring; DIVIDE AND
    CONQUER ◆ 68
  software development roles, as tool for increasing
    responsiveness; COUPLING DECREASES LATENCY ◆ 69
  sub-system, in multi-team distributed system development;
    LOOSE INTERFACES ◆ 94
  TOOL AND MATERIAL COUPLING ◆ 110
  of tools and materials; TOOL AND MATERIAL COUPLING ◆ 110
COUPLING DECREASES LATENCY ◆ 69
course
  See Also education
  development, iterative strategies for; ITERATIVE COURSE
    DEVELOPMENT ◆ 116
  ITERATIVE COURSE DEVELOPMENT ◆ 116
CPU
  See processors
Cranor, C. D.
  [Schmidt+96]; 194
    HALF-SYNC/HALF-ASYNC ◆ 71
CRC cards
  design validation; GROUP VALIDATION ◆ 66
CREATE ABSTRACT SUPERCLASS ◆ 85
CREATING AND UPDATING BUSINESS OBJECTS ◆ 91
CREATING REPORTS WITH QUERY OBJECTS ◆ 40
  [Brant+99]; 183
creation
  of abstract classes; LIFE CYCLE AND REFACTORING PATTERNS
    THAT SUPPORT EVOLUTION AND REUSE ◆ 84
  CREATE ABSTRACT SUPERCLASS ◆ 85
    ABSTRACT CLASS relationship to; CREATE ABSTRACT
      SUPERCLASS ◆ 85
  CREATING AND UPDATING BUSINESS OBJECTS ◆ 91
    CLIENT/SERVER FRAMEWORK relationship to;
      CLIENT/SERVER FRAMEWORK ◆ 91
    DEPENDENCY relationship to; CREATING AND UPDATING
      BUSINESS OBJECTS ◆ 91
    MATERIALIZATION relationship to; CREATING AND
      UPDATING BUSINESS OBJECTS ◆ 91
  CREATING REPORTS WITH QUERY OBJECTS ◆ 40
  creational patterns (GOF)
    ABSTRACT FACTORY; ABSTRACT FACTORY ◆ 2
    BUILDER; BUILDER ◆ 23
    FACTORY METHOD; FACTORY METHOD ◆ 56

CREATOR AS SOLE OWNER ◆ 85
  SEQUENCE OF OWNERS relationship to; SEQUENCE OF
    OWNERS ◆ 85
  SHARED OWNERSHIP relationship to; SHARED
    OWNERSHIP ◆ 86
CREATOR-REVIEWER ◆ 119
  MULTIPLE COMPETING DESIGNS relationship to; MULTIPLE
    COMPETING DESIGNS ◆ 118
of data products; HANDLERS ◆ 95
of dynamic objects, lifetime control issues; CREATOR AS SOLE
  OWNER ◆ 85
interfaces, for groups of related objects; ABSTRACT
  FACTORY ◆ 2
of layered architecture, strategies for; PEDESTAL ◆ 123
OBJECT CREATION ◆ 15
objects; OBJECT CREATION ◆ 15
  with context-determined subtypes; VIRTUAL
    CONSTRUCTOR ◆ 25
of objects, in an encapsulated class tree; LATE CREATION ◆ 120
off objects, messages use; SHORTCUT CONSTRUCTOR
  METHOD ◆ 152
sessions; ABSTRACT SESSION ◆ 2
CREATOR AS SOLE OWNER ◆ 85
CREATOR-REVIEWER ◆ 119
credits
  LEAKY BUCKET OF CREDITS ◆ 102
criteria
  for performance
    achievement determination; THRESHOLD SWITCH ◆ 82
    establishing; PERFORMANCE CRITERIA ◆ 82
  PERFORMANCE CRITERIA ◆ 82
critical
  CRITICAL REGION PROTECTION ◆ 31
    CONCURRENT THREADS OF EXECUTION relationship to;
      CRITICAL REGION PROTECTION ◆ 31
    SELECTING LOCKING DESIGNS FOR PARALLEL PROGRAMS
      relationship to; CRITICAL REGION PROTECTION ◆ 31
    SELECTING LOCKING PRIMITIVES FOR PARALLEL
      PROGRAMMING relationship to; CRITICAL REGION
      PROTECTION ◆ 31
    SHAPE OF PROGRAM relationship to; CRITICAL REGION
      PROTECTION ◆ 31
  CRITICAL-SECTION FUSING ◆ 148
  CRITICAL-SECTION PARTITIONING ◆ 148
  sections
    fusing, as performance enhancement; CRITICAL-SECTION
      FUSING ◆ 148
    partitioning, as performance enhancement;
      CRITICAL-SECTION PARTITIONING ◆ 148
CRITICAL REGION PROTECTION ◆ 31
CRITICAL-SECTION FUSING ◆ 148
CRITICAL-SECTION PARTITIONING ◆ 148
CROSSING CHASMS
  CROSSING CHASMS: A PATTERN LANGUAGE FOR
    OBJECT-RDBMS INTEGRATION ◆ 41
  RELATIONAL DATABASE ACCESS LAYER relationship to;
    RELATIONAL DATABASE ACCESS LAYER ◆ 3
  THREE-TIER ARCHITECTURE relationship to; THREE-TIER
    ARCHITECTURE ◆ 15

CROSSING CHASMS: A PATTERN LANGUAGE FOR
  OBJECT-RDBMS INTEGRATION ♦ 41
  [Brown+96b]; 183
Cryczan, G.
  [Baumer+97]; 184
    ROLE OBJECT ♦ 146
cryptography
  software architecture; TROPYC: A PATTERN LANGUAGE FOR
    CRYPTOGRAPHIC SOFTWARE ♦ 174
  TROPYC: A PATTERN LANGUAGE FOR CRYPTOGRAPHIC
    SOFTWARE ♦ 174
CULT OF PERSONALITY ♦ 130
  PEACEMAKER relationship to; PEACEMAKER ♦ 131
Cunningham, W.
  [Cunningham95]; 186
    CHECKS: PATTERN LANGUAGE OF INFORMATION
      INTEGRITY ♦ 32
  [Cunningham96]; 186
    EPISODES: A PATTERN LANGUAGE OF COMPETITIVE
      DEVELOPMENT ❖ 51
CURIOUSLY RECURRING TEMPLATE ♦ 43
  [Coplien95a]; 185
currency
  options relationship to; OPTIONS ♦ 14
CUSTOMER CONTACT ♦ 23
CUSTOMER INTERACTION PATTERNS ♦ 43
  [Rising99]; 193
CUSTOMER MEETINGS: GO EARLY, STAY LATE ♦ 44
CUSTOMER RAPPORT ♦ 140
customer(s)
  architect interaction with; ENGAGE CUSTOMERS ♦ 66
  architect's role, in relation to developers and; ARCHITECT
    CONTROLS PRODUCT ♦ 65
  assessing the total performance cost relative to each feature;
    FUNCTIONALITY ALA CARTE ♦ 61
  building trust with; BUILD TRUST ♦ 43
  business relationship, representation of; CUSTOMER
    CONTACT ♦ 23
  CUSTOMER CONTACT ♦ 23
    ASSOCIATION OBJECT relationship to; CUSTOMER
      CONTACT ♦ 23
    EVENT LOGGING relationship to; CUSTOMER CONTACT ♦ 23
  CUSTOMER INTERACTION PATTERNS ♦ 43
    CUSTOMER RAPPORT relationship to; CUSTOMER
      RAPPORT ♦ 140
    ENGAGE CUSTOMERS relationship to; ENGAGE
      CUSTOMERS ♦ 66
  CUSTOMER MEETINGS: GO EARLY, STAY LATE ♦ 44
    BUILD TRUST relationship to; BUILD TRUST ♦ 43, CUSTOMER
      MEETINGS: GO EARLY, STAY LATE ♦ 44
    IT'S A RELATIONSHIP, NOT A SALE relationship to;
      CUSTOMER MEETINGS: GO EARLY, STAY LATE ♦ 44
    KNOW THE CUSTOMER relationship to; KNOW THE
      CUSTOMER ♦ 43, CUSTOMER MEETINGS: GO EARLY, STAY
      LATE ♦ 44
  CUSTOMER RAPPORT ♦ 140
    CUSTOMER INTERACTION PATTERNS relationship to;
      CUSTOMER RAPPORT ♦ 140

    ENGAGE CUSTOMERS relationship to; ENGAGE
      CUSTOMERS ♦ 66
    PROTOTYPES relationship to; CUSTOMER RAPPORT ♦ 140
  demonstrations
    archiving scenarios; ARCHIVE SCENARIOS ♦ 48
    feature selection criteria; JUDICIOUS FIREWORKS ♦ 47
    lightweight user interfaces use; LIGHTWEIGHT USER
      INTERFACES ♦ 47
    preparation for; DEMO PREP: A PATTERN LANGUAGE FOR
      THE PREPARATION OF SOFTWARE DEMONSTRATIONS ♦ 46
    programming requirements for; MUTABLE CODE ♦ 47
    prototyping language use; PROTOTYPING LANGUAGES ♦ 47
  developer interaction with; ENGAGE CUSTOMERS ♦ 66
  developing rapport with; IT'S A RELATIONSHIP, NOT A
    SALE ♦ 43
  ENGAGE CUSTOMERS ♦ 66
  importance of integrity in dealing with; SHOW PERSONAL
    INTEGRITY ♦ 44
  importance of listening to; LISTEN, LISTEN, LISTEN ♦ 44
  importance of respect for boundaries; BE AWARE OF
    BOUNDARIES ♦ 44
  importance of responsiveness; BE RESPONSIVE ♦ 44
  KNOW THE CUSTOMER ♦ 43
  learning about; KNOW THE CUSTOMER ♦ 43
  MANAGING AND MEETING CUSTOMER EXPECTATIONS ♦ 140
  meeting protocol; CUSTOMER MEETINGS: GO EARLY, STAY
    LATE ♦ 44
  protocol, components of; MIND YOUR MANNERS ♦ 44
  relationships, strategies for maintaining; CUSTOMER
    RAPPORT ♦ 140
  requirements
    classifying; MANAGING AND MEETING CUSTOMER
      EXPECTATIONS ♦ 140
    early customer demonstration use for establishing;
      CATALYTIC SCENARIOS ♦ 47
  requirements identification role; BUILDING THE RIGHT
    THINGS ♦ 140
  testing from the perspective of; END USER VIEWPOINT ♦ 127
Cybulski, J. L.
  [Cybulski+99]; 186
    COMPOSING MULTIMEDIA ARTIFACTS FOR REUSE ♦ 36
cyclic dependencies
  avoiding; EVENTHANDLER ♦ 55
  eliminating; ACYCLIC VISITOR ♦ 6
  templates and inheritance; CURIOUSLY RECURRING
    TEMPLATE ♦ 43

Dagermo, P.
  [Dagermo+98]; 186
Dahab, R.
  [Braga+99]; 183
    TROPYC: A PATTERN LANGUAGE FOR CRYPTOGRAPHIC
      SOFTWARE ❖ 174
DasNeves, R.
  [DasNeves+98]; 186
    BODYGUARD ♦ 22
data
  ANIMATE THE DATA ♦ 70
  change analysis; TIME THREAD ANALYSIS ♦ 71

DATA ABSTRACTION OR OBJECT-ORIENTED ♦ 125
DATA KNOWS ITS ROOTS ♦ 31
DATA LOCKING ♦ 147
  CODE LOCKING relationship to; DATA LOCKING ♦ 147
  HIERARCHICAL LOCKING relationship to; HIERARCHICAL
    LOCKING ♦ 148
  TEST-AND-SET LOCK relationship to; TEST-AND-SET
    LOCK ♦ 148
DATA OWNERSHIP ♦ 147
  ACTIVE OBJECT relationship to; DATA OWNERSHIP ♦ 147
  TEST-AND-SET LOCK relationship to; TEST-AND-SET
    LOCK ♦ 148
DATA PUMP ♦ 135
  PERIODIC OBJECT relationship to; PERIODIC OBJECT ♦ 134,
    DATA PUMP ♦ 135
  POINT relationship to; POINT ♦ 134
DEFINE THE DATA STRUCTURE ♦ 70
entry
  deferrring; DEFERRED VALIDATION ♦ 33
  feedback; ECHO BACK ♦ 32
flow, stream processing; STREAMS ♦ 167
locking, as performance enhancement over code locking;
  DATA LOCKING ♦ 147
members, determining where to place; STATE MEMBER ♦ 166
model
  causality flow tracing; TIME THREAD ANALYSIS ♦ 71
  creation strategies; ANIMATE THE DATA ♦ 70
  defining; DEFINE THE DATA STRUCTURE ♦ 70
  domain view use in a relational database; HIERARCHICAL
    VIEW ♦ 3
  integrating into implementation; INTRODUCE VIRTUAL
    ATTRIBUTES ♦ 70
projecting implications of; INSTANT PROJECTION ♦ 33
reference, for software development; REFERENCE DATA ♦ 54
REFERENCE DATA ♦ 54
representation
  by abstract data types; DATA ABSTRACTION OR
    OBJECT-ORIENTED ♦ 125
  by abstract data types, handling multiple implementations
    with; ENVELOPE/LETTER ♦ 25
stream
  converting into objects; PARSER/BUILDER ♦ 94
  data product generation strategies; HANDLERS ♦ 95
  factory hierarchy control by; HIERARCHY OF FACTORIES ♦ 94
  pipeline processing of; PIPELINE ♦ 125
streams, for pipes and filters; PIPES & FILTERS ♦ 132
structures
  defining for distributed systems; DEFINE THE DATA
    STRUCTURE ♦ 70
  repositories; REPOSITORY ♦ 125
validation, CHECKS pattern language for; CHECKS:
  PATTERN LANGUAGE OF INFORMATION INTEGRITY ♦ 32
DATA ABSTRACTION OR OBJECT-ORIENTED ♦ 125
DATA KNOWS ITS ROOTS ♦ 31
DATA LOCKING ♦ 147
DATA OWNERSHIP ♦ 147
DATA PUMP ♦ 135

data types
abstract
  data representation by; DATA ABSTRACTION OR
    OBJECT-ORIENTED ♦ 125
  multiple implementations, handling;
    ENVELOPE/LETTER ♦ 25
algebraic, inheritance hierarchy for; ALGEBRAIC
  HIERARCHY ♦ 25
CONCRETE DATA TYPE ♦ 25
promotion
  between different but related C++ types; TYPE
    PROMOTION ♦ 26
  encapsulation of how; PROMOTION LADDER ♦ 26
  in heterogeneous addition; PROMOTE AND ADD ♦ 26
subtypes, domain rule enforcement with in abstract models;
  ABSTRACT MODELS WITH CONSTRAINTS IN SUBTYPES ♦ 4
supertypes, abstracting either-or-both relationship into;
  PARTY ♦ 4, PARTY ♦ 6
DATABASE INTERACTION ♦ 15
database(s)
access layers
  connecting; QUERY BROKER ♦ 4
  in relational databases; ACCESSING RELATIONAL DATABASES
    pattern language ♦ 3, RELATIONAL DATABASE ACCESS
    LAYER ♦ 3
ACCESSING RELATIONAL DATABASES ❖ 3
architecture
  connecting access layers; QUERY BROKER ♦ 4
  defining access layers; ACCESSING RELATIONAL DATABASES
    pattern language ♦ 3, RELATIONAL DATABASE ACCESS
    LAYER ♦ 3
  defining domain views; HIERARCHICAL VIEW ♦ 3
  defining physical views; PHYSICAL VIEW ♦ 3
collection representation in; REPRESENTING COLLECTIONS
  IN A RELATIONAL DATABASE ♦ 42, REPRESENTING
  COLLECTIONS ♦ 107
DATABASE INTERACTION ♦ 15
  THREE-TIER ARCHITECTURE relationship to; DATABASE
    INTERACTION ♦ 15
decoupling from domain-specific application components;
  BROKER ♦ 108
design, behavioral analysis role; TABLE DESIGN TIME ♦ 42
designing tables that represent object models; TABLE DESIGN
  TIME ♦ 107
dynamic query and report generation; CREATING REPORTS
  WITH QUERY OBJECTS ♦ 40
establishing unique references, account number use for;
  ACCOUNT NUMBER ♦ 4
hierarchical view; HIERARCHICAL VIEW ♦ 3
inheritance representation in; REPRESENTING INHERITANCE IN
  A RELATIONAL DATABASE ♦ 42, SURROGATE ♦ 168
layer, handling, in three-tier architecture; DATABASE
  INTERACTION ♦ 15
mapping objects to relational databases; CROSSING
  CHASMS: A PATTERN LANGUAGE FOR OBJECT-RDBMS
  INTEGRATION ♦ 41, OBJECTS FROM RECORDS ♦ 90,
  PATTERN LANGUAGE FOR SMALLTALK & RELATIONAL

database(s) *continued*

mapping objects to relational databases; Crossing Chasms: A Pattern Language for Object-RDBMS Integration, Objects from Records, Pattern Language for Smalltalk & Relational Databases, Representing Objects as Tables *continued* Databases ♦ 106, Representing Objects as Tables ♦ 107

metadata use for; Object Metadata ♦ 108

non-database object representation, foreign key use; Foreign Key References ♦ 43, Foreign Key References ♦ 108

object relationship representation in; Representing Object Relationships ♦ 42

Pattern Language for Smalltalk & Relational Databases ♦ 106

pattern languages, Accessing Relational Databases; Accessing Relational Databases pattern language ♦ 3

Query Optimized Database ♦ 165

Relational Database Access Layer ♦ 3

Representing Collections in a Relational Database ♦ 42

Representing Inheritance in a Relational Database ♦ 42

shared
client-server application, three-tier; Three-Tier Architecture ♦ 15
client-server application, two-tier; Two-Tier Architecture ♦ 14
Stars: A Pattern Language for Query-Optimized Schemas; Stars: A Pattern Language for Query-Optimized Schemas ♦ 164

synchronizing, with clients; Client Synchronization ♦ 109

tables, accessing; Physical View ♦ 3

as three-tier application layer; Three-Tier Architecture ♦ 15

unique object identifier use in; Object Identifier ♦ 42

Day Care ♦ 170

Sacrifice One Person relationship to; Sacrifice One Person ♦ 170

Someone Always Makes Progress relationship to; Day Care ♦ 170

Team per Task relationship to; Someone Always Makes Progress ♦ 169, Team per Task ♦ 169

Debrief After Activities ♦ 118

Simulation Games relationship to; Debrief After Activities ♦ 118

DeBruler, D.

[DeBruler95]; 186

Generative Pattern Language for Distributed Processing ❖ 70

Debug Printing Method ♦ 154

debugging

Debug Printing Method ♦ 154

inspector, encapsulating; Detachable Inspector ♦ 49

print method creation; Debug Printing Method ♦ 154

tools, for framework use; Language Tools ♦ 123

Decision Deferral and Capture Pattern Language ♦ 45

[Hopley96]; 188

Decision Document ♦ 118
Decision Maker's Role ♦ 30
Decision-Based Models ♦ 45
decisions

Decision Deferral and Capture Pattern Language ♦ 45

Decision Document ♦ 118
Multiple Competing Designs relationship to; Multiple Competing Designs ♦ 118, Decision Document ♦ 118

Decision Maker's Role ♦ 30
Human Interface Role is a Special Interface Role relationship to; Decision Maker's Role ♦ 30
Interface's Role relationship to; Decision Maker's Role ♦ 30
Shape of Program relationship to; Decision Maker's Role ♦ 30
Strategy relationship to; Decision Maker's Role ♦ 30
Workers' Role relationship to; Decision Maker's Role ♦ 30

Decision-Based Models ♦ 45
Appropriate Living Models relationship to; Decision-Based Models ♦ 45

model design based on; Decision-Based Models ♦ 45

support systems, query schema for; Stars: A Pattern Language for Query-Optimized Schemas ♦ 164

Decomposing Message ♦ 154

decomposition

of complex behavior, as simplification strategy; To Simplify Complex Behavior, Use Decomposition ♦ 88

of complex enterprise; Enterprise Segment ♦ 9

of computation, self use for; Decomposing Message ♦ 154

Decomposing Message ♦ 154

of distributed software systems; Generative Pattern Language for Distributed Processing ♦ 70

of expressions; Explaining Temporary Variable ♦ 158

recursion use for; Object Recursion ♦ 92

of software into levels of abstraction; Layers ♦ 81

of software systems, for distributed processing; Generative Pattern Language for Distributed Processing ♦ 70

of system requirements, into a layered architecture; Patterns for Generating a Layered Architecture ♦ 123

To Simplify Complex Behavior, Use Decomposition ♦ 88

Decorator ♦ 46

Adapter relationship to; Adapter ♦ 6, Decorator ♦ 46

[Alpert+98]; 182

Composable Query Objects relationship to; Composable Query Objects ♦ 41

Composite relationship to; Composite ♦ 37, Decorator ♦ 46

Detachable Inspector relationship to; Detachable Inspector ♦ 49

Extension Object relationship to; Extension Object ♦ 55

External Polymorphism relationship to; External Polymorphism ♦ 56

[Gamma+95]; 188

Object Recovery relationship to; Object Recovery ♦ 92

Programming-by-Difference relationship to; Programming-by-Difference ♦ 150

Proxy relationship to; Decorator ♦ 46, Proxy ♦ 139

Type Object relationship to; Type Object ♦ 176

DECOUPLE EXECUTION AND OUTPUT ◆ 76
decoupling
See Also encapsulation; isolation; layering
active initialization, from services provided; CONNECTOR ◆ 40
business rules, from transaction-processing software; EXPLICIT
    BUSINESS RULES ◆ 173
caller/provider modules, in a hierarchy of control layers;
    VISIBILITY AND COMMUNICATION BETWEEN CONTROL
    MODULES ◆ 61
clients
    from products; PRODUCT TRADER ◆ 138
    from servers; ABSTRACT CLIENT ◆ 2, APPROACHES FOR
        SEPARATING CLIENTS FROM SERVERS ◆ 16
code that changes from code that doesn't; HOT SPOTS ◆ 122
components, extensible mechanisms for;
    TRANSCEIVER-PARCEL ◆ 133
control from behavior, in finite state machines; THREE-LEVEL
    FSM ◆ 172
DECOUPLE EXECUTION AND OUTPUT ◆ 76
    EVENT QUEUE relationship to; EVENT QUEUE ◆ 76,
        DECOUPLE EXECUTION AND OUTPUT ◆ 76
    HANDLE ARTIFICIAL EVENTS relationship to; DECOUPLE
        EXECUTION AND OUTPUT ◆ 76
    MERGE COMPATIBLE EVENTS relationship to; DECOUPLE
        EXECUTION AND OUTPUT ◆ 76
    OBSERVER relationship to; DECOUPLE EXECUTION AND
        OUTPUT ◆ 76
DECOUPLE STAGES ◆ 68
distributed system components; BROKER ◆ 22
domain-specific from database-specific application
    components; BROKER ◆ 108
editing changes from commit; EDITS INSIDE ◆ 136
hypermedia navigation, from navigation record;
    NAVIGATIONOBSERVER ◆ 48
implementation
    from abstractions; BRIDGE ◆ 22
    from interface, in C++ objects; HANDLE/BODY ◆ 24
    from proposed actions; PROPOSED AND IMPLEMENTED
        ACTION ◆ 12
initialization, from services provided; ACCEPTOR ◆ 3
link activation from endpoint computation;
    NAVIGATIONSTRATEGY ◆ 48
locking workload; PARALLEL FASTPATH ◆ 147
method invocation from method execution; ACTIVE
    OBJECT ◆ 6
model updating from display output; DECOUPLE EXECUTION
    AND OUTPUT ◆ 76
models and ValueModels; USE A BUFFEREDVALUEHOLDER TO
    DELAY THE COMMIT OF A NEW VALUE ◆ 177
multiple input and output sources; ROUTER ◆ 146
objects from classes; TYPE OBJECT ◆ 176
operational and knowledge levels; ACCOUNTABILITY
    KNOWLEDGE LEVEL ◆ 5, ACCOUNTABILITY KNOWLEDGE
    LEVEL ◆ 7
peers from underlying communication mechanisms, in
    peer-to-peer interaction models; FORWARDER-RECEIVER ◆ 60
persistence from object recovery, strategies for; OBJECT
    RECOVERY ◆ 92

of producers and consumers; PATTERN FOR SEPARATING
    ASSEMBLY AND PROCESSING ◆ 97
readers from writers, in locking strategies; READER/WRITER
    LOCKING ◆ 147
representation from construction; BUILDER ◆ 23
sender from receiver of a request; CHAIN OF
    RESPONSIBILITY ◆ 32
service request from execution; COMMAND PROCESSOR ◆ 36
software development stages; DECOUPLE STAGES ◆ 68
    vs. responsiveness; HUB, SPOKE, AND RIM ◆ 68
state transition
    logic from object behavior, in an FSM; LAYERED
        ORGANIZATION ◆ 59
    from reaction; FOR STATE MACHINES, USE TRANSITION
        METHODS ◆ 88
synchronization
    from functionality; OBJECT SYNCHRONIZER ◆ 92
    from object recovery; OBJECT RECOVERY ◆ 92
tool, functional parts from interface parts; SEPARATION OF
    POWERS ◆ 110
of tools, from materials; MATERIALS ◆ 109
transactions, archival vs. active processing; SEPARATE
    TRANSACTION PROCESSING FROM ARCHIVAL ◆ 173
user interface, from persistent subsystem; DOMAIN
    INTERCEPTS ◆ 137
user interface from application; APPLICATION
    BOUNDARY ◆ 136
DEFAULT STATE ◆ 167
DEFAULT VALUE METHOD ◆ 157
DEFAULT VISITOR ◆ 46
[Norberg98]; 191
defaults
DEFAULT STATE ◆ 167
DEFAULT VALUE METHOD ◆ 157
    DEFINE DEFAULT VALUES VIA EXPLICIT PROTOCOL
        relationship to; DEFINE DEFAULT VALUES VIA EXPLICIT
        PROTOCOL ◆ 146, DEFAULT VALUE METHOD ◆ 157
    LAZY INITIALIZATION relationship to; LAZY
        INITIALIZATION ◆ 157
DEFAULT VISITOR ◆ 46
    EXTRINSIC VISITOR relationship to; DEFAULT VISITOR ◆ 46,
        EXTRINSIC VISITOR ◆ 56
    VISITOR relationship to; DEFAULT VISITOR ◆ 46
as reusability strategy; WORKS OUT OF THE BOX ◆ 150
state, initializing; OWNER-DRIVEN TRANSITIONS ◆ 167
values
    defining; DEFINE DEFAULT VALUES VIA EXPLICIT
        PROTOCOL ◆ 146
    representation; DEFAULT VALUE METHOD ◆ 157
DEFER IDENTIFICATION OF STATE VARIABLES ◆ 145
DEFERRED VALIDATION ◆ 33
deferring
actions; SUSPENSION ◆ 12
class instantiation to subclasses; FACTORY METHOD ◆ 56
DECISION DEFERRAL AND CAPTURE PATTERN LANGUAGE ◆ 45
DEFER IDENTIFICATION OF STATE VARIABLES ◆ 145
    IDENTIFY MESSAGE LAYERS relationship to; DEFER
        IDENTIFICATION OF STATE VARIABLES ◆ 145

deferring *continued*
  DEFERRED VALIDATION ♦ 33
    ECHO BACK relationship to; DEFERRED VALIDATION ♦ 33
    HYPOTHETICAL PUBLICATION relationship to;
      HYPOTHETICAL PUBLICATION ♦ 33
    WHOLE VALUE relationship to; DEFERRED VALIDATION ♦ 33
  validation, of data entry; DEFERRED VALIDATION ♦ 33
DEFINE AND RUN PRESENTATION ♦ 36
DEFINE CLASSES BY BEHAVIOR, NOT STATE ♦ 145
DEFINE DEFAULT VALUES VIA EXPLICIT PROTOCOL ♦ 146
DEFINE THE DATA STRUCTURE ♦ 70
DEFINING REQUIREMENTS ♦ 140
definition
  of algorithm family; STRATEGY ♦ 167
  of business terms, for requirements process; DEFINING
    REQUIREMENTS ♦ 140
  of data stuctures, for distributed systems; DEFINE THE DATA
    STRUCTURE ♦ 70
  of default values, in class design; DEFINE DEFAULT VALUES
    VIA EXPLICIT PROTOCOL ♦ 146
  DEFINE AND RUN PRESENTATION ♦ 36
  DEFINE CLASSES BY BEHAVIOR, NOT STATE ♦ 145
    IDENTIFY MESSAGE LAYERS relationship to; IDENTIFY
      MESSAGE LAYERS ♦ 145
    IMPLEMENT BEHAVIOR WITH ABSTRACT STATE relationship
      to; IMPLEMENT BEHAVIOR WITH ABSTRACT STATE ♦ 145
  DEFINE DEFAULT VALUES VIA EXPLICIT PROTOCOL ♦ 146
    DEFAULT VALUE METHOD relationship to; DEFINE DEFAULT
      VALUES VIA EXPLICIT PROTOCOL ♦ 146, DEFAULT VALUE
      METHOD ♦ 157
  DEFINE THE DATA STRUCTURE ♦ 70
    ANIMATE THE DATA relationship to; ANIMATE THE
      DATA ♦ 70
    FACTOR OUT COMMON ATTRIBUTES relationship to; DEFINE
      THE DATA STRUCTURE ♦ 70
    IDENTIFY PROBLEM DOMAIN RELATIONSHIPS relationship to;
      DEFINE THE DATA STRUCTURE ♦ 70
    IDENTIFY THE NOUNS relationship to; DEFINE THE DATA
      STRUCTURE ♦ 70, IDENTIFY THE NOUNS ♦ 70
    INTRODUCE VIRTUAL ATTRIBUTES relationship to;
      INTRODUCE VIRTUAL ATTRIBUTES ♦ 70
    NORMALIZE THE ROLES relationship to; DEFINE THE DATA
      STRUCTURE ♦ 70
    TIME THREAD ANALYSIS relationship to; TIME THREAD
      ANALYSIS ♦ 71
  DEFINING REQUIREMENTS ♦ 140
    BEHAVIORAL REQUIREMENTS relationship to; DEFINING
      REQUIREMENTS ♦ 140
    PROBLEM DOMAIN ANAYSIS relationship to; DEFINING
      REQUIREMENTS ♦ 140
    REQUIREMENTS VALIDATION relationship to; DEFINING
      REQUIREMENTS ♦ 140
  FINDING AND DEFINING THE DOMAIN OBJECTS ♦ 141
  SCENARIOS DEFINE PROBLEM ♦ 66
DeLano, D. E.
  [Delano+98]; 186
  PATTERNS FOR SYSTEM TESTING ♦ 126
DELEGATION ♦ 155

delegation
  See Also composition
  ARTIFICIAL DELEGATION ♦ 164
  DELEGATION ♦ 155
  generalization implementation with; IMPLEMENTING
    GENERALIZATIONS ♦ 15
  as implementation sharing, without inheritance;
    DELEGATION ♦ 155
  self; SELF DELEGATION ♦ 155
  SELF DELEGATION ♦ 155
  setting up for a prototype; ARTIFICIAL DELEGATION ♦ 164
  simple; SIMPLE DELEGATION ♦ 155
  SIMPLE DELEGATION ♦ 155
deliverables
  See Also products
  DELIVERABLES TO GO ♦ 27
  EARLY AND REGULAR DELIVERY ♦ 168
  OWNER PER DELIVERABLE ♦ 169
DELIVERABLES TO GO ♦ 27
**DEMO PREP: A PATTERN LANGUAGE FOR THE PREPARATION
  OF SOFTWARE DEMONSTRATIONS ❖ 46**
  [Coram96]; 186
demonstrations
  See Also presentations
  customer
    archiving scenarios; ARCHIVE SCENARIOS ♦ 48
    feature selection criteria; JUDICIOUS FIREWORKS ♦ 47
    lightweight user interfaces use; LIGHTWEIGHT USER
      INTERFACES ♦ 47
    programming requirements for; MUTABLE CODE ♦ 47
    prototyping language use; PROTOTYPING LANGUAGES ♦ 47
  DEMO PREP: A PATTERN LANGUAGE FOR THE PREPARATION
    OF SOFTWARE DEMONSTRATIONS ♦ 46
  idenifying key elements for; ELEMENT IDENTIFICATION ♦ 46
demultiplexing
  asynchronous completion events; PROACTOR ♦ 137
  multiple event handlers; REACTOR ♦ 143
dependencies
  See Also reference counting
  between models and their views, managing; DEPENDENCY ♦ 91
  client-server, managing; INTELLIGENT CHILDREN ♦ 16,
    ABSTRACT SERVER ♦ 16, ADAPTED SERVER ♦ 17
  component, reducing; LAYERED AND SECTIONED
    ARCHITECTURE ♦ 96
  cycles
    avoiding; EVENTHANDLER ♦ 55
    eliminating; ACYCLIC VISITOR ♦ 6
    templates and inheritance; CURIOUSLY RECURRING
      TEMPLATE ♦ 43
  DEPENDENCY ♦ 91
    CREATING AND UPDATING BUSINESS OBJECTS relationship
      to; CREATING AND UPDATING BUSINESS OBJECTS ♦ 91
    FINALIZATION relationship to; FINALIZATION ♦ 90
    MODEL-VIEW-CONTROLLER relationship to;
      DEPENDENCY ♦ 91
    OBSERVER relationship to; DEPENDENCY ♦ 91
    VIEWING relationship to; VIEWING ♦ 91
  in a fire alarm system, representation of; DEVIATION ♦ 134

location, minimizing in a network management system; Remote Operation ♦ 115

network, consistent update of objects in; Propagator: A Family of Patterns ♦ 138

of objects, garbage collection use; Finalization ♦ 90

one-to-many, state change management with; Observer ♦ 94

protocol relationships defined in terms of; Protocol ♦ 13

Dependency ♦ 91

derived classes

circular dependency issues, with templates; Curiously Recurring Template ♦ 43

Design by Team ♦ 95

Design Patterns for Object-Oriented Hypermedia Applications ❖ 48

[Rossi+96]; 194

Designers Are Our Friends ♦ 126

designs/designing

application, testing relationship to; Application Design is Bounded by Test Design ♦ 66

Application Design is Bounded by Test Design ♦ 66

business system; Accountability and Organizational Structures pattern language ♦ 4

change mechanism characteristics; Metamorphosis ♦ 55

class

hierarchies, interfaces use for; Abstract Class ♦ 2

inheritance-based; Reusability Through Self-Encapsulation ♦ 145

client-server system, layering approach to; Four-Layer Architecture ♦ 106

competing, decision making strategies; Decision Document ♦ 118

Concurrent Programming in Java: Design Principles and Patterns, 2nd ed. ❖ 37

conflict handling; Subclass per Team ♦ 136

cryptographic software, flexibility and reusability strategies; Secure-Channel Communication ♦ 174

Design by Team ♦ 95

Designers Are Our Friends relationship to; Designers Are Our Friends ♦ 126

Diversity of Membership relationship to; Design by Team ♦ 95

Lock 'em Up Together relationship to; Design by Team ♦ 95

Unity of Purpose relationship to; Design by Team ♦ 95

Validation by Teams relationship to; Design by Team ♦ 95

Designers Are Our Friends ♦ 126

Adopt-A-Problem relationship to; Adopt-A-Problem ♦ 128

Design by Team relationship to; Designers Are Our Friends ♦ 126

Document the Problem relationship to; Designers Are Our Friends ♦ 126, Document the Problem ♦ 128

Engage QA relationship to; Engage QA ♦ 66

Get Involved Early relationship to; Designers Are Our Friends ♦ 126, Get Involved Early ♦ 126

Take Time relationship to; Take Time ♦ 126

Time to Test relationship to; Time to Test ♦ 126

distributed systems

data structure definition; Define the Data Structure ♦ 70

naming system attributes, values, and roles; Identify the Nouns ♦ 70

documentation

system testing use; Get Involved Early ♦ 126

technical memos as strategy for; Technical Memo ♦ 54

fault-tolerant systems, interactive telecommunications switching system; Input and Output Pattern Language ♦ 76

of information space navigation; Patterns for Designing Navigable Information Spaces ♦ 119

inheritance structure, factoring common attributes; Factor Out Common Attributes ♦ 70

of interactive

application structures; Model-View-Controller ♦ 87

systems, low-level design issues; Improving Responsiveness in Interactive Applications Using Queues ♦ 76

layered architecture creation; Pedestal ♦ 123

Multiple Competing Designs ♦ 118

organization; Accountability and Organizational Structures pattern language ♦ 4

parallel programs, locking; Selecting Locking Designs for Parallel Programs ♦ 147

of pattern languages, writing strategies; Pattern Language ♦ 102

of patterns and pattern languages, writing strategies; Pattern Language for Pattern Writing ♦ 102

Patterns for Designing in Teams ♦ 118

Patterns for Designing Navigable Information Spaces ♦ 119

principles, for short-term code; Throwaway Code ♦ 21

Prioritizing Forces in Software Design ♦ 135

project, technical writing role; Mercenary Analyst ♦ 67

Prototype a First-Pass Design ♦ 84

of relational database tables, that represent object models; Table Design Time ♦ 107

Selecting Locking Designs for Parallel Programs ♦ 147

small projects, team size; Solo Virtuoso ♦ 64

software

prioritizing forces in; Prioritizing Forces in Software Design ♦ 135

prototyping role; Prototype a First-Pass Design ♦ 84

team skill level consideration; Generics and Specifics ♦ 136

of state-dependent objects, design and implementation strategies; MOODS: Models for Object-Oriented Design of State ♦ 87

strategies, for non-deterministic systems; Blackboard ♦ 22

system

normalizing roles; Normalize the Roles ♦ 70

planning for extensibility; Hook Method ♦ 73

testing importance; Designers Are Our Friends ♦ 126

Table Design Time ♦ 42, ♦ 107

teams

strategies for bulding a team; Design by Team ♦ 95

designs/designing *continued*

teams *continued*

strategies for ensuring effective; MULTIPLE COMPETING
DESIGNS ♦ 118

transformation from analysis; CATERPILLAR'S FATE: A
PATTERN LANGUAGE FOR THE TRANSFORMATION FROM
ANALYSIS TO DESIGN ♦ 28

understanding, as developer role; DEVELOPER CONTROLS
PROCESS ♦ 65

user interface, team skill level consideration; GENERIC UI,
SPECIFIC UI ♦ 136

validation

as software development responsibility; GROUP
VALIDATION ♦ 66

of software development teams; VALIDATION BY TEAMS ♦ 96

of work packet internals; WORK PACKET CONTENTS ♦ 28

WWW text pages; PATTERN LANGUAGE FOR AN ESSAY-BASED
WEB SITE ♦ 97

destroying

objects; OBJECT DESTRUCTION ♦ 15

destruction

OBJECT DESTRUCTION ♦ 15

DETACHABLE INSPECTOR ♦ 49

DECORATOR relationship to; DETACHABLE INSPECTOR ♦ 49

LAYERS relationship to; DETACHABLE INSPECTOR ♦ 49

[Sane+96a]; 194

SINGLETON relationship to; DETACHABLE INSPECTOR ♦ 49

VISITOR relationship to; DETACHABLE INSPECTOR ♦ 49

DETACHED COUNTED BODY ♦ 24

DETECT ♦ 160

detection

DETECT ♦ 160

LOOKUP CACHE relationship to; LOOKUP CACHE ♦ 161

of errors

diagnostic query mechanism for; DIAGNOSTIC QUERY ♦ 33

hypothetical modeling use for; HYPOTHETICAL
PUBLICATION ♦ 33

event, design issues; EVENT ACQUISITION ♦ 31

of message modification, as cryptographic strategy; MESSAGE
INTEGRITY ♦ 174

DETERMINE THE ACTORS ♦ 71

ANIMATE THE DATA relationship to; ANIMATE THE DATA ♦ 70

Devarakonda, M.

[Islam+96]; 188

RECOVERABLE DISTRIBUTOR ♦ 143

DEVELOPER CONTROLS PROCESS ♦ 65

DEVELOPING IN PAIRS ♦ 69

DEVELOPMENT EPISODE ♦ 53

development of courses

ITERATIVE COURSE DEVELOPMENT ♦ 116

development of software

architect

responsibilities for; ARCHITECT ALSO IMPLEMENTS ♦ 65

role in relation to developers and customers; ARCHITECT
CONTROLS PRODUCT ♦ 65

team role, strategies for ensuring coherence; LOCK 'EM UP
TOGETHER ♦ 95

change mechanism characteristics; METAMORPHOSIS ♦ 55

code ownership guidelines; CODE OWNERSHIP ♦ 66

configuration management systems, ENVY/Developer;
PARTITIONING SMALLTALK CODE INTO ENVY/DEVELOPER
COMPONENTS ♦ 96

DEVELOPER CONTROLS PROCESS ♦ 65

developer role(s); DEVELOPER CONTROLS PROCESS ♦ 65

DEVELOPING IN PAIRS ♦ 69

DEVELOPMENT EPISODE relationship to; DEVELOPMENT
EPISODE ♦ 53

INFORMAL LABOR PLAN relationship to; INFORMAL LABOR
PLAN ♦ 53

DEVELOPMENT EPISODE ♦ 53

DEVELOPING IN PAIRS relationship to; DEVELOPMENT
EPISODE ♦ 53

INFORMAL LABOR PLAN relationship to; INFORMAL LABOR
PLAN ♦ 53

REFERENCE DATA relationship to; REFERENCE DATA ♦ 54

SELF-SELECTING TEAM relationship to; SELF-SELECTING
TEAM ♦ 63

for distributed control systems; OBJECT-ORIENTED DESIGN
PATTERNS IN REACTIVE SYSTEMS ♦ 92

flexible foundation importance; FLEXIBLE FOUNDATIONS ♦ 55

forces, reflective systems relationship to; EVOLUTION,
ARCHITECTURE, AND METAMORPHOSIS ♦ 55

frameworks evolution; PATTERNS FOR EVOLVING
FRAMEWORKS ♦ 121

gatekeeper interface to rest of world; GATEKEEPER ♦ 67

GENERATIVE DEVELOPMENT-PROCESS PATTERN LANGUAGE;
GENERATIVE DEVELOPMENT-PROCESS PATTERN
LANGUAGE ♦ 63

high-level manager/champion role; PATRON ♦ 65

identifying product functionality; IMPLIED
REQUIREMENTS ♦ 52

integration timing; NAMED STABLE BASES ♦ 68

interactive systems, low-level structure design; IMPROVING
RESPONSIVENESS IN INTERACTIVE APPLICATIONS USING
QUEUES ♦ 76

life cycle; LIFE CYCLE AND REFACTORING PATTERNS THAT
SUPPORT EVOLUTION AND REUSE ♦ 84

30-day periods; SPRINT ♦ 146

decoupling stages of; DECOUPLE STAGES ♦ 68

decoupling stages of vs. responsiveness; HUB, SPOKE, AND
RIM ♦ 68

management

strategies; CAPABLE, PRODUCTIVE, AND SATISFIED ♦ 26

of unequal communication distribution; THREE TO SEVEN
HELPERS PER ROLE ♦ 68

a managers guide; SURVIVING OBJECT-ORIENTED PROJECTS:
A MANAGER'S GUIDE ♦ 168

market structure impact on team organization structure;
ORGANIZATION FOLLOWS MARKET ♦ 65

OBSERVER pattern implementation strategies;
IMPLEMENTATION PATTERNS FOR THE OBSERVER
PATTERN ♦ 74

organization structure for; EPISODES: A PATTERN LANGUAGE
OF COMPETITIVE DEVELOPMENT ♦ 51

pair programming advantages; DEVELOPING IN PAIRS ♦ 69

prioritizing forces in; PRIORITIZING FORCES IN SOFTWARE
DESIGN ♦ 135

problem-solving techniques; PROBLEM-ORIENTED TEAM ♦ 27

prototyping
evolving into a product; FROM PROTOTYPE TO REALITY ♦ 61, PROTOTYPE AND REALITY ♦ 63
role; PROTOTYPE ♦ 69, PROTOTYPE A FIRST-PASS DESIGN ♦ 84
quality assurance relationship to; ENGAGE QA ♦ 66
release cycle pacing; DELIVERABLES TO GO ♦ 27
resource management strategies; INTERRUPTS UNJAM BLOCKING ♦ 69, DON'T INTERRUPT AN INTERRUPT ♦ 69
restricted memory
cultivating habits for dealing with; THINK SMALL ♦ 72
strategies for dealing with; HIGH-LEVEL AND PROCESS PATTERNS FROM THE MEMORY PRESERVATION SOCIETY ♦ 71
roles
determination; FORM FOLLOWS FUNCTION ♦ 64
value of communication among; COUPLING DECREASES LATENCY ♦ 69
schedule
determination; SIZE THE SCHEDULE ♦ 64
management; TAKE NO SMALL SLIPS ♦ 69
SCRUM: A PATTERN LANGUAGE FOR HYPERPRODUCTIVE SOFTWARE DEVELOPMENT ♦ 146
Scrum strategy; SCRUM: A PATTERN LANGUAGE FOR HYPERPRODUCTIVE SOFTWARE DEVELOPMENT ♦ 146
shift from custom to component integration; PATTERN-BASED INTEGRATION ARCHITECTURES ♦ 115
skill utilization strategies; DEVELOPMENT EPISODE ♦ 53
strategies for; PATTERNS ON THE FLY ♦ 130
team
building; BOOTSTRAPPING ♦ 26
customer interaction with; ENGAGE CUSTOMERS ♦ 66
distractions, protection against; FIRE WALLS ♦ 67
hiring strategies; PHASING IT IN ♦ 64
interaction, structures that support; SHAPING CIRCULATION REALMS ♦ 67
location impact on architecture; ORGANIZATION FOLLOWS LOCATION ♦ 64
matching human capabilities to tasks; ROUND PEGS FOR ROUND HOLES ♦ 27
motivation; COMPENSATE SUCCESS ♦ 69
organization strategies; ORGANIZATIONAL PATTERNS FOR TEAMS ♦ 95
selection; SIZE THE ORGANIZATION ♦ 63, SELF-SELECTING TEAM ♦ 63, SOLO VIRTUOSO ♦ 64
team skill level consideration; GENERIC UI, SPECIFIC UI ♦ 136, GENERICS AND SPECIFICS ♦ 136
teams, strategies for effective use; PATTERNS FOR DESIGNING IN TEAMS ♦ 118
technical writing role; MERCENARY ANALYST ♦ 67
training strategies; APPRENTICE ♦ 64
use cases role in functionality validation; SCENARIOS DEFINE PROBLEM ♦ 66
work flow; WORK FLOWS INWARD ♦ 68
deviation
DEVIATION ♦ 134
POINTS AND DEVIATIONS: PATTERN LANGUAGE OF FIRE ALARM SYSTEMS ♦ 133

DEVIATION ♦ 134
POINT relationship to; DEVIATION ♦ 134
POOL relationship to; DEVIATION ♦ 134, POOL ♦ 134
Devos, M.
[Beedle+99]; 182
SCRUM: A PATTERN LANGUAGE FOR HYPERPRODUCTIVE SOFTWARE DEVELOPMENT ❖ 146
DIAGNOSTIC CONTEXT ♦ 124
DIAGNOSTIC LOGGER ♦ 124
DIAGNOSTIC QUERY ♦ 33
diagnostics
See Also debugging; errors
context, establishing; DIAGNOSTIC CONTEXT ♦ 124
DIAGNOSTIC CONTEXT ♦ 124
COMMAND PROCESSOR relationship to; DIAGNOSTIC CONTEXT ♦ 124
DIAGNOSTIC LOGGER relationship to; DIAGNOSTIC CONTEXT ♦ 124
TYPED diagnostics relationship to; TYPED diagnostics ♦ 124
DIAGNOSTIC LOGGER ♦ 124
DIAGNOSTIC CONTEXT relationship to; DIAGNOSTIC CONTEXT ♦ 124
SINGLETON relationship to; DIAGNOSTIC LOGGER ♦ 124
TYPED diagnostics relationship to; TYPED diagnostics ♦ 124
DIAGNOSTIC QUERY ♦ 33
message, logging of; PATTERNS FOR LOGGING DIAGNOSTIC MESSAGES ♦ 124
PATTERNS FOR LOGGING DIAGNOSTIC MESSAGES ♦ 124
queries, as error detection and correction mechanism; DIAGNOSTIC QUERY ♦ 33
TYPED diagnostics ♦ 124
dialogs
between objects, managing; WORK ACCOMPLISHED THROUGH DIALOGS ♦ 30
WORK ACCOMPLISHED THROUGH DIALOGS ♦ 30
dictionaries
DICTIONARY ♦ 159
LOOKUP CACHE relationship to; LOOKUP CACHE ♦ 161
mapping objects with; DICTIONARY ♦ 159
relationship implementation with; KEYED MAPPING ♦ 16
DICTIONARY ♦ 159
digital libraries
information retrieval issues, feature extraction algorithm assistance; FEATURE EXTRACTION—A PATTERN FOR INFORMATION RETRIEVAL ♦ 58
DIMENSION ROLL-UP ♦ 165
dimensions
business, modeling; DIMENSION ROLL-UP ♦ 165
decomposing an enterprise into; ENTERPRISE SEGMENT ♦ 9
DIMENSION ROLL-UP ♦ 165
TRANSACTION HISTORY relationship to; DIMENSION ROLL-UP ♦ 165
WHOLE BUSINESS ENTITIES relationship to; DIMENSION ROLL-UP ♦ 165
USE A SCROLLVALUEHOLDER TO HOLD A POSITION IN n-DIMENSIONAL SPACE ♦ 178

Dinh, T.
  [Barkataki+98]; 182
DIRECT VARIABLE ACCESS ♦ 157
directories
  NATURAL TEXT DIRECTORIES ♦ 98
DISPATCHED INTERPRETATION ♦ 155
dispatching
  CLIENT-DISPATCHER-SERVER ♦ 34
  client/server role; CLIENT-DISPATCHER-SERVER ♦ 34
  DISPATCHED INTERPRETATION ♦ 155
  double; DOUBLE DISPATCH ♦ 155
  DOUBLE DISPATCH ♦ 155
  multiple event handlers; REACTOR ♦ 143
display(ing)
  See Also GUI
  decoupling model updating from; DECOUPLE EXECUTION AND
    OUTPUT ♦ 76
  device selection, in fault-tolerant systems; WHO ASKED? ♦ 78
  DISPLAY LIST ♦ 49
    PAINTER'S ALGORITHM relationship to; DISPLAY LIST ♦ 49
    REQUEST UPDATE relationship to; DISPLAY LIST ♦ 49
  DISPLAY MAINTENANCE ♦ 49
  lazy redrawing; LAZY REDRAW ♦ 50
  objects, restricting the size of; MEGA-SCROLLING ♦ 90
  objects at a client, in object-oriented framework/legacy system
    interactions; MATERIALIZATION ♦ 90
  selective, of properties; PARALLEL APPLICATION AND DOMAIN
    HIERARCHIES ♦ 14
  sequence of panels; PANEL STATES ♦ 96
  updating
    consolidating requests; CONSOLIDATE REQUESTS ♦ 50
    double buffering use; DOUBLE BUFFER ♦ 50
    page swapping; PAGE FLIP ♦ 50
  updating requests for; REQUEST UPDATE ♦ 49
DISPLAY LIST ♦ 49
DISPLAY MAINTENANCE ♦ 49
  [Towell99]; 197
DISTINCTIVE HEADINGS CONVEY STRUCTURE ♦ 106
distractions
  software development
    handling; SOMEONE ALWAYS MAKES PROGRESS ♦ 169, TEAM
      PER TASK ♦ 169, SACRIFICE ONE PERSON ♦ 170
    protecting a team from; FIRE WALLS ♦ 67
DISTRIBUTED PROCESSES ♦ 51
  [Shaw+96]; 196
DISTRIBUTED READER/WRITER LOCK ♦ 149
distributed systems
  See Also concurrency
  access control, without system-level support;
    BODYGUARD ♦ 22
  ACTIVE OBJECT support for; ACTIVE OBJECT ♦ 6
  architectures for; DISTRIBUTED PROCESSES ♦ 51
  associating state with asynchronous operation completion;
    ASYNCHRONOUS COMPLETION TOKEN ♦ 19
  asynchronous completion event demultiplexing;
    PROACTOR ♦ 137
  attribute validation; ESSENCE ♦ 54
  brokers; BROKER AS DIVORCE ATTORNEY ♦ 133
  callbacks use; OBJECTS WITH REMOTE CONTROL ♦ 93

  collaboration, without system-level support; BODYGUARD ♦ 22
  concurrent control systems, software development strategies;
    OBJECT-ORIENTED DESIGN PATTERNS IN REACTIVE
    SYSTEMS ♦ 92
  control module partitioning; DISTRIBUTION OF CONTROL
    MODULES ♦ 63
  decoupling components; BROKER ♦ 22
  decoupling components for; TRANSCEIVER-PARCEL ♦ 133
  decoupling initialization, from services provided;
    ACCEPTOR ♦ 3
  design
    data structure definition; DEFINE THE DATA STRUCTURE ♦ 70
    naming system attributes, values, and roles; IDENTIFY THE
      NOUNS ♦ 70
    pattern language for; GENERATIVE PATTERN LANGUAGE FOR
      DISTRIBUTED PROCESSING ♦ 70
  DISTRIBUTED PROCESSES ♦ 51
  DISTRIBUTED READER/WRITER LOCK ♦ 149
  event demultiplexing and dispatching; REACTOR ♦ 143
  event-driven remote method call use; EVENT-DRIVEN
    RPC ♦ 94
  GENERATIVE PATTERN LANGUAGE FOR DISTRIBUTED
    PROCESSING; GENERATIVE PATTERN LANGUAGE FOR
    DISTRIBUTED PROCESSING ♦ 70, ♦ 70
  load sharing; RESOURCE EXCHANGER ♦ 144
  local and global data relationships in; RECOVERABLE
    DISTRIBUTOR ♦ 143
  location dependencies, minimizing in a network management
    system; REMOTE OPERATION ♦ 115
  in manufacturing, G++ pattern language; G++: A
    PATTERN LANGUAGE FOR COMPUTER-INTEGRATED
    MANUFACTURING ♦ 61
  microkernel architecture as mechanism for managing;
    MICROKERNEL ♦ 87
  multimedia sessions, managing; SESSION CONTROL &
    OBSERVATION ♦ 151
  network management interfaces; PATTERN SYSTEM FOR
    NETWORK MANAGEMENT INTERFACES ♦ 114
  object-oriented architecture, fire alarm system family; POINTS
    AND DEVIATIONS: PATTERN LANGUAGE OF FIRE ALARM
    SYSTEMS ♦ 133
  object-oriented finite state machine use; OBJECT-ORIENTED
    STATE MACHINE ♦ 129
  ORGANIZATIONAL MULTIPLEXING: PATTERNS FOR PROCESSING
    SATELLITE TELEMETRY WITH DISTRIBUTED TEAMS ♦ 94
  project architecture strategies that reflect a distributed team;
    ORGANIZATION FOLLOWS LOCATION ♦ 64
  remote control of; REMOTE CONTROL ♦ 144
  security in, without system-level support; BODYGUARD ♦ 22
  sharing objects, without system-level support;
    BODYGUARD ♦ 22
  software and organizational development strategies;
    ORGANIZATIONAL MULTIPLEXING: PATTERNS FOR
    PROCESSING SATELLITE TELEMETRY WITH DISTRIBUTED
    TEAMS ♦ 94
distribution
  of control modules, in distributed systems; DISTRIBUTION OF
    CONTROL MODULES ♦ 63

DISTRIBUTION OF CONTROL MODULES ♦ 63
  EVENT-DRIVEN RPC relationship to; EVENT-DRIVEN
    RPC ♦ 94
DISTRIBUTION OF CONTROL MODULES ♦ 63
diversity
  DIVERSITY OF MEMBERSHIP ♦ 95
    GET INVOLVED EARLY relationship to; DIVERSITY OF
      MEMBERSHIP ♦ 95
    HOLISTIC DIVERSITY relationship to; HOLISTIC
      DIVERSITY ♦ 169
  HOLISTIC DIVERSITY ♦ 169
DIVERSITY OF MEMBERSHIP ♦ 95
DIVIDE AND CONQUER ♦ 68
divide-and-conquor strategy
  DIVIDE AND CONQUER ♦ 68
  FORK/JOIN, as parallel computation verion; FORK/JOIN ♦ 40
  form development; SUBFORM ♦ 99
  project tasks; WORK SPLIT ♦ 53
Do ♦ 160
Doble, G. J.
  [Doble+99]; 186
    SMALLTALK SCAFFOLDING PATTERNS ❖ 163
  [Doble96]; 186
    SHOPPER ♦ 152
  [Meszaros+98]; 191
    PATTERN LANGUAGE FOR PATTERN WRITING ❖ 102
DOCUMENT THE PROBLEM ♦ 128
documentation
  AMBIGUOUS DOCUMENTATION ♦ 127
  DECISION DOCUMENT ♦ 118
  design
    decision making strategies using; DECISION
      DOCUMENT ♦ 118
    system testing use; GET INVOLVED EARLY ♦ 126,
      AMBIGUOUS DOCUMENTATION ♦ 127
  diagnostic messages, logging of; PATTERNS FOR LOGGING
    DIAGNOSTIC MESSAGES ♦ 124
  DOCUMENT THE PROBLEM ♦ 128
    ADOPT-A-PROBLEM relationship to; ADOPT-A-
      PROBLEM ♦ 128
    DESIGNERS ARE OUR FRIENDS relationship to;
      DESIGNERS ARE OUR FRIENDS ♦ 126, DOCUMENT THE
      PROBLEM ♦ 128
    GET INVOLVED EARLY relationship to; DOCUMENT THE
      PROBLEM ♦ 128
  headings, pattern language structuring tool; DISTINCTIVE
    HEADINGS CONVEY STRUCTURE ♦ 106
  of methods; METHOD COMMENT ♦ 154
  NEW DOCUMENT NOTIFICATION ♦ 99
  organization, on WWW; NATURAL TEXT DIRECTORIES ♦ 98
  of performance tuning experiements; EXPERIMENT ♦ 82
  problem reports, system testing use; USE OLD PROBLEM
    REPORTS ♦ 127
  project
    technical memos as strategy for; TECHNICAL MEMO ♦ 54
    technical writing role; MERCENARY ANALYST ♦ 67
  sources, for software development; REFERENCE DATA ♦ 54
  of system test problems; DOCUMENT THE PROBLEM ♦ 128
  WORKSHEET DOCUMENTS ♦ 98

domain
  attributes, identifying; ELABORATION OF THE DOMAIN
    OBJECTS ♦ 141
  CLASSIFYING, ASSOCIATING, AND GROUPING THE DOMAIN
    OBJECTS ♦ 141
  constraints, identifying; ELABORATION OF THE DOMAIN
    OBJECTS ♦ 141
  decoupling from database-specific application components;
    BROKER ♦ 108
  details, decoupling rules from; ACCOUNTABILITY KNOWLEDGE
    LEVEL ♦ 5, ACCOUNTABILITY KNOWLEDGE LEVEL ♦ 7
  DOMAIN EXPERTISE IN ROLES ♦ 64
  DOMAIN INTERCEPTS ♦ 137
  ELABORATION OF THE DOMAIN OBJECTS ♦ 141
  for example selection, in teachng; ACQUAINTANCE
    EXAMPLES ♦ 117
  examples, pattern language writing use; RUNNING
    EXAMPLE ♦ 106
  expertise, priority in role assignment; DOMAIN EXPERTISE IN
    ROLES ♦ 64
  experts, pattern writers as; AUTHORS ARE EXPERTS ♦ 111
  FINDING AND DEFINING THE DOMAIN OBJECTS ♦ 141
  IDENTIFY PROBLEM DOMAIN RELATIONSHIPS ♦ 70
  as interface, betwen user interface and persistent subsystem;
    DOMAIN INTERCEPTS ♦ 137
  layered architecture role; PEDESTAL ♦ 123
  model
    decoupling from application model; TWO APPLICATIONS ♦ 97
    decoupling user interface from, in application layer;
      PRESENTATION AND APPLICATION LOGIC ♦ 15
    with general accounting patterns; SPECIALIZED ACCOUNT
      MODEL ♦ 12
    as Smalltalk client-server system layer; FOUR-LAYER
      ARCHITECTURE ♦ 106
  objects
    analyzing the relationships among; CLASSIFYING,
      ASSOCIATING, AND GROUPING THE DOMAIN
      OBJECTS ♦ 141
    identifying; FINDING AND DEFINING THE DOMAIN
      OBJECTS ♦ 141
    identifying life cycle; ELABORATION OF THE DOMAIN
      OBJECTS ♦ 141
    as persistent component; MODEL HIERARCHY ♦ 136
  PARALLEL APPLICATION AND DOMAIN HIERARCHIES ♦ 14
  problem, analysis; PROBLEM DOMAIN ANALYSIS ♦ 141
  PROBLEM DOMAIN ANALYSIS ♦ 141
  product, identifying relationships in; IDENTIFY PROBLEM
    DOMAIN RELATIONSHIPS ♦ 70
  relating to objects in the software; WHOLE BUSINESS
    ENTITIES ♦ 165
  role of objects in; OBJECT STEREOTYPES ♦ 141
  rules, identifying; ELABORATION OF THE DOMAIN
    OBJECTS ♦ 141
  as software architecture subsystem; THREE SUBSYSTEMS ♦ 135
  state change, requirements analysis; OBJECT AGING ♦ 141
  as three-tier application layer; THREE-TIER
    ARCHITECTURE ♦ 15

domain *continued*
  understanding, pattern writing importance; Clear
    Target Audience ♦ 104, Terminology Tailored to
    Audience ♦ 105
  use cases, software design functionality use; Scenarios
    Define Problem ♦ 66
  value relationships, displaying; Visible Implication ♦ 33
  value representation; Whole Value ♦ 32
    outside the normal range; Exceptional Value ♦ 32
  views, creating for a relational database; Hierarchical
    View ♦ 3
Domain Expertise in Roles ♦ 64
Domain Intercepts ♦ 137
Don't Interrupt an Interrupt ♦ 69
Don't Let Them Forget ♦ 79
Don't Trust Simulations ♦ 127
Don't xxx
  Don't Interrupt an Interrupt ♦ 69
  Don't Let Them Forget ♦ 79
    Audible Alarm relationship to; Don't Let Them
    Forget ♦ 79
  Don't Trust Simulations ♦ 127
Doormat ♦ 131
  Sacrificial Lamb relationship to; Doormat ♦ 131
double
  buffering, display update use; Double Buffer ♦ 50
  dispatching; Double Dispatch ♦ 155
  Double Buffer ♦ 50
    Page Flip relationship to; Double Buffer ♦ 50, Page
    Flip ♦ 50
    Painter's Algorithm relationship to; Painter's
    Algorithm ♦ 50
  Double Check ♦ 38
  Double Dispatch ♦ 155
  Double-Checked Locking ♦ 51
    Session relationship to; Session ♦ 17
    Thread-Specific Storage relationship to;
    Thread-Specific Storage ♦ 172
Double Buffer ♦ 50
Double Check ♦ 38
Double Dispatch ♦ 155
Double-Checked Locking ♦ 51
  [Schmidt+98]; 194
Downward Changes ♦ 45
driver
  Driver Duty ♦ 51
    Cascade relationship to; Cascade ♦ 28, Driver
    Duty ♦ 51
    Composite relationship to; Driver Duty ♦ 51
  Driver Duty Builder, Cascade relationship to;
    Cascade ♦ 28
  Driver Duty Constructor ♦ 51
  duty
    construction; Driver Duty Constructor ♦ 51
    definition; Driver Duty ♦ 51
Driver Duty ♦ 51
  [Zhao+98a]; 199
Driver Duty Constructor ♦ 51
  [Zhao+99]; 199

Dual Time Record ♦ 9
  Observation relationship to; Dual Time Record ♦ 9
Duell, M.
  [Duell98]; 187
Duplicate Removing Set ♦ 161
duplication
  Duplicate Removing Set ♦ 161
  removing from a collection; Duplicate Removing Set ♦ 161
duty
  Driver Duty ♦ 51
  Driver Duty Constructor ♦ 51
dynamic
  addition of responsibilities to an object; Decorator ♦ 46
  Dynamic State Instantiation ♦ 60
  formula generation for reports; Formula Objects ♦ 41
  Localized Ownership: Managing Dynamic Objects in
    C++ ♦ 85
  object representation, prototype-based object systems;
    Prototype-Based Object System ♦ 139
  objects
    lifetime management; Localized Ownership: Managing
    Dynamic Objects in C++ ♦ 85
    sharing ownership; Shared Ownership ♦ 86
    transfer from creator; Sequence of Owners ♦ 85
  queries
    design strategies; Query Objects ♦ 41
    query component use; Composable Query Objects ♦ 41
  report generation, design strategies; Report Objects ♦ 41
  resources, selecting from a set of; Sponsor-Selector ♦ 164
  specification, of product types; Pluggable Factory ♦ 132
  state creation, in finite state machine; Dynamic State
    Instantiation ♦ 60
Dynamic State Instantiation ♦ 60
Dyson, P
  [Dyson+98]; 187
    State Patterns ❖ 166

e-commerce
  identification of new material; News ♦ 120
  shopping basket, hypermedia design strategies; Basket ♦ 120
Eager Firing
  term description; Posting Rule Execution ♦ 11
Early and Regular Delivery ♦ 168
  Clear the Fog relationship to; Early and Regular
    Delivery ♦ 168
Echo Back ♦ 32
  Deferred Validation relationship to; Deferred
    Validation ♦ 33
  Visible Implication relationship to; Visible
    Implication ♦ 33
Edition ♦ 34
Edits Inside ♦ 136
education
  classroom, patterns for; Patterns for Classroom
    Education ♦ 116
  Patterns for Classroom Education ♦ 116
Edwards, S. H.
  [Edwards95]; 187
    Streams ♦ 167

EFFECTIVE HANDOVER ◆ 27
either-or-both relationship
  abstracting into a supertype; PARTY ◆ 4, PARTY ◆ 6
elaboration
  ELABORATION OF THE DOMAIN OBJECTS ◆ 141
    BUSINESS RULES relationship to; ELABORATION OF THE
      DOMAIN OBJECTS ◆ 141
    INFORMATION NEEDS relationship to; ELABORATION OF THE
      DOMAIN OBJECTS ◆ 141
    OBJECT AGAING relationship to; ELABORATION OF THE
      DOMAIN OBJECTS ◆ 141
    PROBLEM DOMAIN ANALYSIS relationship to; PROBLEM
      DOMAIN ANALYSIS ◆ 141
ELABORATION OF THE DOMAIN OBJECTS ◆ 141
ELEMENT IDENTIFICATION ◆ 46
elements
  ELEMENT IDENTIFICATION ◆ 46
    CATALYTIC SCENARIOS relationship to; ELEMENT
      IDENTIFICATION ◆ 46
    LIGHTWEIGHT USER INTERFACES relationship to; ELEMENT
      IDENTIFICATION ◆ 46
    PROTOTYPING LANGUAGES relationship to; ELEMENT
      IDENTIFICATION ◆ 46
  OPTIONAL ELEMENTS WHEN HELPFUL ◆ 103
ELEVATE REFERENCES TO ENHANCE REUSE ◆ 124
  BASIC RELATIONSHIP PATTERNS relationship to; ELEVATE
    REFERENCES TO ENHANCE REUSE ◆ 124
  WORK ACCOMPLISHED THROUGH DIALOG relationship to;
    ELEVATE REFERENCES TO ENHANCE REUSE ◆ 124
Elia, G.
  [Aarsten+95]; 181
    G++: A PATTERN LANGUAGE FOR COMPUTER-INTEGRATED
      MANUFACTURING ❖ 61
empty
  IS EMPTY ◆ 160
  testing collections for; IS EMPTY ◆ 160
ENCAPSULATE CONCRETE STATE ◆ 145
ENCAPSULATE SENDERS OF VALUE AND VALUE: ◆ 177
ENCAPSULATED STATE ◆ 60
encapsulation
  accessing state without violating; MEMENTO ◆ 87
  of aggregation elements, while sequentially processing the
    members; ITERATOR ◆ 80
  of behavior
    into an accountability relationship; ACCOUNTABILITY
      ABSTRACTION ◆ 5
    state classes use for; FOR OBJECTS WITH MOODS, USE
      STATE CLASSES ◆ 88
  of big ball of mud code, as control strategy; SWEEPING IT
    UNDER THE RUG ◆ 21
  of class trees; PATTERNS FOR ENCAPSULATING CLASS
    TREES ◆ 120
  of communication interfaces, from legacy clients;
    REQUEST ◆ 90
  of complexity, as reusability strategy; LOW
    SURFACE-TO-VOLUME RATIO ◆ 150
  of components, in a network management system;
    MANAGER-AGENT ◆ 114
  of concrete state; ENCAPSULATE CONCRETE STATE ◆ 145

of data structures; WRAPPER FACADE ◆ 179
of debugging tools; DETACHABLE INSPECTOR ◆ 49
of diagnostic message categories; TYPED DIAGNOSTICS ◆ 124
ENCAPSULATE CONCRETE STATE ◆ 145
ENCAPSULATE SENDERS OF VALUE AND VALUE: ◆ 177
ENCAPSULATED STATE ◆ 60
of events
  in distributed systems; REMOTE CONTROL ◆ 144
  in event-driven system development; OBJECTIFY THE
    EVENTS ◆ 93
of functions; WRAPPER FACADE ◆ 179
of instance management; MANAGER ◆ 86
layering, of programs; SHAPE OF PROGRAM ◆ 29
of measurements; MEASUREMENT ◆ 8
message sender; ENCAPSULATE SENDERS OF VALUE AND
  VALUE: ◆ 177
method, in concurrent programs; SESSION ◆ 37
of network interactions, minimizing location dependencies by;
  REMOTE OPERATION ◆ 115
of object interaction; MEDIATOR ◆ 86
of object rendering, in object-oriented framework/legacy
  system interactions; MATERIALIZATION ◆ 90
of organizational structures; ORGANIZATIONAL
  STRUCTURE-TYPED RELATIONSHIP ◆ 5
of pattern essense, separating essential from optional material;
  SKIPPABLE SECTIONS ◆ 103
PATTERNS FOR ENCAPSULATING CLASS TREES ◆ 120
of physical database tables; PHYSICAL VIEW ◆ 3
pluggable objects, framework development use; PLUGGABLE
  OBJECTS ◆ 122
of resources, client/server/service model;
  CLIENT/SERVER/SERVICE ◆ 62
REUSABILITY THROUGH SELF-ENCAPSULATION ◆ 145
of services, client/server/service model;
  CLIENT/SERVER/SERVICE ◆ 62
of state
  for clients; ABSTRACT SESSION ◆ 2
  in an object; STATE OBJECT ◆ 166
of state change, in finite state machine; ENCAPSULATED
  STATE ◆ 60
of state-transition logic, in finite state machines; INTERFACE
  ORGANIZATION ◆ 59
of system state; OBJECTIFY SYSTEM STATE ◆ 93
of user interface; HUMAN INTERFACE ROLE IS A SPECIAL
  INTERFACE ROLE ◆ 31, APPLICATION BOUNDARY ◆ 136
encryption
  message, secret key use with; INFORMATION SECRECY ◆ 174
  of message, verification of sender identity; SECRECY WITH
    INTEGRITY ◆ 175
END USER VIEWPOINT ◆ 127
ENGAGE CUSTOMERS ◆ 66
ENGAGE QA ◆ 66
engagement
  ENGAGE CUSTOMERS ◆ 66
    CUSTOMER INTERACTION PATTERNS relationship to; ENGAGE
      CUSTOMERS ◆ 66
    CUSTOMER RAPPORT relationship to; ENGAGE
      CUSTOMERS ◆ 66

engagement *continued*
  Engage QA ♦ 66
    Designers Are Our Friends relationship to; Engage
      QA ♦ 66
    Time to Test relationship to; Engage QA ♦ 66
Engel, R.
  [Huni+95]; 188
engineering
  Messaging Engineering Model ♦ 18
  model
    batch, for batch processing; Batch Engineering
      Model ♦ 19
    messaging, forasynchronous interactive support; Messaging
      Engineering Model ♦ 18
    for online interactive systems; Online Engineering
      Model ♦ 18
    stream, for support of batch, interactive, and messaging
      systems; Stream I-O Engineering Model ♦ 19
  models, software architecture definition by; Architecture
    Patterns for Business Systems ♦ 18
  Online Engineering Model ♦ 18
  Stream I-O Engineering Model ♦ 19
**Ensure That All Objects Sharing a Value Use the
  Same ValueModel ♦ 177**
enterprise
  See Also business; customer(s); organization management
  decomposition of; Enterprise Segment ♦ 9
  Enterprise Segment ♦ 9
  modeling, patterns for; Accountability and
    Organizational Structures pattern language ♦ 4
  segment, representing; Enterprise Segment ♦ 9
Enterprise Segment ♦ 9
entities
  modeling, in a transaction processing system; People,
    Places, and Things ♦ 165
  Whole Business Entities ♦ 165
entries
  account
    recording for a transaction; Sources of an Entry ♦ 12
    selecting; Choosing Entries ♦ 11
  booking to multiple accounts; Booking Entries to
    Multiple Accounts ♦ 12
  Choosing Entries ♦ 11
  data
    deferrring validation of; Deferred Validation ♦ 33
    feedback; Echo Back ♦ 32
  Entry Point ♦ 16
    Manager relationship to; Entry Point ♦ 16
  Sources of an Entry ♦ 12
Entry Point ♦ 16
Enumeration ♦ 160
enumeration
  block, parameters, naming; Simple Enumeration
    Parameter ♦ 163
  as collection access technique; Enumeration Method ♦ 158
  Enumeration ♦ 160
  Enumeration Method ♦ 158
  Simple Enumeration Parameter ♦ 163
Enumeration Method ♦ 158

Envelope/Letter ♦ 25
  Algebraic Hierarchy relationship to;
    Envelope/Letter ♦ 25
  Counted Body relationship to; Envelope/Letter ♦ 25
  Envelope/Letter, Handle/Body; Handle/Body ♦ 24
  Handle/Body relationship to; Envelope/Letter ♦ 25
  Promotion Ladder relationship to; Envelope/Letter ♦ 25
  State relationship to; Envelope/Letter ♦ 25
  Virtual Constructor relationship to;
    Envelope/Letter ♦ 25, Virtual Constructor ♦ 25
Environment ♦ 110
environment
  authoring, multimedia; Composing Multimedia Artifacts
    for Reuse ♦ 36
  Environment; Environment ♦ 110, ♦ 110
  multiple platform, system testing on; Multiple
    Processors ♦ 128
  pattern writers workshops, physical arrangements; Sitting in
    a Circle ♦ 112
  relationship of tools and materials to; Environment ♦ 110
  safe, as pattern writers workshop priority; Safe
    Setting ♦ 111
  software development
    importance for optimal human performance; Team
      Space ♦ 27
    Scrum process use; Scrum: A Pattern Language for
      Hyperproductive Software Development ♦ 146
  system testing; Busy System ♦ 127
    simulation unreliability; Don't Trust Simulations ♦ 127
Envisioning ♦ 142
  Information Needs relationship to; Information
    Needs ♦ 141
ENVY/Developer
  components, partitioning into code for; Partitioning
    Smalltalk Code into ENVY/Developer
    Components ♦ 96
  Partitioning Smalltalk Code into ENVY/Developer
    Components ♦ 96
episode
  See Also human relationships; scheduling; software,
    development; time
  development, skill utilization strategies; Development
    Episode ♦ 53
  Development Episode ♦ 53
  Episodes: A Pattern Language of Competitive
    Development ♦ 51
  programming, scheduling strategies; Programming
    Episode ♦ 54
  Programming Episode ♦ 54
**Episodes: A Pattern Language of Competitive
  Development ♦ 51**
  [Cunningham96]; 186
equality
  See Also comparison
  defining methods for; Equality Method ♦ 159
  Equality Method ♦ 159
  Object Equivalence ♦ 10
  relationship
    between account views; Corresponding Account ♦ 12

creating; OBJECT EQUIVALENCE ◆ 10

EQUALITY METHOD ◆ 159

erosion

   of system architecture, handling piecemeal growth without;
      PIECEMEAL GROWTH ◆ 21

error(s)

   classifying into condition hierarchies; EXCEPTION ◆ 89

   detection

      diagnostic query mechanism for; DIAGNOSTIC QUERY ◆ 33

      hypothetical modeling use for; HYPOTHETICAL
         PUBLICATION ◆ 33

   diagnostic message logging

      strategies for; DIAGNOSTIC LOGGER ◆ 124

      in transaction-oriented systems; PATTERNS FOR LOGGING
         DIAGNOSTIC MESSAGES ◆ 124

   FULL VIEW WITH ERRORS ◆ 18

   handling

      backup strategies use for; BACKUP ◆ 19

      dealing with message flooding; FIVE MINUTES OF NO
         ESCALATION MESSAGES ◆ 57

      in fault-tolerant systems, alternative hardware selection
         strategies; TRY ALL HARDWARE COMBOS ◆ 58

      human overrides use; PEOPLE KNOW BEST ◆ 57

      multiphase cancellation; MULTIPHASE CANCELLATION ◆ 39

      roll state back to consistent state; ROLLBACK ◆ 38

      rolling forward when rollback is impossible;
         ROLL-FORWARD ◆ 39

      synchronization of illegal value checking; DOUBLE
         CHECK ◆ 38

   interactive recognition of, engineering model for; ONLINE
      ENGINEERING MODEL ◆ 18

   latent, handling, in fault-tolerant systems; FOOL ME
      ONCE ◆ 58

   in learning concepts, prevention strategies; PITFALL DIAGNOSIS
      AND PREVENTION ◆ 116

   message display, as illegal operation handling method; FULL
      VIEW WITH ERRORS ◆ 18

   messages

      ordering of, in fault-tolerant systems; TIMESTAMP ◆ 77

      strategies for overload handling; GEORGE WASHINGTON IS
         STILL DEAD ◆ 78, FIVE MINUTES OF NO ESCALATION
         MESSAGES ◆ 78

   minimizing, in telecommunications systems; MINIMIZE
      HUMAN INTERVENTION ◆ 57

   observation, handling of; REJECTED OBSERVATION ◆ 9

   override of silenced alarms; DON'T LET THEM FORGET ◆ 79

   prevention, through view limitation; LIMITED VIEW ◆ 18

   reporting

      output direction, fault-tolerant systems; MIND YOUR OWN
         BUSINESS ◆ 77

      prioritizing errors, in fault-tolerant systems; IO TRIAGE ◆ 77

      transient, handling, in fault-tolerant systems; RIDING OVER
         TRANSIENTS ◆ 57

ESSENCE ◆ 54

   [Carlson99]; 184

   OBJECT MERGE relationship to; OBJECT MERGE ◆ 10

Estepp, S.

   [Carlson+99]; 184

   TEMPORAL PATTERNS ❖ 171

estimation

   project time, strategies for; COMPARABLE WORK ◆ 52

evaluation

   of patterns, open review forum advantages; OPEN
      REVIEW ◆ 111

   of performance; PERFORMANCE ASSESSMENT ◆ 81

   sensor, data push handling; DATA PUMP ◆ 135

   of systems; PATTERNS FOR SYSTEM TESTING ◆ 126

   of technical papers

      program committee selection process; IDENTIFY THE
         CHAMPION PATTERN LANGUAGE ◆ 73

      strategies for handling conflicts; IDENTIFY THE
         CONFLICTS ◆ 74

EVENT ACQUISITION ◆ 31

EVENT MECHANISM ◆ 110

EVENT NOTIFICATION ◆ 54

   [Riehle96a]; 193

EVENT QUEUE ◆ 76

EVENT ROUTING ◆ 31

event(s)

   acquisition, design issues; EVENT ACQUISITION ◆ 31

   actions triggered by, in complex concurrent systems; ACTIONS
      TRIGGERED BY EVENTS ◆ 62

   ACTIONS TRIGGERED BY EVENTS ◆ 62

   analysis of, as system design tool; TIME THREAD
      ANALYSIS ◆ 71

   architecture design centered around; EVENT-CENTERED
      ARCHITECTURE ◆ 129

   asynchronous completion, demultiplexing and dispatching;
      PROACTOR ◆ 137

   buffering event queues with artificial events; HANDLE
      ARTIFICIAL EVENTS ◆ 76

   classes, design levels; CLASSES OF EVENT OBJECTS ◆ 129

   CLASSES OF EVENT OBJECTS ◆ 129

   classification, fine-grained; FINE-GRAINED CLASSIFICATION
      OF EVENTS ◆ 129

   as complex behavior cause, management strategies; WHEN
      EVENTS CAUSE MOODS, USE STATE MACHINE ◆ 88

   decoupling rules from; ACCOUNTABILITY KNOWLEDGE
      LEVEL ◆ 5, ACCOUNTABILITY KNOWLEDGE LEVEL ◆ 7

   demultiplexing and dispatching; REACTOR ◆ 143

   display update requests, consolidating; CONSOLIDATE
      REQUESTS ◆ 50

   distributed system encapsulation of; REMOTE CONTROL ◆ 144

   driven systems

      callbacks use; OBJECTS WITH REMOTE CONTROL ◆ 93

      software development strategies; OBJECT-ORIENTED DESIGN
         PATTERNS IN REACTIVE SYSTEMS ◆ 92

   encapsulation of, in event-driven system development;
      OBJECTIFY THE EVENTS ◆ 93

   EVENT ACQUISITION ◆ 31

      PATTERNS OF EVENTS relationship to; EVENT
         ACQUISITION ◆ 31

      SHAPE OF PROGRAM relationship to; EVENT
         ACQUISITION ◆ 31

      SYSTEM CITIZEN'S ROLE relationship to; SYSTEM CITIZEN'S
         ROLE ◆ 29

   EVENT LOGGING, CUSTOMER CONTACT relationship to;
      CUSTOMER CONTACT ◆ 23

event(s) *continued*

EVENT MECHANISM ♦ 110

EVENT NOTIFICATION relationship to; EVENT
MECHANISM ♦ 110

OBSERVER relationship to; EVENT MECHANISM ♦ 110

TOOL COMPOSITION relationship to; TOOL
COMPOSITION ♦ 110

EVENT NOTIFICATION ♦ 54

EVENT MECHANISM relationship to; EVENT
MECHANISM ♦ 110

EVENT QUEUE ♦ 76

COMMAND relationship to; EVENT QUEUE ♦ 76

DECOUPLE EXECUTION AND OUTPUT relationship to; EVENT
QUEUE ♦ 76, DECOUPLE EXECUTION AND OUTPUT ♦ 76

HANDLE ARTIFICIAL EVENTS relationship to; EVENT
QUEUE ♦ 76

MERGE COMPATIBLE EVENTS relationship to; EVENT
QUEUE ♦ 76, MERGE COMPATIBLE EVENTS ♦ 76

SINGLETON relationship to; EVENT QUEUE ♦ 76

EVENT ROUTING ♦ 31

SYSTEM CITIZEN'S ROLE relationship to; SYSTEM CITIZEN'S
ROLE ♦ 29

EVENT-CENTERED ARCHITECTURE ♦ 129

CLASSES OF EVENT OBJECTS relationship to; CLASSES OF
EVENT OBJECTS ♦ 129

OBJECT-ORIENTED STATE MACHINE relationship to;
OBJECT-ORIENTED STATE MACHINE ♦ 129

EVENT-DRIVEN I/O ♦ 39

EVENT-DRIVEN RPC; EVENT-DRIVEN RPC ♦ 94, ♦ 94

DISTRIBUTION OF CONTROL MODULES relationship to;
EVENT-DRIVEN RPC ♦ 94

OBJECT-ORIENTED SIMULATION relationship to;
EVENT-DRIVEN RPC ♦ 94

EVENTHANDLER ♦ 55

CHAIN OF RESPONSIBILITY relationship to; CHAIN OF
RESPONSIBILITY ♦ 32, EVENTHANDLER ♦ 55

FINE-GRAINED CLASSIFICATION OF EVENTS ♦ 129

finite state machine output triggering; MEALLY ♦ 59,
HYBRID ♦ 59

grouping messages about the same kind of, in fault-tolerant
systems; BOTTOM LINE ♦ 78

HANDLE ARTIFICIAL EVENTS ♦ 76

handling; EVENTHANDLER ♦ 55

callbacks use; DETERMINE THE ACTORS ♦ 71

design strategies for; CHAIN OF RESPONSIBILITY ♦ 32

in distributed systems; PATTERNS OF EVENTS ♦ 129

finite state machine use; DETERMINE THE ACTORS ♦ 71

in finite state machines; INTERFACE ORGANIZATION ♦ 59

mechanisms for; IMPLICIT INVOCATION OR
EVENT-BASED ♦ 125

object blocking use; SERVICES 'WAITING FOR' ♦ 62

in real-time control and information systems; PATTERNS OF
EVENTS ♦ 129

in a software tools environment; EVENT MECHANISM ♦ 110

IMPLICIT INVOCATION OR EVENT-BASED ♦ 125

isolating, from rest of the model; PUT FREQUENTLY VARYING
STRUCTURES IN INSTANCES ♦ 5

MERGE COMPATIBLE EVENTS ♦ 76

notification; EVENT NOTIFICATION ♦ 54

OBJECTIFY THE EVENTS ♦ 93

option relationship to; SUBTYPE STATE MACHINES ♦ 14

output, decoupling model updating from; DECOUPLE
EXECUTION AND OUTPUT ♦ 76

overload

handling strategies; MERGE COMPATIBLE EVENTS ♦ 76

strategies for handling, HANDLE ARTIFICIAL EVENTS ♦ 76

PATTERNS OF EVENTS ♦ 129

prototype handling of; SELECTOR SYNTHESIS ♦ 164

queues, interactive application use; EVENT QUEUE ♦ 76

reaction, decoupling from state transition; FOR STATE
MACHINES, USE TRANSITION METHODS ♦ 88

representation, in distributed systems; OBJECT-ORIENTED
STATE MACHINE ♦ 129

representation of fire alarm; DEVIATION ♦ 134

routing, design issues; EVENT ROUTING ♦ 31

saving object state; HISTORY ON SELF ♦ 35

state relationship, capturing in an edition; EDITION ♦ 34

state relationships, capturing; COLLECTION OF HISTORY
PATTERNS ♦ 34

EVENT-CENTERED ARCHITECTURE ♦ 129

EVENT-DRIVEN I/O ♦ 39

EVENT-DRIVEN RPC ♦ 94

EVENTHANDLER ♦ 55

[Jackson99]; 188

evidence

chain of, in a diagnosis, encapsulating; ASSOCIATED
OBSERVATION ♦ 9

EVOCATIVE PATTERN NAME ♦ 104

MEANINGFUL METAPHOR NAME relationship to; EVOCATIVE
PATTERN NAME ♦ 104, MEANINGFUL METAPHOR
NAME ♦ 104

NOUN PHRASE NAME relationship to; EVOCATIVE PATTERN
NAME ♦ 104, NOUN PHRASE NAME ♦ 104

PATTERN THUMBNAIL relationship to; PATTERN
THUMBNAIL ♦ 104

SINGLE-PASS READABLE relationship to; SINGLE-PASS
READABLE ♦ 103

evolution

of classroom courses; ITERATIVE COURSE
DEVELOPMENT ♦ 116

CONSOLIDATE THE PROGRAM TO SUPPORT EVOLUTION AND
REUSE ♦ 85

EVOLUTION, ARCHITECTURE, AND METAMORPHOSIS ♦ 55

EVOLVE AGGREGATIONS FROM INHERITANCE
HIERARCHIES ♦ 85

of frameworks, patterns for; PATTERNS FOR EVOLVING
FRAMEWORKS ♦ 121

of inheritance into aggregations; EVOLVE AGGREGATIONS
FROM INHERITANCE HIERARCHIES ♦ 85

LIFECYCLE AND REFACTORING PATTERNS THAT SUPPORT
EVOLUTION AND REUSE ♦ 84

PATTERNS FOR EVOLVING FRAMEWORKS ♦ 121

product, event-centered architecture support of;
EVENT-CENTERED ARCHITECTURE ♦ 129

of prototype

to product; FROM PROTOTYPE TO REALITY ♦ 61, PROTOTYPE
AND REALITY ♦ 63, OBJECT-ORIENTED DESIGN PATTERNS
IN REACTIVE SYSTEMS ♦ 92

as software development stage; EXPAND THE INITIAL
PROTOTYPE ◆ 84

software
refactoring as stage in; CONSOLIDATE THE PROGRAM TO
SUPPORT EVOLUTION AND REUSE ◆ 85
transition strategies; OBJECT-ORIENTED SIMULATION ◆ 93
of software, strategies and phases; LIFE CYCLE AND
REFACTORING PATTERNS THAT SUPPORT EVOLUTION AND
REUSE ◆ 84

EVOLUTION, ARCHITECTURE, AND METAMORPHOSIS ◆ 55
[Foote+96]; 187

EVOLVE AGGREGATIONS FROM INHERITANCE
HIERARCHIES ◆ 85

EXAMPLE LASTS ONE WEEK ◆ 117

examples
ACQUAINTANCE EXAMPLES ◆ 117
domain, pattern language writing use; RUNNING
EXAMPLE ◆ 106
domain selection for, in teaching; ACQUAINTANCE
EXAMPLES ◆ 117
duration of, in teaching; EXAMPLE LASTS ONE WEEK ◆ 117
EXAMPLE LASTS ONE WEEK ◆ 117
ACQUAINTANCE EXAMPLES relationship to; EXAMPLE LASTS
ONE WEEK ◆ 117
frameworks development based on; THREE EXAMPLES ◆ 121
REFERENCE EXAMPLES ◆ 117
running, pattern language writing use; RUNNING
EXAMPLE ◆ 106
as teaching strategy; MODULE'S STORY ◆ 116
THREE EXAMPLES ◆ 121
working, as reusability strategy; WORKS OUT OF THE
BOX ◆ 150

EXCEPTION ◆ 89

exception(s)
See Also errors
classifying error conditions into hierarchies use of;
EXCEPTION ◆ 89
EXCEPTION ◆ 89
EXCEPTIONAL VALUE ◆ 32
WHOLE VALUE relationship to; EXCEPTIONAL VALUE ◆ 32

EXCEPTIONAL VALUE ◆ 32

exchange
options relationship to exchange rate; OPTIONS ◆ 14
RESOURCE EXCHANGER ◆ 144

exclusion
mutual, conflict set representation of; CONFLICT SETS ◆ 39

EXECUTABLE MODELS ◆ 45

EXECUTE AROUND METHOD ◆ 154

execution
CONCURRENT THREADS OF EXECUTION ◆ 28
DECOUPLE EXECUTION AND OUTPUT ◆ 76
EXECUTABLE MODELS ◆ 45
PROTOTYPE A FIRST-PASS DESIGN relationship to;
EXECUTABLE MODELS ◆ 45
PROTOTYPE relationship to; EXECUTABLE MODELS ◆ 45
PROTOTYPING LANGUAGES relationship to; EXECUTABLE
MODELS ◆ 45
EXECUTE AROUND METHOD ◆ 154
POSTING RULE EXECUTION ◆ 11

EXHAUSTION TEST ◆ 73
MEMORY OVERDRAFT relationship to; MEMORY
OVERDRAFT ◆ 72
THINK SMALL relationship to; THINK SMALL ◆ 72

EXPAND THE INITIAL PROTOTYPE ◆ 84

expansion
EXPAND THE INITIAL PROTOTYPE ◆ 84
of prototype, as software development stage; EXPAND THE
INITIAL PROTOTYPE ◆ 84

expectations
MANAGING AND MEETING CUSTOMER EXPECTATIONS ◆ 140

EXPERIMENT ◆ 82

experimentation
EXPERIMENT ◆ 82
HOT SPOT relationship to; EXPERIMENT ◆ 82
PERFORMANCE CRITERIA relationship to; EXPERIMENT ◆ 82
as performance tuning strategy; EXPERIMENT ◆ 82

experts
domain
pattern writers as; AUTHORS ARE EXPERTS ◆ 111
priority in role assignment; DOMAIN EXPERTISE IN
ROLES ◆ 64
DOMAIN EXPERTISE IN ROLES ◆ 64
EXPERTS REVIEW PAPERS ◆ 73
IDENTIFY THE CHAMPION relationship to; EXPERTS REVIEW
PAPERS ◆ 73
mentoring responsibilities, management of; DAY CARE ◆ 170

EXPLAINING TEMPORARY VARIABLE ◆ 158

explicit
EXPLICIT BUSINESS RULES ◆ 173
EXPLICIT INITIALIZATION ◆ 156

EXPLICIT BUSINESS RULES ◆ 173

EXPLICIT INITIALIZATION ◆ 156

EXPOSABLE GUTS ◆ 98

EXPOSED STATE ◆ 166

exposure
EXPOSABLE GUTS, WORKSHEET DOCUMENTS relationship to;
WORKSHEET DOCUMENTS ◆ 98
EXPOSED STATE ◆ 166

expressions
CACHEABLE EXPRESSION ◆ 82
caching, as optimization technique; CACHEABLE
EXPRESSION ◆ 82
conditional, formatting; CONDITIONAL EXPRESSION ◆ 163
CONDITIONAL EXPRESSION ◆ 163
decomposition into subexpressions; EXPLAINING TEMPORARY
VARIABLE ◆ 158
reusing; REUSING TEMPORARY VARIABLE ◆ 158

EXTENDING SUPER ◆ 155

extensibility
ARTIFICIAL ACCESSORS, EXTENSIBLE ATTRIBUTES relationship
to; EXTENSIBLE ATTRIBUTES ◆ 163
attributes, creating; EXTENSIBLE ATTRIBUTES ◆ 163
CACHED EXTENSIBILITY ◆ 164
command interpreter, architecture of; FLEXIBLE COMMAND
INTERPRETER ◆ 60
decoupling components using; TRANSCEIVER-PARCEL ◆ 133
EXTENDING SUPER ◆ 155

extensibility *continued*

EXTENSIBLE ATTRIBUTES ♦ 163
ARTIFICIAL ACCESSORS relationship to; EXTENSIBLE
ATTRIBUTES ♦ 163, ARTIFICIAL ACCESSORS ♦ 163
CACHED EXTENSIBILITY relationship to; EXTENSIBLE
ATTRIBUTES ♦ 163
GENERATED ACCESSORS relationship to; GENERATED
ACCESSORS ♦ 164
VARIABLE STATE relationship to; VARIABLE STATE ♦ 156,
EXTENSIBLE ATTRIBUTES ♦ 163
EXTENSION OBJECT ♦ 55
DECORATOR relationship to; EXTENSION OBJECT ♦ 55
VISITER relationship to; EXTENSION OBJECT ♦ 55
microkernel architecture as mechanism for facilitating;
MICROKERNEL ♦ 87
prototype-based object systems; PROTOTYPE-BASED OBJECT
SYSTEM ♦ 139
references use for, in teaching; REFERENCE EXAMPLES ♦ 117
system design that facilitates; HOOK METHOD ♦ 73
uninvasive extension, of class functionality; EXTENSION
OBJECT ♦ 55
EXTENSIBLE ATTRIBUTES ♦ 163
EXTENSION OBJECT ♦ 55
[Gamma98]; 188
external
EXTERNAL POLYMORPHISM ♦ 56
ADAPTER relationship to; EXTERNAL POLYMORPHISM ♦ 56
DECORATOR relationship to; EXTERNAL POLYMORPHISM ♦ 56
EXTERNAL POLYMORPHISM ♦ 56
[Cleeland+98a]; 184
[Cleeland+98b]; 184
extraction
FEATURE EXTRACTION—A PATTERN FOR INFORMATION
RETRIEVAL ♦ 58
EXTRINSIC VISITOR ♦ 56
ACYCLIC VISITOR relationship to; EXTRINSIC VISITOR ♦ 56
DEFAULT VISITOR relationship to; DEFAULT VISITOR ♦ 46,
EXTRINSIC VISITOR ♦ 56
[Nordberg98]; 191
VISITOR relationship to; EXTRINSIC VISITOR ♦ 56

FACADE ♦ 56, ♦ 137
[Alpert+98]; 182
[Gamma+95]; 188
facades
See Also wrappers
FACADE ♦ 56, ♦ 137
ABSTRACT FACTORY relationship to; FACADE ♦ 56
ADAPTER relationship to; ADAPTER ♦ 6, FACADE ♦ 56
HALF-SYNC/HALF-ASYNC relationship to;
HALF-SYNC/HALF-ASYNC ♦ 71
INTERFACE'S ROLE relationship to; INTERFACE'S ROLE ♦ 30
(LEGACY) WRAPPER relationship to; (LEGACY)
WRAPPER ♦ 115
MEDIATOR relationship to; MEDIATOR ♦ 86
PRESENTATION AND APPLICATION LOGIC relationship to;
PRESENTATION AND APPLICATION LOGIC ♦ 15
PROGRAMMING-BY-DIFFERENCE relationship to;
PROGRAMMING-BY-DIFFERENCE ♦ 150

WHOLE-PART relationship to; WHOLE-PART ♦ 179
WRAPPER FACADE relationship to; WRAPPER FACADE ♦ 179
WRAPPER FACADE ♦ 179
FACTOR OUT COMMON ATTRIBUTES ♦ 70
factories
ABSTRACT FACTORY ♦ 2
deferring operations to subclasses; FACTORY METHOD ♦ 56
FACTORY METHOD ♦ 56, ♦ 91
ABSTRACT FACTORY relationship to; ABSTRACT FACTORY ♦ 2
ABSTRACT SESSION relationship to; ABSTRACT SESSION ♦ 2
ACCEPTOR relationship to; ACCEPTOR ♦ 3
CONNECTOR relationship to; CONNECTOR ♦ 40
ITERABLE CONTAINER relationship to; ITERABLE
CONTAINER ♦ 80
NAVIGATIONSTRATEGY relationship to;
NAVIGATIONSTRATEGY ♦ 48
OBJECT CREATION relationship to; OBJECT CREATION ♦ 15
PARSER/BUILDER relationship to; PARSER/BUILDER ♦ 94
PLUGGABLE FACTORY relationship to; PLUGGABLE
FACTORY ♦ 132
SERIALIZER relationship to; SERIALIZER ♦ 151
TEMPLATE METHOD relationship to; TEMPLATE
METHOD ♦ 171
WHITE-BOX FRAMEWORKS relationship to; WHITE-BOX
FRAMEWORKS ♦ 121
hierarchy of, stream data control; HIERARCHY OF
FACTORIES ♦ 94
HIERARCHY OF FACTORIES ♦ 94
in legacy system/object-oriented framework interactions;
FACTORY METHOD ♦ 91
multimedia; PLUGGABLE FACTORY ♦ 132
PLUGGABLE FACTORY ♦ 132
factoring
See encapsulating/encapsulation
common code, in framework development; HOT SPOTS ♦ 122
common problems, when writing a pattern language; COMMON
PROBLEMS HIGHLIGHTED ♦ 106
FACTOR OUT COMMON ATTRIBUTES ♦ 70
DEFINE THE DATA STRUCTURE relationship to; DEFINE THE
DATA STRUCTURE ♦ 70
IDENTIFY PROBLEM DOMAIN RELATIONSHIPS relationship to;
IDENTIFY PROBLEM DOMAIN RELATIONSHIPS ♦ 70
IDENTIFY THE NOUNS relationship to; FACTOR OUT
COMMON ATTRIBUTES ♦ 70
NORMALIZE THE ROLES relationship to; NORMALIZE THE
ROLES ♦ 70
FACTORY METHOD ♦ 56, ♦ 91
[Alpert+98]; 182
[Gamma+95]; 188
failure
See Also errors; exception(s); fault-tolerant systems
avoidance, in real-time reactive systems; SHED LOAD ♦ 101
out-of-memory
handling; PARTIAL FAILURE ♦ 72, CAPTAIN OATES ♦ 72
testing for; EXHAUSTION TEST ♦ 73
STRICT PROPAGATOR WITH FAILURE ♦ 138
unforeseen, writing robust code in the face of; MEANINGLESS
BEHAVIOR ♦ 32

family
SMALL FAMILY SYSTEMS ◆ 30
fastpath
PARALLEL FASTPATH ◆ 147
fault-tolerant systems
failure alternative selection strategies; TRY ALL HARDWARE COMBOS ◆ 58
FAULT-TOLERANT TELECOMMUNICATION SYSTEM PATTERNS ◆ 57
INPUT AND OUTPUT PATTERN LANGUAGE; INPUT AND OUTPUT PATTERN LANGUAGE ◆ 76
latent error handling; FOOL ME ONCE ◆ 58
local and global data relationships in; RECOVERABLE DISTRIBUTOR ◆ 143
object recovery in; OBJECT RECOVERY ◆ 92
PATTERN LANGUAGE FOR IMPROVING THE CAPACITY OF REACTIVE SYSTEMS; PATTERN LANGUAGE FOR IMPROVING THE CAPACITY OF REACTIVE SYSTEMS ◆ 100
service replication strategies; MASTER-SLAVE ◆ 86
System Integrity Control Program priority; SICO FIRST AND ALWAYS ◆ 58
in telecommunications systems; FAULT-TOLERANT TELECOMMUNICATION SYSTEM PATTERNS ◆ 57
transient errors
handling; RIDING OVER TRANSIENTS ◆ 57
handling, counter use for; LEAKY BUCKET COUNTERS ◆ 57
FAULT-TOLERANT TELECOMMUNICATION SYSTEM PATTERNS ◆ 57
[Adams+96]; 181
FEATURE EXTRACTION—A PATTERN FOR INFORMATION RETRIEVAL ◆ 58
[Manolescu99]; 190
features
adding to a relationship; OBJECTIFY ASSOCIATIONS ◆ 5
FEATURE EXTRACTION—A PATTERN FOR INFORMATION RETRIEVAL ◆ 58
feedback
in data entry; ECHO BACK ◆ 32
POSITIVE FEEDBACK FIRST ◆ 113
Feiler, P.
[Feiler+99]; 187
PROPAGATOR: A FAMILY OF PATTERNS ❖ 138
Fiksdal-King, I.
[Alexander+77]; 182
filter(ing)
collections; SELECT/REJECT ◆ 160
pipeline connection of; PIPELINE ◆ 125
pipes and, for data streams; PIPES & FILTERS ◆ 132
FINALIZATION ◆ 90
finalization
FINALIZATION ◆ 90
DEPENDENCY relationship to; FINALIZATION ◆ 90
phase, when to start; FINALIZATION ◆ 90
FINDABLE SECTIONS ◆ 103
finding
FINDABLE SECTIONS ◆ 103
MANDATORY ELEMENTS PRESENT relationship to; FINDABLE SECTIONS ◆ 103

OPTIONAL ELEMENTS WHEN HELPFUL relationship to; FINDABLE SECTIONS ◆ 103
SINGLE-PASS READABLE relationship to; SINGLE-PASS READABLE ◆ 103, FINDABLE SECTIONS ◆ 103
SKIPPABLE SECTIONS relationship to; FINDABLE SECTIONS ◆ 103
FINDING AND DEFINING THE DOMAIN OBJECTS ◆ 141
PROBLEM DOMAIN ANALYSIS relationship to; PROBLEM DOMAIN ANALYSIS ◆ 141
SCENARIOS DEFINE PROBLEM relationship to; FINDING AND DEFINING THE DOMAIN OBJECTS ◆ 141
FINDING AND DEFINING THE DOMAIN OBJECTS ◆ 141
fine-grained
event classification; FINE-GRAINED CLASSIFICATION OF EVENTS ◆ 129
FINE-GRAINED CLASSIFICATION OF EVENTS ◆ 129
FINE-GRAINED OBJECTS ◆ 122
BLACK-BOX FRAMEWORK relationship to; FINE-GRAINED OBJECTS ◆ 122, BLACK-BOX FRAMEWORK ◆ 122
COMPONENT LIBRARY relationship to; FINE-GRAINED OBJECTS ◆ 122
HOT SPOTS relationship to; HOT SPOTS ◆ 122
FINE-GRAINED CLASSIFICATION OF EVENTS ◆ 129
FINE-GRAINED OBJECTS ◆ 122
FINISH WORK IN PROGRESS ◆ 101
SHED LOAD relationship to; SHED LOAD ◆ 101
FINITE STATE MACHINE PATTERNS ◆ 58
[Yacoub+99]; 198
finite state machines (FSM)
See Also state
communication issues; INTERFACE ORGANIZATION ◆ 59
dynamic state creation; DYNAMIC STATE INSTANTIATION ◆ 60
event handling use; DETERMINE THE ACTORS ◆ 71
event-based complex behavior handling; WHEN EVENTS CAUSE MOODS, USE STATE MACHINE ◆ 88
FINITE STATE MACHINE PATTERNS ◆ 58
MOODS: MODELS FOR OBJECT-ORIENTED DESIGN OF STATE relationship to; MOODS: MODELS FOR OBJECT-ORIENTED DESIGN OF STATE ◆ 87
OBJECT AGING relationship to; OBJECT AGING ◆ 141
STATE PATTERNS relationship to; FINITE STATE MACHINE PATTERNS ◆ 58
STATE relationship to; STATE ◆ 166
THREE-LEVEL FSM relationship to; FINITE STATE MACHINE PATTERNS ◆ 58
FOR STATE MACHINES, USE TRANSITION METHODS ◆ 88
layering the system structure; LAYERED ORGANIZATION ◆ 59
managing multiple kinds of services with; IMPLEMENTATION OF 'MULTIPLE KINDS OF SERVICES' CONTROL MODULES ◆ 62
object-oriented, event representation in; OBJECT-ORIENTED STATE MACHINE ◆ 129
OBJECT-ORIENTED STATE MACHINE ◆ 129
output
event triggering; MEALLY ◆ 59, HYBRID ◆ 59
state entry triggering; MOORE ◆ 59, HYBRID ◆ 59
STATE PATTERNS; STATE PATTERNS ◆ 166
SUBTYPE STATE MACHINES; SUBTYPE STATE MACHINES ◆ 14, ◆ 14

finite state machines (FSM) *continued*
   three level; THREE-LEVEL FSM ♦ 172
   THREE-LEVEL FSM ♦ 172
   transition method use, in managing complex behavior; FOR
      STATE MACHINES, USE TRANSITION METHODS ♦ 88
   WHEN EVENTS CAUSE MOODS, USE STATE MACHINE ♦ 88
fire alarms
   object-oriented architecture; POINTS AND DEVIATIONS:
      PATTERN LANGUAGE OF FIRE ALARM SYSTEMS ♦ 133
   POINTS AND DEVIATIONS: PATTERN LANGUAGE OF FIRE
      ALARM SYSTEMS ♦ 133
FIRE WALLS ♦ 67
firewalls
   FIRE WALLS ♦ 67
      SACRIFICE ONE PERSON relationship to; SACRIFICE ONE
         PERSON ♦ 170
   FIREWALL PROXY, PROXY DESIGN PATTERN REVISITED
      relationship to; PROXY DESIGN PATTERN REVISITED ♦ 139
first class citizens
   development tools, characteristics of; FLEXIBLE
      FOUNDATIONS ♦ 55
   frameworks, characteristics of; FLEXIBLE FOUNDATIONS ♦ 55
   languages, characteristics of; FLEXIBLE FOUNDATIONS ♦ 55
   links as; EVENT NOTIFICATION ♦ 54
   media, in a session; PARTIES & MEDIA AS FIRST CLASS
      CITIZENS ♦ 96
   parties, in a session; PARTIES & MEDIA AS FIRST CLASS
      CITIZENS ♦ 96
   PARTIES & MEDIA AS FIRST CLASS CITIZENS ♦ 96
   representation, of class semantics, class clause use; CLASS
      CLAUSE ♦ 121
   state changes as; EVENT NOTIFICATION ♦ 54
FIRST ONE'S FREE ♦ 151
   SELFISH CLASS relationship to; SELFISH CLASS ♦ 150
FIVE MINUTES OF NO ESCALATION MESSAGES ♦ 57, ♦ 78
   AUDIBLE ALARM relationship to; FIVE MINUTES OF NO
      ESCALATION MESSAGES ♦ 78
   BOTTOM LINE relationship to; BOTTOM LINE ♦ 78, FIVE
      MINUTES OF NO ESCALATION MESSAGES ♦ 78
   GEORGE WASHINGTON IS STILL DEAD relationship to; GEORGE
      WASHINGTON IS STILL DEAD ♦ 78, FIVE MINUTES OF NO
      ESCALATION MESSAGES ♦ 78
   IO TRIAGE relationship to; FIVE MINUTES OF NO ESCALATION
      MESSAGES ♦ 78
   PEOPLE KNOW BEST relationship to; FIVE MINUTES OF NO
      ESCALATION MESSAGES ♦ 57
Fletcher, B.
   [Bradac+98]; 183
      PATTERN LANGUAGE FOR DEVELOPING FORM STYLE
         WINDOWS ❖ 99
flexibility
   as abstract model advantage; ABSTRACT MODELS WITH
      CONSTRAINTS IN SUBTYPES ♦ 4
   in cryptographic software design; SECURE-CHANNEL
      COMMUNICATION ♦ 174
   as decoupling tools from materials advantage;
      MATERIALS ♦ 109
   extensible command interpreter; FLEXIBLE COMMAND
      INTERPRETER ♦ 60

FLEXIBLE COMMAND INTERPRETER ♦ 60
   INTERPRETER relationship to; FLEXIBLE COMMAND
      INTERPRETER ♦ 60
   STRATEGY relationship to; FLEXIBLE COMMAND
      INTERPRETER ♦ 60
FLEXIBLE FOUNDATIONS ♦ 55
   SOFTWARE TECTONICS relationship to; SOFTWARE
      TECTONICS ♦ 55
   memory management, providing user controls for; MAKE THE
      USER WORRY ♦ 72
   requirements change handling, handling; SOFTWARE
      TECTONICS ♦ 55
FLEXIBLE COMMAND INTERPRETER ♦ 60
   [Portner95]; 192
FLEXIBLE FOUNDATIONS ♦ 55
flipping
   pages, as display update technique; PAGE FLIP ♦ 50
flow
   control
      in an fire alarm system; DATA PUMP ♦ 135
      source code indications; INDENTED CONTROL FLOW ♦ 162
   data, stream processing; STREAMS ♦ 167
   FLOW NETWORKS ♦ 40
   INDENTED CONTROL FLOW ♦ 162
   messages, strategies for coding; REVERSING METHOD ♦ 153
   NATURAL TEXT FLOW ♦ 98
   networks, one-way message handling; FLOW NETWORKS ♦ 40
   text, WWW writing style issues; NATURAL TEXT FLOW ♦ 98
   tracing, data modeling of; TIME THREAD ANALYSIS ♦ 71
   work
      management; WORK FLOW MANAGER ♦ 115
      in software development projects; WORK FLOWS
         INWARD ♦ 68
   WORK FLOW MANAGER ♦ 115
   WORK FLOWS INWARD ♦ 68
FLOW NETWORKS ♦ 40
FLY ON THE WALL ♦ 112
   AUTHOR READS SELECTION relationship to; FLY ON THE
      WALL ♦ 112
   POSITIVE FEEDBACK FIRST relationship to; FLY ON THE
      WALL ♦ 112
   SUGGESTIONS FOR IMPROVEMENT relationship to; FLY ON THE
      WALL ♦ 112
   VOLUNTEER SUMMARIZES THE WORK relationship to; FLY
      ON THE WALL ♦ 112, VOLUNTEER SUMMARIZES THE
      WORK ♦ 113
FLYWEIGHT ♦ 60
   [Alpert+98]; 182
   COMPOSITE relationship to; FLYWEIGHT ♦ 60
   [Gamma+95]; 188
   INTERPRETER relationship to; INTERPRETER ♦ 80
   STATE relationship to; FLYWEIGHT ♦ 60, STATE ♦ 166
   STRATEGY relationship to; FLYWEIGHT ♦ 60
FOOL ME ONCE ♦ 58
   TRY ALL HARDWARE COMBOS relationship to; FOOL ME
      ONCE ♦ 58

Foote, B.
[Foote+95]; 187
LIFE CYCLE AND REFACTORING PATTERNS THAT SUPPORT
EVOLUTION AND REUSE ❖ 84
[Foote+96]; 187
EVOLUTION, ARCHITECTURE, AND METAMORPHOSIS ❖ 55
[Foote+98]; 187
SELFISH CLASS PATTERN LANGUAGE ❖ 149
[Foote+99]; 187
BIG BALL OF MUD PATTERN LANGUAGE ❖ 20
[PLoPD4]; 192
FOR COMPLEX MOODS, USE A MOOD ALTERNATOR ♦ 89
FOR OBJECTS WITH MOODS, USE STATE CLASSES ♦ 88
FOR STATE MACHINES, USE TRANSITION METHODS ♦ 88
FOR xxx
FOR COMPLEX MOODS, USE A MOOD ALTERNATOR ♦ 89
FOR OBJECTS WITH MOODS, USE STATE CLASSES ♦ 88
FOR STATE MACHINES, USE TRANSITION METHODS ♦ 88
forces
See Alsocomplexity; Alsocost; Alsoflexibility;
Alsoperformance; Alsoscalability; Alsosize; Alsotime
complexity, in relationship patterns; RELATIONSHIP
OBJECT ♦ 20
consistency, Mutual Friends; MUTUAL FRIENDS ♦ 20
pattern writing; VISIBLE FORCES ♦ 103
PRIORITIZING FORCES IN SOFTWARE DESIGN ♦ 135
in software design, prioritizing; PRIORITIZING FORCES IN
SOFTWARE DESIGN ♦ 135
VISIBLE FORCES ♦ 103
forecast
confirmation; FORECAST CONFIRMATION ♦ 33
FORECAST CONFIRMATION ♦ 33
hypothetical, error detection use; HYPOTHETICAL
PUBLICATION ♦ 33
FORECAST CONFIRMATION ♦ 33
FOREIGN KEY REFERENCES ♦ 43, ♦ 108
FOREIGN KEY VERSUS DIRECT REFERENCE ♦ 43
foreign keys
FOREIGN KEY REFERENCES ♦ 43, ♦ 108
FOREIGN KEY REFERENCES relationship to; FOREIGN KEY
REFERENCES ♦ 108
FOREIGN KEY VERSUS DIRECT REFERENCE relationship to;
FOREIGN KEY VERSUS DIRECT REFERENCE ♦ 43
REPRESENTING OBJECT RELATIONSHIPS relationship to;
REPRESENTING OBJECT RELATIONSHIPS ♦ 42
REPRESENTING OBJECTS AS TABLES relationship to;
REPRESENTING OBJECTS AS TABLES ♦ 42, REPRESENTING
OBJECTS AS TABLES ♦ 107
FOREIGN KEY VERSUS DIRECT REFERENCE ♦ 43
FOREIGN KEY REFERENCES relationship to; FOREIGN KEY
VERSUS DIRECT REFERENCE ♦ 43
PROXY relationship to; FOREIGN KEY VERSUS DIRECT
REFERENCE ♦ 43
non-database object representation with; FOREIGN KEY
REFERENCES ♦ 43
vs. pointers, representation issues; FOREIGN KEY VERSUS
DIRECT REFERENCE ♦ 43
FORK/JOIN ♦ 40

forking
as divide-and-conquor strategy for parallel processes;
FORK/JOIN ♦ 40
FORK/JOIN ♦ 40
FORM FOLLOWS FUNCTION ♦ 64
formatting
conversion; CONVERSION ♦ 153
messages; INLINE MESSAGE PATTERN ♦ 162
source code
blocks; RECTANGULAR BLOCK ♦ 162
conditional expressions; CONDITIONAL EXPRESSION ♦ 163
conditions; GUARD CLAUSE ♦ 162
indenting; INDENTED CONTROL FLOW ♦ 162
messages; INLINE MESSAGE PATTERN ♦ 162
multiple messages; CASCADE ♦ 163
forms
divide and conquor strategy; SUBFORM ♦ 99
FORM FOLLOWS FUNCTION ♦ 64
online, development strategies; PATTERN LANGUAGE FOR
DEVELOPING FORM STYLE WINDOWS ♦ 99
PATTERN LANGUAGE FOR DEVELOPING FORM STYLE
WINDOWS ♦ 99
subforms
deselecting; SUBFORM MISMATCH ♦ 100
developing alternative versions; ALTERNATIVE
SUBFORMS ♦ 99
divide and conquor strategy; SUBFORM ♦ 99
selection criteria; SUBFORM SELECTION ♦ 99
state change basis for selection; SUBFORM MATCH ♦ 100
FORMULA OBJECTS ♦ 41
formulas
FORMULA OBJECTS ♦ 41
CONSTRAINT OBSERVER relationship to; FORMULA
OBJECTS ♦ 41, CONSTRAINT OBSERVER ♦ 41
REPORT OBJECTS relationship to; REPORT OBJECTS ♦ 41
updating, constraints use for; CONSTRAINT OBSERVER ♦ 41
forward
contracts, time dependencies; FORWARD CONTRACTS ♦ 13
FORWARD CONTRACTS ♦ 13
CONTRACT relationship to; FORWARD CONTRACTS ♦ 13
FORWARDER-RECEIVER ♦ 60
CLIENT-DISPATCHER-SERVER relationship
to; CLIENT-DISPATCHER-SERVER ♦ 34,
FORWARDER-RECEIVER ♦ 60
FORWARD CONTRACTS ♦ 13
FORWARDER-RECEIVER
[Buschmann+96]; 183
Foster, T.
[Foster+97]; 187
[Foster+98]; 187
[Foster+99]; 187
CASCADE ♦ 28
[Zhao+98a]; 199
DRIVER DUTY ♦ 51
[Zhao+98b]; 199
PATTERN LANGUAGE OF TRANSPORT SYSTEMS (POINT AND
ROUTE) ❖ 114
[Zhao+99]; 199
DRIVER DUTY CONSTRUCTOR ♦ 51

foundations
FLEXIBLE FOUNDATIONS ♦ 55
software, flexibility importance; FLEXIBLE FOUNDATIONS ♦ 55
FOUR-LAYER ARCHITECTURE ♦ 106
HIERARCHY OF CONTROL LAYERS relationship to; HIERARCHY OF CONTROL LAYERS ♦ 61, FOUR-LAYER ARCHITECTURE ♦ 106
LAYERED AND SECTIONED ARCHITECTURE relationship to; LAYERED AND SECTIONED ARCHITECTURE ♦ 96, FOUR-LAYER ARCHITECTURE ♦ 106
LAYERED ARCHITECTURE relationship to; FOUR-LAYER ARCHITECTURE ♦ 106, LAYERED ARCHITECTURE ♦ 125
LAYERED ORGANIZATION relationship to; LAYERED ORGANIZATION ♦ 59, FOUR-LAYER ARCHITECTURE ♦ 106
LAYERS relationship to; LAYERS ♦ 81, FOUR-LAYER ARCHITECTURE ♦ 106
PEDESTAL relationship to; FOUR-LAYER ARCHITECTURE ♦ 106, PEDESTAL ♦ 123
SHAPE OF PROGRAM relationship to; SHAPE OF PROGRAM ♦ 29, FOUR-LAYER ARCHITECTURE ♦ 106
THREE-TIER ARCHITECTURE relationship to; THREE-TIER ARCHITECTURE ♦ 15, FOUR-LAYER ARCHITECTURE ♦ 106
Fowler, M.
[Fowler96]; 187
ACCOUNTABILITY AND ORGANIZATIONAL STRUCTURES ♦ 4
[Fowler97]; 187
ANALYSIS PATTERNS ♦ 6
[Fowler98]; 188
Fox, E. A.
[Wake+96]; 197
IMPROVING RESPONSIVENESS IN INTERACTIVE APPLICATIONS USING QUEUES ❖ 76
frameworks
BLACK-BOX FRAMEWORK ♦ 122
CLIENT/SERVER FRAMEWORK ♦ 91
evolving, patterns for; PATTERNS FOR EVOLVING FRAMEWORKS ♦ 121
legacy system relationships; NEW CLIENTS WITH OLD SERVERS: A PATTERN LANGUAGE FOR CLIENT/SERVER FRAMEWORKS ♦ 89
NEW CLIENTS WITH OLD SERVERS: A PATTERN LANGUAGE FOR CLIENT/SERVER FRAMEWORKS ♦ 89
PATTERNS FOR EVOLVING FRAMEWORKS ♦ 121
single occurance of objects in; SOLITAIRE ♦ 89
ValueModel, strategies for defining and using; UNDERSTANDING AND USING THE VALUEMODEL FRAMEWORK IN VISUALWORKS SMALLTALK ♦ 176
visual programming language use; VISUAL BUILDER ♦ 123
white-box, initial framework development use; WHITE-BOX FRAMEWORKS ♦ 121
WHITE-BOX FRAMEWORKS ♦ 121
FRESH WORK BEFORE STALE ♦ 101
MATCH PROGRESS WORK WITH NEW relationship to; FRESH WORK BEFORE STALE ♦ 101, MATCH PROGRESS WORK WITH NEW ♦ 101
SHED LOAD relationship to; SHED LOAD ♦ 101
friends
MUTUAL FRIENDS ♦ 20

FROM PROTOTYPE TO REALITY ♦ 61
[Aarsten+96a]; 181
ADAPTER relationship to; FROM PROTOTYPE TO REALITY ♦ 61
BRIDGE relationship to; FROM PROTOTYPE TO REALITY ♦ 61
PROTOTYPE AND REALITY relationship to; FROM PROTOTYPE TO REALITY ♦ 61, PROTOTYPE AND REALITY ♦ 63
FSM
See finite state machines (FSM)
FULL VIEW WITH ERRORS ♦ 18
CHECKS relationship to; FULL VIEW WITH ERRORS ♦ 18
LIMITED VIEW relationship to; FULL VIEW WITH ERRORS ♦ 18, LIMITED VIEW ♦ 18
FUNCTION OWNERS/COMPONENT OWNERS ♦ 169
functionality
FORM FOLLOWS FUNCTION ♦ 64
FUNCTIONALITY ALA CARTE ♦ 61
as software design priority, in big ball of mud system avoidance strategy; BIG BALL OF MUD ♦ 21
FUNCTIONALITY ALA CARTE ♦ 61
[Adams95]; 181
functions
FUNCTION OWNERS/COMPONENT OWNERS ♦ 169
OWNER PER DELIVERABLE relationship to; FUNCTION OWNERS/COMPONENT OWNERS ♦ 169
TEAM PER TASK relationship to; TEAM PER TASK ♦ 169
functional accessors, for attributes; GENERATED ACCESSORS ♦ 164
outcome, protocols linked to observations through; OUTCOME AND START FUNCTIONS ♦ 13
OUTCOME AND START FUNCTIONS ♦ 13
ownership of; FUNCTION OWNERS/COMPONENT OWNERS ♦ 169
start, protocols linked to observations through; OUTCOME AND START FUNCTIONS ♦ 13

G++: A PATTERN LANGUAGE FOR COMPUTER-INTEGRATED MANUFACTURING ♦ 61
[Aarsten+95]; 181
OBJECT-ORIENTED DESIGN PATTERNS IN REACTIVE SYSTEMS relationship to; OBJECT-ORIENTED DESIGN PATTERNS IN REACTIVE SYSTEMS ♦ 92
games
SIMULATION GAMES ♦ 117
Gamma, E.
[Gamma+95]; 188
ABSTRACT FACTORY ♦ 2
BRIDGE ♦ 22
BUILDER ♦ 23
CHAIN OF RESPONSIBILITY ♦ 32
COMMAND ♦ 35
COMPOSITE ♦ 37
DECORATOR ♦ 46
FACADE ♦ 56
FACTORY METHOD ♦ 56
FLYWEIGHT ♦ 60
HOOK METHOD ♦ 73
ITERATOR ♦ 80
MEDIATOR ♦ 86
MEMENTO ♦ 87

OBSERVER ♦ 94
PROTOTYPER ♦ 138
PROXY ♦ 139
SINGLETON ♦ 152
STATE ♦ 166
STRATEGY ♦ 167
TEMPLATE METHOD ♦ 171
VISITOR ♦ 179
[Gamma+95], INTERPRETER ♦ 80
[Gamma+99]; 188
[Gamma98]; 188
EXTENSION OBJECT ♦ 55
Gamoke, R.
[Adams+96]; 181
FAULT-TOLERANT TELECOMMUNICATION SYSTEM
PATTERNS ❖ 57
garbage collection
See Also memory
of objects, FINALIZATION use for; FINALIZATION ♦ 90
Garlan, D.
[Shaw+96]; 196
DISTRIBUTED PROCESSES ♦ 51
PIPES & FILTERS ♦ 132
PROCESS CONTROL ♦ 137
STATE TRANSITION SYSTEMS ♦ 167
Garrido, G. A.
BODYGUARD ♦ 22
[DasNeves+98]; 186
DESIGN PATTERNS FOR OBJECT-ORIENTED HYPERMEDIA
APPLICATIONS ❖ 48
[Rossi+96]; 194
gatekeepers
GATEKEEPER ♦ 67
SACRIFICE ONE PERSON relationship to; SACRIFICE ONE
PERSON ♦ 170
I/O, in telecommunications system design; IO
GATEKEEPER ♦ 77
IO GATEKEEPER ♦ 77
generalizations
See Also abstract/abstractions
implementing; IMPLEMENTING GENERALIZATIONS ♦ 15
IMPLEMENTING GENERALIZATIONS ♦ 15
PARTY TYPE GENERALIZATIONS ♦ 7
generation
of code, modifying just once; GENERATION GAP ♦ 63
data products, from data stream packets; HANDLERS ♦ 95
GENERATED ACCESSORS ♦ 164
EXTENSIBLE ATTRIBUTES relationship to; GENERATED
ACCESSORS ♦ 164
GENERATION GAP ♦ 63
GENERATIVE DEVELOPMENT-PROCESS PATTERN
LANGUAGE ♦ 63
GENERATIVE PATTERN LANGUAGE FOR DISTRIBUTED
PROCESSING ♦ 70
PATTERNS FOR GENERATING A LAYERED ARCHITECTURE ♦ 123
GENERATION GAP ♦ 63
[Vlissides98a]; 197

GENERATIVE DEVELOPMENT-PROCESS PATTERN
LANGUAGE ♦ 63
[Coplien95b]; 185
**GENERATIVE PATTERN LANGUAGE FOR DISTRIBUTED
PROCESSING ♦ 70**
[DeBruler95]; 186
generic
GENERIC UI, SPECIFIC UI ♦ 136
GENERICS AND SPECIFICS ♦ 136
GENERIC UI, SPECIFIC UI ♦ 136
GENTLE LEARNING CURVE ♦ 150
LOW SURFACE-TO-VOLUME RATIO relationship to; LOW
SURFACE-TO-VOLUME RATIO ♦ 150
SELFISH CLASS relationship to; SELFISH CLASS ♦ 150
WORKS OUT OF THE BOX relationship to; GENTLE LEARNING
CURVE ♦ 150
geometry
See architecture; shape; structure
GEORGE WASHINGTON IS STILL DEAD ♦ 78
BOTTOM LINE relationship to; GEORGE WASHINGTON IS STILL
DEAD ♦ 78, BOTTOM LINE ♦ 78
FIVE MINUTES OF NO ESCALATION MESSAGES relationship to;
GEORGE WASHINGTON IS STILL DEAD ♦ 78
IO GATEKEEPER relationship to; GEORGE WASHINGTON IS
STILL DEAD ♦ 78
IO TRIAGE relationship to; IO TRIAGE ♦ 77, GEORGE
WASHINGTON IS STILL DEAD ♦ 78
MML relationship to; MML ♦ 77
SHUT UP AND LISTEN relationship to; GEORGE WASHINGTON
IS STILL DEAD ♦ 78, SHUT UP AND LISTEN ♦ 79
GET INVOLVED EARLY ♦ 126
APPLICATION DESIGN IS BOUNDED BY TEST DESIGN
relationship to; APPLICATION DESIGN IS BOUNDED BY TEST
DESIGN ♦ 66
BUILD TRUST relationship to; GET INVOLVED EARLY ♦ 126
DESIGNERS ARE OUR FRIENDS relationship to; DESIGNERS ARE
OUR FRIENDS ♦ 126, GET INVOLVED EARLY ♦ 126
DIVERSITY OF MEMBERSHIP relationship to; DIVERSITY OF
MEMBERSHIP ♦ 95
DOCUMENT THE PROBLEM relationship to; DOCUMENT THE
PROBLEM ♦ 128
ITS'S A RELATIONSHIP, NOT A SALE relationship to; GET
INVOLVED EARLY ♦ 126
PRAGMATIC EXTERNAL REQUIREMENTS relationship to;
PRAGMATIC EXTERNAL REQUIREMENTS ♦ 142
TAKE TIME relationship to; TAKE TIME ♦ 126
TIME TO TEST relationship to; TIME TO TEST ♦ 126
GETTING METHOD ♦ 157
INDIRECT VARIABLE ACCESS relationship to; INDIRECT
VARIABLE ACCESS ♦ 157
LAZY INITIALIZATION relationship to; LAZY
INITIALIZATION ♦ 157
global
GLOBAL UPDATE ♦ 49
PAGE FLIP relationship to; PAGE FLIP ♦ 50
REQUEST UPDATE relationship to; GLOBAL UPDATE ♦ 49
one-to-one relationships, ACTIVE VALUE; ACTIVE VALUE ♦ 20
updating, of graphical displays; GLOBAL UPDATE ♦ 49
GLOBAL UPDATE ♦ 49

glossary
   of business term definitions, requirements process use;
      DEFINING REQUIREMENTS ♦ 140
GLOSSARY ♦ 106
   SINGLE-PASS READABLE relationship to; SINGLE-PASS
      READABLE ♦ 103
   TERMINOLOGY TAILORED TO AUDIENCE relationship to;
      TERMINOLOGY TAILORED TO AUDIENCE ♦ 105
GLUE ♦ 36
glue
   in evolutionary software development, ADAPTER use for;
      OBJECT-ORIENTED SIMULATION ♦ 93
   GLUE ♦ 36
GO EARLY, STAY LATE
   BUILD TRUST relationship to; BUILD TRUST ♦ 43
   KNOW THE CUSTOMER relationship to; KNOW THE
      CUSTOMER ♦ 43
GOLD RUSH ♦ 169
   HOLISTIC DIVERSITY relationship to; GOLD RUSH ♦ 169
grammar
   representation of; INTERPRETER ♦ 80
granularity
   categorizing objects with respect to, in complex concurrent
      systems; CATEGORIZE OBJECTS FOR CONCURRENCY ♦ 62
   degrees of, encapsulating; ENTERPRISE SEGMENT ♦ 9
   of events, fine-grained; FINE-GRAINED CLASSIFICATION OF
      EVENTS ♦ 129
   fine, FLYWEIGHT management of; FLYWEIGHT ♦ 60
   of locking, hierarchical locking strategy; HIERARCHICAL
      LOCKING ♦ 148
   of objects, framework development considerations;
      FINE-GRAINED OBJECTS ♦ 122
graphical
   application builders, black-box framework use; VISUAL
      BUILDER ♦ 123
grid
   position in, tracking; USE A SCROLLVALUEHOLDER TO HOLD
      A POSITION IN n-DIMENSIONAL SPACE ♦ 178
group(ing)
   accounts; SUMMARY ACCOUNT ♦ 11
   GROUP VALIDATION ♦ 66
   messages, update, into packets; MESSAGE PACKET ♦ 75
   messages about the same kind of event, in fault-tolerant
      systems; BOTTOM LINE ♦ 78
   system components with similar change rates; SHEARING
      LAYERS ♦ 21
   WORK GROUP ♦ 52
GROUP VALIDATION ♦ 66
growth
   piecemeal, handling without erosion of system architecture;
      PIECEMEAL GROWTH ♦ 21
GUARD CLAUSE ♦ 162
GUI (graphical user interface)
   See Also interface(s); UI (user interface)
   clipping hidden regions; CLIP REQUESTS ♦ 50
   design issues; DISPLAY MAINTENANCE ♦ 49
   displaying, relationships between basic and derived values;
      VISIBLE IMPLICATION ♦ 33
   feedback, data entry; ECHO BACK ♦ 32

   form-style, development strategies; PATTERN LANGUAGE FOR
      DEVELOPING FORM STYLE WINDOWS ♦ 99
   Java panel interaction with; PLUGGABLE VIEW
      CONTROLLER ♦ 132
   lazy redrawing; LAZY REDRAW ♦ 50
   panels, displaying a sequence of; PANEL STATES ♦ 96
   rendering algorithms; PAINTER'S ALGORITHM ♦ 50
   screen update, in multimedia presentations; RESOURCE
      EXCHANGER ♦ 144
   viewing relationship, in legacy system/object-oriented
      framework interactions; VIEWING ♦ 91
   views, managing; VIEW HANDLER ♦ 178
GURU DOES ALL ♦ 130
   PEACEMAKER relationship to; PEACEMAKER ♦ 131

half
   HALF-OBJECT + PROTOCOL ♦ 71
   HALF-SYNC/HALF-ASYNC ♦ 71
      ACTIVE OBJECT relationship to; HALF-SYNC/HALF-
         ASYNC ♦ 71
      FACADE relationship to; HALF-SYNC/HALF-ASYNC ♦ 71
      MEDIATOR relationship to; HALF-SYNC/HALF-ASYNC ♦ 71
      REACTOR relationship to; HALF-SYNC/HALF-ASYNC ♦ 71
HALF-OBJECT + PROTOCOL ♦ 71
   [Meszaros95]; 191
HALF-SYNC/HALF-ASYNC
   [Schmidt+96]; 194
hand-off protocol
   sessions use to manage; SESSION ♦ 37
HANDLE ARTIFICIAL EVENTS ♦ 76
HANDLE/BODY ♦ 24
HANDLE/BODY HIERARCHY ♦ 24
HANDLERS ♦ 95
handles
   HANDLE/BODY ♦ 24
      COUNTED BODY; HANDLE/BODY ♦ 24
      ENVELOPE/LETTER; HANDLE/BODY ♦ 24
      ENVELOPE/LETTER relationship to; ENVELOPE/LETTER ♦ 25
      HANDLE/BODY HIERARCHY; HANDLE/BODY ♦ 24
      VIRTUAL CONSTRUCTOR relationship to; VIRTUAL
         CONSTRUCTOR ♦ 25
   HANDLE/BODY HIERARCHY ♦ 24
      HANDLE/BODY; HANDLE/BODY ♦ 24
handling
   complex behavior, stategies for; FOR OBJECTS WITH MOODS,
      USE STATE CLASSES ♦ 88
   errors
      in fault-tolerant systems, alternative hardware selection
         strategies; TRY ALL HARDWARE COMBOS ♦ 58
      human overrides use; PEOPLE KNOW BEST ♦ 57
      transient, in fault-tolerant systems; RIDING OVER
         TRANSIENTS ♦ 57
   events; EVENTHANDLER ♦ 55
      callbacks use; DETERMINE THE ACTORS ♦ 71
      design issues; EVENT ACQUISITION ♦ 31, EVENT
         ROUTING ♦ 31
      design strategies for; CHAIN OF RESPONSIBILITY ♦ 32
      finite state machine use; DETERMINE THE ACTORS ♦ 71
      in finite state machines; INTERFACE ORGANIZATION ♦ 59

mechanisms for; IMPLICIT INVOCATION OR
EVENT-BASED ◆ 125
in real-time systems; PATTERNS OF EVENTS ◆ 129
in a software tools environment; EVENT MECHANISM ◆ 110
HANDLE ARTIFICIAL EVENTS ◆ 76
DECOUPLE EXECUTION AND OUTPUT relationship to;
DECOUPLE EXECUTION AND OUTPUT ◆ 76
EVENT QUEUE relationship to; EVENT QUEUE ◆ 76
HANDLERS ◆ 95
PATTERN FOR SEPARATING ASSEMBLY AND PROCESSING
relationship to; HANDLERS ◆ 95
PIPES & FILTERS relationship to; HANDLERS ◆ 95
information, requirements process identification of needs;
INFORMATION NEEDS ◆ 141
VIEW HANDLER ◆ 178

handover
of responsibilities, effective mechanisms for; EFFECTIVE
HANDOVER ◆ 27

Hanmer, R.
[Adams+96]; 181
FAULT-TOLERANT TELECOMMUNICATION SYSTEM
PATTERNS ❖ 57
[Hanmer+99]; 188
INPUT AND OUTPUT PATTERN LANGUAGE ◆ 76

hardware
in fault-tolerant systems, failure alternative selection
strategies; TRY ALL HARDWARE COMBOS ◆ 58

Harrison, N. B.
[Harrison96]; 188
ORGANIZATIONAL PATTERNS FOR TEAMS ❖ 95
[Harrison98]; 188
PATTERNS FOR LOGGING DIAGNOSTIC MESSAGES ❖ 124
[PLoPD4]; 192

Harrison, T. H.
[Cleeland+98b]; 185
EXTERNAL POLYMORPHISM ◆ 56
[Pyarali+98]; 193
ASYNCHRONOUS COMPLETION TOKEN ◆ 19
[Pyarali+99]; 193
PROACTOR ◆ 137
[Schmidt+98]; 194
DOUBLE-CHECKED LOCKING ◆ 51
[Schmidt+99]; 195
THREAD-SPECIFIC STORAGE ◆ 172

Harte, S.
[Barkataki+98]; 182

hashing
defining methods for; HASHING METHOD ◆ 159
HASHING METHOD ◆ 159
HASHING METHOD ◆ 159

headings
DISTINCTIVE HEADINGS CONVEY STRUCTURE ◆ 106

Helm, R.
[Gamma+95]; 188
ABSTRACT FACTORY ◆ 2
BRIDGE ◆ 22
BUILDER ◆ 23
CHAIN OF RESPONSIBILITY ◆ 32
COMMAND ◆ 35

COMPOSITE ◆ 37
DECORATOR ◆ 46
FACADE ◆ 56
FACTORY METHOD ◆ 56
FLYWEIGHT ◆ 60
HOOK METHOD ◆ 73
ITERATOR ◆ 80
MEDIATOR ◆ 86
MEMENTO ◆ 87
OBSERVER ◆ 94
PROTOTYPER ◆ 138
PROXY ◆ 139
SINGLETON ◆ 152
STATE ◆ 166
STRATEGY ◆ 167
TEMPLATE METHOD ◆ 171
VISITOR ◆ 179
[Gamma+95], INTERPRETER ◆ 80

helpers
THREE TO SEVEN HELPERS PER ROLE ◆ 68

heterogeneous
addition; PROMOTE AND ADD ◆ 26

HIERARCHIC ACCOUNTABILITY ◆ 7
HIERARCHICAL LOCKING ◆ 148
HIERARCHICAL VIEW ◆ 3

hierarchies
ALGEBRAIC HIERARCHY ◆ 25
CHAIN OF RESPONSIBILITY as a design strategy for; CHAIN OF
RESPONSIBILITY ◆ 32
condition, classifying errors into; EXCEPTION ◆ 89
of control layers, decoupling caller/provider modules;
VISIBILITY AND COMMUNICATION BETWEEN CONTROL
MODULES ◆ 61
of cooperating agents, as interactive system structure;
PRESENTATION-ABSTRACTION-CONTROL ◆ 135
of diagnostic message types; TYPED DIAGNOSTICS ◆ 124
of elements, representing enterprise dimensions as;
ENTERPRISE SEGMENT ◆ 9
event classes, relationship modeling with; FINE-GRAINED
CLASSIFICATION OF EVENTS ◆ 129
HANDLE/BODY HIERARCHY ◆ 24
HIERARCHIC ACCOUNTABILITY ◆ 7
HIERARCHICAL LOCKING ◆ 148
CODE LOCKING relationship to; HIERARCHICAL
LOCKING ◆ 148
DATA LOCKING relationship to; HIERARCHICAL
LOCKING ◆ 148
TEST-AND-SET LOCK relationship to; TEST-AND-SET
LOCK ◆ 148
HIERARCHICAL VIEW ◆ 3
uses QUERY BROKER; HIERARCHICAL VIEW ◆ 3
HIERARCHY OF CONTROL LAYERS ◆ 61
FOUR-LAYER ARCHITECTURE relationship to; HIERARCHY OF
CONTROL LAYERS ◆ 61
LAYERED AND SECTIONED ARCHITECTURE relationship to;
HIERARCHY OF CONTROL LAYERS ◆ 61, LAYERED AND
SECTIONED ARCHITECTURE ◆ 96
LAYERED ARCHITECTURE relationship to; HIERARCHY OF
CONTROL LAYERS ◆ 61, LAYERED ARCHITECTURE ◆ 125

hierarchies *continued*
  Hierarchy of Control Layers *continued*
    Layered Organization relationship to; Layered
      Organization ◆ 59, Hierarchy of Control
      Layers ◆ 61
    Layers relationship to; Hierarchy of Control
      Layers ◆ 61, Layers ◆ 81
    Pedestal relationship to; Hierarchy of Control
      Layers ◆ 61, Pedestal ◆ 123
    Shape of Program relationship to; Shape of
      Program ◆ 29, Hierarchy of Control Layers ◆ 61
    Three-Tier Architecture relationship to; Three-Tier
      Architecture ◆ 15, Hierarchy of Control
      Layers ◆ 61
  Hierarchy of Factories ◆ 94
    Builder relationship to; Hierarchy of Factories ◆ 94
    Loose Interfaces relationship to; Loose Interfaces ◆ 94
    Parser/Builder relationship to; Hierarchy of
      Factories ◆ 94
  inheritance
    abstract class use for cleanup of; Create Abstract
      Superclass ◆ 85
    for algebraic types; Algebraic Hierarchy ◆ 25
    container membership management use; Member
      Container ◆ 86
    linear interation of containers in; Iterable Container ◆ 80
  layering system functions into; Hierarchy of Control
    Layers ◆ 61
  locking, as parallelism performance strategy; Hierarchical
    Locking ◆ 148
  Model Hierarchy ◆ 136
  multiple, in matrix organizations; Multiple Hierarchic
    Associations ◆ 4
  Multiple Hierarchic Associations ◆ 4
  Organization Hierarchies ◆ 7
  organizational
    modeling; Organization Hierarchies ◆ 7
    recursion use to represent; Recursive Structures for
      Organizations ◆ 4
  Parallel Application and Domain Hierarchies ◆ 14
  part-whole, representation of; Composite ◆ 37
  of persistent domain classes; Model Hierarchy ◆ 136
  responsibilities, creating an accounability type for;
    Hierarchic Accountability ◆ 7
  of services, architecture for; Layered Architecture ◆ 125
  structures, for client interaction; Bureaucracy ◆ 23
  of tool components, building software tools from; Tool
    Composition ◆ 110
  views
    connecting with physical view; Query Broker ◆ 4
    of a relational database; Hierarchical View ◆ 3
Hierarchy of Control Layers ◆ 61
Hierarchy of Factories ◆ 94
high
  High-Level and Process Patterns from the Memory
    Preservation Society ◆ 71
  high-level manager/champion role, for project continuity;
    Patron ◆ 65
  runner, optimization; Optimize High-Runner Cases ◆ 100

**High-Level and Process Patterns from the Memory
  Preservation Society ◆ 71**
  [Noble+99]; 191
Historic Mapping ◆ 16
history
  action, decoupling proposed and implemented; Proposed and
    Implemented Action ◆ 12
  capture, designing for; Data Knows its Roots ◆ 31
  capturing, in an organizational structure; Organizational
    Structure-Typed Relationship ◆ 5
  change, creating accounts to record; Account ◆ 10
  Collection of History Patterns ◆ 34
  Historic Mapping ◆ 16
    Association Object relationship to; Association
      Object ◆ 23
    History On Association relationship to; History On
      Association ◆ 34
    Temporal Property relationship to; Temporal
      Property ◆ 171
  History, History On Association relationship to; History
    On Association ◆ 34
  History On Association ◆ 34
    Historic Mapping relationship to; History On
      Association ◆ 34
    History relationship to; History On Association ◆ 34
  History On Self ◆ 35
    Memento Child relationship to; Memento Child ◆ 35
  History On Tree ◆ 35
    Composite relationship to; History On Tree ◆ 35
  hypermedia navigation, user guides;
    NavigationObserver ◆ 48
  object state, saving; History On Self ◆ 35
  of objects, dictionary use for; Historic Mapping ◆ 16
  recording; Collection of History Patterns ◆ 34
  Transaction History ◆ 165
  transaction posting; Posting ◆ 35
  of transactions, maintaining; Transaction History ◆ 165
History On Association ◆ 34
History On Self ◆ 35
History On Tree ◆ 35
Holistic Diversity ◆ 169
  Diversity of Membership relationship to; Holistic
    Diversity ◆ 169
  Gold Rush relationship to; Gold Rush ◆ 169
  Owner per Deliverable relationship to; Holistic
    Diversity ◆ 169
homogeneous
  Homogeneous Addition ◆ 25
    Algebraic Hierarchy relationship to; Algebraic
      Hierarchy ◆ 25, Homogeneous Addition ◆ 25
    Non-Hierarchical Addition relationship to;
      Non-Hierarchical Addition ◆ 26
    Promote and Add relationship to; Homogeneous
      Addition ◆ 25, Promote and Add ◆ 26
Homogeneous Addition ◆ 25
Hook Method ◆ 73
  [Alpert+98]; 182
  [Gamma+95]; 188
  [Pree94]; 192

SECURE-CHANNEL COMMUNICATION relationship to;
SECURE-CHANNEL COMMUNICATION ♦ 174
TEMPLATE METHOD relationship to; HOOK METHOD ♦ 73

Hopley, A.
[Hopley96]; 188
DECISION DEFERRAL AND CAPTURE PATTERN
LANGUAGE ♦ 45

host
relay of message to helpers by; PASS-THROUGH HOST ♦ 38

HOT SPOT ♦ 82

HOT SPOTS ♦ 122

hot spots
HOT SPOT ♦ 82
EXPERIMENT relationship to; EXPERIMENT ♦ 82
HOT SPOTS relationship to; HOT SPOTS ♦ 122
PERFORMANCE CRITERIA relationship to; HOT SPOT ♦ 82
PERFORMANCE MEASUREMENT relationship to; HOT
SPOT ♦ 82
HOT SPOTS ♦ 122
BLACK-BOX FRAMEWORK relationship to; HOT SPOTS ♦ 122,
BLACK-BOX FRAMEWORK ♦ 122
COMPONENT LIBRARY relationship to; COMPONENT
LIBRARY ♦ 122, HOT SPOTS ♦ 122
FINE-GRAINED OBJECTS relationship to; HOT SPOTS ♦ 122
HOT SPOT relationship to; HOT SPOTS ♦ 122
PLUGGABLE OBJECTS relationship to; PLUGGABLE
OBJECTS ♦ 122

HUB, SPOKE, AND RIM ♦ 68

human
errors, minimizing chances for, intelecommunications
systems; MINIMIZE HUMAN INTERVENTION ♦ 57
HUMAN INTERFACE ROLE IS A SPECIAL INTERFACE ROLE ♦ 31
importance, in system testing; TESTER'S MORE IMPORTANT
THAN THE TEST CASES ♦ 126
machine interface
design strategies for large and complex systems; MML ♦ 77
error message overload handling; FIVE MINUTES OF NO
ESCALATION MESSAGES ♦ 57
MINIMIZE HUMAN INTERVENTION ♦ 57
overrides
of error system; SHUT UP AND LISTEN ♦ 79
provision for in fault-tolerant systems; PEOPLE KNOW
BEST ♦ 57

**HUMAN INTERFACE ROLE IS A SPECIAL INTERFACE
ROLE ♦ 31**

human relationships
CUSTOMER INTERACTION PATTERNS ♦ 43
customer interaction with software development team;
ENGAGE CUSTOMERS ♦ 66
HUMAN INTERFACE ROLE IS A SPECIAL INTERFACE ROLE
DECISION MAKER'S ROLE relationship to; DECISION
MAKER'S ROLE ♦ 30
SMALL FAMILY SYSTEMS relationship to; SMALL FAMILY
SYSTEMS ♦ 30
interaction, structures that support; SHAPING CIRCULATION
REALMS ♦ 67

pattern writers workshop protocols; PATTERN LANGUAGE FOR
WRITERS' WORKSHOPS ♦ 111
treating pattern writers as experts; AUTHORS ARE
EXPERTS ♦ 111
running the PC meeting, speaker priorities; CHAMPIONS SPEAK
FIRST ♦ 74
software development team; CAPABLE, PRODUCTIVE, AND
SATISFIED ♦ 26
communication support; BUFFALO MOUNTAIN ♦ 67
gatekeeper interface to rest of world; GATEKEEPER ♦ 67
motivating; COMPENSATE SUCCESS ♦ 69
optimal environment for; TEAM SPACE ♦ 27
between system test and design, strategies for managing; GET
INVOLVED EARLY ♦ 126
technical paper acceptance process; IDENTIFY THE CHAMPION
PATTERN LANGUAGE ♦ 73

Huni, H.
[Huni+95]; 188

HYBRID ♦ 59

hypermedia
DESIGN PATTERNS FOR OBJECT-ORIENTED HYPERMEDIA
APPLICATIONS ❖ 48
NATURAL TEXT HYPERLINKS ♦ 98
navigation
information space design; PATTERNS FOR DESIGNING
NAVIGABLE INFORMATION SPACES ♦ 119
set-based; SET-BASED NAVIGATION ♦ 119
strategies for; NAVIGATIONSTRATEGY ♦ 48
user guides; NAVIGATIONOBSERVER ♦ 48
nodes, hypermedia navigation strategies for different contexts;
NODES IN CONTEXT ♦ 119
orientation
persistent landmarks use for; LANDMARK ♦ 120
references use for; ACTIVE REFERENCE ♦ 120
writing and organizing Web essays; PATTERN LANGUAGE FOR
AN ESSAY-BASED WEB SITE ♦ 97

HYPOTH-A-SIZED COLLECTION ♦ 84

hypotheses
ACTIVE OBSERVATION, HYPOTHESIS, AND PROJECTION ♦ 9
assurance level of; ACTIVE OBSERVATION, HYPOTHESIS, AND
PROJECTION ♦ 9
HYPOTH-A-SIZED COLLECTION ♦ 84
CONCATENATING STREAM relationship to; CONCATENATING
STREAM ♦ 84, CONCATENATING STREAM ♦ 162
HYPOTHETICAL PUBLICATION ♦ 33
DEFERRED VALIDATION relationship to; HYPOTHETICAL
PUBLICATION ♦ 33
INSTANT PROJECTION relationship to; INSTANT
PROJECTION ♦ 33, HYPOTHETICAL PUBLICATION ♦ 33

HYPOTHETICAL PUBLICATION ♦ 33

I/O
event-driven, session handling; EVENT-DRIVEN I/O ♦ 39
EVENT-DRIVEN I/O ♦ 39
gatekeeper, in telecommunications system design; IO
GATEKEEPER ♦ 77
INPUT AND OUTPUT PATTERN LANGUAGE ♦ 76
IO GATEKEEPER ♦ 77
BOTTOM LINE relationship to; BOTTOM LINE ♦ 78

I/O *continued*
IO GATEKEEPER *continued*
GEORGE WASHINGTON IS STILL DEAD relationship to;
GEORGE WASHINGTON IS STILL DEAD ♦ 78
IO TRIAGE relationship to; IO TRIAGE ♦ 77
MIND YOUR OWN BUSINESS relationship to; MIND YOUR
OWN BUSINESS ♦ 77
RAW IO relationship to; RAW IO ♦ 80
STRING A WIRE relationship to; STRING A WIRE ♦ 80
IO TRIAGE ♦ 77
AUDIBLE ALARM relationship to; IO TRIAGE ♦ 77, AUDIBLE
ALARM ♦ 79
BOTTOM LINE relationship to; IO TRIAGE ♦ 77
GEORGE WASHINGTON IS STILL DEAD relationship to; IO
TRIAGE ♦ 77, GEORGE WASHINGTON IS STILL DEAD ♦ 78
IO GATEKEEPER relationship to; IO TRIAGE ♦ 77
MML relationship to; MML ♦ 77
SHUT UP AND LISTEN relationship to; SHUT UP AND
LISTEN ♦ 79
TIMESTAMP relationship to; IO TRIAGE ♦ 77,
TIMESTAMP ♦ 77
WHO ASKED? relationship to; WHO ASKED? ♦ 78
models, integrating synchronous and asynchronous;
HALF-SYNC/HALF-ASYNC ♦ 71
pseudo, subsystem communication use; PSEUDO-IO ♦ 79
raw, as fault-tolerant mechanisms for sending urgent
messages; RAW IO ♦ 80
RAW IO ♦ 80
STREAM I-O ENGINEERING MODEL ♦ 19
streams, defining; STREAMS ♦ 167
virtual, subsystem communication use; PSEUDO-IO ♦ 79
identification
DEFER IDENTIFICATION OF STATE VARIABLES ♦ 145
ELEMENT IDENTIFICATION ♦ 46
IDENTIFICATION SCHEME ♦ 10
OBJECT IDENTIFIER relationship to; OBJECT IDENTIFIER ♦ 42,
OBJECT IDENTIFIER ♦ 107
IDENTIFY MESSAGE LAYERS ♦ 145
DEFER IDENTIFICATION OF STATE VARIABLES relationship to;
DEFER IDENTIFICATION OF STATE VARIABLES ♦ 145
DEFINE CLASSES BY BEHAVIOR, NOT STATE relationship to;
IDENTIFY MESSAGE LAYERS ♦ 145
IMPLEMENT BEHAVIOR WITH ABSTRACT STATE relationship
to; IDENTIFY MESSAGE LAYERS ♦ 145
IDENTIFY MISSING CHAMPIONS ♦ 74
IDENTIFY PROBLEM DOMAIN RELATIONSHIPS ♦ 70
DEFINE THE DATA STRUCTURE relationship to; DEFINE THE
DATA STRUCTURE ♦ 70
FACTOR OUT COMMON ATTRIBUTES relationship to;
IDENTIFY PROBLEM DOMAIN RELATIONSHIPS ♦ 70
IDENTIFY THE NOUNS relationship to; IDENTIFY PROBLEM
DOMAIN RELATIONSHIPS ♦ 70
NORMALIZE THE ROLES relationship to; IDENTIFY PROBLEM
DOMAIN RELATIONSHIPS ♦ 70
IDENTIFY THE CHAMPION ♦ 73
CHAMPIONS REVIEW PAPERS relationship to; CHAMPIONS
REVIEW PAPERS ♦ 74
EXPERTS REVIEW PAPERS relationship to; EXPERTS REVIEW
PAPERS ♦ 73

IDENTIFY THE CHAMPION PATTERN LANGUAGE ❖ 73
IDENTIFY THE CONFLICTS ♦ 74
CHAMPIONS SPEAK FIRST relationship to; CHAMPIONS SPEAK
FIRST ♦ 74
MAKE CHAMPIONS EXPLICIT relationship to; IDENTIFY THE
CONFLICTS ♦ 74
IDENTIFY THE NOUNS ♦ 70
DEFINE THE DATA STRUCTURE relationship to; DEFINE THE
DATA STRUCTURE ♦ 70, IDENTIFY THE NOUNS ♦ 70
FACTOR OUT COMMON ATTRIBUTES relationship to; FACTOR
OUT COMMON ATTRIBUTES ♦ 70
IDENTIFY PROBLEM DOMAIN RELATIONSHIPS relationship to;
IDENTIFY PROBLEM DOMAIN RELATIONSHIPS ♦ 70
IMPLEMENT BEHAVIOR WITH ABSTRACT STATE, IDENTIFY
MESSAGE LAYERS relationship to; IDENTIFY MESSAGE
LAYERS ♦ 145
of key demostation elements; ELEMENT IDENTIFICATION ♦ 46
of problem domain relationships; IDENTIFY PROBLEM DOMAIN
RELATIONSHIPS ♦ 70
of technical paper champion, as program committee selection
strategy; IDENTIFY THE CHAMPION ♦ 73
IDENTIFICATION SCHEME ♦ 10
identifier
creating; NAME ♦ 10
IDENTIFICATION SCHEME ♦ 10
as interface, handle use as; HANDLE/BODY ♦ 24
object, unique, relational database use; OBJECT
IDENTIFIER ♦ 42
OBJECT IDENTIFIER ♦ 42, ♦ 107
unique, defining conventions for; IDENTIFICATION
SCHEME ♦ 10
IDENTIFY MESSAGE LAYERS ♦ 145
IDENTIFY MISSING CHAMPIONS ♦ 74
IDENTIFY PROBLEM DOMAIN RELATIONSHIPS ♦ 70
IDENTIFY THE CHAMPION ♦ 73
IDENTIFY THE CHAMPION PATTERN LANGUAGE ♦ 73, ❖ 73
[Nierstrasz99]; 191
IDENTIFY THE CONFLICTS ♦ 74
IDENTIFY THE NOUNS ♦ 70
identity
IDENTITY MANAGEMENT ♦ 90
of message sender, validation of; SIGNATURE ♦ 175
objects
managing uniqueness of; IDENTITY MANAGEMENT ♦ 90
preserving in a relational database; OBJECT
IDENTIFIER ♦ 107
IDENTITY MANAGEMENT ♦ 90
IMPLEMENT BEHAVIOR WITH ABSTRACT STATE ♦ 145
implementation
ARCHITECT ALSO IMPLEMENTS ♦ 65
architects responsibilities for; ARCHITECT ALSO
IMPLEMENTS ♦ 65
of behavior, with abstract state; IMPLEMENT BEHAVIOR WITH
ABSTRACT STATE ♦ 145
decoupling interface from, in C++ objects;
HANDLE/BODY ♦ 24
IMPLEMENT BEHAVIOR WITH ABSTRACT STATE ♦ 145
DEFINE CLASSES BY BEHAVIOR, NOT STATE relationship to;
IMPLEMENT BEHAVIOR WITH ABSTRACT STATE ♦ 145

IMPLEMENTATION OF 'MULTIPLE KINDS OF SERVICES' CONTROL MODULES ♦ 62
IMPLEMENTATION PATTERNS FOR THE OBSERVER PATTERN ♦ 74
OBSERVER relationship to; IMPLEMENTATION PATTERNS FOR THE OBSERVER PATTERN ♦ 74, OBSERVER ♦ 94
IMPLEMENTING ASSOCIATIONS ♦ 15
BASIC RELATIONSHIP PATTERNS relationship to; IMPLEMENTING ASSOCIATIONS ♦ 15
IMPLEMENTING CONSTRAINTS ♦ 16
TEMPLATE METHOD relationship to; IMPLEMENTING CONSTRAINTS ♦ 16
IMPLEMENTING GENERALIZATIONS ♦ 15
ABSTRACT CLASS relationship to; IMPLEMENTING GENERALIZATIONS ♦ 15
STATE relationship to; IMPLEMENTING GENERALIZATIONS ♦ 15
of new classes, inheritance use; REUSABILITY THROUGH SELF-ENCAPSULATION ♦ 145
of OBSERVER, patterns for; IMPLEMENTATION PATTERNS FOR THE OBSERVER PATTERN ♦ 74
pattern, code sample importance; CODE SAMPLES ♦ 105
separating policy making from; DECISION MAKER'S ROLE ♦ 30
sharing, without inheritance; DELEGATION ♦ 155
small projects, team size; SOLO VIRTUOSO ♦ 64
of state update, for information sent to an observer; CONDUIT OF SUBJECT CHANGE ♦ 75
IMPLEMENTATION OF 'MULTIPLE KINDS OF SERVICES' CONTROL MODULES ♦ 62
IMPLEMENTATION PATTERNS FOR THE OBSERVER PATTERN ♦ 74
[Kim+96]; 189
IMPLEMENTING ASSOCIATIONS ♦ 15
IMPLEMENTING CONSTRAINTS ♦ 16
IMPLEMENTING GENERALIZATIONS ♦ 15
implications
between basic and derived values, displaying; VISIBLE IMPLICATION ♦ 33
data, projecting; INSTANT PROJECTION ♦ 33
IMPLICIT INVOCATION OR EVENT-BASED ♦ 125
IMPLIED REQUIREMENTS ♦ 52
MARKET WALK-THROUGH relationship to; MARKET WALK-THROUGH ♦ 52, IMPLIED REQUIREMENTS ♦ 52
PRODUCT INITIATIVE relationship to; IMPLIED REQUIREMENTS ♦ 52
REQUIREMENT WALK-THROUGH relationship to; REQUIREMENT WALK-THROUGH ♦ 54
WORK QUEUE relationship to; IMPLIED REQUIREMENTS ♦ 52
VISIBLE IMPLICATION ♦ 33
IMPLICIT INVOCATION OR EVENT-BASED ♦ 125
IMPLIED REQUIREMENTS ♦ 52
improvement
IMPROVING RESPONSIVENESS IN INTERACTIVE APPLICATIONS USING QUEUES ♦ 76
SUGGESTIONS FOR IMPROVEMENT ♦ 113
IMPROVING RESPONSIVENESS IN INTERACTIVE APPLICATIONS USING QUEUES ♦ 76
[Wake+96]; 197

INCLUDES: ♦ 160
income statement
distinguishing balance sheet from; BALANCE SHEET AND INCOME STATEMENT ♦ 12
increment
INCREMENTAL INTEGRATION ♦ 170
NAMED STABLE BASES relationship to; INCREMENTAL INTEGRATION ♦ 170
PRIVATE VERSIONING relationship to; INCREMENTAL INTEGRATION ♦ 170
INCREMENTAL INTEGRATION ♦ 170
indentation
INDENTED CONTROL FLOW ♦ 162
INDENTED CONTROL FLOW ♦ 162
independent
change, as model design guideline; APPROPRIATE LIVING MODELS ♦ 45
hierarchical structures, for client interaction; BUREAUCRACY ♦ 23
INDEPENDENT WORKSPACES ♦ 171
NAMED STABLE BASES relationship to; INDEPENDENT WORKSPACES ♦ 171
objects, interaction handling; MEDIATING PROTOCOL ♦ 155
INDEPENDENT WORKSPACES ♦ 171
index
USE AN INDEXEDADAPTOR TO HOLD A SINGLE INDEX IN A COLLECTION ♦ 177
INDIRECT VARIABLE ACCESS ♦ 157
GETTING METHOD relationship to; INDIRECT VARIABLE ACCESS ♦ 157
SETTING METHOD relationship to; INDIRECT VARIABLE ACCESS ♦ 157
INDIVIDUAL INSTANCE METHOD ♦ 11
SINGLETON relationship to; INDIVIDUAL INSTANCE METHOD ♦ 11
STRATEGY relationship to; INDIVIDUAL INSTANCE METHOD ♦ 11
INFORMAL LABOR PLAN ♦ 53
DEVELOPING IN PAIRS relationship to; INFORMAL LABOR PLAN ♦ 53
DEVELOPMENT EPISODE relationship to; INFORMAL LABOR PLAN ♦ 53
PROGRAMMING EPISODE relationship to; INFORMAL LABOR PLAN ♦ 53
information
CHECKS: PATTERN LANGUAGE OF INFORMATION INTEGRITY ♦ 32
handling needs, requirements process identification of; INFORMATION NEEDS ♦ 141
INFORMATION NEEDS ♦ 141
CLASSIFYING, ASSOCIATING, AND GROUPING THE DOMAIN OBJECTS relationship to; CLASSIFYING, ASSOCIATING, AND GROUPING THE DOMAIN OBJECTS ♦ 141
ELABORATION OF THE DOMAIN OBJECTS relationship to; ELABORATION OF THE DOMAIN OBJECTS ♦ 141
ENVISIONING relationship to; INFORMATION NEEDS ♦ 141
PROBLEM DOMAIN ANALYSIS relationship to; PROBLEM DOMAIN ANALYSIS ♦ 141
PROTOTYPES relationship to; INFORMATION NEEDS ♦ 141

information *continued*
  INFORMATION NEEDS *continued*
    USER INTERFACE REQUIREMENTS relationship to;
      INFORMATION NEEDS ♦ 141
  INFORMATION SECRECY ♦ 174
    SECRECY WITH INTEGRITY relationship to; INFORMATION
      SECRECY ♦ 174
    SECRECY WITH SENDER AUTHENTICATION relationship to;
      INFORMATION SECRECY ♦ 174, SECRECY WITH SENDER
      AUTHENTICATION ♦ 175
    SECRECY WITH SIGNATURE relationship to; INFORMATION
      SECRECY ♦ 174, SECRECY WITH SIGNATURE ♦ 175
    SECRECY WITH SIGNATURE WITH APPENDIX relationship to;
      SECRECY WITH SIGNATURE WITH APPENDIX ♦ 175
  INFORMATIONAL ROLE ♦ 30
    INTERFACE'S ROLE relationship to; INFORMATIONAL
      ROLE ♦ 30
    SHAPE OF PROGRAM relationship to; INFORMATIONAL
      ROLE ♦ 30
    VISITOR relationship to; INFORMATIONAL ROLE ♦ 30
  loss, avoiding in multi-level models; UPWARD
    TRACEABILITY ♦ 45
  PATTERNS FOR DESIGNING NAVIGABLE INFORMATION
    SPACES ♦ 119
  representation, feature extraction algorithms; FEATURE
    EXTRACTION—A PATTERN FOR INFORMATION
    RETRIEVAL ♦ 58
  retrieval, feature extraction algorithms; FEATURE
    EXTRACTION—A PATTERN FOR INFORMATION
    RETRIEVAL ♦ 58
  sources, for software development; REFERENCE DATA ♦ 54
  spaces, navigation design for; PATTERNS FOR DESIGNING
    NAVIGABLE INFORMATION SPACES ♦ 119
INFORMATION NEEDS ♦ 141
INFORMATION SECRECY ♦ 174
INFORMATIONAL ROLE ♦ 30
infrastructure
  as Smalltalk client-server system layer; FOUR-LAYER
    ARCHITECTURE ♦ 106
  as software architecture subsystem; THREE SUBSYSTEMS ♦ 135
inheritance
  adding a level to VISITOR; DEFAULT VISITOR ♦ 46
  circular dependencies; CURIOUSLY RECURRING
    TEMPLATE ♦ 43
  EVOLVE AGGREGATIONS FROM INHERITANCE
    HIERARCHIES ♦ 85
  evolving software to aggregations from; LIFE CYCLE AND
    REFACTORING PATTERNS THAT SUPPORT EVOLUTION AND
    REUSE ♦ 84, EVOLVE AGGREGATIONS FROM INHERITANCE
    HIERARCHIES ♦ 85
  in framework development, composition vs.; BLACK-BOX
    FRAMEWORK ♦ 122
  generalization implementation with; IMPLEMENTING
    GENERALIZATIONS ♦ 15
  HANDLE/BODY impact on; HANDLE/BODY ♦ 24
  hierarchies
    abstract class use for cleanup of; CREATE ABSTRACT
      SUPERCLASS ♦ 85
    separation of; HANDLE/BODY HIERARCHY ♦ 24

  hierarchy
    for algebraic types; ALGEBRAIC HIERARCHY ♦ 25
    container membership management use; MEMBER
      CONTAINER ♦ 86
    diagnostic message types; TYPED DIAGNOSTICS ♦ 124
    linear interation of containers in; ITERABLE CONTAINER ♦ 80
    implementation sharing with; DELEGATION ♦ 155
    implementing new classes with; REUSABILITY THROUGH
      SELF-ENCAPSULATION ♦ 145
    loop writing use; WRITE A LOOP ONCE ♦ 179
    parent, communication with; SUPER ♦ 155
    polymorphism outside of; EXTERNAL POLYMORPHISM ♦ 56
    promotion encapsulation; PROMOTION LADDER ♦ 26
    representation, in a relational database; REPRESENTING
      INHERITANCE IN A RELATIONAL DATABASE ♦ 42,
      SURROGATE ♦ 168
    REPRESENTING INHERITANCE IN A RELATIONAL
      DATABASE ♦ 42
    runtime control, replacing message to self; CLIENT-SPECIFIED
      SELF ♦ 34
    structure design, factoring common attributes; FACTOR OUT
      COMMON ATTRIBUTES ♦ 70
    white-box frameworks based on; WHITE-BOX
      FRAMEWORKS ♦ 121
initialization
  active, decoupling from services provided; CONNECTOR ♦ 40
  EXPLICIT INITIALIZATION ♦ 156
  of instance variables; EXPLICIT INITIALIZATION ♦ 156
  lazy; LAZY INITIALIZATION ♦ 157
    class design use; USE LAZY INITIALIZATION ♦ 145
  LAZY INITIALIZATION ♦ 157
  passive, decoupling from services provided; ACCEPTOR ♦ 3
  USE LAZY INITIALIZATION ♦ 145
initiative
  PRODUCT INITIATIVE ♦ 52
INJECT:INTO: ♦ 161
inline
  INLINE MESSAGE PATTERN ♦ 162
INLINE MESSAGE PATTERN ♦ 162
input
  INPUT AND OUTPUT PATTERN LANGUAGE ♦ 76
  multiple, decoupling from multiple output; ROUTER ♦ 146
  remote control of; REMOTE CONTROL ♦ 144
  validation, splitting into two steps; SPLIT VALIDATION ♦ 136
INPUT AND OUTPUT PATTERN LANGUAGE ♦ 76
  [Hanmer+99]; 188
inspector
  debugging, encapsulating; DETACHABLE INSPECTOR ♦ 49
  DETACHABLE INSPECTOR ♦ 49
  object, creating a print method for; DEBUG PRINTING
    METHOD ♦ 154
  tools, for framework use; LANGUAGE TOOLS ♦ 123
instances
  attaching methods to; INDIVIDUAL INSTANCE METHOD ♦ 11
  DYNAMIC STATE INSTANTIATION ♦ 60
  INDIVIDUAL INSTANCE METHOD ♦ 11
  ROLE SUGGESTING INSTANCE VARIABLE NAME ♦ 158
  USE A SLOTADAPTOR TO HOLD A SINGLE INSTANCE
    VARIABLE ♦ 178

variables
  setting from parameters; CONSTRUCTOR PARAMETER
    METHOD ♦ 152
  wrapping ValueModel behavior around; USE A
    SLOTADAPTOR TO HOLD A SINGLE INSTANCE
    VARIABLE ♦ 178
INSTANT PROJECTION ♦ 33
  HYPOTHETICAL PUBLICATION relationship to; INSTANT
    PROJECTION ♦ 33, HYPOTHETICAL PUBLICATION ♦ 33
  VISIBLE IMPLICATION relationship to; INSTANT
    PROJECTION ♦ 33
instrumentation
  debugging, encapsulating; DETACHABLE INSPECTOR ♦ 49
integration
  INCREMENTAL INTEGRATION ♦ 170
  PATTERN-BASED INTEGRATION ARCHITECTURES ♦ 115
  shift from custom to component-based; PATTERN-BASED
    INTEGRATION ARCHITECTURES ♦ 115
  software, timing of; NAMED STABLE BASES ♦ 68
  of vision, in teams, strategies for developing; UNITY OF
    PURPOSE ♦ 95
integrity
  CHECKS: PATTERN LANGUAGE OF INFORMATION
    INTEGRITY ♦ 32
  encrypted message, verification of; SECRECY WITH
    INTEGRITY ♦ 175
  importance in customer relations; SHOW PERSONAL
    INTEGRITY ♦ 44
  MESSAGE INTEGRITY ♦ 174
  of messages, strategies for ensuring; MESSAGE
    INTEGRITY ♦ 174
  SECRECY WITH INTEGRITY ♦ 175
  of software artifact, preserving; PROGRAMMING-BY-
    DIFFERENCE ♦ 150
  system, protecting from change; PROTECTED
    VARIATIONS ♦ 135
INTELLIGENT CHILDREN ♦ 16
  ABSTRACT SERVER relationship to; INTELLIGENT
    CHILDREN ♦ 16, ABSTRACT SERVER ♦ 16
  ADAPTED SERVER relationship to; INTELLIGENT
    CHILDREN ♦ 16, ADAPTED SERVER ♦ 17
INTENT CATALOG ♦ 104
  PATTERN THUMBNAIL relationship to; INTENT CATALOG ♦ 104
  PROBLEM/SOLUTION SUMMARY relationship to;
    PROBLEM/SOLUTION SUMMARY ♦ 105
INTENTION REVEALING MESSAGE ♦ 154
INTENTION REVEALING SELECTOR ♦ 154
interaction
  applications, architectural design; MODEL-VIEW-
    CONTROLLER ♦ 87
  asynchronous, architecture for; MESSAGING ENGINEERING
    MODEL ♦ 18
  client, creating a hierarchical structure for; BUREAUCRACY ♦ 23
  in customer demonstrations, lightweight user interfaces use;
    LIGHTWEIGHT USER INTERFACES ♦ 47
  CUSTOMER INTERACTION PATTERNS ♦ 43
  with customers; CUSTOMER INTERACTION PATTERNS ♦ 43
  DATABASE INTERACTION ♦ 15
  engineering model for; ONLINE ENGINEERING MODEL ♦ 18

hierarchy of cooperating agents; PRESENTATION-
    ABSTRACTION-CONTROL ♦ 135
  human, structures that support; SHAPING CIRCULATION
    REALMS ♦ 67
IMPROVING RESPONSIVENESS IN INTERACTIVE APPLICATIONS
    USING QUEUES ♦ 76
  between independent objects; MEDIATING PROTOCOL ♦ 155
  lazy redrawing facilitation of; LAZY REDRAW ♦ 50
  low-level structure design; IMPROVING RESPONSIVENESS IN
    INTERACTIVE APPLICATIONS USING QUEUES ♦ 76
  object, encapsulation of; MEDIATOR ♦ 86
  peer-to-peer interaction models, decoupling peers
    from underlying communication mechanisms;
    FORWARDER-RECEIVER ♦ 60
  stream engineering model support of; STREAM I-O
    ENGINEERING MODEL ♦ 19
  system, encapsulating as a session; SESSION ♦ 17
  teaching strategies for
    quiz games use; QUIZ GAMES ♦ 118
    simulation games use; SIMULATION GAMES ♦ 117
  undo/redo, strategies for; OBJECT RECOVERY ♦ 92
interception
  DOMAIN INTERCEPTS ♦ 137
INTERESTING RETURN VALUE ♦ 163
interests
  USE onChangeSend:to: TO REGISTER INTERESTS ON A
    VALUE ♦ 176
INTERFACE ORGANIZATION ♦ 59
interface(s)
  See Also GUI (graphical user interface); UI (user interface)
  adding to a class; EXTENSION OBJECT ♦ 55
  common, providing for mulitple interfaces in a subsystem;
    FACADE ♦ 56
  communication, hiding from legacy clients; REQUEST ♦ 90
  creating, for groups of related objects; ABSTRACT FACTORY ♦ 2
  decoupling
    functional parts from; SEPARATION OF POWERS ♦ 110
    implementation from, in C++ objects; HANDLE/BODY ♦ 24
  designing class hierarchies with; ABSTRACT CLASS ♦ 2
  for different object collections, development strategies;
    MANAGED OBJECT ♦ 115
  encapsulation of, in a software tools environment; IP/FP PLUG
    IN ♦ 111
  finite state machine use; INTERFACE ORGANIZATION ♦ 59
  HUMAN INTERFACE ROLE IS A SPECIAL INTERFACE ROLE ♦ 31
  between I/O and logical behavior, representation of;
    POINT ♦ 134
  identifier as, handle use for; HANDLE/BODY ♦ 24
  INTERFACE ORGANIZATION ♦ 59
    STATE-DRIVEN TRANSITION relationship to; INTERFACE
      ORGANIZATION ♦ 59
  INTERFACE TO CONTROL MODULES ♦ 62
  INTERFACE'S ROLE ♦ 30
    BRIDGE relationship to; INTERFACE'S ROLE ♦ 30
    DECISION MAKER'S ROLE relationship to; DECISION
      MAKER'S ROLE ♦ 30
    FACADE relationship to; INTERFACE'S ROLE ♦ 30
    INFORMATIONAL ROLE relationship to; INFORMATIONAL
      ROLE ♦ 30

interface(s) *continued*
INTERFACE'S ROLE *continued*
SHAPE OF PROGRAM relationship to; INTERFACE'S ROLE ♦ 30
layers, Smalltalk client-server determination; FOUR-LAYER
ARCHITECTURE ♦ 106
LOOSE INTERFACES ♦ 94
multiple view use, by a relational database; HIERARCHICAL
VIEW ♦ 3
network management; PATTERN SYSTEM FOR NETWORK
MANAGEMENT INTERFACES ♦ 114
for physical database tables; PHYSICAL VIEW ♦ 3
between program and the rest of the world, creating;
INTERFACE'S ROLE ♦ 30
software development team, gatekeeper role;
GATEKEEPER ♦ 67
sub-system, in multi-team distributed system development;
LOOSE INTERFACES ♦ 94
third-party, testing of; 'UNCHANGED' INTERFACES ♦ 127
'UNCHANGED' INTERFACES ♦ 127
user, encapsulating; HUMAN INTERFACE ROLE IS A SPECIAL
INTERFACE ROLE ♦ 31
volatile, single entry point to; FACADE ♦ 137
INTERFACE TO CONTROL MODULES ♦ 62
INTERFACE'S ROLE ♦ 30
interpretation
DISPATCHED INTERPRETATION ♦ 155
FLEXIBLE COMMAND INTERPRETER ♦ 60
interpreter
as architectural pattern; INTERPRETER ♦ 125
command, grammar-independent; FLEXIBLE COMMAND
INTERPRETER ♦ 60
INTERPRETER ♦ 80, ♦ 125
COMPOSABLE QUERY OBJECTS relationship to; COMPOSABLE
QUERY OBJECTS ♦ 41
COMPOSITE relationship to; INTERPRETER ♦ 80
FLEXIBLE COMMAND INTERPRETER relationship to;
FLEXIBLE COMMAND INTERPRETER ♦ 60
FLYWEIGHT relationship to; INTERPRETER ♦ 80
ITERATOR relationship to; INTERPRETER ♦ 80
OBJECT RECURSION relationship to; OBJECT RECURSION ♦ 92
PARSER/BUILDER relationship to; PARSER/BUILDER ♦ 94
PROGRAMMING-BY-DIFFERENCE relationship to;
PROGRAMMING-BY-DIFFERENCE ♦ 150
VISITOR relationship to; INTERPRETER ♦ 80
INTERPRETER ♦ 80, ♦ 125
[Alpert+98]; 182
[Gamma+95]; 188
interrupts
See Also event(s)
DON'T INTERRUPT AN INTERRUPT ♦ 69
INTERRUPTS UNJAM BLOCKING ♦ 69
INTERRUPTS UNJAM BLOCKING ♦ 69
INTERVAL ♦ 160
interval
INTERVAL ♦ 160
SHORTCUT CONSTRUCTOR METHOD relationship to;
INTERVAL ♦ 160
intervention
MINIMIZE HUMAN INTERVENTION ♦ 57

INTRODUCE VIRTUAL ATTRIBUTES ♦ 70
DEFINE THE DATA STRUCTURE relationship to; INTRODUCE
VIRTUAL ATTRIBUTES ♦ 70
invocation
IMPLICIT INVOCATION OR EVENT-BASED ♦ 125
messages use for; MESSAGE ♦ 154
selecting among alternative; CHOOSING MESSAGE ♦ 154
inward
WORK FLOWS INWARD ♦ 68
IO GATEKEEPER ♦ 77
IO TRIAGE ♦ 77
IP/FP PLUG IN ♦ 111
TOOL COMPOSITION relationship to; IP/FP PLUG IN ♦ 111
IS EMPTY ♦ 160
Ishikawa, S.
[Alexander+75]; 181
[Alexander+77]; 182
Islam, N.
[Islam+96]; 188
RECOVERABLE DISTRIBUTOR ♦ 143
isolation
See Also encapsulation
big ball of mud code, as control strategy; SWEEPING IT UNDER
THE RUG ♦ 21
of frequent changes; PUT FREQUENTLY VARYING STRUCTURES
IN INSTANCES ♦ 5
of predicted variations; PROTECTED VARIATIONS ♦ 135
IT'S A RELATIONSHIP, NOT A SALE ♦ 43
BE AWARE OF BOUNDARIES relationship to; BE AWARE OF
BOUNDARIES ♦ 44
BE RESPONSIVE relationship to; BE RESPONSIVE ♦ 44
BUILD TRUST relationship to; BUILD TRUST ♦ 43
BUILD TRUST relationship with; IT'S A RELATIONSHIP, NOT A
SALE ♦ 43
CUSTOMER MEETINGS: GO EARLY, STAY LATE relationship to;
CUSTOMER MEETINGS: GO EARLY, STAY LATE ♦ 44
GET INVOLVED EARLY relationship to; GET INVOLVED
EARLY ♦ 126
KNOW THE CUSTOMER relationship to; KNOW THE
CUSTOMER ♦ 43
KNOW THE CUSTOMER relationship with; IT'S A RELATIONSHIP,
NOT A SALE ♦ 43
LISTEN, LISTEN, LISTEN relationship to; LISTEN, LISTEN,
LISTEN ♦ 44
MIND YOUR MANNERS relationship to; MIND YOUR
MANNERS ♦ 44
SHOW PERSONAL INTEGRITY relationship to; SHOW PERSONAL
INTEGRITY ♦ 44
ITERABLE CONTAINER ♦ 80
[Martin95b]; 190
iteration
over collections; DO ♦ 160
ITERABLE CONTAINER ♦ 80
FACTORY METHOD relationship to; ITERABLE
CONTAINER ♦ 80
PROTOTYPE relationship to; ITERABLE CONTAINER ♦ 80
STRATEGY relationship to; ITERABLE CONTAINER ♦ 80

ITERATIVE COURSE DEVELOPMENT ◆ 116
  PITFALL DIAGNOSIS AND PREVENTION relationship to;
    PITFALL DIAGNOSIS AND PREVENTION ◆ 116
ITERATOR ◆ 80
  COMPOSITE relationship to; COMPOSITE ◆ 37
  INTERPRETER relationship to; INTERPRETER ◆ 80
  OBJECT RECURSION relationship to; OBJECT RECURSION ◆ 92
  SHOPPER relationship to; SHOPPER ◆ 152
  in teaching
    course development for heterogeneous backgrounds;
      ITERATIVE COURSE DEVELOPMENT ◆ 116
    of interdependent concepts; CHICKEN AND EGG ◆ 116
    new material introduction; MIX NEW AND OLD ◆ 116
ITERATIVE COURSE DEVELOPMENT ◆ 116
ITERATOR ◆ 80
  [Alpert+98]; 182
  [Gamma+95]; 188

Jackson, E.W.
  [Jackson99]; 188
    EVENTHANDLER ◆ 55
Jacobson, M.
  [Alexander+77]; 182
Jain, P.
  [Jain+97]; 188
    SERVICE CONFIGURATOR ◆ 151
Janoff, N.
  [Janoff98]; 189
Java language
  concurrency patterns; CONCURRENT PROGRAMMING IN JAVA:
    DESIGN PRINCIPLES AND PATTERNS, 2ND ED. ◆ 37
  CONCURRENT PROGRAMMING IN JAVA: DESIGN PRINCIPLES
    AND PATTERNS, 2ND ED. ❖ 37
  panels, view control; PLUGGABLE VIEW CONTROLLER ◆ 132
Johnson, R. E.
  [Gamma+95]; 188
    ADAPTER ◆ 6
    BRIDGE ◆ 22
    BUILDER ◆ 23
    CHAIN OF RESPONSIBILITY ◆ 32
    COMMAND ◆ 35
    COMPOSITE ◆ 37
    DECORATOR ◆ 46
    FACADE ◆ 56
    FACTORY METHOD ◆ 56
    FLYWEIGHT ◆ 60
    HOOK METHOD ◆ 73
    ITERATOR ◆ 80
    MEDIATOR ◆ 86
    MEMENTO ◆ 87
    OBSERVER ◆ 94
    PROTOTYPER ◆ 138
    PROXY ◆ 139
    SINGLETON ◆ 152
    STATE ◆ 166
    STRATEGY ◆ 167
    TEMPLATE METHOD ◆ 171
    VISITOR ◆ 179
  [Gamma+95], INTERPRETER ◆ 80

  [Huni+95]; 188
  [Johnson+98]; 189
    TYPE OBJECT ◆ 176
  [Johnson94a]; 189
  [Johnson94b]; 189
  [Johnson95]; 189
  [Johnson96]; 189
    TRANSACTIONS AND ACCOUNTS ❖ 172
  [Roberts+98]; 194
    PATTERNS FOR EVOLVING FRAMEWORKS ❖ 121
joining
  as divide-and-conquer strategy for parallel processes;
    FORK/JOIN ◆ 40
  FORK/JOIN ◆ 40
Jordan, T. D
  [Pyarali+99]; 193
    PROACTOR ◆ 137
journeyman
  MASTER-JOURNEYMAN ◆ 119
JUDGE ◆ 81
  [Metsker98]; 191
    STRATEGY relationship to; JUDGE ◆ 81
JUDICIOUS FIREWORKS ◆ 47
  ARCHIVE SCENARIOS relationship to; JUDICIOUS
    FIREWORKS ◆ 47
  LIGHTWEIGHT USER INTERFACES relationship to; JUDICIOUS
    FIREWORKS ◆ 47
  PROTOTYPING LANGUAGES relationship to; PROTOTYPING
    LANGUAGES ◆ 47

KEEP IT WORKING ◆ 21
Keeve, F.
  [Adams+96]; 181
    FAULT-TOLERANT TELECOMMUNICATION SYSTEM
      PATTERNS ❖ 57
Keller, R. K.
  [Keller+98a]; 189
Keller, W.
  [Keller+98b]; 189
    ACCESSING RELATIONAL DATABASES ❖ 3
kernel
  identifying, in class design; IDENTIFY MESSAGE LAYERS ◆ 145
  layer identifying, in class design; IDENTIFY MESSAGE
    LAYERS ◆ 145
  micro, as system architecture manager; MICROKERNEL ◆ 87
  of software artifact, preserving; PROGRAMMING-BY-
    DIFFERENCE ◆ 150
Kerth, N. L.
  [Kerth95] ◆ 28, 189
  [PLoPD2]; 192
KEY BUSINESS ACTIVITIES AND INFLUENCES ◆ 165
key(s)
  See Also foreign keys
  FOREIGN KEY REFERENCES ◆ 43, ◆ 108
  FOREIGN KEY VERSUS DIRECT REFERENCE ◆ 43
  KEY BUSINESS ACTIVITIES AND INFLUENCES ◆ 165
    PEOPLE, PLACES, AND THINGS relationship to; PEOPLE,
      PLACES, AND THINGS ◆ 165

key(s) *continued*
 Key Business Activities and Influences *continued*
  Query Optimized Database relationship to; Query
   Optimized Database ♦ 165
  Transaction History relationship to; Transaction
   History ♦ 165
  Whole Business Entities relationship to; Key Business
   Activities and Influences ♦ 165
 Keyed Mapping; Keyed Mapping ♦ 16
 secret, message encryption use with; Information
  Secrecy ♦ 174
Killer Test ♦ 128
Kim, J. J.
 [Kim+96]; 189
 Implementation Patterns for the Observer
  Pattern ❖ 74
Kircher, M.
 [Kircher+99]; 189
Knoll, R.
 [Baumer+97]; 184
 Role Object ♦ 146
Know the Customer ♦ 43
knowledge
 Accountability Knowledge Level ♦ 5
 decoupling from domain facts; Accountability Knowledge
  Level ♦ 5, Accountability Knowledge Level ♦ 7
 Know the Customer ♦ 43
  Be Aware of Boundaries relationship to; Be Aware of
   Boundaries ♦ 44
  Be Responsive relationship to; Know the Customer ♦ 43,
   Be Responsive ♦ 44
  Customer Meetings: Go Early, Stay Late relationship
   to; Know the Customer ♦ 43, Customer Meetings:
   Go Early, Stay Late ♦ 44
  Go Early, Stay Late relationship to; Know the
   Customer ♦ 43
  It's a Relationship, Not a Sale relationship to; It's
   a Relationship, Not a Sale ♦ 43, Know the
   Customer ♦ 43
  Listen, Listen, Listen relationship to; Know the
   Customer ♦ 43, Listen, Listen, Listen ♦ 44
  Mind Your Manners relationship to; Mind Your
   Manners ♦ 44
  Show Personal Integrity relationship to; Show
   Personal Integrity ♦ 44
 Knowledge Level ♦ 5
 level, system modification from; Reflection ♦ 144
 modeling, separately from domain operations; Knowledge
  Level ♦ 5
Knowledge Level ♦ 5
Knutsson, P. J.
 [Dagermo+98]; 186

ladder
 Promotion Ladder ♦ 26
lamb
 Sacrificial Lamb ♦ 131
Landmark ♦ 120
Language Tools ♦ 123

languages
 See Also C++ language; Java language; pattern languages and
  collections; Smalltalk language; Tcl language
 independent pattern writing; Code Samples as Bonus ♦ 105
 Language Tools ♦ 123
  Visual Builder; Language Tools ♦ 123
  Visual Builder relationship to; Visual Builder ♦ 123
 prototyping, customer demonstration use; Prototyping
  Languages ♦ 47
 Prototyping Languages ♦ 47
 visual, creation of; Visual Builder ♦ 123
 XLisp language
Late Creation ♦ 120
 Class Clause relationship to; Late Creation ♦ 120
 Class Semantics relationship to; Class Semantics ♦ 121
 Class Specification relationship to; Class
  Specification ♦ 121
latency
 Coupling Decreases Latency ♦ 69
 errors, handling, in fault-tolerant systems; Fool Me
  Once ♦ 58
 product development, reduction of; Coupling Decreases
  Latency ♦ 69
 software development, resource management strategies;
  Interrupts Unjam Blocking ♦ 69
Lavender, R. G.
 [Lavender+96]; 190
 Active Object ♦ 6
Layer in an Application ♦ 96
Layered and Sectioned Architecture ♦ 96
Layered Architecture ♦ 125
Layered Organization ♦ 59
layering
 See Also decoupling; encapsulation
 access layers
  in relational database design; Accessing Relational
   Databases pattern language ♦ 3
  in relational databases; Relational Database Access
   Layer ♦ 3
 application, decoupling user interface from domain model;
  Presentation and Application Logic ♦ 15
 architecture
  communication in; Bridge ♦ 123
  generation of; Patterns for Generating a Layered
   Architecture ♦ 123
 client-server applications
  four-tier; Four-Layer Architecture ♦ 106
  three-tier; Three-Tier Architecture ♦ 15
  two-tier; Two-Tier Architecture ♦ 14
 complex domain applications; Cascade ♦ 28
 components, for driver duty definition; Driver Duty ♦ 51
 database, handling, in three-tier architecture; Database
  Interaction ♦ 15
 finite state machines; Layered Organization ♦ 59
 Hierarchy of Control Layers ♦ 61
  Four-Layer Architecture relationship to; Four-Layer
   Architecture ♦ 106
 Identify Message Layers ♦ 145

identifying kernel layer, in class design; IDENTIFY MESSAGE
LAYERS ♦ 145

LAYER IN AN APPLICATION ♦ 96
  LAYERED AND SECTIONED ARCHITECTURE relationship to;
    LAYER IN AN APPLICATION ♦ 96

LAYERED AND SECTIONED ARCHITECTURE ♦ 96
  FOUR-LAYER ARCHITECTURE relationship to; LAYERED
    AND SECTIONED ARCHITECTURE ♦ 96, FOUR-LAYER
    ARCHITECTURE ♦ 106
  HIERARCHY OF CONTROL LAYERS relationship to;
    HIERARCHY OF CONTROL LAYERS ♦ 61, LAYERED AND
    SECTIONED ARCHITECTURE ♦ 96
  LAYER IN AN APPLICATION relationship to; LAYER IN AN
    APPLICATION ♦ 96
  LAYERED ARCHITECTURE relationship to; LAYERED
    AND SECTIONED ARCHITECTURE ♦ 96, LAYERED
    ARCHITECTURE ♦ 125
  LAYERED ORGANIZATION relationship to; LAYERED
    ORGANIZATION ♦ 59, LAYERED AND SECTIONED
    ARCHITECTURE ♦ 96
  LAYERS relationship to; LAYERS ♦ 81, LAYERED AND
    SECTIONED ARCHITECTURE ♦ 96
  PEDESTAL relationship to; LAYERED AND SECTIONED
    ARCHITECTURE ♦ 96, PEDESTAL ♦ 123
  SECTION IN A SUBAPPLICATION relationship to; SECTION IN
    A SUBAPPLICATION ♦ 97
  SHAPE OF PROGRAM relationship to; SHAPE OF
    PROGRAM ♦ 29, LAYERED AND SECTIONED
    ARCHITECTURE ♦ 96
  THREE-TIER ARCHITECTURE relationship to; LAYERED AND
    SECTIONED ARCHITECTURE ♦ 96

LAYERED AND SECTIONEDARCHITECTURE, THREE-TIER
  ARCHITECTURE relationship to; THREE-TIER
  ARCHITECTURE ♦ 15

LAYERED ARCHITECTURE ♦ 125
  FOUR-LAYER ARCHITECTURE; LAYERED
    ARCHITECTURE ♦ 125
  FOUR-LAYER ARCHITECTURE relationship to; FOUR-LAYER
    ARCHITECTURE ♦ 106
  HIERARCHY OF CONTROL LAYERS; LAYERED
    ARCHITECTURE ♦ 125
  HIERARCHY OF CONTROL LAYERS relationship to;
    HIERARCHY OF CONTROL LAYERS ♦ 61
  LAYERED AND SECTIONED ARCHITECTURE; LAYERED
    ARCHITECTURE ♦ 125
  LAYERED AND SECTIONED ARCHITECTURE relationship to;
    LAYERED AND SECTIONED ARCHITECTURE ♦ 96
  LAYERED ORGANIZATION; LAYERED ARCHITECTURE ♦ 125
  LAYERED ORGANIZATION relationship to; LAYERED
    ORGANIZATION ♦ 59
  LAYERS; LAYERED ARCHITECTURE ♦ 125
  LAYERS relationship to; LAYERS ♦ 81
  PEDESTAL; LAYERED ARCHITECTURE ♦ 125
  PEDESTAL relationship to; PEDESTAL ♦ 123
  SECURE ACCESS LAYER relationship to; SECURE ACCESS
    LAYER ♦ 18
  SHAPE OF PROGRAM; LAYERED ARCHITECTURE ♦ 125
  SHAPE OF PROGRAM relationship to; SHAPE OF
    PROGRAM ♦ 29

THREE-TIER ARCHITECTURE; LAYERED
  ARCHITECTURE ♦ 125
THREE-TIER ARCHITECTURE relationship to; THREE-TIER
  ARCHITECTURE ♦ 15

LAYERED ORGANIZATION ♦ 59
  FOUR-LAYER ARCHITECTURE relationship to; LAYERED
    ORGANIZATION ♦ 59, FOUR-LAYER ARCHITECTURE ♦ 106
  HIERARCHY OF CONTROL LAYERS relationship to; LAYERED
    ORGANIZATION ♦ 59, HIERARCHY OF CONTROL
    LAYERS ♦ 61
  LAYERED AND SECTIONED ARCHITECTURE relationship to;
    LAYERED ORGANIZATION ♦ 59, LAYERED AND SECTIONED
    ARCHITECTURE ♦ 96
  LAYERED ARCHITECTURE relationship to; LAYERED
    ORGANIZATION ♦ 59, LAYERED ARCHITECTURE ♦ 125
  LAYERS relationship to; LAYERED ORGANIZATION ♦ 59,
    LAYERS ♦ 81
  PEDESTAL relationship to; LAYERED ORGANIZATION ♦ 59,
    PEDESTAL ♦ 123
  SHAPE OF PROGRAM relationship to; SHAPE OF
    PROGRAM ♦ 29, LAYERED ORGANIZATION ♦ 59
  THREE-LEVEL FSM relationship to; LAYERED
    ORGANIZATION ♦ 59
  THREE-TIER ARCHITECTURE relationship to; THREE-TIER
    ARCHITECTURE ♦ 15, LAYERED ORGANIZATION ♦ 59

LAYERS ♦ 81
  DETACHABLE INSPECTOR relationship to; DETACHABLE
    INSPECTOR ♦ 49
  FOUR-LAYER ARCHITECTURE relationship to; LAYERS ♦ 81,
    FOUR-LAYER ARCHITECTURE ♦ 106
  HIERARCHY OF CONTROL LAYERS relationship to;
    HIERARCHY OF CONTROL LAYERS ♦ 61, LAYERS ♦ 81
  LAYERED AND SECTIONED ARCHITECTURE relationship
    to; LAYERS ♦ 81, LAYERED AND SECTIONED
    ARCHITECTURE ♦ 96
  LAYERED ARCHITECTURE relationship to; LAYERS ♦ 81,
    LAYERED ARCHITECTURE ♦ 125
  LAYERED ORGANIZATION relationship to; LAYERED
    ORGANIZATION ♦ 59, LAYERS ♦ 81
  MICROKERNEL relationship to; LAYERS ♦ 81
  PEDESTAL relationship to; LAYERS ♦ 81, PEDESTAL ♦ 123
  PRESENTATION-ABSTRACTION-CONTROL relationship to;
    LAYERS ♦ 81
  SECURE ACCESS LAYER relationship to; SECURE ACCESS
    LAYER ♦ 18
  SHAPE OF PROGRAM relationship to; SHAPE OF
    PROGRAM ♦ 29, LAYERS ♦ 81
  SHEARING LAYERS relationship to; SHEARING LAYERS ♦ 21
  THREE-TIER ARCHITECTURE relationship to; THREE-TIER
    ARCHITECTURE ♦ 15, LAYERS ♦ 81

models and ValueModels; USE A BUFFEREDVALUEHOLDER TO
  DELAY THE COMMIT OF A NEW VALUE ♦ 177
open containers; OPEN CONTAINERS ♦ 38
PATTERNS FOR GENERATING A LAYERED ARCHITECTURE ♦ 123
program; SHAPE OF PROGRAM ♦ 29
RELATIONAL DATABASE ACCESS LAYER ♦ 3
secure access, as security integration tool; SECURE ACCESS
  LAYER ♦ 18
SECURE ACCESS LAYER ♦ 18

layering *continued*
  storing layers in applications; LAYER IN AN APPLICATION ♦ 96
  system evolution handling through; SHEARING LAYERS ♦ 21
  of system functions, into a hierarchy; HIERARCHY OF CONTROL
    LAYERS ♦ 61
  systems, into base and meta levels; REFLECTION ♦ 144
  term description; LAYERS ♦ 81
LAYERS ♦ 81
  [Buschmann+96]; 183
layout
  COMPONENTS LAYOUT ♦ 36
  of multimedia artifacts; COMPONENTS LAYOUT ♦ 36
lazy
  initialization; LAZY INITIALIZATION ♦ 157
    class design use; USE LAZY INITIALIZATION ♦ 145
  LAZY INITIALIZATION ♦ 157
    CACHING STATE VARIABLE relationship to; CACHING STATE
      VARIABLE ♦ 83
    DEFAULT VALUE METHOD relationship to; LAZY
      INITIALIZATION ♦ 157
    GETTING METHOD relationship to; LAZY
      INITIALIZATION ♦ 157
  LAZY OPTIMIZATION ♦ 81
    PERFORMANCE CRITERIA relationship to; LAZY
      OPTIMIZATION ♦ 81
    PERFORMANCE MEASUREMENT relationship to; LAZY
      OPTIMIZATION ♦ 81
  LAZY OPTIMIZATION: PATTERNS FOR EFFICIENT SMALLTALK
    PROGRAMMING ♦ 81
  LAZY PROPAGATOR ♦ 138
  LAZY REDRAW ♦ 50
    REQUEST UPDATE relationship to; REQUEST UPDATE ♦ 49,
      LAZY REDRAW ♦ 50
  LAZY STATE ♦ 134
    POINT relationship to; POINT ♦ 134, LAZY STATE ♦ 134
    POOL relationship to; LAZY STATE ♦ 134
    STATE relationship to; LAZY STATE ♦ 134
  optimization
    of Smalltalk programs; LAZY OPTIMIZATION: PATTERNS FOR
      EFFICIENT SMALLTALK PROGRAMMING ♦ 81
    strategies for; LAZY OPTIMIZATION ♦ 81
  redrawing; LAZY REDRAW ♦ 50
  USE LAZY INITIALIZATION ♦ 145
LAZY INITIALIZATION ♦ 157
LAZY OPTIMIZATION ♦ 81
LAZY OPTIMIZATION: PATTERNS FOR EFFICIENT SMALLTALK
  PROGRAMMING ♦ 81
  [Auer+96]; 182
LAZY PROPAGATOR ♦ 138
LAZY REDRAW ♦ 50
LAZY STATE ♦ 134
Lea, D.
  [Lea95]; 190
  [Lea99]; 190
    CONCURRENT PROGRAMMING IN JAVA: DESIGN PRINCIPLES
      AND PATTERNS, 2ND ED. ❖ 37
leadership role
  in pattern writers workshops; MODERATOR GUIDES THE
    WORKSHOP ♦ 112

LEAKY BUCKET COUNTERS ♦ 57
leaky buckets ♦ 102
  LEAKY BUCKET COUNTERS ♦ 57
    RIDING OVER TRANSIENTS relationship to; RIDING OVER
      TRANSIENTS ♦ 57, LEAKY BUCKET COUNTERS ♦ 57
  LEAKY BUCKET OF CREDITS ♦ 102
    LEAKY BUCKET COUNTERS relationship to; LEAKY BUCKET
      OF CREDITS ♦ 102
    WORK SHED AT PERIPHERY relationship to; WORK SHED AT
      PERIPHERY ♦ 102
learning curve
  See Also training
  GENTLE LEARNING CURVE ♦ 150
legacy
  access maintenance; (LEGACY) WRAPPER ♦ 115
  code, hopeless big ball of mud, solution for;
    RECONSTRUCTION ♦ 21
  (LEGACY) WRAPPER
    ADAPTER relationship to; (LEGACY) WRAPPER ♦ 115
    BROKER relationship to; (LEGACY) WRAPPER ♦ 115
    FACADE relationship to; (LEGACY) WRAPPER ♦ 115
  systems, object-oriented framework relationships with; NEW
    CLIENTS WITH OLD SERVERS: A PATTERN LANGUAGE FOR
    CLIENT/SERVER FRAMEWORKS ♦ 89
(LEGACY) WRAPPER ♦ 115
LET'S PLAY TEAM ♦ 131
levels
  3-LEVEL ORDER ♦ 24
  ACCOUNTABILITY KNOWLEDGE LEVEL ♦ 5
  of business activity, modeling; DIMENSION ROLL-UP ♦ 165
  MULTIPLE ACCESS LEVELS TO A PACKAGE ♦ 14
  THREE-LEVEL FSM ♦ 172
library
  COMPONENT LIBRARY ♦ 122
  of components, framework development use; COMPONENT
    LIBRARY ♦ 122
life cycle
  of domain object, identifying; ELABORATION OF THE DOMAIN
    OBJECTS ♦ 141
  LIFE CYCLE AND REFACTORING PATTERNS THAT SUPPORT
    EVOLUTION AND REUSE ♦ 84
  software; LIFE CYCLE AND REFACTORING PATTERNS THAT
    SUPPORT EVOLUTION AND REUSE ♦ 84
  30-day development periods; SPRINT ♦ 146
LIFE CYCLE AND REFACTORING PATTERNS THAT SUPPORT
  EVOLUTION AND REUSE ♦ 84
  [Foote+95]; 187
lifetime
  decoupling from scope; CONCRETE DATA TYPE ♦ 25
  of dynamic objects
    creator as owner of; CREATOR AS SOLE OWNER ♦ 85
    management of; LOCALIZED OWNERSHIP: MANAGING
      DYNAMIC OBJECTS IN C++ ♦ 85
LIFO queue
  workload management; FRESH WORK BEFORE STALE ♦ 101
LIGHTWEIGHT USER INTERFACES ♦ 47
  ELEMENT IDENTIFICATION relationship to; ELEMENT
    IDENTIFICATION ♦ 46

Prototyping Languages relationship to; Prototyping Languages ♦ 47

Lilienthal, C.
[Baumer+97]; 184
Role Object ♦ 146

Limited View ♦ 18
CHECKS relationship to; Limited View ♦ 18
Full View with Errors relationship to; Full View with Errors ♦ 18, Limited View ♦ 18

Linden, T.
[Cybulski+99]; 186
Composing Multimedia Artifacts for Reuse ♦ 36

links
activation, decoupling from endpoint computation; NavigationStrategy ♦ 48
as first class objects; Event Notification ♦ 54
representation, in hypermedia; NavigationStrategy ♦ 48
writing style for WWW links; Natural Text Hyperlinks ♦ 98

Listen, Listen, Listen ♦ 44
Be Aware of Boundaries relationship to; Listen, Listen, Listen ♦ 44
Build Trust relationship to; Build Trust ♦ 43, Listen, Listen, Listen ♦ 44
It's a Relationship, Not a Sale relationship to; Listen, Listen, Listen ♦ 44
Know the Customer relationship to; Know the Customer ♦ 43, Listen, Listen, Listen ♦ 44
Mind Your Manners relationship to; Listen, Listen, Listen ♦ 44
Show Personal Integrity relationship to; Listen, Listen, Listen ♦ 44

lists
See Also collections
display, visible component occlusion management; Display List ♦ 49
Display List ♦ 49
selecting items from; Use SelectionInList to Hold a List and Its Selection ♦ 178
Use SelectionInList to Hold a List and Its Selection ♦ 178

literals
searching for; Searching Literal ♦ 161
Searching Literal ♦ 161

Liu, C.
[Wolf+95]; 198
New Clients with Old Servers: A Pattern Language for Client/Server Frameworks ❖ 89

load
Share the Load ♦ 101
sharing, in distributed systems; Resource Exchanger ♦ 144

localization
Localized Ownership: Managing Dynamic Objects in C++ ♦ 85

Localized Ownership: Managing Dynamic Objects in C++ ♦ 85
[Cargill96b]; 184

location
of alarms, in fault-tolerant systems; Alarm Grid ♦ 79

dependencies, minimizing in a network management system; Remote Operation ♦ 115
geographical, teams, impact on project architecture; Organization Follows Location ♦ 64
of objects; Entry Point ♦ 16
Organization Follows Location ♦ 64
transparency
dispatcher provision of; Client-Dispatcher-Server ♦ 34
for interoperating applications; Broker ♦ 115

Lock 'em Up Together ♦ 95
locking
aggressive, decoupling from conservative locking; Parallel Fastpath ♦ 147
code; Code Locking ♦ 147
Code Locking ♦ 147
Counter Reader/Writer Lock ♦ 149
data, as performance enhancement over code locking; Data Locking ♦ 147
Data Locking ♦ 147
decoupling readers from writers; Reader/Writer Locking ♦ 147
designs, for parallel programs; Selecting Locking Designs for Parallel Programs ♦ 147
Distributed Reader/Writer Lock ♦ 149
double-checked; Double-Checked Locking ♦ 51
Double-Checked Locking ♦ 51
Hierarchical Locking ♦ 148
hierarchies, as parallelism performance strategy; Hierarchical Locking ♦ 148
issues, open container handling; Open Containers ♦ 38
Lock 'em Up Together ♦ 95
Architect Also Implements relationship to; Lock 'em Up Together ♦ 95
Architect Controls Product relationship to; Lock 'em Up Together ♦ 95
Design by Team relationship to; Design by Team ♦ 95
Review the Architecture relationship to; Lock 'em Up Together ♦ 95
memory allocation strategies; Allocator Caches ♦ 148
memory constraint strategies; Test-and-Set Lock ♦ 148
primitives
queued; Queued Lock ♦ 149
selecting; Selecting Locking Primitives for Parallel Programming ♦ 148
test-and-set; Test-and-Set Lock ♦ 148
Queued Lock ♦ 149
Queued Reader/Writer Lock ♦ 149
Reader/Writer Locking ♦ 147
readers
counter lock; Counter Reader/Writer Lock ♦ 149
distributed lock; Distributed Reader/Writer Lock ♦ 149
queued locks; Queued Reader/Writer Lock ♦ 149
Review the Architecture, Lock 'em Up Together relationship to; Lock 'em Up Together ♦ 95
Selecting Locking Designs for Parallel Programs ♦ 147
Selecting Locking Primitives for Parallel Programming ♦ 148
Test-and-Set Lock ♦ 148

Index

locking *continued*
  writers
    counter lock; COUNTER READER/WRITER LOCK ◆ 149
    distributed lock; DISTRIBUTED READER/WRITER LOCK ◆ 149
    queued locks; QUEUED READER/WRITER LOCK ◆ 149
logging
  DIAGNOSTIC LOGGER ◆ 124
  diagnostic messages
    strategeis for; DIAGNOSTIC LOGGER ◆ 124
    in transaction-oriented systems; PATTERNS FOR LOGGING
      DIAGNOSTIC MESSAGES ◆ 124
  PATTERNS FOR LOGGING DIAGNOSTIC MESSAGES ◆ 124
logic(al)
  behavior, interface between I/O and; POINT ◆ 134
  PRESENTATION AND APPLICATION LOGIC ◆ 15
Long, P.
  [Long99]; 190
LONG POLE IN THE TENT ◆ 131
lookup
  LOOKUP CACHE ◆ 161
    DETECT relationship to; LOOKUP CACHE ◆ 161
    DICTIONARY relationship to; LOOKUP CACHE ◆ 161
    SELECT/REJECT relationship to; LOOKUP CACHE ◆ 161
    SELECT/REJECT, LOOKUP CACHE relationship to; LOOKUP
      CACHE ◆ 161
  tables, relationship implementation with; KEYED
    MAPPING ◆ 16
LOOKUP CACHE ◆ 161
loops
  strategies for writing; WRITE A LOOP ONCE ◆ 179
  WRITE A LOOP ONCE ◆ 179
loose
  LOOSE INTERFACES ◆ 94
    HIERARCHY OF FACTORIES relationship to; LOOSE
      INTERFACES ◆ 94
    PARSER/BUILDER relationship to; LOOSE INTERFACES ◆ 94
LOOSE INTERFACES ◆ 94
LOW SURFACE-TO-VOLUME RATIO ◆ 150
  GENTLE LEARNING CURVE relationship to; LOW
    SURFACE-TO-VOLUME RATIO ◆ 150
  PROGRAMMING-BY-DIFFERENCE relationship to;
    PROGRAMMING-BY-DIFFERENCE ◆ 150
  SELFISH CLASS relationship to; SELFISH CLASS ◆ 150
Lyardet, F.
  [Rossi+99]; 194
    PATTERNS FOR DESIGNING NAVIGABLE INFORMATION
      SPACES ❖ 119

MAC (Message Authentication Codes)
  message sender authentication use; SENDER
    AUTHENTICATION ◆ 174
  sender authentication use; SECRECY WITH SENDER
    AUTHENTICATION ◆ 175
machine-human communication
  design strategies for large and complex systems; MML ◆ 77
MAIN PLUS SUBROUTINES ◆ 125
main program
  as control flow mechanism; MAIN PLUS SUBROUTINES ◆ 125
  MAIN PLUS SUBROUTINES ◆ 125

MAINTAIN CONSISTENT VALUEMODELVALUETYPES ◆ 177
maintainance
  MAINTAIN CONSISTENT VALUEMODELVALUETYPES ◆ 177
maintenance
  DISPLAY MAINTENANCE ◆ 49
  handling without system erosion; KEEP IT WORKING ◆ 21
  reduction, in telecommunications systems; FAULT-TOLERANT
    TELECOMMUNICATION SYSTEM PATTERNS ◆ 57, MINIMIZE
    HUMAN INTERVENTION ◆ 57
MAKE CHAMPIONS EXPLICIT ◆ 74
  CHAMPIONS REVIEW PAPERS relationship to; CHAMPIONS
    REVIEW PAPERS ◆ 74
  IDENTIFY THE CONFLICTS relationship to; IDENTIFY THE
    CONFLICTS ◆ 74
MAKE THE USER WORRY ◆ 72
  MEMORY BUDGET relationship to; MAKE THE USER
    WORRY ◆ 72
  MEMORY OVERDRAFT relationship to; MEMORY
    OVERDRAFT ◆ 72
  THINK SMALL relationship to; THINK SMALL ◆ 72
MANAGED OBJECT ◆ 115
management
  of Big Ball of Mud code, through isolation; SWEEPING IT
    UNDER THE RUG ◆ 21
  cache, in a relational database; CACHE MANAGEMENT ◆ 109
  CACHE MANAGEMENT ◆ 109
  of class instances; MANAGER ◆ 86
  of components, in a network management system;
    MANAGER-AGENT ◆ 114
  IDENTITY MANAGEMENT ◆ 90
  LOCALIZED OWNERSHIP: MANAGING DYNAMIC OBJECTS IN
    C++ ◆ 85
  MANAGED OBJECT ◆ 115
  MANAGER ◆ 86
    BROKER relationship to; MANAGER ◆ 86
    CLIENT-DISPATCHER-SERVER relationship to;
      MANAGER ◆ 86
    MANAGER-AGENT relationship to; MANAGER-AGENT ◆ 114
    POOL relationship to; POOL ◆ 134
  MANAGER-AGENT ◆ 114
    ADAPTER relationship to; MANAGER-AGENT ◆ 114
    BROKER relationship to; MANAGER-AGENT ◆ 114
    MANAGER relationship to; MANAGER-AGENT ◆ 114
    MEDIATOR relationship to; MANAGER-AGENT ◆ 114
    REMOTE OPERATION relationship to;
      MANAGER-AGENT ◆ 114
  MANAGING AND MEETING CUSTOMER EXPECTATIONS ◆ 140
    BEHAVIORAL REQUIREMENTS relationship to; MANAGING
      AND MEETING CUSTOMER EXPECTATIONS ◆ 140
    PRAGMATIC EXTERNAL REQUIREMENTS relationship
      to; MANAGING AND MEETING CUSTOMER
      EXPECTATIONS ◆ 140
    PROTOTYPES relationship to; MANAGING AND MEETING
      CUSTOMER EXPECTATIONS ◆ 140
  MEDIATOR, MANAGER-AGENT relationship to;
    MANAGER-AGENT ◆ 114
  of memory, strategies for; HIGH-LEVEL AND PROCESS
    PATTERNS FROM THE MEMORY PRESERVATION SOCIETY ◆ 71

network management interfaces; Pattern System for
Network Management Interfaces ♦ 114
of organizations, configuration management strategies applied
to; Teamwork and Configuration Management ♦ 170
Pattern System for Network Management
Interfaces ♦ 114
of resources, in distributed systems; Resource
Exchanger ♦ 144
software development; Surviving Object-Oriented
Projects: A Manager's Guide ♦ 168
distractions, handling; Someone Always Makes
Progress ♦ 169, Team per Task ♦ 169, Sacrifice One
Person ♦ 170
distractions, protecting against; Fire Walls ♦ 67
Scrum process; Scrum: A Pattern Language for
Hyperproductive Software Development ♦ 146
Surviving Object-Oriented Projects: A Manager's
Guide ♦ 168
Teamwork and Configuration Management ♦ 170
of work flow, integration components use; Work Flow
Manager ♦ 115
Work Flow Manager ♦ 115
Manager ♦ 86
[Sommerlad98]; 196
Manager-Agent ♦ 114
Managing and Meeting Customer Expectations ♦ 140
Mandatory Elements Present ♦ 102
Findable Sections relationship to; Findable
Sections ♦ 103
Pattern relationship to; Pattern ♦ 102
Readable References to Patterns relationship to;
Readable References to Patterns ♦ 104
Single-Pass Readable relationship to; Single-Pass
Readable ♦ 103
manners
See Also human relationships
Mind Your Manners ♦ 44
Manolescu, D. A.
[Manolescu99]; 190
Feature Extraction—A Pattern for Information
Retrieval ♦ 58
manufacturing
computer-integrated, G++ pattern language; G++: A
Pattern Language for Computer-Integrated
Manufacturing ♦ 61
G++: A Pattern Language for Computer-Integrated
Manufacturing ♦ 61
many-to-many relationships
designing, Relationship Object; Relationship
Object ♦ 20
problem domain, identifying; Identify Problem Domain
Relationships ♦ 70
transaction posting; Posting ♦ 35
many-to-one relationships
Chain of Responsibility as a design strategy for; Chain of
Responsibility ♦ 32
classifying similar associations; Typed Relationship ♦ 5
establishing a unique reference, account number use for;
Account Number ♦ 4

mapping
Historic Mapping ♦ 16
keyed, as relationship implementation; Keyed Mapping ♦ 16
objects, dictionary use for; Dictionary ♦ 159
objects to relational databases; Crossing Chasms: A Pattern
Language for Object-RDBMS Integration ♦ 41,
Objects from Records ♦ 90, Pattern Language
for Smalltalk & Relational Databases ♦ 106,
Representing Objects as Tables ♦ 107
metadata use for; Object Metadata ♦ 108
state classes, to objects with multiple states; For Complex
Moods, Use a Mood Alternator ♦ 89
market(ing)
Market Walk-through ♦ 52
Implied Requirements relationship to; Market
Walk-through ♦ 52, Implied Requirements ♦ 52
Product Initiative relationship to; Product
Initiative ♦ 52
Sponsor Objectives relationship to; Sponsor
Objectives ♦ 140
Organization Follows Market ♦ 65
segments, impact on team organization structure;
Organization Follows Market ♦ 65
state, scenario representation of; Scenario ♦ 13
strategies, for software artifacts; First One's Free ♦ 151,
Winning Team ♦ 151
Market Walk-through ♦ 52
Marques, J. A.
[Silva+98]; 196
Object Recovery ♦ 92
[Silva+99]; 196
Object Synchronizer ♦ 92
Martin, J.
[Martin+98]; 190
Martin, R. C.
[Martin95a]; 190
[Martin95b]; 190
Abstract Client ♦ 2
Iterable Container ♦ 80
Member Container ♦ 86
Three-Level FSMe ♦ 172
Write a Loop Once ♦ 179
[Martin95c]; 190
Approaches for separating clients from servers ♦ 16,
❖ 16
[Martin98]; 190
Acyclic Visitor ♦ 6
[PLoPD3]; 192
master
Master-Journeyman ♦ 119
Master-Slave ♦ 86
Master-Journeyman ♦ 119
Master-Slave ♦ 86
[Buschmann+96]; 183
[Buschmann95]; 183
Masuda, G. M.
[Masuda+98]; 190

match
  MATCH PROGRESS WORK WITH NEW ♦ 101
    FRESH WORK BEFORE STALE relationship to; FRESH WORK
      BEFORE STALE ♦ 101, MATCH PROGRESS WORK WITH
      NEW ♦ 101
    SHED LOAD relationship to; SHED LOAD ♦ 101, MATCH
      PROGRESS WORK WITII NEW ♦ 101
    SUBFORM MATCH ♦ 100
MATCH PROGRESS WORK WITH NEW ♦ 101
MATERIAL CONTAINER ♦ 111
material(s)
  constraints
    coordinating changes with tools; TOOL COORDINATOR ♦ 111
    separating from tools; MATERIAL CONTAINER ♦ 111
  decoupling from tools; MATERIALS ♦ 109
  grouping into containers; MATERIAL CONTAINER ♦ 111
  MATERIAL CONTAINER ♦ 111
  MATERIALIZATION ♦ 90
    CREATING AND UPDATING BUSINESS OBJECTS relationship
      to; CREATING AND UPDATING BUSINESS OBJECTS ♦ 91
    OBJECTS FROM RECORDS relationship to;
      MATERIALIZATION ♦ 90
    PROXY relationship to; MATERIALIZATION ♦ 90
    REQUEST relationship to; MATERIALIZATION ♦ 90
  MATERIALS ♦ 109
    ASPECTS relationship to; MATERIALS ♦ 109, ASPECTS ♦ 109
    TOOLS relationship to; MATERIALS ♦ 109
  relationship
    to aspects; ASPECTS ♦ 109
    of environment to; ENVIRONMENT ♦ 110
    to tools; TOOLS ♦ 109
    to tools, representation of; TOOL AND MATERIAL
      COUPLING ♦ 110
  TOOL AND MATERIAL COUPLING ♦ 110
  Tools and Materials Metaphor; PATTERN LANGUAGE FOR TOOL
    CONSTRUCTION AND INTEGRATION BASED ON THE TOOLS
    AND MATERIALS METAPHOR ♦ 109
MATERIALIZATION ♦ 90
MATERIALS ♦ 109
mathematics
  See Also addition; algebra
  algebraic types, C++ IDIOMS pattern language; C++
    IDIOMS ♦ 24
  conversion ratio, between units, defining; CONVERSION
    RATIO ♦ 8
  quantity representation; QUANTITY ♦ 8
matrix organizations
  modeling; MULTIPLE HIERARCHIC ASSOCIATIONS ♦ 4
Mayfield, M.
  [Coad95]; 185
McKenney, P. E.
  [McKenney96a]; 190
    SELECTING LOCKING DESIGNS FOR PARALLEL
      PROGRAMS ❖ 147
  [McKenney96b]; 191
    SELECTING LOCKING PRIMITIVES FOR PARALLEL
      PROGRAMMING ❖ 148

MDC (Modification Detection Code)
  memory requirement reduction use; SIGNATURE WITH
    APPENDIX ♦ 175
  for message integrity; MESSAGE INTEGRITY ♦ 174
    with secrecy preservation use; SECRECY WITH
      INTEGRITY ♦ 175
MEALLY ♦ 59
MEANINGFUL METAPHOR NAME ♦ 104
  EVOCATIVE PATTERN NAME relationship to; EVOCATIVE
    PATTERN NAME ♦ 104, MEANINGFUL METAPHOR
    NAME ♦ 104
  NOUN PHRASE NAME relationship to; NOUN PHRASE
    NAME ♦ 104, MEANINGFUL METAPHOR NAME ♦ 104
MEANINGLESS BEHAVIOR ♦ 32
  EXCEPTIONAL VALUE relationship to; MEANINGLESS
    BEHAVIOR ♦ 32
  VISIBLE IMPLICATION relationship to; VISIBLE
    IMPLICATION ♦ 33
  WHOLE VALUE relationship to; MEANINGLESS BEHAVIOR ♦ 32
MEASUREMENT ♦ 8
MEASUREMENT PROTOCOL ♦ 9
measurements
  categorizing; RANGE ♦ 9
  encapsulating; MEASUREMENT ♦ 8
  MEASUREMENT ♦ 8
    OBSERVATION relationship to; OBSERVATION ♦ 8
    SUBTYPING OBSERVATION CONCEPTS relationship to;
      SUBTYPING OBSERVATION CONCEPTS ♦ 8
  MEASUREMENT PROTOCOL ♦ 9
  of performance, strategies for; PERFORMANCE
    MEASUREMENT ♦ 82
  PERFORMANCE MEASUREMENT ♦ 82
  protocols, in corporate analysis; MEASUREMENT
    PROTOCOL ♦ 9
mechanisms
  EVENT MECHANISM ♦ 110
media
  as first class object, in a session; PARTIES & MEDIA AS FIRST
    CLASS CITIZENS ♦ 96
  PARTIES & MEDIA AS FIRST CLASS CITIZENS ♦ 96
MEDIATING PROTOCOL ♦ 155
mediation
  MEDIATING PROTOCOL ♦ 155
  MEDIATOR ♦ 86
    ABSTRACT SESSION relationship to; ABSTRACT SESSION ♦ 2
    FACADE relationship to; MEDIATOR ♦ 86
    HALF-SYNC/HALF-ASYNC relationship to;
      HALF-SYNC/HALF-ASYNC ♦ 71
    NavigationObserver relationship to;
      NavigationObserver ♦ 48
    OBSERVER relationship to; MEDIATOR ♦ 86, OBSERVER ♦ 94
MEDIATOR ♦ 86
  [Alpert+98]; 182
  [Gamma+95]; 188
medical
  See health care
meeting(s)
  CUSTOMER MEETINGS: GO EARLY, STAY LATE ♦ 44
  MANAGING AND MEETING CUSTOMER EXPECTATIONS ♦ 140

RECOMMITMENT MEETING ♦ 53
SCRUM MEETING ♦ 147
MEGA-SCROLLING ♦ 90
Megert, D.
 [Riehle+98]; 193
  SERIALIZER ♦ 151
MEMBER CONTAINER ♦ 86
 [Martin95b]; 190
members
 data, determining where to place; STATE MEMBER ♦ 166
 MEMBER CONTAINER ♦ 86
 STATE MEMBER ♦ 166
membership
 DIVERSITY OF MEMBERSHIP ♦ 95
MEMENTO ♦ 87
 [Alpert+98]; 182
 [Gamma+95]; 188
memento
 MEMENTO ♦ 87
  ASYNCHRONOUS COMPLETION TOKEN relationship to;
   ASYNCHRONOUS COMPLETION TOKEN ♦ 19
  COMMAND relationship to; COMMAND ♦ 35, MEMENTO ♦ 87
  OBJECT RECOVERY relationship to; OBJECT RECOVERY ♦ 92
  ROLLBACK relationship to; ROLLBACK ♦ 38
 MEMENTO CHILD ♦ 35
  HISTORY ON SELF relationship to; MEMENTO CHILD ♦ 35
MEMENTO CHILD ♦ 35
MEMO ACCOUNT ♦ 11
memory
 allocation, performance strategies; ALLOCATOR CACHES ♦ 148
 budget, establishing for restricted memory software
  development; MEMORY BUDGET ♦ 72
 HIGH-LEVEL AND PROCESS PATTERNS FROM THE MEMORY
  PRESERVATION SOCIETY ♦ 71
 management
  handling unpredictable demands on; MAKE THE USER
   WORRY ♦ 72
  providing user controls for; MAKE THE USER WORRY ♦ 72
  reference counting use; COUNTED POINTER ♦ 40
  strategies for; HIGH-LEVEL AND PROCESS PATTERNS FROM
   THE MEMORY PRESERVATION SOCIETY ♦ 71
 MEMORY BUDGET ♦ 72
  MAKE THE USER WORRY relationship to; MAKE THE USER
   WORRY ♦ 72
  MEMORY OVERDRAFT relationship to; MEMORY
   OVERDRAFT ♦ 72
  THINK SMALL relationship to; THINK SMALL ♦ 72
 MEMORY OVERDRAFT ♦ 72
  CAPTAIN OATES relationship to; MEMORY OVERDRAFT ♦ 72
  EXHAUSTION TEST relationship to; MEMORY
   OVERDRAFT ♦ 72
  MAKE THE USER WORRY relationship to; MEMORY
   OVERDRAFT ♦ 72
  MEMORY BUDGET relationship to; MEMORY
   OVERDRAFT ♦ 72
 MEMORY PERFORMANCE ASSESSMENT ♦ 73
  THINK SMALL relationship to; THINK SMALL ♦ 72

 requirements, reducing in cryptographic systems; SIGNATURE
  WITH APPENDIX ♦ 175, SECRECY WITH SIGNATURE WITH
  APPENDIX ♦ 175
 restrictions
  development software development culture for handling;
   THINK SMALL ♦ 72
  handling unpredictable demands on; MEMORY
   OVERDRAFT ♦ 72
  performance considerations; MEMORY PERFORMANCE
   ASSESSMENT ♦ 73
  strategies for handling; HIGH-LEVEL AND PROCESS
   PATTERNS FROM THE MEMORY PRESERVATION
   SOCIETY ♦ 71
  test-and-set locking use in the face of; TEST-AND-SET
   LOCK ♦ 148
  testing out-of-memory conditions; EXHAUSTION TEST ♦ 73
 running out of, handling; PARTIAL FAILURE ♦ 72, CAPTAIN
  OATES ♦ 72
MEMORY BUDGET ♦ 72
MEMORY OVERDRAFT ♦ 72
MEMORY PERFORMANCE ASSESSMENT ♦ 73
memos
 accounts, creating; MEMO ACCOUNT ♦ 11
 MEMO ACCOUNT ♦ 11
  Account relationship to; MEMO ACCOUNT ♦ 11
  BOOKING ENTRIES TO MULTIPLE ACCOUNTS relationship to;
   BOOKING ENTRIES TO MULTIPLE ACCOUNTS ♦ 12
  TRANSACTION relationship to; MEMO ACCOUNT ♦ 11
 technical, as design documentation; TECHNICAL MEMO ♦ 54
 TECHNICAL MEMO ♦ 54
Menga, G.
 [Aarsten+95]; 181
  G++: A PATTERN LANGUAGE FOR COMPUTER-INTEGRATED
   MANUFACTURING ❖ 61
 [Aarsten+96a]; 181
  FROM PROTOTYPE TO REALITY ♦ 61
 [Aarsten+96b]; 181
  OBJECT-ORIENTED DESIGN PATTERNS IN REACTIVE
   SYSTEMS ❖ 92
  REMOTE CONTROL ♦ 144
mentoring
 in team training strategy; APPRENTICE ♦ 64
MERCENARY ANALYST ♦ 67
 SACRIFICE ONE PERSON relationship to; SACRIFICE ONE
  PERSON ♦ 170
MERGE COMPATIBLE EVENTS ♦ 76
merging
 MERGE COMPATIBLE EVENTS ♦ 76
  DECOUPLE EXECUTION AND OUTPUT relationship to;
   DECOUPLE EXECUTION AND OUTPUT ♦ 76
  EVENT QUEUE relationship to; EVENT QUEUE ♦ 76, MERGE
   COMPATIBLE EVENTS ♦ 76
 OBJECT MERGE ♦ 10
MESSAGE ♦ 154
MESSAGE INTEGRITY ♦ 174
MESSAGE PACKET ♦ 75
messages/messaging
 authentication of, as cryptographic strategy; SENDER
  AUTHENTICATION ♦ 174

messages/messaging *continued*
  cascade
    formatting; CASCADE ♦ 163
    using; YOURSELF ♦ 163
  as computation invocation mechansims; MESSAGE ♦ 154
  cooperating object use; DISPATCHED INTERPRETATION ♦ 155
  DECOMPOSING MESSAGE ♦ 154
  diagnostic
    logging of; PATTERNS FOR LOGGING DIAGNOSTIC
      MESSAGES ♦ 124
    logging of, strategies for; DIAGNOSTIC LOGGER ♦ 124
  as distrbuted system communication device; BROKER ♦ 22
  encrypted, verification of; SECRECY WITH INTEGRITY ♦ 175
  encryption, secret key use with; INFORMATION SECRECY ♦ 174
  engineering model, for asynchronous interactive support;
    MESSAGING ENGINEERING MODEL ♦ 18
  error
    ordering of, in fault-tolerant systems; TIMESTAMP ♦ 77
    strategies for overload handling; GEORGE WASHINGTON IS
      STILL DEAD ♦ 78, FIVE MINUTES OF NO ESCALATION
      MESSAGES ♦ 78
  flow, strategies for coding; REVERSING METHOD ♦ 153
  formatting; INLINE MESSAGE PATTERN ♦ 162
  formatting multiple; CASCADE ♦ 163
  IDENTIFY MESSAGE LAYERS ♦ 145
  indenting; INDENTED CONTROL FLOW ♦ 162
  INLINE MESSAGE PATTERN ♦ 162
  instance creation use; SHORTCUT CONSTRUCTOR
    METHOD ♦ 152
  integrity, strategies for ensuring; MESSAGE INTEGRITY ♦ 174
  INTENTION REVEALING MESSAGE ♦ 154
  MESSAGE ♦ 154
  Message Authentication Codes (MAC)
    message sender authentication use; SENDER
      AUTHENTICATION ♦ 174
    sender authentication use; SECRECY WITH SENDER
      AUTHENTICATION ♦ 175
  MESSAGE INTEGRITY ♦ 174
  MESSAGE PACKET ♦ 75
    OBSERVER relationship to; MESSAGE PACKET ♦ 75
  MESSAGING ENGINEERING MODEL ♦ 18
    BATCH ENGINEERING MODEL relationship to; BATCH
      ENGINEERING MODEL ♦ 19
    ONLINE ENGINEERING MODEL relationship to; MESSAGING
      ENGINEERING MODEL ♦ 18
    STREAM I-O ENGINEERING MODEL relationship to; STREAM
      I-O ENGINEERING MODEL ♦ 19
  modification, detection of, as cryptographic strategy; MESSAGE
    INTEGRITY ♦ 174
  object value access, encapsulation of; ENCAPSULATE SENDERS
    OF VALUE AND VALUE: ♦ 177
  OBSERVER UPDATE MESSAGE ♦ 75
  one-way designs
    concurrency mechanisms; THREAD-PER-MESSAGE ♦ 39
    flow network handling; FLOW NETWORKS ♦ 40
  optimization, in state update information transmission;
    OPTIMIZED MESSAGES PER CHANGE REQUEST ♦ 75
  OPTIMIZED MESSAGES PER CHANGE REQUEST ♦ 75
  PATTERNS FOR LOGGING DIAGNOSTIC MESSAGES ♦ 124
  replacing message to self, with messages to an argument;
    CLIENT-SPECIFIED SELF ♦ 34
  routing, without I/O channel blocking; ROUTER ♦ 146
  selecting multiple alternative computations with; CHOOSING
    MESSAGE ♦ 154
  sender, encapsulation; ENCAPSULATE SENDERS OF VALUE AND
    VALUE: ♦ 177
  sender identity validation; SIGNATURE ♦ 175
  sending to self
    when intention is simple; INTENTION REVEALING
      MESSAGE ♦ 154
    to invoke parts of computation; DECOMPOSING
      MESSAGE ♦ 154
  signature, secrecy preservation; SECRECY WITH
    SIGNATURE ♦ 175
  stream engineering model support of; STREAM I-O
    ENGINEERING MODEL ♦ 19
  THREAD-PER-MESSAGE ♦ 39
  urgent
    fault-tolerant mechanisms for sending; STRING A WIRE ♦ 80
    as fault-tolerant mechanisms for sending; RAW IO ♦ 80
MESSAGING ENGINEERING MODEL ♦ 18
Meszaros, G.
  [Meszaros+98]; 191
    PATTERN LANGUAGE FOR PATTERN WRITING ❖ 102
  [Meszaros95]; 191
    HALF-OBJECT + PROTOCOL ♦ 71
  [Meszaros96]; 191
    PATTERN LANGUAGE FOR IMPROVING THE CAPACITY OF
      REACTIVE SYSTEMS ❖ 100
meta level
  See knowledge level
metadata
  object, mapping objects to relational database schemas;
    OBJECT METADATA ♦ 108
  OBJECT METADATA ♦ 108
  system control by; REFLECTION ♦ 144
METAMORPHOSIS ♦ 55
metamorphosis
  See Also CATERPILLAR'S FATE: A PATTERN LANGUAGE
    FOR THE TRANSFORMATION FROM ANALYSIS TO DESIGN;
    evolution; software, development; transformation
  EVOLUTION, ARCHITECTURE, AND METAMORPHOSIS ♦ 55
  METAMORPHOSIS ♦ 55
    PROTOTYPE-BASED OBJECT SYSTEM relationship to;
      PROTOTYPE-BASED OBJECT SYSTEM ♦ 139
    SOFTWARE TECTONICS relationship to; SOFTWARE
      TECTONICS ♦ 55
metaphors
  MEANINGFUL METAPHOR NAME ♦ 104
  PATTERN LANGUAGE FOR TOOL CONSTRUCTION AND
    INTEGRATION BASED ON THE TOOLS AND MATERIALS
    METAPHOR ♦ 109
  Tools and Materials Metaphor; PATTERN LANGUAGE FOR TOOL
    CONSTRUCTION AND INTEGRATION BASED ON THE TOOLS
    AND MATERIALS METAPHOR ♦ 109
METHOD ADAPTERS ♦ 37
METHOD COMMENT ♦ 154
METHOD OBJECT ♦ 153

methods
adapters, before and after methods; METHOD ADAPTERS ♦ 37
attaching to instances; INDIVIDUAL INSTANCE METHOD ♦ 11
COLLECTION ACCESSOR METHOD ♦ 157
commenting; METHOD COMMENT ♦ 154
COMPARING METHOD ♦ 153
COMPOSED METHOD ♦ 152
CONSTANT METHOD ♦ 157
CONSTRUCTOR METHOD ♦ 152
CONSTRUCTOR PARAMETER METHOD ♦ 152
CONVERTER CONSTRUCTOR METHOD ♦ 153
CONVERTER METHOD ♦ 153
creating objects for; METHOD OBJECT ♦ 153
DEBUG PRINTING METHOD ♦ 154
DEFAULT VALUE METHOD ♦ 157
encapsulation, in concurrent programs; SESSION ♦ 37
ENUMERATION METHOD ♦ 158
EQUALITY METHOD ♦ 159
EXECUTE AROUND METHOD ♦ 154
FOR STATE MACHINES, USE TRANSITION METHODS ♦ 88
GETTING METHOD ♦ 157
HASHING METHOD ♦ 159
HOOK METHOD ♦ 73
INDIVIDUAL INSTANCE METHOD ♦ 11
METHOD ADAPTERS ♦ 37
METHOD COMMENT ♦ 154
METHOD OBJECT ♦ 153
    CONSTRUCTOR METHOD relationship to; METHOD
    OBJECT ♦ 153
naming; INTENTION REVEALING SELECTOR ♦ 154
overriding, in superclass; EXTENDING SUPER ♦ 155,
    MODIFYING SUPER ♦ 155
performance improvement, caching use; CACHING TEMPORARY
    VARIABLE ♦ 158
polymorphic, adding to unrelated classes; EXTERNAL
    POLYMORPHISM ♦ 56
QUERY METHOD ♦ 153
REVERSING METHOD ♦ 153
SETTING METHOD ♦ 157
SHORTCUT CONSTRUCTOR METHOD ♦ 152
stateless
    open call use; OPEN CALLS ♦ 38
    passing messages through a host to a helper; PASS-THROUGH
    HOST ♦ 38
task composition of; COMPOSED METHOD ♦ 152
TEMPLATE METHOD ♦ 171
that contain each other, coding; EXECUTE AROUND
    METHOD ♦ 154
Metsker, S. J.
[Metsker98]; 191
    JUDGE ♦ 81
Meunier, R.
[Buschmann+96]; 183
    BLACKBOARD ♦ 22
    BROKER ♦ 22
    CLIENT-DISPATCHER-SERVER ♦ 34
    COMMAND PROCESSOR ♦ 36
    COUNTED POINTER ♦ 40
    FORWARDER-RECEIVER ♦ 60

    LAYERS ♦ 81
    MASTER-SLAVE ♦ 86
    MICROKERNEL ♦ 87
    MODEL-VIEW-CONTROLLER ♦ 87
    PIPES & FILTERS ♦ 132
    PRESENTATION-ABSTRACTION-CONTROL ♦ 135
    PROXY ♦ 139
    PUBLISHER-SUBSCRIBER ♦ 139
    REFLECTION ♦ 144
    VIEW HANDLER ♦ 178
    WHOLE-PART ♦ 179
[Meunier95]; 191
    PIPES & FILTERS ♦ 132
MICROCOSM ♦ 168
CLEAR THE FOG relationship to; CLEAR THE FOG ♦ 168,
    MICROCOSM ♦ 168
MICROKERNEL ♦ 87
BROKER relationship to; MICROKERNEL ♦ 87
[Buschmann+96]; 183
LAYERS relationship to; LAYERS ♦ 81
REFLECTION relationship to; MICROKERNEL ♦ 87,
    REFLECTION ♦ 144
Microsoft software
See BIG BALL OF MUD PATTERN LANGUAGE
middleware
network management interfaces; PATTERN SYSTEM FOR
    NETWORK MANAGEMENT INTERFACES ♦ 114
MIND xxx
MIND YOUR MANNERS ♦ 44
    BE AWARE OF BOUNDARIES relationship to; BE AWARE OF
    BOUNDARIES ♦ 44
    BE RESPONSIVE relationship to; BE RESPONSIVE ♦ 44
    BUILD TRUST relationship to; MIND YOUR MANNERS ♦ 44
    IT'S A RELATIONSHIP, NOT A SALE relationship to; MIND
    YOUR MANNERS ♦ 44
    KNOW THE CUSTOMER relationship to; MIND YOUR
    MANNERS ♦ 44
    LISTEN, LISTEN, LISTEN relationship to; LISTEN, LISTEN,
    LISTEN ♦ 44
    SHOW PERSONAL INTEGRITY relationship to; MIND YOUR
    MANNERS ♦ 44
MIND YOUR OWN BUSINESS ♦ 77
    BELTLINE TERMINAL relationship to; MIND YOUR OWN
    BUSINESS ♦ 77, BELTLINE TERMINAL ♦ 79
    IO GATEKEEPER relationship to; MIND YOUR OWN
    BUSINESS ♦ 77
    MML relationship to; MML ♦ 77
    PSEUDO-IO relationship to; PSEUDO-IO ♦ 79
    WHO ASKED? relationship to; WHO ASKED? ♦ 78
MIND YOUR MANNERS ♦ 44
MIND YOUR OWN BUSINESS ♦ 77
MINIMIZE HUMAN INTERVENTION ♦ 57
PEOPLE KNOW BEST relationship to; MINIMIZE HUMAN
    INTERVENTION ♦ 57, PEOPLE KNOW BEST ♦ 57
mining
pattern, writing patterns from results of; PATTERN ♦ 102
mismatch
SUBFORM MISMATCH ♦ 100
MIX NEW AND OLD ♦ 116

mixture
   Mix New and Old ◆ 116
   Skill Mix ◆ 135
MML ◆ 77
   Bottom Line relationship to; MML ◆ 77
   George Washington is Still Dead relationship to;
     MML ◆ 77
   IO Triage relationship to; MML ◆ 77
   Mind Your Own Business relationship to; MML ◆ 77
   Pseudo-IO relationship to; MML ◆ 77
   Who Asked relationship to; MML ◆ 77
Model Hierarchy ◆ 136
Model-View-Controller ◆ 87
   [Buschmann+96]; 183
models/modeling
   See Also relationships
   abstract, domain rule enforcement with subtypes; Abstract
     Models with Constraints in Subtypes ◆ 4
   Abstract Models with Constraints in Subtypes ◆ 4
   application
     decoupling from domain model; Two Applications ◆ 97
     as Smalltalk client-server system layer; Four-Layer
       Architecture ◆ 106
   Appropriate Living Models ◆ 45
   behavior, event-centered architecture; Event-Centered
     Architecture ◆ 129
   behavioral, database design role; Table Design Time ◆ 42
   business systems, architectural characteristics of;
     Architecture Patterns for Business Systems ◆ 18
   for call processing, design issues; Decision Deferral and
     Capture Pattern Language ◆ 45
   change independence, as design guideline; Appropriate
     Living Models ◆ 45
   client/server/service model, resource and service
     standardization; Client/Server/Service ◆ 62
   computer, validation of; Forecast Confirmation ◆ 33
   data
     causality flow tracing; Time Thread Analysis ◆ 71
     creation strategies; Animate the Data ◆ 70
     defining; Define the Data Structure ◆ 70
     integrating into implementation; Introduce Virtual
       Attributes ◆ 70
   defining content based on decisions captured by the model;
     Decision-Based Models ◆ 45
   domain
     decoupling from application model; Two Applications ◆ 97
     decoupling user interface from, in application layer;
       Presentation and Application Logic ◆ 15
     with general accounting patterns; Specialized Account
       Model ◆ 12
     as Smalltalk client-server system layer; Four-Layer
       Architecture ◆ 106
   engineering
     batch, for batch processing; Batch Engineering
       Model ◆ 19
     messaging, forasynchronous interactive support; Messaging
       Engineering Model ◆ 18
     for online interactive systems; Online Engineering
       Model ◆ 18

     software architecture definition by; Architecture
       Patterns for Business Systems ◆ 18
     stream, for support of batch, interactive, and messaging
       systems; Stream I-O Engineering Model ◆ 19
   Executable Models ◆ 45
   hypothetical, error detection use; Hypothetical
     Publication ◆ 33
   I/O, integrating synchronous and asynchronous;
     Half-Sync/Half-Async ◆ 71
   interaction, peer-to-peer, decoupling peers from underlying
     communication mechanisms; Forwarder-Receiver ◆ 60
   Java panel interaction with; Pluggable View
     Controller ◆ 132
   matrix organizations; Multiple Hierarchic
     Associations ◆ 4
   Messaging Engineering Model ◆ 18
   Model Hierarchy ◆ 136
   Model-View-Controller ◆ 87
     Online Engineering Model relationship to; Online
       Engineering Model ◆ 18
     Pluggable View Controller relationship to; Pluggable
       View Controller ◆ 132
     Presentation-Abstraction-Control relationship to;
       Model-View-Controller ◆ 87
     Session Control & Observation relationship to;
       Model-View-Controller ◆ 87
   multi-level
     change propagation; Downward Changes ◆ 45
     communication among different levels; Upward
       Traceability ◆ 45
   object
     defining a database schema to support; Pattern Language
       for Smalltalk & Relational Databases ◆ 106
     designing relational database tables that represent; Table
       Design Time ◆ 107
   object change; Temporal Property ◆ 171
   Online Engineering Model ◆ 18
   organizations
     hierarchies, recursion use for; Organization
       Hierarchies ◆ 7
     patterns for; Accountability and Organizational
       Structures pattern language ◆ 4
   people, in a transaction processing system; People, Places,
     and Things ◆ 165
   places, in a transaction processing system; People, Places,
     and Things ◆ 165
   Presentation-Abstraction-Control,
     Model-View-Controller relationship to;
     Model-View-Controller ◆ 87
   prototyping as design tool for; Executable Models ◆ 45
   related object groups, with Abstract Factorys; Abstract
     Factory ◆ 2
   of relationships, in OO programs; Basic Relationship
     Patterns ◆ 19
   relationships, between two objects; Elevate References to
     Enhance Reuse ◆ 124
   responsibilities; Accountability ◆ 7
   shared information, integration mechanism for; Shared
     Repository ◆ 115

Specialized Account Model ♦ 12
state changes, FSM use; Basic FSM ♦ 58
Stream I-O Engineering Model ♦ 19
things, in a transaction processing system; People, Places, and Things ♦ 165

moderator
Moderator Guides the Workshop ♦ 112
   Open Review relationship to; Moderator Guides the Workshop ♦ 112
   Safe Setting relationship to; Safe Setting ♦ 111, Moderator Guides the Workshop ♦ 112
   role, in pattern writers workshops; Moderator Guides the Workshop ♦ 112
Moderator Guides the Workshop ♦ 112
modifications
message, detection of, as cryptographic strategy; Message Integrity ♦ 174
Modification Detection Code (MDC)
   memory requirement reduction use; Signature with Appendix ♦ 175
   message integrity; Message Integrity ♦ 174
   with message integrity, with secrecy preservation use; Secrecy with Integrity ♦ 175
Modifying Super ♦ 155
Request Screen Modification ♦ 144
to transactions, handling; Adjusting Transactions ♦ 173
Modifying Super ♦ 155
Module's Story ♦ 116
modules/modularity
code, ownership guidelines; Code Ownership ♦ 66
Distribution of Control Modules ♦ 63
Interface to Control Modules ♦ 62
languages without support for, architectural structures for; Main Plus Subroutines ♦ 125
Module's Story ♦ 116
   Acquaintance Examples relationship to; Module's Story ♦ 116
   Visible Checklist relationship to; Module's Story ♦ 116, Visible Checklist ♦ 117
Visibility and Communication between Control Modules ♦ 61
Molin, P.
[Molin+98]; 191
   Points and Deviations: Pattern Language of Fire Alarm Systems ♦ 133
money
options relationship to; Options ♦ 14
representing; Quantity ♦ 8
Month End Closing ♦ 173
Continuous Processing relationship to; Continuous Processing ♦ 174
MOODS: Models for Object-Oriented Design of State ♦ 87
See Also change, state
Finite State Machine Patterns relationship to; MOODS: Models for Object-Oriented Design of State ♦ 87
For Complex MOODS, Use a MOOD Alternator ♦ 89
[Ran96]; 193

State Object relationship to; MOODS: Models for Object-Oriented Design of State ♦ 87
State Patterns relationship to; MOODS: Models for Object-Oriented Design of State ♦ 87
State relationship to; MOODS: Models for Object-Oriented Design of State ♦ 87, State ♦ 166
When Events Cause MOODS, Use State Machine ♦ 88
When There Are Many MOODS, Use MOOD Classifier ♦ 89
Moore ♦ 59
morale
team, high-level manager/champion role; Patron ♦ 65
Mosconi, L.
[Aarsten+96b]; 181
   Object-Oriented Design Patterns in Reactive Systems ❖ 92
   Remote Control ♦ 144
motivation
of software development teams; Compensate Success ♦ 69
Move Responsibilities ♦ 67
moving
Move Responsibilities ♦ 67
Mularz, D. E.
[Mularz95]; 191
   Pattern-Based Integration Architectures ❖ 115
multimedia
artifacts
   composition for reusability; Composing Multimedia Artifacts for Reuse ♦ 36
   gluing together; Glue ♦ 36
   laying out; Components Layout ♦ 36
Composing Multimedia Artifacts for Reuse ♦ 36
factories; Pluggable Factory ♦ 132
presentation, update; Request Screen Modification ♦ 144
presentations
   defining and running; Define and Run Presentation ♦ 36
   synchronizing; Synchronize Channels ♦ 37
sessions, managing; Session Control & Observation ♦ 151
templates, defining; Template ♦ 36
Multiphase Cancellation ♦ 39
multiple
accounts
   booking entries to; Booking Entries to Multiple Accounts ♦ 12
   grouping; Summary Account ♦ 11
   posting rule handling; Posting Rules for Many Accounts ♦ 11
Multiple Access Levels to a Package ♦ 14
Multiple Competing Designs ♦ 118
   Creator-Reviewer relationship to; Multiple Competing Designs ♦ 118
   Decision Document relationship to; Multiple Competing Designs ♦ 118, Decision Document ♦ 118
Multiple Hierarchic Associations ♦ 4
   Recursive Structures for Organizations relationship to; Multiple Hierarchic Associations ♦ 4
Multiple Processors ♦ 128
package access levels, handling; Multiple Access Levels to a Package ♦ 14

multiple *continued*
  processors
    See Also distributed systems
    overload communication among; Leaky Bucket of Credits ◆ 102
Multiple Access Levels to a Package ◆ 14
Multiple Competing Designs ◆ 118
Multiple Hierarchic Associations ◆ 4
Multiple Processors ◆ 128
multiplexing
  Organizational Multiplexing: Patterns for Processing Satellite Telemetry with Distributed Teams ◆ 94
multithreading
  See Also threads
  Active Object support for; Active Object ◆ 6
  sessions use of; Session ◆ 17
Mutable Code ◆ 47
  Catalytic Scenarios relationship to; Mutable Code ◆ 47
  Lightweight User Interfaces relationship to; Mutable Code ◆ 47
  Prototyping Languages relationship to; Mutable Code ◆ 47
mutex
  See locking
mutual
  exclusion, conflict set representation of; Conflict Sets ◆ 39
  Mutual Friends ◆ 20
    Collection Object relationship to; Mutual Friends ◆ 20
    Relationship As Attribute relationship to; Relationship As Attribute ◆ 20, Mutual Friends ◆ 20
    Relationship Object relationship to; Mutual Friends ◆ 20
  Mutual Visibility ◆ 14
Mutual Friends ◆ 20
Mutual Visibility ◆ 14
MVC (Model-View-Controller)
  managing model-view relationships, in legacy system/object-oriented framework interactions; Dependency ◆ 91
  Model-View-Controller ◆ 87
    Dependency relationship to; Dependency ◆ 91
    Presentation-Abstraction-Control relationship to; Presentation-Abstraction-Control ◆ 135
    Session Control & Observation relationship to; Session Control & Observation ◆ 151
    View Handler relationship to; View Handler ◆ 178

Name ◆ 10
Named Stable Bases ◆ 68
naming
  attributes, as system design task; Identify the Nouns ◆ 70
  conventions, defining; Identification Scheme ◆ 10
  enumeration block parameters; Simple Enumeration Parameter ◆ 163
  Meaningful Metaphor Name ◆ 104
  methods; Intention Revealing Selector ◆ 154
  Name ◆ 10

Named Stable Bases ◆ 68
  Configuration Management relationship to; Named Stable Bases ◆ 68
  Incremental Integration relationship to; Incremental Integration ◆ 170
  Independent Workspaces relationship to; Independent Workspaces ◆ 171
  Teamwork relationship to; Named Stable Bases ◆ 68
Noun Phrase Name ◆ 104
parameters; Type Suggesting Parameter Name ◆ 162
patterns; Evocative Pattern Name ◆ 104, Noun Phrase Name ◆ 104, Meaningful Metaphor Name ◆ 104
Qualified Subclass Name ◆ 162
Role Suggesting Instance Variable Name ◆ 158
Role Suggesting Temporary Variable Name ◆ 158
roles, as system design task; Identify the Nouns ◆ 70
service, dispatcher provision of; Client-Dispatcher-Server ◆ 34
Simple Superclass Name ◆ 162
subclasses; Qualified Subclass Name ◆ 162
superclasses; Simple Superclass Name ◆ 162
Type Suggesting Parameter Name ◆ 162
values, as system design task; Identify the Nouns ◆ 70
variables; Role Suggesting Instance Variable Name ◆ 158, Role Suggesting Temporary Variable Name ◆ 158
narrative
  as teaching strategy; Module's Story ◆ 116
natural
  Natural Text Directories ◆ 98
    Natural Text Flow relationship to; Natural Text Flow ◆ 98, Natural Text Directories ◆ 98
    Natural Text Hyperlinks relationship to; Natural Text Directories ◆ 98
  Natural Text Flow ◆ 98
    Natural Text Directories relationship to; Natural Text Flow ◆ 98, Natural Text Directories ◆ 98
    Natural Text Hyperlinks relationship to; Natural Text Flow ◆ 98, Natural Text Hyperlinks ◆ 98
  Natural Text Hyperlinks ◆ 98
    Natural Text Directories relationship to; Natural Text Directories ◆ 98
    Natural Text Flow relationship to; Natural Text Flow ◆ 98, Natural Text Hyperlinks ◆ 98
Natural Text Flow ◆ 98
Natural Text Hyperlinks ◆ 98
navigation
  hypermedia
    information space design; Patterns for Designing Navigable Information Spaces ◆ 119
  strategies for; NavigationStrategy ◆ 48
  user guides; NavigationObserver ◆ 48
  NavigationObserver ◆ 48
    Mediator relationship to; NavigationObserver ◆ 48
    Observer relationship to; NavigationObserver ◆ 48
    Singleton relationship to; NavigationObserver ◆ 48
  NavigationStrategy ◆ 48
    Abstract Factory relationship to; NavigationStrategy ◆ 48

ACCEPTOR relationship to; NAVIGATIONSTRATEGY ◆ 48
FACTORY METHOD relationship to;
NAVIGATIONSTRATEGY ◆ 48
STRATEGY relationship to; NAVIGATIONSTRATEGY ◆ 48
TEMPLATE METHOD relationship to;
NAVIGATIONSTRATEGY ◆ 48
PATTERNS FOR DESIGNING NAVIGABLE INFORMATION
SPACES ◆ 119
strategies, set-based; SET-BASED NAVIGATION ◆ 119
WWW
link organization; NATURAL TEXT DIRECTORIES ◆ 98
related material; REFERENCE SECTION ◆ 98

NavigationObserver ◆ 48

NavigationStrategy ◆ 48

needs
See Also requirements
INFORMATION NEEDS ◆ 141

nested
containment relationships, management of; OBSERVER
UPDATE MESSAGE ◆ 75

networks
dependency, consistent update of objects in; PROPAGATOR: A
FAMILY OF PATTERNS ◆ 138
encapsulating client state, in a Session object; ABSTRACT
SESSION ◆ 2
flow, one-way message handling; FLOW NETWORKS ◆ 40
FLOW NETWORKS ◆ 40
management interfaces; PATTERN SYSTEM FOR NETWORK
MANAGEMENT INTERFACES ◆ 114
PATTERN LANGUAGE OF TRANSPORT SYSTEMS (POINT AND
ROUTE); PATTERN LANGUAGE OF TRANSPORT SYSTEMS
(POINT AND ROUTE) ◆ 114
PATTERN SYSTEM FOR NETWORK MANAGEMENT
INTERFACES ◆ 114
transportation, building; PATTERN LANGUAGE OF TRANSPORT
SYSTEMS (POINT AND ROUTE) ◆ 114

**New Clients with Old Servers: A Pattern Language
for Client/Server Frameworks ◆ 89**
[Wolf+95]; 198

New Document Notification ◆ 99

New xxx
EXPOSABLE GUTS, NEW DOCUMENT NOTIFICATION
relationship to; NEW DOCUMENT NOTIFICATION ◆ 99
NEW CLIENTS WITH OLD SERVERS: A PATTERN LANGUAGE
FOR CLIENT/SERVER FRAMEWORKS ◆ 89
NEW DOCUMENT NOTIFICATION ◆ 99
EXPOSABLE GUTS relationship to; NEW DOCUMENT
NOTIFICATION ◆ 99

News ◆ 120

Nicodemus, K.
[Adams+96]; 181
FAULT-TOLERANT TELECOMMUNICATION SYSTEM
PATTERNS ❖ 57

Nierstrasz, O.
[Nierstrasz99]; 191
IDENTIFY THE CHAMPION PATTERN LANGUAGE ❖ 73

No Subapplications ◆ 97

no-op
null object use; NULL OBJECT ◆ 91

Noble, J.
[Noble+99]; 191
HIGH-LEVEL AND PROCESS PATTERNS FROM THE MEMORY
PRESERVATION SOCIETY ❖ 71
[Noble99a]; 191
BASIC RELATIONSHIP PATTERNS ◆ 19
[Noble99b]; 191
PROTOTYPE-BASED OBJECT SYSTEM ◆ 139

nodes
hypermedia, hypermedia navigation strategies for different
contexts; NODES IN CONTEXT ◆ 119
NODES IN CONTEXT ◆ 119
SET-BASED NAVIGATION relationship to; NODES IN
CONTEXT ◆ 119
transportation network, representation of; POINT ◆ 114

Nodes in Context ◆ 119

non-deterministic
systems, design strategies; BLACKBOARD ◆ 22

Non-Hierarchical Addition ◆ 26
ALGEBRAIC HIERARCHY relationship to; ALGEBRAIC
HIERARCHY ◆ 25
HOMOGENEOUS ADDITION relationship to; NON-HIERARCHICAL
ADDITION ◆ 26
PROMOTE AND ADD relationship to; PROMOTE AND ADD ◆ 26
PROMOTION LADDER relationship to; NON-HIERARCHICAL
ADDITION ◆ 26

Nordberg, M.
[Nordberg98]; 191
DEFAULT VISITOR ◆ 46
EXTRINSIC VISITOR ◆ 56

normalization
NORMALIZE THE ROLES ◆ 70
DEFINE THE DATA STRUCTURE relationship to; DEFINE THE
DATA STRUCTURE ◆ 70
FACTOR OUT COMMON ATTRIBUTES relationship to;
NORMALIZE THE ROLES ◆ 70
IDENTIFY PROBLEM DOMAIN RELATIONSHIPS relationship to;
IDENTIFY PROBLEM DOMAIN RELATIONSHIPS ◆ 70
of roles, as system design strategy; NORMALIZE THE
ROLES ◆ 70

Normalize the Roles ◆ 70

North, M
[Coad95]; 185

notation
See Also terminology
clarification, pattern writing importance; UNDERSTOOD
NOTATIONS ◆ 105
UNDERSTOOD NOTATIONS ◆ 105

notification
event; EVENT NOTIFICATION ◆ 54
mechanisms, audible alarms use; AUDIBLE ALARM ◆ 79
NEW DOCUMENT NOTIFICATION ◆ 99
of objects, when values change; USE ONCHANGESEND:TO: TO
REGISTER INTERESTS ON A VALUE ◆ 176

notifications
EVENT NOTIFICATION ◆ 54

Noun Phrase Name ◆ 104

nouns
IDENTIFY THE NOUNS ◆ 70

nouns *continued*

Noun Phrase Name ♦ 104

Evocative Pattern Name relationship to; Evocative Pattern Name ♦ 104, Noun Phrase Name ♦ 104

Meaningful Metaphor Name relationship to; Noun Phrase Name ♦ 104, Meaningful Metaphor Name ♦ 104

Null Object ♦ 91

Proxy relationship to; Null Object ♦ 91

Singleton relationship to; Null Object ♦ 91

[Woolf98]; 198

numbers

conversion of, automatic recalculation; Use a RangeAdaptor to Channel a Number's Range ♦ 177

sequence of, coding; Interval ♦ 160

Use a RangeAdaptor to Channel a Number's Range ♦ 177

Object Aging ♦ 141

Object Creation ♦ 15

Object Destruction ♦ 15

Object Equivalence ♦ 10

Object Identifier ♦ 42, ♦ 107

Object Merge ♦ 10

Object Metadata ♦ 108

Object Recovery ♦ 92

[Silva+98]; 196

Object Recursion ♦ 92

[Woolf99b]; 198

object(s)

Active Object ♦ 6

adding responsibilities to, dynamically; Decorator ♦ 46

archiving; Historic Mapping ♦ 16

aspects, retrieving and storing; Use an AspectAdaptor to Hold an Aspect of an Object ♦ 177

Association Object ♦ 23

behavior

change relative to state change; State ♦ 166

modeling, mapping tool for relational database design; Table Design Time ♦ 42

parameterization of; Pluggable Behavior ♦ 156

Business Patterns of Association Objects ♦ 23

Categorize Objects for Concurrency ♦ 62

change, over time, strategies for handling; Temporal Patterns ♦ 171

change notification; Use onChangeSend:to: to Register Interests on a Value ♦ 176

Classes of Event Objects ♦ 129

Classifying, Associating, and Grouping the Domain Objects ♦ 141

collaboration among, support for; Use a ValueModel to Generalize an Object's Aspect ♦ 176

collection, uniform interface development; Managed Object ♦ 115

Collection Object ♦ 20

comparing; Comparing Method ♦ 153

Composable Query Objects ♦ 41

conversion of

different protocol; Converter Constructor Method ♦ 153

same protocol; Converter Method ♦ 153

stream data into; Parser/Builder ♦ 94

cooperating, message use; Dispatched Interpretation ♦ 155

Creating and Updating Business Objects ♦ 91

Creating Reports with Query Objects ♦ 40

creation; Object Creation ♦ 15

with context-determined subtypes; Virtual Constructor ♦ 25

messages use; Shortcut Constructor Method ♦ 152

decoupling classes from; Type Object ♦ 176

dependencies, garbage collection use; Finalization ♦ 90

destroying; Object Destruction ♦ 15

domain

analyzing the relationships among; Classifying, Associating, and Grouping the Domain Objects ♦ 141

identifying; Finding and Defining the Domain Objects ♦ 141

dynamic

lifetime management; Localized Ownership: Managing Dynamic Objects in C++ ♦ 85

sharing ownership; Shared Ownership ♦ 86

transfer from creator; Sequence of Owners ♦ 85

Elaboration of the Domain Objects ♦ 141

encapsulated class tree, creating; Late Creation ♦ 120

Extension Object ♦ 55

Finding and Defining the Domain Objects ♦ 141

Fine-Grained Objects ♦ 122

For Objects with MOODS, Use State Classes ♦ 88

format conversion; Conversion ♦ 153

Formula Objects ♦ 41

granularity of, framework development considerations; Fine-Grained Objects ♦ 122

identity

managing uniqueness of; Identity Management ♦ 90

preserving in a relational database; Object Identifier ♦ 107

independent, interaction handling; Mediating Protocol ♦ 155

inspection tools, for framework use; Language Tools ♦ 123

interaction, encapsulation of; Mediator ♦ 86

Localized Ownership: Managing Dynamic Objects in C++ ♦ 85

locating; Entry Point ♦ 16

Managed Object ♦ 115

mapping to relational databases; Crossing Chasms: A Pattern Language for Object-RDBMS Integration ♦ 41, Objects from Records ♦ 90, Pattern Language for Smalltalk & Relational Databases ♦ 106, Representing Objects as Tables ♦ 107

metadata, mapping objects to relational database schemas; Object Metadata ♦ 108

Method Object ♦ 153

methods, representation as; Method Object ♦ 153

models, designing relational database tables that represent; TABLE DESIGN TIME ♦ 107

in multiple address spaces, handling; HALF-OBJECT + PROTOCOL ♦ 71

NULL OBJECT ♦ 91

OBJECT AGAING, ELABORATION OF THE DOMAIN OBJECTS relationship to; ELABORATION OF THE DOMAIN OBJECTS ♦ 141

OBJECT AGING ♦ 141
  BEHAVIORAL REQUIREMENTS relationship to; OBJECT AGING ♦ 141
  FINITE STATE MACHINE PATTERNS relationship to; OBJECT AGING ♦ 141
  PROBLEM DOMAIN ANALYSIS relationship to; PROBLEM DOMAIN ANALYSIS ♦ 141
  STATE PATTERNS relationship to; OBJECT AGING ♦ 141
  STATE relationship to; OBJECT AGING ♦ 141

OBJECT CREATION ♦ 15
  FACTORY METHOD relationship to; OBJECT CREATION ♦ 15

OBJECT DESTRUCTION ♦ 15

OBJECT EQUIVALENCE ♦ 10
  BASIC RELATIONSHIP PATTERNS relationship to; OBJECT EQUIVALENCE ♦ 10

OBJECT IDENTIFIER ♦ 42, ♦ 107
  IDENTIFICATION SCHEME relationship to; OBJECT IDENTIFIER ♦ 42, OBJECT IDENTIFIER ♦ 107
  OBJECT IDENTIFIER relationship to; OBJECT IDENTIFIER ♦ 107
  REPRESENTING OBJECTS AS TABLES relationship to; REPRESENTING OBJECTS AS TABLES ♦ 42, REPRESENTING OBJECTS AS TABLES ♦ 107

OBJECT MERGE ♦ 10
  ESSENCE relationship to; OBJECT MERGE ♦ 10

OBJECT METADATA ♦ 108
  QUERY OBJECT relationship to; QUERY OBJECT ♦ 108

OBJECT METATDATA ♦ 108
  BROKER relationship to; BROKER ♦ 108, OBJECT METADATA ♦ 108
  PROXY relationship to; OBJECT METADATA ♦ 108
  QUERY OBJECT relationship to; OBJECT METADATA ♦ 108

OBJECT RECOVERY ♦ 92
  COMMAND PROCESSOR relationship to; OBJECT RECOVERY ♦ 92
  COMMAND relationship to; OBJECT RECOVERY ♦ 92
  DECORATOR relationship to; OBJECT RECOVERY ♦ 92
  MEMENTO relationship to; OBJECT RECOVERY ♦ 92
  OBJECT SYNCHRONIZER relationship to; OBJECT SYNCHRONIZER ♦ 92
  RECOVERABLE DISTRIBUTER relationship to; OBJECT RECOVERY ♦ 92
  STRATEGY relationship to; OBJECT RECOVERY ♦ 92

OBJECT RECURSION ♦ 92
  CHAIN OF RESPONSIBILITY relationship to; CHAIN OF RESPONSIBILITY ♦ 32, OBJECT RECURSION ♦ 92
  INTERPRETER relationship to; OBJECT RECURSION ♦ 92
  ITERATOR relationship to; OBJECT RECURSION ♦ 92
  PROXY relationship to; OBJECT RECURSION ♦ 92

OBJECT STEREOTYPES ♦ 141

OBJECT SYNCHRONIZER ♦ 92
  ACTIVE OBJECT relationship to; OBJECT SYNCHRONIZER ♦ 92
  OBJECT RECOVERY relationship to; OBJECT SYNCHRONIZER ♦ 92
  PROXY relationship to; OBJECT SYNCHRONIZER ♦ 92
  STRATEGY relationship to; OBJECT SYNCHRONIZER ♦ 92

OBJECT TRANSFORMATION ♦ 83
  TRANSIENT REDUCTION relationship to; TRANSIENT REDUCTION ♦ 83, OBJECT TRANSFORMATION ♦ 83

OBJECT-ORIENTED DESIGN PATTERNS IN REACTIVE SYSTEMS ♦ 92
  G++ relationship to; OBJECT-ORIENTED DESIGN PATTERNS IN REACTIVE SYSTEMS ♦ 92

OBJECT-ORIENTED SIMULATION ♦ 93
  ADAPTER relationship to; OBJECT-ORIENTED SIMULATION ♦ 93
  EVENT-DRIVEN RPC relationship to; EVENT-DRIVEN RPC ♦ 94
  OBJECTS WITH REMOTE CONTROL relationship to; OBJECTS WITH REMOTE CONTROL ♦ 93

OBJECT-ORIENTED STATE MACHINE ♦ 129
  EVENT-CENTERED ARCHITECTURE relationship to; OBJECT-ORIENTED STATE MACHINE ♦ 129

OBJECTIFY ASSOCIATIONS ♦ 5

OBJECTIFY SYSTEM STATE ♦ 93
  OBJECTS WITH REMOTE CONTROL relationship to; OBJECTS WITH REMOTE CONTROL ♦ 93
  PROTOTYPE AND REALITY relationship to; OBJECTIFY SYSTEM STATE ♦ 93

OBJECTIFY THE EVENTS ♦ 93
  OBJECTS WITH REMOTE CONTROL relationship to; OBJECTIFY THE EVENTS ♦ 93, OBJECTS WITH REMOTE CONTROL ♦ 93

OBJECTS FROM RECORDS ♦ 90
  MATERIALIZATION relationship to; MATERIALIZATION ♦ 90

OBJECTS WITH REMOTE CONTROL ♦ 93
  OBJECT-ORIENTED SIMULATION relationship to; OBJECTS WITH REMOTE CONTROL ♦ 93
  OBJECTIFY SYSTEM STATE relationship to; OBJECTS WITH REMOTE CONTROL ♦ 93
  OBJECTIFY THE EVENTS relationship to; OBJECTIFY THE EVENTS ♦ 93, OBJECTS WITH REMOTE CONTROL ♦ 93
  PROTOTYPE AND REALITY relationship to; OBJECTS WITH REMOTE CONTROL ♦ 93

PERIODIC OBJECT ♦ 134

pluggable, framework development use; PLUGGABLE OBJECTS ♦ 122

PLUGGABLE OBJECTS ♦ 122

problem domain role of; OBJECT STEREOTYPES ♦ 141

properties, testing; QUERY METHOD ♦ 153

prototyping, strategies for; PROTOTYPE ♦ 138

proxies, strategies for creating; PROXY ♦ 139

QUERY OBJECT ♦ 108

QUERY OBJECTS ♦ 41

recovery, strategies for; OBJECT RECOVERY ♦ 92

RELATIONSHIP OBJECT ♦ 20

relationships
  preserving in a relational database; PATTERN LANGUAGE FOR SMALLTALK & RELATIONAL DATABASES ♦ 106

object(s) *continued*

relationships *continued*

representation in; REPRESENTING OBJECT
RELATIONSHIPS ♦ 42

representing; REPRESENTING OBJECT RELATIONSHIPS ♦ 107

tracking change over time; TEMPORAL ASSOCIATION ♦ 172

rendering at the client, in object-oriented framework/legacy
system interactions; MATERIALIZATION ♦ 90

REPORT OBJECTS ♦ 41

representation

evolutionary software development issues;
OBJECT-ORIENTED SIMULATION ♦ 93

as relational database tables; REPRESENTING OBJECTS AS
TABLES ♦ 107

as tables; REPRESENTING OBJECTS AS TABLES ♦ 42

REPRESENTING OBJECT RELATIONSHIPS ♦ 42, ♦ 107

REPRESENTING OBJECTS AS TABLES ♦ 42, ♦ 107

reuse strategies; SELFISH CLASS PATTERN LANGUAGE ♦ 149

ROLE OBJECT ♦ 146

as roles; ROLE OBJECT ♦ 146

SEARCHING FOR BUSINESS OBJECTS ♦ 90

serialization of; SERIALIZER ♦ 151

sharing values between; USE A VALUEMODEL TO SHARE A
VALUE ♦ 176

single occurence, in frameworks, making explicit;
SOLITAIRE ♦ 89

software development projects, a managers guide; SURVIVING
OBJECT-ORIENTED PROJECTS: A MANAGER'S GUIDE ♦ 168

SQL representation as; QUERY OBJECT ♦ 108

STATE OBJECT ♦ 166

state-dependent representation, design and implementation
strategies; MOODS: MODELS FOR OBJECT-ORIENTED
DESIGN OF STATE ♦ 87

structure, creating a print method for; DEBUG PRINTING
METHOD ♦ 154

synchronization of; OBJECT SYNCHRONIZER ♦ 92

systems, prototype-based; PROTOTYPE-BASED OBJECT
SYSTEM ♦ 139

transformation of, as optimization techique; OBJECT
TRANSFORMATION ♦ 83

TYPE OBJECT ♦ 176

unique identifiers, relational database use; OBJECT
IDENTIFIER ♦ 42

updating

in a dependency network; PROPAGATOR: A FAMILY OF
PATTERNS ♦ 138

in legacy system/object-oriented framework interactions;
CREATING AND UPDATING BUSINESS OBJECTS ♦ 91

USE A PLUGGABLEADAPTOR TO HOLD SOME PART OF AN
OBJECT ♦ 178

USE A VALUEHOLDER TO HOLD A STAND-ALONE
OBJECT ♦ 177

USE AN ASPECTADAPTOR TO HOLD AN ASPECT OF AN
OBJECT ♦ 177

WHEN STATES ARE ASSOCIATIONS, USE STATE OBJECTS ♦ 89

with multiple states, mapping to state classes; FOR COMPLEX
MOODS, USE A MOOD ALTERNATOR ♦ 89

wrapping ValueModel behavior around an portion of; USE
A PLUGGABLEADAPTOR TO HOLD SOME PART OF AN
OBJECT ♦ 178

OBJECT STEREOTYPES ♦ 141

OBJECT SYNCHRONIZER ♦ 92

[Silva+99]; 196

OBJECT TRANSFORMATION ♦ 83

**OBJECT-ORIENTED DESIGN PATTERNS IN REACTIVE
SYSTEMS ♦ 92**

[Aarsten+96b]; 181

OBJECT-ORIENTED SIMULATION ♦ 93

OBJECT-ORIENTED STATE MACHINE ♦ 129

OBJECTIFY ASSOCIATIONS ♦ 5

OBJECTIFY THE EVENTS ♦ 93

objectives

software development, clarifying; CLEAR THE FOG ♦ 168

SPONSOR OBJECTIVES ♦ 140

OBJECTS FROM RECORDS ♦ 90

OBJECTS WITH REMOTE CONTROL ♦ 93

OBSERVATION ♦ 8

observations

ACTIVE OBSERVATION, HYPOTHESIS, AND PROJECTION ♦ 9

ASSOCIATED OBSERVATION ♦ 9

assurance level of; ACTIVE OBSERVATION, HYPOTHESIS, AND
PROJECTION ♦ 9

CONSTRAINT OBSERVER ♦ 41

encapsulating; PROCESS OF OBSERVATION ♦ 9

protocol relationships; PROTOCOL ♦ 8

IMPLEMENTATION PATTERNS FOR THE OBSERVER
PATTERN ♦ 74

linking to

phenomena; SUBTYPING OBSERVATION CONCEPTS ♦ 8

protocols, through outcome and start functions; OUTCOME
AND START FUNCTIONS ♦ 13

navigation, as user interface tool; NAVIGATIONOBSERVER ♦ 48

NAVIGATIONOBSERVER ♦ 48

OBSERVATION ♦ 8

DUAL TIME RECORD relationship to; DUAL TIME RECORD ♦ 9

MEASUREMENT relationship to; OBSERVATION ♦ 8

OBSERVER relationship to; OBSERVATION ♦ 8,
OBSERVER ♦ 94

REJECTED OBSERVATION relationship to; REJECTED
OBSERVATION ♦ 9

OBSERVER ♦ 94

COMPOSABLE QUERY OBJECTS relationship to; COMPOSABLE
QUERY OBJECTS ♦ 41

CONDUIT OF SUBJECT CHANGE relationship to; CONDUIT OF
SUBJECT CHANGE ♦ 75

DECOUPLE EXECUTION AND OUTPUT relationship to;
DECOUPLE EXECUTION AND OUTPUT ♦ 76

DEPENDENCY relationship to; DEPENDENCY ♦ 91

EVENT MECHANISM relationship to; EVENT
MECHANISM ♦ 110

implementation patterns for; IMPLEMENTATION PATTERNS
FOR THE OBSERVER PATTERN ♦ 74

IMPLEMENTATION PATTERNS FOR THE OBSERVER PATTERN
relationship to; IMPLEMENTATION PATTERNS FOR THE
OBSERVER PATTERN ♦ 74, OBSERVER ♦ 94

MEDIATOR relationship to; MEDIATOR ♦ 86, OBSERVER ♦ 94

MESSAGE PACKET relationship to; MESSAGE PACKET ♦ 75
NAVIGATIONOBSERVER relationship to;
  NAVIGATIONOBSERVER ♦ 48
OBSERVATION relationship to; OBSERVATION ♦ 8,
  OBSERVER ♦ 94
OBSERVER UPDATE MESSAGE relationship to; OBSERVER
  UPDATE MESSAGE ♦ 75, OBSERVER ♦ 94
ONE MESSAGE PER AFFECTED OBJECT relationship to; ONE
  MESSAGE PER AFFECTED OBJECT ♦ 75
ONE MESSAGE PER CHANGE REQUEST relationship to; ONE
  MESSAGE PER CHANGE REQUEST ♦ 75
PROACTOR relationship to; PROACTOR ♦ 137
PROPAGATOR: A FAMILY OF PATTERNS relationship to;
  PROPAGATOR: A FAMILY OF PATTERNS ♦ 138
PUBLISHER-SUBSCRIBER relationship to; OBSERVER ♦ 94,
  PUBLISHER-SUBSCRIBER ♦ 139
RECOVERABLE DISTRIBUTOR relationship to; RECOVERABLE
  DISTRIBUTOR ♦ 143
SUBTYPING OBSERVATION CONCEPTS relationship to;
  SUBTYPING OBSERVATION CONCEPTS ♦ 8
OBSERVER UPDATE MESSAGE ♦ 75
CONDUIT OF SUBJECT CHANGE relationship to; CONDUIT OF
  SUBJECT CHANGE ♦ 75
OBSERVER relationship to; OBSERVER UPDATE
  MESSAGE ♦ 75, OBSERVER ♦ 94
ONE MESSAGE PER CHANGE REQUEST relationship to; ONE
  MESSAGE PER CHANGE REQUEST ♦ 75
PROCESS OF OBSERVATION ♦ 9
rejected, handling of; REJECTED OBSERVATION ♦ 9
SESSION CONTROL & OBSERVATION ♦ 151
SUBTYPING OBSERVATION CONCEPTS ♦ 8
time recording, in dual records; DUAL TIME RECORD ♦ 9
OBSERVER ♦ 94
  [Alpert+98]; 182
  [Gamma+95]; 188
OBSERVER UPDATE MESSAGE ♦ 75
occlusion
  of graphical components, display list management of; DISPLAY
    LIST ♦ 49
Odell, J. J.
  [Martin+98]; 190
offer
  quote representation of; QUOTE ♦ 13
OFFICE ALARMS ♦ 79
  AUDIBLE ALARM relationship to; AUDIBLE ALARM ♦ 79
Ohlsson, L.
  [Molin+98]; 191
    POINTS AND DEVIATIONS: PATTERN LANGUAGE OF FIRE
      ALARM SYSTEMS ♦ 133
Olson, D. S.
  [Olson98a]; 191
    PATTERNS ON THE FLY ♦ 130
  [Olson98b]; 192
    POCKET-SIZED BROKER ❖ 133
OLTP (online transaction processing)
  query optimization for; QUERY OPTIMIZED DATABASE ♦ 165

one message
  ONE MESSAGE PER AFFECTED OBJECT ♦ 75
    CONDUIT OF SUBJECT CHANGE relationship to; ONE
      MESSAGE PER AFFECTED OBJECT ♦ 75
    OBSERVER relationship to; ONE MESSAGE PER AFFECTED
      OBJECT ♦ 75
    ONE MESSAGE PER CHANGE REQUEST relationship to; ONE
      MESSAGE PER AFFECTED OBJECT ♦ 75
  ONE MESSAGE PER CHANGE REQUEST ♦ 75
    CONDUIT OF SUBJECT CHANGE relationship to; ONE
      MESSAGE PER CHANGE REQUEST ♦ 75
    OBSERVER relationship to; ONE MESSAGE PER CHANGE
      REQUEST ♦ 75
    OBSERVER UPDATE MESSAGE relationship to; ONE MESSAGE
      PER CHANGE REQUEST ♦ 75
    ONE MESSAGE PER AFFECTED OBJECT relationship to; ONE
      MESSAGE PER AFFECTED OBJECT ♦ 75
ONE MESSAGE PER CHANGE REQUEST ♦ 75
one-off problems
  design principles, that avoid trashy code; THROWAWAY
    CODE ♦ 21
one-to-many relationships
  dependencies, state change management with; OBSERVER ♦ 94
  designing; COLLECTION OBJECT ♦ 20
  representation of; COLLECTION ♦ 159
one-to-one relationships
  communication between objects in; WORK ACCOMPLISHED
    THROUGH DIALOGS ♦ 30
  designing; RELATIONSHIP AS ATTRIBUTE ♦ 20
  owner and software deliverable; OWNER PER
    DELIVERABLE ♦ 169
one-way messaging designs
  flow network handling; FLOW NETWORKS ♦ 40
  thread handling; THREAD-PER-MESSAGE ♦ 39
ONLINE ENGINEERING MODEL ♦ 18
  BATCH ENGINEERING MODEL relationship to; BATCH
    ENGINEERING MODEL ♦ 19
  MESSAGING ENGINEERING MODEL relationship to; MESSAGING
    ENGINEERING MODEL ♦ 18
  MODEL-VIEW-CONTROLLER relationship to; ONLINE
    ENGINEERING MODEL ♦ 18
  STREAM I-O ENGINEERING MODEL relationship to; STREAM
    I-O ENGINEERING MODEL ♦ 19
  TRANSACTION relationship to; ONLINE ENGINEERING
    MODEL ♦ 18
Opdyke, W.F.
  [Foote+95]; 187
    LIFE CYCLE AND REFACTORING PATTERNS THAT SUPPORT
      EVOLUTION AND REUSE ❖ 84
open
  calls, stateless method use with; OPEN CALLS ♦ 38
  OPEN CALLS ♦ 38
  OPEN CONTAINERS ♦ 38
  OPEN REVIEW ♦ 111
    AUTHORS ARE EXPERTS relationship to; AUTHORS ARE
      EXPERTS ♦ 111
    COMMUNITY OF TRUST relationship to; OPEN REVIEW ♦ 111,
      COMMUNITY OF TRUST ♦ 112

open *continued*
  Open Review *continued*
    Moderator Guides the Workshop relationship to;
      Moderator Guides the Workshop ◆ 112
    Reading Just Before Reviewing relationship to;
      Reading Just Before Reviewing ◆ 112
    Safe Setting relationship to; Open Review ◆ 111, Safe
      Setting ◆ 111
    Sitting in a Circle relationship to; Sitting in a
      Circle ◆ 112
Open Calls ◆ 38
Open Containers ◆ 38
Open Review ◆ 111
Operating Scope ◆ 7
operations
  Operating Scope ◆ 7
  Remote Operation ◆ 115
  representation of, for object manipulation; Visitor ◆ 179
optimization
  of collection searching; Lookup Cache ◆ 161
  of display update requests; Consolidate Requests ◆ 50,
    Lazy Redraw ◆ 50, Clip Requests ◆ 50
  lazy
    of Smalltalk programs; Lazy Optimization: Patterns for
      Efficient Smalltalk Programming ◆ 81
    strategies for; Lazy Optimization ◆ 81
  Lazy Optimization ◆ 81
  Lazy Optimization: Patterns for Efficient Smalltalk
    Programming ◆ 81
  of messages, in state update information transmission;
    Optimized Messages per Change Request ◆ 75
  Optimize High-Runner Cases ◆ 100
  Optimized Messages per Change Request ◆ 75
    Conduit of Subject Change relationship to; Optimized
      Messages per Change Request ◆ 75
  Query Optimized Database ◆ 165
  safe simplification techniques; Simplification ◆ 83
  Stars: A Pattern Language for Query-Optimized
    Schemas ◆ 164
  system throughput
    finishing work in progress first; Finish Work in
      Progress ◆ 101
    overload handling strategies; Work Shed at
      Periphery ◆ 102
    user request classifying for; Shed Load ◆ 101
Optimize High-Runner Cases ◆ 100
Optimized Messages per Change Request ◆ 75
option(s)
  barrier, option relationship to; Subtype State
    Machines ◆ 14
  Optional Elements When Helpful ◆ 103
    Findable Sections relationship to; Findable
      Sections ◆ 103
    Pattern relationship to; Pattern ◆ 102
    Skippable Sections relationship to; Skippable
      Sections ◆ 103
  optional sections, pattern writing use; Skippable
    Sections ◆ 103

Options ◆ 14
  Contract relationship to; Options ◆ 14
  term description; Options ◆ 14
Optional Elements When Helpful ◆ 103
  Skippable Sections relationship to; Skippable
    Sections ◆ 103
Options ◆ 14
Ordered Collection ◆ 159
ordering
  See Also comparison
  3-Level Order ◆ 24
  collections, providing multiple sort orders; Temporarily
    Sorted Collection ◆ 161
  components, for driver duty definition; Driver Duty ◆ 51
  of error messages; Timestamp ◆ 77
  of event queues, in interactive applications; Event
    Queue ◆ 76
  multimedia presentations; Define and Run
    Presentation ◆ 36
  objects; Comparing Method ◆ 153
  Ordered Collection ◆ 159
  Stack relationship to; Stack ◆ 161
orders
  business, representation of; 3-Level Order ◆ 24
Orenstein, R.
  [Orenstein96]; 192
    Pattern Language for an Essay-Based Web Site ◆ 97
organization
  abstracting either-or-both relationship into a supertype;
    Party ◆ 4, Party ◆ 6
  Accountability and Organizational Structures ◆ 4
  analysis patterns, patterns for; Accountability and
    Organizational Structures pattern language ◆ 4
  communication among software development roles, as tool
    for increasing responsiveness; Coupling Decreases
    Latency ◆ 69
  coupling related roles, in organizational restructuring; Divide
    and Conquer ◆ 68
  document, on WWW; Natural Text Directories ◆ 98
  Generative Development-Process Pattern Language;
    Generative Development-Process Pattern
    Language ◆ 63
  hierarchies, modeling; Organization Hierarchies ◆ 7
  Interface Organization ◆ 59
  Layered Organization ◆ 59
  management of, configuration management strategies applied
    to; Teamwork and Configuration Management ◆ 170
  matching human capabilities to tasks; Round Pegs for
    Round Holes ◆ 27
  matrix, modeling; Multiple Hierarchic Associations ◆ 4
  Organization Follows Location ◆ 64
  Organization Follows Market ◆ 65
  Organization Hierarchies ◆ 7
  Organization Structure ◆ 7
  Organizational Multiplexing: Patterns for Processing
    Satellite Telemetry with Distributed Teams ◆ 94
  Organizational Patterns for Teams ◆ 95
  Organizational Structure-Typed Relationship ◆ 5

of pattern writers workshops; PATTERN LANGUAGE FOR
WRITERS' WORKSHOPS ◆ 111
RECURSIVE STRUCTURES FOR ORGANIZATIONS ◆ 4
role relative to architecture; CONWAY'S LAW ◆ 65
size, for software development teams; SIZE THE
ORGANIZATION ◆ 63
SIZE THE ORGANIZATION ◆ 63
structures
defining relationships in; ORGANIZATION STRUCTURE ◆ 7
for software development; EPISODES: A PATTERN
LANGUAGE OF COMPETITIVE DEVELOPMENT ◆ 51
subdomain organization; AESTHETIC PATTERN ◆ 68
team; PEACEMAKER ◆ 131
ORGANIZATION FOLLOWS LOCATION ◆ 64
ORGANIZATION HIERARCHIES ◆ 7
ORGANIZATION STRUCTURE ◆ 7
**ORGANIZATIONAL MULTIPLEXING: PATTERNS FOR
PROCESSING SATELLITE TELEMETRY WITH DISTRIBUTED
TEAMS ◆ 94**
[Berczuk96]; ORGANIZATIONAL MULTIPLEXING: PATTERNS
FOR PROCESSING SATELLITE TELEMETRY WITH DISTRIBUTED
TEAMS ◆ 94
ORGANIZATIONAL PATTERNS FOR TEAMS ◆ 95
[Harrison96]; 188
ORGANIZATIONAL STRUCTURE-TYPED RELATIONSHIP ◆ 5
orientation
information space
persistent landmarks use for; LANDMARK ◆ 120
references use for; ACTIVE REFERENCE ◆ 120
OUTCOME AND START FUNCTIONS ◆ 13
outcome functions
OUTCOME AND START FUNCTIONS ◆ 13
protocols linked to observations through; OUTCOME AND
START FUNCTIONS ◆ 13
output
classification, in fault-tolerant systems; MIND YOUR OWN
BUSINESS ◆ 77
DECOUPLE EXECUTION AND OUTPUT ◆ 76
direction, in fault-tolerant systems; WHO ASKED? ◆ 78
events, decoupling model updating from; DECOUPLE
EXECUTION AND OUTPUT ◆ 76
finite state machine
event triggering; MEALLY ◆ 59, HYBRID ◆ 59
state entry triggering; MOORE ◆ 59, HYBRID ◆ 59
INPUT AND OUTPUT PATTERN LANGUAGE ◆ 76
multiple, decoupling from multiple input; ROUTER ◆ 146
remote control of; REMOTE CONTROL ◆ 144
overdraft
MEMORY OVERDRAFT ◆ 72
overload
of error messages, handling; FIVE MINUTES OF NO
ESCALATION MESSAGES ◆ 57
error messages, strategies for handling; GEORGE WASHINGTON
IS STILL DEAD ◆ 78, FIVE MINUTES OF NO ESCALATION
MESSAGES ◆ 78
events, strategies for handling; MERGE COMPATIBLE
EVENTS ◆ 76, HANDLE ARTIFICIAL EVENTS ◆ 76
handling
in real-time reactive systems; SHED LOAD ◆ 101

strategies for; WORK SHED AT PERIPHERY ◆ 102
inter-processor communication; LEAKY BUCKET OF
CREDITS ◆ 102
override
human
in fault-tolerant systems; SHUT UP AND LISTEN ◆ 79
provision for in fault-tolerant systems; PEOPLE KNOW
BEST ◆ 57
methods, in superclass; EXTENDING SUPER ◆ 155, MODIFYING
SUPER ◆ 155
of silenced alarms; DON'T LET THEM FORGET ◆ 79
overview
pattern language, as pattern writing strategy; PATTERN
LANGUAGE SUMMARY ◆ 105
owner
CODE OWNERSHIP ◆ 66
components, importance for software development control;
FUNCTION OWNERS/COMPONENT OWNERS ◆ 169
CREATOR AS SOLE OWNER ◆ 85
DATA OWNERSHIP ◆ 147
of dynamic object, creator as; CREATOR AS SOLE OWNER ◆ 85
of dynamic objects
sharing ownership; SHARED OWNERSHIP ◆ 86
transfer from creator; SEQUENCE OF OWNERS ◆ 85
FUNCTION OWNERS/COMPONENT OWNERS ◆ 169
functions, importance for software development control;
FUNCTION OWNERS/COMPONENT OWNERS ◆ 169
LOCALIZED OWNERSHIP: MANAGING DYNAMIC OBJECTS IN
C++ ◆ 85
OWNER PER DELIVERABLE ◆ 169
DAY CARE relationship to; OWNER PER DELIVERABLE ◆ 169
FUNCTION OWNERS/COMPONENT OWNERS relationship
to; OWNER PER DELIVERABLE ◆ 169, FUNCTION
OWNERS/COMPONENT OWNERS ◆ 169
HOLISTIC DIVERSITY relationship to; HOLISTIC
DIVERSITY ◆ 169
SACRIFICE ONE PERSON relationship to; SACRIFICE ONE
PERSON ◆ 170
TEAM PER TASK relationship to; OWNER PER
DELIVERABLE ◆ 169
OWNER-DRIVEN TRANSITIONS ◆ 167
SEQUENCE OF OWNERS ◆ 85
SHARED OWNERSHIP ◆ 86
software deliverable, one-to-one relationship; OWNER PER
DELIVERABLE ◆ 169
OWNER PER DELIVERABLE ◆ 169
OWNER-DRIVEN TRANSITIONS ◆ 167

PAC (Presentation-Abstraction-Control) agent
VIEW HANDLER relationship to; VIEW HANDLER ◆ 178
packages
MULTIPLE ACCESS LEVELS TO A PACKAGE ◆ 14
selective use; MULTIPLE ACCESS LEVELS TO A PACKAGE ◆ 14
separate, subtype visibility; SUBTYPING PACKAGES ◆ 14
SUBTYPING PACKAGES ◆ 14
visibility between, permitting; MUTUAL VISIBILITY ◆ 14
packets
COLLABORATIVE WORK PACKETS ◆ 28
data stream, generating data products from; HANDLERS ◆ 95

packets *continued*
grouping update messages into; MESSAGE PACKET ♦ 75
MESSAGE PACKET ♦ 75
WORK PACKET CONTENTS ♦ 28
WORK PACKET PRIORITY ♦ 29
WORK PACKET SECURITY ♦ 29
WORK PACKET STATUS REPORT ♦ 29

page
PAGE FLIP ♦ 50
DOUBLE BUFFER relationship to; DOUBLE BUFFER ♦ 50,
PAGE FLIP ♦ 50
GLOBAL UPDATE relationship to; PAGE FLIP ♦ 50
swapping, as display update technique; PAGE FLIP ♦ 50

PAGE FLIP ♦ 50
PAINTER'S ALGORITHM ♦ 50
painting
PAINTER'S ALGORITHM ♦ 50
DISPLAY LIST relationship to; DISPLAY LIST ♦ 49
DOUBLE BUFFER relationship to; PAINTER'S
ALGORITHM ♦ 50

pair programming
DEVELOPING IN PAIRS ♦ 69
software development advantages; DEVELOPING IN PAIRS ♦ 69

PANEL STATES ♦ 96
[Spall98]; 196

panels
displaying a sequence of; PANEL STATES ♦ 96
PANEL STATES ♦ 96
PLUGGABLE VIEW CONTROLLER relationship to; PANEL
STATES ♦ 96
STATE relationship to; PANEL STATES ♦ 96

Pang, C.
[Pang99]; 192
SURROGATE ♦ 168

paradigm shift
custom to component integration; PATTERN-BASED
INTEGRATION ARCHITECTURES ♦ 115

PARALLEL APPLICATION AND DOMAIN HIERARCHIES ♦ 14
PARALLEL FASTPATH ♦ 147
parallelism
See Also concurrency
coordinating independent processes; COMMUNICATING
PROCESSES ♦ 36
locking designs for; SELECTING LOCKING DESIGNS FOR
PARALLEL PROGRAMS ♦ 147
PARALLEL APPLICATION AND DOMAIN HIERARCHIES ♦ 14
PARALLEL FASTPATH ♦ 147
TEST-AND-SET LOCK relationship to; TEST-AND-SET
LOCK ♦ 148
SELECTING LOCKING DESIGNS FOR PARALLEL
PROGRAMS ♦ 147
selecting locking primitives; SELECTING LOCKING PRIMITIVES
FOR PARALLEL PROGRAMMING ♦ 148
SELECTING LOCKING PRIMITIVES FOR PARALLEL
PROGRAMMING ♦ 148
work load sharing, as system throughput optimization; SHARE
THE LOAD ♦ 101

parameterization
of behavior; PLUGGABLE BEHAVIOR ♦ 156, PLUGGABLE
BLOCK ♦ 156
COLLECTING PARAMETER ♦ 156
COMMAND support of; COMMAND ♦ 35
CONSTRUCTOR PARAMETER METHOD ♦ 152
of diagnostic message type; TYPED DIAGNOSTICS ♦ 124
instance variable setting from; CONSTRUCTOR PARAMETER
METHOD ♦ 152
message flow coding use; REVERSING METHOD ♦ 153
naming parameters; TYPE SUGGESTING PARAMETER
NAME ♦ 162
enumeration block; SIMPLE ENUMERATION
PARAMETER ♦ 163
of objects, framework development use; PLUGGABLE
OBJECTS ♦ 122
return of collections use; COLLECTING PARAMETER ♦ 156
SIMPLE ENUMERATION PARAMETER ♦ 163
TYPE SUGGESTING PARAMETER NAME ♦ 162

parent
change of, recording previous reference; MEMENTO
CHILD ♦ 35
communication with; SUPER ♦ 155

PARSER/BUILDER ♦ 94
parsing
PARSER/BUILDER ♦ 94
BUILDER relationship to; PARSER/BUILDER ♦ 94
FACTORY METHOD relationship to; PARSER/BUILDER ♦ 94
HIERARCHY OF FACTORIES relationship to; HIERARCHY OF
FACTORIES ♦ 94
INTERPRETER relationship to; PARSER/BUILDER ♦ 94
LOOSE INTERFACES relationship to; LOOSE INTERFACES ♦ 94
PARSING STREAM ♦ 161
strategies for; PARSING STREAM ♦ 161
stream data, into objects; PARSER/BUILDER ♦ 94

PARSING STREAM ♦ 161
PARTIAL FAILURE ♦ 72
CAPTAIN OATES relationship to; PARTIAL FAILURE ♦ 72,
CAPTAIN OATES ♦ 72

parties
as first class object, in a session; PARTIES & MEDIA AS FIRST
CLASS CITIZENS ♦ 96
PARTIES & MEDIA AS FIRST CLASS CITIZENS ♦ 96
SESSION CONTROL & OBSERVATION relationship to; SESSION
CONTROL & OBSERVATION ♦ 151
PARTY ♦ 4, ♦ 6
PARTY TYPE GENERALIZATIONS ♦ 7

PARTIES & MEDIA AS FIRST CLASS CITIZENS ♦ 96
[VandenBroecke+97]; 197

partitioning
client-server applications
three-tier; THREE-TIER ARCHITECTURE ♦ 15
two-tier; TWO-TIER ARCHITECTURE ♦ 14
data, as parallelism management strategy; DATA
OWNERSHIP ♦ 147
PARTITIONING SMALLTALK CODE INTO ENVY/DEVELOPER
COMPONENTS ♦ 96
subtypes, in a matrix organization; MULTIPLE HIERARCHIC
ASSOCIATIONS ♦ 4

PARTITIONING SMALLTALK CODE INTO ENVY/DEVELOPER COMPONENTS ♦ 96
  [Woolf96]; 198
parts
  part-whole hierarchies, representing; COMPOSITE ♦ 37
  USE A PLUGGABLEADAPTOR TO HOLD SOME PART OF AN OBJECT ♦ 178
  WHOLE-PART ♦ 179
PARTY ♦ 4, ♦ 6
PARTY TYPE GENERALIZATIONS ♦ 7
PASS-THROUGH HOST ♦ 38
  OPEN CALLS relationship to; PASS-THROUGH HOST ♦ 38
PATRON ♦ 65
PATTERN ♦ 102
PATTERN AS A CLASS ♦ 97
  [Soukup95]; 196
PATTERN FOR SEPARATING ASSEMBLY AND PROCESSING ♦ 97
  [Berczuk95]; 182
PATTERN LANGUAGE ♦ 102
PATTERN LANGUAGE FOR AN ESSAY-BASED WEB SITE ♦ 97
  [Orenstein96]; 192
PATTERN LANGUAGE FOR DEVELOPING FORM STYLE WINDOWS ♦ 99
  [Bradac+98]; 183
PATTERN LANGUAGE FOR IMPROVING THE CAPACITY OF REACTIVE SYSTEMS ♦ 100
  [Meszaros96]; 191
PATTERN LANGUAGE FOR PATTERN WRITING ♦ 102
  [Meszaros+98]; 191
PATTERN LANGUAGE FOR SMALLTALK & RELATIONAL DATABASES ♦ 106
  [Brown+96a]; 183
PATTERN LANGUAGE FOR TOOL CONSTRUCTION AND INTEGRATION BASED ON THE TOOLS AND MATERIALS METAPHOR ♦ 109
  [Riehle95]; 193
PATTERN LANGUAGE FOR WRITERS' WORKSHOPS ♦ 111
  [Coplien97]; 185
PATTERN LANGUAGE OF TRANSPORT SYSTEMS (POINT AND ROUTE) ♦ 114
  [Zhao+98b]; 199
PATTERN LANGUAGE SUMMARY ♦ 105
pattern languages and collections
  ACCESSING RELATIONAL DATABASES; ACCESSING RELATIONAL DATABASES pattern language ♦ 3
  ACCOUNTABILITY AND ORGANIZATIONAL STRUCTURES; ACCOUNTABILITY AND ORGANIZATIONAL STRUCTURES pattern language ♦ 4
  ANALYSIS PATTERNS; ANALYSIS PATTERNS ♦ 6
  APPROACHES FOR SEPARATING CLIENTS FROM SERVERS; APPROACHES FOR SEPARATING CLIENTS FROM SERVERS ♦ 16
  ARCHITECTURAL PATTERNS FOR ENABLING APPLICATION SECURITY; ARCHITECTURAL PATTERNS FOR ENABLING APPLICATION SECURITY ♦ 17
  ARCHITECTURE PATTERNS FOR BUSINESS SYSTEMS; ARCHITECTURE PATTERNS FOR BUSINESS SYSTEMS ♦ 18
  BASIC RELATIONSHIP PATTERNS; BASIC RELATIONSHIP PATTERNS ♦ 19

BIG BALL OF MUD PATTERN LANGUAGE; BIG BALL OF MUD PATTERN LANGUAGE ♦ 20
BUSINESS PATTERNS OF ASSOCIATION OBJECTS; BUSINESS PATTERNS OF ASSOCIATION OBJECTS ♦ 23
C++ IDIOMS; C++ IDIOMS ♦ 24
CAPABLE, PRODUCTIVE, AND SATISFIED; CAPABLE, PRODUCTIVE, AND SATISFIED ♦ 26
CATERPILLAR'S FATE; CATERPILLAR'S FATE: A PATTERN LANGUAGE FOR THE TRANSFORMATION FROM ANALYSIS TO DESIGN ♦ 28
CHECKS: PATTERN LANGUAGE OF INFORMATION INTEGRITY; CHECKS: PATTERN LANGUAGE OF INFORMATION INTEGRITY ♦ 32
COLLECTION OF HISTORY PATTERNS; COLLECTION OF HISTORY PATTERNS ♦ 34
COMPOSING MULTIMEDIA ARTIFACTS FOR REUSE; COMPOSING MULTIMEDIA ARTIFACTS FOR REUSE ♦ 36
CONCURRENT PROGRAMMING IN JAVA: DESIGN PRINCIPLES AND PATTERNS, 2ND ED.; CONCURRENT PROGRAMMING IN JAVA: DESIGN PRINCIPLES AND PATTERNS, 2ND ED. ♦ 37
CREATING REPORTS WITH QUERY OBJECTS ♦ 40, CREATING REPORTS WITH QUERY OBJECTS ♦ 40
CROSSING CHASMS; CROSSING CHASMS: A PATTERN LANGUAGE FOR OBJECT-RDBMS INTEGRATION ♦ 41
CUSTOMER INTERACTION; CUSTOMER INTERACTION PATTERNS ♦ 43
DECISION DEFERRAL AND CAPTURE; DECISION DEFERRAL AND CAPTURE PATTERN LANGUAGE ♦ 45
DEMO PREP; DEMO PREP: A PATTERN LANGUAGE FOR THE PREPARATION OF SOFTWARE DEMONSTRATIONS ♦ 46
DISPLAY MAINTENANCE; DISPLAY MAINTENANCE ♦ 49
EPISODES; EPISODES: A PATTERN LANGUAGE OF COMPETITIVE DEVELOPMENT ♦ 51
EVOLUTION, ARCHITECTURE, AND METAPHORPHOSIS; SOFTWARE TECTONICS ♦ 55
FAULT-TOLERANT TELECOMMUNICATION SYSTEM; FAULT-TOLERANT TELECOMMUNICATION SYSTEM PATTERNS ♦ 57
FINITE STATE MACHINE PATTERNS; FINITE STATE MACHINE PATTERNS ♦ 58
G++; G++: A PATTERN LANGUAGE FOR COMPUTER-INTEGRATED MANUFACTURING ♦ 61
GENERATIVE DEVELOPMENT-PROCESS; GENERATIVE DEVELOPMENT-PROCESS PATTERN LANGUAGE ♦ 63
GENERATIVE PATTERN LANGUAGE FOR DISTRIBUTED PROCESSING; GENERATIVE PATTERN LANGUAGE FOR DISTRIBUTED PROCESSING ♦ 70
headings, as structuring tool; DISTINCTIVE HEADINGS CONVEY STRUCTURE ♦ 106
HIGH-LEVEL AND PROCESS PATTERNS FROM THE MEMORY PRESERVATION SOCIETY; HIGH-LEVEL AND PROCESS PATTERNS FROM THE MEMORY PRESERVATION SOCIETY ♦ 71
IDENTIFY THE CHAMPION; IDENTIFY THE CHAMPION PATTERN LANGUAGE ♦ 73
IMPLEMENTATION PATTERNS FOR THE OBSERVER PATTERN; IMPLEMENTATION PATTERNS FOR THE OBSERVER PATTERN ♦ 74

pattern languages and collections *continued*

IMPROVING RESPONSIVENESS IN INTERACTIVE APPLICATIONS USING QUEUES; IMPROVING RESPONSIVENESS IN INTERACTIVE APPLICATIONS USING QUEUES ♦ 76

INPUT AND OUTPUT PATTERN LANGUAGE; INPUT AND OUTPUT PATTERN LANGUAGE ♦ 76

LAZY OPTIMIZATION; LAZY OPTIMIZATION: PATTERNS FOR EFFICIENT SMALLTALK PROGRAMMING ♦ 81

LIFECYCLE; LIFE CYCLE AND REFACTORING PATTERNS THAT SUPPORT EVOLUTION AND REUSE ♦ 84

LOCALIZED OWNERSHIP: MANAGING DYNAMIC OBJECTS IN C++; LOCALIZED OWNERSHIP: MANAGING DYNAMIC OBJECTS IN C++ ♦ 85

MOODS: MODELS FOR OBJECT-ORIENTED DESIGN OF STATE; MOODS: MODELS FOR OBJECT-ORIENTED DESIGN OF STATE ♦ 87

NEW CLIENTS WITH OLD SERVERS; NEW CLIENTS WITH OLD SERVERS: A PATTERN LANGUAGE FOR CLIENT/SERVER FRAMEWORKS ♦ 89

ORGANIZATIONAL MULTIPLEXING; ORGANIZATIONAL MULTIPLEXING: PATTERNS FOR PROCESSING SATELLITE TELEMETRY WITH DISTRIBUTED TEAMS ♦ 94

ORGANIZATIONAL PATTERNS FOR TEAMS; ORGANIZATIONAL PATTERNS FOR TEAMS ♦ 95

PARTITIONING SMALLTALK CODE INTO ENVY/DEVELOPER COMPONENTS; PARTITIONING SMALLTALK CODE INTO ENVY/DEVELOPER COMPONENTS ♦ 96

PATTERN LANGUAGE FOR AN ESSAY-BASED WEB SITE; PATTERN LANGUAGE FOR AN ESSAY-BASED WEB SITE ♦ 97

PATTERN LANGUAGE FOR DEVELOPING FORM STYLE WINDOWS; PATTERN LANGUAGE FOR DEVELOPING FORM STYLE WINDOWS ♦ 99

PATTERN LANGUAGE FOR IMPROVING THE CAPACITY OF REACTIVE SYSTEMS; PATTERN LANGUAGE FOR IMPROVING THE CAPACITY OF REACTIVE SYSTEMS ♦ 100

PATTERN LANGUAGE FOR PATTERNWRITING; PATTERN LANGUAGE FOR PATTERN WRITING ♦ 102

PATTERN LANGUAGE FOR SMALLTALK & RELATIONAL DATABASES ♦ 106, PATTERN LANGUAGE FOR SMALLTALK & RELATIONAL DATABASES ♦ 106

PATTERN LANGUAGE FOR TOOL CONSTRUCTION AND INTEGRATION BASED ON THE TOOLS AND MATERIALS METAPHOR ♦ 109, PATTERN LANGUAGE FOR TOOL CONSTRUCTION AND INTEGRATION BASED ON THE TOOLS AND MATERIALS METAPHOR ♦ 109

PATTERN LANGUAGE FOR WRITERS' WORKSHOPS ♦ 111, PATTERN LANGUAGE FOR WRITERS' WORKSHOPS ♦ 111

PATTERN LANGUAGE OF TRANSPORT SYSTEMS (POINT AND ROUTE) ♦ 114, PATTERN LANGUAGE OF TRANSPORT SYSTEMS (POINT AND ROUTE) ♦ 114

PATTERN LANGUAGE SUMMARY ♦ 105

PROBLEM/SOLUTION SUMMARY relationship to; PATTERN LANGUAGE SUMMARY ♦ 105

RUNNING EXAMPLE relationship to; PATTERN LANGUAGE SUMMARY ♦ 105

PATTERN SYSTEM FOR NETWORK MANAGEMENT INTERFACES; PATTERN SYSTEM FOR NETWORK MANAGEMENT INTERFACES ♦ 114

PATTERN-BASED INTEGRATION ARCHITECTURES; PATTERN-BASED INTEGRATION ARCHITECTURES ♦ 115

PATTERNS FOR CLASSROOM EDUCATION; PATTERNS FOR CLASSROOM EDUCATION ♦ 116

PATTERNS FOR DESIGNING IN TEAMS; PATTERNS FOR DESIGNING IN TEAMS ♦ 118

PATTERNS FOR DESIGNING NAVIGABLE INFORMATION SPACES; PATTERNS FOR DESIGNING NAVIGABLE INFORMATION SPACES ♦ 119

PATTERNS FOR ENCAPSULATING CLASS TREES; PATTERNS FOR ENCAPSULATING CLASS TREES ♦ 120

PATTERNS FOR EVOLVING FRAMEWORKS; PATTERNS FOR EVOLVING FRAMEWORKS ♦ 121

PATTERNS FOR GENERATING A LAYERED ARCHITECTURE; PATTERNS FOR GENERATING A LAYERED ARCHITECTURE ♦ 123

PATTERNS FOR SOFTWARE ARCHITECTURES; PATTERNS FOR SOFTWARE ARCHITECTURES ♦ 124

PATTERNS FOR SYSTEM TESTING; PATTERNS FOR SYSTEM TESTING ♦ 126

PATTERNS OF EVENTS; PATTERNS OF EVENTS ♦ 129

POCKET-SIZED BROKER; POCKET-SIZED BROKER ♦ 133

POINTS AND DEVIATIONS: PATTERN LANGUAGE OF FIRE ALARM SYSTEMS ♦ 133, POINTS AND DEVIATIONS: PATTERN LANGUAGE OF FIRE ALARM SYSTEMS ♦ 133

PRIORITIZING FORCES IN SOFTWARE DESIGN; PRIORITIZING FORCES IN SOFTWARE DESIGN ♦ 135

problem summary; PROBLEM/SOLUTION SUMMARY ♦ 105

PROBLEM/SOLUTION SUMMARY, PATTERN LANGUAGE SUMMARY relationship to; PATTERN LANGUAGE SUMMARY ♦ 105

PROPAGATOR; PROPAGATOR: A FAMILY OF PATTERNS ♦ 138

RAPPeL: A REQUIREMENTS-ANALYSIS PROCESS PATTERN LANGUAGE FOR OBJECT-ORIENTED DEVELOPMENT; RAPPeL: A REQUIREMENTS-ANALYSIS PROCESS PATTERN LANGUAGE FOR OBJECT-ORIENTED DEVELOPMENT ♦ 140

REUSABILITY THROUGH SELF-ENCAPSULATION; REUSABILITY THROUGH SELF-ENCAPSULATION ♦ 145

RUNNING EXAMPLE, PATTERN LANGUAGE SUMMARY relationship to; PATTERN LANGUAGE SUMMARY ♦ 105

SCRUM; SCRUM: A PATTERN LANGUAGE FOR HYPERPRODUCTIVE SOFTWARE DEVELOPMENT ♦ 146

SELECTING LOCKING DESIGNS FOR PARALLEL PROGRAMS; SELECTING LOCKING DESIGNS FOR PARALLEL PROGRAMS ♦ 147

SELECTING LOCKING PRIMITIVES FOR PARALLEL PROGRAMMING; SELECTING LOCKING PRIMITIVES FOR PARALLEL PROGRAMMING ♦ 148

SELFISH CLASS PATTERN LANGUAGE; SELFISH CLASS PATTERN LANGUAGE ♦ 149

SMALLTALK SCAFFOLDING PATTERNS ♦ 163, SMALLTALK SCAFFOLDING PATTERNS ♦ 163

solution summary; PROBLEM/SOLUTION SUMMARY ♦ 105

STARS; STARS: A PATTERN LANGUAGE FOR QUERY-OPTIMIZED SCHEMAS ♦ 164

STATE PATTERNS; STATE PATTERNS ♦ 166

structures

headings as tool for conveying; DISTINCTIVE HEADINGS CONVEY STRUCTURE ♦ 106

intents catalog use for pattern referencing; Intent Catalog ♦ 104

Surviving Object-Oriented Projects: A Manager's Guide; Surviving Object-Oriented Projects: A Manager's Guide ♦ 168

Teamwork and Configuration Management; Teamwork and Configuration Management ♦ 170

Temporal Patterns; Temporal Patterns ♦ 171

Transactions and Accounts; Transactions and Accounts ♦ 172

Tropyc: A Pattern Language for Cryptographic Software; Tropyc: A Pattern Language for Cryptographic Software ♦ 174

understanding, overview importance for; Pattern Language Summary ♦ 105

Understanding and Using the ValueModel Framework in VisualWorks Smalltalk; Understanding and Using the ValueModel Framework in VisualWorks Smalltalk ♦ 176

writing
  design strategies; Pattern Language ♦ 102
  domain example use; Running Example ♦ 106
  factoring common problems; Common Problems Highlighted ♦ 106
  glossary; Glossary ♦ 106
  overview importance; Pattern Language Summary ♦ 105
  problem summary; Problem/Solution Summary ♦ 105
  solution summary; Problem/Solution Summary ♦ 105
  strategies for; Pattern Language for Pattern Writing ♦ 102

Pattern System for Network Management Interfaces ♦ 114
  [Keller+98a]; 189

Pattern Thumbnail ♦ 104

Pattern-Based Integration Architectures ♦ 115
  [Mularz95]; 191

patterns
  Aesthetic Pattern ♦ 68
  Analysis Patterns ♦ 6
  implementation, code sample importance; Code Samples ♦ 105
  naming; Evocative Pattern Name ♦ 104, Noun Phrase Name ♦ 104, Meaningful Metaphor Name ♦ 104
  Pattern ♦ 102
    Mandatory Elements Present relationship to; Pattern ♦ 102
    Optional Elements When Helpful relationship to; Pattern ♦ 102
    Pattern Language relationship to; Pattern Language ♦ 102
    Pattern Thumbnail relationship to; Pattern Thumbnail ♦ 104
  Pattern as a Class ♦ 97
  Pattern for Separating Assembly and Processing ♦ 97
    Abstract Factory relationship to; Pattern for Separating Assembly and Processing ♦ 97
    Handlers relationship to; Handlers ♦ 95
  Pattern Language ♦ 102
    Pattern relationship to; Pattern Language ♦ 102

Pattern Language for an Essay-Based Web Site ♦ 97

Pattern Language for Developing Form Style Windows ♦ 99

Pattern Language for Improving the Capacity of Reactive Systems ♦ 100

Pattern Language for Pattern Writing ♦ 102

Pattern Language Summary, Single-Pass Readable relationship to; Single-Pass Readable ♦ 103

Pattern System for Network Management Interfaces ♦ 114

Pattern Thumbnail ♦ 104
  Evocative Pattern Name relationship to; Pattern Thumbnail ♦ 104
  Pattern relationship to; Pattern Thumbnail ♦ 104
  Readable References to Patterns relationship to; Readable References to Patterns ♦ 104
  Single-Pass Readable relationship to; Single-Pass Readable ♦ 103

pattern writers workshops, structures and protocols; Pattern Language for Writers' Workshops ♦ 111

Pattern-Based Integration Architectures ♦ 115

Patterns for Classroom Education ♦ 116

Patterns for Designing in Teams ♦ 118
  Capable, Productive, and Satisfied relationship to; Patterns for Designing in Teams ♦ 118

Patterns for Designing Navigable Information Spaces ♦ 119

Patterns for Encapsulating Class Trees ♦ 120
  Wrapper Facade relationship to; Wrapper Facade ♦ 179

Patterns for Evolving Frameworks ♦ 121

Patterns for Generating a Layered Architecture ♦ 123

Patterns for Logging Diagnostic Messages ♦ 124

Patterns for Software Architectures ♦ 124

Patterns for System Testing ♦ 126

Patterns of Events ♦ 129
  Event Acquisition relationship to; Event Acquisition ♦ 31

Patterns on the Fly ♦ 130

relationships among
  pattern writing strategies for conveying semantics; Pattern Thumbnail ♦ 104
  pattern writing strategies for identifying; Relationships to Other Patterns ♦ 103

representing as classes; Pattern as a Class ♦ 97

reviewing
  author reads selection; Author Reads Selection ♦ 112
  author request for clarification; Author Asks for Clarification ♦ 113
  author role; Workshop Comprises Authors ♦ 112
  author role during the review; Fly on the Wall ♦ 112
  closing the review on a positive note; Positive Closure ♦ 113
  closing the workshop; Clearing the Palate ♦ 113
  group composition; Community of Trust ♦ 112
  improvement suggestions order; Suggestions for Improvement ♦ 113
  incorporating feedback; Selective Changes ♦ 114
  moderator role; Moderator Guides the Workshop ♦ 112
  open review forum advantages; Open Review ♦ 111

patterns *continued*
reviewing *continued*
pattern writers as experts; Authors are Experts ◆ 111
pattern writers workshop structures and protocols; Pattern Language for Writers' Workshops ◆ 111
physical arrangements; Sitting in a Circle ◆ 112, Authors' Circle ◆ 112
positive feedback order; Positive Feedback First ◆ 113
preparation for review; Reading Just Before Reviewing ◆ 112
safe setting importance; Safe Setting ◆ 111
summarizing the pattern; Volunteer Summarizes the Work ◆ 113
thanking the author; Thank the Author ◆ 113
structures of
design components that support searching; Findable Sections ◆ 103
separating essential from optional material; Skippable Sections ◆ 103
Temporal Patterns ◆ 171
writing
clarification of notation; Understood Notations ◆ 105
code samples; Code Samples ◆ 105
domain-specific terminology; Terminology Tailored to Audience ◆ 105
forces; Visible Forces ◆ 103
handling pattern references; Readable References to Patterns ◆ 104
initial stage; Pattern ◆ 102
intents catalog; Intent Catalog ◆ 104
language independence importance; Code Samples as Bonus ◆ 105
naming strategies; Evocative Pattern Name ◆ 104, Noun Phrase Name ◆ 104, Meaningful Metaphor Name ◆ 104
necessary information to include; Mandatory Elements Present ◆ 102
optional elements; Optional Elements When Helpful ◆ 103
optional sections; Skippable Sections ◆ 103
pattern relationship specification; Relationships to Other Patterns ◆ 103
semantics of referenced patterns; Pattern Thumbnail ◆ 104
strategies for; Pattern Language for Pattern Writing ◆ 102
strategies for minimizing time to read; Single-Pass Readable ◆ 103
target audience identification; Clear Target Audience ◆ 104
Patterns for Classroom Education ◆ 116
[Anthony96]; 182
Patterns for Designing in Teams ◆ 118
[Weir98]; 197
Patterns for Designing Navigable Information Spaces ◆ 119
[Rossi+99]; 194
Patterns for Encapsulating Class Trees ◆ 120
[Riehle96b]; 193

Patterns for Evolving Frameworks ◆ 121
[Roberts+98]; 194
Patterns for Generating a Layered Architecture ◆ 123
[Rubel95]; 194
Patterns for Logging Diagnostic Messages ◆ 124
[Harrison98]; 188
Patterns for Software Architectures ◆ 124
[Shaw95]; 196
Patterns for System Testing ◆ 126
[DeLano+98]; 186
Patterns of Events ◆ 129
[Ran95]; 193
Patterns on the Fly ◆ 130
[Olson98a]; 191
Peacemaker ◆ 131
Cult of Personality relationship to; Peacemaker ◆ 131
Guru Does All relationship to; Peacemaker ◆ 131
Sacrificial Lamb relationship to; Peacemaker ◆ 131
Pedestal ◆ 123
Bridge relationship to; Bridge ◆ 123
Four-Layer Architecture relationship to; Four-Layer Architecture ◆ 106, Pedestal ◆ 123
Hierarchy of Control Layers relationship to; Hierarchy of Control Layers ◆ 61, Pedestal ◆ 123
Layered and Sectioned Architecture relationship to; Layered and Sectioned Architecture ◆ 96, Pedestal ◆ 123
Layered Architecture relationship to; Pedestal ◆ 123, Layered Architecture ◆ 125
Layered Organization relationship to; Layered Organization ◆ 59, Pedestal ◆ 123
Layers relationship to; Layers ◆ 81, Pedestal ◆ 123
Shape of Program relationship to; Pedestal ◆ 123
Symmetrical Reuse relationship to; Symmetrical Reuse ◆ 123
Three-Tier Architecture relationship to; Three-Tier Architecture ◆ 15, Pedestal ◆ 123
peer-to-peer
interaction models, decoupling peers from underlying communication mechanisms; Forwarder-Receiver ◆ 60
people
See Also customer(s); human; human relationships; teams
modeling, in a transaction processing system; People, Places, and Things ◆ 165
People Know Best ◆ 57
Alarm Grid relationship to; Alarm Grid ◆ 79
Audible Alarm relationship to; Audible Alarm ◆ 79
Five Minutes of No Escalation Messages relationship to; Five Minutes of No Escalation Messages ◆ 57
Minimize Human Intervention relationship to; Minimize Human Intervention ◆ 57, People Know Best ◆ 57
People, Places, and Things ◆ 165
Key Business Activities and Influences relationship to; People, Places, and Things ◆ 165
Sacrifice One Person ◆ 170
People Know Best ◆ 57
People, Places, and Things ◆ 165

Pereira, J. D.
  [Silva+98]; 196
    OBJECT RECOVERY ◆ 92
  [Silva+99]; 196
    OBJECT SYNCHRONIZER ◆ 92
performance
  assessing the total cost relative to each feature;
    FUNCTIONALITY ALA CARTE ◆ 61
  assessment, software development; PRODUCTION
    POTENTIAL ◆ 26
  bottleneck analysis; HOT SPOT ◆ 82
  broker improvement; BROKER AS MATCHMAKER ◆ 133
  collection searching optimization; LOOKUP CACHE ◆ 161
  concatenating collections into streams for; CONCATENATING
    STREAM ◆ 162
  concurrency vs.; PERIODIC OBJECT ◆ 134
  criteria
    achievement determination; THRESHOLD SWITCH ◆ 82
    establishing; PERFORMANCE CRITERIA ◆ 82
  data locking vs. code locking; DATA LOCKING ◆ 147
  database, layering advantages for; RELATIONAL DATABASE
    ACCESS LAYER ◆ 3
  enhancement, in cryptographic systems; SECRECY WITH
    SIGNATURE WITH APPENDIX ◆ 175
  evaluation strategies; PERFORMANCE ASSESSMENT ◆ 81
  lazy optimzation, of Smalltalk programs; LAZY
    OPTIMIZATION: PATTERNS FOR EFFICIENT SMALLTALK
    PROGRAMMING ◆ 81
  measurement, strategies for; PERFORMANCE
    MEASUREMENT ◆ 82
  memory allocation strategies; ALLOCATOR CACHES ◆ 148
  MEMORY PERFORMANCE ASSESSMENT ◆ 73
  memory restrictions vs.; MEMORY PERFORMANCE
    ASSESSMENT ◆ 73
  methods, caching use; CACHING TEMPORARY VARIABLE ◆ 158
  parallel programs
    critical section fusing, as performance enhancement;
      CRITICAL-SECTION FUSING ◆ 148
    critical section partitioning; CRITICAL-SECTION
      PARTITIONING ◆ 148
    decoupling aggressive from conservative locking sections;
      PARALLEL FASTPATH ◆ 147
    hierarchical locking; HIERARCHICAL LOCKING ◆ 148
  PERFORMANCE ASSESSMENT ◆ 81
    PERFORMANCE CRITERIA relationship to; PERFORMANCE
      ASSESSMENT ◆ 81
  PERFORMANCE CRITERIA ◆ 82
    EXPERIMENT relationship to; EXPERIMENT ◆ 82
    HOT SPOT relationship to; HOT SPOT ◆ 82
    LAZY OPTIMIZATION relationship to; LAZY
      OPTIMIZATION ◆ 81
    PERFORMANCE ASSESSMENT relationship to; PERFORMANCE
      ASSESSMENT ◆ 81
    PERFORMANCE MEASUREMENT relationship to;
      PERFORMANCE CRITERIA ◆ 82
    THRESHOLD SWITCH relationship to; PERFORMANCE
      CRITERIA ◆ 82
  PERFORMANCE MEASUREMENT ◆ 82
    HOT SPOT relationship to; HOT SPOT ◆ 82

    LAZY OPTIMIZATION relationship to; LAZY
      OPTIMIZATION ◆ 81
    PERFORMANCE CRITERIA relationship to; PERFORMANCE
      CRITERIA ◆ 82
    THRESHOLD SWITCH relationship to; THRESHOLD
      SWITCH ◆ 82, PERFORMANCE MEASUREMENT ◆ 82
  prioritization of problem areas; HOT SPOT ◆ 82
  software development
    environment importance for; TEAM SPACE ◆ 27
    management strategies; CAPABLE, PRODUCTIVE, AND
      SATISFIED ◆ 26
  software development life-cycle rhythms; PULSE ◆ 27
  threads, access strategies for multiple threads;
    THREAD-SPECIFIC STORAGE ◆ 172
  tuning, systematic handling; EXPERIMENT ◆ 82
PERFORMANCE ASSESSMENT ◆ 81
PERFORMANCE CRITERIA ◆ 82
PERFORMANCE MEASUREMENT ◆ 82
PERIODIC OBJECT ◆ 134
periodicity
  PERIODIC OBJECT ◆ 134
    COMPOSITE relationship to; PERIODIC OBJECT ◆ 134
    DATA PUMP relationship to; PERIODIC OBJECT ◆ 134, DATA
      PUMP ◆ 135
    POINT relationship to; POINT ◆ 134
periphery
  WORK SHED AT PERIPHERY ◆ 102
Perl language
  as prototyping language, customer demonstration use;
    PROTOTYPING LANGUAGES ◆ 47
permissions
  user, encapsulating as roles; ROLES ◆ 17
persistence
  See Also databases
  of accessors, client-server application use; PERSISTENCE
    ACCESSORS ◆ 135
  PERSISTENCE ACCESSORS ◆ 135
  as persistent domain object component; MODEL
    HIERARCHY ◆ 136
  storage, integration mechanism for; SHARED
    REPOSITORY ◆ 115
  subsystem, decoupling from user interface; DOMAIN
    INTERCEPTS ◆ 137
PERSISTENCE ACCESSORS ◆ 135
PET PEEVE ◆ 129
  ADOPT-A-PROBLEM relationship to; ADOPT-A-PROBLEM ◆ 128,
    PET PEEVE ◆ 129
  DESIGNERS ARE OUR FRIENDS relationship to; PET
    PEEVE ◆ 129
  DOCUMENT THE PROBLEM relationship to; PET PEEVE ◆ 129
Peterson, S.
  [Peterson95]; 192
    STARS: A PATTERN LANGUAGE FOR QUERY-OPTIMIZED
      SCHEMAS ◆ 164
PHASING IT IN ◆ 64
phenomena
  linking ranges to; PHENOMENON WITH RANGE ◆ 10
  PHENOMENON WITH RANGE ◆ 10
    RANGE relationship to; RANGE ◆ 9

phenomena *continued*

    qualitative, encapsulating; Observation ◆ 8

    quantitative, encapsulating; Measurement ◆ 8

    subtyping; Subtyping Observation Concepts ◆ 8

Phenomenon with Range ◆ 10

phrases

    Noun Phrase Name ◆ 104

physical

    Physical View ◆ 3

    view

        accessing physical database tables with; Physical View ◆ 3

        connecting with domain views; Query Broker ◆ 4

Physical View ◆ 3

Piecemeal Growth ◆ 21

Piehler, M.

    [Piehler99]; 192

Pipeline ◆ 125

pipes

    filters and, for data streams; Pipes & Filters ◆ 132

    Pipeline ◆ 125

    Pipes & Filters ◆ 132

        Handlers relationship to; Handlers ◆ 95

        Streams relationship to; Streams ◆ 167

    as software architecture mechanism; Pipeline ◆ 125

Pipes & Filters ◆ 132

    [Buschmann+96]; 183

    [Meunier95]; 191

    [Shaw+96]; 196

Pitfall Diagnosis and Prevention ◆ 116

    Iterative Course Development relationship to; Pitfall Diagnosis and Prevention ◆ 116

    Quiz Games relationship to; Quiz Games ◆ 118

    Simulation Games relationship to; Pitfall Diagnosis and Prevention ◆ 116

    Visible Checklist relationship to; Pitfall Diagnosis and Prevention ◆ 116

placeholders

    for objects, strategies for creating; Proxy ◆ 139

places

    See Also location

    modeling, in a transaction processing system; People, Places, and Things ◆ 165

Plan ◆ 13

plan

    Plan ◆ 13

    term description; Plan ◆ 13

planning

    pilot studies use; Microcosm ◆ 168

platforms

    marketing importance of; Winning Team ◆ 151

    multiple, system testing on; Multiple Processors ◆ 128

plug-ins

    Pluggable Behavior ◆ 156

        Pluggable Block relationship to; Pluggable Block ◆ 156

    Pluggable Block ◆ 156

        Composed Method relationship to; Pluggable Block ◆ 156

        Pluggable Behavior relationship to; Pluggable Block ◆ 156

        Role Suggesting Instance Variable Name relationship to; Pluggable Block ◆ 156

    Pluggable Factory ◆ 132

        Abstract Factory relationship to; Pluggable Factory ◆ 132

        Factory Method relationship to; Pluggable Factory ◆ 132

        Product Trader relationship to; Pluggable Factory ◆ 132

        Prototype relationship to; Pluggable Factory ◆ 132

    Pluggable Objects ◆ 122

        Black-Box Framework relationship to; Black-Box Framework ◆ 122

        Component Library relationship to; Pluggable Objects ◆ 122

        Hot Spots relationship to; Pluggable Objects ◆ 122

    Pluggable Selector ◆ 156

        Composed Method relationship to; Pluggable Selector ◆ 156

        Role Suggesting Instance Variable Name relationship to; Pluggable Selector ◆ 156

    Pluggable View Controller ◆ 132

        Model-View-Controller relationship to; Pluggable View Controller ◆ 132

        Panel States relationship to; Panel States ◆ 96

    Tools and Materials Metaphor use; IP/FP Plug In ◆ 111

    Use a PluggableAdaptor to Hold Some Part of an Object ◆ 178

Pluggable Behavior ◆ 156

Pluggable Block ◆ 156

Pluggable Factory ◆ 132

    [VandenBroecke+97]; 197

    [Vlissides98b]; 197

    [Vlissides99]; 197

Pluggable Objects ◆ 122

Pluggable View Controller ◆ 132

    [Spall98]; 196

Pocket-Sized Broker ◆ 133

    [Olson98b]; 192

Point ◆ 114, ◆ 134

point

    Entry Point ◆ 16

    Pattern Language of Transport Systems (Point and Route) ◆ 114

    Point ◆ 114, ◆ 134

        Bridge relationship to; Point ◆ 134

        Data Pump relationship to; Point ◆ 134

        Deviation relationship to; Deviation ◆ 134

        Lazy State relationship to; Point ◆ 134

        Periodic Object relationship to; Point ◆ 134

        State relationship to; Point ◆ 114

    Points and Deviations: Pattern Language of Fire Alarm Systems ◆ 133

    position in space, tracking; Use a ScrollValueHolder to Hold a Position in n-Dimensional Space ◆ 178

    Single Access Point ◆ 17

pointers
COUNTED POINTER ◆ 40
vs. foreign keys, representation issues; FOREIGN KEY VERSUS
DIRECT REFERENCE ◆ 43
**POINTS AND DEVIATIONS: PATTERN LANGUAGE OF FIRE
ALARM SYSTEMS ◆ 133**
[Molin+98]; 191
policies
creating, separating support services from; DECISION MAKER'S
ROLE ◆ 30
work packets
priority; WORK PACKET PRIORITY ◆ 29
security; WORK PACKET SECURITY ◆ 29
polymorphism
adding an inheritance level to VISITOR; DEFAULT VISITOR ◆ 46
adding to unrelated classes; EXTERNAL POLYMORPHISM ◆ 56
EXTERNAL POLYMORPHISM ◆ 56
representation, in a relational database; SURROGATE ◆ 168
POOL ◆ 134
DEVIATION relationship to; DEVIATION ◆ 134, POOL ◆ 134
MANAGER relationship to; POOL ◆ 134
PORTFOLIO ◆ 13
portfolio
PORTFOLIO ◆ 13
CONTRACT relationship to; PORTFOLIO ◆ 13
term description; PORTFOLIO ◆ 13
Portner, N.
[Portner95]; 192
FLEXIBLE COMMAND INTERPRETER ◆ 60
position
responsibilities of, modeling; POST ◆ 7
USE A SCROLLVALUEHOLDER TO HOLD A POSITION IN
N-DIMENSIONAL SPACE ◆ 178
positive
POSITIVE CLOSURE ◆ 113
AUTHOR ASKS FOR CLARIFICATION relationship to; AUTHOR
ASKS FOR CLARIFICATION ◆ 113
SAFE SETTING relationship to; SAFE SETTING ◆ 111
SUGGESTIONS FOR IMPROVEMENT relationship to; POSITIVE
CLOSURE ◆ 113
POSITIVE FEEDBACK FIRST ◆ 113
FLY ON THE WALL relationship to; FLY ON THE WALL ◆ 112
SAFE SETTING relationship to; SAFE SETTING ◆ 111
SUGGESTIONS FOR IMPROVEMENT relationship to;
SUGGESTIONS FOR IMPROVEMENT ◆ 113
VOLUNTEER SUMMARIZES THE WORK relationship to;
POSITIVE FEEDBACK FIRST ◆ 113
POSITIVE CLOSURE ◆ 113
POSITIVE FEEDBACK FIRST ◆ 113
POST ◆ 7
POSTING ◆ 35
posting
POST ◆ 7
POSTING ◆ 35
ACCOUNT relationship to; POSTING ◆ 35
POSTING RULES relationship to; POSTING ◆ 35
TRANSACTION relationship to; POSTING ◆ 35
POSTING RULE EXECUTION ◆ 11

POSTING RULES ◆ 11
ACCOUNTING PRACTICE relationship to; ACCOUNTING
PRACTICE ◆ 12
POSTING relationship to; POSTING ◆ 35
POSTING RULES FOR MANY ACCOUNTS ◆ 11
ACCOUNT relationship to; POSTING RULES FOR MANY
ACCOUNTS ◆ 11
ACCOUNTABILITY KNOWLEDGE LEVEL relationship to;
POSTING RULES FOR MANY ACCOUNTS ◆ 11
SUMMARY ACCOUNT relationship to; POSTING RULES FOR
MANY ACCOUNTS ◆ 11
rules
for many accounts, handling; POSTING RULES FOR MANY
ACCOUNTS ◆ 11
creating a structure for; ACCOUNTING PRACTICE ◆ 12
decoupling strategy from; POSTING RULE EXECUTION ◆ 11
recording for a transaction; SOURCES OF AN ENTRY ◆ 12
POSTING RULE EXECUTION ◆ 11
POSTING RULES ◆ 11
POSTING RULES FOR MANY ACCOUNTS ◆ 11
potential
PRODUCTION POTENTIAL ◆ 26
powers
SEPARATION OF POWERS ◆ 110
practice
ACCOUNTING PRACTICE ◆ 12
SMALLTALK BEST PRACTICE PATTERNS ◆ 152
PRAGMATIC EXTERNAL REQUIREMENTS ◆ 142
GET INVOLVED EARLY relationship to; PRAGMATIC EXTERNAL
REQUIREMENTS ◆ 142
MANAGING AND MEETING CUSTOMER EXPECTATIONS
relationship to; MANAGING AND MEETING CUSTOMER
EXPECTATIONS ◆ 140
REQUIREMENTS VALIDATION relationship to; PRAGMATIC
EXTERNAL REQUIREMENTS ◆ 142
Prantzalos, D.
[Price+99]; 192
predictions
WHEN STATES ARE CONDITIONS, USE PREDICATIVE STATE
CLASSES ◆ 88
Pree, W.
[Pree94]; 192
HOOK METHOD ◆ 73
PRESENTATION AND APPLICATION LOGIC ◆ 15
PRESENTATION-ABSTRACTION-CONTROL ◆ 135
[Buschmann+96]; 183
presentations
See Also demonstrations
decoupling from domain model, in application layer;
PRESENTATION AND APPLICATION LOGIC ◆ 15
DEFINE AND RUN PRESENTATION ◆ 36
multimedia
defining and running; DEFINE AND RUN PRESENTATION ◆ 36
synchronizing; SYNCHRONIZE CHANNELS ◆ 37
updating; REQUEST SCREEN MODIFICATION ◆ 144
PRESENTATION AND APPLICATION LOGIC ◆ 15
FACADE relationship to; PRESENTATION AND APPLICATION
LOGIC ◆ 15

presentations *continued*
  PRESENTATION AND APPLICATION LOGIC *continued*
    PRESENTATION-ABSTRACTION-CONTROL relationship to;
      PRESENTATION AND APPLICATION LOGIC ♦ 15
    THREE-TIER ARCHITECTURE relationship to; PRESENTATION
      AND APPLICATION LOGIC ♦ 15
  PRESENTATION-ABSTRACTION-CONTROL ♦ 135
    LAYERS relationship to; LAYERS ♦ 81
    MODEL-VIEW-CONTROLLER relationship to;
      PRESENTATION-ABSTRACTION-CONTROL ♦ 135
    PRESENTATION AND APPLICATION LOGIC relationship to;
      PRESENTATION AND APPLICATION LOGIC ♦ 15
    VIEW HANDLER relationship to; VIEW HANDLER ♦ 178
preserving
  values, of simple variables, in a change log; CHANGE LOG ♦ 34
preventing
  redundancy, in complex systems; OBJECT MERGE ♦ 10
Price, M.
  [Price+99]; 192
primitives
  SELECTING LOCKING PRIMITIVES FOR PARALLEL
    PROGRAMMING ♦ 148
printing
  debug print method; DEBUG PRINTING METHOD ♦ 154
  DEBUG PRINTING METHOD ♦ 154
priorities
  among error alarms, in fault-tolerant systems; IO TRIAGE ♦ 77
  in fault-tolerant systems, human override; SHUT UP AND
    LISTEN ♦ 79
  fault-tolerant systems, System Integrity Control Program
    importance; SICO FIRST AND ALWAYS ♦ 58
  meeting speakers; CHAMPIONS SPEAK FIRST ♦ 74
  performance bottlenecks; HOT SPOT ♦ 82
  PRIORITIZING FORCES IN SOFTWARE DESIGN ♦ 135
  project, strategies for scheduling; WORK QUEUE ♦ 52
  software design, as big ball of mud system avoidance strategy;
    BIG BALL OF MUD ♦ 21
  software development forces; PRIORITIZING FORCES IN
    SOFTWARE DESIGN ♦ 135
  of software development tasks, strategies for; BACKLOG ♦ 146
  WORK PACKET PRIORITY ♦ 29
  work packets, establishing policies for; WORK PACKET
    PRIORITY ♦ 29
PRIORITIZING FORCES IN SOFTWARE DESIGN ♦ 135
  [Cockburn96]; 185
PRIVATE VERSIONING ♦ 170
  CODE OWNERSHIP relationship to; PRIVATE VERSIONING ♦ 170
  INCREMENTAL INTEGRATION relationship to; INCREMENTAL
    INTEGRATION ♦ 170
PROACTOR ♦ 137
  ACTIVE OBJECT relationship to; PROACTOR ♦ 137
  ASYNCHRONOUS COMPLETION TOKEN relationship
    to; ASYNCHRONOUS COMPLETION TOKEN ♦ 19,
    PROACTOR ♦ 137
  CHAIN OF RESPONSIBILITY relationship to; PROACTOR ♦ 137
  OBSERVER relationship to; PROACTOR ♦ 137
  [Pyarali+99]; 193
  REACTOR relationship to; PROACTOR ♦ 137
PROBLEM AREA ♦ 127

PROBLEM DOMAIN ANALYSIS ♦ 141
PROBLEM/SOLUTION SUMMARY ♦ 105
problems
  ADOPT-A-PROBLEM ♦ 128
  common, factoring, when writing a pattern language; COMMON
    PROBLEMS HIGHLIGHTED ♦ 106
  COMMON PROBLEMS HIGHLIGHTED ♦ 106
  DOCUMENT THE PROBLEM ♦ 128
  documentation, system testing use; USE OLD PROBLEM
    REPORTS ♦ 127, DOCUMENT THE PROBLEM ♦ 128
  domain
    analysis; PROBLEM DOMAIN ANALYSIS ♦ 141
    role of objects in; OBJECT STEREOTYPES ♦ 141
  IDENTIFY PROBLEM DOMAIN RELATIONSHIPS ♦ 70
  one-off, design principles that avoid trashy code; THROWAWAY
    CODE ♦ 21
  pattern language summary of; PROBLEM/SOLUTION
    SUMMARY ♦ 105
  PROBLEM AREA ♦ 127
    AMBIGUOUS DOCUMENTATION relationship to; PROBLEM
      AREA ♦ 127
    USE OLD PROBLEM REPORTS relationship to; PROBLEM
      AREA ♦ 127
  PROBLEM DOMAIN ANALYSIS ♦ 141
    BEHAVIORAL REQUIREMENTS relationship to; PROBLEM
      DOMAIN ANALYSIS ♦ 141
    BUSINESS RULES relationship to; PROBLEM DOMAIN
      ANALYSIS ♦ 141
    CLASSIFYING, ASSOCIATING, AND GROUPING THE
      DOMAIN OBJECTS relationship to; PROBLEM DOMAIN
      ANALYSIS ♦ 141
    ELABORATION OF THE DOMAIN OBJECTS relationship to;
      PROBLEM DOMAIN ANALYSIS ♦ 141
    FINDING AND DEFINING THE DOMAIN OBJECTS relationship
      to; PROBLEM DOMAIN ANALYSIS ♦ 141
    INFORMATION NEEDS relationship to; PROBLEM DOMAIN
      ANALYSIS ♦ 141
    OBJECT AGING relationship to; PROBLEM DOMAIN
      ANALYSIS ♦ 141
    REQUIREMENTS SPECIFICATION relationship to;
      REQUIREMENTS SPECIFICATION ♦ 142
  PROBLEM DOMAIN ANAYSIS, DEFINING REQUIREMENTS
    relationship to; DEFINING REQUIREMENTS ♦ 140
  PROBLEM-ORIENTED TEAM ♦ 27
    BOOTSTRAPPING relationship to; BOOTSTRAPPING ♦ 26
  PROBLEM/SOLUTION SUMMARY ♦ 105
    INTENT CATALOG relationship to; PROBLEM/SOLUTION
      SUMMARY ♦ 105
  quick fix, design principles that avoid trashy code;
    THROWAWAY CODE ♦ 21
  resolving, in system testing; PET PEEVE ♦ 129
  SCENARIOS DEFINE PROBLEM ♦ 66
  selecting, for system test; PROBLEM AREA ♦ 127
  unresolved, system test handling; ADOPT-A-PROBLEM ♦ 128
  USE OLD PROBLEM REPORTS ♦ 127
PROCESS CONTROL ♦ 137
  [Shaw+96]; 196
process(ing)
  See Also handling

COMMAND PROCESSOR ♦ 36

COMMUNICATING PROCESSES ♦ 36

CONTINUOUS PROCESSING ♦ 174

control system; PROCESS CONTROL ♦ 137

cost, optimization strategies; OPTIMIZE HIGH-RUNNER
CASES ♦ 100

data stream packets, into data products; HANDLERS ♦ 95

DEVELOPER CONTROLS PROCESS ♦ 65

distributed, distributed system architectures; DISTRIBUTED
PROCESSES ♦ 51

DISTRIBUTED PROCESSES ♦ 51

forking; FORK/JOIN ♦ 40

HIGH-LEVEL AND PROCESS PATTERNS FROM THE MEMORY
PRESERVATION SOCIETY ♦ 71

independent, coordinating; COMMUNICATING PROCESSES ♦ 36

interprocess communication, providing transparency in;
FORWARDER-RECEIVER ♦ 60

interprocess protocols, distributed system architecture use;
DISTRIBUTED PROCESSES ♦ 51

PATTERN FOR SEPARATING ASSEMBLY AND PROCESSING ♦ 97

power, as limiting factor, strategies for dealing with;
PROCESSING CAPACITY ♦ 100

PROCESS CONTROL ♦ 137

PROCESS OF OBSERVATION ♦ 9

ASSOCIATED OBSERVATION relationship to; PROCESS OF
OBSERVATION ♦ 9

process-oriented systems, architecture for; MESSAGING
ENGINEERING MODEL ♦ 18

PROCESSING CAPACITY ♦ 100

OPTIMIZE HIGH-RUNNER CASES relationship to; PROCESSING
CAPACITY ♦ 100

SHARE THE LOAD relationship to; PROCESSING
CAPACITY ♦ 100

SHED LOAD relationship to; PROCESSING CAPACITY ♦ 100

SEPARATE TRANSACTION PROCESSING FROM ARCHIVAL ♦ 173

PROCESS OF OBSERVATION ♦ 9

PROCESSING CAPACITY ♦ 100

processors

data ownership, as parallelism management strategy; DATA
OWNERSHIP ♦ 147

distributing locks among; DISTRIBUTED READER/WRITER
LOCK ♦ 149

multiple

See Also distributed systems

overload communication among; LEAKY BUCKET OF
CREDITS ♦ 102

system testing on; MULTIPLE PROCESSORS ♦ 128

MULTIPLE PROCESSORS ♦ 128

producers

consumer separation from; PATTERN FOR SEPARATING
ASSEMBLY AND PROCESSING ♦ 97

PRODUCT ♦ 14

PRODUCT INITIATIVE ♦ 52

PRODUCT TRADER ♦ 138

[Baumer+98]; 184

production

functionality, identifying; IMPLIED REQUIREMENTS ♦ 52

PRODUCTION POTENTIAL ♦ 26

BOOTSTRAPPING relationship to; PRODUCTION
POTENTIAL ♦ 26

PULSE relationship to; PRODUCTION POTENTIAL ♦ 26

ROUND PEGS FOR ROUND HOLES relationship to;
PRODUCTION POTENTIAL ♦ 26

SCRUM: A PATTERN LANGUAGE FOR HYPERPRODUCTIVE
SOFTWARE DEVELOPMENT ♦ 146

PRODUCTION POTENTIAL ♦ 26

products

ARCHITECT CONTROLS PRODUCT ♦ 65

customer expectations, classifying; MANAGING AND MEETING
CUSTOMER EXPECTATIONS ♦ 140

decoupling clients from; PRODUCT TRADER ♦ 138

domain, identifying relationships in; IDENTIFY PROBLEM
DOMAIN RELATIONSHIPS ♦ 70

evolution of, event-centered architecture support of;
EVENT-CENTERED ARCHITECTURE ♦ 129

evolving a prototype into; FROM PROTOTYPE TO REALITY ♦ 61,
PROTOTYPE AND REALITY ♦ 63, OBJECT-ORIENTED DESIGN
PATTERNS IN REACTIVE SYSTEMS ♦ 92

improvement, defining an initiative for; PRODUCT
INITIATIVE ♦ 52

as performance measurement tool; PERFORMANCE
MEASUREMENT ♦ 82

PRODUCT ♦ 14

CONTRACT relationship to; PRODUCT ♦ 14

PRODUCT INITIATIVE ♦ 52

IMPLIED REQUIREMENTS relationship to; IMPLIED
REQUIREMENTS ♦ 52

MARKET WALK-THROUGH relationship to; PRODUCT
INITIATIVE ♦ 52

RECOMMITMENT MEETING relationship to; RECOMMITMENT
MEETING ♦ 53

PRODUCT TRADER ♦ 138

PLUGGABLE FACTORY relationship to; PLUGGABLE
FACTORY ♦ 132

SERIALIZER relationship to; SERIALIZER ♦ 151

requirements specification, team composition for; DIVERSITY
OF MEMBERSHIP ♦ 95

term description; PRODUCT ♦ 14

types, dynamic specification of; PLUGGABLE FACTORY ♦ 132

profiles

security, encapsulating; ROLES ♦ 17

program committee (PC)

running the PC meeting, speaker priorities; CHAMPIONS SPEAK
FIRST ♦ 74

technical paper acceptance process; IDENTIFY THE CHAMPION
PATTERN LANGUAGE ♦ 73

programming

See Also code

episode, scheduling strategies; PROGRAMMING EPISODE ♦ 54

minimizing, for customer demonstrations; MUTABLE
CODE ♦ 47

pair, software development advantages; DEVELOPING IN
PAIRS ♦ 69

PROGRAMMING EPISODE ♦ 54

INFORMAL LABOR PLAN relationship to; INFORMAL LABOR
PLAN ♦ 53

programming *continued*

PROGRAMMING-BY-DIFFERENCE ♦ 150

ADAPTER relationship to; PROGRAMMING-BY-
DIFFERENCE ♦ 150

COMPOSITE relationship to; PROGRAMMING-BY-
DIFFERENCE ♦ 150

DECORATOR relationship to; PROGRAMMING-BY-
DIFFERENCE ♦ 150

FACADE relationship to; PROGRAMMING-BY-
DIFFERENCE ♦ 150

INTERPRETER relationship to; PROGRAMMING-BY-
DIFFERENCE ♦ 150

LOW SURFACE-TO-VOLUME RATIO relationship to;
PROGRAMMING-BY-DIFFERENCE ♦ 150

SELFISH CLASS relationship to; SELFISH CLASS ♦ 150

WORKS OUT OF THE BOX relationship to;
PROGRAMMING-BY-DIFFERENCE ♦ 150

PROGRAMMING EPISODE ♦ 54

PROGRAMMING-BY-DIFFERENCE ♦ 150

programs

roles, establishing; SYSTEM CITIZEN'S ROLE ♦ 29

SEQUENTIAL PROGRAM ♦ 147

progress

FINISH WORK IN PROGRESS ♦ 101

projections

ACTIVE OBSERVATION, HYPOTHESIS, AND PROJECTION ♦ 9

assurance level of; ACTIVE OBSERVATION, HYPOTHESIS, AND
PROJECTION ♦ 9

data implications; INSTANT PROJECTION ♦ 33

INSTANT PROJECTION ♦ 33

projects

building, as team training technique; TRIAL PROJECT ♦ 130

champion, software development role; PATRON ♦ 65

continuity, high-level manager/champion role; PATRON ♦ 65

design, technical writing role; MERCENARY ANALYST ♦ 67

documentation, technical memos as strategy for; TECHNICAL
MEMO ♦ 54

scheduling

delay handling strategies; RECOMMITMENT MEETING ♦ 53

divide-and-conquor strategy; WORK SPLIT ♦ 53

programming episode strategy; PROGRAMMING EPISODE ♦ 54

requirements development plan strategies; REQUIREMENT
WALK-THROUGH ♦ 54

short term work plan strategies; INFORMAL LABOR
PLAN ♦ 53

status tracking; WORK QUEUE REPORT ♦ 52

strategies for; WORK QUEUE ♦ 52

SURVIVING OBJECT-ORIENTED PROJECTS: A MANAGER'S
GUIDE ♦ 168

time estimation strategies; COMPARABLE WORK ♦ 52

estimation strategies; COMPLETION HEADROOM ♦ 53

TRIAL PROJECT ♦ 130

troubled; CULT OF PERSONALITY ♦ 130

strategies for handling; GURU DOES ALL ♦ 130, CULT OF
PERSONALITY ♦ 130, CARGO CULT ♦ 131, CONTAINMENT
BUILDING ♦ 131

PROMOTE AND ADD ♦ 26

promotion

See Also conversion

data type, between different but related C++ types; TYPE
PROMOTION ♦ 26

data types, encapsulation of how; PROMOTION LADDER ♦ 26

non-hierarchical; NON-HIERARCHICAL ADDITION ♦ 26

PROMOTE AND ADD ♦ 26

ALGEBRAIC HIERARCHY relationship to; ALGEBRAIC
HIERARCHY ♦ 25, PROMOTE AND ADD ♦ 26

HOMOGENEOUS ADDITION relationship to; HOMOGENEOUS
ADDITION ♦ 25, PROMOTE AND ADD ♦ 26

NON-HIERARCHICAL ADDITION relationship to; PROMOTE
AND ADD ♦ 26

PROMOTION LADDER relationship to; PROMOTE AND
ADD ♦ 26, PROMOTION LADDER ♦ 26

PROMOTION LADDER ♦ 26

ALGEBRAIC HIERARCHY relationship to; ALGEBRAIC
HIERARCHY ♦ 25

ENVELOPE/LETTER relationship to; ENVELOPE/LETTER ♦ 25

NON-HIERARCHICAL ADDITION relationship to;
NON-HIERARCHICAL ADDITION ♦ 26

PROMOTE AND ADD relationship to; PROMOTE AND
ADD ♦ 26, PROMOTION LADDER ♦ 26

TYPE PROMOTION ♦ 26

proof of concept code

design principles, that avoid trashy code; THROWAWAY
CODE ♦ 21

propagation

ADAPTIVE PROPAGATOR ♦ 138

LAZY PROPAGATOR ♦ 138

PROPAGATOR: A FAMILY OF PATTERNS ♦ 138

OBSERVER relationship to; PROPAGATOR: A FAMILY OF
PATTERNS ♦ 138

PUBLISHER-SUBSCRIBER relationship to; PROPAGATOR: A
FAMILY OF PATTERNS ♦ 138

STRICT PROPAGATOR ♦ 138

STRICT PROPAGATOR WITH FAILURE ♦ 138

of updates

adaptively; ADAPTIVE PROPAGATOR ♦ 138

with delegation; LAZY PROPAGATOR ♦ 138

in a dependency network; PROPAGATOR: A FAMILY OF
PATTERNS ♦ 138

with failure marking; STRICT PROPAGATOR WITH
FAILURE ♦ 138

immediately; STRICT PROPAGATOR ♦ 138

one-way; PUBLISHER-SUBSCRIBER ♦ 139

PROPAGATOR: A FAMILY OF PATTERNS ♦ 138

[Feiler+99]; 187

properties

See Also attributes

boolean, setting; BOOLEAN PROPERTY SETTING
METHOD ♦ 158

BOOLEAN PROPERTY SETTING METHOD ♦ 158

change over time; TEMPORAL PROPERTY ♦ 171

class, class clause representation of; CLASS CLAUSE ♦ 121

concealing, during object list display; PARALLEL APPLICATION
AND DOMAIN HIERARCHIES ♦ 14

object, testing; QUERY METHOD ♦ 153

TEMPORAL PROPERTY ♦ 171

topological, of distributed systems; DISTRIBUTED
PROCESSES ♦ 51

PROPOSED AND IMPLEMENTED ACTION ♦ 12

PROTECTED VARIATIONS ♦ 135

protection

CRITICAL REGION PROTECTION ♦ 31

PROTECTED VARIATIONS ♦ 135

PROTECTION PROXY, PROXY DESIGN PATTERN REVISITED
relationship to; PROXY DESIGN PATTERN REVISITED ♦ 139

of shared resources; CRITICAL REGION PROTECTION ♦ 31

PROTOCOL ♦ 8, ♦ 13

protocols

See Also rules

customer, components of; MIND YOUR MANNERS ♦ 44

DEFINE DEFAULT VALUES VIA EXPLICIT PROTOCOL ♦ 146

different, object conversion; CONVERTER CONSTRUCTOR
METHOD ♦ 153

encapsulating; PROTOCOL ♦ 8

HALF-OBJECT + PROTOCOL ♦ 71

hand-off, sessions use to manage; SESSION ♦ 37

interprocess, distributed system architecture use; DISTRIBUTED
PROCESSES ♦ 51

linking to observations, through outcome and start functions;
OUTCOME AND START FUNCTIONS ♦ 13

measurement, in corporate analysis; MEASUREMENT
PROTOCOL ♦ 9

MEASUREMENT PROTOCOL ♦ 9

MEDIATING PROTOCOL ♦ 155

object coordination, in multiple address spaces; HALF-OBJECT
+ PROTOCOL ♦ 71

pattern writers workshops; PATTERN LANGUAGE FOR
WRITERS' WORKSHOPS ♦ 111

PROTOCOL ♦ 8, ♦ 13

same, object conversion with; CONVERTER METHOD ♦ 153

system citizens, establishing for programs; SYSTEM CITIZEN'S
ROLE ♦ 29

term description; PROTOCOL ♦ 13

PROTOTYPE ♦ 69, ♦ 138, ♦ 168

[Alpert+98]; 182

[Gamma+95]; 188

PROTOTYPE A FIRST-PASS DESIGN ♦ 84

PROTOTYPE AND REALITY ♦ 63

PROTOTYPE-BASED OBJECT SYSTEM ♦ 139

[Noble99b]; 191

PROTOTYPES ♦ 142

prototyping

as customer requirements identification tool;
PROTOTYPES ♦ 142

design principles, that avoid trashy code; THROWAWAY
CODE ♦ 21

dynamic specification, of product types; PLUGGABLE
FACTORY ♦ 132

as early-stage software development tool

discovering what works; PROTOTYPE ♦ 168

uncovering development issues; EARLY AND REGULAR
DELIVERY ♦ 168

uncovering domain issues; CLEAR THE FOG ♦ 168

evolving the final product from; FROM PROTOTYPE TO
REALITY ♦ 61, PROTOTYPE AND REALITY ♦ 63,
OBJECT-ORIENTED DESIGN PATTERNS IN REACTIVE
SYSTEMS ♦ 92

EXPAND THE INITIAL PROTOTYPE ♦ 84

expanding, as software development stage; EXPAND THE
INITIAL PROTOTYPE ♦ 84

FROM PROTOTYPE TO REALITY ♦ 61

languages, customer demonstration use; PROTOTYPING
LANGUAGES ♦ 47

as model design tool; EXECUTABLE MODELS ♦ 45

object systems based on; PROTOTYPE-BASED OBJECT
SYSTEM ♦ 139

objects, strategies for; PROTOTYPE ♦ 138

performance evaluation role; PERFORMANCE ASSESSMENT ♦ 81

product transition strategies; OBJECT-ORIENTED
SIMULATION ♦ 93

project planning, pilot studies use; MICROCOSM ♦ 168

PROTOTYPE ♦ 69, ♦ 138, ♦ 168

ABSTRACT FACTORY relationship to; ABSTRACT FACTORY ♦ 2

CLEAR THE FOG relationship to; CLEAR THE FOG ♦ 168,
PROTOTYPE ♦ 168

COMMAND relationship to; COMMAND ♦ 35

EXECUTABLE MODELS relationship to; EXECUTABLE
MODELS ♦ 45

ITERABLE CONTAINER relationship to; ITERABLE
CONTAINER ♦ 80

PLUGGABLE FACTORY relationship to; PLUGGABLE
FACTORY ♦ 132

PROTOTYPE A FIRST PASS DESIGN relationship to;
PROTOTYPE ♦ 69

PROTOTYPE a FIRST-PASS DESIGN relationship to;
PROTOTYPE a FIRST-PASS DESIGN ♦ 84

PROTOTYPE A FIRST-PASS DESIGN relationship to;
PROTOTYPE ♦ 168

PROTOTYPES relationship to; PROTOTYPE ♦ 69,
PROTOTYPES ♦ 142, PROTOTYPE ♦ 168

PROTOTYPE A FIRST PASS DESIGN, PROTOTYPE relationship to;
PROTOTYPE ♦ 69

PROTOTYPE a FIRST-PASS DESIGN ♦ 84

EXECUTABLE MODELS relationship to; EXECUTABLE
MODELS ♦ 45

PROTOTYPE relationship to; PROTOTYPE a FIRST-PASS
DESIGN ♦ 84

PROTOTYPES relationship to; PROTOTYPE a FIRST-PASS
DESIGN ♦ 84

PROTOTYPE A FIRST-PASS DESIGN, PROTOTYPE relationship to;
PROTOTYPE ♦ 168

PROTOTYPE AND REALITY ♦ 63

ADAPTER relationship to; PROTOTYPE AND REALITY ♦ 63

BRIDGE relationship to; PROTOTYPE AND REALITY ♦ 63

FROM PROTOTYPE TO REALITY relationship to; FROM
PROTOTYPE TO REALITY ♦ 61, PROTOTYPE AND
REALITY ♦ 63

OBJECTIFY SYSTEM STATE relationship to; OBJECTIFY
SYSTEM STATE ♦ 93

OBJECTS WITH REMOTE CONTROL relationship to; OBJECTS
WITH REMOTE CONTROL ♦ 93

PROTOTYPE-BASED OBJECT SYSTEM ♦ 139

METAMORPHOSIS relationship to; PROTOTYPE-BASED OBJECT
SYSTEM ♦ 139

REFLECTION relationship to; PROTOTYPE-BASED OBJECT
SYSTEM ♦ 139, REFLECTION ♦ 144

prototyping *continued*
  PROTOTYPE-BASED OBJECT SYSTEM *continued*
    TYPE OBJECT relationship to; PROTOTYPE-BASED OBJECT
      SYSTEM ♦ 139
  PROTOTYPES ♦ 142
    CUSTOMER RAPPORT relationship to; CUSTOMER
      RAPPORT ♦ 140
    INFORMATION NEEDS relationship to; INFORMATION
      NEEDS ♦ 141
    MANAGING AND MEETING CUSTOMER EXPECTATIONS
      relationship to; MANAGING AND MEETING CUSTOMER
      EXPECTATIONS ♦ 140
    PROTOTYPE A FIRST-PASS DESIGN relationship to;
      PROTOTYPE A FIRST-PASS DESIGN ♦ 84
    PROTOTYPE relationship to; PROTOTYPE ♦ 69,
      PROTOTYPES ♦ 142, PROTOTYPE ♦ 168
    REQUIREMENTS VALIDATION relationship to; REQUIREMENTS
      VALIDATION ♦ 143
    USER INTERFACE REQUIREMENTS relationship to; USER
      INTERFACE REQUIREMENTS ♦ 142
  PROTOTYPING LANGUAGES ♦ 47
    CATALYTIC SCENARIOS relationship to; PROTOTYPING
      LANGUAGES ♦ 47
    ELEMENT IDENTIFICATION relationship to; ELEMENT
      IDENTIFICATION ♦ 46
    EXECUTABLE MODELS relationship to; EXECUTABLE
      MODELS ♦ 45
    JUDICIOUS FIREWORKS relationship to; PROTOTYPING
      LANGUAGES ♦ 47
    LIGHTWEIGHT USER INTERFACES relationship to;
      PROTOTYPING LANGUAGES ♦ 47
  Smalltalk patterns for; SMALLTALK SCAFFOLDING
    PATTERNS ♦ 163
  software development; PROTOTYPE ♦ 69
PROTOTYPING LANGUAGES ♦ 47
proxies
  distributed system control use; REMOTE CONTROL ♦ 144
  for objects, strategies for creating; PROXY ♦ 139
  PROXY ♦ 139
    ADAPTER relationship to; ADAPTER ♦ 6, PROXY ♦ 139
    BACKUP relationship to; BACKUP ♦ 19
    BODYGUARD relationship to; BODYGUARD ♦ 22
    BROKER AS DIVORCE ATTORNEY relationship to; BROKER AS
      DIVORCE ATTORNEY ♦ 133
    BROKER relationship to; BROKER ♦ 108
    DECORATOR relationship to; DECORATOR ♦ 46, PROXY ♦ 139
    FOREIGN KEY VERSUS DIRECT REFERENCE relationship to;
      FOREIGN KEY VERSUS DIRECT REFERENCE ♦ 43
    MATERIALIZATION relationship to; MATERIALIZATION ♦ 90
    NULL OBJECT relationship to; NULL OBJECT ♦ 91
    OBJECT METADATA relationship to; OBJECT
      METADATA ♦ 108
    OBJECT RECURSION relationship to; OBJECT RECURSION ♦ 92
    OBJECT SYNCHRONIZER relationship to; OBJECT
      SYNCHRONIZER ♦ 92
    QUERY OBJECT relationship to; QUERY OBJECT ♦ 108
    RECOVERABLE DISTRIBUTOR relationship to; RECOVERABLE
      DISTRIBUTOR ♦ 143

    REMOTE OPERATION relationship to; REMOTE
      OPERATION ♦ 115
    SPONSOR-SELECTOR relationship to; SPONSOR-
      SELECTOR ♦ 164
    THREAD-SPECIFIC STORAGE relationship to;
      THREAD-SPECIFIC STORAGE ♦ 172
  PROXY DESIGN PATTERN REVISITED ♦ 139
  variants on PROXY; PROXY DESIGN PATTERN REVISITED ♦ 139
PROXY ♦ 139
  [Alpert+98]; 182
  [Buschmann+96]; 183
  [Gamma+95]; 188
PROXY DESIGN PATTERN REVISITED ♦ 139
  [Rohner96]; 194
Pryce, N.
  [Pryce99]; 193
    ABSTRACT SESSION ♦ 2
  [Schmidt+99]; 195
    THREAD-SPECIFIC STORAGE ♦ 172
PSEUDO-IO ♦ 79
  MIND YOUR OWN BUSINESS relationship to; PSEUDO-IO ♦ 79
  MML relationship to; MML ♦ 77
publication
  hypothetical, error detection use; HYPOTHETICAL
    PUBLICATION ♦ 33
  HYPOTHETICAL PUBLICATION ♦ 33
PUBLISHER-SUBSCRIBER ♦ 139
  [Buschmann+96]; 183
publishing
  PUBLISHER-SUBSCRIBER ♦ 139
    OBSERVER relationship to; OBSERVER ♦ 94,
      PUBLISHER-SUBSCRIBER ♦ 139
    PROPAGATOR: A FAMILY OF PATTERNS relationship to;
      PROPAGATOR: A FAMILY OF PATTERNS ♦ 138
PULSE ♦ 27
  PRODUCTION POTENTIAL relationship to; PRODUCTION
    POTENTIAL ♦ 26
pump
  DATA PUMP ♦ 135
pure
  PURE STATE ♦ 166
  state objects; PURE STATE ♦ 166
PURE STATE ♦ 166
purpose
  UNITY OF PURPOSE ♦ 95
PUT FREQUENTLY VARYING STRUCTURES IN INSTANCES ♦ 5
Pyarali, I.
  [Pyarali+98]; 193
    ASYNCHRONOUS COMPLETION TOKEN ♦ 19
  [Pyarali+99]; 193
    PROACTOR ♦ 137

QA (quality assurance)
  ENGAGE QA ♦ 66
  software development role; ENGAGE QA ♦ 66
  testing strategies for; PATTERNS FOR SYSTEM TESTING ♦ 126
qualification
  QUALIFIED SUBCLASS NAME ♦ 162
QUALIFIED SUBCLASS NAME ♦ 162

qualitative phenomena
  encapsulating, encapsulating; Observation ♦ 8
quantities
  large, Flyweight management of; Flyweight ♦ 60
  quantitative phenomena, encapsulating; Measurement ♦ 8
  Quantity ♦ 8
    Conversion Ratio relationship to; Conversion Ratio ♦ 8
    Whole Value relationship to; Quantity ♦ 8
  representation of; Whole Value ♦ 32
    outside the normal range; Exceptional Value ♦ 32
Quantity ♦ 8
queries
  composable, dynamic query generation use; Composable Query Objects ♦ 41
  Composable Query Objects ♦ 41
  Creating Reports with Query Objects ♦ 40
  database, dynamic generation of; Creating Reports with Query Objects ♦ 40
  for decision support systems; Stars: A Pattern Language for Query-Optimized Schemas ♦ 164
  diagnostic, as error detection and correction mechanism; Diagnostic Query ♦ 33
  Diagnostic Query ♦ 33
  dynamic, design strategies; Query Objects ♦ 41
  for OLTP system; Query Optimized Database ♦ 165
  Query Broker ♦ 4
    Broker relationship to; Query Broker ♦ 4
    used by Hierarchical View; Hierarchical View ♦ 3
    used by Relational Database Access Layer; Relational Database Access Layer ♦ 3
  Query Method ♦ 153
  Query Object ♦ 108
    Broker relationship to; Broker ♦ 108, Query Object ♦ 108
    Object Metadata relationship to; Object Metadata ♦ 108, Query Object ♦ 108
    Proxy relationship to; Query Object ♦ 108
  Query Objects ♦ 41
    Composable Query Objects relationship to; Composable Query Objects ♦ 41
    Report Objects relationship to; Report Objects ♦ 41, Query Objects ♦ 41
  Query Optimized Database ♦ 165
    Key Business Activities and Influences relationship to; Query Optimized Database ♦ 165
    Whole Business Entities relationship to; Whole Business Entities ♦ 165
  query-before-write, as cache management strategy; Cache Management ♦ 109
  SQL, representation of; Query Object ♦ 108
  Stars: A Pattern Language for Query-Optimized Schemas ♦ 164
Query Broker ♦ 4
Query Method ♦ 153
Query Object ♦ 108
Query Objects ♦ 41
Query Optimized Database ♦ 165
Queue ♦ 161
Queued Lock ♦ 149

Queued Reader/Writer Lock ♦ 149
queues
  event
    interactive application use; Event Queue ♦ 76
    overload handling strategies; Merge Compatible Events ♦ 76, Handle Artificial Events ♦ 76
  Event Queue ♦ 76
  implementing; Queue ♦ 161
  Improving Responsiveness in Interactive Applications Using Queues ♦ 76
  LIFO, workload management; Fresh Work Before Stale ♦ 101
  lock, reader/writer; Queued Reader/Writer Lock ♦ 149
  locks; Queued Lock ♦ 149
  Ordered Collection, Queue relationship to; Queue ♦ 161
  Queue ♦ 161
    Ordered Collection relationship to; Queue ♦ 161
  Queued Lock ♦ 149
    Test-and-Set Lock relationship to; Queued Lock ♦ 149
  Queued Reader/Writer Lock ♦ 149
  shared, object blocking use; Services 'Waiting For' ♦ 62
  Test-and-Set Lock, Queued Lock relationship to; Queued Lock ♦ 149
  Work Queue ♦ 52
  Work Queue Report ♦ 52
quick fix problems
  design principles, that avoid trashy code; Throwaway Code ♦ 21
Quiz Games ♦ 118
  Pitfall Diagnosis and Prevention relationship to; Quiz Games ♦ 118
  Simulation Games relationship to; Simulation Games ♦ 117
  Visible Checklist relationship to; Quiz Games ♦ 118
Quote ♦ 13
quotes
  Quote ♦ 13
    Scenario relationship to; Scenario ♦ 13
  scenario as collection of; Scenario ♦ 13
  term description; Quote ♦ 13

Ramirez, R. L.
  [Ramirez95]; 193
Ran, A. S.
  [Ran95]; 193
    Patterns of Events ❖ 129
  [Ran96]; 193
    MOODS: Models for Object-Oriented Design of State ♦ 87
Range ♦ 9
ranges
  linking to phenomena; Phenomenon with Range ♦ 10
  of measurements, defining; Range ♦ 9
  Phenomenon with Range ♦ 10
  Range ♦ 9
    Phenomenon with Range relationship to; Range ♦ 9
    Temporal Property relationship to; Temporal Property ♦ 171

Index

ranges *continued*
   Use a RangeAdaptor to Channel a Number's
      Range ♦ 177
   values outside of, representation; Exceptional Value ♦ 32
**RAPPeL: A Requirements-Analysis Process Pattern
Language for Object-Oriented Development ♦ 140**
   [Whitenack95]; 197
ratio
   conversion, between units, defining; Conversion Ratio ♦ 8
   Conversion Ratio ♦ 8
   Low Surface-to-Volume Ratio ♦ 150
Raw IO ♦ 80
   IO Gatekeeper relationship to; Raw IO ♦ 80
   String a Wire relationship to; String a Wire ♦ 80, Raw
      IO ♦ 80
reaction
   See Also interaction; real-time systems
   event, decoupling from state transition; For State Machines,
      Use Transition Methods ♦ 88
   improving the capacity and reliability of reactive systems;
      Pattern Language for Improving the Capacity of
      Reactive Systems ♦ 100
   Object-Oriented Design Patterns in Reactive
      Systems ♦ 92
   Pattern Language for Improving the Capacity of
      Reactive Systems ♦ 100
   reactive systems, software development strategies;
      Object-Oriented Design Patterns in Reactive
      Systems ♦ 92
   Reactor ♦ 143
      Bodyguard relationship to; Bodyguard ♦ 22
      Connector relationship to; Connector ♦ 40
      Facade relationship to; Reactor ♦ 143
      Factory Method relationship to; Reactor ♦ 143
      Half-Sync/Half-Async relationship to;
         Half-Sync/Half-Async ♦ 71
      Pipes & Filters relationship to; Reactor ♦ 143
      Proactor relationship to; Proactor ♦ 137
      Router relationship to; Router ♦ 146
      Template Method relationship to; Reactor ♦ 143
Reactor ♦ 143
   [Schmidt95]; 195
Reader/Writer Locking ♦ 147
Readers and Writers ♦ 39
Reading Just Before Reviewing ♦ 112
reading/readers
   Counter Reader/Writer Lock ♦ 149
   decoupling from writers, in locking strategies;
      Reader/Writer Locking ♦ 147
   Distributed Reader/Writer Lock ♦ 149
   locking
      counter lock; Counter Reader/Writer Lock ♦ 149
      distributed lock; Distributed Reader/Writer Lock ♦ 149
      queued locks; Queued Reader/Writer Lock ♦ 149
   pattern readability, strategies for enhancing; Single-Pass
      Readable ♦ 103
   Queued Reader/Writer Lock ♦ 149

Readable References to Patterns ♦ 104
   Mandatory Elements Present relationship to;
      Readable References to Patterns ♦ 104
   Pattern Thumbnail relationship to; Readable
      References to Patterns ♦ 104
Reader/Writer Locking ♦ 147
Readers and Writers ♦ 39
Reading Just Before Reviewing ♦ 112
   Author Reads Selection relationship to; Author Reads
      Selection ♦ 112
   Open Review relationship to; Reading Just Before
      Reviewing ♦ 112
   Safe Setting relationship to; Reading Just Before
      Reviewing ♦ 112
   Single-Pass Readable ♦ 103
   writers and, relationship among; Readers and Writers ♦ 39
real-time systems
   See Also fault-tolerant systems; reaction
   concurrent control systems, software development strategies;
      Object-Oriented Design Patterns in Reactive
      Systems ♦ 92
   improving the capacity and reliability of; Pattern Language
      for Improving the Capacity of Reactive Systems ♦ 100
   recursive control of; Recursive Control ♦ 143
reality
   From Prototype to Reality ♦ 61
   Prototype and Reality ♦ 63
rebirth
   as hopeless big ball of mud solution; Reconstruction ♦ 21
receivables
   as business order component, representation of; 3-Level
      Order ♦ 24
receiving
   Forwarder-Receiver ♦ 60
Recommitment Meeting ♦ 53
   Completion Headroom relationship to; Completion
      Headroom ♦ 53, Size the Schedule ♦ 64
   Product Initiative relationship to; Recommitment
      Meeting ♦ 53
   Size the Schedule relationship to; Size the Schedule ♦ 64
   Work Queue relationship to; Recommitment Meeting ♦ 53
   Work Queue Report relationship to; Recommitment
      Meeting ♦ 53
Reconstruction ♦ 21
recording
   time, in dual records; Dual Time Record ♦ 9
records
   mapping to objects; Objects from Records ♦ 90
   Objects from Records ♦ 90
Recoverable Distributor ♦ 143
   [Islam+96]; 188
recovery
   object, strategies for; Object Recovery ♦ 92
   Object Recovery ♦ 92
   Recoverable Distributer, Object Recovery relationship
      to; Object Recovery ♦ 92
   Recoverable Distributor ♦ 143
      Bridge relationship to; Recoverable Distributor ♦ 143

OBSERVER relationship to; RECOVERABLE
  DISTRIBUTOR ♦ 143
PROXY relationship to; RECOVERABLE DISTRIBUTOR ♦ 143
STRATEGY relationship to; RECOVERABLE
  DISTRIBUTOR ♦ 143
RECTANGULAR BLOCK ♦ 162
recursion
  collection snapshot use; HISTORY ON TREE ♦ 35
  modeling, organizational hierarchies; ORGANIZATION
    HIERARCHIES ♦ 7
  OBJECT RECURSION ♦ 92
  organizational hierarchy represenation; RECURSIVE
    STRUCTURES FOR ORGANIZATIONS ♦ 4
  over a structure; OBJECT RECURSION ♦ 92
  real-time system control; RECURSIVE CONTROL ♦ 143
  RECURSIVE CONTROL ♦ 143
  RECURSIVE STRUCTURES FOR ORGANIZATIONS ♦ 4
    ABSTRACT MODELS WITH CONSTRAINTS IN SUBTYPES
      relationship to; RECURSIVE STRUCTURES FOR
      ORGANIZATIONS ♦ 4
    MULTIPLE HIERARCHIC ASSOCIATIONS relationship to;
      MULTIPLE HIERARCHIC ASSOCIATIONS ♦ 4
    used by MULTIPLE HIERARCHIC ASSOCIATIONS; MULTIPLE
      HIERARCHIC ASSOCIATIONS ♦ 4
    uses ABSTRACT MODELS WITH CONSTRAINTS IN SUBTYPES;
      RECURSIVE STRUCTURES FOR ORGANIZATIONS ♦ 4
RECURSIVE CONTROL ♦ 143
  [Selic98]; 195
RECURSIVE STRUCTURES FOR ORGANIZATIONS ♦ 4
redirection
  output, in fault-tolerant systems; MIND YOUR OWN
    BUSINESS ♦ 77
redrawing
  lazy; LAZY REDRAW ♦ 50
  LAZY REDRAW ♦ 50
reduction
  of component dependencies; LAYERED AND SECTIONED
    ARCHITECTURE ♦ 96
  TRANSIENT REDUCTION ♦ 83
  of transients, as optimization technique; TRANSIENT
    REDUCTION ♦ 83
redundancy
  designing for; BACKUP ♦ 19
  eliminating, in complex systems; OBJECT MERGE ♦ 10
refactoring
  See Also factoring
  inheritance-based strategies; REUSABILITY THROUGH
    SELF-ENCAPSULATION ♦ 145
  LIFE CYCLE AND REFACTORING PATTERNS THAT SUPPORT
    EVOLUTION AND REUSE ♦ 84
  as piecemeal growth management tool; PIECEMEAL
    GROWTH ♦ 21
  software, strategies for; CONSOLIDATE THE PROGRAM TO
    SUPPORT EVOLUTION AND REUSE ♦ 85
  as software development strategy; LIFE CYCLE AND
    REFACTORING PATTERNS THAT SUPPORT EVOLUTION AND
    REUSE ♦ 84
  systems into layers, handling uneven changes by; SHEARING
    LAYERS ♦ 21

REFERENCE DATA ♦ 54
REFERENCE EXAMPLES ♦ 117
reference(s)
  ACTIVE REFERENCE ♦ 120
  counting
    See Also dependency
    copying use of; COUNTED BODY ♦ 24
    copying use with immutable classes; DETACHED COUNTED
      BODY ♦ 24
    memory management use; COUNTED POINTER ♦ 40
    of objects; FINALIZATION ♦ 90
  data, for software development; REFERENCE DATA ♦ 54
  ELEVATE REFERENCES TO ENHANCE REUSE ♦ 124
  as extensible teaching strategy; REFERENCE EXAMPLES ♦ 117
  FOREIGN KEY REFERENCES ♦ 43, ♦ 108
  FOREIGN KEY VERSUS DIRECT REFERENCE ♦ 43
  foreign keys, vs. pointers, representation issues; FOREIGN KEY
    VERSUS DIRECT REFERENCE ♦ 43
  information space navigation use; ACTIVE REFERENCE ♦ 120
  to objects not in a database, foreign key representation;
    FOREIGN KEY REFERENCES ♦ 43, FOREIGN KEY
    REFERENCES ♦ 108
  READABLE REFERENCES TO PATTERNS ♦ 104
  REFERENCE DATA ♦ 54
    DEVELOPMENT EPISODE relationship to; REFERENCE
      DATA ♦ 54
    REQUIREMENT WALK-THROUGH relationship to; REFERENCE
      DATA ♦ 54
  REFERENCE EXAMPLES ♦ 117
    ACQUAINTANCE EXAMPLES relationship to; ACQUAINTANCE
      EXAMPLES ♦ 117
  REFERENCE SECTION ♦ 98
    WORKSHEET DOCUMENTS relationship to; WORKSHEET
      DOCUMENTS ♦ 98
  WWW, commenting reasons for inclusion; EXPOSABLE
    GUTS ♦ 98
  WWW cross references to related material; REFERENCE
    SECTION ♦ 98
REFERENCE SECTION ♦ 98
REFLECTION ♦ 144
  [Buschmann+96]; 183
  [Buschmann96]; 184
reflection
  REFLECTION ♦ 144
    MICROKERNEL relationship to; MICROKERNEL ♦ 87,
      REFLECTION ♦ 144
    PROTOTYPE-BASED OBJECT SYSTEM relationship
      to; PROTOTYPE-BASED OBJECT SYSTEM ♦ 139,
      REFLECTION ♦ 144
    SPONSOR-SELECTOR relationship to; SPONSOR-
      SELECTOR ♦ 164
  software development forces impact on; EVOLUTION,
    ARCHITECTURE, AND METAMORPHOSIS ♦ 55
  system self-modification using; REFLECTION ♦ 144
region
  CRITICAL REGION PROTECTION ♦ 31
REJECTED OBSERVATION ♦ 9
  OBSERVATION relationship to; REJECTED OBSERVATION ♦ 9

Index

rejection
  SELECT/REJECT ♦ 160
RELATIONAL DATABASE ACCESS LAYER ♦ 3
  See Also database(s); LAYERED ARCHITECTURE; LAYERS
  CROSSING CHASMS relationship to; RELATIONAL DATABASE
    ACCESS LAYER ♦ 3
  QUERY BROKER relationship to; RELATIONAL DATABASE
    ACCESS LAYER ♦ 3
RELATIONSHIP AS ATTRIBUTE ♦ 20
RELATIONSHIP OBJECT ♦ 20
relationships
  See Also associations; collections; modeling
  abstracting, into types; OBJECTIFY ASSOCIATIONS ♦ 5
  accountability, creating from similar associations;
    ACCOUNTABILITY ABSTRACTION ♦ 5
  among activities and entities, defining; KEY BUSINESS
    ACTIVITIES AND INFLUENCES ♦ 165
  between aggregate and its parts; WHOLE-PART ♦ 179
  among basic and derived values, displaying; VISIBLE
    IMPLICATION ♦ 33
  BASIC RELATIONSHIP PATTERNS; BASIC RELATIONSHIP
    PATTERNS ♦ 19
  business and customer, representation of; CUSTOMER
    CONTACT ♦ 23
  among classes, managing; JUDGE ♦ 81
  classifying; TYPED RELATIONSHIP ♦ 5
  creating types for; ASSOCIATIVE TYPE ♦ 16
  customer, strategies for maintaining; CUSTOMER
    RAPPORT ♦ 140
  defining
    in organizational structures; ORGANIZATION STRUCTURE ♦ 7
    among party types; PARTY TYPE GENERALIZATIONS ♦ 7
  among domain objects, analyzing; CLASSIFYING, ASSOCIATING,
    AND GROUPING THE DOMAIN OBJECTS ♦ 141
  amount domain operations, configuring with a knowledge
    level model; KNOWLEDGE LEVEL ♦ 5
  either-or-both, abstracting into a supertype; PARTY ♦ 4,
    PARTY ♦ 6
  enforcing, rules use for; ORGANIZATION HIERARCHIES ♦ 7
  equivalence
    between account views; CORRESPONDING ACCOUNT ♦ 12
    creating; OBJECT EQUIVALENCE ♦ 10
  IDENTIFY PROBLEM DOMAIN RELATIONSHIPS ♦ 70
  implementing, with keyed mapping; KEYED MAPPING ♦ 16
  among local and global data, in distributed and/or fault-tolerant
    systems; RECOVERABLE DISTRIBUTOR ♦ 143
  many-to-many
    identifying for problem domain; IDENTIFY PROBLEM
      DOMAIN RELATIONSHIPS ♦ 70
    modeling; RELATIONSHIP OBJECT ♦ 20
    transaction posting; POSTING ♦ 35
  modeling, between two objects; ELEVATE REFERENCES TO
    ENHANCE REUSE ♦ 124
  nested containment, management of; OBSERVER UPDATE
    MESSAGE ♦ 75
  object
    preserving in a relational database; PATTERN LANGUAGE
      FOR SMALLTALK & RELATIONAL DATABASES ♦ 106

    representation in a relational database; REPRESENTING
      OBJECT RELATIONSHIPS ♦ 42
    representing; REPRESENTING OBJECT RELATIONSHIPS ♦ 107
  between object-oriented frameworks and legacy systems; NEW
    CLIENTS WITH OLD SERVERS: A PATTERN LANGUAGE FOR
    CLIENT/SERVER FRAMEWORKS ♦ 89
  among objects
    ABSTRACT FACTORY represenation of; ABSTRACT
      FACTORY ♦ 2
    tracking change over time; TEMPORAL ASSOCIATION ♦ 172
  among observations, in a diagnosis, encapsulating;
    ASSOCIATED OBSERVATION ♦ 9
  one-to-many
    COLLECTION OBJECT; COLLECTION OBJECT ♦ 20
    representation of; COLLECTION ♦ 159
    state change management with; OBSERVER ♦ 94
  one-to-one
    communication between objects in; WORK ACCOMPLISHED
      THROUGH DIALOGS ♦ 30
    global, modeling with ACTIVE VALUE; ACTIVE VALUE ♦ 20
    modeling with RELATIONSHIP AS ATTRIBUTE; RELATIONSHIP
      AS ATTRIBUTE ♦ 20
    owner and software deliverable; OWNER PER
      DELIVERABLE ♦ 169
  organizational, encapsulating; ORGANIZATIONAL
    STRUCTURE-TYPED RELATIONSHIP ♦ 5
  ORGANIZATIONAL STRUCTURE-TYPED RELATIONSHIP ♦ 5
  among patterns
    pattern writing strategies for conveying semantics; PATTERN
      THUMBNAIL ♦ 104
    pattern writing strategies for identifying; RELATIONSHIPS TO
      OTHER PATTERNS ♦ 103
  problem domain, identifying; IDENTIFY PROBLEM DOMAIN
    RELATIONSHIPS ♦ 70
  among readers and writers; READERS AND WRITERS ♦ 39
  RELATIONSHIP AS ATTRIBUTE ♦ 20
    ACTIVE VALUE relationship to; RELATIONSHIP AS
      ATTRIBUTE ♦ 20
    COLLECTION OBJECT relationship to; RELATIONSHIP AS
      ATTRIBUTE ♦ 20
    MUTUAL FRIENDS relationship to; RELATIONSHIP AS
      ATTRIBUTE ♦ 20, MUTUAL FRIENDS ♦ 20
    RELATIONSHIP OBJECT relationship to; RELATIONSHIP AS
      ATTRIBUTE ♦ 20, RELATIONSHIP OBJECT ♦ 20
  RELATIONSHIP OBJECT ♦ 20
    ACTIVE VALUE relationship to; RELATIONSHIP OBJECT ♦ 20
    ASSOCIATION OBJECT relationship to; RELATIONSHIP
      OBJECT ♦ 20
    COLLECTION OBJECT relationship to; RELATIONSHIP
      OBJECT ♦ 20
    MUTUAL FRIENDS relationship to; MUTUAL FRIENDS ♦ 20
    RELATIONSHIP AS ATTRIBUTE relationship to; RELATIONSHIP
      AS ATTRIBUTE ♦ 20, RELATIONSHIP OBJECT ♦ 20
  RELATIONSHIPS TO OTHER PATTERNS; RELATIONSHIPS TO
    OTHER PATTERNS ♦ 103, ♦ 103
  REPRESENTING OBJECT RELATIONSHIPS ♦ 42, ♦ 107
  state/event
    capturing; COLLECTION OF HISTORY PATTERNS ♦ 34
    capturing in an edition; EDITION ♦ 34

among states, management strategies; FOR STATE MACHINES, USE TRANSITION METHODS ♦ 88, WHEN STATES ARE CONDITIONS, USE PREDICATIVE STATE CLASSES ♦ 88, WHEN STATES ARE ASSOCIATIONS, USE STATE OBJECTS ♦ 89

time-based, association object representation of; BUSINESS PATTERNS OF ASSOCIATION OBJECTS ♦ 23

of tools to materials; TOOLS ♦ 109

and aspects; ASPECTS ♦ 109

and environment; ENVIRONMENT ♦ 110

representation of; TOOL AND MATERIAL COUPLING ♦ 110

two-way

modeling; MUTUAL FRIENDS ♦ 20

Mutual Friends pattern; MUTUAL FRIENDS ♦ 20

TYPED RELATIONSHIP ♦ 5

unique, account number use to establish; ACCOUNT NUMBER ♦ 4

RELATIONSHIPS TO OTHER PATTERNS ♦ 103

release cycle

software development, pacing; DELIVERABLES TO GO ♦ 27

reliability

enhancing, with backup strategies; BACKUP ♦ 19

handling maintenance needs without system erosion; KEEP IT WORKING ♦ 21

of reactive systems, improving; PATTERN LANGUAGE FOR IMPROVING THE CAPACITY OF REACTIVE SYSTEMS ♦ 100

of real-time systems, improving; PATTERN LANGUAGE FOR IMPROVING THE CAPACITY OF REACTIVE SYSTEMS ♦ 100

system testing, simulations unsuited for; DON'T TRUST SIMULATIONS ♦ 127

in telecommunications systems; FAULT-TOLERANT TELECOMMUNICATION SYSTEM PATTERNS ♦ 57

remote

connections, for error handling; BELTLINE TERMINAL ♦ 79

OBJECTS WITH REMOTE CONTROL ♦ 93

REMOTE CONTROL ♦ 144

REMOTE OPERATION ♦ 115

MANAGER-AGENT relationship to; MANAGER-AGENT ♦ 114

PROXY relationship to; REMOTE OPERATION ♦ 115

REMOTE PROXY, PROXY DESIGN PATTERN REVISITED relationship to; PROXY DESIGN PATTERN REVISITED ♦ 139

REMOTE CONTROL ♦ 144

[Aarsten+96b]; 181

REMOTE OPERATION ♦ 115

removing

DUPLICATE REMOVING SET ♦ 161

rendering

algorithms; PAINTER'S ALGORITHM ♦ 50

objects at a client, in object-oriented framework/legacy system interactions; MATERIALIZATION ♦ 90

replication

service, management of, in fault-tolerant systems; MASTER-SLAVE ♦ 86

REPORT OBJECTS ♦ 41

reports/reporting

business activity level, creating structures for; DIMENSION ROLL-UP ♦ 165

completion, work packets; WORK PACKET COMPLETION REPORT ♦ 29

configurable, design strategies; REPORT OBJECTS ♦ 41

CREATING REPORTS WITH QUERY OBJECTS ♦ 40

database, dynamic generation of; CREATING REPORTS WITH QUERY OBJECTS ♦ 40

dynamic formula generation for; FORMULA OBJECTS ♦ 41

errors

output direction, fault-tolerant systems; MIND YOUR OWN BUSINESS ♦ 77

prioritizing errors, in fault-tolerant systems; IO TRIAGE ♦ 77

problem, system testing use; USE OLD PROBLEM REPORTS ♦ 127

REPORT OBJECTS ♦ 41

FORMULA OBJECTS relationship to; REPORT OBJECTS ♦ 41

QUERY OBJECTS relationship to; REPORT OBJECTS ♦ 41, QUERY OBJECTS ♦ 41

status, for work packets, designing; WORK PACKET STATUS REPORT ♦ 29

USE OLD PROBLEM REPORTS ♦ 127

WORK PACKET COMPLETION REPORT ♦ 29

WORK PACKET STATUS REPORT ♦ 29

WORK QUEUE REPORT ♦ 52

repositories

creating objects from; PLUGGABLE FACTORY ♦ 132

REPOSITORY ♦ 125

BLACKBOARD relationship to; REPOSITORY ♦ 125

shared, integration mechanism for; SHARED REPOSITORY ♦ 115

SHARED REPOSITORY ♦ 115

structures and operations; REPOSITORY ♦ 125

REPOSITORY ♦ 125

representation

of behavior, for object manipulation; VISITOR ♦ 179

of class semantics, class clause use; CLASS CLAUSE ♦ 121, CLASS SEMANTICS ♦ 121

of collections

with a fixed number of elements; ARRAY ♦ 159

in a relational database; REPRESENTING COLLECTIONS IN A RELATIONAL DATABASE ♦ 42, REPRESENTING COLLECTIONS ♦ 107

with unique elements; SET ♦ 159

of control modules, in complex concurrent systems; CATEGORIZE OBJECTS FOR CONCURRENCY ♦ 62

of data, by abstract data types; DATA ABSTRACTION OR OBJECT-ORIENTED ♦ 125

data, by abstract data types, handling multiple implementations with; ENVELOPE/LETTER ♦ 25

decoupling from construction; BUILDER ♦ 23

of default values; DEFAULT VALUE METHOD ♦ 157

of domain-specific values; WHOLE VALUE ♦ 32

outside the normal range; EXCEPTIONAL VALUE ♦ 32

of enterprise components; ENTERPRISE SEGMENT ♦ 9

of events, in distributed systems; OBJECT-ORIENTED STATE MACHINE ♦ 129

of fire alarms; DEVIATION ♦ 134

information, feature extraction algorithms; FEATURE EXTRACTION—A PATTERN FOR INFORMATION RETRIEVAL ♦ 58

of inheritance, in a relational database; REPRESENTING INHERITANCE IN A RELATIONAL DATABASE ♦ 42, SURROGATE ♦ 168

representation *continued*
of instance creation; CONSTRUCTOR METHOD ♦ 152,
    SHORTCUT CONSTRUCTOR METHOD ♦ 152
issues, in evolutionary software development;
    OBJECT-ORIENTED SIMULATION ♦ 93
of language grammars; INTERPRETER ♦ 80
of links, in hypermedia; NAVIGATIONSTRATEGY ♦ 48
of methods, as objects; METHOD OBJECT ♦ 153
mutual exclusion, conflict set use; CONFLICT SETS ♦ 39
of object models, in the design of relational database; TABLE
    DESIGN TIME ♦ 107
of object relationships; REPRESENTING OBJECT
    RELATIONSHIPS ♦ 107
    in a relational database; REPRESENTING OBJECT
        RELATIONSHIPS ♦ 42
of objects
    as relational database tables; OBJECTS FROM RECORDS ♦ 90,
        PATTERN LANGUAGE FOR SMALLTALK & RELATIONAL
        DATABASES ♦ 106, REPRESENTING OBJECTS AS
        TABLES ♦ 107
    as tables; REPRESENTING OBJECTS AS TABLES ♦ 42
of objects not in a database, foreign key representation;
    FOREIGN KEY REFERENCES ♦ 43, FOREIGN KEY
    REFERENCES ♦ 108
of one-to-many relationships; COLLECTION ♦ 159
of patterns, as classes; PATTERN AS A CLASS ♦ 97
of polymorphism, in a relational database; SURROGATE ♦ 168
of quantity; QUANTITY ♦ 8
of relationship between tools and materials; TOOL AND
    MATERIAL COUPLING ♦ 110
REPRESENTING COLLECTIONS ♦ 107
    REPRESENTING COLLECTIONS IN A RELATIONAL DATABASE
        relationship to; REPRESENTING COLLECTIONS ♦ 107
    REPRESENTING OBJECT RELATIONSHIPS relationship to;
        REPRESENTING OBJECT RELATIONSHIPS ♦ 107
    REPRESENTING OBJECTS AS TABLES relationship to;
        REPRESENTING OBJECTS AS TABLES ♦ 42, REPRESENTING
        OBJECTS AS TABLES ♦ 107
    TABLE DESIGN TIME relationship to; TABLE DESIGN
        TIME ♦ 42, TABLE DESIGN TIME ♦ 107
REPRESENTING COLLECTIONS IN A RELATIONAL
    DATABASE ♦ 42
    REPRESENTING COLLECTIONS relationship to; REPRESENTING
        COLLECTIONS ♦ 107
REPRESENTING INHERITANCE IN A RELATIONAL
    DATABASE ♦ 42
    REPRESENTING OBJECT RELATIONSHIPS relationship to;
        REPRESENTING OBJECT RELATIONSHIPS ♦ 107
    SURROGATE relationship to; SURROGATE ♦ 168
    TABLE DESIGN TIME relationship to; TABLE DESIGN
        TIME ♦ 42, TABLE DESIGN TIME ♦ 107
REPRESENTING OBJECT RELATIONSHIPS ♦ 42, ♦ 107
    FOREIGN KEY REFERENCES relationship to; REPRESENTING
        OBJECT RELATIONSHIPS ♦ 42
    REPRESENTING COLLECTIONS relationship to; REPRESENTING
        OBJECT RELATIONSHIPS ♦ 107
    REPRESENTING INHERITANCE IN A RELATIONAL
        DATABASE relationship to; REPRESENTING OBJECT
        RELATIONSHIPS ♦ 107

    TABLE DESIGN TIME relationship to; TABLE DESIGN
        TIME ♦ 42, TABLE DESIGN TIME ♦ 107
    REPRESENTING OBJECTS AS TABLES ♦ 42, ♦ 107
        FOREIGN KEY REFERENCES relationship to; REPRESENTING
            OBJECTS AS TABLES ♦ 42, REPRESENTING OBJECTS AS
            TABLES ♦ 107
        OBJECT IDENTIFIER relationship to; REPRESENTING
            OBJECTS AS TABLES ♦ 42, REPRESENTING OBJECTS AS
            TABLES ♦ 107
        REPRESENTING COLLECTIONS relationship to; REPRESENTING
            OBJECTS AS TABLES ♦ 42, REPRESENTING OBJECTS AS
            TABLES ♦ 107
        REPRESENTING OBJECTS AS TABLES relationship to;
            REPRESENTING OBJECTS AS TABLES ♦ 107
        TABLE DESIGN TIME relationship to; TABLE DESIGN
            TIME ♦ 42, TABLE DESIGN TIME ♦ 107
of resources, in network management system; MANAGED
    OBJECT ♦ 115
of SQL; QUERY OBJECT ♦ 108
of state; COMMON STATE ♦ 156, VARIABLE STATE ♦ 156
state-dependent objects, design and implementation strategies;
    MOODS: MODELS FOR OBJECT-ORIENTED DESIGN OF
    STATE ♦ 87
of time-based relationships, with association objects;
    BUSINESS PATTERNS OF ASSOCIATION OBJECTS ♦ 23
of transportation network
    nodes; POINT ♦ 114
    routes; ROUTE ♦ 114
**REPRESENTING INHERITANCE IN A RELATIONAL
    DATABASE ♦ 42**
REPRESENTING OBJECT RELATIONSHIPS ♦ 42, ♦ 107
REPRESENTING OBJECTS AS TABLES ♦ 42, ♦ 107
REQUEST ♦ 90
REQUEST SCREEN MODIFICATION ♦ 144
    [Towell95]; 196
REQUEST UPDATE ♦ 49
requests
    cancellation, strategies for handling; MATCH PROGRESS WORK
        WITH NEW ♦ 101
    change
        handling optiminzation; OPTIMIZED MESSAGES PER CHANGE
            REQUEST ♦ 75
        strategies for handling; ONE MESSAGE PER CHANGE
            REQUEST ♦ 75
    CLIP REQUESTS ♦ 50
    clipping hidden regions; CLIP REQUESTS ♦ 50
    CONSOLIDATE REQUESTS ♦ 50
    decoupling from execution; COMMAND PROCESSOR ♦ 36
    encapsulation as a object; COMMAND ♦ 35
    ONE MESSAGE PER CHANGE REQUEST ♦ 75
    OPTIMIZED MESSAGES PER CHANGE REQUEST ♦ 75
    processing cost, optimization strategies; OPTIMIZE
        HIGH-RUNNER CASES ♦ 100
    REQUEST ♦ 90
        MATERIALIZATION relationship to; MATERIALIZATION ♦ 90
    REQUEST SCREEN MODIFICATION ♦ 144
    REQUEST UPDATE ♦ 49
        CLIP REQUESTS relationship to; REQUEST UPDATE ♦ 49

Consolidate Requests relationship to; Request Update ♦ 49, Consolidate Requests ♦ 50

Display List relationship to; Display List ♦ 49

Lazy Redraw relationship to; Request Update ♦ 49, Lazy Redraw ♦ 50

updating

consolidating; Consolidate Requests ♦ 50

global redraw of display; Global Update ♦ 49

removing hidden regions; Clip Requests ♦ 50

for visual component display; Request Update ♦ 49

Requirement Walk-through ♦ 54

requirements

analysis

for object-oriented development; RAPPeL: A Requirements-Analysis Process Pattern Language for Object-Oriented Development ♦ 140

prototyping role; Prototype ♦ 69

behavior, analysis of; Behavioral Requirements ♦ 142

business, identifying; Sponsor Objectives ♦ 140

business term definitions; Defining Requirements ♦ 140

change

handling; Software Tectonics ♦ 55

microkernel architecture as mechanism for handling; Microkernel ♦ 87

customer, classifying; Managing and Meeting Customer Expectations ♦ 140

Defining Requirements ♦ 140

design and planning relationship to; Gold Rush ♦ 169

identifying sources for; Building the Right Things ♦ 140

implied, identifying; Implied Requirements ♦ 52

Implied Requirements ♦ 52

memory, reducing in cryptographic systems; Signature with Appendix ♦ 175, Secrecy with Signature with Appendix ♦ 175

planning, early customer demonstration use; Catalytic Scenarios ♦ 47

product, defining an initiative for; Product Initiative ♦ 52

project scheduling strategies; Requirement Walk-through ♦ 54

Requirement Walk-through ♦ 54

Implied Requirements relationship to; Requirement Walk-through ♦ 54

Reference Data relationship to; Reference Data ♦ 54

Work Group relationship to; Requirement Walk-through ♦ 54

Requirements Specification ♦ 142

Behavioral Requirements relationship to; Requirements Specification ♦ 142

Problem Domain Analysis relationship to; Requirements Specification ♦ 142

Requirements Validation relationship to; Requirements Specification ♦ 142

Requirements Validation ♦ 143

Defining Requirements relationship to; Defining Requirements ♦ 140

Pragmatic External Requirements relationship to; Pragmatic External Requirements ♦ 142

Prototypes relationship to; Requirements Validation ♦ 143

Requirements Specification relationship to; Requirements Specification ♦ 142

specification, team composition for; Diversity of Membership ♦ 95

specification of; Requirements Specification ♦ 142

system

decomposing into a layered architecture; Patterns for Generating a Layered Architecture ♦ 123

system testing use; Get Involved Early ♦ 126

understanding, as developer role; Developer Controls Process ♦ 65

user interface, identifying; User Interface Requirements ♦ 142

User Interface Requirements ♦ 142

validation; Requirements Validation ♦ 143

Requirements Specification ♦ 142

Requirements Validation ♦ 143

research

WWW sources, commenting reasons for inclusion; Exposable Guts ♦ 98

Resource Allocation ♦ 13

Resource Exchanger ♦ 144

[Sane+96b]; 194

resources

allocation of; Resource Allocation ♦ 13

limited

as big ball of mud system force; Big Ball of Mud ♦ 21

capacity, strategies for dealing with; Capacity Bottleneck ♦ 100

high-cost request optimization strategies; Optimize High-Runner Cases ♦ 100

processing power, strategies for dealing with; Processing Capacity ♦ 100

management, in software development; Interrupts Unjam Blocking ♦ 69, Don't Interrupt an Interrupt ♦ 69

managing, in distributed systems; Resource Exchanger ♦ 144

minimizing pattern read time, pattern writing strategies that support; Single-Pass Readable ♦ 103

representation of, in network management system; Managed Object ♦ 115

Resource Allocation ♦ 13

Resource Exchanger ♦ 144

selecting, from a dynamically changing set; Sponsor-Selector ♦ 164

shared, management heterogeneous pool of; Implementation of 'Multiple Kinds of Services' Control Modules ♦ 62

sharing, identifying objects involved with; Critical Region Protection ♦ 31

responsibilities

determining, for software development projects; Form Follows Function ♦ 64

of domain object, identifying; Elaboration of the Domain Objects ♦ 141

hierarchical, creating an accounability type for; Hierarchic Accountability ♦ 7

management of, structures that support; Move Responsibilities ♦ 67

Index

responsibilities *continued*
Move Responsibilities ♦ 67
object, dynamic attachment; Decorator ♦ 46
of a position, modeling; Post ♦ 7
subtyping the diverse operating scopes of; Operating
Scope ♦ 7
responsiveness
importance in customer relations; Be Responsive ♦ 44
Improving Responsiveness in Interactive Applications
Using Queues ♦ 76
vs. stage decoupling, in software development management;
Hub, Spoke, and Rim ♦ 68
restrictions
memory
development software development culture for handling;
Think Small ♦ 72
handling unpredictable demands on; Memory
Overdraft ♦ 72
performance considerations; Memory Performance
Assessment ♦ 73
strategies for handling; High-Level and Process
Patterns from the Memory Preservation
Society ♦ 71
test-and-set locking use in the face of; Test-and-Set
Lock ♦ 148
testing out-of-memory conditions; Exhaustion Test ♦ 73
retrieving
See Also access(ing)
Class Retrieval ♦ 120
classes
class specification use; Class Specification ♦ 121
from encapsulated class trees; Class Retrieval ♦ 120
Feature Extraction—A Pattern for Information
Retrieval ♦ 58
object; Entry Point ♦ 16
aspects; Use an AspectAdaptor to Hold an Aspect of
an Object ♦ 177
return
of collections; Collecting Parameter ♦ 156
Interesting Return Value ♦ 163
value, explicit specification of; Interesting Return
Value ♦ 163
reusability
in class hierarchy design; Abstract Class ♦ 2
Composing Multimedia Artifacts for Reuse ♦ 36
Consolidate the Program to Support Evolution and
Reuse ♦ 85
in cryptographic software design; Secure-Channel
Communication ♦ 174
of customer demonstrations
archiving scenarios for; Archive Scenarios ♦ 48
code, issues and possibilities; Mutable Code ♦ 47
defaults role in; Works Out of the Box ♦ 150
determining potential for; Symmetrical Reuse ♦ 123
Elevate References to Enhance Reuse ♦ 124
of expressions; Reusing Temporary Variable ♦ 158
Life Cycle and Refactoring Patterns that Support
Evolution and Reuse ♦ 84

in manufacturing systems, G++ pattern language; G++:
A Pattern Language for Computer-Integrated
Manufacturing ♦ 61
multimedia artifacts, composition for; Composing
Multimedia Artifacts for Reuse ♦ 36
object, strategies for; Selfish Class Pattern
Language ♦ 149
Reusability Through Self-Encapsulation ♦ 145
Reusing Temporary Variable ♦ 158
software, strategies that encourage; Selfish Class ♦ 150
strategies
capability subsetting; Gentle Learning Curve ♦ 150
complexity encapsulation; Low Surface-to-Volume
Ratio ♦ 150
strategies that enhance
evolving software from inheritance to aggregations; Evolve
Aggregations from Inheritance Hierarchies ♦ 85
refactoring software to support; Consolidate the
Program to Support Evolution and Reuse ♦ 85
Symmetrical Reuse ♦ 123
Reusability Through Self-Encapsulation ♦ 145
[Auer95]; 182
Reusing Temporary Variable ♦ 158
Reversing Method ♦ 153
Review the Architecture ♦ 65
reviewing
architecture, strategies for; Review the Architecture ♦ 65
checklist use for; Visible Checklist ♦ 117
code, design validation use; Group Validation ♦ 66
Creator-Reviewer ♦ 119
open; Open Review ♦ 111
Open Review ♦ 111
of patterns, open review forum advantages; Open
Review ♦ 111
reading just before, in a pattern writers workshop; Reading
Just Before Reviewing ♦ 112
Reading Just Before Reviewing ♦ 112
reading patterns just before a; Reading Just Before
Reviewing ♦ 112
Review the Architecture ♦ 65
teaching strategies for
checklist use for continuity and review; Visible
Checklist ♦ 117
open-ended review; Debrief After Activities ♦ 118
quiz games; Quiz Games ♦ 118
technical papers
acceptance process; Identify the Champion Pattern
Language ♦ 73
selecting reviewers for; Experts Review Papers ♦ 73
strategies for encouraging champions; Champions Review
Papers ♦ 74
Riding Over Transients ♦ 57
Leaky Bucket Counters relationship to; Riding Over
Transients ♦ 57, Leaky Bucket Counters ♦ 57
Riehle, D.
[Baumer+97]; 184
Role Object ♦ 146
[Baumer+98]; 184
Product Trader ♦ 138

[Baumer+99]; 184
> Role Object ◆ 146

[PLoPD3]; 192

[Riehle+95]; 193
> Pattern Language for Tool Construction and Integration Based on the Tools and Materials Metaphor ❖ 109

[Riehle+98]; 193
> Serializer ◆ 151

[Riehle96a]; 193

[Riehle96a] Event Notification ◆ 54

[Riehle96b]; 193
> Patterns for Encapsulating Class Trees ❖ 120

[Riehle98]; 193
> Bureaucracy ◆ 23

ring
as distributed system topological properties; Distributed Processes ◆ 51

Rising, L.
[Delano+98]; 186
[DeLano+98], Patterns for System Testing ◆ 126
[PHand]; 192
[Rising99]; 193
> Customer Interaction Patterns ◆ 43

Roberts, D.
[Roberts+98]; 194
> Patterns for Evolving Frameworks ❖ 121

robots
cooperative autonomous mobile, software development strategies; Object-Oriented Design Patterns in Reactive Systems ◆ 92

Rohnert, H.
[Buschmann+96]; 183
> Blackboard ◆ 22
> Broker ◆ 22
> Client-Dispatcher-Server ◆ 34
> Command Processor ◆ 36
> Counted Pointer ◆ 40
> Forwarder-Receiver ◆ 60
> Layers ◆ 81
> Master-Slave ◆ 86
> Microkernel ◆ 87
> Model-View-Controller ◆ 87
> Pipes & Filters ◆ 132
> Presentation-Abstraction-Control ◆ 135
> Proxy ◆ 139
> Publisher-Subscriber ◆ 139
> Reflection ◆ 144
> View Handler ◆ 178
> Whole-Part ◆ 179

[PLoPD4]; 192

[Rohnert96]; 194
> Proxy Design Pattern Revisited ◆ 139

Role ◆ 17
Role Object ◆ 146
[Baumer+97]; 184
[Baumer+99]; 184

Role Suggesting Instance Variable Name ◆ 158
Role Suggesting Temporary Variable Name ◆ 158

roles
of author, in pattern writers workshops; Workshop Comprises Authors ◆ 112

Decision Maker's Role ◆ 30

determining, for software development projects; Form Follows Function ◆ 64

developer; Developer Controls Process ◆ 65

domain expertise importance; Domain Expertise in Roles ◆ 64

Domain Expertise in Roles ◆ 64

encapsulating security profiles as; Roles ◆ 17

of expert, in technical paper review; Experts Review Papers ◆ 73

Human Interface Role is a Special Interface Role ◆ 31

information delivery, encapsulating; Informational Role ◆ 30

Informational Role ◆ 30

interface, encapsulating; Interface's Role ◆ 30

Interface's Role ◆ 30

modeling; Post ◆ 7

of moderator, in pattern writers workshops; Moderator Guides the Workshop ◆ 112

naming, as system design task; Identify the Nouns ◆ 70

Normalize the Roles ◆ 70

normalizing, as system design strategy; Normalize the Roles ◆ 70

of objects, in problem domain; Object Stereotypes ◆ 141

objects as; Role Object ◆ 146

policy making
> policy-maker creation; Decision Maker's Role ◆ 30
> worker creation; Workers' Role ◆ 30

related, coupling, in organizational restructuring; Divide and Conquer ◆ 68

Role ◆ 17

Role Object ◆ 146
> Cascade relationship to; Cascade ◆ 28
> Decorator relationship to; Role Object ◆ 146
> Product Trader relationship to; Role Object ◆ 146

Role Suggesting Instance Variable Name ◆ 158
> Pluggable Block relationship to; Pluggable Block ◆ 156
> Pluggable Selector relationship to; Pluggable Selector ◆ 156

Role Suggesting Temporary Variable Name ◆ 158

software development, value of communication among; Coupling Decreases Latency ◆ 69

in system, of programs; System Citizen's Role ◆ 29

System Citizen's Role ◆ 29

Three to Seven Helpers per Role ◆ 68

Workers' Role ◆ 30

Roll-forward ◆ 39
roll-ups
Dimension Roll-Up ◆ 165

Rollback ◆ 38
rollback
object recovery, strategies for; Object Recovery ◆ 92

Rollxxx
  Roll-forward ♦ 39
    Rollback relationship to; Rollback ♦ 38,
      Roll-forward ♦ 39
  Rollback ♦ 38
    Memento relationship to; Rollback ♦ 38
    Roll-Forward relationship to; Rollback ♦ 38
Rossi, G.
  [Rossi+96]; 194
    Design Patterns for Object-Oriented Hypermedia
      Applications ❖ 48
  [Rossi+99]; 194
    Patterns for Designing Navigable Information
      Spaces ❖ 119
Round Pegs for Round Holes ♦ 27
  Bootstrapping relationship to; Bootstrapping ♦ 26
  Production Potential relationship to; Production
    Potential ♦ 26
Route ♦ 114
route(ing)
  Event Routing ♦ 31
  events, design issues; Event Routing ♦ 31
  Pattern Language of Transport Systems (Point and
    Route) ♦ 114
  Route ♦ 114
    Cascade relationship to; Cascade ♦ 28
    Composite relationship to; Route ♦ 114
  Router ♦ 146
    Reactor relationship to; Router ♦ 146
  in a transportation network, representation of; Route ♦ 114
Router ♦ 146
  [Schmidt96b]; 195
RPC (remote procedure call)
  Event-Driven RPC ♦ 94
  event-driven system use; Event-Driven RPC ♦ 94
RTTI (run-time type identification)
  heterogeneous addition use; Promote and Add ♦ 26
Rubel, B
  [Rubel95]; 194
    Patterns for Generating a Layered
      Architecture ❖ 123
Rubira, C. M. F.
  [Braga+99]; 183
    Tropyc: A Pattern Language for Cryptographic
      Software ❖ 174
rules
  See Also protocol
  business
    decoupling from transaction-processing software; Explicit
      Business Rules ♦ 173
    defining and capturing; Business Rules ♦ 142
  as business order component, representation of; 3-Level
    Order ♦ 24
  Business Rules ♦ 142
  decoupling from domain specifics; Accountability
    Knowledge Level ♦ 5, Accountability Knowledge
    Level ♦ 7
  domain object, identifying; Elaboration of the Domain
    Objects ♦ 141

Explicit Business Rules ♦ 173
posting
  for many accounts, handling; Posting Rules for Many
    Accounts ♦ 11
  creating a structure for; Accounting Practice ♦ 12
  decoupling strategy from; Posting Rule Execution ♦ 11
  recording for a transaction; Sources of an Entry ♦ 12
Posting Rule Execution ♦ 11
Posting Rules ♦ 11
Posting Rules for Many Accounts ♦ 11
relationship enforcement, in organizational hierarchies;
  Organization Hierarchies ♦ 7
for transfering between accounts; Posting Rules ♦ 11
Run Array ♦ 159
run(ing)
  Define and Run Presentation ♦ 36
  example, pattern language writing use; Running
    Example ♦ 106
  multimedia presentations; Define and Run
    Presentation ♦ 36
  Run Array ♦ 159
  Running Example ♦ 106
  value, keeping for a collection; Inject:into: ♦ 161
Running Example ♦ 106
runtime inheritance control
  replacing message to self; Client-Specified Self ♦ 34

sacrifice
  Sacrifice One Person ♦ 170
    Day Care relationship to; Sacrifice One Person ♦ 170
    Fire Walls relationship to; Sacrifice One Person ♦ 170
    Gatekeeper relationship to; Sacrifice One Person ♦ 170
    Mercenary Analyst relationship to; Sacrifice One
      Person ♦ 170
    Owner per Deliverable relationship to; Sacrifice One
      Person ♦ 170
    Someone Always Makes Progress relationship to;
      Sacrifice One Person ♦ 170
    Team per Task relationship to; Team per Task ♦ 169,
      Sacrifice One Person ♦ 170
  Sacrificial Lamb ♦ 131
    Cargo Cult relationship to; Cargo Cult ♦ 131
    Doormat relationship to; Doormat ♦ 131
    Peacemaker relationship to; Peacemaker ♦ 131
  Someone Always Makes Progress, Sacrifice One Person
    relationship to; Sacrifice One Person ♦ 170
Sacrifice One Person ♦ 170
Sacrificial Lamb ♦ 131
Safe Setting ♦ 111
safety
  See Also security
  Safe Setting ♦ 111
    Authors are Experts relationship to; Authors are
      Experts ♦ 111
    Authors' Circle relationship to; Safe Setting ♦ 111
    Community of Trust relationship to; Community of
      Trust ♦ 112

MODERATOR GUIDES THE WORKSHOP relationship to;
SAFE SETTING ♦ 111, MODERATOR GUIDES THE
WORKSHOP ♦ 112

OPEN REVIEW relationship to; OPEN REVIEW ♦ 111, SAFE
SETTING ♦ 111

POSITIVE CLOSURE relationship to; SAFE SETTING ♦ 111

POSITIVE FEEDBACK FIRST relationship to; SAFE
SETTING ♦ 111

READING JUST BEFORE REVIEWING relationship to;
READING JUST BEFORE REVIEWING ♦ 112

SITTING IN A CIRCLE relationship to; SITTING IN A
CIRCLE ♦ 112

SUGGESTIONS FOR IMPROVEMENT relationship to; SAFE
SETTING ♦ 111

THANK THE AUTHOR relationship to; SAFE SETTING ♦ 111

WORKSHOP COMPRISES AUTHORS relationship to; SAFE
SETTING ♦ 111, WORKSHOP COMPRISES AUTHORS ♦ 112

Sakamoto, G. N.
[Masuda+98]; 190

samples
CODE SAMPLES ♦ 105
CODE SAMPLES AS BONUS ♦ 105

Sane, A.
[Sane+96a]; 194
DETACHABLE INSPECTOR ♦ 49
[Sane+96b]; 194
RESOURCE EXCHANGER ♦ 144

satellite telemetry systems
software and organizational development strategies;
ORGANIZATIONAL MULTIPLEXING: PATTERNS FOR
PROCESSING SATELLITE TELEMETRY WITH DISTRIBUTED
TEAMS ♦ 94

saving
values, for method use; TEMPORARY VARIABLE ♦ 158

scaffolding
SMALLTALK SCAFFOLDING PATTERNS ♦ 163

SCENARIO ♦ 13

scenarios
ARCHIVE SCENARIOS ♦ 48
archiving; ARCHIVE SCENARIOS ♦ 48
CATALYTIC SCENARIOS ♦ 47
customer demonstrations, requirements planning use;
CATALYTIC SCENARIOS ♦ 47
SCENARIO ♦ 13
QUOTE relationship to; SCENARIO ♦ 13
SCENARIOS DEFINE PROBLEM ♦ 66
FINDING AND DEFINING THE DOMAIN OBJECTS relationship
to; FINDING AND DEFINING THE DOMAIN OBJECTS ♦ 141
term description; SCENARIO ♦ 13

SCENARIOS DEFINE PROBLEM ♦ 66

SCHEDULE CHICKEN ♦ 132

scheduling
development, determination of; SIZE THE SCHEDULE ♦ 64
project
delay handling strategies; RECOMMITMENT MEETING ♦ 53
divide-and-conquor strategy; WORK SPLIT ♦ 53
programming episode strategy; PROGRAMMING EPISODE ♦ 54
requirements development plan strategies; REQUIREMENT
WALK-THROUGH ♦ 54

short term work plan strategies; INFORMAL LABOR
PLAN ♦ 53
strategies for; WORK QUEUE ♦ 52

SCHEDULE CHICKEN ♦ 132

SIZE THE SCHEDULE ♦ 64

software development
resource management strategies; INTERRUPTS UNJAM
BLOCKING ♦ 69, DON'T INTERRUPT AN INTERRUPT ♦ 69
schedule management; TAKE NO SMALL SLIPS ♦ 69
status tracking; WORK QUEUE REPORT ♦ 52

schemas
STARS: A PATTERN LANGUAGE FOR QUERY-OPTIMIZED
SCHEMAS ♦ 164

Schmid, H. A.
[Schmid95]; 194
[Schmid96]; 194

Schmidt, D. C.
[Cleeland+98a]; 184
EXTERNAL POLYMORPHISM ♦ 56
[Cleeland+98b]; 185
EXTERNAL POLYMORPHISM ♦ 56
[Jain+97]; 188
SERVICE CONFIGURATOR ♦ 151
[Kircher+99]; 189
[Lavender+96]; 190
ACTIVE OBJECT ♦ 6
[PLoPD1]; 192
[Pyarali+98]; 193
ASYNCHRONOUS COMPLETION TOKEN ♦ 19
[Pyarali+99]; 193
PROACTOR ♦ 137
[Schmidt+95]; 194
[Schmidt+96]; 194
HALF-SYNC/HALF-ASYNC ♦ 71
[Schmidt+98]; 194
DOUBLE-CHECKED LOCKING ♦ 51
[Schmidt+99]; 195
THREAD-SPECIFIC STORAGE ♦ 172
[Schmidt95]; 195
REACTOR ♦ 143
[Schmidt96a]; 195
[Schmidt96b]; 195
ROUTER ♦ 146
[Schmidt97]; 195
[Schmidt98a]; 195
[Schmidt98b]; 195
ACCEPTOR ♦ 3
CONNECTOR ♦ 40
[Schmidt99]; 195
WRAPPER FACADE ♦ 179

Schwabe, D.
[Rossi+99]; 194
PATTERNS FOR DESIGNING NAVIGABLE INFORMATION
SPACES ❖ 119

Schwaber, K.
[Beedle+99]; 182
SCRUM: A PATTERN LANGUAGE FOR HYPERPRODUCTIVE
SOFTWARE DEVELOPMENT ❖ 146

Index

scope
  decoupling from lifetime; CONCRETE DATA TYPE ♦ 25
  of operations, modeling for Accountability; OPERATING
    SCOPE ♦ 7
SCRATCH 'N SNIFF ♦ 128
screens
  REQUEST SCREEN MODIFICATION ♦ 144
scripting
  languages, customer demonstration use; PROTOTYPING
    LANGUAGES ♦ 47
scrolling
  as collection display management tool; MEGA-SCROLLING ♦ 90
  as position in space tracker; USE A SCROLLVALUEHOLDER TO
    HOLD A POSITION IN n-DIMENSIONAL SPACE ♦ 178
  USE A SCROLLVALUEHOLDER TO HOLD A POSITION IN
    n-DIMENSIONAL SPACE ♦ 178
**SCRUM: A PATTERN LANGUAGE FOR HYPERPRODUCTIVE
SOFTWARE DEVELOPMENT ♦ 146**
  [Beedle+99]; 182
SCRUM MEETING ♦ 147
searching
  for collection elements; INCLUDES: ♦ 160
  collections; DETECT ♦ 160
    optimization of; LOOKUP CACHE ♦ 161
  encapsulation, in legacy system/object-oriented framework
    interactions; SEARCHING FOR BUSINESS OBJECTS ♦ 90
  for literals; SEARCHING LITERAL ♦ 161
  pattern design structures that support; FINDABLE
    SECTIONS ♦ 103
  SEARCHING FOR BUSINESS OBJECTS ♦ 90
    CLIENT/SERVER FRAMEWORK relationship to;
      CLIENT/SERVER FRAMEWORK ♦ 91
  SEARCHING LITERAL ♦ 161
SEARCHING FOR BUSINESS OBJECTS ♦ 90
SEARCHING LITERAL ♦ 161
secrecy
  INFORMATION SECRECY ♦ 174
  message
    encryption and secret key use; INFORMATION SECRECY ♦ 174
    preserving while verifying sender identity; SECRECY WITH
      INTEGRITY ♦ 175
  SECRECY WITH INTEGRITY ♦ 175
    INFORMATION SECRECY relationship to; INFORMATION
      SECRECY ♦ 174
  SECRECY WITH SENDER AUTHENTICATION ♦ 175
    INFORMATION SECRECY relationship to; INFORMATION
      SECRECY ♦ 174, SECRECY WITH SENDER
      AUTHENTICATION ♦ 175
    SENDER AUTHENTICATION relationship to; SECRECY WITH
      SENDER AUTHENTICATION ♦ 175
  SECRECY WITH SIGNATURE ♦ 175
    INFORMATION SECRECY relationship to; INFORMATION
      SECRECY ♦ 174, SECRECY WITH SIGNATURE ♦ 175
    SIGNATURE relationship to; SECRECY WITH
      SIGNATURE ♦ 175
  SECRECY WITH SIGNATURE WITH APPENDIX ♦ 175
    INFORMATION SECRECY relationship to; SECRECY WITH
      SIGNATURE WITH APPENDIX ♦ 175

    SIGNATURE WITH APPENDIX relationship to; SECRECY WITH
      SIGNATURE WITH APPENDIX ♦ 175
  SENDER AUTHENTICATION, SECRECY WITH SENDER
    AUTHENTICATION relationship to; SECRECY WITH SENDER
    AUTHENTICATION ♦ 175
SECRECY WITH INTEGRITY ♦ 175
SECRECY WITH SENDER AUTHENTICATION ♦ 175
SECRECY WITH SIGNATURE ♦ 175
SECRECY WITH SIGNATURE WITH APPENDIX ♦ 175
SECTION IN A SUBAPPLICATION ♦ 97
sections
  architecture, reducing component dependencies with;
    LAYERED AND SECTIONED ARCHITECTURE ♦ 96
  critical
    fusing, as performance enhancement; CRITICAL-SECTION
      FUSING ♦ 148
    partitioning, as performance enhancement;
      CRITICAL-SECTION PARTITIONING ♦ 148
  CRITICAL-SECTION FUSING ♦ 148
  CRITICAL-SECTION PARTITIONING ♦ 148
  evolving from applications; NO SUBAPPLICATIONS ♦ 97
  FINDABLE SECTIONS ♦ 103
  LAYERED AND SECTIONED ARCHITECTURE ♦ 96
  optional, pattern writing use; SKIPPABLE SECTIONS ♦ 103
  pattern, search cues for; FINDABLE SECTIONS ♦ 103
  REFERENCE SECTION ♦ 98
  SECTION IN A SUBAPPLICATION ♦ 97
    LAYERED AND SECTIONED ARCHITECTURE relationship to;
      SECTION IN A SUBAPPLICATION ♦ 97
  storing in subapplications; SECTION IN A SUBAPPLICATION ♦ 97
  subapplication representation of; NO SUBAPPLICATIONS ♦ 97
SECURE ACCESS LAYER ♦ 18
SECURE-CHANNEL COMMUNICATION ♦ 174
security
  See Also access control
  architectural patterns for; ARCHITECTURAL PATTERNS FOR
    ENABLING APPLICATION SECURITY ♦ 17
  ARCHITECTURAL PATTERNS FOR ENABLING APPLICATION
    SECURITY ♦ 17
  concealing properties, during object list display; PARALLEL
    APPLICATION AND DOMAIN HIERARCHIES ♦ 14
  in distributed systems, without system-level support;
    BODYGUARD ♦ 22
  emotional, as pattern writers workshop priority; SAFE
    SETTING ♦ 111
  SECURE ACCESS LAYER ♦ 18
    LAYERED ARCHITECTURE relationship to; SECURE ACCESS
      LAYER ♦ 18
    LAYERS relationship to; SECURE ACCESS LAYER ♦ 18
  SECURE-CHANNEL COMMUNICATION ♦ 174
    HOOK METHOD relationship to; SECURE-CHANNEL
      COMMUNICATION ♦ 174
  work packet, establishing policies for; WORK PACKET
    SECURITY ♦ 29
  WORK PACKET SECURITY ♦ 29
segment
  enterprise, representing; ENTERPRISE SEGMENT ♦ 9
  ENTERPRISE SEGMENT ♦ 9
SELECT/REJECT ♦ 160

selecting
SELECTIVE CHANGES ♦ 114
SELECTING LOCKING DESIGNS FOR PARALLEL PROGRAMS ♦ 147
[McKenney96a]; 190
SELECTING LOCKING PRIMITIVES FOR PARALLEL PROGRAMMING ♦ 148
[McKenney96b]; 191
selection
of account entries; CHOOSING ENTRIES ♦ 11
INTENTION REVEALING SELECTOR ♦ 154
PLUGGABLE SELECTOR ♦ 156
resources, dynamic; SPONSOR-SELECTOR ♦ 164
SELECT/REJECT ♦ 160
SELECTING LOCKING DESIGNS FOR PARALLEL PROGRAMMING,
SELECTING LOCKING PRIMITIVES FOR PARALLEL PROGRAMS
relationship to; SELECTING LOCKING PRIMITIVES FOR
PARALLEL PROGRAMMING ♦ 148
SELECTING LOCKING DESIGNS FOR PARALLEL
PROGRAMS ♦ 147
CRITICAL REGION PROTECTION relationship to; CRITICAL
REGION PROTECTION ♦ 31
SELECTING LOCKING PRIMITIVES FOR PARALLEL
PROGRAMMING ♦ 148
CRITICAL REGION PROTECTION relationship to; CRITICAL
REGION PROTECTION ♦ 31
SELECTING LOCKING DESIGNS FOR PARALLEL PROGRAMS
relationship to; SELECTING LOCKING PRIMITIVES FOR
PARALLEL PROGRAMMING ♦ 148
SELECTIVE CHANGES ♦ 114
SELECTOR SYNTHESIS ♦ 164
SPONSOR-SELECTOR ♦ 164
SUBFORM SELECTION ♦ 99
subforms
criteria for; SUBFORM SELECTION ♦ 99
state change basis for; SUBFORM MATCH ♦ 100
state change basis for deselecting; SUBFORM
MISMATCH ♦ 100
USE SELECTIONINLIST TO HOLD A LIST AND ITS
SELECTION ♦ 178
SELECTIVE CHANGES ♦ 114
SELECTOR SYNTHESIS ♦ 164
self
CLIENT-SPECIFIED SELF ♦ 34
HISTORY ON SELF ♦ 35
modification, by meta level data; REFLECTION ♦ 144
reference, in delegation; SELF DELEGATION ♦ 155
replacing message to, with messages to an argument;
CLIENT-SPECIFIED SELF ♦ 34
SELF DELEGATION ♦ 155
SELF-SELECTING TEAM ♦ 63
DEVELOPMENT EPISODE relationship to; SELF-SELECTING
TEAM ♦ 63
UNITY OF PURPOSE relationship to; UNITY OF PURPOSE ♦ 95
SELFISH CLASS ♦ 150
FIRST ONE'S FREE relationship to; SELFISH CLASS ♦ 150
GENTLE LEARNING CURVE relationship to; SELFISH
CLASS ♦ 150

LOW SURFACE-TO-VOLUME RATIO relationship to; SELFISH
CLASS ♦ 150
PROGRAMMING-BY-DIFFERENCE relationship to; SELFISH
CLASS ♦ 150
WINNING TEAM relationship to; SELFISH CLASS ♦ 150
WORKS OUT OF THE BOX relationship to; SELFISH
CLASS ♦ 150
SELFISH CLASS PATTERN LANGUAGE ♦ 149
sending messages to; DECOMPOSING MESSAGE ♦ 154
when intention is simple; INTENTION REVEALING
MESSAGE ♦ 154
SELF DELEGATION ♦ 155
SELF-SELECTING TEAM ♦ 63
SELFISH CLASS ♦ 150
SELFISH CLASS PATTERN LANGUAGE ♦ 149
[Foote+98]; 187
Selic, B.
[Selic98]; 195
RECURSIVE CONTROL ♦ 143
selling
contract use in; CONTRACT ♦ 13
price, quote representation of; QUOTE ♦ 13
semantics
class, class clause representation of; CLASS SEMANTICS ♦ 121
CLASS SEMANTICS ♦ 121
membership, for containers, managing; MEMBER
CONTAINER ♦ 86
representation of, class clause use; CLASS CLAUSE ♦ 121
semaphores
as object blocking mechanism; SERVICES 'WAITING FOR' ♦ 62
sender
authentication
as cryptographic strategy; SENDER AUTHENTICATION ♦ 174
secrecy; SECRECY WITH SENDER AUTHENTICATION ♦ 175
ENCAPSULATE SENDERS OF VALUE AND VALUE: ♦ 177
message, encapsulation; ENCAPSULATE SENDERS OF VALUE
AND VALUE: ♦ 177
SECRECY WITH SENDER AUTHENTICATION ♦ 175
SENDER AUTHENTICATION ♦ 174
SENDER AUTHENTICATION ♦ 174
**SEPARATE TRANSACTION PROCESSING FROM
ARCHIVAL ♦ 173**
separation
See Also decoupling; encapsulation
of access layers, QUERY BROKER use for; RELATIONAL
DATABASE ACCESS LAYER ♦ 3, HIERARCHICAL VIEW ♦ 3
APPROACHES FOR SEPARATING CLIENTS FROM SERVERS ♦ 16
of information delivery from rest of system; INFORMATIONAL
ROLE ♦ 30
of inheritance hierarchies; HANDLE/BODY HIERARCHY ♦ 24
of interface
from rest of system; INTERFACE'S ROLE ♦ 30
from tool functional parts; SEPARATION OF POWERS ♦ 110
of material constraints from tools; MATERIAL
CONTAINER ♦ 111
PATTERN FOR SEPARATING ASSEMBLY AND PROCESSING ♦ 97
of policy making from support services for
policy-maker role creation; DECISION MAKER'S ROLE ♦ 30
worker role creation; WORKERS' ROLE ♦ 30

Index

separation *continued*

of sender from receiver of a request; CHAIN OF
  RESPONSIBILITY ♦ 32

SEPARATE TRANSACTION PROCESSING FROM ARCHIVAL ♦ 173

  BUSINESS TRANSACTIONS relationship to; BUSINESS
    TRANSACTIONS ♦ 173, SEPARATE TRANSACTION
    PROCESSING FROM ARCHIVAL ♦ 173

SEPARATION OF POWERS ♦ 110

  TOOL COMPOSITION relationship to; TOOL
    COMPOSITION ♦ 110, SEPARATION OF POWERS ♦ 110

SEPARATION OF POWERS ♦ 110

sequence

of numbers, coding; INTERVAL ♦ 160

of proposed actions, plan defined as; PLAN ♦ 13

SEQUENCE OF OWNERS ♦ 85

  CREATOR AS SOLE OWNER relationship to; SEQUENCE OF
    OWNERS ♦ 85

  SHARED OWNERSHIP relationship to; SEQUENCE OF
    OWNERS ♦ 85, SHARED OWNERSHIP ♦ 86

SEQUENTIAL PROGRAM ♦ 147

SHARED OWNERSHIP, SEQUENCE OF OWNERS relationship to;
  SEQUENCE OF OWNERS ♦ 85

SEQUENCE OF OWNERS ♦ 85

SEQUENTIAL PROGRAM ♦ 147

serialization

of objects; SERIALIZER ♦ 151

SERIALIZER ♦ 151

  FACTORY METHOD relationship to; SERIALIZER ♦ 151

  PRODUCT TRADER relationship to; SERIALIZER ♦ 151

  STRATEGY relationship to; SERIALIZER ♦ 151

STRATEGY, SERIALIZER relationship to; SERIALIZER ♦ 151

SERIALIZER ♦ 151

[Riehle+98]; 193

server(s)

abstract class implementation by, in client-server dependency
  management; ABSTRACT SERVER ♦ 16, ADAPTED
  SERVER ♦ 17

ABSTRACT SERVER ♦ 16

ADAPTED SERVER ♦ 17

APPROACHES FOR SEPARATING CLIENTS FROM SERVERS ♦ 16

CLIENT-DISPATCHER-SERVER ♦ 34

client-server architecture

  as distributed system architecture; DISTRIBUTED
    PROCESSES ♦ 51

  four-tier; FOUR-LAYER ARCHITECTURE ♦ 106

  frameworks, legacy system relationships with; NEW
    CLIENTS WITH OLD SERVERS: A PATTERN LANGUAGE FOR
    CLIENT/SERVER FRAMEWORKS ♦ 89

  in legacy system/object-oriented framework interactions;
    CLIENT/SERVER FRAMEWORK ♦ 91

  partitioning, two-tier; TWO-TIER ARCHITECTURE ♦ 14

  three-tier; THREE-TIER ARCHITECTURE ♦ 15

CLIENT/SERVER FRAMEWORK ♦ 91

CLIENT/SERVER/SERVICE ♦ 62

client/server/service model, resource and service
  standardization; CLIENT/SERVER/SERVICE ♦ 62

decoupling clients from, from; ABSTRACT CLIENT ♦ 2

decoupling from clients; APPROACHES FOR SEPARATING
  CLIENTS FROM SERVERS ♦ 16

dispatcher as intermediary between clients and;
  CLIENT-DISPATCHER-SERVER ♦ 34

encapsulating client state, in a Session object; ABSTRACT
  SESSION ♦ 2

NEW CLIENTS WITH OLD SERVERS: A PATTERN LANGUAGE
  FOR CLIENT/SERVER FRAMEWORKS ♦ 89

physical database views as; QUERY BROKER ♦ 4

SERVICE CONFIGURATOR ♦ 151

[Jain+97]; 188

services

client/server/service model, resource and service
  standardization; CLIENT/SERVER/SERVICE ♦ 62

configuring; SERVICE CONFIGURATOR ♦ 151

multiple kinds, management of; IMPLEMENTATION OF
  'MULTIPLE KINDS OF SERVICES' CONTROL MODULES ♦ 62

replication of, management of, in fault-tolerant systems;
  MASTER-SLAVE ♦ 86

SERVICE CONFIGURATOR ♦ 151

  ACTIVE OBJECT relationship to; SERVICE
    CONFIGURATOR ♦ 151

  CONNECTOR relationship to; CONNECTOR ♦ 40

  HOOK METHODS relationship to; SERVICE
    CONFIGURATOR ♦ 151

  MANAGER relationship to; SERVICE CONFIGURATOR ♦ 151

  REACTOR relationship to; SERVICE CONFIGURATOR ♦ 151

SERVICES 'WAITING FOR' ♦ 62

SERVICES 'WAITING FOR' ♦ 62

SESSION ♦ 17, ♦ 37

SESSION CONTROL & OBSERVATION ♦ 151

[VandenBroecke+97]; 197

sessions

ABSTRACT SESSION ♦ 2

cache management use; CACHE MANAGEMENT ♦ 109

creating; ABSTRACT SESSION ♦ 2

managing a hand-off protocol with; SESSION ♦ 37

multimedia, managing; SESSION CONTROL &
  OBSERVATION ♦ 151

parties as first class objects in; PARTIES & MEDIA AS FIRST
  CLASS CITIZENS ♦ 96

SESSION ♦ 17, ♦ 37

  ABSTRACT SESSION relationship to; ABSTRACT SESSION ♦ 2

  DOUBLE-CHECKED LOCKING relationship to; SESSION ♦ 17

  SINGLE ACCESS POINT relationship to; SINGLE ACCESS
    POINT ♦ 17

  THREAD-SPECIFIC STORAGE relationship to; SESSION ♦ 17

SESSION CONTROL & OBSERVATION ♦ 151

  BUILDER relationship to; SESSION CONTROL &
    OBSERVATION ♦ 151

  COMMAND relationship to; SESSION CONTROL &
    OBSERVATION ♦ 151

  MODEL-VIEW-CONTROLLER relationship to;
    MODEL-VIEW-CONTROLLER ♦ 87

  PARTIES & MEDIA AS FIRST CLASS CITIZENS relationship to;
    SESSION CONTROL & OBSERVATION ♦ 151

  SESSION CONTROL & OBSERVATION MODEL-VIEW-
    CONTROLLER relationship to; SESSION CONTROL &
    OBSERVATION ♦ 151

SET ♦ 159

set(s)
See Also collections
Conflict Sets ♦ 39
creating; Set ♦ 159
Duplicate Removing Set ♦ 161
of objects, traversing; Shopper ♦ 152
operations, container use; Member Container ♦ 86
Set ♦ 159
Set-based Navigation ♦ 119
   Nodes in Context relationship to; Nodes in
      Context ♦ 119
Set-based Navigation ♦ 119
setting
boolean properties; Boolean Property Setting
   Method ♦ 158
instance variables
   directly; Direct Variable Access ♦ 157
   setting from parameters; Constructor Parameter
      Method ♦ 152
safe, as pattern writers workshop priority; Safe
   Setting ♦ 111
Safe Setting ♦ 111
Setting Method ♦ 157
   Indirect Variable Access relationship to; Indirect
      Variable Access ♦ 157
   variables; Setting Method ♦ 157
   indirectly; Indirect Variable Access ♦ 157
Setting Method ♦ 157
seven
Seven Parts ♦ 116
   Visible Checklist relationship to; Visible
      Checklist ♦ 117
Three to Seven Helpers per Role ♦ 68
Seven Parts ♦ 116
Shape of Program ♦ 29
See Also geometry; shape; structure
Concurrent Threads of Execution relationship to;
   Concurrent Threads of Execution ♦ 28
Critical Region Protection relationship to; Critical
   Region Protection ♦ 31
Decision Maker's Role relationship to; Decision Maker's
   Role ♦ 30
Event Acquisition relationship to; Event Acquisition ♦ 31
Four-Layer Architecture relationship to; Shape of
   Program ♦ 29, Four-Layer Architecture ♦ 106
Hierarchy of Control Layers relationship to; Shape of
   Program ♦ 29, Hierarchy of Control Layers ♦ 61
Informational Role relationship to; Informational
   Role ♦ 30
Interface's Role relationship to; Interface's Role ♦ 30
Layered and Sectioned Architecture relationship to;
   Shape of Program ♦ 29, Layered and Sectioned
   Architecture ♦ 96
Layered Architecture relationship to; Shape of
   Program ♦ 29
   Layered Architecture relationship to; Layered
      Architecture ♦ 125
Layered Organization relationship to; Shape of
   Program ♦ 29, Layered Organization ♦ 59

Layers relationship to; Shape of Program ♦ 29,
   Layers ♦ 81
Pedestal relationship to; Shape of Program ♦ 29,
   Pedestal ♦ 123
relationship to; Shape of Program ♦ 29
Small Family Systems relationship to; Shape of
   Program ♦ 29, Small Family Systems ♦ 30
System Citizen's Role relationship to; System Citizen's
   Role ♦ 29
Three-Tier Architecture relationship to; Three-Tier
   Architecture ♦ 15, Shape of Program ♦ 29
Work Accomplished Through Dialogs relationship to;
   Shape of Program ♦ 29
Work Packet Completion Report relationship to; Work
   Packet Completion Report ♦ 29
Work Packet Priority relationship to; Work Packet
   Priority ♦ 29
Workers' Role relationship to; Workers' Role ♦ 30
Shaping Circulation Realms ♦ 67
Share the Load ♦ 101
Shared Ownership ♦ 86
Shared Repository ♦ 115
shared/sharing
database
   client-server application, three-tier; Three-Tier
      Architecture ♦ 15
   client-server application use; Two-Tier Architecture ♦ 14
in distributed systems, without system-level support;
   Bodyguard ♦ 22
Ensure That All Objects Sharing a Value Use the
   Same ValueModel ♦ 177
implementation, without inheritance; Delegation ♦ 155
load, in distributed systems; Resource Exchanger ♦ 144
multimedia components, defining a template for;
   Template ♦ 36
object value, type conversion use; Use a TypeConverter to
   Convert a Value Between Types ♦ 178
objects, reference counting management of; Counted
   Pointer ♦ 40
pure state objects; Pure State ♦ 166
queues, object blocking use; Services 'Waiting For' ♦ 62
repository, integration mechanism for; Shared
   Repository ♦ 115
resources
   Active Object support for; Active Object ♦ 6
   identifying objects involved with; Critical Region
      Protection ♦ 31
   management heterogeneous pool of; Implementation of
      'Multiple Kinds of Services' Control Modules ♦ 62
Share the Load ♦ 101
Shared Ownership ♦ 86
   Creator as Sole Owner relationship to; Shared
      Ownership ♦ 86
   Sequence of Owners relationship to; Shared
      Ownership ♦ 86
Shared Repository ♦ 115
as support for large numbers of small objects; Flyweight ♦ 60
Use a ValueModel to Share a Value ♦ 176

shared/sharing *continued*
  values
    between objects; USE A VALUEMODEL TO SHARE A
      VALUE ◆ 176
    single reference guarentees; ENSURE THAT ALL OBJECTS
      SHARING A VALUE USE THE SAME VALUEMODEL ◆ 177
  variable access control, encapsulating as a session;
    SESSION ◆ 17
Sharon, Y.
  [Beedle+99]; 182
    SCRUM: A PATTERN LANGUAGE FOR HYPERPRODUCTIVE
      SOFTWARE DEVELOPMENT ❖ 146
Shaw, M.
  [Shaw+96]; 196
    DISTRIBUTED PROCESSES ◆ 51
    PIPES & FILTERS ◆ 132
    PROCESS CONTROL ◆ 137
    STATE TRANSITION SYSTEMS ◆ 167
  [Shaw95]; 196
    PATTERNS FOR SOFTWARE ARCHITECTURES ❖ 124
  [Shaw96]; 196
    COMMUNICATING PROCESSES ◆ 36
SHEARING LAYERS ◆ 21
  LAYERS relationship to; SHEARING LAYERS ◆ 21
SHED LOAD ◆ 101
  FINISH WORK IN PROGRESS relationship to; SHED LOAD ◆ 101
  FRESH WORK BEFORE STALE relationship to; SHED
    LOAD ◆ 101
  MATCH PROGRESS WORK WITH NEW relationship to; SHED
    LOAD ◆ 101, MATCH PROGRESS WORK WITH NEW ◆ 101
  WORK SHED AT PERIPHERY relationship to; SHED LOAD ◆ 101,
    WORK SHED AT PERIPHERY ◆ 102
SHOPPER ◆ 152
  [Doble96]; 186
shopping
  basket, for e-commerce, hypermedia design strategies;
    BASKET ◆ 120
  SHOPPER ◆ 152
    CHAIN OF RESPONSIBILITY relationship to; SHOPPER ◆ 152
    ITERATOR relationship to; SHOPPER ◆ 152
    STRATEGY relationship to; SHOPPER ◆ 152
  STRATEGY, SHOPPER relationship to; SHOPPER ◆ 152
SHORTCUT CONSTRUCTOR METHOD ◆ 152
  CONSTRUCTOR METHOD relationship to; SHORTCUT
    CONSTRUCTOR METHOD ◆ 152
  INTERVAL relationship to; INTERVAL ◆ 160
SHOW PERSONAL INTEGRITY ◆ 44
  BE AWARE OF BOUNDARIES relationship to; BE AWARE OF
    BOUNDARIES ◆ 44, SHOW PERSONAL INTEGRITY ◆ 44
  BE RESPONSIVE relationship to; BE RESPONSIVE ◆ 44
  BUILD TRUST relationship to; SHOW PERSONAL
    INTEGRITY ◆ 44
  IT'S A RELATIONSHIP, NOT A SALE relationship to; SHOW
    PERSONAL INTEGRITY ◆ 44
  KNOW THE CUSTOMER relationship to; SHOW PERSONAL
    INTEGRITY ◆ 44
  LISTEN, LISTEN, LISTEN relationship to; LISTEN, LISTEN,
    LISTEN ◆ 44

  MIND YOUR MANNERS relationship to; MIND YOUR
    MANNERS ◆ 44
SHUT UP AND LISTEN ◆ 79
  BOTTOM LINE relationship to; BOTTOM LINE ◆ 78, SHUT UP
    AND LISTEN ◆ 79
  GEORGE WASHINGTON IS STILL DEAD relationship to;
    GEORGE WASHINGTON IS STILL DEAD ◆ 78, SHUT UP AND
    LISTEN ◆ 79
  IO TRIAGE relationship to; SHUT UP AND LISTEN ◆ 79
Siberski, W.
  [Riehle+98]; 193
    SERIALIZER ◆ 151
SICO FIRST AND ALWAYS ◆ 58
SICO (System Integrity Control Program)
  SICO FIRST AND ALWAYS ◆ 58
SIGNATURE ◆ 175
signature
  message, secrecy preservation; SECRECY WITH
    SIGNATURE ◆ 175
  SECRECY WITH SIGNATURE ◆ 175
  SECRECY WITH SIGNATURE WITH APPENDIX ◆ 175
  SIGNATURE ◆ 175
    SECRECY WITH SIGNATURE relationship to; SECRECY WITH
      SIGNATURE ◆ 175
  SIGNATURE WITH APPENDIX ◆ 175
    MESSAGE INTEGRITY relationship to; SIGNATURE WITH
      APPENDIX ◆ 175
    SECRECY WITH SIGNATURE WITH APPENDIX relationship to;
      SECRECY WITH SIGNATURE WITH APPENDIX ◆ 175
    SIGNATURE relationship to; SIGNATURE WITH
      APPENDIX ◆ 175
SIGNATURE WITH APPENDIX ◆ 175
Silva, A. R.
  [Silva+98]; 196
    OBJECT RECOVERY ◆ 92
  [Silva+99]; 196
    OBJECT SYNCHRONIZER ◆ 92
Silverstein, M.
  [Alexander+75]; 181
  [Alexander+77]; 182
simple
  SIMPLE DELEGATION ◆ 155
  SIMPLE ENUMERATION PARAMETER ◆ 163
  SIMPLE SUPERCLASS NAME ◆ 162
SIMPLE DELEGATION ◆ 155
SIMPLE ENUMERATION PARAMETER ◆ 163
SIMPLE SUPERCLASS NAME ◆ 162
SIMPLIFICATION ◆ 83
simplification
  of complex behavior, decomposition use; TO SIMPLIFY
    COMPLEX BEHAVIOR, USE DECOMPOSITION ◆ 88
  of expressions; EXPLAINING TEMPORARY VARIABLE ◆ 158
  safe optimization techniques; SIMPLIFICATION ◆ 83
  simple delegation; SIMPLE DELEGATION ◆ 155
  SIMPLIFICATION ◆ 83
simularity
  searching, feature extraction algorithm assistance;
    FEATURE EXTRACTION—A PATTERN FOR INFORMATION
    RETRIEVAL ◆ 58

SIMULATION GAMES ◆ 117
simulations
  DON'T TRUST SIMULATIONS ◆ 127
  OBJECT-ORIENTED SIMULATION ◆ 93
  SIMULATION GAMES ◆ 117
    COLORFUL ANALOGY relationship to; COLORFUL ANALOGY ◆ 117
    DEBRIEF AFTER ACTIVITIES relationship to; DEBRIEF AFTER ACTIVITIES ◆ 118
    PITFALL DIAGNOSIS AND PREVENTION relationship to; PITFALL DIAGNOSIS AND PREVENTION ◆ 116
    QUIZ GAMES relationship to; SIMULATION GAMES ◆ 117
  system test distrust of; DON'T TRUST SIMULATIONS ◆ 127
simultaneous access
  protection mechanisms; CRITICAL REGION PROTECTION ◆ 31
single
  instance of a class, guaranteeing; SINGLETON ◆ 152
  occurence of an object in a framework, making explicit; SOLITAIRE ◆ 89
  reference, shared values, guarenteeing; ENSURE THAT ALL OBJECTS SHARING A VALUE USE THE SAME VALUEMODEL ◆ 177
  SINGLE ACCESS POINT ◆ 17
    CHECK POINT relationship to; SINGLE ACCESS POINT ◆ 17
    SESSION relationship to; SINGLE ACCESS POINT ◆ 17
    SINGLETON relationship to; SINGLE ACCESS POINT ◆ 17
  SINGLE-PASS READABLE ◆ 103
    EVOCATIVE PATTERN NAME relationship to; SINGLE-PASS READABLE ◆ 103
    FINDABLE SECTIONS relationship to; SINGLE-PASS READABLE ◆ 103, FINDABLE SECTIONS ◆ 103
    GLOSSARY relationship to; SINGLE-PASS READABLE ◆ 103
    MANDATORY ELEMENTS PRESENT relationship to; SINGLE-PASS READABLE ◆ 103
    PATTERN LANGUAGE SUMMARY relationship to; SINGLE-PASS READABLE ◆ 103
    PATTERN THUMBNAIL relationship to; SINGLE-PASS READABLE ◆ 103
    SKIPPABLE SECTIONS relationship to; SINGLE-PASS READABLE ◆ 103, SKIPPABLE SECTIONS ◆ 103
    VISIBLE FORCES relationship to; SINGLE-PASS READABLE ◆ 103
  SINGLETON ◆ 152
    DETACHABLE INSPECTOR relationship to; DETACHABLE INSPECTOR ◆ 49
    DIAGNOSTIC LOGGER relationship to; DIAGNOSTIC LOGGER ◆ 124
    EVENT QUEUE relationship to; EVENT QUEUE ◆ 76
    INDIVIDUAL INSTANCE METHOD relationship to; INDIVIDUAL INSTANCE METHOD ◆ 11
    NavigationObserver relationship to; NavigationObserver ◆ 48
    NULL OBJECT relationship to; NULL OBJECT ◆ 91
    SINGLE ACCESS POINT relationship to; SINGLE ACCESS POINT ◆ 17
    SINGLETON relationship to; SOLITAIRE ◆ 89
    SOLITAIRE relationship to; SOLITAIRE ◆ 89
    SYSTEM CITIZEN'S ROLE relationship to; SYSTEM CITIZEN'S ROLE ◆ 29

    THREAD-SPECIFIC STORAGE relationship to; THREAD-SPECIFIC STORAGE ◆ 172
    USE A SlotAdaptor TO HOLD A SINGLE INSTANCE VARIABLE ◆ 178
    USE AN IndexedAdaptor TO HOLD A SINGLE INDEX IN A COLLECTION ◆ 177
SINGLE ACCESS POINT ◆ 17
SINGLE-PASS READABLE ◆ 103
  SKIPPABLE SECTIONS relationship to; SKIPPABLE SECTIONS ◆ 103
SINGLETON ◆ 152
  [Alpert+98]; 182
  [Gamma+95]; 188
SITTING IN A CIRCLE ◆ 112
  AUTHORS' CIRCLE relationship to; AUTHORS' CIRCLE ◆ 112
  OPEN REVIEW relationship to; SITTING IN A CIRCLE ◆ 112
  SAFE SETTING relationship to; SITTING IN A CIRCLE ◆ 112
  VOLUNTEER SUMMARIZES THE WORK relationship to; VOLUNTEER SUMMARIZES THE WORK ◆ 113
size
  collection
    dynamic determination of; ORDERED COLLECTION ◆ 159
    sufficient initial allocation, as optimization technique; HYPOTH-A-SIZED COLLECTION ◆ 84
  SIZE THE ORGANIZATION ◆ 63
  SIZE THE SCHEDULE ◆ 64
    RECOMMITMENT MEETING relationship to; SIZE THE SCHEDULE ◆ 64
  small, FLYWEIGHT management of; FLYWEIGHT ◆ 60
  teams
    recommendations; SIZE THE ORGANIZATION ◆ 63
    small projects; SOLO VIRTUOSO ◆ 64
  training module; SEVEN PARTS ◆ 116
SIZE THE ORGANIZATION ◆ 63
SIZE THE SCHEDULE ◆ 64
SKILL MIX ◆ 135
skills
  human, system testing importance; TESTER'S MORE IMPORTANT THAN THE TEST CASES ◆ 126
  SKILL MIX ◆ 135
    CONWAY'S LAW relationship to; SKILL MIX ◆ 135
  team
    software design considerations; GENERIC UI, SPECIFIC UI ◆ 136, GENERICS AND SPECIFICS ◆ 136
    subsystem design that accomodates; SKILL MIX ◆ 135
SKIPPABLE SECTIONS ◆ 103
  FINDABLE SECTIONS relationship to; FINDABLE SECTIONS ◆ 103
  OPTIONAL ELEMENTS WHEN HELPFUL relationship to; SKIPPABLE SECTIONS ◆ 103
  SINGLE-PASS READABLE relationship to; SINGLE-PASS READABLE ◆ 103, SKIPPABLE SECTIONS ◆ 103
slave
  MASTER-SLAVE ◆ 86
slots
  USE A SlotAdaptor TO HOLD A SINGLE INSTANCE VARIABLE ◆ 178

Index

small

groups of objects, architectural structure; SMALL FAMILY SYSTEMS ♦ 30

SMALL FAMILY SYSTEMS ♦ 30

HUMAN INTERFACE ROLE IS A SPECIAL INTERFACE ROLE relationship to; SMALL FAMILY SYSTEMS ♦ 30

SHAPE OF PROGRAM relationship to; SHAPE OF PROGRAM ♦ 29, SMALL FAMILY SYSTEMS ♦ 30

SMALL FAMILY SYSTEMS ♦ 30

SMALLTALK BEST PRACTICE PATTERNS ♦ 152

[Beck97]; 182

Smalltalk language

best practice; SMALLTALK BEST PRACTICE PATTERNS ♦ 152

collections, representing in a relational database; REPRESENTING COLLECTIONS IN A RELATIONAL DATABASE ♦ 42

database query and report generation; CREATING REPORTS WITH QUERY OBJECTS ♦ 40

lazy optimzation; LAZY OPTIMZATION: PATTERNS FOR EFFICIENT SMALLTALK PROGRAMMING ♦ 81

partitioning code into ENVY/Developer components; PARTITIONING SMALLTALK CODE INTO ENVY/DEVELOPER COMPONENTS ♦ 96

PARTITIONING SMALLTALK CODE INTO ENVY/DEVELOPER COMPONENTS ♦ 96

PATTERN LANGUAGE FOR SMALLTALK & RELATIONAL DATABASES ♦ 106

relational databases and; PATTERN LANGUAGE FOR SMALLTALK & RELATIONAL DATABASES ♦ 106

SMALLTALK BEST PRACTICE PATTERNS ♦ 152

SMALLTALK SCAFFOLDING PATTERNS ♦ 163

ValueModel framework, strategies for defining and using; UNDERSTANDING AND USING THE VALUEMODEL FRAMEWORK IN VISUALWORKS SMALLTALK ♦ 176

SMALLTALK SCAFFOLDING PATTERNS ♦ 163

[Doble+99]; 186

SNAPSHOT ♦ 172

snapshot

of collection, saving; HISTORY ON TREE ♦ 35

market, scenario representation of; SCENARIO ♦ 13

properties, for information systems; SNAPSHOT ♦ 172

relationships, for information systems; SNAPSHOT ♦ 172

SNAPSHOT ♦ 172

TEMPORAL PROPERTY relationship to; TEMPORAL PROPERTY ♦ 171

software

architecture; PATTERNS FOR SOFTWARE ARCHITECTURES ♦ 124

adapting to changing system requirements; MICROKERNEL ♦ 87

big ball of mud system analysis and solutions; BIG BALL OF MUD PATTERN LANGUAGE ♦ 20

debugging tools, for framework use; LANGUAGE TOOLS ♦ 123

DEMO PREP: A PATTERN LANGUAGE FOR THE PREPARATION OF SOFTWARE DEMONSTRATIONS ♦ 46

design, prototyping role; PROTOTYPE A FIRST-PASS DESIGN ♦ 84

development, See development of software

evolution of, strategies and phases; LIFE CYCLE AND REFACTORING PATTERNS THAT SUPPORT EVOLUTION AND REUSE ♦ 84

PATTERNS FOR SOFTWARE ARCHITECTURES ♦ 124

PRIORITIZING FORCES IN SOFTWARE DESIGN ♦ 135

refactoring, strategies for; CONSOLIDATE THE PROGRAM TO SUPPORT EVOLUTION AND REUSE ♦ 85

reusability, strategies that encourage; SELFISH CLASS ♦ 150

SCRUM: A PATTERN LANGUAGE FOR HYPERPRODUCTIVE SOFTWARE DEVELOPMENT ♦ 146

SOFTWARE TECTONICS ♦ 55

See Also BIG BALL OF MUD

FLEXIBLE FOUNDATIONS relationship to; SOFTWARE TECTONICS ♦ 55

METAMORPHOSIS relationship to; SOFTWARE TECTONICS ♦ 55

SOFTWARE TECTONICS ♦ 55

SOLITAIRE ♦ 89

SOLO VIRTUOSO ♦ 64

solutions

pattern language summary of; PROBLEM/SOLUTION SUMMARY ♦ 105

SOMEONE ALWAYS MAKES PROGRESS ♦ 169

DAY CARE relationship to; SOMEONE ALWAYS MAKES PROGRESS ♦ 169

SACRIFICE ONE PERSON relationship to; SOMEONE ALWAYS MAKES PROGRESS ♦ 169

TEAM PER TASK relationship to; SOMEONE ALWAYS MAKES PROGRESS ♦ 169, TEAM PER TASK ♦ 169

Sommerlad, P.

[Buschmann+96]; 183

BLACKBOARD ♦ 22

BROKER ♦ 22

CLIENT-DISPATCHER-SERVER ♦ 34

COMMAND PROCESSOR ♦ 36

COUNTED POINTER ♦ 40

FORWARDER-RECEIVER ♦ 60

LAYERS ♦ 81

MASTER-SLAVE ♦ 86

MICROKERNEL ♦ 87

MODEL-VIEW-CONTROLLER ♦ 87

PIPES & FILTERS ♦ 132

PRESENTATION-ABSTRACTION-CONTROL ♦ 135

PROXY ♦ 139

PUBLISHER-SUBSCRIBER ♦ 139

REFLECTION ♦ 144

VIEW HANDLER ♦ 178

WHOLE-PART ♦ 179

[Sommerlad+96]; 196

CLIENT-DISPATCHER-SERVER ♦ 34

[Sommerlad96]; 196

COMMAND PROCESSOR ♦ 36

[Sommerlad98]; 196

MANAGER ♦ 86

SOP (standard operating procedure)

See protocol

SORTED COLLECTION ♦ 159

sorting
  collections; SORTED COLLECTION ♦ 159
    providing multiple sort orders; TEMPORARILY SORTED
      COLLECTION ♦ 161
  SORTED COLLECTION ♦ 159
  TEMPORARILY SORTED COLLECTION ♦ 161
Soukup, J.
  [Soukup95]; 196
    PATTERN AS A CLASS ♦ 97
source code
  formatting
    blocks; RECTANGULAR BLOCK ♦ 162
    conditional expressions; CONDITIONAL EXPRESSION ♦ 163
    conditions; GUARD CLAUSE ♦ 162
    indenting; INDENTED CONTROL FLOW ♦ 162
    messages; INLINE MESSAGE PATTERN ♦ 162
    multiple messages; CASCADE ♦ 163
sources
  SOURCES OF AN ENTRY ♦ 12
    CHAIN OF RESPONSIBILITY relationship to; SOURCES OF AN
      ENTRY ♦ 12
    POSTING RULES relationship to; SOURCES OF AN ENTRY ♦ 12
    TRANSACTION relationship to; SOURCES OF AN ENTRY ♦ 12
  of WWW references, commenting reasons for inclusion;
    EXPOSABLE GUTS ♦ 98
SOURCES OF AN ENTRY ♦ 12
space
  address, multiple, handling objects in; HALF-OBJECT +
    PROTOCOL ♦ 71
  position in, tracking; USE A SCROLLVALUEHOLDER TO HOLD
    A POSITION IN n-DIMENSIONAL SPACE ♦ 178
  TEAM SPACE ♦ 27
  USE A SCROLLVALUEHOLDER TO HOLD A POSITION IN
    n-DIMENSIONAL SPACE ♦ 178
spaghetti code systems
  analysis and solutions; BIG BALL OF MUD PATTERN
    LANGUAGE ♦ 20
Spall, R.
  [Spall98]; 196
    PANEL STATES ♦ 96
    PLUGGABLE VIEW CONTROLLER ♦ 132
SPECIALIZED ACCOUNT MODEL ♦ 12
specific
  GENERICS AND SPECIFICS ♦ 136
specification
  class, retrieving classes with; CLASS SPECIFICATION ♦ 121
  CLASS SPECIFICATION ♦ 121
  dynamic, of product types; PLUGGABLE FACTORY ♦ 132
  of requirements; REQUIREMENTS SPECIFICATION ♦ 142
    team composition for; DIVERSITY OF MEMBERSHIP ♦ 95
  REQUIREMENTS SPECIFICATION ♦ 142
spiral
  teaching strategies; MIX NEW AND OLD ♦ 116
SPLIT VALIDATION ♦ 136
splitting
  SPLIT VALIDATION ♦ 136
  WORK SPLIT ♦ 53

sponsor
  SPONSOR OBJECTIVES ♦ 140
    MARKET WALK-THROUGH relationship to; SPONSOR
      OBJECTIVES ♦ 140
  SPONSOR-SELECTOR ♦ 164
    BLACKBOARD relationship to; SPONSOR-SELECTOR ♦ 164
    BROKER relationship to; SPONSOR-SELECTOR ♦ 164
    CLIENT-DISPATCHER-SERVER relationship to;
      SPONSOR-SELECTOR ♦ 164
    PROXY relationship to; SPONSOR-SELECTOR ♦ 164
    REFLECTION relationship to; SPONSOR-SELECTOR ♦ 164
    STRATEGY relationship to; SPONSOR-SELECTOR ♦ 164
  STRATEGY, SPONSOR-SELECTOR relationship to;
    SPONSOR-SELECTOR ♦ 164
SPONSOR OBJECTIVES ♦ 140
SPONSOR-SELECTOR ♦ 164
  [Wallingford98]; 197
SPRINT ♦ 146
SQL (Structured Query Language)
  representation; QUERY OBJECT ♦ 108
Srinivasan, S.
  [Srinivasan99]; 196
stability
  NAMED STABLE BASES ♦ 68
STACK ♦ 161
stacks
  implementing; STACK ♦ 161
  STACK ♦ 161
    ORDERED COLLECTION relationship to; STACK ♦ 161
stages
  DECOUPLE STAGES ♦ 68
Stal, M.
  [Buschmann+96]; 183
    BLACKBOARD ♦ 22
    BROKER ♦ 22
    CLIENT-DISPATCHER-SERVER ♦ 34
    COMMAND PROCESSOR ♦ 36
    COUNTED POINTER ♦ 40
    FORWARDER-RECEIVER ♦ 60
    LAYERS ♦ 81
    MASTER-SLAVE ♦ 86
    MICROKERNEL ♦ 87
    MODEL-VIEW-CONTROLLER ♦ 87
    PIPES & FILTERS ♦ 132
    PRESENTATION-ABSTRACTION-CONTROL ♦ 135
    PROXY ♦ 139
    PUBLISHER-SUBSCRIBER ♦ 139
    REFLECTION ♦ 144
    VIEW HANDLER ♦ 178
    WHOLE-PART ♦ 179
  [Sommerlad+96]; 196
    CLIENT-DISPATCHER-SERVER ♦ 34
stand-alone
  USE A VALUEHOLDER TO HOLD A STAND-ALONE
    OBJECT ♦ 177
standardization
  of resources, client/server/service model;
    CLIENT/SERVER/SERVICE ♦ 62

Index

standardization *continued*
   of services, client/server/service model;
      CLIENT/SERVER/SERVICE ♦ 62

stars
   as distributed system topological properties; DISTRIBUTED
      PROCESSES ♦ 51
   STARS: A PATTERN LANGUAGE FOR QUERY-OPTIMIZED
      SCHEMAS ♦ 164

**STARS: A PATTERN LANGUAGE FOR QUERY-OPTIMIZED
SCHEMAS ♦ 164**
   [Peterson95]; 192

start functions
   OUTCOME AND START FUNCTIONS ♦ 13
   protocols linked to observations through; OUTCOME AND
      START FUNCTIONS ♦ 13

state
   abstract, behavior implementation with; IMPLEMENT
      BEHAVIOR WITH ABSTRACT STATE ♦ 145
   accessing, without violation of encapsulation; MEMENTO ♦ 87
   action, decoupling proposed and implemented; PROPOSED AND
      IMPLEMENTED ACTION ♦ 12
   associating with asynchronous operation completion;
      ASYNCHRONOUS COMPLETION TOKEN ♦ 19
   as associations, management strategies; WHEN STATES ARE
      ASSOCIATIONS, USE STATE OBJECTS ♦ 89
   behavior vs., in defining new classes; DEFINE CLASSES BY
      BEHAVIOR, NOT STATE ♦ 145
   business
      tracking with business accounts; BUSINESS ACCOUNTS ♦ 173
      transaction capture of; BUSINESS TRANSACTIONS ♦ 173
   CACHING STATE VARIABLE ♦ 83
   change
      behavior modeling, FSM use; BASIC FSM ♦ 58
      changing state objects to reflect; STATE-DRIVEN
         TRANSITIONS ♦ 167
      in domain objects, requirements analysis; OBJECT
         AGING ♦ 141
      encapsulating in a finite state machine; DYNAMIC STATE
         INSTANTIATION ♦ 60
      event notification; EVENT NOTIFICATION ♦ 54
      moderating reports about; FIVE MINUTES OF NO
         ESCALATION MESSAGES ♦ 78
      object behavior modification relative to; STATE ♦ 166
      one-to-many dependency relationship management of;
         OBSERVER ♦ 94
      strategies for detecting; GEORGE WASHINGTON IS STILL
         DEAD ♦ 78
      subform selection based on; SUBFORM MATCH ♦ 100
   changes, handling, in a software tools environment; EVENT
      MECHANISM ♦ 110
   classes
      classification of; WHEN THERE ARE MANY MOODS, USE
         MOOD CLASSIFIER ♦ 89
      managing complex dynamic behavior with; FOR OBJECTS
         WITH MOODS, USE STATE CLASSES ♦ 88
      mapping objects with multiple states to; FOR COMPLEX
         MOODS, USE A MOOD ALTERNATOR ♦ 89
   COMMON STATE ♦ 156

   computation, when state-dependent behavior is invoked; LAZY
      STATE ♦ 134
   concrete, encapsulation of; ENCAPSULATE CONCRETE
      STATE ♦ 145
   as conditions, management strategies; WHEN STATES ARE
      CONDITIONS, USE PREDICATIVE STATE CLASSES ♦ 88
   default, initializing; OWNER-DRIVEN TRANSITIONS ♦ 167
   DEFAULT STATE ♦ 167
   DEFER IDENTIFICATION OF STATE VARIABLES ♦ 145
   deferring use of, in subclass design; DEFER IDENTIFICATION
      OF STATE VARIABLES ♦ 145
   DEFINE CLASSES BY BEHAVIOR, NOT STATE ♦ 145
   dependent object representation, design and implementation
      strategies; MOODS: MODELS FOR OBJECT-ORIENTED
      DESIGN OF STATE ♦ 87
   driven transitions, mechanisms for; STATE-DRIVEN
      TRANSITION ♦ 59
   dynamic creation, in finite state machine; DYNAMIC STATE
      INSTANTIATION ♦ 60
   DYNAMIC STATE INSTANTIATION ♦ 60
   ENCAPSULATE CONCRETE STATE ♦ 145
   ENCAPSULATED STATE ♦ 60
   encapsulation
      for clients; ABSTRACT SESSION ♦ 2
      in an object; STATE OBJECT ♦ 166
   entry, finite state machine output triggering; MOORE ♦ 59,
      HYBRID ♦ 59
   event relationships
      capturing; COLLECTION OF HISTORY PATTERNS ♦ 34
      capturing in an edition; EDITION ♦ 34
   EXPOSED STATE ♦ 166
   finite state machines (FSM), development patterns; FINITE
      STATE MACHINE PATTERNS ♦ 58
   fire alarm system, representation of; DEVIATION ♦ 134
   FOR OBJECTS WITH MOODS, USE STATE CLASSES ♦ 88
   FOR STATE MACHINES, USE TRANSITION METHODS ♦ 88
   IMPLEMENT BEHAVIOR WITH ABSTRACT STATE ♦ 145
   input/output, representation of; POINT ♦ 134
   lazy; LAZY STATE ♦ 134
   LAZY STATE ♦ 134
   market, scenario representation of; SCENARIO ♦ 13
   MOODS: MODELS FOR OBJECT-ORIENTED DESIGN OF
      STATE ♦ 87
   multimedia session, managing; SESSION CONTROL &
      OBSERVATION ♦ 151
   multiple, mapping to state classes; FOR COMPLEX MOODS,
      USE A MOOD ALTERNATOR ♦ 89
   object, saving; HISTORY ON SELF ♦ 35
   OBJECT-ORIENTED STATE MACHINE ♦ 129
   OBJECTIFY SYSTEM STATE ♦ 93
   objects
      access control; EXPOSED STATE ♦ 166
      changing; STATE-DRIVEN TRANSITIONS ♦ 167
      reducing the number of; PURE STATE ♦ 166
   PANEL STATES ♦ 96
   preservation
      atomic commitment use; ATOMIC COMMITMENT ♦ 38
      rollback in response to an error; ROLLBACK ♦ 38

rolling forward when rollback is impossible;
ROLL-FORWARD ♦ 39

prototype handling of; SELECTOR SYNTHESIS ♦ 164

PURE STATE ♦ 166

refinements to the STATE pattern; STATE PATTERNS ♦ 166

relationships, management strategies; FOR STATE MACHINES,
USE TRANSITION METHODS ♦ 88, WHEN STATES ARE
CONDITIONS, USE PREDICATIVE STATE CLASSES ♦ 88,
WHEN STATES ARE ASSOCIATIONS, USE STATE OBJECTS ♦ 89

representation; COMMON STATE ♦ 156, VARIABLE
STATE ♦ 156

selecting a panel to display based on; PANEL STATES ♦ 96

STATE ♦ 166

   ALGEBRAIC HIERARCHY relationship to; ALGEBRAIC
   HIERARCHY ♦ 25

   BACKUP relationship to; BACKUP ♦ 19

   BASIC FSM relationship to; BASIC FSM ♦ 58

   ENVELOPE/LETTER relationship to; ENVELOPE/LETTER ♦ 25

   FLYWEIGHT relationship to; STATE ♦ 166

   IMPLEMENTING GENERALIZATIONS relationship to;
   IMPLEMENTING GENERALIZATIONS ♦ 15

   MOODS: MODELS FOR OBJECT-ORIENTED DESIGN OF STATE
   relationship to; MOODS: MODELS FOR OBJECT-ORIENTED
   DESIGN OF STATE ♦ 87

   MOODS relationship to; STATE ♦ 166

   OBJECT AGING relationship to; OBJECT AGING ♦ 141

   PANEL STATES relationship to; PANEL STATES ♦ 96

   POINT relationship to; POINT ♦ 114

   STATE OBJECT relationship to; STATE OBJECT ♦ 166

   STATE PATTERNS relationship to; STATE ♦ 166, STATE
   PATTERNS ♦ 166

   STATE-DRIVEN TRANSITION relationship to; STATE-DRIVEN
   TRANSITION ♦ 59

   SUBFORM MATCH relationship to; SUBFORM MATCH ♦ 100

   THREE-LEVEL FSM relationship to; THREE-LEVEL
   FSM ♦ 172

   TYPE OBJECT relationship to; TYPE OBJECT ♦ 176

STATE MEMBER; STATE MEMBER ♦ 166, ♦ 166

STATE OBJECT ♦ 166

   MOODS: MODELS FOR OBJECT-ORIENTED DESIGN OF STATE
   relationship to; MOODS: MODELS FOR OBJECT-ORIENTED
   DESIGN OF STATE ♦ 87

   STATE relationship to; STATE OBJECT ♦ 166

STATE PATTERNS ♦ 166

   BASIC FSM relationship to; BASIC FSM ♦ 58

   FINITE STATE MACHINE PATTERNS relationship to; FINITE
   STATE MACHINE PATTERNS ♦ 58

   MOODS: MODELS FOR OBJECT-ORIENTED DESIGN OF STATE
   relationship to; MOODS: MODELS FOR OBJECT-ORIENTED
   DESIGN OF STATE ♦ 87

   OBJECT AGING relationship to; OBJECT AGING ♦ 141

   STATE relationship to; STATE ♦ 166, STATE PATTERNS ♦ 166

STATE TRANSITION SYSTEMS ♦ 167

STATE-DRIVEN TRANSITION ♦ 59

   STATE relationship to; STATE-DRIVEN TRANSITION ♦ 59

   STATE-DRIVEN TRANSITIONS relationship to; STATE-DRIVEN
   TRANSITION ♦ 59

STATE-DRIVEN TRANSITIONS ♦ 167

   STATE-DRIVEN TRANSITION relationship to; STATE-DRIVEN
   TRANSITION ♦ 59

stateless methods

   open call use; OPEN CALLS ♦ 38

   passing messages through a host to a helper; PASS-THROUGH
   HOST ♦ 38

stateless objects, SINGLETON use; NULL OBJECT ♦ 91

subform selection based on; ALTERNATIVE SUBFORMS ♦ 99

SUBTYPE STATE MACHINES ♦ 14

system, encapsulation of; OBJECTIFY SYSTEM STATE ♦ 93

transition

   behavior modeling, FSM use; BASIC FSM ♦ 58

   decoupling from reaction; FOR STATE MACHINES, USE
   TRANSITION METHODS ♦ 88

transition logic, decoupling from object behavior, in an FSM;
LAYERED ORGANIZATION ♦ 59

transitions, moving from one state to another by; STATE
TRANSITION SYSTEMS ♦ 167

undo/redo management, in conjunction with COMMAND;
MEMENTO ♦ 87

update, with nested containment relationships; OBSERVER
UPDATE MESSAGE ♦ 75

updating

   grouping messages into packets; MESSAGE PACKET ♦ 75

   optiminzation of; OPTIMIZED MESSAGES PER CHANGE
   REQUEST ♦ 75

   sending information to an observer; CONDUIT OF SUBJECT
   CHANGE ♦ 75

   strategies for; ONE MESSAGE PER CHANGE REQUEST ♦ 75,
   ONE MESSAGE PER AFFECTED OBJECT ♦ 75

VARIABLE STATE ♦ 156

variables, caching, as optimization technique; CACHING STATE
VARIABLE ♦ 83

WHEN STATES ARE ASSOCIATIONS, USE STATE OBJECTS ♦ 89

WHEN STATES ARE CONDITIONS, USE PREDICATIVE STATE
CLASSES ♦ 88

STATE ♦ 166
   [Alpert+98]; 182
   [Gamma+95]; 188

STATE MEMBER ♦ 166

STATE OBJECT ♦ 166

STATE PATTERNS ♦ 166
   [Dyson+98]; 187

STATE TRANSITION SYSTEMS ♦ 167
   [Shaw+96]; 196

STATE-DRIVEN TRANSITION ♦ 59

STATE-DRIVEN TRANSITIONS ♦ 167

status
   report, for work packets, designing; WORK PACKET STATUS
   REPORT ♦ 29
   WORK PACKET STATUS REPORT ♦ 29

Stephenson, P.
   [Schmidt+95]; 194

stereotypes
   OBJECT STEREOTYPES ♦ 141

Sternbach, E.
   [Zhang+96a]; 198
   [Zhang+96b]; 198

Index

Sternbach, E. *continued*
[Zhang+96c]; 199
storage
THREAD-SPECIFIC STORAGE ♦ 172
strategies
NAVIGATIONSTRATEGY ♦ 48
of posting rules, decoupling from the rules; POSTING RULE
    EXECUTION ♦ 11
STRATEGY ♦ 167
    ABSTRACT SERVER relationship to; ABSTRACT SERVER ♦ 16
    DECISION MAKER'S ROLE relationship to; DECISION
        MAKER'S ROLE ♦ 30
    FLEXIBLE COMMAND INTERPRETER relationship to;
        FLEXIBLE COMMAND INTERPRETER ♦ 60
    INDIVIDUAL INSTANCE METHOD relationship to; INDIVIDUAL
        INSTANCE METHOD ♦ 11
    ITERABLE CONTAINER relationship to; ITERABLE
        CONTAINER ♦ 80
    JUDGE relationship to; JUDGE ♦ 81
    NavigationStrategy relationship to;
        NAVIGATIONSTRATEGY ♦ 48
    OBJECT RECOVERY relationship to; OBJECT RECOVERY ♦ 92
    OBJECT SYNCHRONIZER relationship to; OBJECT
        SYNCHRONIZER ♦ 92
    RECOVERABLE DISTRIBUTOR relationship to; RECOVERABLE
        DISTRIBUTOR ♦ 143
    STATE relationship to; STATE ♦ 166
    TEMPLATE METHOD relationship to; TEMPLATE
        METHOD ♦ 171
    TYPE OBJECT relationship to; TYPE OBJECT ♦ 176
    VIRTUAL CONSTRUCTOR relationship to; VIRTUAL
        CONSTRUCTOR ♦ 25
STRATEGY ♦ 167
[Gamma+95]; 188
STREAM I-O ENGINEERING MODEL ♦ 19
stream(ing)
concatenating, as optimization technique; CONCATENATING
    STREAM ♦ 84
concatenating collections into; CONCATENATING
    STREAM ♦ 162
CONCATENATING STREAM ♦ 84, ♦ 162
data
    architecture for; PIPES & FILTERS ♦ 132
    converting into objects; PARSER/BUILDER ♦ 94
    data product generation strategies; HANDLERS ♦ 95
    factory hierarchy control by; HIERARCHY OF FACTORIES ♦ 94
    pipeline processing of; PIPELINE ♦ 125
defining; STREAMS ♦ 167
engineering model, for support of batch, interactive, and
    messaging systems; STREAM I-O ENGINEERING MODEL ♦ 19
objects, into data structures; SERIALIZER ♦ 151
PARSING STREAM ♦ 161
STREAM I-O ENGINEERING MODEL ♦ 19
    BATCH ENGINEERING MODEL relationship to; STREAM I-O
        ENGINEERING MODEL ♦ 19
    MESSAGING ENGINEERING MODEL relationship to; STREAM
        I-O ENGINEERING MODEL ♦ 19
    ONLINE ENGINEERING MODEL relationship to; STREAM I-O
        ENGINEERING MODEL ♦ 19

STREAMS ♦ 167
    PIPES & FILTERS relationship to; STREAMS ♦ 167
STREAMS ♦ 167
[Edwards95]; 187
stress testing
as system test strategy; KILLER TEST ♦ 128
strict
propagation
    failure marking; STRICT PROPAGATOR WITH FAILURE ♦ 138
    immediate updating; STRICT PROPAGATOR ♦ 138
STRICT PROPAGATOR ♦ 138
    STRICT PROPAGATOR WITH FAILURE relationship to; STRICT
        PROPAGATOR WITH FAILURE ♦ 138
STRICT PROPAGATOR WITH FAILURE ♦ 138
    STRICT PROPAGATOR relationship to; STRICT PROPAGATOR
        WITH FAILURE ♦ 138
STRICT PROPAGATOR ♦ 138
STRICT PROPAGATOR WITH FAILURE ♦ 138
STRING A WIRE ♦ 80
    IO GATEKEEPER relationship to; STRING A WIRE ♦ 80
    RAW IO relationship to; STRING A WIRE ♦ 80, RAW IO ♦ 80
structures
accounting rules; ACCOUNTING PRACTICE ♦ 12
data
    defining, for distributed systems; DEFINE THE DATA
        STRUCTURE ♦ 70
    repositories; REPOSITORY ♦ 125
decomposing software into levels of abstraction; LAYERS ♦ 81
decoupling abstractions from implementation; BRIDGE ♦ 22
DEFINE THE DATA STRUCTURE ♦ 70
DISTINCTIVE HEADINGS CONVEY STRUCTURE ♦ 106
document, on WWW; NATURAL TEXT DIRECTORIES ♦ 98
of frequent changes, isolating from rest of model; PUT
    FREQUENTLY VARYING STRUCTURES IN INSTANCES ♦ 5
hierarchical
    for client interaction; BUREAUCRACY ♦ 23
    recursion use to represent; RECURSIVE STRUCTURES FOR
        ORGANIZATIONS ♦ 4
inheritance, factoring common attributes; FACTOR OUT
    COMMON ATTRIBUTES ♦ 70
of interactive, applications; MODEL-VIEW-CONTROLLER ♦ 87
interactive, systems, ow-level design; IMPROVING
    RESPONSIVENESS IN INTERACTIVE APPLICATIONS USING
    QUEUES ♦ 76
market, impact on team organization structure; ORGANIZATION
    FOLLOWS MARKET ♦ 65
object, creating a print method for; DEBUG PRINTING
    METHOD ♦ 154
organization
    defining relationships in; ORGANIZATION STRUCTURE ♦ 7
    encapsulating history in; ORGANIZATIONAL
        STRUCTURE-TYPED RELATIONSHIP ♦ 5
    patterns for; ACCOUNTABILITY AND ORGANIZATIONAL
        STRUCTURES pattern language ♦ 4
    software development; EPISODES: A PATTERN LANGUAGE
        OF COMPETITIVE DEVELOPMENT ♦ 51
ORGANIZATION STRUCTURE ♦ 7
ORGANIZATIONAL STRUCTURE-TYPED RELATIONSHIP ♦ 5

pattern language

  headings as tool for conveying; DISTINCTIVE HEADINGS CONVEY STRUCTURE ♦ 106

  intents catalog use for pattern referencing; INTENT CATALOG ♦ 104

  of pattern writers workshops; PATTERN LANGUAGE FOR WRITERS' WORKSHOPS ♦ 111

  pattern writers workshops, physical arrangements; SITTING IN A CIRCLE ♦ 112, AUTHORS' CIRCLE ♦ 112

  of patterns

    design components that support searching; FINDABLE SECTIONS ♦ 103

    separating essential from optional material; SKIPPABLE SECTIONS ♦ 103

  recursion over; OBJECT RECURSION ♦ 92

RECURSIVE STRUCTURES FOR ORGANIZATIONS ♦ 4

responsibility management support; MOVE RESPONSIBILITIES ♦ 67

software development team

  communication support; BUFFALO MOUNTAIN ♦ 67

  interaction; SHAPING CIRCULATION REALMS ♦ 67

structural patterns (GOF)

  ADAPTER; ADAPTER ♦ 6

  BRIDGE; BRIDGE ♦ 22

  COMPOSITE; COMPOSITE ♦ 37

  DECORATOR; DECORATOR ♦ 46

  FLYWEIGHT; FLYWEIGHT ♦ 60

subdomain, organization strategies; AESTHETIC PATTERN ♦ 68

WWW

  See Also spaghetti code systems

  design; PATTERN LANGUAGE FOR AN ESSAY-BASED WEB SITE ♦ 97

  related material; REFERENCE SECTION ♦ 98

style

  PATTERN LANGUAGE FOR DEVELOPING FORM STYLE WINDOWS ♦ 99

stylesheets

  multimedia, defining templates for; TEMPLATE ♦ 36

Stymfal, G.

  [Hanmer+99]; 188

  INPUT AND OUTPUT PATTERN LANGUAGE ♦ 76

subapplication

  SECTION IN A SUBAPPLICATION ♦ 97

subclass(ing)

  alternatives to; DECORATOR ♦ 46

  deferring class instantiation to subclasses; FACTORY METHOD ♦ 56

  design strategies; DEFER IDENTIFICATION OF STATE VARIABLES ♦ 145

  naming; QUALIFIED SUBCLASS NAME ♦ 162

  QUALIFIED SUBCLASS NAME ♦ 162

  SUBCLASS PER TEAM ♦ 136

SUBCLASS PER TEAM ♦ 136

SUBFORM ♦ 99

SUBFORM MATCH ♦ 100

SUBFORM MISMATCH ♦ 100

SUBFORM SELECTION ♦ 99

subforms

  ALTERNATIVE SUBFORMS ♦ 99

  deselecting; SUBFORM MISMATCH ♦ 100

  development criteria; ALTERNATIVE SUBFORMS ♦ 99

  divide and conquer strategy; SUBFORM ♦ 99

  selection criteria; SUBFORM SELECTION ♦ 99

  state change basis for; SUBFORM MATCH ♦ 100

  SUBFORM ♦ 99

    ALTERNATIVE SUBFORMS relationship to; ALTERNATIVE SUBFORMS ♦ 99

  SUBFORM MATCH ♦ 100

    STATE relationship to; SUBFORM MATCH ♦ 100

    SUBFORM MISMATCH relationship to; SUBFORM MISMATCH ♦ 100

    SUBFORM SELECTION relationship to; SUBFORM MATCH ♦ 100

  SUBFORM MISMATCH ♦ 100

    SUBFORM MATCH relationship to; SUBFORM MISMATCH ♦ 100

  SUBFORM SELECTION ♦ 99

    ALTERNATIVE SUBFORMS relationship to; ALTERNATIVE SUBFORMS ♦ 99, SUBFORM SELECTION ♦ 99

    SUBFORM MATCH relationship to; SUBFORM MATCH ♦ 100

Subramanian, S.

  [Subramanian+96]; 196

  BACKUP ♦ 19

subrontines

  languages without support for modularity use of; MAIN PLUS SUBROUTINES ♦ 125

subroutines

  MAIN PLUS SUBROUTINES ♦ 125

subscribing

  PUBLISHER-SUBSCRIBER ♦ 139

subsetting

  as complexity management strategy; GENTLE LEARNING CURVE ♦ 150

subsystems

  persistent, decoupling from user interface; DOMAIN INTERCEPTS ♦ 137

  THREE SUBSYSTEMS ♦ 135

  for workstation application software; THREE SUBSYSTEMS ♦ 135

subtype(ing)

  ABSTRACT MODELS WITH CONSTRAINTS IN SUBTYPES ♦ 4

  domain rule enforcement with, in abstract models; ABSTRACT MODELS WITH CONSTRAINTS IN SUBTYPES ♦ 4

  partitioning of, in a matrix organization; MULTIPLE HIERARCHIC ASSOCIATIONS ♦ 4

  SUBTYPE STATE MACHINES ♦ 14

  SUBTYPING OBSERVATION CONCEPTS ♦ 8

    MEASUREMENT relationship to; SUBTYPING OBSERVATION CONCEPTS ♦ 8

    OBSERVER relationship to; SUBTYPING OBSERVATION CONCEPTS ♦ 8

  SUBTYPING PACKAGES ♦ 14

SUBTYPE STATE MACHINES ♦ 14

SUBTYPING OBSERVATION CONCEPTS ♦ 8

SUBTYPING PACKAGES ♦ 14

SUGGESTIONS FOR IMPROVEMENT ♦ 113

  FLY ON THE WALL relationship to; FLY ON THE WALL ♦ 112

  POSITIVE CLOSURE relationship to; POSITIVE CLOSURE ♦ 113

Index

SUGGESTIONS FOR IMPROVEMENT *continued*
    POSITIVE FEEDBACK FIRST relationship to; SUGGESTIONS FOR
        IMPROVEMENT ◆ 113
    SAFE SETTING relationship to; SAFE SETTING ◆ 111
summaries
    account, creating; SUMMARY ACCOUNT ◆ 11
    of messages about the same kind of event, in fault-tolerant
        systems; BOTTOM LINE ◆ 78
    pattern, during pattern review; VOLUNTEER SUMMARIZES THE
        WORK ◆ 113
    SUMMARY ACCOUNT ◆ 11
        POSTING RULES FOR MANY ACCOUNTS relationship to;
            POSTING RULES FOR MANY ACCOUNTS ◆ 11
    VOLUNTEER SUMMARIZES THE WORK ◆ 113
SUMMARY ACCOUNT ◆ 11
SUPER ◆ 155
superclass
    communication with; SUPER ◆ 155
    CREATE ABSTRACT SUPERCLASS ◆ 85
    EXTENDING SUPER ◆ 155
    MODIFYING SUPER ◆ 155
    naming; SIMPLE SUPERCLASS NAME ◆ 162
    overriding methods in; EXTENDING SUPER ◆ 155, MODIFYING
        SUPER ◆ 155
    SIMPLE SUPERCLASS NAME ◆ 162
    SUPER ◆ 155
supertypes
    abstracting either-or-both relationship into; PARTY ◆ 4,
        PARTY ◆ 6
support
    of policy decision-making, encapsulation of; WORKERS'
        ROLE ◆ 30
SURROGATE ◆ 168
    [Pang99]; 192
surrogates
    for objects, strategies for creating; PROXY ◆ 139
    SURROGATE ◆ 168
        REPRESENTING INHERITANCE IN A RELATIONAL DATABASE
            relationship to; SURROGATE ◆ 168
**SURVIVING OBJECT-ORIENTED PROJECTS: A MANAGER'S
    GUIDE ◆ 168**
    [Cockburn98]; 185
suspending
    actions; SUSPENSION ◆ 12
    SUSPENSION ◆ 12
SUSPENSION ◆ 12
Sutherland, J.
    [Beedle+99]; 182
    SCRUM: A PATTERN LANGUAGE FOR HYPERPRODUCTIVE
        SOFTWARE DEVELOPMENT ❖ 146
swapping
    pages, as display update technique; PAGE FLIP ◆ 50
SWEEPING IT UNDER THE RUG ◆ 21
switching
    telecommunications systems, fault-tolerant interactive systems
        design; INPUT AND OUTPUT PATTERN LANGUAGE ◆ 76
SYMMETRICAL REUSE ◆ 123
symmetry
    as reuse criteria; SYMMETRICAL REUSE ◆ 123

SYMMETRICAL REUSE ◆ 123
    PEDESTAL relationship to; SYMMETRICAL REUSE ◆ 123
synchronization
    ACTIVE OBJECT support for; ACTIVE OBJECT ◆ 6
    CLIENT SYNCHRONIZATION ◆ 109
    of clients, with databases; CLIENT SYNCHRONIZATION ◆ 109
    computation completion management, with Futures;
        FUTURES ◆ 40
    elimination of, as complexity management strategy;
        SEQUENTIAL PROGRAM ◆ 147
    I/O models, integrating asynchronous and;
        HALF-SYNC/HALF-ASYNC ◆ 71
    of illegal value checking; DOUBLE CHECK ◆ 38
    initialization, decoupling from services provided;
        CONNECTOR ◆ 40
    of multimedia presentations; SYNCHRONIZE CHANNELS ◆ 37
    of mutually exclusive actions, conflict set use; CONFLICT
        SETS ◆ 39
    object recovery decoupling from, strategies for; OBJECT
        RECOVERY ◆ 92
    OBJECT SYNCHRONIZER ◆ 92
    of objects; OBJECT SYNCHRONIZER ◆ 92
    overhead, reduction, double-checked locking use;
        DOUBLE-CHECKED LOCKING ◆ 51
    of shared resources, identifying objects involved with;
        CRITICAL REGION PROTECTION ◆ 31
    SYNCHRONIZATION OF CONCURRENT THREADS ◆ 28
        CONCURRENT THREADS OF EXECUTION relationship
            to; CONCURRENT THREADS OF EXECUTION ◆ 28,
            SYNCHRONIZATION OF CONCURRENT THREADS ◆ 28
        WORK PACKET COMPLETION REPORT relationship to; WORK
            PACKET COMPLETION REPORT ◆ 29
    SYNCHRONIZATION PROXY, PROXY DESIGN PATTERN
        REVISITED relationship to; PROXY DESIGN PATTERN
        REVISITED ◆ 139
    SYNCHRONIZE CHANNELS ◆ 37
    of threads; SYNCHRONIZATION OF CONCURRENT
        THREADS ◆ 28
SYNCHRONIZATION OF CONCURRENT THREADS ◆ 28
SYNCHRONIZE CHANNELS ◆ 37
synthesis
    SELECTOR SYNTHESIS ◆ 164
SYSTEM CITIZEN'S ROLE ◆ 29
system(s)
    See Also distributed systems; fault-tolerant systems
    BUSY SYSTEM ◆ 127
    chaotic, analysis and solutions; BIG BALL OF MUD PATTERN
        LANGUAGE ◆ 20
    concurrent, controling complexity through layering system
        functions into hierarchies; HIERARCHY OF CONTROL
        LAYERS ◆ 61
    information, navigation design for; PATTERNS FOR DESIGNING
        NAVIGABLE INFORMATION SPACES ◆ 119
    modification, by meta level data; REFLECTION ◆ 144
    OBJECTIFY SYSTEM STATE ◆ 93
    PATTERNS FOR SYSTEM TESTING ◆ 126
    reactive
        control of; OBJECT-ORIENTED DESIGN PATTERNS IN
            REACTIVE SYSTEMS ◆ 92

improving the capacity and reliability of; PATTERN
    LANGUAGE FOR IMPROVING THE CAPACITY OF REACTIVE
    SYSTEMS ◆ 100
real-time
    concurrent control systems, software development strategies;
        OBJECT-ORIENTED DESIGN PATTERNS IN REACTIVE
        SYSTEMS ◆ 92
    improving the capacity and reliability of; PATTERN
        LANGUAGE FOR IMPROVING THE CAPACITY OF REACTIVE
        SYSTEMS ◆ 100
    recursive control of; RECURSIVE CONTROL ◆ 143
SMALL FAMILY SYSTEMS ◆ 30
spaghetti code, analysis and solutions; BIG BALL OF MUD
    PATTERN LANGUAGE ◆ 20
state, encapsulation of; OBJECTIFY SYSTEM STATE ◆ 93
STATE TRANSITION SYSTEMS ◆ 167
SYSTEM CITIZEN'S ROLE ◆ 29
    CONCURRENT THREADS OF EXECUTION relationship to;
        SYSTEM CITIZEN'S ROLE ◆ 29
    EVENT ACQUISITION relationship to; SYSTEM CITIZEN'S
        ROLE ◆ 29
    EVENT ROUTING relationship to; SYSTEM CITIZEN'S
        ROLE ◆ 29
    SHAPE OF PROGRAM relationship to; SYSTEM CITIZEN'S
        ROLE ◆ 29
    SINGLETON relationship to; SYSTEM CITIZEN'S ROLE ◆ 29
telemetry
    ORGANIZATIONAL MULTIPLEXING: PATTERNS FOR
        PROCESSING SATELLITE TELEMETRY WITH DISTRIBUTED
        TEAMS; ORGANIZATIONAL MULTIPLEXING: PATTERNS FOR
        PROCESSING SATELLITE TELEMETRY WITH DISTRIBUTED
        TEAMS ◆ 94
    PATTERN FOR SEPARATING ASSEMBLY AND PROCESSING;
        PATTERN FOR SEPARATING ASSEMBLY AND
        PROCESSING ◆ 97
    testing; PATTERNS FOR SYSTEM TESTING ◆ 126
    transportation, building; PATTERN LANGUAGE OF TRANSPORT
        SYSTEMS (POINT AND ROUTE) ◆ 114
    unstructured, analysis and solutions; BIG BALL OF MUD
        PATTERN LANGUAGE ◆ 20

TABLE DESIGN TIME ◆ 42, ◆ 107
tables
    representing objects as; REPRESENTING OBJECTS AS
        TABLES ◆ 42, REPRESENTING OBJECTS AS TABLES ◆ 107
    REPRESENTING OBJECTS AS TABLES ◆ 42, ◆ 107
    TABLE DESIGN TIME ◆ 42, ◆ 107
        REPRESENTING COLLECTIONS relationship to; TABLE DESIGN
            TIME ◆ 42, TABLE DESIGN TIME ◆ 107
        REPRESENTING INHERITANCE IN A RELATIONAL DATABASE
            relationship to; TABLE DESIGN TIME ◆ 42, TABLE DESIGN
            TIME ◆ 107
        REPRESENTING OBJECT RELATIONSHIPS relationship to;
            TABLE DESIGN TIME ◆ 42, TABLE DESIGN TIME ◆ 107
        REPRESENTING OBJECTS AS TABLES relationship to; TABLE
            DESIGN TIME ◆ 42, TABLE DESIGN TIME ◆ 107
TAKE NO SMALL SLIPS ◆ 69
    COMPLETION HEADROOM relationship to; COMPLETION
        HEADROOM ◆ 53, TAKE NO SMALL SLIPS ◆ 69

WORK QUEUE REPORT relationship to; TAKE NO SMALL
    SLIPS ◆ 69
TAKE TIME ◆ **126**
    DESIGNERS ARE OUR FRIENDS relationship to; TAKE
        TIME ◆ 126
    GET INVOLVED EARLY relationship to; TAKE TIME ◆ 126
    TIME TO TEST relationship to; TIME TO TEST ◆ 126, TAKE
        TIME ◆ 126
TAKE YOUR LICKS ◆ **44**
target audience
    identification, pattern writing importance; CLEAR TARGET
        AUDIENCE ◆ 104
task(s)
    decomposition, into methods; COMPOSED METHOD ◆ 152
    TEAM PER TASK ◆ 169
Taylor, P.
    [Taylor99]; 196
    CAPABLE, PRODUCTIVE, AND SATISFIED ◆ 26
Tcl language
    as prototyping language, customer demonstration use;
        PROTOTYPING LANGUAGES ◆ 47
teaching
    classroom, patterns for; PATTERNS FOR CLASSROOM
        EDUCATION ◆ 116
    strategies
        analogies use for teaching concepts; COLORFUL
            ANALOGY ◆ 117
        checklist use for continuity and review; VISIBLE
            CHECKLIST ◆ 117
        error prevention; PITFALL DIAGNOSIS AND
            PREVENTION ◆ 116
        example domain selection; ACQUAINTANCE EXAMPLES ◆ 117
        example duration; EXAMPLE LASTS ONE WEEK ◆ 117
        interdependent concepts; CHICKEN AND EGG ◆ 116
        open-ended review; DEBRIEF AFTER ACTIVITIES ◆ 118
        presenting a coherant whole; MODULE'S STORY ◆ 116
        references use to extend a course; REFERENCE
            EXAMPLES ◆ 117
        reviewing; QUIZ GAMES ◆ 118
        simulation games; SIMULATION GAMES ◆ 117
        size of a module; SEVEN PARTS ◆ 116
        spiral approach to introducing new material; MIX NEW AND
            OLD ◆ 116
TEAM PER TASK ◆ **169**
TEAM SPACE ◆ **27**
teams
    See Also human; human relationships
    architecture development by, strategies for ensuring coherance;
        LOCK 'EM UP TOGETHER ◆ 95
    building, in software development; BOOTSTRAPPING ◆ 26
    composition of; HOLISTIC DIVERSITY ◆ 169
    customer interaction with software development; ENGAGE
        CUSTOMERS ◆ 66
    DESIGN BY TEAM ◆ 95
    design conflict handling; SUBCLASS PER TEAM ◆ 136
    design validation strategies; VALIDATION BY TEAMS ◆ 96
    distributed system development, software and organizational
        development strategies; ORGANIZATIONAL MULTIPLEXING:

teams *continued*
  distributed system development, software and organizational development strategies; ORGANIZATIONAL MULTIPLEXING: PATTERNS FOR PROCESSING SATELLITE TELEMETRY WITH DISTRIBUTED TEAMS *continued*
    PATTERNS FOR PROCESSING SATELLITE TELEMETRY WITH DISTRIBUTED TEAMS ◆ 94
  gatekeeper interface to rest of world; GATEKEEPER ◆ 67
  GENERATIVE DEVELOPMENT-PROCESS PATTERN LANGUAGE; GENERATIVE DEVELOPMENT-PROCESS PATTERN LANGUAGE ◆ 63
  geographical location, impact on project architecture; ORGANIZATION FOLLOWS LOCATION ◆ 64
  hiring strategies, long term; PHASING IT IN ◆ 64
  ineffective behaviors; LET'S PLAY TEAM ◆ 131, LONG POLE IN THE TENT ◆ 131
  integration strategies for building effective teams; DESIGN BY TEAM ◆ 95
  interaction, structures that support; SHAPING CIRCULATION REALMS ◆ 67
  leadership roles; GURU DOES ALL ◆ 130, CULT OF PERSONALITY ◆ 130, PEACEMAKER ◆ 131
  LET'S PLAY TEAM ◆ 131
  management strategies; CAPABLE, PRODUCTIVE, AND SATISFIED ◆ 26, DOORMAT ◆ 131
    daily meetings; SCRUM MEETINGS ◆ 147
    a managers guide; SURVIVING OBJECT-ORIENTED PROJECTS: A MANAGER'S GUIDE ◆ 168
    Scrum process; SCRUM: A PATTERN LANGUAGE FOR HYPERPRODUCTIVE SOFTWARE DEVELOPMENT ◆ 146
  matching human capabilities to tasks; ROUND PEGS FOR ROUND HOLES ◆ 27
  morale, high-level manager/champion role; PATRON ◆ 65
  motivating; COMPENSATE SUCCESS ◆ 69
  of objects, architectural structure; SMALL FAMILY SYSTEMS ◆ 30
  organization of; PEACEMAKER ◆ 131
  organization strategies; ORGANIZATIONAL PATTERNS FOR TEAMS ◆ 95
  ORGANIZATIONAL MULTIPLEXING: PATTERNS FOR PROCESSING SATELLITE TELEMETRY WITH DISTRIBUTED TEAMS ◆ 94
  ORGANIZATIONAL PATTERNS FOR TEAMS ◆ 95
  PATTERNS FOR DESIGNING IN TEAMS ◆ 118
  performance cycles, managing; PULSE ◆ 27
  PROBLEM-ORIENTED TEAM ◆ 27
  problem-solving techniques for; PROBLEM-ORIENTED TEAM ◆ 27
  project difficulty handling; CULT OF PERSONALITY ◆ 130, CARGO CULT ◆ 131, CONTAINMENT BUILDING ◆ 131, SACRIFICIAL LAMB ◆ 131, SCHEDULE CHICKEN ◆ 132
  requirements specification; DIVERSITY OF MEMBERSHIP ◆ 95
  role determination; FORM FOLLOWS FUNCTION ◆ 64
  selection criteria for; SELF-SELECTING TEAM ◆ 63
  SELF-SELECTING TEAM ◆ 63
  size
    recommendations; SIZE THE ORGANIZATION ◆ 63
    small projects; SOLO VIRTUOSO ◆ 64
  skill level, software design considerations; GENERIC UI, SPECIFIC UI ◆ 136, GENERICS AND SPECIFICS ◆ 136
  skill utilization strategies; DEVELOPMENT EPISODE ◆ 53
  software development; PATTERNS FOR DESIGNING IN TEAMS ◆ 118
    configuration management strategies; TEAMWORK AND CONFIGURATION MANAGEMENT ◆ 170
    distractions, handling; SOMEONE ALWAYS MAKES PROGRESS ◆ 169, TEAM PER TASK ◆ 169, SACRIFICE ONE PERSON ◆ 170
    organization structure for; EPISODES: A PATTERN LANGUAGE OF COMPETITIVE DEVELOPMENT ◆ 51
    protecting against distractions; FIRE WALLS ◆ 67
    work assignment strategies; WORK GROUP ◆ 52
  strategies for ensuring effective design work; MULTIPLE COMPETING DESIGNS ◆ 118
  SUBCLASS PER TEAM ◆ 136
  tasks between projects; CASUAL DUTY ◆ 130
  TEAM PER TASK ◆ 169
    DAY CARE relationship to; TEAM PER TASK ◆ 169
    FUNCTION OWNERS/COMPONENT OWNERS relationship to; TEAM PER TASK ◆ 169
    SACRIFICE ONE PERSON relationship to; TEAM PER TASK ◆ 169, SACRIFICE ONE PERSON ◆ 170
    SOMEONE ALWAYS MAKES PROGRESS relationship to; TEAM PER TASK ◆ 169
    TEAM PER TASK relationship to; SOMEONE ALWAYS MAKES PROGRESS ◆ 169
  TEAM SPACE ◆ 27
  TEAMWORK, NAMED STABLE BASES relationship to; NAMED STABLE BASES ◆ 68
  TEAMWORK AND CONFIGURATION MANAGEMENT ◆ 170
  training
    building initial projects; TRIAL PROJECT ◆ 130
    in relevant technologies; TRAIN HARD FIGHT EASY ◆ 130, TRAIN THE TRAINER ◆ 130
  training strategies, apprenticeship program; APPRENTICE ◆ 64
  VALIDATION BY TEAMS ◆ 96
  volatile, subsystem design that accomodates; SKILL MIX ◆ 135
  WINNING TEAM ◆ 151
TEAMWORK AND CONFIGURATION MANAGEMENT ◆ 170
[Berczuk97]; 183
technical
  memos, as project documentation; TECHNICAL MEMO ◆ 54
  papers
    acceptance process; IDENTIFY THE CHAMPION PATTERN LANGUAGE ◆ 73
    evaluation conflicts, strategies for handling; IDENTIFY THE CONFLICTS ◆ 74
    selecting reviewers for; EXPERTS REVIEW PAPERS ◆ 73
    selecting reviewers for, strategies for encouraging champions; CHAMPIONS REVIEW PAPERS ◆ 74
    selection criteria; CONSENSUS ON PC PAPERS ◆ 74
  TECHNICAL MEMO ◆ 54
  writing, project design role; MERCENARY ANALYST ◆ 67
TECHNICAL MEMO ◆ 54
tectonics
  software
    See Also BIG BALL OF MUD
    change management in response to requirements change; SOFTWARE TECTONICS ◆ 55

Software Tectonics ◆ 55

telecommunications
fault-tolerant systems for; Fault-Tolerant
Telecommunication System Patterns ◆ 57
Fault-Tolerant Telecommunication System
Patterns ◆ 57
human interaction system design; Input and Output
Pattern Language ◆ 76
Pattern Language for Improving the Capacity of
Reactive Systems; Pattern Language for Improving
the Capacity of Reactive Systems ◆ 100

telemetry systems
Organizational Multiplexing: Patterns for Processing
Satellite Telemetry with Distributed Teams ◆ 94
Pattern for Separating Assembly and Processing;
Pattern for Separating Assembly and Processing ◆ 97

Template ◆ 36
Template Method ◆ 171
[Alpert+98]; 182
[Gamma+95]; 188

templates
algorithm definition use; Template Method ◆ 171
circular dependencies; Curiously Recurring
Template ◆ 43
Curiously Recurring Template; Curiously Recurring
Template ◆ 43, ◆ 43
multimedia, defining; Template ◆ 36
Template ◆ 36
Template Method ◆ 171
Acceptor relationship to; Acceptor ◆ 3
Connector relationship to; Connector ◆ 40
Factory Method relationship to; Template
Method ◆ 171
Hook Method relationship to; Hook Method ◆ 73
NavigationStrategy relationship to;
NavigationStrategy ◆ 48
Strategy relationship to; Template Method ◆ 171
White-Box Frameworks relationship to; White-Box
Frameworks ◆ 121

temporal
See Also time
Temporal Association ◆ 172
Association Object relationship to; Temporal
Association ◆ 172
Temporal Property relationship to; Temporal
Property ◆ 171, Temporal Association ◆ 172
Temporal Patterns ◆ 171
Temporal Property ◆ 171
Historic Mapping relationship to; Temporal
Property ◆ 171
Range relationship to; Temporal Property ◆ 171
Snapshot relationship to; Temporal Property ◆ 171
Temporal Association relationship to; Temporal
Property ◆ 171, Temporal Association ◆ 172
Temporal Association ◆ 172
Temporal Patterns ◆ 171
[Carlson+99]; 184
Temporal Property ◆ 171
Temporarily Sorted Collection ◆ 161

temporary
Temporarily Sorted Collection ◆ 161
Temporary Variable ◆ 158
variables, caching, as optimization technique; Caching
Temporary Variable ◆ 83
Temporary Variable ◆ 158
terminals
Beltline Terminal ◆ 79
terminology
See Also naming
defining, for requirements process; Defining
Requirements ◆ 140
domain, pattern writing importance; Terminology Tailored
to Audience ◆ 105
Terminology Tailored to Audience ◆ 105
Clear Target Audience relationship to; Terminology
Tailored to Audience ◆ 105
Glossary relationship to; Terminology Tailored to
Audience ◆ 105
unfamiliar, including in a pattern language glossary;
Glossary ◆ 106
Terminology Tailored to Audience ◆ 105
territoriality
human, in software development; Arranging the
Furniture ◆ 27
Tessier, J.
[Keller+98a]; 189
Pattern System for Network Management
Interfaces ❖ 114
[Keller+98b], Accessing Relational Databases pattern
language ◆ 3
Test-and-Set Lock ◆ 148
Tester's More Important Than the Test Cases ◆ 126
testing
14.4 Kbps Testing ◆ 99
Application Design is Bounded by Test Design ◆ 66
application design relationship to; Application Design is
Bounded by Test Design ◆ 66
collections, for emptiness; Is Empty ◆ 160
determining which test case to run; Scratch 'n Sniff ◆ 128
Exhaustion Test ◆ 73
Killer Test ◆ 128
object properties; Query Method ◆ 153
out-of-memory conditions; Exhaustion Test ◆ 73
Patterns for System Testing ◆ 126
as requirements specification component, team composition
for; Diversity of Membership ◆ 95
stress, as system test strategy; Killer Test ◆ 128
system; Patterns for System Testing ◆ 126
collaboration with designers; Designers Are Our
Friends ◆ 126
Test-and-Set Lock ◆ 148
Allocator Caches relationship to; Test-and-Set
Lock ◆ 148
Data Locking relationship to; Test-and-Set Lock ◆ 148
Data Ownership relationship to; Test-and-Set
Lock ◆ 148
Hierarchical Locking relationship to; Test-and-Set
Lock ◆ 148

Index

testing *continued*
    TEST-AND-SET LOCK *continued*
        PARALLEL FASTPATH relationship to; TEST-AND-SET
            LOCK ♦ 148
    TESTER'S MORE IMPORTANT THAN THE TEST CASES ♦ 126
    when to start; TIME TO TEST ♦ 126
text
    flow, WWW writing style issues; NATURAL TEXT FLOW ♦ 98
    NATURAL TEXT DIRECTORIES ♦ 98
    NATURAL TEXT FLOW ♦ 98
    NATURAL TEXT HYPERLINKS ♦ 98
THANK THE AUTHOR ♦ 113
    AUTHOR ASKS FOR CLARIFICATION relationship to; THANK
        THE AUTHOR ♦ 113
    SAFE SETTING relationship to; SAFE SETTING ♦ 111
thin clients
    engineering model for; ONLINE ENGINEERING MODEL ♦ 18
THINK SMALL ♦ 72
    CAPTAIN OATES relationship to; THINK SMALL ♦ 72
    EXHAUSTON TEST relationship to; THINK SMALL ♦ 72
    MAKE THE USER WORRY relationship to; THINK SMALL ♦ 72
    MEMORY BUDGET relationship to; THINK SMALL ♦ 72
    MEMORY PERFORMANCE ASSESSMENT relationship to; THINK
        SMALL ♦ 72
thrashing
    software development, resource management strategies;
        DON'T INTERRUPT AN INTERRUPT ♦ 69
THREAD-PER-MESSAGE ♦ 39
THREAD-SPECIFIC STORAGE ♦ 172
    [Schmidt+99]; 195
threads
    See Also
    ACTIVE OBJECT support for; ACTIVE OBJECT ♦ 6
    CONCURRENT THREADS OF EXECUTION ♦ 28
    data ownership, as parallelism management strategy; DATA
        OWNERSHIP ♦ 147
    efficient use of, event-driven mechanisms; EVENT-DRIVEN
        I/O ♦ 39
    identifying; CONCURRENT THREADS OF EXECUTION ♦ 28
    multiple, access strategies; THREAD-SPECIFIC STORAGE ♦ 172
    one-way messaging design use, concurrency mechannisms;
        THREAD-PER-MESSAGE ♦ 39
    synchronization of; SYNCHRONIZATION OF CONCURRENT
        THREADS ♦ 28
    SYNCHRONIZATION OF CONCURRENT THREADS ♦ 28
    THREAD-PER-MESSAGE ♦ 39
    THREAD-SPECIFIC STORAGE ♦ 172
        DOUBLE-CHECKED LOCKING relationship to;
            THREAD-SPECIFIC STORAGE ♦ 172
        PROXY relationship to; THREAD-SPECIFIC STORAGE ♦ 172
        SESSION relationship to; SESSION ♦ 17
        SINGLETON relationship to; THREAD-SPECIFIC
            STORAGE ♦ 172
    TIME THREAD ANALYSIS ♦ 71
    worker, unrelated task handling by; WORKER THREADS ♦ 39
    WORKER THREADS ♦ 39
three
    3-LEVEL ORDER ♦ 24

third-party interfaces, testing of; 'UNCHANGED'
    INTERFACES ♦ 127
THREE EXAMPLES ♦ 121
    WHITE-BOX FRAMEWORKS relationship to; THREE
        EXAMPLES ♦ 121, WHITE-BOX FRAMEWORKS ♦ 121
THREE SUBSYSTEMS ♦ 135
THREE TO SEVEN HELPERS PER ROLE ♦ 68
three-legged transactions, term description; TRANSACTION ♦ 10
THREE-LEVEL FSM ♦ 172
    FINITE STATE MACHINE PATTERNS relationship to; FINITE
        STATE MACHINE PATTERNS ♦ 58
    LAYERED ORGANIZATION relationship to; LAYERED
        ORGANIZATION ♦ 59
    STATE relationship to; THREE-LEVEL FSM ♦ 172
THREE-TIER ARCHITECTURE ♦ 15
    ACCESSING RELATIONAL DATABASES relationship to;
        THREE-TIER ARCHITECTURE ♦ 15
    CROSSING CHASMS relationship to; THREE-TIER
        ARCHITECTURE ♦ 15
    DATABASE INTERACTION relationship to; DATABASE
        INTERACTION ♦ 15
    FOUR-LAYER ARCHITECTURE relationship to; THREE-TIER
        ARCHITECTURE ♦ 15, FOUR-LAYER ARCHITECTURE ♦ 106
    HIERARCHY OF CONTROL LAYERS relationship to;
        THREE-TIER ARCHITECTURE ♦ 15, HIERARCHY OF
        CONTROL LAYERS ♦ 61
    LAYERED AND SECTIONED ARCHITECTURE relationship to;
        LAYERED AND SECTIONED ARCHITECTURE ♦ 96
    LAYERED AND SECTIONEDARCHITECTURE relationship to;
        THREE-TIER ARCHITECTURE ♦ 15
    LAYERED ARCHITECTURE relationship to; THREE-TIER
        ARCHITECTURE ♦ 15, LAYERED ARCHITECTURE ♦ 125
    LAYERED ORGANIZATION relationship to; THREE-TIER
        ARCHITECTURE ♦ 15
    LAYERS relationship to; THREE-TIER ARCHITECTURE ♦ 15,
        LAYERS ♦ 81
    PEDESTAL relationship to; THREE-TIER ARCHITECTURE ♦ 15,
        PEDESTAL ♦ 123
    PRESENTATION AND APPLICATION LOGIC relationship to;
        PRESENTATION AND APPLICATION LOGIC ♦ 15
    SHAPE OF PROGRAM relationship to; THREE-TIER
        ARCHITECTURE ♦ 15, SHAPE OF PROGRAM ♦ 29
THREE EXAMPLES ♦ 121
THREE SUBSYSTEMS ♦ 135
THREE TO SEVEN HELPERS PER ROLE ♦ 68
THREE-LEVEL FSM ♦ 172
THREE-LEVEL FSMe
    [Martin95b]; 190
THREE-TIER ARCHITECTURE ♦ 15
THRESHOLD SWITCH ♦ 82
    PERFORMANCE CRITERIA relationship to; PERFORMANCE
        CRITERIA ♦ 82
    PERFORMANCE MEASUREMENT relationship to; THRESHOLD
        SWITCH ♦ 82, PERFORMANCE MEASUREMENT ♦ 82
throughput
    optimization
        finishing work in progress first; FINISH WORK IN
            PROGRESS ♦ 101

overload handling strategies; WORK SHED AT
    PERIPHERY ♦ 102
    user request classifying for; SHED LOAD ♦ 101
software development, resource management strategies;
    INTERRUPTS UNJAM BLOCKING ♦ 69
THROWAWAY CODE ♦ 21
thumbnail
    PATTERN THUMBNAIL ♦ 104
Tichy, W.
    [Feiler+99]; 187
    PROPAGATOR: A FAMILY OF PATTERNS ❖ 138
tiers
    See Also layering
    THREE-TIER ARCHITECTURE ♦ 15
    TWO-TIER ARCHITECTURE ♦ 14
TIME ♦ 165
time
    See Also temporal
    access control over, encapsulating as a session; SESSION ♦ 17
    archiving objects; HISTORIC MAPPING ♦ 16
    association object handling; ASSOCIATION OBJECT ♦ 23
    based relationships, association object representation of;
        BUSINESS PATTERNS OF ASSOCIATION OBJECTS ♦ 23
    capturing
        in an organizational structure; ORGANIZATIONAL
            STRUCTURE-TYPED RELATIONSHIP ♦ 5
        in a transaction processing system; TIME ♦ 165
    collection snapshot, saving; HISTORY ON TREE ♦ 35
    container change, recording previous reference; MEMENTO
        CHILD ♦ 35
    development schedule, determination of; SIZE THE
        SCHEDULE ♦ 64
    estimation, in system testing; TAKE TIME ♦ 126
    as event queue ordering mechanism, interactive application
        use; EVENT QUEUE ♦ 76
    example duration, in teaching; EXAMPLE LASTS ONE
        WEEK ♦ 117
    future, forward contracts use in; FORWARD CONTRACTS ♦ 13
    history capture, designing for; DATA KNOWS ITS ROOTS ♦ 31
    limited, as big ball of mud system force; BIG BALL OF
        MUD ♦ 21
    market snapshot, scenario representation of; SCENARIO ♦ 13
    minimizing pattern read time, pattern writing strategies that
        support; SINGLE-PASS READABLE ♦ 103
    object change
        strategies for handling; TEMPORAL PATTERNS ♦ 171
        tracking; TEMPORAL PROPERTY ♦ 171
    object relationship change, tracking; TEMPORAL
        ASSOCIATION ♦ 172
    project, estimation strategies; COMPARABLE WORK ♦ 52,
        COMPLETION HEADROOM ♦ 53
    project scheduling
        delay handling strategies; RECOMMITMENT MEETING ♦ 53
        programming episode strategy; PROGRAMMING EPISODE ♦ 54
        requirements development plan strategies; REQUIREMENT
            WALK-THROUGH ♦ 54
    recording, in dual records; DUAL TIME RECORD ♦ 9
    recording history of state and events; COLLECTION OF HISTORY
        PATTERNS ♦ 34

saving object state; HISTORY ON SELF ♦ 35
saving variable values
    complex, in an edition object; HISTORY ON
        ASSOCIATION ♦ 34
    simple, in a change log; CHANGE LOG ♦ 34
software development
    early-stage strategies; EARLY AND REGULAR
        DELIVERY ♦ 168
    schedule management; TAKE NO SMALL SLIPS ♦ 69
software integration; NAMED STABLE BASES ♦ 68
synchronizing multimedia presentations; SYNCHRONIZE
    CHANNELS ♦ 37
system impact, handling without destroying system
    architecture; PIECEMEAL GROWTH ♦ 21
TABLE DESIGN TIME ♦ 42, ♦ 107
TAKE TIME ♦ 126
thread analysis, as system design tool; TIME THREAD
    ANALYSIS ♦ 71
TIME ♦ 165
TIME THREAD ANALYSIS ♦ 71
    ANIMATE THE DATA relationship to; ANIMATE THE
        DATA ♦ 70, TIME THREAD ANALYSIS ♦ 71
    CATERPILLAR'S FATE relationship to; TIME THREAD
        ANALYSIS ♦ 71
    DEFINE THE DATA STRUCTURE relationship to; TIME
        THREAD ANALYSIS ♦ 71
TIME TO TEST
    DESIGNERS ARE OUR FRIENDS relationship to; TIME TO
        TEST ♦ 126
    ENGAGE QA relationship to; ENGAGE QA ♦ 66
    GET INVOLVED EARLY relationship to; TIME TO TEST ♦ 126
    TAKE TIME relationship to; TIME TO TEST ♦ 126, TAKE
        TIME ♦ 126
time-out as overload handling strategy, in real-time reactive
    systems; SHED LOAD ♦ 101
TIMED ASSOCIATION, ASSOCIATION OBJECT relationship to;
    ASSOCIATION OBJECT ♦ 23
timers as object blocking mechanism; SERVICES 'WAITING
    FOR' ♦ 62
TIMESTAMP ♦ 77
    IO TRIAGE relationship to; IO TRIAGE ♦ 77, TIMESTAMP ♦ 77
transaction posting; POSTING ♦ 35
UNUSUAL TIMING ♦ 128
unusual timings, testing for; UNUSUAL TIMING ♦ 128
TIME THREAD ANALYSIS ♦ 71
TIMESTAMP ♦ 77
**TO SIMPLIFY COMPLEX BEHAVIOR, USE
    DECOMPOSITION ♦ 88**
TOOL AND MATERIAL COUPLING ♦ 110
TOOL COMPOSITION ♦ 110
TOOL COORDINATOR ♦ 111
TOOLS ♦ 109
tools
    coordination material constraint changes with; TOOL
        COORDINATOR ♦ 111
    decoupling, functional parts from interface parts; SEPARATION
        OF POWERS ♦ 110
    decoupling from materials; MATERIALS ♦ 109
    encapsulation, of functional parts; IP/FP PLUG IN ♦ 111

tools *continued*
encapsulation of, in a software tools environment; IP/FP PLUG
IN ♦ 111
hierarchy, building software tools from; TOOL
COMPOSITION ♦ 110
language, for framework use; LANGUAGE TOOLS ♦ 123
LANGUAGE TOOLS ♦ 123
PATTERN LANGUAGE FOR TOOL CONSTRUCTION AND
INTEGRATION BASED ON THE TOOLS AND MATERIALS
METAPHOR ♦ 109
relationship
to aspects; ASPECTS ♦ 109
to environment; ENVIRONMENT ♦ 110
to materials; TOOLS ♦ 109
to materials, representation of; TOOL AND MATERIAL
COUPLING ♦ 110
TOOL AND MATERIAL COUPLING ♦ 110
ASPECTS relationship to; ASPECTS ♦ 109, TOOL AND
MATERIAL COUPLING ♦ 110
TOOL COMPOSITION ♦ 110
BUREAUCRACY relationship to; TOOL COMPOSITION ♦ 110
EVENT MECHANISM relationship to; TOOL
COMPOSITION ♦ 110
SEPARATION OF POWERS relationship to; TOOL
COMPOSITION ♦ 110, SEPARATION OF POWERS ♦ 110
TOOLS relationship to; TOOLS ♦ 109, TOOL
COMPOSITION ♦ 110
TOOL COORDINATOR ♦ 111
MATERIALS relationship to; TOOL COORDINATOR ♦ 111
TOOLS relationship to; TOOL COORDINATOR ♦ 111
TOOLS ♦ 109
ASPECTS relationship to; TOOLS ♦ 109, ASPECTS ♦ 109
TOOL COMPOSITION relationship to; TOOLS ♦ 109, TOOL
COMPOSITION ♦ 110
Tools and Materials Metaphor; PATTERN LANGUAGE FOR TOOL
CONSTRUCTION AND INTEGRATION BASED ON THE TOOLS
AND MATERIALS METAPHOR ♦ 109
topological properties
of distributed systems; DISTRIBUTED PROCESSES ♦ 51
Towell, D.
[Towell95]; 196
REQUEST SCREEN MODIFICATION ♦ 144
[Towell99]; 197
DISPLAY MAINTENANCE ♦ 49
tracing
diagnostic, as error detection and correction mechanism;
DIAGNOSTIC QUERY ♦ 33
information through different model levels; UPWARD
TRACEABILITY ♦ 45
UPWARD TRACEABILITY ♦ 45
tracking
project schedule status; WORK QUEUE REPORT ♦ 52
trader
PRODUCT TRADER ♦ 138
trading
contract description of; CONTRACT ♦ 13
TRAIN HARD FIGHT EASY ♦ 130
TRAIN THE TRAINER ♦ 130

training
in team development strategy; APPRENTICE ♦ 64
teams
building initial projects; TRIAL PROJECT ♦ 130
in relevant technologies; TRAIN HARD FIGHT EASY ♦ 130,
TRAIN THE TRAINER ♦ 130
TRAIN HARD FIGHT EASY ♦ 130
TRAIN THE TRAINER relationship to; TRAIN THE
TRAINER ♦ 130
TRAIN THE TRAINER ♦ 130
TRAIN HARD FIGHT EASY relationship to; TRAIN THE
TRAINER ♦ 130
TRANSACTION ♦ 10
TRANSACTION HISTORY ♦ 165
transactions
ADJUSTING TRANSACTIONS ♦ 173
adjustment, handling; ADJUSTING TRANSACTIONS ♦ 173
analysis of, as system design tool; TIME THREAD
ANALYSIS ♦ 71
business purposes for; BUSINESS TRANSACTIONS ♦ 173
BUSINESS TRANSACTIONS ♦ 173
composite, handling; COMPOSITE TRANSACTIONS ♦ 173
COMPOSITE TRANSACTIONS ♦ 173
continuous processing of; CONTINUOUS PROCESSING ♦ 174
decoupling, archival vs. active processing; SEPARATE
TRANSACTION PROCESSING FROM ARCHIVAL ♦ 173
maintaining a history of; TRANSACTION HISTORY ♦ 165
-oriented systems, diagnostic message logging in; PATTERNS
FOR LOGGING DIAGNOSTIC MESSAGES ♦ 124
posting; POSTING ♦ 35
processing systems, strategies for; TRANSACTIONS AND
ACCOUNTS ♦ 172
SEPARATE TRANSACTION PROCESSING FROM ARCHIVAL ♦ 173
source rule and entry recording; SOURCES OF AN ENTRY ♦ 12
TRANSACTION ♦ 10
ACCOUNT relationship to; TRANSACTION ♦ 10
MEMO ACCOUNT relationship to; MEMO ACCOUNT ♦ 11
ONLINE ENGINEERING MODEL relationship to; ONLINE
ENGINEERING MODEL ♦ 18
POSTING relationship to; POSTING ♦ 35
SOURCES OF AN ENTRY relationship to; SOURCES OF AN
ENTRY ♦ 12
TRANSACTION HISTORY ♦ 165
DIMENSION ROLL-UP relationship to; DIMENSION
ROLL-UP ♦ 165
KEY BUSINESS ACTIVITIES AND INFLUENCES relationship to;
TRANSACTION HISTORY ♦ 165
TRANSACTIONS AND ACCOUNTS ♦ 172
COMMAND relationship to; COMMAND ♦ 35
TRANSACTIONS AND ACCOUNTS ♦ 172
[Johnson96]; 189
TRANSCEIVER-PARCEL ♦ 133
BROKER AS INTERMEDIARY relationship to; BROKER AS
INTERMEDIARY ♦ 133
VISITOR relationship to; TRANSCEIVER-PARCEL ♦ 133
transfering
between accounts, rules for; POSTING RULES ♦ 11

transformation
> from analysis to design; CATERPILLAR'S FATE: A PATTERN
> > LANGUAGE FOR THE TRANSFORMATION FROM ANALYSIS TO
> > DESIGN ◆ 28
>
> OBJECT TRANSFORMATION ◆ 83
>
> of objects, as optimization techique; OBJECT
> > TRANSFORMATION ◆ 83

TRANSIENT REDUCTION ◆ 83

transient(s)
> errors, handling, in fault-tolerant systems; RIDING OVER
> > TRANSIENTS ◆ 57
>
> reducing, as optimization technique; TRANSIENT
> > REDUCTION ◆ 83
>
> RIDING OVER TRANSIENTS ◆ 57
>
> TRANSIENT REDUCTION ◆ 83
> > CACHING ARGUMENT relationship to; TRANSIENT
> > > REDUCTION ◆ 83
> >
> > CONCATENATING STREAM relationship to; TRANSIENT
> > > REDUCTION ◆ 83
> >
> > OBJECT TRANSFORMATION relationship to; TRANSIENT
> > > REDUCTION ◆ 83, OBJECT TRANSFORMATION ◆ 83

transitions
> *See Also* finite state machines (FSM); state
>
> FOR STATE MACHINES, USE TRANSITION METHODS ◆ 88
>
> OWNER-DRIVEN TRANSITIONS ◆ 167
>
> state
> > behavior modeling, FSM use; BASIC FSM ◆ 58
> >
> > changing state objects; STATE-DRIVEN TRANSITIONS ◆ 167
> >
> > decoupling from reaction; FOR STATE MACHINES, USE
> > > TRANSITION METHODS ◆ 88
> >
> > moving from one state to another by; STATE TRANSITION
> > > SYSTEMS ◆ 167
>
> state transition logic, decoupling from object behavior, in an
> > FSM; LAYERED ORGANIZATION ◆ 59
>
> STATE TRANSITION SYSTEMS ◆ 167
>
> state-driven, mechanisms for; STATE-DRIVEN
> > TRANSITION ◆ 59
>
> STATE-DRIVEN TRANSITION ◆ 59
>
> STATE-DRIVEN TRANSITIONS ◆ 167

transparency
> in inter-process communication; FORWARDER-RECEIVER ◆ 60
>
> location
> > dispatcher provision of; CLIENT-DISPATCHER-SERVER ◆ 34
> >
> > for interoperating applications; BROKER ◆ 115

transportation
> driver duty
> > construction; DRIVER DUTY CONSTRUCTOR ◆ 51
> >
> > definition; DRIVER DUTY ◆ 51
>
> networks, complexity management; CASCADE ◆ 28
>
> PATTERN LANGUAGE OF TRANSPORT SYSTEMS (POINT AND
> > ROUTE) ◆ 114
>
> systems, building; PATTERN LANGUAGE OF TRANSPORT
> > SYSTEMS (POINT AND ROUTE) ◆ 114

traversal
> of object set; SHOPPER ◆ 152

trees
> class
> > creating objects from; LATE CREATION ◆ 120
>
> > encapsulation of; PATTERNS FOR ENCAPSULATING CLASS
> > > TREES ◆ 120
> >
> > retrieval of information from; CLASS RETRIEVAL ◆ 120
>
> HISTORY ON TREE ◆ 35
>
> PATTERNS FOR ENCAPSULATING CLASS TREES ◆ 120
>
> representing part-whole hierarchies as; COMPOSITE ◆ 37

triage
> IO TRIAGE ◆ 77
>
> as overload handling strategy
> > in fault-tolerant systems; IO TRIAGE ◆ 77
> >
> > in real-time reactive systems; SHED LOAD ◆ 101

TRIAL PROJECT ◆ 130

triggering
> ACTIONS TRIGGERED BY EVENTS ◆ 62

**TROPYC: A PATTERN LANGUAGE FOR CRYPTOGRAPHIC
SOFTWARE ◆ 174**
> [Braga+99]; 183

trust
> BUILD TRUST ◆ 43
>
> building
> > in customer relationships; BUILD TRUST ◆ 43
> >
> > in pattern writers workshops; WORKSHOP COMPRISES
> > > AUTHORS ◆ 112, COMMUNITY OF TRUST ◆ 112
> >
> > between system designers and testers; GET INVOLVED
> > > EARLY ◆ 126
>
> COMMUNITY OF TRUST ◆ 112
>
> DON'T TRUST SIMULATIONS ◆ 127
>
> unwarrented, in simulations; DON'T TRUST
> > SIMULATIONS ◆ 127

TRY ALL HARDWARE COMBOS ◆ 58
> FOOL ME ONCE relationship to; FOOL ME ONCE ◆ 58

Tsai, W.
> [Subramanian+96]; 196
>
> BACKUP ◆ 19

turnover
> key people, effective transfer of knowledge; EFFECTIVE
> > HANDOVER ◆ 27

two
> TWO APPLICATIONS ◆ 97
>
> two-legged transactions, term description; TRANSACTION ◆ 10
>
> TWO-TIER ARCHITECTURE ◆ 14
>
> two-way relationships, designing; MUTUAL FRIENDS ◆ 20

TWO APPLICATIONS ◆ 97

TWO-TIER ARCHITECTURE ◆ 14

type(ing)
> *See Also* abstract data types; data types
>
> ASSOCIATIVE TYPE ◆ 16
>
> consistency, maintaining for objects; MAINTAIN CONSISTENT
> > VALUEMODELVALUETYPES ◆ 177
>
> conversion, in object value sharing; USE A TYPECONVERTER
> > TO CONVERT A VALUE BETWEEN TYPES ◆ 178
>
> diagnostic messages; TYPED DIAGNOSTICS ◆ 124
>
> PARTY TYPE GENERALIZATIONS ◆ 7
>
> product, dynamic specification of; PLUGGABLE
> > FACTORY ◆ 132
>
> TYPE OBJECT ◆ 176
> > DECORATOR relationship to; TYPE OBJECT ◆ 176
> >
> > PROTOTYPE-BASED OBJECT SYSTEM relationship to;
> > > PROTOTYPE-BASED OBJECT SYSTEM ◆ 139

type(ing) *continued*
Type Object *continued*
State relationship to; Type Object ♦ 176
Strategy relationship to; Type Object ♦ 176
Type Promotion ♦ 26
Algebraic Hierarchy relationship to; Algebraic
Hierarchy ♦ 25
Type Suggesting Parameter Name ♦ 162
Typed diagnostics ♦ 124
Diagnostic Context relationship to; Typed
diagnostics ♦ 124
Diagnostic Logger relationship to; Typed
diagnostics ♦ 124
Typed Relationship ♦ 5
Use a TypeConverter to Convert a Value Between
Types ♦ 178
Type Object ♦ 176
[Johnson+98]; 189
Type Promotion ♦ 26
Type Suggesting Parameter Name ♦ 162
Typed diagnostics ♦ 124
Typed Relationship ♦ 5

UI (user interface)
See user interface (UI)
'Unchanged' Interfaces ♦ 127
understanding
algorithms, as developer role; Developer Controls
Process ♦ 65
design, as developer role; Developer Controls
Process ♦ 65
of domain, pattern writing importance; Clear Target
Audience ♦ 104
domain, pattern writing importance; Terminology Tailored
to Audience ♦ 105
of notation, pattern writing importance; Understood
Notations ♦ 105
of pattern language, overview importance for; Pattern
Language Summary ♦ 105
requirements, as developer role; Developer Controls
Process ♦ 65
terminology, pattern language glossary use for;
Glossary ♦ 106
Understanding and Using the ValueModel Framework
in VisualWorks Smalltalk ♦ 176
Understood Notations ♦ 105
Clear Target Audience relationship to; Understood
Notations ♦ 105
**Understanding and Using the ValueModel
Framework in VisualWorks Smalltalk ♦ 176**
[Woolf95]; 198
Understood Notations ♦ 105
undo/redo
Command Processor support of; Command Processor ♦ 36
Command support of; Command ♦ 35
object recovery, strategies for; Object Recovery ♦ 92
state management, in conjunction with Command;
Memento ♦ 87

unique
identifier
defining conventions for; Identification Scheme ♦ 10
relational database use; Object Identifier ♦ 42
object identity, managing; Identity Management ♦ 90
relationship, account number use to establish; Account
Number ♦ 4
unit(s)
atomic, term description; Compound Units ♦ 8
compound, term description; Compound Units ♦ 8
testing, as developer role; Developer Controls
Process ♦ 65
unity
Unity of Purpose ♦ 95
Design by Team relationship to; Design by Team ♦ 95
Self-Selecting Team relationship to; Unity of
Purpose ♦ 95
Unity of Purpose ♦ 95
unstructured systems
analysis and solutions; Big Ball of Mud Pattern
Language ♦ 20
Unusual Timing ♦ 128
updating
adaptively; Adaptive Propagator ♦ 138
copy-on-write; Copy-on-Write ♦ 38
Creating and Updating Business Objects ♦ 91
with delegation; Lazy Propagator ♦ 138
displays, page swapping; Page Flip ♦ 50
with failure marking; Strict Propagator with
Failure ♦ 138
formulas, constraints use for; Constraint Observer ♦ 41
Global Update ♦ 49
immediately; Strict Propagator ♦ 138
multimedia presentations; Request Screen
Modification ♦ 144
object, one-to-many dependency relationship management of;
Observer ♦ 94
objects
in a dependency network; Propagator: A Family of
Patterns ♦ 138
in legacy system/object-oriented framework interactions;
Creating and Updating Business Objects ♦ 91
Observer Update Message ♦ 75
Request Update ♦ 49
requests
consolidating; Consolidate Requests ♦ 50
global redraw of display; Global Update ♦ 49
for visual component display; Request Update ♦ 49
simple strategies for; Use ValueModel Chains Instead of
onChangeSend:to: ♦ 176
state
optiminzation of; Optimized Messages per Change
Request ♦ 75
with nested containment relationships; Observer Update
Message ♦ 75
state information sent to an observer
implementation mechanisms; Conduit of Subject
Change ♦ 75

strategies for; ONE MESSAGE PER CHANGE REQUEST ♦ 75, ONE MESSAGE PER AFFECTED OBJECT ♦ 75

transaction processing system accounts, strategies for; TRANSACTIONS AND ACCOUNTS ♦ 172

upward
UPWARD TRACEABILITY ♦ 45

UPWARD TRACEABILITY ♦ 45

urgent messages
fault-tolerant mechanisms for sending; STRING A WIRE ♦ 80, RAW IO ♦ 80

USE A BUFFEREDVALUEHOLDER TO DELAY THE COMMIT OF A NEW VALUE ♦ 177

USE A PLUGGABLEADAPTOR TO HOLD SOME PART OF AN OBJECT ♦ 178

USE A RANGEADAPTOR TO CHANNEL A NUMBER'S RANGE ♦ 177

USE A SCROLLVALUEHOLDER TO HOLD A POSITION IN n-DIMENSIONAL SPACE ♦ 178

USE A SLOTADAPTOR TO HOLD A SINGLE INSTANCE VARIABLE ♦ 178

USE A TYPECONVERTER TO CONVERT A VALUE BETWEEN TYPES ♦ 178

USE A VALUEHOLDER TO HOLD A STAND-ALONE OBJECT ♦ 177

USE A VALUEMODEL TO SHARE A VALUE ♦ 176

USE AN ASPECTADAPTOR TO HOLD AN ASPECT OF AN OBJECT ♦ 177

USE AN INDEXEDADAPTOR TO HOLD A SINGLE INDEX IN A COLLECTION ♦ 177

use cases
business rule constaints on; BUSINESS RULES ♦ 142

customer requirement prototyping vs.; PROTOTYPES ♦ 142

defining; ENVISIONING ♦ 142

software design functionality use; SCENARIOS DEFINE PROBLEM ♦ 66

user interface requirements identification with; USER INTERFACE REQUIREMENTS ♦ 142

USE LAZY INITIALIZATION ♦ 145

USE OLD PROBLEM REPORTS ♦ 127

USE onChangeSend:to: TO REGISTER INTERESTS ON A VALUE ♦ 176

USE SELECTIONINLIST TO HOLD A LIST AND ITS SELECTION ♦ 178

USE VALUEMODEL CHAINS INSTEAD OF onChangeSend:to: ♦ 176

USER INTERFACE REQUIREMENTS ♦ 142

user interface (UI)
See Also GUI (graphical user interface); interface(s)
decoupling
from application; APPLICATION BOUNDARY ♦ 136
from domain model, in application layer; PRESENTATION AND APPLICATION LOGIC ♦ 15
from persistent subsystem; DOMAIN INTERCEPTS ♦ 137
deferring data entry validation; DEFERRED VALIDATION ♦ 33
design, team skill level considerations; GENERIC UI, SPECIFIC UI ♦ 136
encapsulating; HUMAN INTERFACE ROLE IS A SPECIAL INTERFACE ROLE ♦ 31
GENERIC UI, SPECIFIC UI ♦ 136

Java panel control of; PLUGGABLE VIEW CONTROLLER ♦ 132

lightweight, customer demonstration use; LIGHTWEIGHT USER INTERFACES ♦ 47

LIGHTWEIGHT USER INTERFACES ♦ 47

memory management, providing user controls for; MAKE THE USER WORRY ♦ 72

patterns
design, search cues for; FINDABLE SECTIONS ♦ 103
helping users to reference a pattern; INTENT CATALOG ♦ 104
requirements, identifying; USER INTERFACE REQUIREMENTS ♦ 142
as software architecture subsystem; THREE SUBSYSTEMS ♦ 135

USER INTERFACE REQUIREMENTS ♦ 142
INFORMATION NEEDS relationship to; INFORMATION NEEDS ♦ 141
PROTOTYPES relationship to; USER INTERFACE REQUIREMENTS ♦ 142

Ushijima, K.
[Masuda+98]; 190

validation
See Also verification
attribute; ESSENCE ♦ 54
of computer models; FORECAST CONFIRMATION ♦ 33
data, CHECKS pattern language for; CHECKS: PATTERN LANGUAGE OF INFORMATION INTEGRITY ♦ 32
DEFERRED VALIDATION ♦ 33
deferring, of data entry; DEFERRED VALIDATION ♦ 33
design, as software development responsibility; GROUP VALIDATION ♦ 66
of designs, by software development teams; VALIDATION BY TEAMS ♦ 96
GROUP VALIDATION ♦ 66
of input, splitting into two steps; SPLIT VALIDATION ♦ 136
as persistent domain object component; MODEL HIERARCHY ♦ 136
requirements; BUILDING THE RIGHT THINGS ♦ 140
of requirements; REQUIREMENTS VALIDATION ♦ 143
REQUIREMENTS VALIDATION ♦ 143
SPLIT VALIDATION ♦ 136
VALIDATION BY TEAMS ♦ 96
CREATOR-REVIEWER relationship to; VALIDATION BY TEAMS ♦ 96
DESIGN BY TEAM relationship to; DESIGN BY TEAM ♦ 95
DIVERSITY OF MEMBERSHIP relationship to; VALIDATION BY TEAMS ♦ 96
REVIEW THE ARCHITECTURE relationship to; VALIDATION BY TEAMS ♦ 96
UNITY OF PURPOSE relationship to; VALIDATION BY TEAMS ♦ 96
of WWW references; EXPOSABLE GUTS ♦ 98

VALIDATION BY TEAMS ♦ 96

value(s)
accessing; GETTING METHOD ♦ 157
ACTIVE VALUE ♦ 20
changing, of variables; SETTING METHOD ♦ 157
collecting; COLLECTING TEMPORARY VARIABLE ♦ 158

value(s) *continued*
default
defining; DEFINE DEFAULT VALUES VIA EXPLICIT
PROTOCOL ◆ 146
representation; DEFAULT VALUE METHOD ◆ 157
DEFAULT VALUE METHOD ◆ 157
DEFINE DEFAULT VALUES VIA EXPLICIT PROTOCOL ◆ 146
ENCAPSULATE SENDERS OF VALUE AND VALUE: ◆ 177
ENSURE THAT ALL OBJECTS SHARING A VALUE USE THE
SAME VALUEMODEL ◆ 177
exceptional, representation of; EXCEPTIONAL VALUE ◆ 32
EXCEPTIONAL VALUE ◆ 32
illegal, synchronization of checking; DOUBLE CHECK ◆ 38
INTERESTING RETURN VALUE ◆ 163
MAINTAIN CONSISTENT VALUEMODELVALUETYPES ◆ 177
message cascade, using; YOURSELF ◆ 163
naming, as system design task; IDENTIFY THE NOUNS ◆ 70
representation of; WHOLE VALUE ◆ 32
return, explicit specification of; INTERESTING RETURN
VALUE ◆ 163
running, keeping for a collection; INJECT:INTO: ◆ 161
saving
complex variables, in an edition object; HISTORY ON
ASSOCIATION ◆ 34
for method use; TEMPORARY VARIABLE ◆ 158
simple variable, in a change log; CHANGE LOG ◆ 34
shared, single reference guarentees; ENSURE THAT
ALL OBJECTS SHARING A VALUE USE THE SAME
VALUEMODEL ◆ 177
sharing, between objects; USE A VALUEMODEL TO SHARE A
VALUE ◆ 176
UNDERSTANDING AND USING THE VALUEMODEL FRAMEWORK
IN VISUALWORKS SMALLTALK ◆ 176
USE A BUFFEREDVALUEHOLDER TO DELAY THE COMMIT OF A
NEW VALUE ◆ 177
USE A TYPECONVERTER TO CONVERT A VALUE BETWEEN
TYPES ◆ 178
USE A VALUEMODEL TO SHARE A VALUE ◆ 176
USE ONCHANGESEND:TO: TO REGISTER INTERESTS ON A
VALUE ◆ 176
USE VALUEMODEL CHAINS INSTEAD OF
ONCHANGESEND:TO: ◆ 176
ValueModel framework, strategies for defining and using;
UNDERSTANDING AND USING THE VALUEMODEL
FRAMEWORK IN VISUALWORKS SMALLTALK ◆ 176
WHOLE VALUE ◆ 32
VandenBroecke, J. A.
[VandenBroecke+97]; 197
PARTIES & MEDIA AS FIRST CLASS CITIZENS ◆ 96
PLUGGABLE FACTORY ◆ 132
SESSION CONTROL & OBSERVATION ◆ 151
variable(s)
accessing; GETTING METHOD ◆ 157
directly; DIRECT VARIABLE ACCESS ◆ 157
indirectly; INDIRECT VARIABLE ACCESS ◆ 157
CACHING STATE VARIABLE ◆ 83
CACHING TEMPORARY VARIABLE ◆ 83, ◆ 158
COLLECTING TEMPORARY VARIABLE ◆ 158

complex, saving values of, saving in an edition object;
HISTORY ON ASSOCIATION ◆ 34
DEFER IDENTIFICATION OF STATE VARIABLES ◆ 145
DIRECT VARIABLE ACCESS ◆ 157
EXPLAINING TEMPORARY VARIABLE ◆ 158
INDIRECT VARIABLE ACCESS ◆ 157
instance
initialization of; EXPLICIT INITIALIZATION ◆ 156
setting from parameters; CONSTRUCTOR PARAMETER
METHOD ◆ 152
wrapping ValueModel behavior around; USE A
SLOTADAPTOR TO HOLD A SINGLE INSTANCE
VARIABLE ◆ 178
naming; ROLE SUGGESTING INSTANCE VARIABLE NAME ◆ 158,
ROLE SUGGESTING TEMPORARY VARIABLE NAME ◆ 158
REUSING TEMPORARY VARIABLE ◆ 158
ROLE SUGGESTING INSTANCE VARIABLE NAME ◆ 158
ROLE SUGGESTING TEMPORARY VARIABLE NAME ◆ 158
setting; SETTING METHOD ◆ 157
simple, saving values of, in a change log; CHANGE LOG ◆ 34
state, caching, as optimization technique; CACHING STATE
VARIABLE ◆ 83
temporary, caching, as optimization technique; CACHING
TEMPORARY VARIABLE ◆ 83
TEMPORARY VARIABLE ◆ 158
USE A SLOTADAPTOR TO HOLD A SINGLE INSTANCE
VARIABLE ◆ 178
VARIABLE STATE ◆ 156
EXTENSIBLE ATTRIBUTES relationship to; VARIABLE
STATE ◆ 156, EXTENSIBLE ATTRIBUTES ◆ 163
VARIABLE STATE ◆ 156
variations
See Also change
predicted, isolating; PROTECTED VARIATIONS ◆ 135
PROTECTED VARIATIONS ◆ 135
verification
See Also validation
check point use for; CHECK POINT ◆ 17
of message sender identity; SIGNATURE ◆ 175
versioning
associating state with events; COLLECTION OF HISTORY
PATTERNS ◆ 34
capturing state/event relationships in an edition; EDITION ◆ 34
cycle, management of; INCREMENTAL INTEGRATION ◆ 170
designing for; DATA KNOWS ITS ROOTS ◆ 31
PRIVATE VERSIONING ◆ 170
software
management of the cycle duration; INCREMENTAL
INTEGRATION ◆ 170
managing individual developer needs vs. team needs;
INDEPENDENT WORKSPACES ◆ 171
team management in relation to; PRIVATE VERSIONING ◆ 170
VETOABLE CHANGES ◆ 39
VIEW HANDLER ◆ 178
[Buschmann+96]; 183
view(s)
See Also MVC
account, equivalence relationship between; CORRESPONDING
ACCOUNT ◆ 12

client-specific, role objects as; ROLE OBJECT ♦ 146
domain
  connecting with physical view; QUERY BROKER ♦ 4
  of a relational database; HIERARCHICAL VIEW ♦ 3
encapsulating, in legacy system/object-oriented framework
  interactions; VIEWING ♦ 91
end-user, testing from the perspective of; END USER
  VIEWPOINT ♦ 127
full, illegal operation handling methods with; FULL VIEW
  WITH ERRORS ♦ 18
FULL VIEW WITH ERRORS ♦ 18
limited, illegal operation prevention with; LIMITED VIEW ♦ 18
LIMITED VIEW ♦ 18
MODEL-VIEW-CONTROLLER ♦ 87
panels, displaying a sequence of; PANEL STATES ♦ 96
physical
  accessing physical database tables with; PHYSICAL VIEW ♦ 3
  connecting with domain views; QUERY BROKER ♦ 4
PLUGGABLE VIEW CONTROLLER ♦ 132
as Smalltalk client-server system layer; FOUR-LAYER
  ARCHITECTURE ♦ 106
software system, managing; VIEW HANDLER ♦ 178
VIEW HANDLER ♦ 178
  MODEL-VIEW-CONTROLLER relationship to; VIEW
    HANDLER ♦ 178
  PRESENTATION-ABSTRACTION-CONTROL relationship to;
    VIEW HANDLER ♦ 178
VIEWING ♦ 91
  CLIENT/SERVER FRAMEWORK relationship to;
    CLIENT/SERVER FRAMEWORK ♦ 91
  DEPENDENCY relationship to; VIEWING ♦ 91
  FACTORY METHOD relationship to; VIEWING ♦ 91
  WINDOW-KEEPING relationship to; VIEWING ♦ 91
VIEWING ♦ 91
Viljamaa, P.
  [Viljamaa95]; 197
    CLIENT-SPECIFIED SELF ♦ 34
virtual
  attributes, navigation assistance; INTRODUCE VIRTUAL
    ATTRIBUTES ♦ 70
  containers, managing distributed system objects with;
    POOL ♦ 134
  data objects, computation completion managment with;
    FUTURES ♦ 40
  I/O, subsystem communication use; PSEUDO-IO ♦ 79
  INTRODUCE VIRTUAL ATTRIBUTES ♦ 70
  VIRTUAL CONSTRUCTOR ♦ 25
    ENVELOPE/LETTER relationship to; ENVELOPE/LETTER ♦ 25,
      VIRTUAL CONSTRUCTOR ♦ 25
    HANDLE/BODY relationship to; VIRTUAL CONSTRUCTOR ♦ 25
    STRATEGY relationship to; VIRTUAL CONSTRUCTOR ♦ 25
  VIRTUAL PROXY REVISITED, PROXY DESIGN PATTERN
    REVISITED relationship to; PROXY DESIGN PATTERN
    REVISITED ♦ 139
VIRTUAL CONSTRUCTOR ♦ 25
visibility
  of graphical components
    display list management of; DISPLAY LIST ♦ 49

    updating request for; REQUEST UPDATE ♦ 49, GLOBAL
      UPDATE ♦ 49
MUTUAL VISIBILITY ♦ 14
between packages
  permitting; MUTUAL VISIBILITY ♦ 14
  subtype visibility; SUBTYPING PACKAGES ♦ 14
pattern design structures that support searching; FINDABLE
  SECTIONS ♦ 103
VISIBILITY AND COMMUNICATION BETWEEN CONTROL
  MODULES ♦ 61
  VISIBILITY AND COMMUNICATION BETWEEN
    CONTROL MODULES relationship to; VISIBILITY AND
    COMMUNICATION BETWEEN CONTROL MODULES ♦ 61
VISIBLE CHECKLIST ♦ 117
  MODULE'S STORY relationship to; MODULE'S STORY ♦ 116,
    VISIBLE CHECKLIST ♦ 117
  PITFALL DIAGNOSIS AND PREVENTION relationship to;
    PITFALL DIAGNOSIS AND PREVENTION ♦ 116
  QUIZ GAMES relationship to; QUIZ GAMES ♦ 118
  SEVEN PARTS relationship to; VISIBLE CHECKLIST ♦ 117
VISIBLE FORCES ♦ 103
  PATTERN LANGUAGE relationship to; VISIBLE FORCES ♦ 103
  PATTERN relationship to; VISIBLE FORCES ♦ 103
  SINGLE-PASS READABLE relationship to; SINGLE-PASS
    READABLE ♦ 103
VISIBLE IMPLICATION ♦ 33
  ECHO BACK relationship to; VISIBLE IMPLICATION ♦ 33
  INSTANT PROJECTION relationship to; INSTANT
    PROJECTION ♦ 33
  MEANINGLESS BEHAVIOR relationship to; VISIBLE
    IMPLICATION ♦ 33
VISUAL BUILDER, BLACK-BOX FRAMEWORK relationship to;
  BLACK-BOX FRAMEWORK ♦ 122
**VISIBILITY AND COMMUNICATION BETWEEN CONTROL
  MODULES ♦ 61**
VISIBLE CHECKLIST ♦ 117
VISIBLE FORCES ♦ 103
VISIBLE IMPLICATION ♦ 33
vision
  common, in teams, strategies for developing; UNITY OF
    PURPOSE ♦ 95
VISITOR ♦ 179
  [Alpert+98]; 182
  [Gamma+95]; 188
visitors
  ACYCLIC VISITOR ♦ 6
  COMPOSITE, VISITOR relationship to; VISITOR ♦ 179
  default implementation addition to VISITOR; DEFAULT
    VISITOR ♦ 46
  DEFAULT VISITOR ♦ 46
  extrinsic; EXTRINSIC VISITOR ♦ 56
  EXTRINSIC VISITOR ♦ 56
  INTERPRETER, VISITOR relationship to; VISITOR ♦ 179
  VISITER, EXTENSION OBJECT relationship to; EXTENSION
    OBJECT ♦ 55
  VISITOR ♦ 179
    COMPOSITE relationship to; COMPOSITE ♦ 37, VISITOR ♦ 179
    DEFAULT VISITOR relationship to; DEFAULT VISITOR ♦ 46
    dependency cycles, eliminating; ACYCLIC VISITOR ♦ 6

visitors *continued*

  Visitor *continued*

    Detachable Inspector relationship to; Detachable Inspector ◆ 49

    Extrinsic Visitor relationship to; Extrinsic Visitor ◆ 56

    Informational Role relationship to; Informational Role ◆ 30

    Interpreter relationship to; Interpreter ◆ 80, Visitor ◆ 179

    Transceiver-Parcel relationship to; Transceiver-Parcel ◆ 133

visual

  programming language, creation of; Visual Builder ◆ 123

  properties, of multimedia artifacts, layout design; Components Layout ◆ 36

  Visual Builder ◆ 123

    Black-Box Framework relationship to; Visual Builder ◆ 123

    Language Tools relationship to; Visual Builder ◆ 123

Visual Builder ◆ 123

Vlissides, J.

  [Gamma+95]; 188

    Adapter ◆ 6

    Bridge ◆ 22

    Builder ◆ 23

    Chain of Responsibility ◆ 32

    Command ◆ 35

    Composite ◆ 37

    Decorator ◆ 46

    Facade ◆ 56

    Factory Method ◆ 56

    Flyweight ◆ 60

    Hook Method ◆ 73

    Iterator ◆ 80

    Mediator ◆ 86

    Memento ◆ 87

    Observer ◆ 94

    Prototyper ◆ 138

    Proxy ◆ 139

    Singleton ◆ 152

    State ◆ 166

    Strategy ◆ 167

    Template Method ◆ 171

    Visitor ◆ 179

  [Gamma+95], Interpreter ◆ 80

  [PLoPD2]; 192

  [Vlissides95]; 197

  [Vlissides98a]; 197

    Generation Gap ◆ 63

  [Vlissides98b]; 197

    Pluggable Factory ◆ 132

  [Vlissides99]; 197

    Pluggable Factory ◆ 132

volatility

  interfaces, single entry point to; Facade ◆ 137

  in team composition, subsystem design that accomodates; Skill Mix ◆ 135

volunteer

  Volunteer Summarizes the Work ◆ 113

    Fly on the Wall relationship to; Fly on the Wall ◆ 112, Volunteer Summarizes the Work ◆ 113

    Positive Feedback First relationship to; Positive Feedback First ◆ 113

    Sitting in a Circle relationship to; Volunteer Summarizes the Work ◆ 113

Volunteer Summarizes the Work ◆ 113

vonBochmann, G.

  [Keller+98a]; 189

    Pattern System for Network Management Interfaces ❖ 114

waiting

  Services 'Waiting For' ◆ 62

Wake, B. D.

  [Wake+96]; 197

    Improving Responsiveness in Interactive Applications Using Queues ❖ 76

Wake, W. C.

  [Wake+96]; 197

    Improving Responsiveness in Interactive Applications Using Queues ❖ 76

  [Wake95]; 197

    Account Number ◆ 4

walkthrough

  product, as software development process; Market Walk-through ◆ 52

  Requirement Walk-through ◆ 54

Wallingford, E.

  [Wallingford98]; 197

    Sponsor-Selector ◆ 164

Weir, C.

  [Noble+99]; 191

    High-Level and Process Patterns from the Memory Preservation Society ❖ 71

  [Weir98]; 197

    Patterns for Designing in Teams ❖ 118

When Events Cause MOODS, Use State Machine ◆ 88

When States are Associations, Use State Objects ◆ 89

When States are Conditions, Use Predicative State Classes ◆ 88

When There Are Many MOODS, Use MOOD Classifier ◆ 89

When xxx

  Finite State Machine Patterns, When Events Cause MOODS, Use State Machine relationship to; When Events Cause MOODS, Use State Machine ◆ 88

  Three-Level FSM, When Events Cause MOODS, Use State Machine relationship to; When Events Cause MOODS, Use State Machine ◆ 88

  When Events Cause MOODS, Use State Machine ◆ 88

    Finite State Machine Patterns relationship to; When Events Cause MOODS, Use State Machine ◆ 88

    Three-Level FSM relationship to; When Events Cause MOODS, Use State Machine ◆ 88

  When States are Associations, Use State Objects ◆ 89

When States are Conditions, Use Predicative State
 Classes ◆ 88
When There Are Many MOODS, Use MOOD
 Classifier ◆ 89
White, I.
 [White96]; 197
White-Box Frameworks ◆ 121
 Black-Box Framework relationship to; White-Box
  Frameworks ◆ 121
 Component Library relationship to; Component
  Library ◆ 122
 Factory Method relationship to; White-Box
  Frameworks ◆ 121
 Template Method relationship to; White-Box
  Frameworks ◆ 121
 Three Examples relationship to; Three Examples ◆ 121,
  White-Box Frameworks ◆ 121
Whitenack, B.
 [Brown+96a]; 183
  Pattern Language for Smalltalk & Relational
   Databases ❖ 106
 [Brown+96b]; 183
  Crossing Chasms: A Pattern Language for
   Object-RDBMS Integration ◆ 41
 [Whitenack95]; 197
  RAPPeL: A Requirements-Analysis Process Pattern
   Language for Object-Oriented Development ❖ 140
Who Asked? ◆ 78
 IO Triage relationship to; Who Asked? ◆ 78
 Mind Your Own Business relationship to; Who Asked? ◆ 78
 MML relationship to; MML ◆ 77
whole
 Whole Business Entities ◆ 165
  Dimension Roll-Up relationship to; Dimension
   Roll-Up ◆ 165
  Key Business Activities and Influences relationship to;
   Key Business Activities and Influences ◆ 165
  Query Optimized Database relationship to; Whole
   Business Entities ◆ 165
 Whole Value ◆ 32
  Deferred Validation relationship to; Deferred
   Validation ◆ 33
  Exceptional Value relationship to; Exceptional
   Value ◆ 32
  Quantity relationship to; Quantity ◆ 8
 Whole-Part ◆ 179
  Composite relationship to; Whole-Part ◆ 179
  Facade relationship to; Whole-Part ◆ 179
Whole Business Entities ◆ 165
Whole Value ◆ 32
Whole-Part ◆ 179
 [Buschmann+96]; 183
Window-Keeping ◆ 91
windows
 See Also GUI
 form-style, development strategies; Pattern Language for
  Developing Form Style Windows ◆ 99
 managing, in legacy system/object-oriented framework
  interactions; Window-Keeping ◆ 91

Window-Keeping ◆ 91
 Viewing relationship to; Viewing ◆ 91
winning
 Winning Team ◆ 151
  Selfish Class relationship to; Selfish Class ◆ 150
Winning Team ◆ 151
Wirfs-Brock, R.
 [Wirfs-Brock93]; 197
Wolf, K.
 [Wolf+95]; 198
  New Clients with Old Servers: A Pattern Language
   for Client/Server Frameworks ❖ 89
Woodward, K. G.
 [Woodward96]; 198
Woolf, B.
 [Alpert+98]; 182
  Abstract Factory ◆ 2
  Adapter ◆ 6
  Bridge ◆ 22
  Builder ◆ 23
  Chain of Responsibility ◆ 32
  Command ◆ 35
  Composite ◆ 37
  Decorator ◆ 46
  Facade ◆ 56
  Factory Method ◆ 56
  Flyweight ◆ 60
  Hook Method ◆ 73
  Iterator ◆ 80
  Mediator ◆ 86
  Memento ◆ 87
  Observer ◆ 94
  Prototype ◆ 138
  Proxy ◆ 139
  Singleton ◆ 152
  State ◆ 166
  Template Method ◆ 171
  Visitor ◆ 179
 [Alpert+98], Interpreter ◆ 80
 [Johnson+98]; 189
  Type Object ◆ 176
 [Woolf95]; 198
  Understanding and Using the ValueModel
   Framework in VisualWorks Smalltalk ❖ 176
 [Woolf96]; 198
  Partitioning Smalltalk Code into ENVY/Developer
   Components ❖ 96
 [Woolf98]; 198
  Null Object ◆ 91
 [Woolf99a]; 198
  Abstract Class ◆ 2
 [Woolf99b]; 198
  Object Recursion ◆ 92
work
 assignment strategies, for software development teams; Work
  Group ◆ 52
 cancellation of user requests, strategies for handling; Match
  Progress Work with New ◆ 101
 Collaborative Work Packets ◆ 28

work *continued*

COMPARABLE WORK ♦ 52

FINISH WORK IN PROGRESS ♦ 101

flow

management; WORK FLOW MANAGER ♦ 115

in software development projects; WORK FLOWS
INWARD ♦ 68

INDEPENDENT WORKSPACES ♦ 171

LIFO queue management of; FRESH WORK BEFORE
STALE ♦ 101

load sharing, as system throughput optimization; SHARE THE
LOAD ♦ 101

packets

collaborative; COLLABORATIVE WORK PACKETS ♦ 28

completion reports; WORK PACKET COMPLETION
REPORT ♦ 29

designing the internals; WORK PACKET CONTENTS ♦ 28

priorities, establishing policies for; WORK PACKET
PRIORITY ♦ 29

security, establishing policies for; WORK PACKET
SECURITY ♦ 29

status report design; WORK PACKET STATUS REPORT ♦ 29

plans, short term, strategies for; INFORMAL LABOR PLAN ♦ 53

in progress, on a website, indications of; WORKSHEET
DOCUMENTS ♦ 98

VOLUNTEER SUMMARIZES THE WORK ♦ 113

WORK ACCOMPLISHED THROUGH DIALOG, ELEVATE
REFERENCES TO ENHANCE REUSE relationship to; ELEVATE
REFERENCES TO ENHANCE REUSE ♦ 124

WORK ACCOMPLISHED THROUGH DIALOGS ♦ 30

SHAPE OF PROGRAM relationship to; SHAPE OF
PROGRAM ♦ 29

WORK FLOW MANAGER ♦ 115

WORK FLOWS INWARD ♦ 68

WORK GROUP ♦ 52

REQUIREMENT WALK-THROUGH relationship to;
REQUIREMENT WALK-THROUGH ♦ 54

WORK QUEUE REPORT relationship to; WORK GROUP ♦ 52

WORK PACKET COMPLETION REPORT ♦ 29

COLLABORATIVE WORK PACKETS relationship to; WORK
PACKET COMPLETION REPORT ♦ 29

SHAPE OF PROGRAM relationship to; WORK PACKET
COMPLETION REPORT ♦ 29

SYNCHRONIZATION OF CONCURRENT THREADS relationship
to; WORK PACKET COMPLETION REPORT ♦ 29

WORK PACKET CONTENTS relationship to; WORK PACKET
CONTENTS ♦ 28, WORK PACKET COMPLETION
REPORT ♦ 29

WORK PACKET CONTENTS ♦ 28

WORK PACKET COMPLETION REPORT relationship to; WORK
PACKET CONTENTS ♦ 28, WORK PACKET COMPLETION
REPORT ♦ 29

WORK PACKET PRIORITY relationship to; WORK PACKET
CONTENTS ♦ 28

WORK PACKET SECURITY relationship to; WORK PACKET
CONTENTS ♦ 28, WORK PACKET SECURITY ♦ 29

WORK PACKET STATUS REPORT relationship to; WORK
PACKET CONTENTS ♦ 28, WORK PACKET STATUS
REPORT ♦ 29

WORK PACKET PRIORITY ♦ 29

COLLABORATIVE WORK PACKETS relationship to; WORK
PACKET PRIORITY ♦ 29

SHAPE OF PROGRAM relationship to; WORK PACKET
PRIORITY ♦ 29

WORK PACKET CONTENTS relationship to; WORK PACKET
CONTENTS ♦ 28

WORK PACKET SECURITY ♦ 29

COLLABORATIVE WORK PACKETS relationship to; WORK
PACKET SECURITY ♦ 29

WORK PACKET CONTENTS relationship to; WORK PACKET
CONTENTS ♦ 28, WORK PACKET SECURITY ♦ 29

WORK PACKET STATUS REPORT ♦ 29

COLLABORATIVE WORK PACKETS relationship to; WORK
PACKET STATUS REPORT ♦ 29

WORK PACKET CONTENTS relationship to; WORK PACKET
CONTENTS ♦ 28, WORK PACKET STATUS REPORT ♦ 29

WORK QUEUE ♦ 52

IMPLIED REQUIREMENTS relationship to; IMPLIED
REQUIREMENTS ♦ 52

RECOMMITMENT MEETING relationship to; RECOMMITMENT
MEETING ♦ 53

WORK SPLITrelationship to; WORK SPLIT ♦ 53

WORK QUEUE REPORT ♦ 52

COMPLETION HEADROOM relationship to; WORK QUEUE
REPORT ♦ 52

RECOMMITMENT MEETING relationship to; RECOMMITMENT
MEETING ♦ 53

WORK GROUP relationship to; WORK GROUP ♦ 52

WORK SHED AT PERIPHERY ♦ 102

LEAKY BUCKET OF CREDITS relationship to; WORK SHED AT
PERIPHERY ♦ 102

SHED LOAD relationship to; SHED LOAD ♦ 101, WORK SHED
AT PERIPHERY ♦ 102

WORK SPLIT ♦ 53

COMPLETION HEADROOMrelationship to; WORK SPLIT ♦ 53

WORK QUEUErelationship to; WORK SPLIT ♦ 53

WORKER THREADS ♦ 39

WORKERS' ROLE ♦ 30

DECISION MAKER'S ROLE relationship to; DECISION
MAKER'S ROLE ♦ 30

SHAPE OF PROGRAM relationship to; WORKERS' ROLE ♦ 30

WORKS OUT OF THE BOX ♦ 150

GENTLE LEARNING CURVE relationship to; GENTLE
LEARNING CURVE ♦ 150

PROGRAMMING-BY-DIFFERENCE relationship to;
PROGRAMMING-BY-DIFFERENCE ♦ 150

SELFISH CLASS relationship to; SELFISH CLASS ♦ 150

WORKSHEET DOCUMENTS ♦ 98

EXPOSABLE GUTS relationship to; WORKSHEET
DOCUMENTS ♦ 98

REFERENCE SECTION relationship to; WORKSHEET
DOCUMENTS ♦ 98

WORK ACCOMPLISHED THROUGH DIALOGS ♦ 30

WORK FLOW MANAGER ♦ 115

WORK FLOWS INWARD ♦ 68

WORK PACKET COMPLETION REPORT ♦ 29

WORK PACKET CONTENTS ♦ 28

WORK PACKET PRIORITY ♦ 29

Work Packet Security ♦ 29
Work Packet Status Report ♦ 29
Work Queue ♦ 52
Work Queue Report ♦ 52
Work Shed at Periphery ♦ 102
Work Split ♦ 53
Worker Threads ♦ 39
workers
　threads, unrelated task handling by; Worker Threads ♦ 39
　Worker Threads ♦ 39
Workers' Role ♦ 30
Works Out of the Box ♦ 150
Worksheet Documents ♦ 98
Workshop Comprises Authors ♦ 112
workshops
　Moderator Guides the Workshop ♦ 112
　Open Review, Workshop Comprises Authors relationship
　　to; Workshop Comprises Authors ♦ 112
　Pattern Language for Writers' Workshops ♦ 111
　pattern writers, structures and protocols; Pattern Language
　　for Writers' Workshops ♦ 111
　Workshop Comprises Authors ♦ 112
　　Open Review relationship to; Workshop Comprises
　　　Authors ♦ 112
　　Safe Setting relationship to; Safe Setting ♦ 111,
　　　Workshop Comprises Authors ♦ 112
workstations
　software architecture; Three Subsystems ♦ 135
Wrapper Facade ♦ 179
　[Schmidt99]; 195
wrappers
　See Also adapters
　encapsulating low-level functions and data structures with;
　　Wrapper Facade ♦ 179
　legacy access maintenance with; (Legacy) Wrapper ♦ 115
　objects, with ValueModel behavior; Use a ValueHolder to
　　Hold a Stand-Alone Object ♦ 177
　Wrapper Facade ♦ 179
　　Facade relationship to; Wrapper Facade ♦ 179
　　Patterns for Encapsulating Class Trees relationship
　　　to; Wrapper Facade ♦ 179
Write a Loop Once ♦ 179
　[Martin95b]; 190
writing/writers
　Copy-on-Write ♦ 38
　copy-on-write updates; Copy-on-Write ♦ 38
　Counter Reader/Writer Lock ♦ 149
　decoupling from readers, in locking strategies;
　　Reader/Writer Locking ♦ 147
　Distributed Reader/Writer Lock ♦ 149
　locking
　　counter lock; Counter Reader/Writer Lock ♦ 149
　　distributed lock; Distributed Reader/Writer Lock ♦ 149
　　queued locks; Queued Reader/Writer Lock ♦ 149
　loops; Write a Loop Once ♦ 179
　Pattern Language for Pattern Writing ♦ 102
　Pattern Language for Writers' Workshops ♦ 111
　pattern languages
　　domain example use; Running Example ♦ 106

　　factoring common problems; Common Problems
　　　Highlighted ♦ 106
　　glossary; Glossary ♦ 106
　　overview importance; Pattern Language Summary ♦ 105
　　problem summary; Problem/Solution Summary ♦ 105
　　solution summary; Problem/Solution Summary ♦ 105
　　strategies for; Pattern Language for Pattern
　　　Writing ♦ 102
　patterns
　　clarification of notation; Understood Notations ♦ 105
　　code samples; Code Samples ♦ 105
　　domain-specific terminology; Terminology Tailored to
　　　Audience ♦ 105
　　forces; Visible Forces ♦ 103
　　handling pattern references; Readable References to
　　　Patterns ♦ 104
　　intents catalog; Intent Catalog ♦ 104
　　language independence importance; Code Samples as
　　　Bonus ♦ 105
　　naming strategies; Evocative Pattern Name ♦ 104,
　　　Noun Phrase Name ♦ 104, Meaningful Metaphor
　　　Name ♦ 104
　　necessary information to include; Mandatory Elements
　　　Present ♦ 102
　　optional elements; Optional Elements When
　　　Helpful ♦ 103
　　optional sections; Skippable Sections ♦ 103
　　pattern relationship specification; Relationships to Other
　　　Patterns ♦ 103
　　semantics of referenced patterns; Pattern
　　　Thumbnail ♦ 104
　　strategies for minimizing time to read; Single-Pass
　　　Readable ♦ 103
　　target audience identification; Clear Target
　　　Audience ♦ 104
　patterns and pattern languages, strategies for; Pattern
　　Language for Pattern Writing ♦ 102
　query-before-write, as cache management strategy; Cache
　　Management ♦ 109
　Queued Reader/Writer Lock ♦ 149
　Reader/Writer Locking ♦ 147
　readers and, relationship among; Readers and Writers ♦ 39
　Readers and Writers ♦ 39
　Web essays; Pattern Language for an Essay-Based Web
　　Site ♦ 97
　workshop structures and protocols; Pattern Language for
　　Writers' Workshops ♦ 111
　Write a Loop Once ♦ 179
　WWW writing style
　　for links; Natural Text Hyperlinks ♦ 98
　　for text; Natural Text Flow ♦ 98
WWW (World-Wide Web)
　See Also hypermedia
　identification of new material; News ♦ 120
　navigation design for; Patterns for Designing Navigable
　　Information Spaces ♦ 119
　notifications
　　new material; New Document Notification ♦ 99
　　work in progress; Worksheet Documents ♦ 98

WWW (World-Wide Web) *continued*
  organization
    links; NATURAL TEXT DIRECTORIES ♦ 98
    related material; REFERENCE SECTION ♦ 98
  orientation, persistent landmarks use for; LANDMARK ♦ 120
  PATTERN LANGUAGE FOR AN ESSAY-BASED WEB SITE ♦ 97
  performance issues; 14.4 KBPS TESTING ♦ 99
  references, commenting reasons for inclusion; EXPOSABLE
    GUTS ♦ 98
  writing and organizing essays for; PATTERN LANGUAGE FOR
    AN ESSAY-BASED WEB SITE ♦ 97
  writing style
    for links; NATURAL TEXT HYPERLINKS ♦ 98
    for text; NATURAL TEXT FLOW ♦ 98

XLisp language
  as prototyping language, customer demonstration use;
    PROTOTYPING LANGUAGES ♦ 47

Yacoub, S
  [Yacoub+99]; 198
    FINITE STATE MACHINE PATTERNS ❖ 58
Yoder, J.
  [Brant+99]; 183
    CREATING REPORTS WITH QUERY OBJECTS ♦ 40
  [Foote+96]; 187
    EVOLUTION, ARCHITECTURE, AND METAMORPHOSIS ❖ 55
  [Foote+98]; 187
    SELFISH CLASS PATTERN LANGUAGE ❖ 149
  [Foote+99]; 187
    BIG BALL OF MUD PATTERN LANGUAGE ♦ 20

  [Yoder+99]; 198
    ARCHITECTURAL PATTERNS FOR ENABLING APPLICATION
      SECURITY ♦ 17
YOURSELF ♦ 163
yourself
  YOURSELF ♦ 163

Zhang, J. Q.
  [Zhang+96a]; 198
  [Zhang+96b]; 198
  [Zhang+96c]; 199
Zhao, L.
  [Foster+97]; 187
  [Foster+98]; 187
  [Foster+99]; 187
    CASCADE ♦ 28
  [Zhao+98a]; 199
    DRIVER DUTY ♦ 51
  [Zhao+98b]; 199
    PATTERN LANGUAGE OF TRANSPORT SYSTEMS (POINT AND
      ROUTE) ❖ 114
  [Zhao+99]; 199
    DRIVER DUTY CONSTRUCTOR ♦ 51
Zullighoven, H.
  [Baumer+97]; 184
    ROLE OBJECT ♦ 146
  [Riehle+95]; 193
    PATTERN LANGUAGE FOR TOOL CONSTRUCTION AND
      INTEGRATION BASED ON THE TOOLS AND MATERIALS
      METAPHOR ❖ 109
  [Riehle+98]; 193
    SERIALIZER ♦ 151